BASIC ACCOUNTING AND COST ACCOUNTING

McGRAW-HILL ACCOUNTING SERIES

NORTON M. BEDFORD, ROBERT K. JAEDICKE, AND
CHARLES E. JOHNSON, *Consulting Editors*

ARKIN—Handbook of Sampling for Auditing and Accounting
BLOCKER AND WELTMER—Cost Accounting
EASTON AND NEWTON—Accounting and Analysis of Financial Data
EDWARDS AND RUSWINCKEL—The Professional CPA Examination: *Volume 1,* Text and Problems, *Volume 2,* Solutions
FOULKE—Practical Financial Statement Analysis
GRANT AND BELL—Basic Accounting and Cost Accounting
HENRICI—Standard Costs for Manufacturing
JENCKS—Auditing Principles
JOHNSON—Accounting Systems in Modern Business
KELLER—Management Accounting for Profit Control
MACFARLAND, AYARS, AND STONE—Accounting Fundamentals
NICKERSON—Managerial Cost Accounting and Analysis
SMITH AND ASHBURNE—Financial and Administrative Accounting
WENTWORTH–MONTGOMERY–GOWEN–HARNELL—The Accounting Process: A Program for Self-instruction

Dean F. H. Elwell of the University of Wisconsin was Consulting Editor of the McGraw-Hill Accounting Series from its inception until his retirement in 1955.

BASIC ACCOUNTING AND COST ACCOUNTING

2d EDITION

Eugene L. Grant
Professor of Economics of Engineering, Emeritus Stanford University

Lawrance F. Bell
Consultant, Manufacturing Education General Electric Company Formerly Acting Associate Professor of Industrial Engineering Stanford University

McGraw-Hill Book Company
New York San Francisco Toronto London

BASIC ACCOUNTING AND COST ACCOUNTING

Library of Congress Catalog Card Number 63-15021

16 17 18 19 20 FGBP 7 9

ISBN 07-024094-9

PREFACE

This book might have been subtitled "Accounting for Non-accountants." For every professional accountant, there are dozens of other persons in industry and government who need to understand the basic concepts of accounting in order to do their jobs properly. In fact, in our modern industrial age of high taxation and of numerous laws that are related to accounting figures, one might almost say that an elementary knowledge of accounting should be viewed as a prerequisite for good citizenship.

The objective of this book is to provide a fundamental knowledge of accounting for persons who do not expect to become accountants but need to understand the basic accounting concepts and to gain some insight into the structure and the operating characteristics of accounting systems. These matters are important to persons who must interpret various accounting reports or make use of data available in the accounting records. There are very few people who do not fall in this category in their business and personal life, if not in their jobs.

The non-accountant needs a sound working knowledge of fundamental concepts, definitions, and terminologies of accounting and the basic techniques and policies commonly employed in accounting systems. But he has a limited amount of time to devote to the study of these matters. Therefore, this book is brief, although it treats both general accounting and cost accounting, together with related topics such as depreciation, budgetary control, and managerial uses of accounting information.

Brevity is accomplished partly by careful selection of topics and of the kinds of transactions and events used to illustrate problems of accounting policy and procedure. Many matters of importance to professional accountants, such as accounting history, philosophy, and theory, are considered less essential for non-accountants and treated as being outside the scope of this book.

Also, considerable effort has been expended in the development and improvement of this book to reduce to a minimum nonproductive clerical work required of the student. This effort has led to many helpful simplifications and to the development of a set of problem-solution forms to eliminate unnecessary writing and permit concentration on learning. (The problem-solution forms are available through the publisher as a supplement to the book.)

The material in this book—both text and problems—has been developed over a period of more than 25 years, starting in syllabus form and progressing to this second-edition form. It has been thoroughly tested by actual classroom use in a course for administrative and technical people in industry as well as in classes for regular college students. This experience has provided strong support for the viewpoint that the best way for a non-accountant to acquire an adequate and lasting understanding of accounting principles is by solving numerical problems. Therefore, this book contains 97 problems, providing considerable selection for individual problem solving and classroom discussion. The majority of these problems are short complete-cycle problems. Many of the others are even shorter problems, dealing with particular matters of accounting policy or method or with the interpretation and use of accounting data. An effective teaching method has been to solve one problem in the classroom (with student participation), following the assignment of the corresponding text example, and then follow through with a related problem for home solution.

The authors wish to express appreciation to the many students, accounting teachers, and other readers of the first edition who have contributed constructive criticism, provided ideas for improving teaching effectiveness, or created a prototype of one or more of the new problems incorporated into this second edition. Particular thanks are given to Paul T. Norton, Jr., Professor Norton M. Bedford, Professor David V. Heebink, and Dean Maurice Moonitz.

Eugene L. Grant

Lawrance F. Bell

CONTENTS

1/FUNDAMENTALS OF FINANCIAL ACCOUNTING

1/ SOME BASIC CONCEPTS

This book on accounting has been written for persons who do not intend to become professional accountants. Anyone who expects to hold a responsible position in business or government needs to understand the principles of accounting and the practicable objectives and the limitations of accounting systems. All supervisory jobs and most technical jobs involve dealing with information which becomes input to the accounting system. Usually persons in such jobs also must interpret and use accounting information. And frequently the results of their efforts and the effectiveness of departments or programs for which they are responsible are measured and judged in the terms of accounting reports.

It is difficult to get a clear understanding of the fundamentals of accounting merely through practical contact with the accounting procedures and reports of a particular enterprise. This is especially true in the common case where such contact is limited to the input and output fringes of the accounting system. There are many complications that tend to obscure the basic principles, and it is easy to confuse the mechanics of clerical procedures and operations with the underlying concepts and objectives of accounting. There is always the danger that knowledge gained by observation and practical contact will involve serious misconceptions of fundamental principles.

IMPORTANCE OF ACCOUNTING TO INDUSTRY. The greater the size of an industrial concern, the more important is accounting from the viewpoint of internal control. In a small concern it is possible for the executive to have personal contact with all its affairs. As the size of the concern increases, executive control becomes less a matter of personal contact and is increasingly dependent on such things as budgets, cost statements, variances, profit and loss statements, and balance sheets. Thus industrial growth has increased the importance of accounting.

Moreover, from the viewpoint of external control of industry the trend of the times is to make accounting more important; governmental bodies are increasingly concerned with the affairs of private business. Income taxes, social security taxes, and sales taxes depend on the evidence of the accounts. The regulation of public utilities is dependent on figures secured from prescribed accounting systems. The regulation of security markets and the administration of laws limiting profits (on government contracts and elsewhere) and of laws prohibiting price differentials not based on cost differences are all intimately connected with accounting. It is significant that, in the attempt to provide a legal form of self-regulation for industry under the National Industrial Recovery Act of 1933, more than three-fourths of the industry codes contained provisions for uniform cost accounting.

SOCIAL IMPORTANCE OF A WIDESPREAD UNDERSTANDING OF ACCOUNTING AND COST ACCOUNTING PRINCIPLES. In modern industrial society, improvements in the general level of material well-being depend in large measure on improvements in the productive use of our resources, both material and human. Accounting and cost accounting are necessary tools of measurement in any effort to improve productivity within a given firm or industry.

Moreover, many of the laws and government regulations based in part on accounting figures have an important impact on industrial productivity. Even when persons responsible for legislation and for the interpretation and enforcement of laws have a good understanding of accounting principles, it may be difficult to avoid certain obstacles to the improvement of industrial productivity. Misunderstandings of accounting principles may be responsible for serious obstacles. In general, the more widespread the understanding of accounting and cost accounting principles, the greater the chance of wise legislation and regulations concerning those matters in which laws are intimately connected with accounting.

IMPORTANCE OF ACCOUNTING KNOWLEDGE TO THE INDIVIDUAL. The importance of accounting as a means of control makes it desirable for everyone occupying a responsible position in industry to understand accounting principles. Even those persons whose activities bring them into contact with only a limited part of the accounting records can act more intelligently if they understand how these records fit into the entire scheme of things. Each promotion to a position of greater administrative responsibility is likely to increase an individual's contacts with accounting. As a result of such promotion, a person is likely to find that he must base many decisions on figures furnished by the accounting system; he may have responsibility for deciding just what accounting records should be kept; his superiors may judge his own performance partly in terms of accounting figures.

Not only should a knowledge of accounting be a help in securing promotion in industry, but it should also be an even greater help in doing an effective job after such promotion. Moreover, there are many positions in industry where it is necessary to combine an intimate knowledge of engineering or manufacturing processes with a good understanding of the system of accounting and budgetary control used by the particular concern. Such jobs frequently are excellent steppingstones to high executive positions.

SUBJECT MATTER OF THIS BOOK. This book presents in concise form the essential principles of both general (i.e., financial) accounting and cost accounting. For anyone who is employed in the field of production, cost accounting is particularly important. Although the main emphasis throughout the book is on the kinds of information one *can* get from the accounting records, some stress is also laid on the kinds of information one *cannot* get from accounting.

When a person has such a general picture of accounting fundamentals as a basis, the details of an actual accounting system become intelligible; without it, they may never really be understood. There is almost infinite variation in accounting practice among industries and even among different concerns in the same industry. Thus an objective of this book is to create a background from which an industrial employee can fill in his own required details in practice and on the basis of which he can develop a critical appreciation of the uses and limitations of accounting.

WHAT IS ACCOUNTING? The Committee on Terminology of the American Institute of Certified Public Accountants has proposed the following definition: "Accounting is the art of recording, classifying and summarizing in a significant manner and in terms of money, transactions and events which are, in part at least, of a financial character, and interpreting the results thereof."[1]

It is evident from this definition that the accounts of an enterprise provide a partial history of its activities—a history in which the recorded facts are generally expressed in terms of money amounts. A study of accounting principles is, in effect, a study of the rules that are used for determining the money figures and for recording, classifying, summarizing, and interpreting them. These rules of accounting have evolved from the practices of accountants over many years and are always undergoing changes and clarifications as to details. Although the details are sometimes technical and complicated, the underlying pattern of accounting principles is fairly simple and easy to understand.

THE BALANCE SHEET VIEWPOINT. A consideration of the balance sheet provides a convenient approach to basic accounting prin-

[1] Quoted by permission of the American Institute of Certified Public Accountants from *Accounting Research and Terminology Bulletins* (Final Edition—1961), Review and Résumé, p. 9, #9.

ciples. The balance sheet is a statement taken from the books of account that gives a picture of the financial condition of a business enterprise on a specified date.[2] By stating in money terms what the enterprise owns (i.e., its assets) and what the enterprise owes (i.e., its liabilities), the balance sheet places a money valuation on the owners' equity in the enterprise. It does this by showing what is left over for the owners after the liabilities have been deducted from the assets. The valuation rule involved here may be expressed in the form of an equation as follows:

Owners' Equity = valuation in the accounts of what the enterprise *owns* minus what the enterprise *owes*

or, expressed more briefly,

Owners' Equity = Assets — Liabilities

"Owners' Equity" (or, more briefly, "Ownership") is used throughout this book to mean the money value placed by the accounts of a business enterprise on the owners' interest in that enterprise. This is given various names by different writers on accounting. "Proprietorship," "Capital," and "Net Worth" are other terms commonly used.

The preceding equation is, in effect, simply a definition of owners' equity. It is important for the student of accounting to understand that owners' equity in the sense used here is a derived figure. It is the valuation that the accounts place on the assets and liabilities that determines the valuation they place on the owners' equity.

LIMITATIONS OF ACCOUNTING VALUATIONS. It should also be recognized that the "values" for assets that are found in balance sheets are figures that result from the application of formal and systematic rules of accounting. In most instances, these valuations are based on the cost of the asset to the business enterprise for which the accounts are kept or on some modification of that cost.

The systematic rules for determining the valuations assigned to assets in the accounts often give figures that are quite different from market values. The market value of the owners' interest in a business enterprise depends on many factors, not all of which can be measured by the formal processes of accounting. It is easy for anyone who does not understand accounting principles to misunderstand balance sheets and other financial statements. Anyone who has mastered even a brief presentation of accounting fundamentals should be less vulnerable to such misunderstandings.

[2] This statement is sometimes titled "Statement of Financial Position" or "Statement of Financial Condition."

COMPUTING THE VALUE OF OWNERS' EQUITY. The way in which Ownership[3] is derived from the figures for Assets and Liabilities can be illustrated by the following simple example:

The Blaine Equipment Company is a corporation that leases storage space for construction equipment not in use and also acts as a broker in the sale of secondhand construction equipment. The accounts show that on March 1, 19____, the company had a balance of \$1,100 in its checking accounts in the First National Bank. It owned land that had cost \$4,000 and a storage shed that had cost \$1,500. It had accounts receivable of \$220 from Mack & Sons and \$680 from Doe Construction Co. It owed *Weekly Construction News* \$120 and Columbia Realty Co. \$1,000. The company had no other assets or liabilities.

The assets can be listed as follows:

Balance in checking account	\$1,100
Account receivable from Mack & Sons	220
Account receivable from Doe Construction Co	680
Land	4,000
Storage shed	1,500
Total assets	\$7,500

The liabilities can be listed as follows:

Account payable to *Weekly Construction News*	\$ 120
Account payable to Columbia Realty Co	1,000
Total liabilities	\$1,120

The owners' equity in the business can be determined by subtraction as follows:

Assets	\$7,500
Liabilities	1,120
Ownership	\$6,380

THE CORPORATE FORM OF BUSINESS ORGANIZATION. The Blaine Equipment Company is a corporation. This is a common form of business organization, often used for small enterprises and nearly always used for large ones. Nearly all the examples and problems in this book refer to corporations. Two other forms of business organization, the sole proprietorship and the partnership, are discussed briefly in Chap. 18. Generally speaking, anyone who understands the fundamentals of accounting as applied to corporations should have no difficulty in understanding accounting principles as applied to other forms of business organization.

The corporation may be thought of as an artificial person, a legal

[3] Hereafter, wherever the total balance sheet figure for assets, liabilities, or ownership is referred to, the word in question will be capitalized. In this connection, *ownership* and *owners' equity* are used interchangeably.

entity created by the granting of a charter from the state. Its ownership is evidenced by shares of stock which are readily transferable. A corporation itself has continued existence, quite independent of the transfer of shares of its stock from one individual to another. Its control is vested in a board of directors elected by the stockholders. A brief discussion of some advantages and disadvantages of the corporate form of organization is given in Chap. 18.

DETERMINATION OF THE RETAINED EARNINGS OR SURPLUS. Another fact about the Blaine Equipment Company, not previously stated, is that the original investment by its stockholders (i.e., its owners) was $5,000. This is represented by 50 shares of stock of $100 par value.

The valuation placed by the books on Ownership has been computed to be $6,380. It is evident that this figure is $1,380 more than the original $5,000 investment made by the stockholders. This $1,380 represents that portion of the past profits that have been left in the business rather than paid out to stockholders as dividends. The accounting name for such a figure is *retained earnings* or *earned surplus.*[4] Whenever the current book value for Ownership is less than the paid-in value of the outstanding stock, the retained earnings figure is negative and the term "deficit" is used in the balance sheet.

A SIMPLE BALANCE SHEET. For purposes of a formal financial statement, it is convenient to rewrite the equation that defined Owners' Equity as the difference between Assets and Liabilities to read as follows:

$$\text{Assets} = \text{Liabilities} + \text{Ownership}$$

This is the common form of the balance sheet equation. The formal balance sheet involves a classification and tabulation of the various items in this equation. This may be illustrated as follows:

BLAINE EQUIPMENT COMPANY
BALANCE SHEET, MARCH 1, 19___

Assets		*Liabilities and Owners' Equity*	
Cash	$1,100	Accounts Payable	$1,120
Accounts Receivable	900	Capital Stock	5,000
Land	4,000	Earned Surplus	1,380
Buildings	1,500		
Total	$7,500	Total	$7,500

[4] *Earned surplus* is the older term; *retained earnings* is more widely used. In the latter term, the word "income" is sometimes used in place of "earnings," and there are numerous other variations using such words as "accumulated," "reinvested," or "employed" together with or in place of the word "retained."

It will be noted that in this statement the individual accounts receivable have been combined into a single figure. This is also true of the accounts payable. The balance in the checking account is referred to as "Cash." The account title Cash is frequently used to refer to a balance in checking accounts in commercial banks.

Reference has already been made to possible limitations on balance sheet valuations. A simple illustration at this point may be obtained by noting that the land is valued at its cost of $4,000. Obviously the present market value might be either more or less than this cost.

The right-hand side of the Blaine Equipment Company's balance sheet is headed Liabilities and Owners' Equity. There is no one standard heading always used in practice for the right-hand side of balance sheets. A common heading is simply Liabilities. By thinking of the business as an entity apart from its owners, one may view Ownership as the amount the business owes its owners; in this way Ownership may be thought of as a liability. Another possible heading is Equities; the liabilities constitute the creditors' equity in the business, and the ownership items constitute the owners' equity.

TECHNICAL MEANING OF "EARNED SURPLUS" OR "RETAINED EARNINGS." The item in the owners' equity section of the balance sheet titled Earned Surplus or Retained Earnings is sometimes misconstrued by a non-accountant to mean cash or liquid assets beyond the amount necessary to provide for the ordinary needs of the business. Of course, this item on the balance sheet has no necessary relation to cash or liquid assets. For example, if the Blaine Equipment Company should spend its $1,100 of cash for more land, the form of the assets would be changed without any change in their total amount. Thus there would be no change in the Owners' Equity. The earned surplus (i.e., retained earnings) would still be $1,380 even though the company had no cash.

The technical accounting meaning of earned surplus is that share of the capital (the difference between assets and liabilities) which has been provided by plowing back profits into the business. Basically, this accounting concept provides a distinction between that part of the owners' equity which was *paid* into the business and that part which is an accumulation of past earnings *left* in the business. To attempt to relate either paid-in capital or retained earnings to any particular asset of the business. such as cash, is, of course, meaningless. This difference between the technical accounting meaning and the popular idea of the term "surplus" is emphasized by the position of Earned Surplus on the right-hand side of the balance sheet, as opposed to the assets, which are shown on the left-hand side.

Surplus is one of several words that have technical accounting meanings quite different from their popular meanings. Such differences in meaning often create unfortunate confusion in the popular interpretation of accounting figures. Sometimes this confusion even extends to the courts in litigated matters related to accounting. The problems created by these dual meanings are widely recognized by the accounting profession and have led to the gradual change to terminologies which are less likely to be misinterpreted. In the case of earned surplus, the trend now is to substitute the more easily interpreted term *retained earnings*. However, the older technical words are still used on many published balance sheets, and it is therefore important that the student of accounting gain a clear understanding of the meanings of all such words.

SUBDIVISION OF ASSETS, LIABILITIES, AND OWNERSHIP INTO ACCOUNTS. In the formal accounts of a business enterprise each asset or group of similar assets will have its own account. So also will each liability and each subdivision of ownership. Thus the Blaine Equipment Company might have accounts entitled Cash, Accounts Receivable, Land, Accounts Payable, Capital Stock, etc. The use of these and other accounts is illustrated in Chap. 2. In a business enterprise that is even moderately complex, the skill with which the classification of accounts is drawn will have a great influence on the usefulness of the information obtainable from the accounting system.

The home of the accounts is called the *ledger*. It is convenient to think of the ledger as a book in which each account has its own page. The ledger page has columns on each side.[5] The left-hand side is called the *debit* side, and the right-hand side is called the *credit* side. When a figure is entered on the left-hand side, we say the account has been debited; when a figure is entered on the right-hand side, we say the account has been credited. Each account in the ledger is algebraic: Debits and credits are treated as having opposite signs, and the balance in the account at any time is the algebraic sum of all previous debits and credits entered in the account.

INTRODUCTION TO DEBIT AND CREDIT. The historical origin of the use of the words "debit" and "credit" in accounting goes back to the days of single-entry bookkeeping in which the chief objective was keeping track of amounts owed by customers (debtors) and amounts owed to creditors. Debit is Latin for "he owes"; credit is Latin for "he trusts." Debiting a customer's account was simply recording an amount that the customer owed us; crediting a vendor's account was recording an amount for which the vendor (creditor) trusted us. It followed that, when the customer paid his bill, his account should be credited; when

[5] This is the historical form of a ledger and is still widely used in accounting systems. Other physical forms for ledgers are mentioned in Chap. 5.

a vendor's bill was paid, his account was debited. The debits and credits to any one account, of course, oppose each other. Subsequently, it became the custom of accounting that debits were shown on the left-hand side of accounts and credits were shown on the right-hand side of accounts.

With the development of double-entry bookkeeping and the elaboration of accounting systems, the original derivation of the words debit and credit lost its significance and became unsatisfactory as a basis for understanding the meaning of these words in modern accounting. There remained only the connotation that debit refers to the left-hand and credit refers to the right-hand. A debit may be defined as an amount of money recorded on the left-hand side of an account; a credit may be defined as an amount of money recorded on the right-hand side of an account.

ABBREVIATIONS AND SYNONYMS FOR DEBIT AND CREDIT. In books of account and in accountants' working papers, debit is frequently abbreviated to "Dr." and credit is similarly abbreviated to "Cr."

The word "charge" is used in accounting as having the same meaning as *debit*. To charge an account with $100 means to debit it with $100. Many accounting forms are headed Charges and Credits rather than Debits and Credits.

There is no other word that has the same meaning as *credit* in the language of accounting.

BASIS OF DOUBLE-ENTRY BOOKKEEPING. Modern double-entry bookkeeping is based on the balance sheet equation. Assets must always equal the sum of Liabilities and Ownership. No transaction or event can disturb this equality. This follows from the definition of Owners' Equity as the derived difference between Assets and Liabilities. Some transactions are merely the exchange of one asset for another, as when office furniture is purchased for cash or when an account receivable from a customer is wiped out by his cash payment. Other transactions may involve an increase in an asset and a corresponding increase in a liability, as occurs when piece of machinery is purchased on credit. But any transaction that alters the difference between Assets and Liabilities necessarily makes a change in Ownership.

Therefore, any event which changes the balance of any asset or liability account necessarily changes the balance in another asset or liability account or in an ownership account. This is the so-called dual character or business transactions that permits double-entry bookkeeping.[6]

[6] Some transactions affect more than two accounts and require *compound* entries with three or more parts. Such entries, of course, also must be balanced with respect to the basic equation.

RULES FOR DEBITING AND CREDITING ACCOUNTS. The basic mechanics of double-entry bookkeeping are embodied in the rules for making entries in the accounts to record the monetary effects of transactions that are made and events that occur. These rules and the conventions that go with them are so drawn that they provide very important checks on the accuracy and completeness with which entries are made into the accounts.

The following conventions are observed with respect to the left-hand and right-hand sides of the accounts:

For asset accounts, the left-hand (debit) side is the plus side of the account and the right-hand (credit) side is the minus side of the account.

For liability and ownership accounts, the right-hand (credit) side is the plus side of the account, and the left-hand (debit) side is the minus side of the account.

From these conventions, together with the requirement of the balance sheet equation, the following rules for debiting and crediting accounts are derived:

Debit

1. If an asset is *increased* by a transaction, *debit* the appropriate asset account.
2. If a liability is *decreased* by a transaction, *debit* the appropriate liability account.
3. If Ownership is *decreased* by a transaction, *debit* the appropriate ownership account (usually an expense account).

Credit

1. If an asset is *decreased* by a transaction, *credit* the appropriate asset account.
2. If a liability is *increased* by a transaction, *credit* the appropriate liability account.
3. If Ownership is *increased* by a transaction, *credit* the appropriate ownership account (usually an income account).

For memory convenience, these rules can be summarized as follows:

Account	If increased	If decreased
Asset......................	Debit the account	Credit the account
Liability or Ownership......	Credit the account	Debit the account

Or inversely, entries in the account may be interpreted as follows:

Account	A debit means	A credit means
Asset......................	An increase	A decrease
Liability or Ownership......	A decrease	An increase

It is convenient to symbolize an account, with its debit and credit sides, in skeleton form as a large T. Using one such T to represent all asset accounts, another to represent all liability accounts, and a third to represent all ownership accounts,. the rules for debiting and crediting can be represented symbolically as follows:

A = L + O

A		L		O	
Dr.	Cr.	Dr.	Cr.	Dr.	Cr.
+	−	−	+	−	+

If the foregoing rules are followed, and if a complete entry is made for each transaction, it follows that every entry made into the ledger will be balanced with respect to the basic accounting equation Assets = Liabilities + Ownership. Also, of course, this equality will then consistently be true for the ledger as a whole.

DEBITS MUST EQUAL CREDITS. Necessarily, if each transaction is properly recorded in accordance with (1) the balance sheet equation and (2) the rules for debiting and crediting, it will also be true that for each transaction the sum of the debits entered in the ledger will be equal to the sum of the credits. This provides a check which can be made for each transaction, and this check will disclose a wide variety of possible mistakes. Also, of course, if for every transaction entered the sum of the debits equals the sum of the credits, this equality will also hold for the ledger as a whole at any time. When an accountant says. "The ledger is in balance," he means that this test was applied to the ledger and did not fail.

ANALYSIS OF CHANGES IN OWNERSHIP. The Blaine Equipment Company's balance sheet shows Ownership represented by only two accounts, Capital Stock and Earned Surplus. These two accounts were sufficient for balance sheet purposes. Together they stated the total valuation that the accounts placed on owners' equity on the balance sheet date. Separately they showed how much of this total came from the contributions of the owners and how much came from profit that had been left in the business.

Nevertheless, from the viewpoint of business evaluation and control it is not enough for the accounting process to place a valuation on ownership on a particular date. It is even more important to determine how ownership changes from one date to another. This is the purpose of the income statement (profit and loss statement) which is prepared for each successive period of time (month, quarter, or year).

In order to accumulate and classify the information necessary to explain the net change in ownership from one balance sheet date to the next, it is necessary to use many ownership accounts in addition to those shown on the balance sheet. These accounts are called income and expense accounts.[7]

The illustrative example in Chap. 2 deals with an artificially simple case in which all incomes and expenses are entered in a single account entitled Profit and Loss. In this first example illustrating the application of the rules for debit and credit, it is desired to show directly the effect on Ownership of various types of transactions. In all subsequent examples and problems and in all actual accounting, a number of separate income and expense accounts are used that classify the various sources of changes in Ownership. These accounts may be thought of as temporary subdivisions of Ownership that are used during an accounting period; at the end of each accounting period, their balances are summarized in the Profit and Loss (or Income and Expense) account, which is then "closed out" into the permanent ownership account Earned Surplus (or Retained Earnings).

SUMMARY. The main points of this chapter can be restated as follows:

1. Because of the importance of accounting as a means of business control and because of the difficulty of learning accounting principles merely through practical contact with the details of an actual accounting system, those who expect to occupy responsible positions in business and industry ought to study the fundamentals of general accounting and cost accounting.
2. A balance sheet is a formal statement showing the money valuations given by the books of account to the assets and liabilities of a business enterprise, and thus indicating the Ownership (the owners' equity in the business) as the difference between the sum of the assets and the sum of the liabilities. Because assets and liabilities are valued by systematic application of formal rules of accounting, the money figures shown in a balance sheet do not necessarily agree with ordinary commercial valuations.
3. The definition of owners' equity as the difference between total assets and total liabilities is the basis for the balance sheet equation Assets = Liabilities + Ownership. No transaction or event can disturb this equality.
4. The books of account of an enterprise subdivide the values assigned to Assets, Liabilities, and Ownership into many separate accounts. Each account has its place in a formal record known as a ledger. Increases on the assets side (the left-hand side) of the balance sheet equation are recorded in the left-hand column of an asset account in the ledger. Increases on the liabilities and ownership side (the right-

[7] Many accountants prefer the word "revenue" as an alternative to the word "income."

hand side) of the balance sheet equation are recorded in the right-hand column of an appropriate account in the ledger. Decreases are recorded in the opposite columns of the accounts, and a ledger account is interpreted algebraically. Thus the balance in an account is determined by the difference between the sum of the figures in the left-hand column and the sum of the figures in the right-hand column.

5. A debit, or charge, is an amount recorded on the left-hand side of an account in a ledger; a credit is an account recorded on the right-hand side. The rules for debiting and crediting accounts can be summarized as follows:

A		=	L		+	O	
Dr.	Cr.		Dr.	Cr.		Dr.	Cr.
+	−		−	+		−	+

6. The rules for debiting and crediting accounts are so devised that, for each entry recording the effects of a transaction, the sum of the debits must equal the sum of the credits. Therefore, unless an error has been made, the sum of the debit account balances in the ledger will equal the sum of the credit account balances in the ledger.

DISCUSSION QUESTIONS

1-A. In what way might each of the following persons employed by an electrical equipment manufacturing company have contact with the accounting system of the company?

1. A young engineer working in the product design department
2. The foreman of the foundry department
3. The union steward in the foundry department
4. The manager of a branch sales office for the company

1-B. Why should it be difficult for the persons mentioned in question 1-A to gain a clear idea of accounting and cost accounting principles merely through their contacts with the accounting aspects of their respective jobs?

1-C. You are the proprietor of a small retail store. In what ways might various governmental departments be concerned with your accounting records? Mention some kinds of information that you might reasonably expect to obtain from your accounts in addition to the information required to satisfy the demands of the governmental departments.

1-D. What are the essential ideas contained in the definition of accounting prepared by the Committee on Terminology of the American Institute of Certified Public Accountants?

1-E. State the balance sheet equation in two forms.

1-F. The market valuation of the owners' equity in a corporation may in some cases be quite different from the valuation of the owners' equity shown in the corporation's balance sheet. Explain this statement. How could you estimate the market valuation of the owners' equity for a corporation whose shares are traded on the New York Stock Exchange?

1G. A corporation's assets are valued at $222,700 in its books of account. Its liabilities are shown as $75,900. The paid-in value of its capital stock is $150,000. Does this corporation have a surplus or a deficit and how much?

1-H. List several kinds of assets you might expect a company like the Blaine Equipment Company to own which would not properly be included in any of the four asset groups shown on the balance sheet on page 8. Also, answer the same question with respect to liabilities.

1-J. Suppose that, after the Blaine Equipment Company balance sheet shown on page 8 was drawn up, the manager pointed out that the following transaction has not been taken into account: On February 27 the company purchased a used quonset hut for $600, to be paid on delivery. Revise the balance sheet to show the effects of this event.

1-K. Explain why the debits are balanced by equal credits in modern double-entry bookkeeping.

1-L. On which side of the balance sheet are the assets conventionally shown? The liabilities? The owners' equity? Would it be possible to present the same information regarding assets, liabilities, and owners' equity without using this conventional form?

1-M. Name some ledger accounts that you would expect usually to have debit balances.

1-N. The balance sheet of a cooperative college bookstore was published in a student newspaper. This financial statement showed assets of approximately $100,000, chiefly merchandise inventory and furniture and fixtures. It showed the original investment by the associated students to be $10,000, liabilities of approximately $10,000, and surplus of about $80,000. A student wrote a letter to the newspaper suggesting that this "huge surplus" should be spent for student scholarships. Does this seem to you to be a practical suggestion? Explain your answer.

PROBLEMS

Problem 1-1. The Miller Lumber Company has 100 shares of stock outstanding at $100 per share. It owns an inventory of lumber which had cost $7,317. Its accounts receivable are $3,710, and it owes its trade creditors $2,280. It owns a secondhand motor truck which it has just purchased for $950. Its checking account at the Merchants' National Bank has a balance of $1,733. It owns a second mortgage of $500 on J. Reed's house. It owes $129 in taxes.

What is this company's earned surplus or deficit as of now? Prepare a balance sheet from the above information.

Problem 1-2. The Hurd Construction Company owns land for which it had paid $800. On this land is a storage shed which cost $300. The company owns a concrete mixer valued on its books at $920, miscellaneous tools valued at $4,350, and a truck valued at $1,100. It still owes $650 on its installment contract on the truck. The balance in its checking account at the State Bank is $1,140, but it owes $1,500 on a promissory note payable to the same bank. It has advanced $150 of next month's salary to G. White, its foreman. It has accounts receivable of $2,190. It owes $800 to suppliers. It has 40 shares of stock outstanding at $100 per share.

What is this company's earned surplus or deficit as of now? Prepare a balance sheet from the above information.

Problem 1-3. At the end of 1962, the Micro Manufacturing Company has machinery and equipment valued on the books at $51,240, tools valued at $6,840, and raw materials and supplies which cost $1,800. Accounts receivable total $9,400, and accounts payable total $880. The company owes a balance of $7,340 on equipment purchase contract notes, $690 in wages payable, $570 in payroll taxes, and an estimated $320 for income taxes for the past year. It has miscellaneous assets, such as utility and rent deposits and insurance (which is paid for in advance), worth $290. Cash in the bank is $900. Employees owe a total of $630 for materials and small tools, cash advances, and other personal dealings with the company.

The company has received $60,000 capital for which 6,000 shares of stock were issued to the owners.

What is the present earned surplus or deficit? Prepare a balance sheet from the above information. What is the "book value" (net ownership) per share of stock outstanding?

Problem 1-4. The following data describe the situation of the Micro Manufacturing Company (of problem 1-3) 1 year later, at the end of 1963. From this information determine the end-of-1963 earned surplus figure and prepare a new balance sheet. Calculate the end-of-1963 "book value per share." Also calculate the change (increase or decrease) in the earned surplus account during the year 1963, and label it profit or loss, whichever is appropriate:

An additional 600 shares of stock were sold early in 1963 at $10 per share, bringing the total in the capital stock account to $66,000. No dividends have been paid to the stockholders. The values in the accounts as of the end of 1963 show machinery and equipment at $57,340, tools at $5,930, a motor vehicle at $2,120, raw materials and supplies at $2,110, accounts receivable at $11,170, accounts payable at $1,080, balance owed on purchase contract notes $7,790, bank note payable of $2,000, wages payable of $770, payroll taxes payable of $610, estimated 1963 income taxes payable of $250, amounts receivable from employees totaling $850, miscellaneous assets of $420, and cash in bank of $460.

2/ A SIMPLE EXAMPLE ILLUSTRATING DEBITS AND CREDITS

This chapter and the following two contain examples involving a complete accounting cycle. These examples start with the account balances for a business enterprise at the beginning of an accounting period (month, quarter, or year) and illustrate the effects on the accounts of the events occurring during the period. The examples conclude with the preparation of a balance sheet at the end of the period and a statement showing the net income or loss for the period. Each example in turn introduces certain new ideas which are important for the student to understand.

SOME DEVICES TO SIMPLIFY THE STUDY OF ACCOUNTING. The application of accounting in a business enterprise involves repetitive tasks, division of labor, and systematic checking for errors and for protection against fraud and embezzlement. However, it is not practical in a brief book designed mainly for non-accountants to treat these system aspects of accounting in a comprehensive way. Therefore, in this book, only the most basic of the methods and devices used in accounting systems are introduced. Also, a number of convenient simplifications are employed so that the attention can be focused primarily on important ideas and the amount of detail work will be minimized.

One expedient used in the examples and problems (except in Chap. 5) is the representation of the ledger on one page with a large T for each account. Although such a T-account ledger is efficient and satisfactory for a one-cycle problem, it would be unsatisfactory for many reasons in a continuously operating accounting system and is never used in actual accounting practice.

One of the important techniques of accounting practice is to record all transactions and events requiring ledger entries first in a *book of original entry* (a *journal*). Entries into ledgers are always made by *posting* from a book of original entry. Except in Chaps. 5 and 6, this normal step of the accounting process is bypassed in the examples and problems and the entries are made directly into the ledgers.

The complete-cycle examples and problems are simplified in various other ways. Only a few representative transactions are included in any example or problem. Also, the money amounts involved are in even dollars and generally round numbers. (In actual accounting practice, accounts ordinarily are kept to the nearest cent or other smallest monetary unit, even though the figures may be rounded off for the purpose of financial statement presentation.) These two simplifications reduce the arithmetic required and permit concentration of attention on principles.

In the interest of simplicity, a number of matters that are important in keeping the accounts of a business enterprise have been omitted from most of the examples and problems. The discussion of income taxes and the related topic of the distribution of profits to the owners of an enterprise is deferred until Chap. 18. Social security taxes and the withholding of income taxes in payrolls are discussed in Chap. 13, but these matters are generally ignored elsewhere in this book. Although the matter of depreciation is first introduced in Chap. 7, discussion of the various methods of computing annual depreciation expense is deferred until Chap. 19. Prior to Chap. 7, the whole matter of accounting for depreciable assets and depreciation expense is avoided or ignored in the examples and problems. In general, in each new complete example or problem, attention is concentrated on certain new ideas introduced in the particular chapter; no attempt is made to illustrate all the complications to be expected in an actual accounting system.

In many of the examples and problems in this book the accounting period is assumed to be 1 month, and it is implied that the books are formally closed and financial statements are prepared at the end of each calendar month. This assumption simplifies the examples and problems in many desirable ways. However, it should be pointed out that for many business enterprises this practice would be unduly expensive, and therefore the formal accounting cycle often runs 3 months, 6 months, or a full year.

ACCOUNTING TERMINOLOGY. In certain areas of accounting, terminology is not entirely standardized; in other areas, it seems to be in a state of change. The selection of accounting terms used in this book has been influenced by the fact that the book has been written for non-accountants. Where accountants may use several words or phrases in the same meaning, those in most common use have been introduced and are used interchangeably. (An example of this is the interchangeable use of *indirect manufacturing expense, manufacturing overhead,* and *factory burden.*) Where terminology is in a state of change, the phrase that is the older of those in more common current use is employed most frequently, but other phrases that are often encountered in accounting also are used occasionally for illustration. (Thus the term *earned surplus* is used more frequently but interchangeably with the term *retained earnings.*)

Throughout this book, whenever reference is made to a specific account, the account title is capitalized.

HOW TO ANALYZE A BUSINESS TRANSACTION IN TERMS OF DEBIT AND CREDIT. In order to determine how to make the entry for a specific transaction, the student should ask himself questions such as: "Has any asset been increased or decreased by this transaction? If so, which asset (e.g., cash, an account receivable from a particular customer, an item of merchandise for sale, etc.) and how much? Has any liability account been increased or decreased by this transaction? If so, which liability (e.g., an account payable to a particular creditor) and how much?"

EXHIBIT 2-1

TRANSACTIONS FOR BLAINE EQUIPMENT COMPANY DURING MARCH, 19___

A. Opening balances on March 1, 19___, were as follows:

Account	*Debit*	*Credit*		
Cash	$1,100		Accounts receivable were:	
Accounts Receivable	900		Mack & Sons	$ 220
Land	4,000		Doe Construction Co.	680
Buildings	1,500		Total	$ 900
Accounts Payable		$1,120	Accounts payable were:	
Capital Stock		5,000	*Weekly Construction News*	$ 120
Earned Surplus		1,380	Columbia Realty Co.	1,000
Totals	$7,500	$7,500	Total	$1,120

B. Received $300 from Doe Construction Co. as a payment on account.
C. Paid account with *Weekly Construction News* in full, $120.
D. Received bill of $320 from the Olson Co. for addition to storage shed.
E. Received $100 from Henry Green for rental of storage space for grading machinery.
F. Paid *Daily Builder* $70 for advertising during March.
G. Received $180 from J. Cobb for commission on sale of concrete mixer.
H. Billed Mack & Sons $370 for commission on sale of power shovel.
I. Paid the Olson Co. $160 on account.
J. Received bill of $90 from *Weekly Construction News* for March advertising.
K. Billed Doe Construction Co. for $150 for current month's rental of space in storage lot and shed.
L. Paid the manager, Sid Adams, his March salary, $520.

In determining whether a change in Ownership has taken place, remember that Ownership = Assets — Liabilities; if the transaction changes the difference between the sum of the assets and the sum of the liabilities, there has been a corresponding change in Ownership. For instance, if a transaction decreases the asset of Cash by $100 and does not change any other asset or any liability, there has been a decrease of $100 in Ownership. A discussion of the topic of classification of changes in Ownership into income and expense accounts is deferred until Chap. 3.

THE BLAINE EQUIPMENT COMPANY EXAMPLE. In Chap. 1, the assets and liabilities of the Blaine Equipment Company on March 1, 19____, were examined and a balance sheet was prepared as of that date. Exhibit 2-1 gives the transactions of this company during March. These transactions illustrate a number of the various possible combinations of changes in assets, liabilities, and ownership.

EXHIBIT 2-2

T-ACCOUNT LEDGER FOR THE BLAINE EQUIPMENT COMPANY SHOWING ENTRIES FOR MARCH, 19____

Assets = *Liabilities* + *Ownership*

Assets

Cash

	Debit	Credit	
A	1,100	120	C
B	300	70	F
E	100	160	I
G	180	520	L

Accounts Receivable

	Debit	Credit	
A	900	300	B
H	370		
K	150		

Land

	Debit	Credit	
A	4,000		

Buildings

	Debit	Credit	
A	1,500		
D	320		

Liabilities

Accounts Payable

	Debit	Credit	
C	120	1,120	A
I	160	320	D
		90	J

Ownership

Capital Stock

	Debit	Credit	
		5,000	A

Earned Surplus

	Debit	Credit	
		1,380	A

Profit and Loss

	Debit	Credit	
F	70	100	E
J	90	180	G
L	520	370	H
		150	K

Exhibit 2-2 is a T-account ledger showing the opening balances as of March 1 and the entries required by all the March transactions. The capital letter shown alongside each figure in the T accounts refers back to the transaction description in Exhibit 2-1. In all the T-account illustrations in this chapter, the debit and credit parts of each entry are identified with each other and referenced to the transaction in this matter. (This technique is recommended to the student for use in solving problems where entries are made directly into a T-account ledger.)

The student should give careful attention to the following explanation of each entry and to the accompanying comments.

Entry A. If our ledger had been used for the preceding accounting period (i.e., February), the opening balances for March would already be in the ledger. In this example, our opening balances are those that were developed at the end of Chap. 1. The asset accounts have debit balances; the liability and ownership accounts have credit balances. With these opening balances entered the T accounts would appear as follows:

Cash	
A 1,100	

Accounts Receivable	
A 900	

Accounts Payable	
	1,120 A

Capital Stock	
	5,000 A

Land	
A 4,000	

Buildings	
A 1,500	

Earned Surplus	
	1,380 A

Note that the sum of the debit amounts is equal to the sum of the credit amounts.

Entry B. Received $300 from the Doe Construction Co. as a payment on account. The account for the asset increased, Cash, is debited with the amount of its increase, $300. The account for the asset decreased, Accounts Receivable, is credited with the amount of its decrease, $300.

After these entries the accounts affected will appear as follows:

Cash	
A 1,100	
B **300**	

Accounts Receivable	
A 900	**300** B

INTERPRETATION OF THE ACCOUNT CASH. As pointed out in Chap. 1, the Blaine Equipment Company's balance in its checking account with the First National Bank was listed in the balance sheet as Cash. The account Cash in any accounting system usually refers to a balance in a commercial account in a bank. The implication is that all receipts, in the form of either checks or currency, are promptly deposited in the bank. Disbursements are presumably by check.

KEEPING TRACK OF INDIVIDUAL ACCOUNTS RECEIVABLE AND ACCOUNTS PAYABLE. In the Blaine Equipment example and in the examples in Chaps. 3 to 5 only one ledger is used, and in that ledger there is only one account for all accounts receivable. Of course, in actual business practice, it is necessary to have a separate record of the account with each individual customer, showing the increases and decreases in sequence and the current balance owed by that customer. The usual accounting practice is to have a *subsidiary ledger* containing these individual accounts receivable. This subsidiary ledger is "controlled" by the account in the general ledger titled Accounts Receivable. Accounts payable are commonly treated in a similar fashion.

The use of such subsidiary ledgers is explained more fully in Chap. 6. Meanwhile, the examples and problems involve only a few trans-

actions, and the maintenance of such subsidiary records would be an unnecessary complication.

Entry C. Paid account with *Weekly Construction News* in full, $120. Here a liability and an asset account are reduced by equal amounts. The account for the liability decreased, Accounts Payable, is debited with the amount of its decrease, $120. The account for the asset decreased, Cash, is credited with the amount of its decrease, $120.

Cash			
A	1,100	**120**	C
B	300		

Accounts Payable			
C	**120**	1,120	A

Entry D. Received bill of $320 from the Olson Co. for addition to storage shed. The addition to the storage shed is something the business owns, i.e., an asset. Hence an asset has been increased, and at the same time a liability has been increased. The account for the asset increased, Buildings, is debited with the amount of its increase, $320. The account for the liability increased, Accounts Payable, is credited with the amount of its increase, $320.

Buildings			
A	1,500		
D	**320**		

Accounts Payable			
C	120	1,120	A
		320	D

TREATMENT OF CHANGES IN OWNERSHIP IN THIS EXAMPLE. The preceding entries have involved changes in assets and liabilities but no change in ownership. In each case, the change in an asset has been offset by an equal change in another asset or in a liability, so that the excess of Assets over Liabilities was unchanged by the transaction.

In all but one of the remaining entries, however, a change in ownership takes place. Some of the entries involve increases in ownership, i.e., incomes. Others involve decreases in ownership, i.e., expenses.

In this example, all these changes in ownership will be entered in a single account entitled Profit and Loss. The two ownership accounts already on our book are Capital Stock and Earned Surplus. Capital Stock (the investment contributed by the stockholders) is obviously unchanged by these incomes and expenses. It follows that Earned Surplus is the account ultimately affected by these changes in ownership. All the incomes and expenses recorded in the Profit and Loss account during the month will enable us to find the net change in Ownership—the profit or the loss—at the end of the month. This net change will then be transferred from the Profit and Loss account to the Earned Surplus account.

In actual accounting, many different accounts are used to classify and record incomes and expenses. Such income and expense accounts are introduced in Chap. 3 and will be used in all subsequent examples and problems in this book.

Entry E. Received $100 from Henry Green for rental of storage space for grading machinery. This is obviously an increase in the asset of cash. The account with the asset increased, Cash, is therefore debited with the amount of its increase, $100. No other asset is changed by this transaction. Neither is there a change in any liability. The excess of Assets over Liabilities is therefore increased by $100. By definition, this is an increase in Ownership, and the appropriate ownership account should be credited. In this example we make this credit entry of $100 to the account Profit and Loss. The accounts affected now appear as follows:

Cash

	Debit	Credit	
A	1,100	120	C
B	300		
E	**100**		

Profit and Loss

	Debit	Credit	
		100	**E**

Note that Accounts Receivable was not affected in entry E. This entry involves a "cash" transaction in the sense that the actual payment by Henry Green took place at the same time as the recognition of his obligation to pay. Thus it was not necessary to make any entry to Accounts Receivable.

If the account receivable were to be shown on the books, two entries would be made in rapid succession, the first (a) showing the increase in Accounts Receivable (debit) and the corresponding increase in Ownership (credit) and the second (b) showing the increase in Cash (debit) and the decrease in Accounts Receivable (credit).

Cash

	Debit	Credit	
b	100		

Accounts Receivable

	Debit	Credit	
a	100	100	b

Profit and Loss

	Debit	Credit	
		100	a

It is evident that the net effect of these two entries would be the same as that of entry E. Since both events, recognition of the rental due and the actual payment, occurred in the same accounting period, it was satisfactory to combine them into one entry.

Entry F. Paid *Daily Builder* $70 for advertising during March. This is a decrease in Ownership, an expense. The asset Cash has been reduced with no change in any other asset or any liability. The excess of Assets over Liabilities is therefore decreased by $70. Because all expenses are debited to Profit and Loss in the present example, the account Profit and Loss is debited $70 to show the decrease in Ownership. The account with the asset decreased, Cash, is credited with the amount of the decrease, $70. The accounts affected now appear as follows:

	Cash				Profit and Loss		
A	1,100	120	C	F	70	100	E
B	300	**70**	**F**				
E	100						

Note that Accounts Payable was not affected by entry F. This transaction, as in the preceding entry E, could be viewed as two separate events. In this case they are (1) recognition of the expense and the obligation to pay and (2) the actual payment. This would imply two entries, the first debiting Profit and Loss and crediting Accounts Payable and the second debiting Accounts Payable and crediting Cash. However, since the expense properly was applicable to March and the payment was made immediately, in March, the one entry F was satisfactory and accomplished the same result that would have been obtained with the two entries.

In many accounting systems, the disbursement procedures require that all obligations be set up as accounts payable before they are paid. Although this practice appears to involve more work, it has certain advantages which are explained in Chap. 6 in connection with the discussion of the invoice register. Meanwhile, in examples and problems prior to Chap. 6, we shall not set up an account payable unless there is a time interval between the recognition of the obligation to pay and the actual payment.

Entry G. Received $180 from J. Cobb for commission on sale of concrete mixer. The asset Cash is increased $180 and therefore is debited with this amount. Ownership is increased by this income, and therefore Profit and Loss is credited $180.

Entry H. Billed Mack & Sons $370 for commission on sale of power shovel. Accounts Receivable is debited $370 to show the increase in this asset. Profit and Loss is credited $370 to show the increase in Ownership.

Entry I. Paid the Olson Co. $160 on account. This involves a decrease in a liability and a decrease in an asset. Accounts Payable is debited and Cash is credited with the amount of the decrease, $160.

Entry J. Received bill of $90 from *Weekly Construction News* for March advertising. Profit and Loss is debited $90 to show the decrease in Ownership, the expense, of that amount. Accounts Payable is credited $90 to show the increase in liabilities connected with the obligation to pay the *Weekly Construction News* that amount. Note the difference between this entry and entry F.

Entry K. Billed Doe Construction Co. $150 for current month's rental of space in storage lot and shed. The increase in the asset, Accounts Receivable, is shown by a debit of $150. The increase in Ownership (income recognized as earned in March) is shown by a credit of $150 to Profit and Loss.

Entry L. Paid the manager, Sid Adams, his March salary, $520. This is an expense, a decrease in Ownership. Profit and Loss is debited $520. The asset Cash is decreased, so this account is credited, $520.

EXHIBIT 2-3
T-ACCOUNT LEDGER FOR THE BLAINE EQUIPMENT COMPANY SHOWING ACCOUNT BALANCES AT THE END OF MARCH, 19__

Cash

Debit	Credit
A 1,100	120 C
B 300	70 F
E 100	160 I
G 180	520 L
1,680	*870*
	810
810	

Accounts Receivable

Debit	Credit
A 900	300 B
H 370	
K 150	
1,420	*300*
	1,120
1,120	

Accounts Payable

Debit	Credit
C 120	1,120 A
I 160	320 D
	90 J
280	*1,530*
1,250	
	1,250

Capital Stock

Debit	Credit
	5,000 A

Earned Surplus

Debit	Credit
	1,380 A

Land

Debit	Credit
A 4,000	

Buildings

Debit	Credit
A 1,500	
D 320	
	1,820
1,820	

Profit and Loss

Debit	Credit
F 70	100 E
J 90	180 G
L 520	370 H
	150 K
680	*800*
120	
	120

RULING AND BALANCING THE ACCOUNTS. Exhibit 2-3 shows the T-account ledger after the entries have been summarized and the balance "brought down" in each account. Note the way this is shown in an account, taking the Cash account for example. The sum of the debits is $1,680; the sum of the credits is $870; these totals were noted in small figures. The difference was determined:

$$\$1,680 - \$870 = \$810$$

This difference, of course, is the balance in the account—a debit balance—and is shown therefore on the debit side below the horizontal ruling. If this same amount, **$810,** is also shown on the credit side, above the line, then the sum of all the credits above the line will equal the sum of all the debits above the line. Therefore, all entries above the ruling can be ignored in subsequent calculations of the account balance. Note that this practice is consistent with the rules for debiting and crediting accounts; in effect, a balanced "entry" is made in the account in this summarizing procedure.[1]

ACCRUAL ACCOUNTING. In the administration of the Federal income tax, the United States Internal Revenue Service makes a sharp distinction between "cash" and "accrual" accounting. When accounts are kept on the accrual basis, income is shown in the accounting period in which it is earned even though it may not be received during that period. Expenses are shown in the accounting period for which they are applicable even though they may not be paid during that period. There is an effort to "match" expenses with the revenues with which they are associated. Related to this is an effort to make the balance sheet prepared for any one date reflect the known assets and liabilities on that date as fully as possible.

The explanation of accrual and adjusting entries in Chaps. 4 and 7 deals with many of the accounting procedures that are employed in realizing these objectives. In general, any formal presentation of accounting principles in a course or a textbook will deal with accrual accounting. All the examples and problems in this book assume accrual accounting. This concept was introduced in the Blaine Equipment example in entries H, J, and K. Entries H and K show a rental and a commission as March income even though in these cases the cash was not yet received as of March 31. Entry J records a $90 advertising item as March expense even though the invoice has not been paid.

THE DISTINCTION BETWEEN AN ASSET AND AN EXPENSE MAY BE A MATTER OF TIMING. It is the final date of the current accounting period that needs to be considered in making a decision regarding the accounting treatment of certain types of transaction. In a sense, at the date of payment the Blaine Equipment Company may be thought of as owning a legal right to the March advertising in the *Daily Builder* and to the March services of Sid Adams, its manager; on first impression, one might perhaps view these as assets. Nevertheless, these legal rights will all expire at the end of March; it would be improper to include them in a statement of assets in a balance sheet dated March 31. It follows that such expenditures are properly viewed as causing decreases in Ownership.

The borderline field between expenditures that are properly viewed

[1] In actual bookkeeping there are a number of ways to show account balances; the choice depends on the ledger form used and the methods employed in posting entries and computing account balances. The practice illustrated in Exhibit 2-3 is recommended to the student for use with skeleton (T) accounts.

as resulting in assets and those properly viewed as expenses will be explored at greater length in subsequent chapters.

TAKING A TRIAL BALANCE. For each transaction entered in the Blaine Equipment Company's ledger (Exhibit 2-3) the debits equaled the credits. Therefore, the total of the debit balances in the ledger should equal the total of the credit balances.

Exhibit 2-4 shows a listing of the account balances and the debit

EXHIBIT 2-4
BLAINE EQUIPMENT COMPANY
TRIAL BALANCE, MARCH 31, 19___

Account	*Debit*	*Credit*
Cash	$ 810	
Accounts Receivable	1,120	
Land	4,000	
Buildings	1,820	
Accounts Payable		$1,250
Capital Stock		5,000
Earned Surplus		1,380
Profit and Loss		120
Totals	$7,750	$7,750

and credit totals—which are equal. Such a listing, called a *trial balance,* is taken at the end of each accounting period. It serves two useful purposes. One is to provide a partial check for any clerical errors in the bookkeeping. The other is to provide a convenient summary of the figures in the ledger. Such a summary gives a large part of the information necessary for preparation of an end-of-period balance sheet and a statement of the profit or loss for the period.

USE OF THE TRIAL BALANCE AS A CHECK ON CLERICAL ERRORS. If the sum of the debits does not equal the sum of the credits, it is certain that some error has been made. Whenever the trial balance fails to balance, it is necessary for the bookkeeper to hunt for the error and to correct it.

In hunting for an error disclosed by a trial balance, it is usually desirable first to make sure that the error has not occurred in the preparation of the trial balance from the accounts. For instance, the debit or credit sum in the trial balance may have been computed incorrectly, an account may have been omitted in the trial balance, or an account balance may have been copied incorrectly or entered in the wrong column. Or an acount balance may have been calculated incorrectly even though all entries in the account were correct.

If the error is not in the calculation of account balances or in the preparation of the trial balance itself, it must be in one or more incorrect entries in the ledger. One side of an entry may have been made and the other side omitted, or a debit may have been entered as a credit or vice versa. Or an incorrect figure may have been entered for one side of a transaction.

Although the trial balance is a necessary check on clerical errors, there are a number of types of such errors that cannot be found by the trial balance. An entire transaction may be omitted from the accounts, an entry may be made to the wrong account, or the same incorrect figure may be entered on both the debit and credit sides. Moreover, sometimes there are compensating errors of other types; if so, errors that would ordinarily be found by a trial balance may remain undetected.

DETERMINING THE PROFIT AND LOSS FOR THE PERIOD. The Profit and Loss account has a credit balance of $120. This indicates a profit for the month of March, a net increase in Ownership during the month. The $120 profit figure is derived from credits in the Profit and Loss account representing incomes totaling $800 and debits representing expenses totaling $680.

From the viewpoint of management, it is important to have more information than this regarding the amounts and types of incomes and expenses that produced this $120 profit. In this simple example with only seven entries in the Profit and Loss account, it would be easy enough to classify the incomes ($550 of commissions and $250 of rentals) and expenses ($520 salary and $160 advertising) to obtain a better picture of the source of the profit. Although such an analysis is easy with only seven entries in the Profit and Loss account, it would not have been practicable if there had been, say, seven thousand such entries. It is clearly desirable to set up a classification of incomes and expenses and to enter changes in Ownership in the ledger according to this classification. Incomes and expense accounts are illustrated in all the remaining examples starting with Chap. 3.

One reservation should be made regarding the appropriateness of this $120 figure for profit. Our accounts have disregarded the fact that the Blaine Equipment Company's storage shed is an asset with a limited life. Some small part of the $1,820 cost of this fixed asset should properly be allotted as an expense to the month of March, 19___. Such an allocation would reduce the $120 profit figure. The important topic of the accounting treatment of the depreciation of fixed assets is deferred until Chaps. 7 and 19.

PUTTING THE LEDGER IN SHAPE TO START THE NEXT ACCOUNTING PERIOD. In this simple example in which all changes in Ownership have been entered in one account, only one entry is necessary to put the accounts in shape to start April. This entry is to transfer the balance in the account Profit and Loss to the account Earned Surplus, by debiting Profit and Loss $120 and crediting the same amount to Earned Surplus. Identifying this entry as M, the two accounts affected now appear as follows:

Profit and Loss

	Debit	Credit	
F	70	100	E
J	90	180	G
L	520	370	H
		150	K
	120		
M	**120**	120	

Earned Surplus

Debit	Credit	
	1,380	A
	120	**M**
1,500		
	1,500	

To use the language of accounting, Profit and Loss is *closed* into Earned Surplus. A line is ruled below the entries in the Profit and Loss account to show that the account now has a zero balance. The balance in the Earned Surplus account is now $1,500, the sum of the $1,380 figure on March 1 and the $120 increase in Ownership during March. The net figure from the temporary ownership account Profit and Loss has been transferred to the permanent ownership account Earned Surplus.

PREPARATION OF AN END-OF-PERIOD BALANCE SHEET. Exhibit 2-5 is a balance sheet showing the condition of the Blaine Equipment Company's business at the end of March. All the information presented in this balance sheet has come from the trial balance. The earned surplus (retained earnings) figure includes the March profit.

EXHIBIT 2-5
BLAINE EQUIPMENT COMPANY
BALANCE SHEET, MARCH 31, 19____

Assets			*Liabilities and Owners' Equity*		
Current Assets:			Liabilities:		
Cash	$ 810		Accounts Payable		$1,250
Accounts Receivable	1,120	$1,930			
Fixed Assets:			Owners' Equity:		
Land	$4,000		Capital Stock	$5,000	
Buildings	1,820	5,820	Earned Surplus	1,500	6,500
Total		$7,750	Total		$7,750

In this balance sheet, the assets have been divided into two general classes, current assets and fixed assets. The current assets consist of cash and other relatively liquid assets that presumably will be converted into cash in the ordinary course of business operations and within a reasonable time. Fixed assets are the relatively long-lived properties of the business. The importance of this distinction will be developed in later chapters and the foregoing definitions will be further explained and illustrated.

SUMMARY. Some of the important points of this chapter are stated as follows:

1. In this brief study of accounting principles, we shall make use of a number of simplifications, such as a ledger consisting of T accounts, and we shall postpone to later chapters consideration of many of the normal practices and techniques used in accounting.
2. The application of the balance sheet equation in analyzing transactions is emphasized throughout this first example by showing all changes in Ownership in a single temporary ownership account, Profit and Loss. At the end of the accounting period, the net profit or loss for the period is transferred from this account to the summary ownership account Earned Surplus.
3. Accounts with persons and corporations are either accounts receivable or accounts payable, depending on whether they normally have debit or credit balances. When the general ledger has only one Accounts Receivable account and one Accounts Payable account, it is usually necessary to maintain subsidiary ledgers containing separate accounts for the individual customers and creditors.
4. In accrual accounting, an effort is made to show incomes and expenses in the accounting periods to which they properly apply regardless of the date of actual payment.
5. The trial balance lists the balances in all accounts at the end of an accounting period. It contains a large part of the information necessary for the preparation of financial statements, and also provides a necessary check on errors.

DISCUSSION QUESTIONS

2-A. What assets are increased or decreased, what liabilities are increased or decreased, and how is the owners' equity changed in each of the following transactions?

1. A customer pays his bill.
2. A creditor's bill is paid.
3. The current month's rent is paid to the landlord.
4. Land is purchased for cash.
5. A customer who owes money on open account gives a promissory note as evidence of his indebtedness.
6. A motor truck to be used for delivery is purchased by giving a cash down payment and an installment note for the balance.
7. An employee's salary for the current month is paid.
8. Money is received from a customer for services rendered to him.

2-B. List a number of possible errors in accounting entries that would cause the trial balance to have unequal debit and credit totals. List a number of possible errors that would not cause the trial balance to have unequal debit and credit totals.

2-C. What is your understanding of the general distinction between current assets and fixed assets? Can you see any reasons why this distinction might be important in the interpretation of balance sheets?

2-D. The assets of the Superior Mercantile Company totaled $40,750 on January 1 and totaled $43,500 on December 31 of the same year. From this information, what, if anything, can you tell about the profit or loss for the year? Explain your answer.

2-E. Prepare a list of the individual accounts payable as of March 31 for the Blaine Equipment Company, showing the name of each creditor and the balance owed. Determine the total, and check this total against the end-of-month balance in the Accounts Payable account in Exhibit 2-3.

2-F. In the Blaine Equipment Company example, three liabilities were lumped in one account, Accounts Payable. Now assume that the $1,000 liability to the Columbia Realty Co. is a promissory note due July 1. Explain why it would be more appropriate to record this liability in another account (perhaps titled Notes Payable) separate from the *Weekly Construction News* and Olson Co. liabilities.

2-G. In the Blaine Equipment Company, entry J, suppose this bill was for advertising which will appear early in April. Would the entry for this as shown in Exihibit 2-3 be appropriate under these circumstances? If not, suggest a satisfactory way of handling the matter.

2-H. In the Blaine Equipment Company example, suppose that the $100 received in entry E was for 2 months' rent—March and April. Suggest an entry that would be appropriate under these altered circumstances.

PROBLEMS[2]

Problem 2-1. Harris and Rolfe, Inc., is a corporation engaged in land surveying. At the start of business on May 1 the company had $1,250 cash in the bank. It had accounts receivable totaling $6,000 as follows: Fish & Sons, $3,600; Myron Realty Co., $2,400. It had accounts payable totaling $550 as follows: Instrument Rental Co., $380; Street Photo Service, $170. Its outstanding capital stock consisted of 50 shares at $100 per share.

Set up T accounts as follows: Cash, Accounts Receivable, Accounts Payable, Capital Stock, Earned Surplus, and Profit and Loss. Make entries for the following transactions directly into the accounts. Use only one account for all accounts receivable and one account for all accounts payable. Enter all changes in Ownership directly to the account Profit and Loss. New asset or liability accounts can be opened as necessary.

A. Determine the earned surplus or deficit and enter the May 1 balances in their respective accounts.

B. Fish & Sons paid $1,800 on account.

[2] In this chapter and throughout the remainder of this book, the problem statements may contain redundant or extraneous information. It should not be assumed that it is necessary to make use of all the information given.

C. Paid Street Photo Service account in full, $170.
D. Received bill from Instrument Rental Co. for May rental of surveying instruments, $350.
E. Received $240 from L. Hudson for resurvey of the boundaries of his farm.
F. Billed Fish & Sons $2,100 for route and grade survey work in May.
G. Paid V. Stein $100 for office rental for May.
H. Accepted two lots in Myron Subdivision in full payment of the $2,400 owed by Myron Realty Co. These lots are to be valued at $1,200 each on the books of account. This is the price at which Myron Realty Co. is offering them for sale.
I. Paid Instrument Rental Co. $400 on account.
J. Paid electric light and power bill for office, $30.
K. Received bill from Street Photo Service for blueprints and photostats, $160.
L. Received $300 from T. Crane in full payment for a survey of his property.
M. Paid month's salaries, $1,850.
N. Sold the two lots in the Myron Subdivision to F. Wiles for $2,250. Wiles paid $250 and gave his promissory note for the remaining $2,000.

Determine and record the balance in each account. Take a trial balance of the ledger. Determine the profit or loss for May. Prepare a balance sheet as of May 31.

Problem 2-2. On January 1, the Walker Delivery Service, a corporation, had cash in the bank of $1,200. It had accounts receivable totaling $1,620 as follows: Bender Electric Shop, $550; Collins Pharmacy, $380; Coombs Florist Shoppe, $270; Plank Grocery, $420. It had accounts payable totaling $550 as follows: Leopard Oil Company, $100; Meek Motor Co., $450. Assume that it had no other assets or liabilities. The shareholders have contributed $2,000 capital.

Set up T accounts as follows: Cash, Accounts Receivable, Accounts Payable, Profit and Loss, Earned Surplus, and Capital Stock. Enter the following transactions directly in the T accounts. Open accounts needed for any new assets or liabilities.

A. Determine the retained earnings or deficit as of January 1, and enter the opening balances in the accounts.
B. Paid Weil Realty Co. $125 for January rent for garage and office space.
C. Received bill from Leopard Oil Company for $90 for gas and oil.
D. Receipts on account from "contract" customers during January, were $1,270: Bender Electric, $300; Collins Pharmacy, $380; Coombs Florist, $170; Plank Grocery, $420.
E. Paid on account $100 to Leopard Oil Company and $240 to Meek Motor Co.
F. Paid Dee-Tee Agency $30 for direct mail advertising.
G. Received bill of $250 from Meek Motor Co. for rental of two delivery trucks during January.
H. Paid miscellaneous monthly bills, $45: telephone, $15; utilities, $20; other, $10.
I. Billings to contract customers for January amounted to $1,360: Bender

Electric, $280; Collins Pharmacy, $360; Coombs Florist, $240; Plank Grocery, $480.

J. Purchased a motor scooter for $560. Paid $260 cash; the balance is due in 30 days.

K. Received $75 from Harry's Hardware for use of a truck and driver for 2 days and $45 from "call-in" customers during January, a total of $120.

L. Paid F. Craig, driver, $420 and H. Baker, manager and driver, $550 January salaries.

Determine the end-of-month balance in each account and take a trial balance of the ledger. Close the Profit and Loss account to Earned Surplus. Prepare a balance sheet as of January 31.

Problem 2-3. This problem is supplementary to problem 2-2. Determine the balance owed to the Walker Delivery Service as of January 31 by each of the four contract customers. Prepare a list of these customers' accounts (name of each customer and balance outstanding as of Janaury 31). Compute the total from this list and check it against the end-of-month balance developed in the Accounts Receivable account in problem 2-2.

Problem 2-4. The See Saw Service, a corporation, leases its shop space and equipment from the See Cabinet Shop. As of the close of business on September 30, See Saw had $540 cash in the bank, $2,330 in accounts receivable, and merchandise which cost $1,110. It owed $690 for merchandise and September services. It had 200 shares of capital stock outstanding at $10 per share.

Set up T accounts titled Cash, Accounts Receivable, Merchandise Stock, Accounts Payable, Capital Stock, Earned Surplus, and Profit and Loss. No other accounts are required in this problem. Make entries for the following events that occurred in October. In this problem customer transactions are treated as if all sales of merchandise and services were on credit.

A. Determine the earned surplus or deficit as of September 30, and enter the opening balances in the accounts.

B. Paid See Cabinet Shop $200 for October rents.

C. Billed customers during the month $1,860 for saw and knife sharpening.

D. Purchased on credit merchandise (saws, blades, etc.) costing $410.

E. Received $2,510 from customers during the month (all payments on account).

F. Paid all bills on hand at the start of the month, $690.

G. Sales of merchandise during October came to $490 (all sales on credit).

H. Paid $90 for October expenses such as telephone and supplies.

I. The merchandise sold in October had cost $300.

J. Paid October wages and salaries of $950.

K. At the end of the month, unpaid bills for other October expenses such as delivery service, advertising, and shop supplies totaled $370.

Determine and record the balance in each account. Take a trial balance of the ledger. What was the profit or loss for October? Prepare a balance sheet as of the end of October.

3/ AN EXAMPLE INTRODUCING INCOME AND EXPENSE ACCOUNTS

As illustrated in the preceding chapter, many of the business transactions that take place in any enterprise involve changes in the valuation that the accounts place on Ownership. These changes are either increases in Ownership, i.e., incomes, or decreases in Ownership, i.e., expenses. To a considerable extent these are temporary changes that offset each other. Business enterprises incur expenses in the expectation of securing incomes somewhat greater than the expenses. It is the possibility of getting this excess of income over expense, or profit, that provides the motive for business activity.

As has been pointed out, it is not sufficient to know at the end of any period merely what the profit or loss has been. Good management requires information regarding the sources of the incomes and the nature of the expenses that, taken together, have resulted in a profit or a loss. One of the primary purposes of accounting is to give this information.

To this end, every accounting system makes use of a number of *income* and *expense* accounts that are really subdivisions of ownership. Such accounts are illustrated in the example of this chapter.

ACCOUNTS FOR A MERCHANDISING BUSINESS. Exhibit 3-1 states the transactions for Buck & Company for May, 19____. Exhibit 3-2 shows a skeleton ledger in T-account form containing the entries required by these transactions.

Buck & Company is a merchandising or trading business. It has the exclusive agency for the sale of Modern Machine Co. electric washing machines and driers in its locality. It rents its store and store fixtures and hires its delivery service and installation service.

This example illustrates the use of perpetual-inventory accounts for merchandise items. Two such accounts are used, one for washing machines and the other for driers. These are the only two items Buck & Company sells.

EXHIBIT 3-1

TRANSACTIONS FOR BUCK & COMPANY DURING MAY, 19____

A. Opening balances on May 1 were as follows:

Account	*Debit*	*Credit*
Cash	$2,100	
Accounts Receivable	1,200	
Washing Machines (10 @ $250)	2,500	
Driers (5 @ $200)	1,000	
Accounts Payable		$1,450
Capital Stock		4,000
Retained Earnings		1,350
Totals	$6,800	$6,800

Accounts receivable were:	
L. Wallace	$ 400
Stone's Washomat	800
Total	$1,200
Accounts payable were:	
Modern Machine Co.	$1,350
N. D. West	100
Total	$1,450

B. Paid May rent for store and store fixtures, $240.
C. Paid Modern Machine Co. $900 on account.
D. Billed L. Wallace $30 for installation charge on washing machine.
E. Sold 6 washing machines for cash at $400 each, a total of $2,400.
F. Purchased 12 washing machines at $250 each and 6 driers at $200 each from Modern Machine Co., all on credit, a total of $4,200.
G. Paid $40 to a local printing shop for advertising circulars.
H. Sold 4 washing machines on credit to Stone's Washomat at $380 each, a total of $1,520.
I. Received $120 from L. Wallace on account.
J. Paid salaries for first half of May, $540.
K. Paid N. D. West in full, $100.
L. Sold on credit to M. Atkins a washing machine for $400 and a drier for $320. Installation charges were $70. Total bill was $790.
M. Received $800 on account from Stone's Washomat.
N. Sold 3 driers for cash at $320 each, a total of $960.
O. Received bill of $80 from *Daily Gazette* for May advertising.
P. Paid $140 to a local trucking company for deliveries during May.
Q. Received bill from N. D. West for $90 for installations made during May.
R. Paid Modern Machine Co., $2,000 on account.
S. Paid salaries for second half of May, $560.

ENTRIES TO EXPENSE ACCOUNTS AND INCOME ACCOUNTS. The expense accounts used by Buck & Company are:

Cost of Goods Sold	Installation Expense
Delivery Expense	Advertising Expense
Rent Expense	Salaries

The account Cost of Goods Sold is used to record the decrease in Ownership (expense) associated with the withdrawal of merchandise from inventory for delivery to customers. The other five expense accounts will provide an appropriate place in which to record each of the various expenses involved in this simple example.

For the accounting system of an enterprise it is important to plan what expense accounts will be needed and to define clearly, by account titles and descriptions, what items of expense should be charged to

EXHIBIT 3-2
T-ACCOUNT LEDGER FOR BUCK & COMPANY
SHOWING ENTRIES FOR MAY, 19___

Assets = *Liabilities* + *Ownership*

Assets and Liabilities

Cash

Debit	Credit
A 2,100	240 B
E 2,400	900 C
I 120	40 G
M 800	540 J
N 960	100 K
	140 P
	2,000 R
	560 S
6,380	*4,520*
	1,860
1,860	

Accounts Receivable

Debit	Credit
A 1,200	120 I
D 30	800 M
H 1,520	
L 790	
3,540	*920*
	2,620
2,620	

Accounts Payable

Debit	Credit
C 900	1,450 A
K 100	4,200 F
R 2,000	80 O
	90 Q
3,000	*5,820*
2,820	
	2,820

Washing Machines

Debit units	Debit amount	Credit units	Credit amount
A 10 @ 250	2,500	6 @ 250	1,500 E
F 12 @ 250	3,000	4 @ 250	1,000 H
		1 @ 250	250 L
22	*5,500*	*11*	*2,750*
		11 @ 250	2,750
11 @ 250	2,750		

Driers

Debit units	Debit amount	Credit units	Credit amount
A 5 @ 200	1,000	1 @ 200	200 L
F 6 @ 200	1,200	3 @ 200	600 N
11	*2,200*	*4*	*800*
		7 @ 200	1,400
7 @ 200	1,400		

(Income Accounts)

Sales

Debit	Credit
	2,400 E
	1,520 H
	720 L
	960 N
	5,600

Installation Income

Debit	Credit
	30 D
	70 L

(Expense Accounts)

Cost of Goods Sold

Debit	Credit
E 1,500	
H 1,000	
L 450	
N 600	
3,550	

Advertising Expense

Debit	Credit
G 40	
O 80	

Delivery Expense

Debit	Credit
P 140	

Installation Expense

Debit	Credit
Q 90	

Rent Expense

Debit	Credit
B 240	

Salaries

Debit	Credit
J 540	
S 560	

(Ownership Summary Accounts)

Capital Stock

Debit	Credit
	4,000 A

Retained Earnings

Debit	Credit
	1,350 A

each account. Obviously, there should be a proper place for every item of expense that is likely to occur. It is also desirable that the available expense accounts provide for the classification and collection of expenses in a consistent and meaningful way. These and related matters are considered more fully in later chapters.

The income accounts used by Buck & Company are Sales and Installation Income. The account Sales is used to record the amounts charged customers for merchandise sold; the account Installation Income is used to record income from customers for installation of washing machines and driers.

Every expense is a decrease in Ownership. *It follows that entries to expense accounts are debit entries.* A credit to an expense account made during an accounting period would be an entry to correct a previous overstatement of the particular expense. When the books are being closed at the end of an accounting period, credit entries to expense accounts are made to transfer their balances to a summary ownership account.

Every income is an increase in Ownership. *It follows that entries to income accounts are credit entries.* A debit to an income account during an accounting period would be an entry to correct a previous overstatement of an income. At the end of an accounting period, debit entries to income accounts are made to transfer their balances to a summary ownership account.

Entry A. This entry in Exhibit 3-2 merely records the opening balances in the various accounts. In a continuing set of books, these balances would all have been carried forward from the preceding month.

Entry B. Paid May rent of store and store fixtures, $240. This is a decrease in Ownership resulting from a decrease in the asset Cash with no change in any other asset or liability. We are now classifying decreases in Ownership into appropriate expense accounts. We therefore debit Rent Expense $240 and credit Cash $240.

Entry C. Paid Modern Machine Co. $900 on account. We debit Accounts Payable to show the decrease of $900 in that liability. We credit the asset Cash with the amount of its decrease, $900.

Entry D. Billed L. Wallace $30 for installation charge on washing machine. Although installations are handled by a separate contractor, in this transaction the sale of the washing machine was on credit, and the credit was extended to cover the installation charge. Accounts Receivable is debited $30 to show the increase in that asset. As there has been no change in any other asset or in any liability, this is an increase in Ownership, an income. We are now classifying increases in Ownership into appropriate income accounts. We therefore credit Installation Income $30.

Note that the *cost* of installation is not involved in this entry. This will be handled as a separate transaction when the bill from the installation contractor is entered in the books (entry Q).

Entry E. Sold six washing machines for cash at $400 each, a total of $2,400. This introduces the important subject of the accounting entries used to record the sale of merchandise. Several different aspects of this subject are explained in the following discussion.

A FIRST APPROACH TO ANALYZING THE ACCOUNTING ENTRY FOR A MERCHANDISE SALE. It is evident in transaction E that one asset, cash, has been increased by $2,400, the selling price of the washing machines. It is also evident, that another asset, the merchandise inventory of washing machines, has been decreased by six machines. These are carried on the books at their cost of $250 each, a total of $1,500. No other assets or liabilities are changed by this transaction. With one asset increased by $2,400 and another decreased by $1,500, it follows that there has been an increase in Ownership of $900.

It would be possible to record this increase in Ownership in a single income account. If this account were entitled Profit on Sales, the entry would be as follows:

Cash	
2,400	

Washing Machines	
	1,500

Profit on Sales	
	900

USE OF THE ACCOUNTS SALES AND COST OF GOODS SOLD. Such an entry is never made even though it would be entirely consistent with the rules for debit and credit given in Chap. 1. The objection to the use of a single account Profit on Sales is that the accounts would fail to supply management with certain necessary information. Management needs to know the total amount of the sales in each accounting period and to know the cost of the merchandise sold. To this end, two accounts, Sales (an income account) and Cost of Goods Sold (an expense account), are used rather than a single account that merely shows the profit (or loss) on the sale. With these accounts, entry E is made as follows:

Cash	
2,400	

Sales	
	2,400

Cost of Goods Sold	
1,500	

Washing Machines	
	1,500

The entry to the income account Sales and the entry to the expense account Cost of Goods Sold need to be viewed together to observe the effect on Ownership of a merchandise sale. Consider these two accounts apart from the others affected by entry E.

Cost of Goods Sold	
1,500	

Sales	
	2,400

These two entries together show an excess of income over expense of $900. That is, Ownership is shown to have been increased by $900, the profit on the sale.

In the study of accounting principles, it is helpful to think of a sale of merchandise as requiring two entries, one at the selling price and the other at the cost price. The entry at the selling price is a debit to the asset increased, usually Cash or an account receivable, and a credit to Sales. The entry at the cost price is a debit to Cost of Goods Sold and a credit to the appropriate merchandise inventory account or accounts.

Cash or Account Receivable	
Selling Price	

Sales	
	Selling Price

Cost of Goods Sold	
Cost Price	

Merchandise Inventory Accounts	
	Cost Price

The account title Cost of Goods Sold is often replaced by the shorter account title Cost of Sales. The two are used interchangeably throughout the remainder of this book.

ACCOUNTING TREATMENT OF MERCHANDISE SALES WHERE PERPETUAL-INVENTORY ACCOUNTS ARE NOT MAINTAINED. Entry E is representative of the accounting treatment of a merchandise sale where there are perpetual-inventory accounts. The accounts show the reduction of the asset of merchandise inventory resulting from each sale or group of sales (such as the six washing machines). The inventory accounts for each class of merchandise show at all times the quantities and costs of the items on hand.

It is simple enough to keep perpetual-inventory accounts for merchandise items if there are only a few large items such as the washing machines and driers. In contrast, where there are many small items of merchandise, the clerical cost of maintaining perpetual-inventory accounts may be prohibitively high.

The example in Chap. 4 illustrates the accounts for a merchandising business that does not maintain perpetual-inventory accounts. In spite of the differences in accounting procedure brought out in these two examples, the foregoing explanation of the accounting treatment of a merchandise sale applies to the enterprise without perpetual-inventory accounts as well as to the one having such accounts. Each sale may still be thought of as involving one entry at the selling price (a debit to Cash or an account receivable and a credit to Sales) and another at the cost price (a debit to Cost of Goods Sold and a credit to Inventory). The essential difference is that in the case without perpetual-inventory accounts, the entries at the cost price are put off until the end of the accounting period. At that time, one entry is made to record the entire Cost of Goods Sold for the accounting period; this takes the place of many entries that would have been needed to record the costs of individual sales when made. This point of view is explained in greater detail in Chap. 4.

SOME PROBLEMS IN USING PERPETUAL–INVENTORY ACCOUNTS. To make an entry such as entry E, it is necessary to have a unit cost figure for the items sold. The perpetual-inventory accounts constitute the source of this needed information on unit costs. To emphasize this point, the T accounts for washing machines and driers in Exhibit 3-2 show quantities and unit prices as well as dollar balances.

A discussion of forms and methods actually used for keeping such accounts is deferred until Chap. 12, which deals with material costs in cost accounting. Perpetual-inventory accounts are important tools of cost accounting.

In the Buck & Company example, no change occurs in the price at which washing machines or driers are purchased. Variations in the prices at which merchandise items are purchased complicate the problem of determining a figure for cost of goods sold. A discussion of this matter is put off until later chapters. Some general aspects of the problem are considered in Chap. 7. The relationship between price fluctuations and perpetual-inventory accounts is explained in Chap. 12.

Entry F. Purchased 12 washing machines at $250 and 6 driers at $200 from Modern Machine Co., all on credit, a total of $4,200. This is an increase in the asset Washing Machines of $3,000 and an increase in the asset Driers of $1,200. We therefore debit these merchandise inventory accounts with their respective increases. The liability account, Accounts Payable, is credited with $4,200, the amount of its increase. Note that in this case two debit entries are balanced by a single credit entry; this is called a *compound* entry.

Entries G through S. These remaining entries are similar to entries already explained in this chapter or in the preceding one. It is suggested that the student consider each transaction in Exhibit 3-1 in turn to decide on the appropriate debit and credit entries. He can then check his analysis by looking at the entries shown in Exhibit 3-2.

A SIX–COLUMN WORK SHEET. In summarizing and analyzing information from the accounts, the accountant uses many *working papers*. Although such papers are not part of the formal books of account, they play an important part in the accounting process. A particularly useful working paper is the 10-column *work sheet* explained in Chap. 4. Such a work sheet is used to combine information from the trial balance and from end-of-period accrual and adjustment entries (introduced in Chap. 4) to secure the figures needed for the profit and loss statement and balance sheet. Work sheets are used in many of the problems in this book; in fact, a number of problems conclude with the preparation of a work sheet.

EXHIBIT 3-3

WORK SHEET FOR BUCK & COMPANY, MAY 31, 19___

Account	Trial balance		Income statement		Balance sheet	
	Debit	Credit	Debit	Credit	Debit	Credit
Cash	1,860				1,860	
Accounts Receivable	2,620				2,620	
Washing Machines	2,750				2,750	
Driers	1,400				1,400	
Accounts Payable		2,820				2,820
Capital Stock		4,000				4,000
Retained Earnings		1,350				1,350
Sales		5,600		5,600		
Installation Income		100		100		
Cost of Goods Sold	3,550		3,550			
Installation Expense	90		90			
Delivery Expense	140		140			
Advertising Expense	120		120			
Rent Expense	240		240			
Salaries	1,100		1,100			
Totals	13,870	13,870	5,240	5,700	8,630	8,170
Profit			460			460
			5,700	5,700	8,630	8,630

Exhibit 3-3 provides an introduction of the work sheet. The first two columns of this sheet contain Buck & Company's trial balance at the end of May. The Buck & Company example is simpler than subsequent examples because its trial balance contains all the information needed to prepare a new balance sheet and a statement showing the profit or loss for the period. In actual practice and in the later examples in this book, it is always necessary to recognize that certain pertinent information has not been included in the trial balance. Because of the greater simplicity of the Buck & Company example, its work sheet requires only six columns rather than the usual ten.

In effect, this six-column work sheet separates the balances in the income and expense accounts from the balances in the asset, liability, and summary ownership accounts. The expense and income figures from the trial balance are copied in the third and fourth columns of the work sheet under the heading Income Statement. The total of the expenses (debits) under this heading is $5,240; the total of the incomes (credits) is $5,700. Because the incomes exceed the expenses, the word "Profit" is entered on the line below the account titles. (If expenses had exceeded incomes, the word "Loss" would have been used.) The amount of the excess of incomes over expenses, $460, is the profit figure entered in the debit column under the heading Income Statement. This figure, added to the $5,240 above, serves to balance the debits and credits in this section of the work sheet.

The two right-hand columns of the work sheet show the balances in the asset, liability, and summary ownership accounts. All these figures are end-of-month balances ready to be used in a formal balance sheet, except the figure for retained earnings (earned surplus), which is the May 1 figure of $1,350. Note that the debit and credit totals at this point disagree by $460. This is the net difference between the credits and debits sorted into the income statement columns and summarized in the single figure of $460 profit. When this figure is "transferred" from the income statement section to the balance sheet section, it appears as a credit (increase in Ownership) in the balance sheet credits column and brings the sum of the credits equal to the sum of the debits. The end-of-month retained earnings figure is not shown in this work sheet; it is $1,810—the sum of the retained earnings at the beginning of the month, $1,350, and the profit for the month, $460.

INCOME STATEMENT OR PROFIT AND LOSS STATEMENT. The third and fourth columns of the work sheet supply the information for Exhibit 3-4. This is a formal statement showing the incomes and

EXHIBIT 3-4
BUCK & COMPANY
INCOME STATEMENT FOR MAY, 19___

Sales		$5,600
Less: Cost of Goods Sold		3,550
Gross Profit on Sales		$2,050
Add: Installation Income		100
		$2,150
Less: Operating Expenses:		
Installation Expense	$ 90	
Delivery Expense	140	
Advertising	120	
Rent	240	
Salaries	1,100	1,690
Net Profit for May		$ 460

expenses for the accounting period and the development of a figure for the net income (profit) or loss for the period. Such a statement is called an *income statement,* an *earnings statement,* or a *profit and loss statement.*[1]

In an income statement for a merchandising business, it is desirable to indicate the *gross profit* made on sales. This gross profit is simply the difference between the selling price and the cost price of the goods sold. If a merchandising enterprise is to be profitable, this excess of selling price over cost must be larger than the total operating expenses of the business. The final figure in any income statement is the *net* profit or loss for the period, the difference between the sum of the incomes and the sum of the expenses.

In the study of accounting, it is sometimes helpful to think of accounting procedures as being aimed at the preparation of the two major financial statements, the income statement and the balance sheet. To use a comparison from photography, a balance sheet is a snapshot of the condition of the business enterprise at a particular moment; an income statement is a motion picture of the activities that took place over a stated period of time.

Nevertheless, although these two financial statements are always end products of accounting procedures, it is much too narrow a view of the matter to think of these statements as the sole objectives of accounting. There are many other important purposes of accounting, a number of which are discussed in the remainder of this book. Chapter 8 deals briefly with certain aspects of the analysis of income statements and balance sheets.

EXHIBIT 3-5
BUCK & COMPANY
BALANCE SHEET, MAY 31, 19___

Assets		*Liabilities and Owners' Equity*		
Current Assets:		Liabilities:		
Cash	$1,860	Accounts Payable		$2,820
Accounts Receivable	2,620	Owners' Equity:		
Merchandise Inventory	4,150	Capital Stock	$4,000	
		Retained Earnings	1,810	5,810
Total	$8,630	Total		$8,630

[1] These three terms are used interchangeably in this book. The oldest term *profit and loss statement* emphasizes the important point that either a profit or a loss is possible in a business enterprise. The term *income statement* is the most widely used in accounting practice and textbooks. The term *earnings statement* appears to be gaining in popularity. The exact titles used on published financial statements are sometimes embellished with additional descriptive words.

END–OF–MONTH BALANCE SHEET. Exhibit 3-5 shows Buck & Company's balance sheet at the close of business on May 31. This balance sheet is based on the figures in the final two columns of the work sheet, Exhibit 3-3. The balance sheet shows only a total figure for merchandise inventory, combining the washing machine and drier inventory accounts for balance sheet purposes.

Buck & Company rents its store, store fixtures, and hires its delivery service and therefore carries on its business without owning any fixed assets. All its assets (cash, receivables, and inventory) are properly classified as current assets.

USE OF THE ACCOUNT PROFIT AND LOSS SUMMARY IN CLOSING THE BOOKS. In the Blaine Equipment Company example in Chap. 2, all the entries for incomes and expenses were made into a single account entitled Profit and Loss. In this artifically simple example, when the end of one accounting period was reached, practically all the accounts were ready to start the next accounting period. The only necessary step was to transfer the balance in the Profit and Loss account into the Earned Surplus account.

Although the Buck & Company example is also an artificially simple one devised for the purpose of explaining accounting principles on a step-by-step basis, some new complications are present in closing the books. There are now a number of income and expense accounts that should start the next accounting period with zero balances. The net change in Owners' Equity during the period needs to be transferred to the summary ownership account, which in this example is titled Retained Earnings.

It is convenient to make the necessary transfers among accounts by the use of an auxiliary account entitled Profit and Loss Summary.[2] Exhibit 3-6 illustrates the use of such an account in closing Buck & Company's books. Only those accounts affected by the closing entries are shown in this exhibit. These are the income accounts, the expense accounts, Profit and Loss Summary, and Retained Earnings.

The entries shown in boldface type are those transferring the balances in the income and expense accounts into Profit and Loss Summary. Each expense account is credited with its respective balance and an equal debit entry is made to Profit and Loss Summary. Each income account is debited with its respective balance and an equal credit entry is made to Profit and Loss Summary.

The entry shown in italics transfers the balance in Profit and Loss Summary into the account Retained Earnings.

[2] An alternative account title is Income and Expense Summary. Another is Revenue and Expense Summary. In each case, the word summary is sometimes omitted.

EXHIBIT 3-6

DIAGRAM ILLUSTRATING CLOSING ENTRIES FOR BUCK & COMPANY

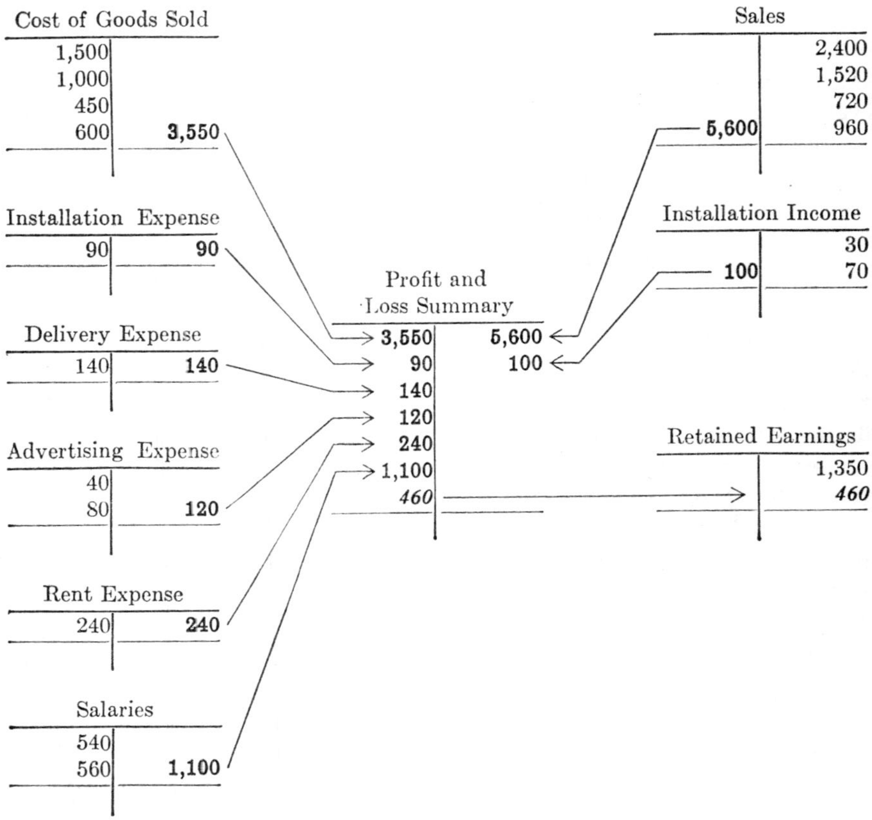

SUMMARY. Some of the important points of this chapter can be restated as follows:

1. The use of income and expense accounts makes it possible to secure a detailed analysis of the various sources of changes in Owners' Equity. These are temporary accounts; their balances are transferred to summary ownership accounts at the end of each accounting period.
2. Expense accounts are debited to show decreases in Owners' Equity. Income accounts are credited to show increases in Owners' Equity.
3. When a merchandise sale is made, two entries are necessary to show the full effect of the sale: One, at the selling price, involves a debit to Cash or to an account receivable and a credit to Sales. The other, at the cost price of the goods sold, involves a debit to Cost of Goods Sold and a credit to the inventory account that shows the cost of the merchandise in stock.

4. The profit and loss statement or income statement shows the amounts of the various incomes and expenses during an accounting period, combined in a way to give useful information to management and to show the profit or loss for the period.
5. A work sheet is an accountant's working paper that starts with a trial balance and concludes with the necessary figures for preparation of a profit and loss statement for the period and an end-of-period balance sheet.

DISCUSSION QUESTIONS

3-A. It is necessary to set up an accounting system for a college athletic association which handles the funds for all competitive sports. What expense accounts would you consider to be appropriate for such an organization? What income accounts? What purposes ought to be served by this accounting system?

3-B. A student has the campus concession for the sale of a certain soft drink. He purchases this beverage from the bottling company in returnable bottles on which he pays a deposit. At various places on the campus there are electrically refrigerated soft-drink dispensers which are owned by the bottling company and rented by the student. Suggest expense and income accounts that this student might use in his accounts for this business enterprise.

3-C. Explain the accounting treatment of a merchandise sale.

3-D. What purposes might be served by the simple work sheet in the Buck & Company example?

3-E. Why are closing entries required at the end of each accounting period?

3-F. Suppose, in the Buck & Company accounting system, that the accounting period was chosen to be a calendar year and the books were formally closed only at the end of each year. Assume that it is desired nevertheless to produce a balance sheet and an income statement each month. Devise a modified work sheet for use in preparing the monthly statements, and illustrate how it would work for the month of May, 19____, using assumed data as necessary. *Hint:* The balance in any income (or expense) account at the end of April, for example, would include all entries made to that account since the start of the year.

3-G. What would be the advantages and disadvantages of preparing financial statements quarterly instead of monthly for Buck & Company?

3-H. Why is it better to have income and expense accounts rather than to record all changes in Ownership in a single account such as the Profit and Loss account used in the Blaine Equipment Company example in Chap. 2?

3-J. List some expenses you might expect to be incurred in the operation of Buck & Company which would not properly belong in any of the six expense accounts illustrated.

3-K. Discuss the relative advantages of changing the title of the Rent Expense account in the Buck & Company system to Store Expense and including therein the costs of rent, utilities, and janitorial service. In contrast to this suggestion, discuss the pros and cons of having an account titled Telephone Expense in which this one expense would be isolated.

3-L. Contrast the information given by the balance sheet with the information given by the profit and loss statement. Discuss possible uses of the two statements by the management personnel of a business enterprise. Does one of these statements seem to you likely to be more useful than the other for managerial purposes? If so, which one and why?

PROBLEMS

Problem 3-1. The S-P-D Scooter Sales Company sells motor scooters. It also handles repairs for its customers, contracting this work to the Tinker Auto Service shop next door. Perpetual-inventory accounts are maintained for SDL (super de luxe) scooters and for DLX (de luxe) scooters. Opening balances on October 1 were as follows:

Account	*Debit*	*Credit*
Cash	$1,880	
Accounts Receivable	1,430	
SDL Scooters (8 @ $300)	2,400	
DLX Scooters (3 @ $240)	720	
Accounts Payable		$1,450
Capital Stock		4,000
Retained Earnings		980
Totals	$6,430	$6,430

Accounts receivable were:	
Baker Blueprint Co.	$ 800
V. McCoy	300
R. Nolan	200
W. Wonka	130
Total	$1,430
Accounts payable were:	
Scat Motor Co.	$1,250
Tinker Auto Service	200
Total	$1,450

Other accounts required are as follows:

Scooter Sales	Advertising Expense
Repair Service Income	Rent Expense
Cost of Goods Sold	Salaries
Repair Service Expense	Income and Expense Summary

Set up T accounts for the accounts listed, and enter the following October transactions directly in these accounts. Maintain the merchandise inventory accounts up to date at all times.

A. Enter the opening balances in their respective accounts.
B. Paid rent for store and store equipment to B. Star, $120.
C. Received $250 from Baker Blueprint Co., $50 from R. Nolan, and $100 from V. McCoy, a total of $400.
D. Sold 3 SDL scooters for cash, $450 each, a total of $1,350.
E. Paid Scat Motor Co. $1,000 on account.
F. Customers' bills for scooter repairs completed during October totaled $300. Of this, $250 was collected in cash; the other $50 was for repairs to a scooter owned by Baker Blueprint Co.

G. Sold a DLX scooter to E. Langford, $350. Langford paid $60 in cash and owes the balance of $290.
H. Received bill for $240 from Tinker Auto Service for October scooter repairs.
I. Purchased on credit from Scat Motor Co. 5 DLX scooters at $240 each, a total cost of $1,200.
J. Paid Tinker Auto Service bill for September, $200.
K. Sold 2 DLX scooters for cash, $350 each, a total of $700.
L. Received bill from *Weekly Clarion* for advertising, $30.
M. Paid salaries for the month, $650.

Determine and record the balance in each T account. Set up a six-column work sheet, and take a trial balance of the ledger. Complete the work sheet. Make the entries in the T accounts necessary to close the ledger. Identify these entries with the letter X. Prepare the new balance sheet and an income statement for October.

Problem 3-2. This problem is supplementary to problem 3-1 concerning the S-P-D Scooter Sales Company. Prepare a list of the individual accounts receivable (name of each customer and balance outstanding) as of October 31. Compute the total from this list, and check it against the end-of-month balance developed in the Accounts Receivable account in problem 3-1. Do the same for Accounts Payable.

Problem 3-3. The Zuni TV Shop sells TV sets and subcontracts installations and repairs to an amateur radio "ham," H. Coffee. Opening balances on May 1 were as follows:

Account	*Debit*	*Credit*
Cash	$ 950	
Accounts Receivable	670	
Portable TV sets (8 @ $100)	800	
Standard TV sets (6 @ $150)	900	
Color TV sets (2 @ $250)	500	
Used TV sets (at cost)	180	
Accounts Payable		$ 750
Capital Stock		3,000
Retained Earnings		250
Totals	$4,000	$4,000

Accounts receivable were:	
C. Chili	$130
El Morro Hotel	390
P. Marel	100
T. Martinez	50
Total	$670

Accounts payable were:	
H. Coffee	$120
Gallup Gazette	30
Horizon TV, Inc	600
Total	$750

Other accounts required are as follows:

Sales	Auto Expense
Repair Service Income	Rent Expense
Cost of Goods Sold	Salaries
Repair Service Expense	Telephone Expense
Advertising Expense	Income and Expense Summary

Set up T accounts for the accounts listed, and make entries for the following May transactions directly in these accounts. Maintain the merchandise inventory accounts up to date at all times. Open any additional asset or liability accounts you think necessary.

A. Enter the opening balances in their respective accounts.
B. Paid Gallup Realty Co. $150 rent for store space and utilities for May.
C. Billed the Tortilla Restaurant $400 for a new color TV set.
D. Purchased a rebuilt TV set from H. Coffee on credit, $40.
E. Collections on account were: C. Chili, $30; El Morro Hotel, $390; P. Marel, $10; a total of $430.
F. Accepted 4 new Navajo rugs in trade for a portable TV set. It is expected that these rugs can be sold for more than the cost of the TV set.
G. Paid *Gallup Gazette* in full, $30. Paid Horizon TV, Inc., $400 on account.
H. Billed El Morro Hotel $70 and the Sand Bar $20 for TV repairs in May.
I. Paid monthly telephone bill, $40. Of this amount, $10 was the monthly charge for the advertisement in the phone book.
J. Sold 5 portable TV sets at $170 each and 2 standard TV sets at $250 each, a total of $1,350. Received $1,320 in cash, allowing one customer $30 for a used TV set he traded in.
K. Traded the 4 rugs acquired in entry F to H. Coffee in full settlement of the balance due him, $160.
L. Purchased on credit from Horizon TV, Inc., 4 portable TV sets at $100 each, 1 standard TV set at $150, and 1 color TV set at $250, a total of $800.
M. Paid Radio Station KLUP $50 for spot commercials during May.
N. Sold 2 used TV sets for a total of $170 cash. These 2 sets were carried in inventory at a total cost of $110.
O. Received bill of $20 from H. Coffee for repairing the used TV set acquired in entry J. This set is now on display for sale at $80 with a 1-year guarantee.
P. Paid the manager, T. Sandervagon, $30 for auto mileage on company business in May.
Q. Received $180 from various cash customers for TV servicing in May.
R. Received bill from H. Coffee for repairs to customers' TV sets during May, $190.
S. Paid month's salaries, $750.

Determine and record the balance in each T account. Set up a six-column work sheet, and take a trial balance of the ledger. Complete the work sheet. Make the entries in the T accounts necessary to close the ledger. Prepare the new balance sheet and an income statement for May.

Problem 3-4. This problem is supplementary to problem 3-3 concerning the Zuni TV Shop. Prepare a list of the individual accounts receivable (name of each customer and balance outstanding) as of May 31. Compute the total from this list, and check it against the end-of-month balance developed in the Accounts Receivable account in problem 3-3. Do the same for Accounts Payable.

Problem 3-5. The Stitcher Shop sells sewing machines. Opening balances on June 1 were as follows:

Account	*Debit*	*Credit*
Cash	$1,000	
Accounts Receivable	1,600	
Standard Machines (10 @ $140)	1,400	
Portable Machines (15 @ $90)	1,350	
Used Machines (1 @ $70)	70	
Accounts Payable		$ 990
Capital Stock		3,000
Retained Earnings		1,430
Totals	$5,420	$5,420

Accounts payable were:

KXTV	$ 90
Webster & Co	900
Total	$990

Other accounts required are as follows:

Sales
Cost of Goods Sold
Advertising Expense
Income and Expense Summary
Salaries
Store Expense
Telephone Expense

Set up T accounts for the accounts listed, and enter the following June transactions directly in these accounts. Maintain the merchandise inventory accounts up to date at all times.

A. Enter the opening balances in their respective accounts.
B. Paid rent for store and store fixtures, $180.
C. Sold a new standard machine for $240. On this sale a used machine was turned in for $70 and the balance of $170 was paid in cash.
D. Paid Webster & Co. $750 on account; paid outstanding KXTV bill, $90.
E. Paid $80 for newspaper advertising which appeared in June.
F. Sales on credit were 2 standard machines at $240 each and 3 portable machines at $150 each, a total of $930.
G. Paid monthly utility bills for the store, $20.
H. Received payments on account from credit customers totaling $360.
I. Received bill from Wells Print Shop for advertising circulars, $30 (June expense).
J. Paid telephone bill, $40, of which $10 is monthly charge for advertisement in phone book.
K. Cash sales of sewing machines were 3 standard machines at $240 each, 8 portable machines at $150 each, and 1 used machine for $60, a total of $1,980.
L. Bought on credit from Webster & Co. 4 standard machines at $140 each and 10 portable machines at $90 each, a total of $1,460.
M. Paid month's salaries, $800.

Set up a six-column work sheet and take a trial balance of the ledger. Complete the work sheet. Make the entries necessary to close the ledger. Prepare the new balance sheet and an income statement for June.

Problem 3-6. The Quiet Lake Boat Co. operates the boathouse and rental concession owned by the Quiet Lake Lodge. It also sells canoes, rowboats, and sailboats and does boat repair work. The lodge owns the land, buildings, equipment, and rental boats. The boat company receives a commission on boat rental and is provided office, boat storage, and repair shop space at a nominal rent of $25 a month.

The opening balances of the boat company on July 1 were as follows:

Account		
Cash	$ 980	
Accounts Receivable	580	
Boat Contracts Receivable	180	
Repair Supplies Inventory	90	
Aluminum Rowboats (4 @ $120)	480	
Fiber glass Rowboats (2 @ $160)	320	
Canoes (2 @ $180)	360	
Used Boats and Canoes	280	
Hand Tools	150	
Accounts Payable		$ 640
Boat Rentals Payable		270
Capital Stock		1,500
Retained Earnings		1,010
Totals	$3,420	$3,420

Accounts receivable were:	
D. Early	$380
K. Lane	120
L. Mead	20
Quiet Lake Lodge	60
Total	$580
Boat contracts receivable were:	
A. Kennedy	$180
Accounts payable were:	
Northern Marine Supply	$ 40
Tippecanoe Co.	180
Waukeegan Boat Works	420
Total	$640

Other accounts required are as follows:

Boat Sales	Repair Service Expense
Repair Service Income	Auto Expense
Rental Commissions Earned	Office Expense
Cost of Boats Sold	Rent Expense
Income and Expense Summary	Salaries

Set up the T accounts indicated and make entries directly into the accounts for the month of July. Maintain the merchandise inventory accounts for canoes and rowboats up to date at all times.

A. Enter the opening balances in their respective accounts.
B. Paid Quiet Lake Lodge $25 rent for July.
C. Sold a used canoe for $140 cash. This canoe had been carried on the books at a cost value of $80.
D. Paid Quiet Lake Lodge $270, representing 75% of the boat rentals collected during June.
E. Received payments from credit customers totaling $280, as follows: Quiet Lake Lodge, $60; D. Early, $180; K. Lane, $40.
F. Sold on credit 2 canoes and 1 fiber glass rowboat to Quiet Lake Lodge for $780 and an aluminum rowboat to T. Moore for $180.
G. Paid Radford Welding Shop $20 for repairs to a metal rowboat owned by the lodge.
H. Received $60 from A. Kennedy as monthly payment on his 90-day contract for a canoe he purchased in June.
I. Payments to vendors on account were as follows: Northern Marine Supply, $40; Tippecanoe Co., $180; Waukeegan Boat Works, $300; a total of $520.
J. Sold a new sailboat to R. Swalm for $450. Swalm paid $150 cash; the balance is payable in three monthly installments of $100 each. Re

ceived an invoice for $300 from Waukeegan Boat Works for this sailboat.

K. Bought a used sailboat for $120 cash.

L. Sold some boat paint and thinner for $10 cash. The cost value was $6.

M. Paid Lake City Stationers $12 for miscellaneous office supplies. Paid Pine Tree Store $15 for various small tools.

N. Invoices for boats purchased in July totaled $1,120: Waukeegan Boat Works, 2 aluminum rowboats at $120 each and 1 fiber glass rowboat at $160; Tippecanoe Co., 4 canoes at $180 each.

P. Sold for cash 1 canoe at $270 and 2 aluminum rowboats at $180 each, a total of $630.

Q. Billed Quiet Lake Lodge $55 and L. Mead $25 for boat and canoe repairs in July.

R. Purchases of repair supplies on credit from Northern Marine Supply during July totaled $60. The cost of repair supplies used during July was estimated to be a total of $70.

S. Received $125 from various cash customers for boat repairs in July.

T. Paid manager B. McNeil $43 as reimbursement of boat company expenses incurred by him during July. The breakdown was as follows: auto mileage, $15; repair supplies purchased, $10; office supplies and expense, $18.

U. Received $420 cash from boat rentals during July; $315 of this total must be paid to the lodge by August 10; the remaining $105 is the boat company's commission.

V. Paid salaries for the month, $750.

Determine and record the balance in each T account. Set up a six-column work sheet, and take a trial balance of the ledger. Complete the work sheet. Make the entries in the T accounts necessary to close the ledger. Prepare the new balance sheet and an income statement for July.

4/ AN EXAMPLE INTRODUCING END-OF-PERIOD ENTRIES

The example in this chapter is the third in a series of three examples aimed at introducing accounting fundamentals prior to a consideration of formal accounting procedure and system. The important new topic in this chapter is the matter of making necessary entries that have not been initiated automatically by the origin or the receipt of a document in the course of routine procedures.

In the preceding examples the trial balance provided all the information necessary for the preparation of the financial statement. Each of the events for which an entry was made involved a transaction with another business entity or individual. For each of these transactions there was an *original evidence* document such as an invoice, a check stub or voucher, a charge sale slip, or a cash register tape. In these artifically simple examples the entries based on these source documents were sufficient to give appropriate valuations for the assets and liabilities for the balance sheet and to find the profit or loss for the period.

In this particular respect, these examples were unrealistic. In addition to entries for *transactions,* it is nearly always necessary to make end-of-period entries which are *recognitions* of revelant matters not already shown in the accounts as the result of current-period transactions. These end-of-period entries are commonly called *adjusting entries.*[1]

Most of the necessary end-of-period entries relate to transactions that occurred during previous accounting periods or are expected to occur in future accounting periods. There are many kinds of transactions that may occur in prior or subsequent accounting periods that properly should affect the current-period income statement and the balance sheet at the end of the current period. In some cases the effect on the current

[1] This is a technical accounting term to which non-accountants often attach incorrect connotations. "Adjusting" does not imply arbitrary manipulation. Nor should it be interpreted as implying that end-of-period entries are of less importance than "original" transaction entries.

period accounting is determined by the passage of time; in other cases the effect depends on events occurring in the current period (e.g., sales consummated). Some examples of adjusting entries for such matters are illustrated in this chapter.

The general category *adjusting entries* includes also entries that *could* be initiated by during-the-period events, such as sale transactions, but for reasons of economy and convenience are handled by one summary entry at the end of the period. An important example of this is the treatment of merchandise purchases and the determination of cost of goods sold in the common situation where perpetual-inventory accounts are not maintained.

Not uncommonly, special-purpose adjusting entries are required to correct mistakes or to modify earlier accounting decisions in the light of new information available. One simple entry of this kind is included in the following example.

A significant point in connection with end-of-period entries is that they are an important part of the business of properly sorting and apportioning incomes and expenses into arbitrary blocks of time (accounting periods) in a systematic and meaningful way. In most cases this is the main purpose of the entry.

CENTRAL HARDWARE CO. EXAMPLE. In this example the business entity is a small corporation engaged in the retail sale of hardware and homeware. For simplification, Central Hardware has no fixed assets; it rents its store and equipment. It extends credit only to business establishments.

The accounts used in the 1-month cycle of this example that have not been introduced in previous examples are as follows:

Notes Receivable	Sales Returns and Allowances
Accrued Interest Receivable	Purchases
Prepaid Insurance	Telephone Expense
Prepaid Advertising	Insurance Expense
Accrued Taxes Payable	Property Tax Expense
Notes Payable	Interest Expense
Accrued Interest Payable	Interest Income

Exhibit 4-1 presents the opening balances and the July transactions. For many of the repetitive transactions, such as sales and purchases, the data given are summaries of numerous similar transactions during the month. Discussion of special journal techniques for developing such totals is deferred until Chap. 6.

Exhibit 4-2 is a skeleton ledger of T accounts showing the entries for the July transactions. Accounts not needed for transaction entries are omitted from this exhibit. End-of-period adjusting and closing entries are presented later in the chapter and are shown in Exhibit 4-7. The following explanations and comments are limited to the entries for those transactions that introduce some new topic.

EXHIBIT 4-1

TRANSACTIONS FOR CENTRAL HARDWARE DURING JULY, 19___

A. The opening balances on July 1 are as follows:

Account	*Debit*	*Credit*
Cash	$ 540	
Accounts Receivable	1,850	
Merchandise Inventory	19,600	
Prepaid Insurance	210	
Accounts Payable		$ 3,950
Capital Stock		12,000
Earned Surplus		6,250
Totals	$22,200	$22,200

Accounts receivable were:	
Micro Mfg. Co	$ 460
See Cabinet Shop	120
Doe Construction Co	380
Tinker Auto Service	50
N. D. West Co	90
Flasch Electric Co	750
Total	$1,850

B. Paid rents for store and equipment, $320.
C. Borrowed $2,000 from the Commerce Trust Co. on a 90-day note at 6% interest.
D. Paid *Morning Herald* $210 for advertising.
E. Sales on credit during the month totaled $1,670. (The breakdown by customer was Micro Mfg. Co., $290; See Cabinet Shop, $130; Doe Construction Co., $1,050; Tinker Auto Service, $70; N. D. West Co., $90; Flasch Electric Co., $40.)
F. Received invoices for merchandise purchased during the month totaling $4,050.
G. Micro Mfg. Co. was allowed $20 credit on an order of brass fittings. (They had asked for bright plated fittings and received unplated ones.)
H. Cash customers were refunded $190 cash for merchandise returned during the month. (This merchandise was all put back into sales stock.)
I. Paid monthly telephone bill, $41, of which $12 is monthly charge for advertisement in phone book.
J. Accepted a promissory note for $750 from Flasch Electric Co. in settlement of their July 1 open account balance. This note is due in 6 months with interest at 8% per annum.
K. Collections from credit customers during the month totaled $870. (The breakdown by customer was Micro Mfg. Co., $460; See Cabinet Shop, $120; Doe Construction Co., $200; N. D. West Co., $90.)
L. Paid $5,100 to merchandise suppliers and other creditors.
M. Cash sales during the month were $5,030.
N. Paid salaries for the month, $1,600.
O. Other unpaid bills on hand at the end of July were Downtown Merchants' Assn., $40 for share of "July Bargain Days" street banner cost; National Service Insurance Co., $72 for renewal of comprehensive liability insurance for 1 year starting July 1.

Entry C. Borrowed $2,000 from the Commerce Trust Co. on a 90-day note at 6% interest. There has been an increase in the asset Cash, which is then debited $2,000. There has been a corresponding increase in liabilities. Because of the 90-day term of the note, this obligation is not properly shown as a current account payable. The appropriate entry is an increase (credit) in the liability account titled Notes Payable.

At this time there is no interest accrued on the note, and therefore no entry is required in this connection. However, the information about the interest rate is recorded for future use.

EXHIBIT 4-2
T-ACCOUNT LEDGER SHOWING ENTRIES IN ACCOUNTS OF CENTRAL HARDWARE FOR JULY, 19___

Cash

Debit	Credit
A 540	320 B
C 2,000	210 D
K 870	190 H
M 5,030	41 I
	5,100 L
	1,600 N
8,440	*7,461*

Notes Receivable

Debit	Credit
J 750	

Merchandise Inventory

Debit	Credit
A 19,600	

Prepaid Insurance

Debit	Credit
A 210	
O 72	
282	

Accounts Receivable

Debit	Credit
A 1,850	20 G
E 1,670	750 J
	870 K
3,520	*1,640*

Accounts Payable

Debit	Credit
L 5,100	3,950 A
	4,050 F
	112 O
5,100	*8,112*

Notes Payable

Debit	Credit
	2,000 C

Capital Stock

Debit	Credit
	12,000 A

Earned Surplus

Debit	Credit
	6,250 A

Sales

Debit	Credit
	1,670 E
	5,030 M
	6,700

Sales Returns and Allowances

Debit	Credit
G 20	
H 190	

Purchases

Debit	Credit
F 4,050	

Advertising Expense

Debit	Credit
D 210	
I 12	
O 40	
262	

Telephone Expense

Debit	Credit
I 29	

Rent Expense

Debit	Credit
B 320	

Salaries

Debit	Credit
N 1,600	

Entry E. Sales on credit during the month totaled $1,670. The appropriate entry for this is to debit Accounts Receivable $1,670 and credit the same amount to Sales. This records in the ledger the increase in Accounts Receivable and the increase in Ownership associated with the selling price side of the credit sale transactions.

Note that, although a lump-sum entry for all such transactions is satisfactory for Central Hardware's financial accounting purposes, detailed information by customer and by transaction would be necessary for the proper conduct of business relations with the various customers. The Central Hardware example is expanded in Chap. 5 to introduce the subsidiary ledger technique of handling such matters.

ENTRIES TO RECORD SALES WHERE NO PREPETUAL INVENTORY ACCOUNTS ARE USED. In Chap. 3 we noted that each sale involved an increase in an asset of cash or an account receivable from a customer and a decrease in one or more assets of merchandise on hand. Where merchandise has been sold at a higher price than was paid for it, there is a net increase in assets which results in an increase in Ownership. We found that, instead of recording this profit in one income account, Profit on Sales, it was desirable to set up an income account, Sales, and an expense account, Cost of Goods Sold; the increase in Ownership resulting from the sale was the difference between the amounts entered in these two accounts. And we found it convenient to think of two entries as being required for each sale—an entry at the selling price debiting Cash or an account receivable and crediting Sales and an entry at cost debiting Cost of Goods Sold and crediting a perpetual-inventory account (such as the Washing Machines account in Chap. 3).

Clearly, it is necessary to record the selling price side of each sale transaction at the time of the sale; the enterprise needs to know at all times the amount due from each customer (credit sale) and also its bank balance (cash sale). In contrast, the cost side of these sale transactions is an internal matter, not affecting financial relations with outside parties. The purpose of the entry at the cost price is to match expense (cost of merchandise sold) with the sales income for the period and to correct the balance-sheet value of the asset Merchandise Inventory. In other words, the cost entry is necessary to permit the preparation of a balance sheet and an income statement.

Balance sheets and income statements are prepared only at stated intervals, usually annually, semiannually, quarterly, or possibly monthly. No obstacle to the preparation of these financial statements is created if the policy is adopted of entering the cost of goods sold only at these same stated intervals. Under this policy, the cost of goods sold is computed from inventories of the merchandise on hand at the start and at the end of each accounting period and from a record of the net purchases during the period. This calculation gives a figure for the total cost of the goods sold during a period; no information is shown in the accounts regarding the cost of the goods sold in each individual sale.

In retail merchandising enterprises that make a large number of small sales, it is obvious that the determination of the cost of goods sold for each sale will involve considerable expense for clerical labor. For this reason, many such enterprises follow the practice of making no record at the cost price for individual sale transactions. The entry recording cost of goods sold is an adjusting entry made at the end of each accounting period. This type of entry is illustrated later in this chapter.

Entry F. Received invoices for merchandise purchased during the month totaling $4,050. Clearly, Accounts Payable should receive a credit showing the increase in liabilities. At first glance it might seem that the account to be debited is Merchandise Inventory—on the premise that this asset has been increased. However, this is not the common practice in systems where perpetual-inventory accounts are not used. One reason is that the account Merchandise Inventory contains an end-of-period figure based on a physical count and pricing of items on hand whereas the figures for merchandise purchased during the period are based on vendors' invoices. For this and other reasons, the debits for merchandise purchases are collected in a "temporary" account titled Purchases, as illustrated in Exhibit 4-2.

Entry G. Micro Mfg. Co. was allowed $20 credit on an order of brass fittings. (They had asked for bright-plated fittings and received unplated ones.) To settle this matter Micro Mfg. Co. retained the fittings but was allowed a price reduction of $20. This might properly be viewed as a decrease in Ownership resulting from the reduction in income previously entered in the sales account. Hence a debit of $20 to Sales would appear to be appropriate.

However, the usefulness to management of the financial statements taken from the accounts can be increased if there is a separate record of sales returns and allowances. It is important to management to know whether such returns and allowances are large or small in relation to total sales and also to know whether they are increasing or decreasing. This needed information would be concealed if returns and allowances were entered directly as debits to Sales. For this reason the debit is made to an account titled Sales Returns and Allowances. The $20 credit is to Accounts Receivable.

A similar account, used in connection with purchases, is Purchase Returns and Allowances. The use of this account is not illustrated here.

Entry H. Cash customers were refunded $190 cash for merchandise returned during the month. (This merchandise was all put back into sales stock.) This entry is similar to entry G to the extent that these are both negative sale transactions. However, in this case the asset Cash is decreased rather than the asset Accounts Receivable. Note that no record is made at the cost price at the time the merchandise is returned. This will automatically be taken into account in the calculation of the end-of-period entry recording the cost of goods sold.

Entry I. Paid monthly telephone bill, $41, of which $12 is the monthly charge for advertisement in phone book. The appropriate entry for this is a credit of $41 to the account Cash, offset by two debits: one for $12 to Advertising Expense and the other for $29 to Telephone Expense. This is an example of a compound entry. The $41 decrease in Ownership is split into two parts in accordance with previous decisions made about the classification of expenses in this system.

Entry J. Accepted a promissory note for $750 from Flasch Electric Co. in settlement of their July 1 open account balance. This note is due in 6 months with interest at 8% per annum. A first impression might be that no entry in the accounts is needed for this transaction. Before the transaction, Flasch Electric owed $750 to Central Hardware; after signing the note, Flasch Electric still owes $750. Nevertheless, the form of the obligation has been changed. From the viewpoint of Central Hardware, this asset is no longer a current account receivable item and is now properly classified as a note receivable. One asset, Accounts Receivable, has been decreased, and another asset, Notes Receivable, has been increased. We therefore debit Notes Receivable and credit Accounts Receivable, $750.

PROMISSORY NOTES. A promissory note is an unconditional written promise by one person, the *maker*, to pay a definite money amount to another person, the *payee*, or to his order at a fixed or determinable future time. Promissory notes are *negotiable instruments.* Legal title to them can readily be transferred. Ordinarily the purchaser of a negotiable instrument can collect from the maker even though the maker may have certain legal defenses that would make it impossible for the payee to collect.

Notes are nearly always used in connection with the loan of funds, as in entry C. They are also frequently used in cases such as entry J where credit is extended for longer than the normal credit period. In such cases, as in entry J, the creditor may decide to charge interest in addition to the regular sale price. In the maker's books, notes are usually listed under the account title Notes Payable and in the payee's books under the title Notes Receivable. It is customary for the amounts listed under these account titles to be limited to the face amount of the notes in question. Any interest due that is in addition to the face amount is listed under a separate account title, as illustrated in the discussion of adjusting entries later in this chapter.

Entries K, L, and M. These entries concern collections from credit customers, amounts paid on account to merchandise suppliers, and cash sales. In each case, numerous transactions that are alike in nature are recorded in the ledger by a single entry. Discussion of methods for obtaining the totals for such entries and for maintaining up-to-date detailed records of the financial relations with customers and suppliers is deferred until Chap. 6.

Entry O. Other unpaid bills on hand at the end of July were Downtown Merchants' Assn., $40 for share of "July Bargain Days" street banner cost; National Service Insurance Co., $72 for renewal of comprehensive liability insurance for 1 year starting July 1. The liability connected with these two invoices should be reflected in the July 31 balance sheet in the value shown for Accounts Payable. Also, both these invoices affect current period expense, although in different ways. The Merchants' Association bill for $40 clearly represents an expense associated with the current accounting period. Therefore, $40 is debited to Advertising Expense. The $72 invoice from National Service Insurance Co. is somewhat different. This is the premium for an insurance policy which will provide certain liability insurance protection for a whole year. It is appropriate to think of the insurance policy as an *asset* that will be used up little by little as time goes on. Therefore the asset account Prepaid Insurance is debited with the amount of its increase, $72. The matter of spreading the cost of the insurance policy over the 12 accounting periods in which it is effective is treated later in this chapter in the explanation of end-of-period adjusting entries.

ADJUSTING ENTRIES FOR CENTRAL HARDWARE CO. EXAMPLE. Exhibit 4-2 shows the condition of the ledger after all the entries for the month's external transactions have been made (entries A to O). The trial balance obtainable from the ledger at this point does not give enough information for the preparation of satisfactory financial statements. Entries must be made for a number of end-of-period recognitions of changes in assets, liabilities, and ownership that have taken place during the accounting period but which have not yet been recorded in the books.

In the remainder of this chapter, seven adjusting entries are introduced and discussed and then presented in T-account form in Exhibit 4-7. Each of these seven was selected to illustrate the need for a different type of end-of-period entry. A more extensive discussion of adjusting entries is given in Chap. 7.

Adjusting entry a. No invoice has been received for a trailer-mounted radial saw delivered and billed to Doe Construction Co. in July. The cost is expected to be $720, including freight. The sales-price side of this transaction between Central Hardware and Doe Construction Co. was included in entry E, crediting Sales and debiting Accounts Receivable. However, because Central Hardware did not receive the vendor's invoice in time, the cost of the saw was not included in entry F, which recorded the cost of merchandise purchased during the month. Someone had to think of this matter and initiate an entry in order for this cost to be included in the cost of goods sold for July and for the liability to be reflected in the balance sheet. The appropriate entry, of course, is like that for entry F: a debit (of $720) to Purchases and a credit (of $720) to Accounts Payable.

Adjusting entry b. The merchandise inventory at the end of July is valued (at cost) at $20,250. This $20,250 figure is based on a physical count of the merchandise on hand at the end of July. Each item on the inventory list was priced at cost. (The various interpretations of "cost" are discussed in Chap. 7, as well as alternative methods of inventory valuation.) This new inventory figure makes possible a calculation of the cost of goods sold for the month as follows:

Cost of merchandise inventory July 1	$19,600
Cost of merchandise purchases during July	4,770
Cost of all merchandise available for sale during July	$24,370
Less: Cost of merchandise unsold at end of July	20,250
Cost of merchandise sold during July	$ 4,120

Using this information, an appropriate compound entry can be constructed with the following reasoning:

1. Ownership has been decreased $4,120; this amount should be debited to an expense account, Cost of Goods Sold.
2. The merchandise inventory valuation should be changed from $19,600 to $20,250. This can be accomplished by the usual accounting practice of crediting the account Merchandise Inventory with the opening inventory figure ($19,600) and debiting it with the closing inventory figure ($20,250).
3. The balance in the temporary account Purchases should be closed out. The merchandise purchased during the period either has been sold or is incorporated in the new end-of-period inventory. To close this account it must be credited $4,770.
4. Check: Is the sum of the debits equal to the sum of the credits?

Account	*Debit*	*Credit*
Cost of Goods Sold	$ 4,120	
Merchandise Inventory	20,250	$19,600
Purchases		4,770
Totals	$24,370	$24,370

This entry appears in the T accounts (Exhibit 4-7) as follows:

Merchandise Inventory

	Debit	Credit	
A	19,600	**19,600**	b
b	**20,250**		

Cost of Goods Sold

	Debit	Credit
b	**4,120**	

Purchases

	Debit	Credit	
F	4,050		
a	720	**4,770**	b

An important observation here is the *derived* nature of the cost of goods sold figure developed in a system in which perpetual-inventory accounts are not maintained. The astute student will notice that any error in the physical count or pricing of the inventory items at the end of an accounting period will result in (1) an incorrect valuation of merchandise inventory on the balance sheet and (2) an incorrect figure for cost of goods sold for the accounting period. Any error in inventory valuation results in an equal and opposite error in the cost of goods sold for the period terminated and a countererror in the cost of goods sold for the period following. Also, of course, any loss by theft or other unrecorded removal of goods from stock will be absorbed into the cost of goods sold. In effect, the value of goods not otherwise accounted for is taken to be the cost of goods sold. This is a first hint at a point that is important for a non-accountant to understand: Accounting figures may be somewhat less accurate and reliable than might be inferred from the fact they are usually reported to the nearest cent.

Another equally important point illustrated here is the conflict between improved accuracy and increased accounting costs. If a perpetual-inventory record were maintained for each inventory item, each delivery of merchandise to a customer could be priced out of inventory at cost and the sum of all such transactions would provide directly a figure for cost of goods sold. It would also be possible to obtain a total for the value of remaining inventory directly from the perpetual-inventory records. This, in turn, could be checked periodically by physically counting actual inventory on hand. However, for retail merchandising businesses, the concensus of accountants is that the expense involved in the perpetual-inventory record approach is not justified by the improved accuracy of the financial statements and the potential benefits of being able to detect significant amounts of inventory theft.

It is also generally too expensive to take a complete and accurate physical inventory at frequent intervals; for monthly and quarterly statements, cost of goods sold is usually estimated as a function of sales. In this respect, the examples and problems that are based on a 1-month accounting period and presume that inventories are counted and "priced out" each month are somewhat unrealistic.

PURCHASE RETURNS AND ALLOWANCES. If any merchandise purchased during the accounting period (or on hand at the start of the period) is returned to the vendor for credit, this must be taken into acount in computing the cost of goods sold for the period. Clearly, such a transaction is the reverse of a purchase and could be handled in the accounts by crediting Purchases and debiting Accounts Payable. However, it is common practice to provide a separate account entitled Purchase Returns and Allowances in which these "negative purchases" are recorded. The word *allowances* in the title of this account indicates it is used also in the case of a vendor allowing credit even though the merchandise involved is not returned. Such an allowance is, in effect, a price reduction for goods previously purchased. Whether the goods involved were returned or not, and whether the goods were purchased in the current period or a prior one, the usual procedure is to include the credit in the calculation of cost of goods sold for the current period.

FREIGHT ON PURCHASES. The cost of transporation of merchandise purchased is usually considered to be part of the cost of the merchandise. Therefore, this cost of "freight-in" is included in the valuation of merchandise inventory and in the cost of goods sold.

If freight charges are paid by the vendor and included in his price, the question of how to handle this cost does not come up. It is automatically included in the debit to Purchases. For cases in which the freight is paid by the purchaser, it is very common to collect the debits in an account called Freight In. The balance in this account at the end of the period is included with the total from the Purchases account in the calculation of cost of goods sold.

Adjusting entry c. The July 1 balance in the Prepaid Insurance account represents the value (at cost) of the remaining 21 months' coverage under a 3-year fire insurance policy on merchandise stock. Also, 1 month's liability insurance has expired. This illustrates the accrual of an expense with the passage of time—in this case insurance expense. An entry should be made recognizing that 1 month's coverage under each of the two policies has expired. The asset Prepaid Insurance should therefore be decreased, and the corresponding decrease in Ownership should be shown by a charge to Insurance Expense for the current accounting period. The amounts involved are $10 for the fire insurance policy and $6 for the liability insurance policy, a total of $16. Thus $16 is credited to Prepaid Insurance and debited to Insurance Expense.

Adjusting entry d. The entry for the $210 paid to the *Morning Herald* was incorrect. The advertising will appear in July, August, and September, and should be allocated one-third to each of these months. The effect of transaction entry D was to show a decrease in Ownership (an expense) in the month of July of $210. It is now recognized that two-thirds of this amount, $140, properly should be viewed as an asset—the right to have the paid-for advertising appear in August and September. Only $70 should be viewed as July expense. The appropriate adjusting entry, therefore, is to credit Advertising Expense $140 and debit the asset account Prepaid Advertising $140.

Note that the entries which must be made at the end of August and the end of September will be in reverse: crediting Prepaid Advertising and debiting Advertising Expense. A more consistent treatment would have been to recognize the multiperiod nature of this expenditure in the first place and, in entry D, debit the entire $210 to Prepaid Advertising. Then the entries at the end of July, August, and September would all be the same, and there would be less chance of a possible mistake. Viewed in this way, entry **d** as shown in Exhibit 4-7 is a corrective rather than an accrual entry.

Adjusting entry e. Accrued interest on the note receivable is $5. Because 1 month has elapsed, Flasch Electric now owes Central Hardware $5 in addition to the face value of the note. An entry should be made recognizing the increase in an asset, Accrued Interest Receivable, and the consequent increase in Ownership. Thus, Accrued Interest Receivable is debited $5, and Interest Income is credited $5.

Adjusting entry f. Accrued interest on the note payable is $10. Here again, due to the passage of time, there has been a change which should be recognized and recorded. A liability has been increased, and Ownership has decreased. Therefore, the liability account Accrued Interest Payable is credited $10 and the ownership account Interest Expense is debited $10.

It is interesting to look ahead to October 1 when the note must be paid off. At that time a disbursement of $2,030 will be required. Meanwhile, accrual entries at the end of August and September will have charged $10 to Interest Expense for August and $10 for September, and the balance in Accrued Interest Payable will have been increased to $30. The entry when the note is paid will be a credit to Cash of $2,030, a debit to Notes Payable of $2,000, and a debit to Accrued Interest Payable of $30. The effect of the three end-of-month accrual entries will have been to allocate properly the $30 interest expense among the three accounting periods, $10 to each.

Adjusting entry g. The estimated property tax on merchandise stock for the year starting July 1 is $300. Although the tax does not have to be paid until November 30, a share of this annual cost properly should be charged to July expense. Also, of course, the obligation to pay these taxes should be reflected in a liability account on the balance sheet at the end of July. An appropriate entry, as shown in Exhibit 4-7, is to debit one-twelfth of the total estimated tax, $25, to Property Tax Expense and credit the same amount to Accrued Taxes Payable.

An alternative view of this matter is to say that, as of July 1, the entire amount of the tax has become a legal liability of the company regardless of future events. This would lead to an entry crediting Accrued Taxes Payable $300 and debiting an account titled Prepaid Property Taxes $300 and another entry immediately then crediting Prepaid Property Taxes $25 and debiting Property Tax Expense $25 for July. In T-account form, this alternative treatment would appear as follows:

Prepaid Property Taxes		Accrued Taxes Payable		Property Tax Expense	
300	25		300	25	

RECORDING ADJUSTING ENTRIES ON A WORK SHEET. Like the 6-column work sheet in Chap. 3, the 10-column work sheet in Exhibit 4-3 provides the necessary figures for the income statement and the new balance sheet. Two of the four new columns contain the ad-

EXHIBIT 4-3

WORK SHEET FOR CENTRAL HARDWARE, JULY 31, 19___

Account	Trial balance		Adjustments		Adjusted trial balance		Income statement		Balance sheet	
	Dr.	Cr.	Dr.	Cr.	Dr.	Cr.	Dr.	Cr.	Dr.	Cr.
Cash	979				979				979	
Accounts Receivable	1,880				1,880				1,880	
Notes Receivable	750				750				750	
Accrued Interest Receivable			(e) 5		5				5	
Merchandise Inventory	19,600		(b) 20,250	19,600 (b)	20,250				20,250	
Prepaid Insurance	282			16 (c)	266				266	
Prepaid Advertising			(d) 140		140				140	
Accounts Payable		3,012		720 (a)		3,732				3,732
Accrued Taxes Payable				25 (g)		25				25
Notes Payable		2,000				2,000				2,000
Accrued Interest Payable				10 (f)		10				10
Capital Stock		12,000				12,000				12,000
Earned Surplus		6,250				6,250				6,250
Sales		6,700				6,700		6,700		
Sales Returns & Allowances	210				210		210			
Purchases	4,050		(a) 720	4,770 (b)						
Cost of Goods Sold			(b) 4,120		4,120		4,120			
Advertising Expense	262			140 (d)	122		122			
Telephone Expense	29				29		29			
Insurance Expense			(c) 16		16		16			
Rent Expense	320				320		320			
Property Tax Expense			(g) 25		25		25			
Interest Expense			(f) 10		10		10			
Salaries	1,600				1,600		1,600			
Interest Income				5 (e)		5		5		
Totals	29,962	29,962	25,286	25,286	30,722	30,722	6,452	6,705	24,270	24,017
Profit							253			253
							6,705	6,705	24,270	24,270

justing entries; the other two contain an adjusted trial balance. The following statements explain the mechanical aspects of a 10-column work sheet.

1. Each line on the work sheet corresponds to an account.
2. The debit or credit figure shown on any line in the columns headed Trial Balance is the balance in that account at the end of the period

after all external transactions have been entered in the ledger but before any adjusting entries have been made.

3. The debit or credit figure shown on a line in the columns headed Adjustments is the debit or credit to that account by reason of an adjusting entry.
4. The adjusted trial balance combines the figures from the Trial Balance and the Adjustments columns. Each line shows the net debit or credit balance in its respective account after adjusting entries have been made. (This adjusted trial balance is useful in student work, particularly in the early stages of learning about work sheets. It is often omitted as a short cut on accountants' work sheets; where it is omitted, 8 columns do the work of the 10 shown in Exhibit 4-3.)
5. Although the totals for the Adjustments columns are not an essential part of the work sheet, they occasionally disclose errors in entering figures in these columns. Whenever the debit and credit totals in the adjusted trial balance fail to agree, some error has been made which should be corrected before completing the work sheet.
6. The balances in the income and expense accounts are transferred from the adjusted trial balance to the columns headed Income Statement. The balances in the asset, liability, and summary ownership accounts are transferred to the columns headed Balance Sheet. This is merely a process of sorting out the figures for the income statement from the figures for the balance sheet.
7. If the credit total exceeds the debit total in the columns headed Income Statement, the difference is the profit. These columns are balanced by adding this profit to the debit total. The columns headed Balance Sheet are balanced by adding the profit to the credit total.
8. If the debit total exceeds the credit total in the columns headed Income Statement, the difference is the loss. These columns are balanced by adding this loss to the credit total. The columns headed Balance Sheet are balanced by adding the loss to the debit total.

Note that, on the "profit" line of the work sheet in Exhibit 4-3, the figure $253 appears as a debit in the income statement section and as a credit in the balance sheet section. On the other hand, the figures transferred from the adjusted trial balance section to the income statement and balance sheet sections are simply "copied over"—debits remaining debits and credits remaining credits. The reason for this will become clear by comparing the figures in the income statement section of the work sheet with those in the T account titled Income and Expense Summary in Exhibit 4-7. Also, compare the "entry" on the profit line of the work sheet with entry j as illustrated in Exhibit 4-7.

As already pointed out, the information needed for a formal balance sheet and income statement can be obtained quickly by means of

EXHIBIT 4-4
CENTRAL HARDWARE CO.
INCOME STATEMENT FOR THE MONTH OF JULY, 19___

Sales		$6,700
Less: Sales Returns & Allowances		210
Net Sales		$6,490
Less: Cost of Goods Sold:		
Inventory July 1	$19,600	
Purchases	4,770	
Total	$24,370	
Less: Inventory July 31	20,250	
Cost of Goods Sold		4,120
Gross Profit on Sales		$2,370
Less: Operating Expenses:		
Salaries	$ 1,600	
Rent Expense	320	
Advertising Expense	122	
Telephone Expense	29	
Insurance Expense	16	
Property Tax Expense	25	
Total Operating Expense		2,112
Net Operating Income		$ 258
Add: Interest Income		5
Total Operating and Other Income		$ 263
Less: Interest Expense		10
Net Income for July		$ 253

EXHIBIT 4-5
CENTRAL HARDWARE CO.
BALANCE SHEET, JULY 31, 19___

Assets			*Liabilities and Stockholders' Equity*		
Current Assets:			Liabilities:		
Cash	$ 979		Accounts Payable	$ 3,732	
Accounts Receivable	1,880		Accrued Taxes	25	
Notes Receivable	750		Notes Payable	2,000	
Accrued Interest Receivable	5		Accrued Interest	10	
Merchandise Inventory	20,250		Total Liabilities		$ 5,767
Total Current Assets		$23,864			
Prepaid Expenses:			Stockholders' Equity:		
Prepaid Insurance	$ 226		Capital Stock	$12,000	
Prepaid Advertising	140		Earned Surplus	6,503	
Total Prepaid Expense		406	Stockholders' Equity		18,503
Total		$24,270	Total		$24,270

a work sheet. As the work sheet can be completed before the adjusting and closing entries are made in the books, its use avoids delays in presenting these financial statements to management. Even though the work sheet is not part of the formal accounts, all work sheets should be preserved. They are generally required by outside auditors in any examination of the books, not only in audits by public accounting firms but also in those made by government tax examiners in connection with income tax returns.

INCOME STATEMENT. Exhibit 4-4 is an income statement (profit and loss statement) for Central Hardware for the month of July. Note that all the information for this statement is obtainable directly from the work sheet. This statement and the one in Exhibit 3-4, for Buck & Company, illustrate a rather traditional arrangement and presentation of the information. Other arrangements which have become quite popular in recent years are illustrated later on in the book.

With respect to content of the income statement, it should be kept in mind that Central Hardware is a small business and that its operations are very simple. Therefore, it is practical to show in the income statement considerable detail of interest to management, such as the derivation of cost of goods sold and the listing of all expenses. For a more complex business, these things are often shown as separate schedules. Another point of detail that is usually omitted in the published income statement for a complex business is the development of net sales as gross sales minus returns and allowances. Such detailed sets of information as these are of considerable interest to the management of the enterprise but are usually considered to be not materially important to the readers of published statements.

BALANCE SHEET. Exhibit 4-5 presents a balance sheet for Central Hardware as of July 31. With respect to arrangement and content this statement is also traditional. Some of the innovations which are becoming quite popular are illustrated in later chapters, particularly Chap. 8.

In the Central Hardware balance sheet, note that the assets and the liabilities are both listed in the general sequence of their liquidity. This is the common practice.

Prepaid insurance and prepaid advertising are shown in this balance sheet under the heading Prepaid Expenses. An alternative accounting term for these assets is *deferred charges.*

CLOSING ENTRIES. The end-of-period entries *h, i,* and *j,* described in Exhibit 4-6 and illustrated in Exhibit 4-7, are the closing entries necessary to put the ledger in shape to start a new accounting period. Note that, after these entries have been made, all the "temporary" accounts have zero balances. These accounts have been closed into "permanent" (balance sheet) accounts. The only accounts showing balances carried forward into August are the asset and liability accounts and the summary ownership accounts Capital Stock and Earned Surplus.

EXHIBIT 4-6

ADJUSTING AND CLOSING ENTRIES FOR CENTRAL HARDWARE

Adjusting entries:

a. No invoice has been received for a trailer-mounted radial saw delivered and billed to Doe Construction Co. in July. The cost is expected to be $720 including freight.

b. The Merchandise inventory at the end of July is valued (at cost) at $20,250.

c. The July 1 balance in the Prepaid Insurance account represents the value (at cost) of the remaining 21 months' coverage under a 3-year fire insurance policy on merchandise stock. Also, 1 month's liability insurance has expired.

d. The entry for the $210 paid to the *Morning Herald* was incorrect. The advertising will appear in July, August, and September and should be allocated one-third to each of these months.

e. Accrued interest on the note receivable is $5.

f. Accrued interest on the note payable is $10.

g. The estimated local property tax on merchandise stock for the year starting July 1 is $300. (This does not have to be paid until November 30.)

Closing entries:

h. Sales, Sales Returns and Allowances, and Cost of Goods Sold are closed into Income and Expense Summary.

i. Other expense accounts and income accounts are closed into Income and Expense Summary.

j. Income and Expense Summary is closed into Earned Surplus.

SUMMARY. Some of the important points of this chapter can be restated as follows:

1. In many merchandising enterprises, the only record made at the time of a sale is at the selling price. No entry at the cost price is made for each sale, but the cost of all the goods sold during an accounting period is determined at the end of the period and recorded on the books in one entry. In such a system, perpetual-inventory accounts for merchandise are not maintained and it is necesary to determine the value of merchandise on hand at the end of each period in order to calculate the cost of goods sold.
2. Adjusting entries are end-of-period recognitions of matters pertinent to the preparation of balance sheets and income statements that have not already been entered in the accounts as the result of business transactions taking place during the accounting period.
3. Where sales are not costed as they are made, an important adjusting entry is the one recording the cost of goods sold. Many of the other adjusting entries relate to the time distribution of expense and income.
4. A 10-column work sheet is a convenient device used by accountants to combine the adjusting entries with the information from the trial

EXHIBIT 4-7
T ACCOUNTS SHOWING ADJUSTING AND CLOSING ENTRIES FOR CENTRAL HARDWARE

Accrued Interest Receivable

	Dr.	Cr.	
e	5		

Merchandise Inventory

	Dr.	Cr.	
A	19,600	19,600	b
b	20,250		

Prepaid Insurance

	Dr.	Cr.	
A	210	16	c
O	72	266	
	266		

Prepaid Advertising

	Dr.	Cr.	
d	140		

Accounts Payable

	Dr.	Cr.	
L	5,100	3,950	A
		4,050	F
		112	O
	5,100	8,112	
	3,732	720	a
		3,732	

Accrued Taxes Payable

	Dr.	Cr.	
		25	g

Accrued Interest Payable

	Dr.	Cr.	
		10	f

Earned Surplus

	Dr.	Cr.	
		6,250	A
	6,503	253	j
		6,503	

Sales

	Dr.	Cr.	
		1,670	E
h	6,700	5,030	M

Sales Returns and Allowances

	Dr.	Cr.	
G	20		
H	190	210	h

Purchases

	Dr.	Cr.	
F	4,050		
a	720	4,770	b

Cost of Goods Sold

	Dr.	Cr.	
b	4,120	4,120	h

Advertising Expense

	Dr.	Cr.	
D	210	140	d
I	12		
O	40	122	i

Telephone Expense

	Dr.	Cr.	
I	29	29	i

Insurance Expense

	Dr.	Cr.	
c	16	16	i

Rent Expense

	Dr.	Cr.	
B	320	320	i

Property Tax Expense

	Dr.	Cr.	
g	25	25	i

Interest Expense

	Dr.	Cr.	
f	10	10	i

Salaries

	Dr.	Cr.	
N	1,600	1,600	i

Interest Income

	Dr.	Cr.	
i	5	5	e

Income and Expense Summary

	Dr.	Cr.	
h	210	6,700	h
h	4,120		
i	122	5	i
i	29		
i	16		
i	320		
i	25		
i	10		
i	1,600		
	6,452	6,705	
	253		
j	253	253	

balance. The balance sheet and profit and loss statement can be prepared directly from the work sheet before the adjusting and closing entries are made in the formal books of account.

5. Closing entries serve to wipe out the balances in income and expense accounts and transfer the net profit or loss to a summary ownership account such as Surplus.

DISCUSSION QUESTIONS

4-A. Explain the accounting treatment of prepaid insurance illustrated in this chapter. Expenditures for fire insurance are typically prepayments for a 3-year period. Can you think of some different methods of accounting treatment of such expenditures? How would these alternative treatments change the month-by-month figures for profit or loss as compared with the treatment illustrated in this chapter?

4-B. Explain the accounting treatment of accrued interest receivable illustrated in this chapter. What other method can you think of for accounting treatment of interest on notes receivable? How would this alternative treatment change the month-by-month figures for profit or loss as compared with the treatment illustrated in this chapter?

4-C. What advantages can you see in completing the work sheet before making adjusting and closing entries in the actual books of account?

4-D. What conclusion is indicated when the total of the debit column exceeds the total of the credit column in the section of the work sheet headed Profit and Loss? How might you complete the work sheet in this case?

4-E. This January 1 inventory of merchandise was $105,000; the net merchandise purchases during the year were $432,500; the December 31 inventory of merchandise was $93,700. Compute the cost of goods sold for the year.

4-F. Review entry G of the Central Hardware example. Assume that Micro Mfg. was originally billed $108 for these fittings. Assume now that, instead of keeping the fittings, Micro Mfg. returned them to Central Hardware who, in turn, returned them to the supplier and received a credit memo for the cost previously billed, $72. Set up appropriate T accounts, and make the necessary entries for this.

4-G. Review adjusting entry **a** in the Central Hardware example. Compute what the profit for the month of July would have appeared to be if no one had thought to make an entry for this matter. Also, explain briefly what the effect of the omission would have been on the August statements.

4-H. Suppose now, in connection with the matter of adjusting entry **a**, that the invoice arrived in August and was paid. Assume that the actual amount of the invoice was $715 and that this figure was used in the entry for the cash disbursement. What is the error thus introduced? How would this error affect the trial balance at the end of August? The income statement for August? The August 31 balance sheet? Suggest one or more ways this error might be discovered.

4-J. Review the calculation of cost of goods sold for entry **b** of the Central Hardware example. Assume now that the start-of-month inventory figure, $19,600, is correct but that, in arriving at the end-of-month figure, $20,250, certain items which cost $250 were overlooked. What would the profit for July have appeared to be if this error had not been made? What effect, if any, will this error have on the August income statement (assuming that the end-of-August inventory is correct)? How was the balance sheet linking these two periods affected by the error?

4-K. Set up T accounts for each of the following accounts: Property Tax Expense, Accrued Taxes Payable, and Cash. Make entries affecting these accounts for 12 successive months, beginning with July, 1962, and ending with June, 1963, using the data given for entry **g** in the Central Hardware example. Follow the precedent of entry g as illustrated in Exhibit 4-7. Assume that the books are closed at the end of each month. Also assume that the actual tax bill, received in October, is for $318 (instead of $300 as estimated in July) and that this amount, $318, is paid in November.

4-L. Repeat question 4-K, but this time make the entries according to the alternative plan suggested in the discussion of entry g.

4-M. Suppose that Central Hardware offered its credit customers a discount of 2% on their monthly bills if payment is made by the tenth of the following month. Assume also that most, but not all, of the customers take advantage of this "cash discount"—taking off 2% and remitting the balance on or before the tenth. Suggest a scheme for handling this matter in the ledger accounts and on the income statement.

PROBLEMS

Problem 4-1. The Sands Company, a merchandising enterprise, does not maintain perpetual-inventory accounts for merchandise but determines cost of goods sold each month on the basis of monthly physical inventories combined with a record of purchases. Opening balances on October 1 were as follows:

Account	*Debit*	*Credit*
Cash	$ 300	
Accounts Receivable	1,340	
Merchandise Inventory	4,710	
Accounts Payable		$ 900
Capital Stock		4,000
Retained Earnings		1,450
Totals	$6,350	$6,350

Accounts receivable were:

H. Bolles	$ 460
C. Carroll	700
E. Hagen	180
Total	$1,340

Other accounts used by this company are as follows:

Sales	Interest Expense
Cost of Goods Sold	Rent Expense
Purchases	Salaries
Delivery Expense	Utilities Expense
Insurance Expense	Income and Expense Summary

Set up T accounts, and enter the following October transactions directly in these accounts. Use one account for all accounts receivable. Open the necessary accounts for any new assets or liabilities. Identify each entry by transaction letter.

A. Enter the figures for the opening balances in their respective accounts.
B. Paid October rent for store and store fixtures, $180.
C. Borrowed 1,000 from A. V. Sands on a 90-day note with interest payable (on the date the note matures) at 6% per annum.
D. Paid all accounts payable, $900.
E. Purchased merchandise from Brown & Green on credit, $1,400.
F. Sale to T. Shoemaker on credit, $770.

G. Paid for fire insurance policy on merchandise stock running 3 years from October 1, $360.
H. Cash sales during the first half of October were $1,280.
I. Paid Brown & Green $1,000 on account.
J. Paid monthly light and power bill, $20
K. Purchased merchandise on credit from Wright Co., $1,450.
L. Sale to E. Hagen on credit, $520.
M. Paid $70 for delivery service for October.
N. Collections on accounts receivable totaled $960: H. Bolles, $460; E. Hagen, $400; C. Carroll, $100.
O. Cash sales for the balance of October were $1,480.
P. Paid October salaries, $840.

Take a trial balance using the first two columns of a 10-column work sheet. Complete the work sheet, making adjustments for the following matters:

a. Merchandise inventory October 31 is $4,870.
b. One month has expired out of the 3-year term of the insurance policy.
c. Accrued interest on the note payable is $5.

Prepare an end-of-month balance sheet and an income statement for October. Make the adjusting and closing entries in the T accounts. Identify these entries with the letter d.

Problem 4-2. Holmes & Co., a merchandising enterprise, does not maintain perpetual inventories but determines cost of goods sold each month on the basis of monthly physical inventories combined with a record of purchases. Opening balances on November 1 were as follows:

Account	*Debit*	*Credit*
Cash	$ 910	
Accounts Receivable	2,700	
Merchandise Inventory	8,630	
Prepaid Insurance	140	
Accounts Payable		$ 1,190
Capital Stock		8,000
Retained Earnings		3,190
Totals	$12,380	$12,380

Accounts receivable were:	
C. Douglas	$ 420
A. Reed	1,500
H. Roberts	250
J. Stone	530
Total	$2,700
Accounts payable were:	
Butler & Co.	$ 750
Hagerman & Sons	440
Total	$1,190

Other accounts used by this company are as follows:

Sales	Insurance Expense
Sales Returns and Allowances	Rent Expense
Cost of Goods Sold	Salaries
Purchases	Interest Income
Advertising Expense	Income and Expense Summary

Set up T accounts, and enter the following November transactions directly in those accounts. Use one account for all accounts receivable and one for all accounts payable. Open the necessary accounts for any new assets or liabilities. Identify each entry by transaction letter.

A. Enter the figures for the opening balances in their respective accounts.

B. Paid November rent for store and store fixtures, $280.
C. Merchandise sales on credit totaling $1,180 were: L. Beach, $670; J. Stone, $510.
D. Accepted a promissory note for $1,500 from A. Reed in settlement of his open account. This note is due in 3 months with interest at 8% per annum.
E. Paid Benchley Publishing Co. $120 for magazine advertising.
F. Cash sales for the first half of November was $1,150.
G. Paid Butler & Co., in full, $750, and Hagerman & Sons $350 on account, a total of $1,100.
H. Sold merchandise on credit to H. Roberts, $580.
I. L. Beach returned goods which he had purchased on credit for $80.
J. Purchased merchandise on credit from Hughes & Taft, $890, and from Butler & Co., $1,050, at total of $1,940.
K. Received bill from *The Daily Bugle* for advertising, $75.
L. Collections on accounts receivable totaled $815: C. Douglas, $300; H. Roberts, $250; J. Stone, $265.
M. Cash sales for the remainder of November were $1,110.
N. Paid November salaries, $1,250.

Take a trial balance using the first two columns of a 10-column work sheet. Complete the work sheet, making adjustments for the following matters:

a. Merchandise Inventory, November 30, is $8,460.
b. On November 1, the fire insurance policy on the merchandise stock had 28 months to run. One of these months has now expired.
c. Accrued interest on the note receivable is $10.
d. The $120 payment to Benchley Publishing Co. included $60 for an advertisement that appeared in November and $60 for one scheduled to appear in December.

Prepare an end-of-month balance sheet and an income statement for November. Make the adjusting and closing entries in the T accounts. Identify the closing entries with the letter e.

Problem 4-3. The Polar Shop sells and rents winter sports equipment and accessories. The shop does not maintain perpetual-inventory accounts but determines cost of goods sold each month on the basis of monthly physical inventories combined with a record of purchases. Opening balances on January 1 were as follows:

Account	*Debit*	*Credit*
Cash	$ 960	
Accounts Receivable	880	
Merchandise Inventory	2,980	
Rental Equipment Inventory	1,350	
Accounts Payable		$1,960
Capital Stock		2,500
Retained Earnings		1,710
Total	$6,170	$6,170

Accounts receivable were:	
V. Perry	$ 360
T. Scott	110
Z. Tracy	410
Total	$ 880
Accounts payable were:	
Mountain Boot Co	$ 260
Telemark Co	1,200
Winter Wear Mfg. Co.	500
Total	$1,960

Other accounts used by this company are as follows:

Merchandise Sales	Advertising Expense
Sales Returns and Allowances	Insurance Expense
Used Equipment Sales	Salaries
Rental Income	Store Expense
Cost of Merchandise Sold	Interest Expense
Cost of Used Equipment Sold	Income and Expense Summary
Merchandise Purchases	

Set up T accounts, and enter the following January transactions directly in these accounts. Use one account for all accounts receivable and one for all accounts payable. Open the necessary accounts for any new assets or liabilities. Identify each entry by transaction letter.

A. Enter the figures for the opening balances in their respective accounts.
B. Paid January rent for store and store fixtures, $275.
C. Borrowed $1,000 from Badger Loan Co., giving a 90-day note bearing interest at 6% payable when the note comes due.
D. Paid the following suppliers on accounts: Mountain Boot Co., $260; Telemark Co., $900; and Winter Wear Mfg. Co., $240; a total of $1,400.
E. Paid *Daily Courier* $35 for advertising.
F. Collections on accounts receivable totaled $610: V. Perry, $270; T. Scott, $110; Z. Tracy, $230.
G. Cash sales of merchandise in the first half of January totaled $840.
H. Purchased equipment from Telemark Co. on credit, $510.
I. Paid for fire insurance policy on merchandise stock, running for 3 years from January 1, $360.
J. Sold used (rental) equipment for $310, cash.
K. Sold merchandise on credit to Z. Tracy for $280 and to D. Werry for $185, a total of $465.
L. Purchased accessories on credit from Winter Wear Mfg. Co., $260, and Mountain Boot Co., $345, a total of $605.
M. Equipment rentals during January totaled $720 (all cash).
N. Customers were refunded a total of $130 cash for merchandise returned during the month. (Assume that the goods returned were still salable as new merchandise.)
O. Sold merchandise to V. Perry on credit, $85.
P. Cash sales of merchandise in the last half of January totaled $910.
Q. Paid January salaries, $1,345.
R. Paid utilities bills for the store, $40.

Take a trial balance of the first two columns of a 10-column work sheet. Complete the work sheet, making adjustments for the following matters:

a. The used rental equipment sold in January had been carried in the Rental Equipment Inventory account at the cost value of $285.
b. During January, new equipment having a cost value of $300 was taken from merchandise stocks for rental use.
c. Merchandise inventory January 31 is $2,725.
d. Accrued interest on the note payable is $5.

e. One month has expired of the 3 years covered by the insurance policy.

Prepare an end-of-month balance sheet and an income statement for January. On the income statement, show gross profit on merchandise sales, gross profit on used equipment sales, and rental income and the total of these three figures.

Make the adjusting and closing entries in the T accounts. Identify these entries with the letter f.

Problem 4-4. The Big Rock Gun Shop sells firearms, ammunition, gun parts, and accessories and does gunsmith (repair) work. The inventories are valued at the end of each quarter by taking physical inventory and applying prices taken from recent purchase invoices. The cost of goods sold for each quarter is calculated for each class of goods using the starting and ending inventory figures together with a summary of purchases (and a record of gun parts used in the repair work). Opening balances on April 1 were as follows:

Account	*Debit*	*Credit*
Cash	$ 500	
Accounts Receivable	820	
Firearms Inventory	2,610	
Merchandise Inventory	3,240	
Prepaid Advertising	30	
Prepaid Insurance	80	
Accounts Payable		$ 730
Notes Payable		600
Capital Stock		4,000
Retained Earnings		1,950
Totals	$7,280	$7,280

Accounts payable were:

Chicago Gun Mart	$390
Cold Firearms Co	125
Remchester Arms Co	180
Big Rock Gazette	35
Total	$730

The accounts receivable consist of personal accounts of about 50 citizens of Big Rock and vicinity. The Merchandise Inventory account includes ammunition, gun accessories, gun parts, and all other merchandise except firearms. Other accounts used by this company are as follows:

Sales—Firearms
Sales—Other Merchandise
Repair Income
Cost of Firearms Sold
Cost of Other Merchandise Sold
Cost of Repair Service
Purchases—Firearms
Purchases—Other Merchandise
Advertising Expense
Insurance Expense
Interest Expense
Rent and Utilities
Telephone Expense
Salaries
Income and Expense Summary

Set up T accounts, and make appropriate entries for the quarter ending June 30 directly into these accounts. Use one account for all accounts payable. Open the necessary accounts for any new assets or liabilities. Identify each entry by transaction letter.

A. Enter the opening balances in their respective accounts.

B. Sales on credit totaled $700, of which $300 was sales of firearms and $400 was sales of other merchandise.

C. Cash sales totaled $5,800, of which $1,700 was sales of firearms and $4,100 was sales of other merchandise.
D. Repair service income was $1,300, of which $250 was billed to charge-account customers and $1,050 was cash business.
E. Received $850 on account from charge-account customers.
F. Purchases, on credit, were as follows:

	Firearms	Other merchandise	Total
Chicago Gun Mart........	$120	$1,680	$1,800
Cold Firearms Co.........	230	70	300
Remchester Arms Co......	440	360	800
Totals.................	$790	$2,110	$2,900

G. An analysis of the check stubs and supporting papers provided the following information about disbursements during the quarter:

Rent (April, May, June)........................		$ 405
Intercity Telephone Co..........................		75
Directory advertising....................	$ 21	
Telephone services......................	54	
Big Rock State Bank (paid $300 on note with interest through June 30).......................		310
Utilities (electricity, water, and oil)...............		80
Accounts payable...............................		2,680
Chicago Gun Mart......................	$1,640	
Cold Firearms Co.......................	325	
Remchester Arms Co....................	680	
Big Rock Gazette......................	35	
Northern Lights Insurance Co....................		240
(Premium for 3-year renewal of fire insurance policy)		
Advertising (May and June)......................		65
Denver Gunsmiths (gun repairs sent out)...........		90
Salaries...		3,600
Repair service labor.....................	$ 600	
Other salary expense....................	3,000	
Total.......................................		$7,545

Take a trial balance using the first two columns of a 10-column sheet Complete the work sheet, making adjustments for the following matters:

a. The value of the inventory of firearms as of June 30 is $2,300.
b. The value of the inventory of other merchandise as of June 30 is $3,03C Parts that cost a total of $270 were taken from this merchandise inventor during the quarter for use in repair work.
c. Of the $80 prepaid insurance at the start of the quarter, $40 worth ha expired. Also, the renewed fire insurance policy, costing $240 for 3 year was effective as of May 15.
d. The following information was compiled from the file of bills on hand an unpaid as of June 30:

Chicago Gun Mart	$550
Cold Firearms Co	100
Remchester Company	300
Denver Gunsmiths	25
Big Rock Merchants' Association	18
Total	$993

The bill from Denver Gunsmiths is for repairs to a customer's gun; the repaired gun was delivered to the customer in June. The Big Rock Merchants' Association bill is for advertising in the July 4 rodeo program.

Prepare an end-of-quarter balance sheet and an income statement for the quarter. Arrange the income statement to show separately the gross profit for each of the three sources of income—firearms sales, other merchandise sales, and repair service. You may omit the details of derivation of the cost of goods sold figures on this statement.

Make the adjusting and closing entries in the T accounts. Identify the closing entries with the letter e.

Problem 4-5. The Hardscelle Sales Co. conducts a wholesale business in a line of bicycles, parts, and accessories. All sales are on credit. Cost of goods sold is determined at the end of each quarter using a physical inventory count and a record of purchases.

The account balances on July 1 were as follows:

Account	*Debit*	*Credit*
Cash	$ 1,400	
Accounts Receivable	4,600	
Notes Receivable	1,000	
Bicycle Inventory	9,500	
Parts Inventory	700	
Accessories Inventory	3,500	
Spoiled Merchandise	200	
Prepaid Insurance	300	
Accounts Payable		$ 3,200
Import Duty Payable		400
Capital Stock		10,000
Retained Earnings		7,600
Totals	$21,200	$21,200

Bicycle inventory details:

Model L26 180 @ $20.00	$3,600
Model S26 200 @ 17.50	3,500
Model S24 150 @ 16.00	2,400
Total	$9,500

Accounts payable were:

Jitensha Boeki K.K.	$1,900
Bike Accessories, Inc	900
Flubber Rubber Co	220
Pacific Freight Clearings	180
Total	$3,200

Other accounts used by this company are as follows:

Sales	Delivery Expense
Sales Returns	Insurance Expense
Cost of Goods Sold	Rent Expense
Purchases	Salaries
Purchase Returns	Telephone Expense
Advertising Expense	Interest Expense
Automobile Expense	Interest Income
Entertainment Expense	Income and Expense Summary

Set up T accounts, and make appropriate entries for the quarter ending September 30 directly into these accounts. Use one account for all three types of bicycles and one account for all accounts payable. Open accounts for any new assets or liabilities as required. Identify each entry by transaction letter.

A. Enter the opening balances in their respective accounts.

B. Borrowed $8,000 from the Golden State Bank on July 31 on a 90-day note.

C. Following is an analysis of merchandise purchases during the quarter. The costs of freight and United States customs duty are to be included in the merchandise value.

Vendor or service	L26	S26	S24	Total bikes	Parts	Accessories	Total
Jitensha Boeki K.K.	$ 8,000	$7,300	$4,200	$19,500	$1,500	......	$21,000
Bike Accessories, Inc.	......	......	......	......	......	$7,600	7,600
Flubber Rubber Co.	......	......	......	......	500	200	700
Pacific Freight Clearings	630	560	310	1,500	100	100	1,700
Totals, trade accounts	$ 8,630	$7,860	$4,510	$21,000	$2,100	$7,900	$31,000
U.S. Customs Department	2,170	1,940	1,090	5,200	300	......	5,500
Totals	$10,800	$9,800	$5,600	$26,200	$2,400	$7,900	$36,500
No. of bicycles received	540	560	350				

D. Sales for the quarter were summarized as follows:

	L26	S26	S24	Total
Bicycles	$8,550	$8,250	$4,600	$21,400
Parts	.....	.....	.....	2,650
Accessories	.....	.....	.....	7,950
Total sales	.....	.....	.....	$32,000

E. Dealers were allowed $430 for accessories returned.

F. Collections on accounts receivable totaled $31,400.

G. Disbursements during the quarter were summarized as follows:

Office and warehouse rents		$ 720
Delivery expense		990
Salaries		5,700
Interstate Telephone Co.		160
Diners' Club (entertainment)		70
Accounts payable		25,500
Jitensha Boeki K.K.	$18,140	
Bike Accessories, Inc.	5,200	
Flubber Rubber Co.	620	
Pacific Freight Clearings	1,540	
U.S. Customs Department (import duty)		5,225
Employees' expense reimbursements		385
Automobile mileage	$ 270	
Telephone	35	
Customer entertainment	80	
Southern Cross Insurance Co. (annual premium)		210
Advertising		880
Total		$39,840

H. Sold to a junk dealer for $180 cash the spoiled merchandise that had been carried on the books at $200. (Charge the $20 difference to Cost of Goods Sold.)

J. Received a credit memo from Bike Accessories, Inc., for $100 for defective accessories returned.

Take a trial balance using the first two columns of a 10-column work sheet. Complete the work sheet, making adjustments for the following matters:

a. The number of bicycles on hand as of September 30 was 420 L26, 430 S26, and 300 S24. The inventories of parts and accessories were $1,375 and $5,700, respectively. These figures were developed from a physical count of salable merchandise on hand in the warehouse on September 30.

b. The accessories returned to Hardscelle by dealers (entry E) had a total original cost value of $300. Part of this merchandise was sent back to Bike Accessories, Inc. (entry J). It is expected that a junk dealer will pay about $60 for the rest of this damaged merchandise. It was not counted in the end-of-quarter inventory of salable merchandise. Assume that the desired end result is that the net loss on this merchandise be included in the cost of goods sold for this quarter. Note that, as things stand after making entries J and **a**, the cost of parts and accessories sold is overstated.

c. Interest accrued on the note receivable is $15 for the quarter.

d. Jitensha Boeki K.K. is to be charged a total of $200 for their share of cooperative advertising expenses incurred by Hardscelle during the quarter. This amount will be deducted from the balance due Jitensha.

e. Prepaid insurance that cost $120 expired during the quarter.

f. Interest accrued on the note payable is $80 for August and September.

Prepare an end-of-quarter balance sheet and an income statement for the quarter. Make the adjusting and closing entries in the T accounts. Identify these entries with the letter g.

5/ INTRODUCTION TO ACCOUNTING SYSTEMS—SIMPLE JOURNALS AND LEDGERS

In the preceding chapters we have used only a simplified representation of a ledger in T-account form, and all entries were made directly into this ledger. We now proceed to an introduction to certain basic techniques and kinds of records employed in actual accounting systems.

Up to this point we have intentionally ignored certain problems that are of great importance in the design and operation of actual accounting systems. Two of these problems, considered in this chapter, are as follows:

1. The figures entered in the ledger accounts are a record of the financial consequences of past events classified by the types of assets, liabilities, and changes in Ownership affected. A fundamental accounting requirement is that it must be feasible to trace back from ledger entries to records disclosing adequate definitive and descriptive information about the transactions and events for which the entries were made. In the language of accountants, an "audit trail" is necessary.

2. It is important to minimize the introduction of errors into the ledger. Once in the ledger, some kinds of errors are likely to remain forever undetected. Protection against these errors must be preventive. For the kinds of errors that are normally detected by a subsequent test (such as a trial balance), an important consideration is the cost of locating and correcting them.

ACCOUNTING SYSTEM INPUT PROCEDURES. Customarily a business transaction will be recorded at least three times:

First, in most cases some original record of the transaction will be written.

Second, it will be entered in a book[1] called a *journal,* in which transactions are recorded in chronological order. A journal shows for

[1] The word "book" is used in the accountants' sense: A book (of account) is not necessarily a bound volume or even a loose-leaf one but may refer to any sort of formal accounting record.

each successive transaction the amounts subsequently debited and credited to different accounts, with explanation as required.

Third, it will be recorded in a book called a *ledger*, in which each account has its own separate place. Each figure in a ledger is *posted* from the corresponding figure in some journal. In the ledger, the accounting information is arranged account by account (whereas in the journal it is recorded transaction by transaction).

CENTRAL HARDWARE EXAMPLE EXPANDED. The Central Hardware Co. example of Chap. 4 is reviewed and extended in this chapter to introduce these new topics of journals and formal ledgers in elementary form. Only one journal and only one ledger are employed by Central Hardware. The use of additional special journals and subsidiary ledgers to improve the efficiency and extend the capabilities of the system is the subject of Chap. 6.

ORIGINAL EVIDENCES. For each business transaction, there is usually some written evidence. The original evidence of a credit sale might be a sales ticket or customer's invoice. The original evidence for a cash sale might be a figure on a cash register tape. The original evidence of a payment by check might be the check itself or perhaps a carbon copy made from it. The original evidence of a purchase of goods on credit might be the vendor's invoice. The original evidence of cash received from a charge customer might be a copy of the receipt given him, and so on.

These original documents are the basis on which journal entries are made. Before making the journal entries, bookkeepers generally examine the original documents with a view to finding any obvious errors in them. The original evidences are often filed as a permanent record of the transactions they represent.

Except for certain original documents that are important in cost accounting, original evidences are not illustrated in this book. The statements of transactions in the examples and problems in this book should be thought of as having been obtained from the appropriate original evidences. In some cases the transaction statements imply that many original evidences for similar transactions have been collected and summarized to obtain totals for all such transactions during the accounting period. How this collecting and summarizing can be accomplished is considered in Chap. 6.

NEED FOR THE USE OF SOME FORM OF JOURNAL. A journal is referred to as a book of original entry. No entry is made in a ledger until it has first been journalized. There are several reasons why it is not desirable to dispense with a journal record and make entries initially into a ledger in the manner illustrated in our simple examples in the preceding chapters.

One important reason is that the journalizing process helps keep errors out of the ledgers. In this process, each event for which an entry should be made is analyzed and interpreted into an accounting entry which conforms to the balance sheet equation and the rules for debiting and crediting. Then, before posting to the ledger, the journal entry is tested to make sure that the sum of the debits is equal to the sum of the credits.

Another reason is that the chronological transaction-by-transaction journal record is helpful in locating errors that do get into the ledgers. Also, without this journal record, which shows in one place the accounts debited and credited for each entry, it would be difficult to relate opposing debits and credits appearing in the ledger.

Journals also provide a link between original evidences and ledger postings. Thus journals facilitate reviewing any one entry with respect to appropriateness and completeness and determining whether or not an entry has been made for a given transaction or event.[2] Moreover, the journal makes it possible to include desirable supplementary information about transactions that cannot be recorded conveniently in an account-by-account record such as a ledger.

EXAMPLE OF A SIMPLE TYPE OF JOURNAL. Exhibit 5-1 shows some of the entries for the Central Hardware example in a simple two-column journal. Note the following conventions that are usually observed for this form of journal entry.

1. Each transaction is fully entered before the next one is started, and a one-line space is left between entries.
2. The date for each entry is recorded in the left-hand column on the first line for that entry.
3. The titles of the accounts to be debited and credited are listed each on a separate line: first, the accounts to be debited and then, indented, the accounts to be credited.
4. On the line for each account listed, the account number and the amount to be debited or credited to that account are recorded in the appropriate columns on the right.
5. The check mark after each debit or credit indicates that it has been posted to the ledger account.
6. Below the listing of the accounts debited and credited is a brief explanation of the nature of the transaction with any pertinent memoranda about it. In cases where the transaction is a routine

[2] This is easily done in most of the problems and examples of this book, where the entire ledger is displayed on one T-account sheet and each debit and credit is referenced to the transaction list by letter. In an actual accounting system, of course, things cannot be so simplified and convenient.

one, so that it is obvious from the accounts debited and credited just what has happened, this explanation can be omitted.

KEEPING ACCOUNTS TO THE SMALLEST MONETARY UNIT. In the preceding chapters, the examples and the accompanying problems were simplified by having all transactions in even dollars, generally in

EXHIBIT 5-1

PAGE FROM CENTRAL HARDWARE CO. JOURNAL

GENERAL JOURNAL No. 19

DATE 19___		DESCRIPTION OF ENTRY	ACCT. NO.	DEBIT AMOUNT	√	CREDIT AMOUNT	√
July	21	Telephone Expense	77	29 30	✓		
		Advertising Expense	70	12 00	✓		
		Cash	01			41 30	✓
	24	Notes Receivable	08	750 —	✓		
		Accounts Receivable	04			750 —	✓
		Note from Flasch Electric Co.					
		Payable Jan. 24, 19—, with 8% interest					
	31	Cash	01	5029 85	✓		
		Sales	55			5029 85	✓
	31	Salaries	75	1600 —	✓		
		Cash	01			1600 —	✓
		July salaries per payroll					
	31	Advertising Expense	70	40 —	✓		
		Prepaid Insurance	30	72 —	✓		
		Accounts Payable	40			112 —	✓
		Downtown Merch. Assn., $40 for banners					
		Nat'l. Service Insur. $72 for liability					
		insurance, 12 mo. starting July 1					
	31	Purchases	65	720 —	✓		
		Accounts Payable	40			720 —	✓
		To setup liability and charge Purchases					
		for radial saw sold to Ore Construction Co.					
	31	Cost of Goods Sold	64	4119 81	✓		
		Merchandise Inventory	10	20250 25	✓		
		Purchases	65			4769 66	✓
		Merchandise Inventory	10			19600 40	✓
		To enter cost of goods sold for July					

round numbers. In contrast, the exhibits in this chapter show all transactions to the nearest cent. (The figures of the Central Hardware example have been slightly modified so that many of the transactions are no longer in even dollars.) This is to illustrate that it is usually necessary in accounting practice to carry accounts involving external financial relationships to the smallest monetary unit and that ordinarily this practice is followed for all the accounts in a system.

In the remainder of this book nearly all the examples and problems are stated in even dollars and usually in round numbers. As in the preceding chapters, this simplification of the arithmetic is to permit concentration on the understanding of principles.

LIMITATIONS AND USES OF THE SIMPLE JOURNAL FORM. Where a large number of similar transactions must be recorded, the simple form of journal illustrated in Exhibit 5-1 requires an excessive amount of clerical labor, both in entering transactions initially and in posting them to the ledger. This form, therefore, is seldom used in practice for the recording of routine transactions. The next chapter illustrates the usual plan of having separate journals with special rulings to record such repetitive items as cash receipts, cash disbursements, sales, and recognitions of obligations to pay.

Variations of this simple journal form are commonly used in actual accounting systems for the *general journal.* The general journal records such transactions as do not occur often enough to justify a special journal of their own and is used for adjusting and closing entries. This simple journal form is also widely used in accounting literature in the discussion of various types of accounting entries to show the accounts debited and credited.

USE OF ACCOUNT NUMBERS. It is common practice to assign numbers to the various ledger accounts in some systematic way. Ordinarily the number of an account will identify it as an asset, liability, or ownership account, and usually the number will also classify the account within that general group. The accounts are arranged in the ledger according to this same classification and are therefore in numerical order. Consequently, having an account number associated with each debit and credit in an entry, as illustrated in Exhibit 5-1, facilitates locating the ledger sheet to which the amount is to be posted.

The account code numbers also provide a much more convenient way to refer to the various accounts in much of the other detailed bookkeeping work. Whereas the account numbers are highly desirable even in simple manual accounting systems, they are, of course, essential in systems utilizing posting, tabulating, and computing machines.

The following numbering scheme, used by the Central Hardware Co., is quite simple in that only the numbers from 1 to 99 are used. In many actual accounting systems, greater flexibility and more detailed classification are obtained by using three-digit account number schemes. In more complex businesses it is not uncommon for the account codes to contain four or more digits or a combination of letters and numbers.

Following are the accounts used in the Central Hardware Co. example with their identifying numbers:

Assets	*Sales and Other Income*
01 Cash	55 Sales
04 Accounts Receivable	56 Sales Returns and Allowances
08 Notes Receivable	59 Interest Income
09 Accrued Interest Receivable	*Cost of Sales*
10 Merchandise Inventory	64 Cost of Goods Sold
30 Prepaid Insurance	65 Purchases
31 Prepaid Advertising	66 Purchase Returns
Liabilities	*Expenses*
40 Accounts Payable	70 Advertising Expense
41 Accrued Taxes Payable	71 Insurance Expense
43 Notes Payable	73 Property Tax Expense
44 Accrued Interest Payable	74 Rent Expense
Owners' Equity	75 Salaries
50 Capital Stock	77 Telephone Expense
51 Earned Surplus	79 Interest Expense
54 Income and Expense Summary	

POSTING TO THE LEDGER. *It is important for the student to recognize that, in actual bookkeeping, no entry is recorded in the ledger until it has first been journalized.* The journal entry is always the basis of the ledger entry; in the language of accounting, every ledger entry is *posted* from one journal entry already made.

Exhibit 5-2 shows how a few selected accounts of the Central Hardware Co. might appear in an actual hand-posted ledger. Journal entries such as those shown in Exhibit 5-1 have been posted on these ledger pages.

Where books are kept in this way with only one journal, each entry in the journal must be posted separately to the ledger. In fact, each journal entry requires at least two postings, one to the account debited and one to the account credited. A compound journal entry may involve postings to three or more accounts. In contrast, where several columnar journals are used, each with a special purpose and with special rulings, the clerical labor of posting is greatly reduced, as it is only necessary to post the column totals that summarize a great many transactions into a few figures. This common plan for simplifying posting is described and illustrated in the next chapter.

Journal entries, of course, can be made at any time during an accounting period. However, the posting to the general ledger is normally done only at the end of an accounting period.

BALANCE-COLUMN LEDGER FORM. The ledger form shown in Exhibit 5-3 is an alternative to the one illustrated in Exhibit 5-2. The third column in which to show the net debit-or-credit balance considerably simplifies the matter of summarizing an account. This is particularly convenient for accounts in which it is desired to com-

EXHIBIT 5-2

SOME PAGES FROM THE CENTRAL HARDWARE LEDGER

ACCOUNT: *Accounts Receivable* No. 04

DATE		EXPLANATION	POST. REF.	DEBIT AMOUNT	DATE		EXPLANATION	POST. REF.	CREDIT AMOUNT
July	1	Balance	✓	1852 15	July	14	Allowance	17	20 —
	31		19	1671 10		24	Prom. note	19	750 —
						31		19	873 25
				3523 25		31	Bal. Fwd.	✓	1643 25 1880 —
				3523 25					3523 25
Aug.	1	Balance	✓	1880 —					

ACCOUNT: *Prepaid Insurance* No. 30

DATE		EXPLANATION	POST. REF.	DEBIT AMOUNT	DATE		EXPLANATION	POST. REF.	CREDIT AMOUNT
July	1	Balance	✓	210 —	July	31		19	16 —
	31	Liability ins.--12 mo.	19	72 —		31	Bal. Fwd.	✓	266 —
Aug.	1	Balance	✓	266 —					

ACCOUNT: *Accounts Payable* No. 40

DATE		EXPLANATION	POST. REF.	DEBIT AMOUNT	DATE		EXPLANATION	POST. REF.	CREDIT AMOUNT
July	31		19	5098 28	July	1	Balance	✓	3949 37
						31		18	4049 66
						31		19	112 —
	31	Bal. Fwd.	✓	3732 75		31		19	8111 03 720 —
				8831 03					8831 03
					Aug.	1	Balance	✓	3732 75

ACCOUNT: *Purchases* No. 65

DATE		EXPLANATION	POST. REF.	DEBIT AMOUNT	DATE		EXPLANATION	POST. REF.	CREDIT AMOUNT
July	31		18	4049 66	July	31		19	4769 66
	31		19	720 —					

pute and show the balance frequently and is quite popular in actual accounting practice.

To reduce the chances of mistaking a debit balance for a credit balance, or vice versa, many such balance-column ledger forms have a space at the left of the balance column for entering Dr. or Cr. Other forms provide four columns: debit amount, credit amount, debit balance, and credit balance, in that order.

OTHER TYPES OF LEDGER FORMS. The two general-purpose ledger forms illustrated in this chapter are widely used in systems where posting is done by hand. For machine-posting systems, the forms are generally patterned after the balance-column type shown in Exhibit 5-3.

There are also many different ledger forms for special purposes. Some of these are discussed in later chapters in connection with cost accounting and fixed-capital accounting. There is great variability in such special-purpose ledger forms. In part, this variability arises because these forms often combine other useful information with the debit and credit entries that are essential in any ledger account.

EXHIBIT 5-3
AN ALTERNATIVE LEDGER FORM

ACCOUNT *Cash*

DATE		EXPLANATION	REF.	DEBIT	CREDIT	BALANCE
						540 35
July	3		18		320 —	220 35
	6	90-day note	18	2000 —		
	6		18		210 40	2009 95
	21		19		41 30	
	31		19		189 70	
	31		19	870 45		
	31		19		5100 15	
	31		19	5029 85		
	31		19		1600 —	979 10

LEDGER AND JOURNAL FORMS USED IN REMAINDER OF THIS BOOK. Because the T account is such a good compact representation of an account, we shall return to the use of T accounts in the examples and problems. Where special-purpose ledger forms are required, these will be illustrated and sometimes a simplified version will be used in an example and the related problems.

Also, after Chap. 6, we shall frequently employ again the short cut of bypassing the journalizing step and making entries directly into the ledgers. However, entries will often be illustrated in the text in two-column journal style. Also, a number of the discussion questions and problems will ask for the analysis of transactions to be presented in this way. Hereafter, whenever a ruled journal form is used, it will have no columns for cents.

SUMMARY. The new ideas introduced in this chapter are restated as follows:

1. An important technique of accounting practice is the journalizing process. An entry for each transaction and event affecting the accounts is made in a book of original entry, a *journal.* The journal entries show all the debits and credits for each transaction in one place. The journal provides a transaction-by-transaction record.
2. Each debit and credit is *posted* from a journal to the ledger account affected. In the ledger, the financial information is classified account

by account. The purpose and meaning of any debit or credit in an account can be reviewed by reference to the journal from which it was posted.

DISCUSSION QUESTIONS

5-A. In the examples and problems in the first four chapters of this book, entries were made directly into a skeleton ledger and no journals were used. Why is this not a practicable scheme of keeping books for an actual business enterprise?

5-B. Explain how the process of journalizing all entries before they are posted helps to keep certain kinds of errors from getting into the general ledger.

5-C. What is meant by *posting?*

5-D. Describe the two types of ledger forms illustrated in this chapter. Which type seems to you to be preferable? Why?

5-E. The ledger contains the same information that has already been recorded in the journal. In spite of this fact, these two books of account are quite different. Explain the two foregoing statements.

5-F. In Exhibit 5-2, illustrating selected pages of a ledger, there are check marks in the "posting reference" columns for certain entries instead of journal page numbers. Describe and explain the purpose of the procedure in which these check marks presumably were made.

PROBLEMS

Problem 5-1. Set up a general journal for the Sands Company of problem 4-1, using two-column journal paper. Journalize the end-of-month entries **a** through **c**.

Problem 5-2. Set up a general journal for Holmes & Co. of problem 4-2, using two-column journal paper. Journalize the end-of-month entries **a** through **d**.

Problem 5-3. Set up the Cash account for the Sands Co. of problem 4-1, using a sheet of ledger paper of the type shown in Exhibit 5-2. Enter the opening balance, and make all postings to this account for the month of October.

Problem 5-4. Solve problem 5-3 for Holmes & Co. of problem 4-2.

Problem 5-5. Solve problem 5-3 for the Polar Shop of problem 4-3.

Problem 5-6. Set up the Prepaid Insurance account shown in Exhibit 5-2 on a sheet of ledger paper of the type shown in Exhibit 5-3 (balance-column form). Make all postings to this account starting with the July 1 balance and continuing for 13 months, through August of the following year. Assume that any insurance policy that expires is promptly renewed and that the premium rate does not change. Assume that no other new policies are started. Refer to the exhibits in Chap. 4 for any information required.

6/ INTRODUCTION TO ACCOUNTING SYSTEMS— COLUMNAR JOURNALS AND SUBSIDIARY LEDGERS

In this chapter the basic elements and the structure of accounting systems are explored further. One objective is to introduce the idea of a subsidiary ledger and its relationship to the general ledger. Another is to introduce columnar journals and indicate the nature of the system problem which arises from the fact that collecting, recording, and processing information for accounting purposes involve repetitive tasks.

COLUMNAR JOURNALS. In the preceding chapters the problem of summarizing data about frequently occurring events such as sales, collections, purchases, and disbursements was intentionally ignored. In the example and the problems of Chap. 5, where a single journal was employed, there were many instances where a single journal entry served to record numerous similar transactions that occurred during a week or a month. The means by which the figures for these entries may have been compiled from original evidence documents was not discussed.

Clearly, it would be tedious and unduly expensive to make a separate entry in a general journal of the type illustrated in Chap. 5 for each different transaction. A better approach is to recognize that a few highly repetitive types of events represent the mainstream of the work. This leads to the accounting technique of providing a special journal for each such basic type of transaction and designing these journals not only for recording the transactions easily but also to facilitate classifying and summarizing the data. Such journals are arranged with columns for collecting money amounts requiring the same accounting treatment. Only the column totals need to be posted from this type of journal to the general ledger accounts. Therefore the number of ledger postings and the probability of errors getting into the ledger are very much reduced.

SPORT SHOP EXAMPLE. The example introduced in this chapter is that of a small corporation engaged in retail merchandising of sporting goods. This company does business under the name The Sport Shop. The account balances at the start of the period, February 1, and the transactions during February are stated in Exhibit 6-1.

EXHIBIT 6-1

TRANSACTIONS FOR THE SPORT SHOP DURING FEBRUARY, 19___

Feb. 1. Opening balances on February 1 were as follows:

General Ledger Account	*Debit*	*Credit*
01 Cash	$ 900	
04 Accounts Receivable	1,890	
10 Merchandise Inventory	9,200	
16 Prepaid Insurance	60	
40 Accounts Payable		$ 1,255
44 Notes Payable		1,200
45 Accrued Interest Payable		12
50 Capital Stock		5,000
51 Earned Surplus		4,583
Totals	$12,050	$12,050

Accounts receivable were:	
T. Berg	$ 390
A. Carlson	240
S. Duffy	480
A. James	600
K. King	180
Total	$1,890

The balance in account 40, Accounts Payable, represents an invoice of a supplier, Hale & Co., for $1,250 less 2% discount for payment by February 6 and a bill from Mercury Delivery Service for January deliveries, $30. These invoices were entered in the invoice register in January and assigned invoice numbers 307 and 308, respectively.

2. Sold merchandise on credit to R. Stone, $140. Received $160 from S. Duffy on account.
3. Received invoice dated February 1 from Smith & Smith for merchandise purchased on credit, $2,000, terms 1% 10 days net 30.
4. Paid Hope Realty Co. February rent on store and equipment, $240. Received on account: $250 from T. Berg and $120 from A. Carlson.
5. Received bill from South Insurance Agency for fire insurance on merchandise stock for 3 years starting February 1, $288.
6. Paid Hale & Co., invoice 307, $1,225, taking advantage of the discount for prompt payment.
7. Cash sales for the week were $1,160.
9. Received bill from Gulf Telephone Company, $60, of which $25 was the monthly charge for directory advertising.
10. Paid Mercury Delivery Service, invoice 308, $30.
11. Received invoice dated February 9 from Hale & Co. for merchandise, $1,500, terms 2% 10 days net 30.
12. Paid South Insurance Agency bill, $288, and telephone company bill, $60.
13. Sold merchandise on credit to A. Tipler, $105.
14. Cash sales for week were $1,240.
16. Accepted a promissory note for $600 from A. James in settlement of his open account. This note is payable in three monthly installments with interest at 8% per annum from February 1.
17. Received $180 from K. King in full payment of his account.
18. Received bill from Super Ads, Inc., $125, for advertising, of which $85 is to be considered February expense and the balance charged to March.

EXHIBIT 6-1 (Continued)

19. Paid Hale & Co. invoice, $1,470, taking the 2% discount.
20. Sold merchandise on credit to B. Wild for $210.
21. Cash sales for the week were $1,480. Received invoice dated February 16 from Alpine Equipment Co. for merchandise, $1,000, terms 2% 10th prox.
23. Paid S. G. & E. Company the monthly gas and electricity bill, $22.
24. Sold goods on credit to K. King, $115. Paid the Smith & Smith invoice at the gross amount, $2,000.
25. Paid Super Ads bill, $125. Received $20 cash from junk dealer for scrap lead and old cartridge brass.
26. Allowed B. Wild $25 credit for repair of defective merchandise he purchased February 20.
27. Received bill from Mercury Delivery Service for February, $60. Sold merchandise on credit to T. Berg, $100.
28. Cash sales for the week were $1,320. Paid salaries as follows: F. D. Ward, $550; V. N. Lee, $700.

JOURNALS USED BY THE SPORT SHOP. In addition to a general journal, four special journals are used. The names of these journals and the types of transaction recorded in each one are as follows:

Invoice register. All recognitions of obligations to pay money on open account are recorded in this journal, regardless of whether payment is to be made later or at once.

Cash receipts journal. As the name implies, all receipts of money are recorded in this journal.

Cash disbursements journal. All disbursements of money are recorded here. In this system, no disbursement can be entered in this journal until the obligation to make the payment has been recorded in the invoice register.

Sales journal. All regular sales of merchandise are recorded in this journal. Cash sales are recorded both here and in the cash receipts journal.

All transactions that do not fall into one of the four special-journal classes are recorded in the general journal, which is used also for adjusting and closing entries. The five journals used in this system are mutually exclusive in the sense that an entry made in one of the journals is not made in any of the others. One exception to this rule is the cash sale which involves two simultaneous events—a sale and a cash receipt.

CLASSIFICATION OF GENERAL LEDGER ACCOUNTS. The general ledger accounts used in the accounting system of The Sport Shop are as follows:

Assets
01 Cash
04 Accounts Receivable
08 Notes Receivable
09 Accrued Interest Receivable
10 Merchandise Inventory
15 Prepaid Advertising
16 Prepaid Insurance

Liabilities
40 Accounts Payable
44 Notes Payable
45 Accrued Interest Payable

Owners' Equity
50 Capital Stock
51 Earned Surplus
52 Profit and Loss Summary

Income and Cost of Sales
53 Sales
54 Sales Returns
57 Interest Income
58 Other Income
61 Cost of Sales
62 Purchases
63 Purchase Returns

Expenses
70 Advertising Expense
71 Delivery Expense
72 Insurance Expense
75 Salaries
76 Store Expense
77 Telephone Expense
83 Interest Expense
85 Purchase Discount Lost

Miscellaneous
99 Cash Sales Clearing

Two new accounts are introduced in this example. One is account 99, Cash Sales Clearing, which is discussed in connection with the use of the special journals. The other is account 85, Purchase Discount Lost, an expense account which is used in connection with the matter of discounts allowed by vendors for prompt payment of their invoices.

DISCOUNT FOR PROMPT PAYMENT. It is common practice in many classes of trade between commercial enterprises for the vendor to offer to the purchaser a discount that is contingent upon payment of the invoice by a certain date. For example, the terms of payment for an invoice might be stated "2% 10 days net 30." This means that the purchaser is entitled to deduct 2% of the face amount of the bill if he makes payment within 10 days of the date of the invoice. The words "net 30" mean that, if the purchaser defers payment beyond the 10-day period he must then pay the full amount, which he is expected to do within 30 days from the date of invoice. There is quite a variety of discount terms in use. The percentage discount may be as small as ½% or more than 2%. The termination of the discount period may be specified as an actual date, as "end-of-month," or as "10th prox." (meaning the tenth day of the following month). Such discounts, which are contingent upon prompt payment, are often referred to as *cash discounts*. From the viewpoint of the purchaser of goods subject to such a discount, it is often referred to as a *purchase discount*. Alternative accounting treatments of purchase discounts are discussed following the Sport Shop example.

USE OF A SUBSIDIARY LEDGER FOR ACCOUNTS RECEIVABLE. In the Sport Shop example as in the other examples, there is only one account in the ledger for all accounts receivable, and entries to this general ledger account need be made only at the end of each accounting period. As demonstrated in the previous chapters, this is all that is necessary for developing an end-of-period figure for the asset Accounts Receivable. However, satisfactory conduct of business with the different customers normally requires that there be available during the accounting period an up-to-date record showing the status and history of each account. Usually it is considered necessary to show each transaction separately in these detailed customer accounts, to make postings to these accounts within a short time after the occurrence of each transaction, and to reference the entries (particularly charges) to the original evidence documents on which they are based.

The individual customer accounts could, of course, be kept in the general ledger in place of the Accounts Receivable account. However, in nearly all accounting systems, these detail accounts are removed to a separate *subsidiary* ledger, which is then represented in the general ledger by the single account titled Accounts Receivable.

Postings to a subsidiary ledger are made periodically (perhaps daily) during the accounting period, and the new balance can be determined and recorded after each posting. Meanwhile, for the general ledger, the same basic transaction data are being collected, and at the end of the accounting period the data are summarized, journalized, and posted to the general ledger in accordance with the double-entry bookkeeping rules. Thus, the debits and credits posted to the general ledger Accounts Receivable account are totals for numerous separate postings made to individual customer accounts in the subsidiary ledger. At the end of an accounting period, if no errors have been made, the total of the balances in all the customer accounts in the subsidiary ledger will be equal to the balance in the general ledger account. In the language of accounting, the subsidiary accounts receivable ledger is *controlled* by the Accounts Receivable account in the general ledger. This relationship between a subsidiary ledger and the general ledger *controlling account* is important.

EXPLANATION OF ENTRIES IN JOURNALS. The February transactions of The Sport Shop are shown in Exhibit 6-2 as they would be entered in the five journals. The accounts receivable ledger is shown in T-account form in Exhibit 6-3.

The following comments about selected entries are intended not only to explain how this simple accounting system works but also to point out some of the alternatives of accounting theory and technique that might be applied in such a system.

Feb. 2. Sold merchandise on credit to R. Stone, $140. As this is a sale of merchandise, it is entered in the sales journal. The ultimate

EXHIBIT 6-2
JOURNALS FOR THE SPORT SHOP

INVOICE REGISTER

DAY Feb.	ACCOUNTS PAYABLE 40 CR	PAYABLE TO	NOTES	DATE DUE	INV. NO.	PAID DATE	PAID CHECK NO.	PURCHASES 62 DR	ADVERTISING EXP. 70 DR	DELIVERY EXPENSE 71 DR	SALARIES 75 DR	STORE EXPENSE 76 DR	MISC. DEBITS ACCT.	MISC. DEBITS AMOUNT	✓
3	1980	Smith & Smith	1% C.D. - $20	2-11	310	2-24	108	1980							
4	240	Hope Realty	Feb. rent		311	2-4	101					240			
5	288	South Insurance Agy.	Fire, 3 yrs/Feb. 1	2-15	312	2-12	104						16	288	✓
9	60	Gulf Telephone Co.			313	2-12	105		25				77	35	✓
11	1470	Hale & Co.	2% C.D. - $30	2-19	314	2-19	106	1470							
18	125	Super Ads., Inc.	Feb. & Mar. ads		315	2-25	109		85				15	40	✓
21	980	Alpine Equip. Co.	2% C.D. - $20	3-10	316			980							
23	22	S. G. & E.	Feb. utilities		317	2-23	107					22			
27	60	Mercury Delivery	Feb. service		318					60					
28	550	F. D. Ward	Feb. salary		319	2-28	110				550				
28	700	M. N. Lee	" "		320	2-28	111				700				
	6475							4430	110	60	1250	262		363	
	✓							✓	✓	✓	✓	✓			

CASH DISBURSEMENTS JOURNAL

CASH 01 CR	PAID DAY Feb.	PAID CHECK NO.	INV. NO.	IN FAVOR OF	ACCOUNTS PAYABLE 40 DR	MISC. DEBITS ACCT.	MISC. DEBITS AMOUNT	✓
240	4	101	311	Hope Realty	240			
1225	6	102	307	Hale & Co.	1225			
30	10	103	308	Mercury Delivery	30			
288	12	104	312	South Insurance	288			
60	12	105	313	Gulf Telephone	60			
1470	19	106	314	Hale & Co.	1470			
22	23	107	317	S. G. & E.	22			
2000	24	108	310	Smith & Smith	1980	85	20	✓
125	25	109	315	Super Ads., Inc.	125			
550	28	110	319	F. D. Ward	550			
700	28	111	320	M. N. Lee	700			
6710 ✓					6690 ✓		20	

GENERAL JOURNAL

DATE 19XX	DESCRIPTION	ACCT. NO.	✓	DEBIT AMOUNT	✓	CREDIT AMOUNT	✓
2-16	Notes Receivable	08		600	✓		
	Accounts Receivable	04	✓			600	✓
	A. James, for open						
	account. 3 mo., 8%						
2-26	Sales Returns	54		25	✓		
	Accounts Receivable	04	✓			25	✓
	B. Wild, allowance						

SALES JOURNAL

DAY Feb.	CASH SALES 99 DR	ACCOUNTS RECEIVABLE 04 DR	✓	SOLD TO	SALES 53 CR
2		140	✓	R. Stone	140
7	1160			cash	1160
13		105	✓	A. Tipler	105
14	1240			cash	1240
20		210	✓	B. Wild	210
21	1480			cash	1480
24		115	✓	K. King	115
27		100	✓	T. Berg	100
28	1320			cash	1320
	5200	670			5870
	✓	✓			✓

CASH RECEIPTS JOURNAL

DAY Feb.	CASH 01 DR	RECEIVED FROM	✓	ACCOUNTS RECEIVABLE 04 CR	CASH SALES 99 CR	MISCELLANEOUS CREDITS ACCT.	MISCELLANEOUS CREDITS AMOUNT	
2	160	S. Duffy	✓	160				
4	250	T. Berg	✓	250				
4	120	A. Carlson	✓	120				
7	1160	sales			1160			
14	1240	sales			1240			
17	180	K. King	✓	180				
21	1480	sales			1480			
25	20	junkman (scrap)				58	20	✓
28	1320	sales			1320			
	5930			710	5200		20	
	✓			✓	✓			

EXHIBIT 6-3

ACCOUNTS RECEIVABLE LEDGER FOR THE SPORT SHOP

T. Berg

	Dr	Cr	
2/1	390	250	2/4
2/27	100	240	
	240		

A. Carlson

	Dr	Cr	
2/1	240	120	2/4
		120	
	120		

S. Duffy

	Dr	Cr	
2/1	480	160	2/2
		320	
	320		

A. James

	Dr	Cr	
2/1	600	600	2/16

K. King

	Dr	Cr	
2/1	180	180	2/17
2/24	115		

R. Stone

	Dr	Cr	
2/2	140		

A. Tipler

	Dr	Cr	
2/13	105		

B. Wild

	Dr	Cr	
2/20	210	25	2/26
		185	
	185		

effect of this journal entry on the general ledger will be that Accounts Receivable will be debited $140 and Sales will be credited $140. However, no posting to the general ledger is made at this time. At the end of the month, when the columns in the several journals are totaled, the *column totals* will be posted to the appropriate general ledger accounts. Meanwhile, any transaction affecting an account receivable is posted to the subsidiary ledger at the time the journal entry is made. In this case the account of R. Stone is debited $140, and the fact that this has been done is shown in the sales journal by a check mark.

Feb. 2. Received $160 from S. Duffy on account. This is recorded in the cash receipts journal. The general ledger accounts affected are Cash (debited) and Accounts Receivable (credited). Here again is an event affecting an account receivable, which therefore requires a posting to the customer's account in the subsidiary ledger. The check mark in the cash receipts journal shows that this was done.

Feb. 3. Received invoice dated Feburary 1 from Smith & Smith for merchandise purchased on credit, $2,000, terms 1% 10 net 30. In the Sport Shop system, obligations are recognized and recorded at the time an invoice is received or at the time payment is made, whichever comes first. In either case, an entry setting up the obligation to pay is made in the invoice register. All entries in this journal result in an increase in Accounts Payable (credit). On the debit side, this journal is the means of obtaining an analysis of the debits to ownership accounts and asset accounts. In this case, the debit is to the account Purchases.

In a system like this, if an invoice is recorded in the invoice register, it is presumed that payment has been properly authorized. In this case the bookkeeper is authorized and expected to prepare a check payable to Smith & Smith in the amount of $1,980 ($2,000 less 1%, assuming that payment will be made by February 11).

The point of view applied in this system concerning the amount to be charged to account 62, Purchases, is that it is presumed that payment of an invoice subject to cash discount will be made within the discount period and therefore the net cost of the purchase will be the gross amount of the invoice minus the allowable discount for prompt payment. The journal form illustrated here is designed to help the person responsible avoid failure to pay an invoice on time. In the case of a "discount invoice," both the percentage and the amount of the discount are recorded, and the discount deadline date is shown in the following column. The invoice number 310 was assigned when the invoice was recorded in the journal; the date paid and the check number were not entered until payment was made on February 24.

Feb. 4. Paid Hope Realty Co. February rent on store and equipment, $240. This obligation has not yet been recorded in the invoice register.

Therefore, two accounting actions are required: recognition of the obligation to pay and payment of that obligation. The procedural rule in the Sport Shop system is that no disbursement on open account will be made except in payment of an obligation recorded in the invoice register.

Having obtained the proper authorization and made the entry in the invoice register, check No. 101 was then drawn to Hope Realty and recorded in the cash disbursements journal. The date of payment and check number were then recorded in the invoice register. The net effect of the two journal entries will be, of course, a credit of $240 to Cash and a debit of $240 to Store Expense.

Feb. 5. Received bill from South Insurance Agency for fire insurance on merchandise stock for 3 years starting February 1, $288. The obligation to pay is recorded in the invoice register. The effect of this will be to credit Accounts Payable and debit the asset account Prepaid Insurance. Information shown on the invoice caused the bookkeeper to note that this invoice should be paid by February 15.

Feb. 6. Paid Hale & Co., invoice 307, $1,255, taking advantage of the discount for prompt payment. The obligation to pay in this case was recorded in the invoice register during the previous month. Therefore what is required now is an entry in the cash disbursements journal debiting Accounts Payable and crediting Cash. The date of payment and check number would, of course, be entered in the invoice register on the line for invoice 307 (not shown in Exhibit 6-2).

Feb. 7. Cash sales for the week were $1,160. It is desirable that all sales be entered in the sales journal and all cash receipts be entered in the cash receipts journal. Clearly, to record the cash sales for the week, Cash should be debited $1,160 and Sales should be credited $1,160. To accomplish this and maintain the basic division between the two journals, a special "clearing" account, Cash Sales Clearing, is used. Note that the debit to Cash Sales Clearing in the sales journal is immediately offset by the credit to Cash Sales Clearing in the cash receipts journal. The purpose of this apparently unnecessary double entry, as will be brought out later on, is to help prevent certain kinds of errors from being introduced into the general ledger.

Feb. 16. Accepted a promissory note for $600 from A. James in settlement of his open account. This note is payable in three monthly installments with interest at 8% per annum from February 1. Clearly, this event is not a routine business transaction, and it does not fit into any one of the four special journals. The entry therefore is made in the general journal.

Because this entry affects an account receivable, it is necessary to post the subsidiary ledger immediately. The fact that this has been done is indicated in the general journal by a check mark in the column next to the account number. This check column not only provides for recording the fact that subsidiary ledger posting has been done; it also serves to remind the bookkeeper that the subsidiary ledger must be posted. The other check marks in this journal, alongside the amounts in the debit and credit columns, indicate that those amounts were posted to the general ledger accounts at the end of the month.

Feb. 18. Received bill from Super Ads, Inc., $125, for advertising, of which $85 is to be considered February expense and the balance charged to March. Recording the obligation to pay in the invoice register will result in a credit to Accounts Payable of $125. This is offset by two debits: one to account 70, Advertising Expense, for that portion of the total that appropriately should be charged to February and the other to account 15, Prepaid Advertising, for that portion of the invoice that properly should be associated with future accounting periods.

Feb. 19. Paid Hale & Co. invoice, $1,470, taking the 2% discount. When this obligation was recorded in the invoice register, it was assumed that it would be paid within the discount time period—which it was—and therefore the debit to Accounts Payable in the cash disbursements journal exactly offsets the credit to Accounts Payable entered on February 11 in the invoice register.

Feb. 24. Paid the Smith & Smith invoice at the gross amount, $2,000. In this case the assumption that was made on February 3 turned out to be incorrect. The invoice was not paid on or before February 11, apparently because of a temporary shortage of cash and consideration of the costs and trouble of short-term borrowing. The view applied by the accountant at this point, in this system, is that the extra $20 that has been paid represents a business expense related to the financial management side of the enterprise rather than the purchasing side. Therefore, the original debit of $1,980 to Purchases is not increased; the $20 is debited to an expense account titled Purchase Discount Lost.

Feb. 25. Received $20 cash from junk dealer from scrap lead and old cartridge brass. The entry for this could have been made in the general journal. However, it is somewhat better system-wise and somewhat easier to make the entry in the cash receipts journal, using the miscellaneous credits column.

Feb. 28. Paid salaries as follows: F. D. Ward, $550; V. N. Lee, $700. Inasmuch as there are only two employees, the appropriate way to handle this matter is as shown in Exhibit 6-2. Devices and techniques for handling payroll matters and the attendant complications are many and diverse. This matter is explored somewhat further in Chap. 13.

SOME OTHER COMMENTS ON THE SPORT SHOP JOURNALS. Each of the four special journals is shown in the end-of-month condition with the columns totaled and "cross-footed." In other words, after the columns have been totaled in preparation for posting to the general ledger, the check is made to see that the sum of the debits is equal to the sum of the credits. The column-total entry posted from the invoice register was, in formal journal form, as follows:

	Account	*Debit*	*Credit*
15	Prepaid Advertising	$ 40	
16	Prepaid Insurance	288	
62	Purchases	4,430	
70	Advertising Expense	110	
71	Delivery Expense	60	
75	Salaries	1,250	
76	Store Expense	262	
77	Telephone Expense	35	
40	Accounts Payable		$6,475
	Totals	$6,475	$6,475

Similarly, summary entries were posted from the cash disbursements journal, sales journal, and the cash receipts journal. Each entry in the general journal was posted separately to the general ledger. Note that, in all the journals, each amount posted to a general ledger account was checked off in the journal at the time of posting.

ACCOUNTS RECEIVABLE LEDGER FOR THE SPORT SHOP. In Exhibit 6-3, the subsidiary accounts receivable ledger is shown in T-account form as it would appear at the end of February 19___. In each account the posting for each sale and each payment on account is identified by the date of the transaction. In an actual ledger, additional information would be recorded to reference each posting to the journal entry and relate each sale (and each sales return) to the source document (charge sale slip or credit slip).

TRIAL BALANCE OF THE GENERAL LEDGER. Exhibit 6-4 shows in T-account form the general ledger of The Sport Shop at the end of February after posting the journal entries for the month's transactions.[1] At this point, before journalizing and posting adjusting and closing entries, a trial balance is taken of the general ledger. This is shown in Exhibit 6-5.

[1] The notations CRJ, CDJ, IR, SJ, and GJ shown in the T accounts of Exhibit 6-4 refer to the journals from which the entries were posted. The notation Bfd means "balance forward." These notations are used here to illustrate the point that T accounts are only convenient representations of actual accounts as shown in Chap. 5. In the ledger exhibits elsewhere in this book, the opening balances and the figures that represent postings from journals are identified by alphabetic characters referring to the statements on which they are based and the Bfd notation is omitted in connection with the account-summarizing entries.

EXHIBIT 6-4
GENERAL LEDGER FOR THE SPORT SHOP

01 Cash

	Debit	Credit	
Bfd	900	6,710	CDJ
CRJ	5,930		
	6,830	*6,710*	
		120	Bfd
Bfd	120		

04 Accounts Receivable

	Debit	Credit	
Bfd	1,890	600	GJ
SJ	670	25	GJ
		710	CRJ
	2,560	*1,335*	
		1,225	Bfd
Bfd	1,225		

08 Notes Receivable

	Debit	Credit	
GJ	600		

10 Merchandise Inventory

	Debit	Credit	
Bfd	9,200		

15 Prepaid Advertising

	Debit	Credit	
IR	40		

16 Prepaid Insurance

	Debit	Credit	
Bfd	60		
IR	288		

40 Accounts Payable

	Debit	Credit	
CDJ	6,690	1,255	Bfd
		6,475	IR
	66,90	77,30	
Bfd	1,040		
		1,040	Bfd

44 Notes Payable

	Debit	Credit	
		1,200	Bfd

45 Accrued Interest Payable

	Debit	Credit	
		12	Bfd

50 Capital Stock

	Debit	Credit	
		5,000	Bfd

51 Earned Surplus

	Debit	Credit	
		4,583	Bfd

53 Sales

	Debit	Credit	
		5,870	SJ

54 Sales Returns

	Debit	Credit	
GJ	25		

58 Other Income

	Debit	Credit	
		20	CRJ

62 Purchases

	Debit	Credit	
IR	4,430		

70 Advertising Expense

	Debit	Credit	
IR	110		

71 Delivery Expense

	Debit	Credit	
IR	60		

75 Salaries

	Debit	Credit	
IR	1,250		

76 Store Expense

	Debit	Credit	
IR	262		

77 Telephone Expense

	Debit	Credit	
IR	35		

85 Purchase Discount Lost

	Debit	Credit	
CDJ	20		

99 Cash Sales Clearing

	Debit	Credit	
SJ	5,200	5,200	CRJ

RECONCILIATION OF ACCOUNTS RECEIVABLE. Having made all entries to the customer's accounts in the subsidiary ledger from day to day, the total in the subsidiary ledger should equal the total developed in the general ledger account, Accounts Receivable, after posting the journal column totals. The balance in the subsidiary ledger can be developed as shown at top of page 103. If this total did not agree with the general ledger account balance (see Exhibit 6-4), the existence of an error would be known.

When the subsidiary ledger balance disagrees with the controlling account, the error might conceivably be in the controlling account, in the subsidiary ledger, or in both. Nevertheless, the reasonable presumption is that the controlling account figure is correct and that the mistake

Customer	*Amount*
T. Berg	$ 240
A. Carlson	120
S. Duffy	320
K. King	115
R. Stone	140
A. Tipler	105
B. Wild	185
Total	$1,225

is somewhere in the subsidiary ledger. There are many chances for an error in the subsidiary ledger for every chance for an error in the controlling account. Moreover, certain checks have already been applied to the controlling account figure before it is compared with the subsidiary ledger balance. Before the column totals from the various journals

EXHIBIT 6-5
TRIAL BALANCE OF THE GENERAL LEDGER
THE SPORT SHOP, FEBRUARY 28, 19—

Account	*Debit*	*Credit*
01 Cash	$ 120	
04 Accounts Receivable	1,225	
08 Notes Receivable	600	
10 Merchandise Inventory	9,200	
15 Prepaid Advertising	40	
16 Prepaid Insurance	348	
40 Accounts Payable		$ 1,040
44 Notes Payable		1,200
45 Accrued Interest Payable		12
50 Capital Stock		5,000
51 Earned Surplus		4,583
53 Sales		5,870
54 Sales Returns	25	
58 Other Income		20
62 Purchases	4,430	
70 Advertising Expense	110	
71 Delivery Expense	60	
75 Salaries	1,250	
76 Store Expense	262	
77 Telephone Expense	35	
85 Purchase Discount Lost	20	
Totals	$17,725	$17,725

were posted to the controlling account, each journal was shown to have equal debits and credits. And the trial balance of the general ledger has been checked.

The Sport Shop example does not illustrate the foregoing points as vividly as would be the case if it had more transactions. If The Sport Shop had 700 customers rather than 7, the sales journal and cash receipts journal would each still furnish only one column total to post to the controlling account Accounts Receivable, even though the number of subsidiary ledger postings would be multiplied one hundredfold.

ADVANTAGES OF A SUBSIDIARY LEDGER. When a subsidiary ledger is used for a group of accounts such as accounts receivable, the operation of the general ledger is simplified considerably. There is only one controlling account in place of many detail accounts; this simplifies taking the trial balance and completing the work sheet. Numerous during-the-period entries to the general ledger are replaced by a few end-of-period entries; this reduces the incidence of errors in the general ledger and permits the physical segregation of this detail work from the general-ledger work.

Also, importantly, the use of a subsidiary ledger aids in locating errors which are made. Many types of errors which may be made in the subsidiary ledger accounts will be detected by the end-of-month reconciliation with the control account. Such errors are compartmented within the subsidiary ledger; the end-of-period work with the general ledger does not need to be held up while such errors are tracked down and corrected in the subsidiary ledger accounts.

Another technical advantage is that the addition of new accounts and the removal of closed accounts in the subsidiary ledger do not change the list of general ledger accounts. Also, the methods and the medium used for maintaining the subsidiary ledger may be different from those used for the general ledger, which may be of great advantage in an operating system.

CONTROL OF ACCOUNTS PAYABLE. In the Sport Shop system, whenever an invoice is paid, this fact is recorded not only in the cash disbursements journal but also in the invoice register, where the date of payment and the check number are noted. The invoice register therefore shows which invoices have been paid and which have not. This provides a convenient and current record of "open" (unpaid) invoices, from which the up-to-date accounts payable balance can be determined at any time.

At the end of an accounting period, the total of the unpaid invoices can be compared against the balance in the general ledger account as a check on the accuracy of the invoice recording and the ledger posting work. In the example, the end-of-month open balance consisted of $980 (invoice 316), plus $60 (invoice 318), a total of $1,040. This total agrees with the balance in general ledger account 40, Accounts Payable (see Exhibit 6-4).

ADJUSTING AND CLOSING ENTRIES IN THE SPORT SHOP SYSTEM. In a system employing special journals, such as illustrated in the Sport Shop example, adjusting and closing entries are entered in the general journal. These end-of-period entries are usually developed on a work sheet before they are recorded in the journal. Inasmuch as these steps would be essentially the same for The Sport Shop as for the Central Hardware Company, they are not illustrated.

As a practical matter, adjusting and closing entries rarely are made at the end of each month; in many systems these entries are made only at the end of each year. Financial statements for interim periods are developed using work-sheet techniques to develop the appropriate adjustments and the income and expense figures for the interim period. These procedures involve considerably less work than is required to journalize and post the adjusting and closing entries to the ledger.

VARIETY IN THE DESIGN OF ACCOUNTING SYSTEMS. Generally speaking, an accounting system ought to be tailor-made to the needs of the particular business enterprise. The Sport Shop example in this chapter is representative of many actual accounting systems for small businesses for which rather straightforward manual bookkeeping methods are appropriate. In such systems the use of several special-purpose journals and the maintenance of a subsidiary ledger for accounts receivable are very common. However, the decisions about what special-purpose journals to use and the design of those journals quite properly differ considerably from one kind of enterprise to another. Also, for many businesses it is appropriate to have more than one subsidiary ledger. Other obvious differences between accounting systems are in the physical form of the journals and ledgers and in the methods and devices used in processing the accounting information.

For systems in which the accounting information is written or printed on paper, as in the Sport Shop example, there is an almost infinite variety of writing methods and devices, forms, and storage equipment. For example, a ledger might be a loose-leaf book or a tray of visible-margin cards that is posted by hand or a file of ledger sheets on which postings are written by an operator-controlled machine.

In some systems the basic information is converted to a mechanical form such as holes or notches in cards or holes in paper tape and processed by machine methods. In other systems, where the volume of information processed is very large, a major part of the accounting work may be carried on in the medium of electric impulses and magnetic bits.

Regardless of the physical form of the accounting records and the methods and equipment used in the system, the accounting principles are the same. The student who understands these principles in terms of manual-method systems has made a good start toward understanding the structure and operation of more complex accounting systems. Discussion of the system aspects of accounting in this book is in terms of manual-method systems except as otherwise indicated.

SOME COMMENTS ON THE USE OF SPECIAL-PURPOSE COLUMNAR JOURNALS. The main benefits of using special-purpose columnar journals lie in reducing the costs of posting the general ledger and determining the account balances and in reducing both the chance of introducing errors into the ledger and the expense of hunting for errors and correcting them. These benefits are derived from the fact that the number of ledger postings is greatly reduced by posting column totals instead of individual transaction figures.

Another set of benefits is derived from the special-purpose nature of the columnar journals, which permit division of labor in the bookkeeping operations. Division of labor is essential when there are a great number of transactions to be recorded. Perhaps equally important are the checks and balances for minimizing the danger of fraud that become possible when the accounting work is divided among different employees in appropriate ways.

RECORDING OBLIGATIONS AND DISBURSEMENTS. In the Sport Shop system the rule was that no disbursement would be made without first setting up the obligation to pay by means of an entry in the invoice register. Therefore, all disbursements "went through" Accounts Payable, including any relatively uncommon events such as retirement of long-term debt or acquisition of long-lived assets.

It is not uncommon to define the events to be recorded in a special journal somewhat less inclusively, restricting the use of the particular journal to a certain class of repetitive transactions. For example, an invoice register might be used only for obligations arising from the purchase of goods and services or only for purchases of merchandise. In the latter case it would probably be called a *purchase* journal and might have a number of debit columns for classifying the purchases by class of merchandise or by department.

In some systems all obligations, whether originating from a purchase invoice or not, are recorded first on a standard form called a *voucher*. Usually, each voucher has an identification and control number and spaces for recording the payee, the amount to be paid, the distribution of debits to the various accounts affected, and one or more dates. The voucher carries the authorization to make the disbursement and also may specify when payment is to be made. It may show cross references to one or more supporting documents, such as a purchase order and a receiving report. In many voucher systems there is a one-for-one correspondence between disbursements and vouchers, but one voucher may cover several invoices of the same creditor. The voucher, in general, serves to systematize and facilitate procedures leading up to the disbursements of funds and helps to provide protection against errors and fraud.

When a voucher scheme is used, the journal for entering the obligation and distributing the debits is called a *voucher register* instead of an invoice register. Usually the rule is that no disbursement is made except on the authority of the voucher. To provide for cases where Accounts Payable is not the appropriate account to credit, a voucher register may have a miscellaneous credits column.

It should be noted that the decisions about the design and use of special journals are necessarily interlocked with the decisions about what accounts are to be in the general ledger and how the contents of those accounts are defined. For example, in the Sport Shop system the balance in Accounts Payable at the end of a period might include obligations for services, wages, and many other things in addition to purchases of merchandise. In other systems, this account is used only for liabilities arising out of merchandise purchases.

RECORDING OBLIGATIONS AT THE TIME OF PAYMENT. In some businesses, particularly small ones, it may not be worthwhile formally to record obligations until the time of payment. In other words, the invoice register (or voucher register) can be omitted. If so, the cash disbursements journal becomes the means for making the distribution of debits. Thus if the invoice register were eliminated in the Sport Shop system, the cash disbursements journal might have six or more additional debit columns. It might also have a miscellaneous credits column for greater flexibility with respect to unusual entries.

In a system like this there will usually be some unpaid invoices on hand at the end of each accounting period for which the debits need to be included in the figures for that period. Also, of course, the balance sheet would be misleading if these liabilities were not recognized. One way to handle this problem is to list the unpaid invoices on hand and make an end-of-period adjustment crediting the total to Accounts Payable and distributing the debits to the appropriate accounts. Subsequently, as each of these invoices is paid, the debit is made to Accounts Payable in the cash disbursements journal.

REVERSING ENTRIES. The foregoing procedure for end-of-period payables creates a bothersome problem. For some disbursements the debit is directly to the ownership or asset account affected; for others the debit is to Accounts Payable (or other liability account). The disbursements journal procedure may be considerably simpler if all cases are treated in the same way. This becomes possible if at the start of each new accounting period the end-of-period adjustment for payables is reversed. In other words, an equal and opposite entry is made, deleting the effects of the adjustment, which was only required temporarily for the purpose of sorting transactions properly between the two accounting periods. This is an illustration of what the accountants call a *reversing entry*. The reversing entry idea is one example of many such tricks used by professional accountants to simplify their work and reduce the chances of mistakes.

A SUBSIDIARY LEDGER FOR ACCOUNTS PAYABLE. If an enterprise does business on credit with a number of vendors, and if many transactions are involved, an accounts payable ledger may be very helpful. This subsidiary ledger contains an account for each creditor and shows the current liability and a detailed record of the events leading to that current balance. Such a record is often helpful in detecting and preventing errors that might cause a monetary loss to the enterprise. Also, because each account is kept up to date, it is possible to keep track of the total of these liabilities on a day-to-day basis. This may be useful in planning both purchases and disbursements of cash.

In the Sport Shop example, adequate control of accounts payable was provided by the invoice register alone because there were only a few creditors and the transactions with each one were relatively well spaced in time. It was not necessary to maintain a creditor-by-creditor record of these obligations. However, there are many situations in which the maintenance of an accounts payable ledger is clearly worthwhile. An alternative to keeping a formal subsidiary ledger for payables is to maintain a file having a folder for each creditor in which the unpaid invoices (or vouchers) are filed. Such a file is, in reality, a subsidiary ledger, with each folder representing a different account. An "account" in such a "ledger" is credited by filing a new invoice in the folder and debited by removing an invoice when it is paid.

CASH IN THE BANK. In the Sport Shop example, all money received was presumably entered in the cash receipts journal and deposited in a commercial bank. All disbursements were made by check drawn on the same bank; each check was recorded in the cash disbursements journal. Whereas these journals are adequate and efficient for general accounting purposes, they are not designed to provide for keeping track of the current bank balance. The current balance is, of course, very helpful in managing the bank account so as to avoid overdrafts and yet not keep an excessive amount of idle money in the bank.

One way to handle this matter is to provide memo-only columns in the cash disbursements journal for recording bank deposits and the current bank balance. The total of the deposits at the end of the period is used only in checking the bank balance; it is not posted to the cash account because this is done from the cash receipts journal.

Another way to accomplish the same thing would be to combine the cash receipts journal and the cash disbursements journal into a single book called a *cash journal* in which there may be a memo column for the bank balance.

PETTY CASH. In most businesses it is desirable to make miscellaneous small disbursements with cash rather than by check. One way to handle this is to establish a *petty cash* fund by drawing a check on the bank account, cashing it, and placing the cash in the custody of a particular employee. (The credit to the account Cash would be offset by a debit to the account Petty Cash.) A record is kept of all disbursements from the petty cash fund (and any miscellaneous small cash receipts). From time to time, a check is drawn to reimburse the petty cash fund for past disbursements (minus receipts), restoring the balance to the original amount. The record of petty cash disbursements (and receipts if any) provides the information necessary for making the appropriate compound entry in the invoice register, debiting the various expense accounts. This is sometimes referred to as the *imprest* system of handling petty cash.

In most retail businesses a comparable scheme is employed with respect to the amount of money that is provided in each cash register for making change. One difference, of course, is that the change fund in each cash register is not depleted like the petty cash fund and does not need to be reimbursed in the same way.

SALES JOURNALS. In most accounting systems the sales journal is somewhat more elaborate than the one shown in Exhibit 6-2. There is often a need for additional debit and credit columns for handling such things as allowances, sales tax, and freight adjustments. Also, it may be desired to obtain a breakdown of sales by department or class of merchandise, requiring a separate credit column for each sales account.

In a business in which most sales are on credit, the cash sales clearing account is usually omitted from the journals and the ledger and all sales are "run through" Accounts Receivable.

SOME OTHER SPECIAL–PURPOSE JOURNALS. In a particular enterprise, if any type of transaction occurs with sufficient frequency, it may be desirable to have a special journal for recording it. Three such journals which are fairly common are a sales returns and allowances journal, a purchase returns and allowances journal, and a payroll journal. Depending on the type of business, it may be appropriate to have special journals for such things as capital stock transfers, notes receivable transactions, or notes payable transactions. Large, complex organizations usually need a variety of special-purpose journals for recording changes and transfers within the company.

In some systems it may appear that certain entries are made in the general ledger without first being recorded in a journal. In all probability the truth is that the source of the postings is a document which has the status of a journal if not the title. A very common example of this is "the payroll," which may serve the purposes of the invoice register and the cash disbursements journal for this specific and limited class of disbursements. If such a document is used as the basis for posting debits and credits to general ledger accounts, the reference noted in those accounts will be to this document and the document itself will be preserved in the same manner as a journal sheet. Another example of an unusual journal is that in which ledger postings are made directly from vouchers. When vouchers are used in this way, in reality they become numbered pages of a loose-leaf journal. They are, of course, preserved as a basis for explanation and justification of the ledger postings.

As modern data-processing equipment becomes more and more widely used, probably it will become more and more difficult for the nonprofessional to identify the journals and ledgers of an accounting system and the journalizing and posting processes that are associated with them. For example, a reel of magnetic tape may be a journal in every sense of the term, a "book" of original entry in which events of monetary significance are recorded in chronological order; in the same system another reel of tape might be the general ledger, in which each successive length of the tape represents a different account. The tasks of journalizing, summarizing, posting, balancing, etc., may all be performed inside a computer very rapidly and invisibly.

THE USE OF JOURNALS IN THE REMAINDER OF THIS BOOK. After this chapter, it will be assumed to be understood that journals are the source of figures posted to ledger accounts. Whenever figures are given which represent summaries of numerous similar transactions, the implication is that such figures were developed through a procedure employing the principles of a columnar journal. However, the chore of journalizing numerous transactions will hereafter be omitted in the examples and problems for the sake of simplicity.

MORE ABOUT SUBSIDIARY LEDGERS. In the examples and problems of Part 1 of this book, the idea of subsidiary ledgers is demonstrated in terms of an accounts receivable ledger. The possibility of subsidiary ledgers for accounts payable and for other assets and liabilities has been mentioned at various times. In Part 2, dealing with cost accounting, considerable stress is laid on the use of subsidiary ledgers for assets such as raw materials, work in process, and finished goods. There are also references to (and examples of) subsidiary ledgers for plant and equipment, for groups of expense accounts, and for different plants or divisions of a complex enterprise.

Somewhat like the famous fleas[2] in De Morgan's "A Budget of Paradoxes," subsidiary ledgers may contain controlling accounts for other

[2] "Great fleas have little fleas upon their backs to bite 'em,
And little fleas have lesser fleas, and so *ad infinitum*. . . ."

subsidiary ledgers, and these, in turn, may contain controlling accounts for their own subsidiary ledgers. In the general ledger of a large corporation, many of the accounts may be controlling accounts for factories, warehouses, branch sales offices, and other company activities at a distance from the central office. The factory ledger for a works may contain controlling accounts for each of the manufacturing divisions within the works. Each manufacturing division may have subsidiary ledgers for stores, work in process, etc.

SUBSIDIARY LEDGER BALANCING. Ordinarily the accounts in a subsidiary ledger for an asset, such as Accounts Receivable, will all have debit balances, and the sum of the account balances will be a debit amount. (In an accounts payable ledger, the account balances and the ledger totals would be credit amounts.) If it is desired to have a subsidiary ledger balance within itself, it is necessary to provide in the subsidiary ledger an additional account entitled General Ledger Control. The amounts posted to this account would be the same summary figures posted to the controlling account in the general ledger. However, a column total entered as a debit in the general ledger would be entered on the credit side of the General Ledger Control account in the subsidiary ledger, and vice versa. Thus, in an accounts receivable ledger, if a set of charge sales are posted as debits to various customers' accounts, the total would be posted as a credit to the General Ledger Control account. Conversely, payments on account would be credited to the various customers' accounts and the total would be debited to the General Ledger Control account. Therefore, for every entry made in the subsidiary ledger the sum of the debits would be equal to the sum of the credits, and the ledger should be in balance at all times.

The use of a General Ledger Control account in a subsidiary ledger so that the ledger will be self-balancing is particularly useful where the subsidiary ledger is maintained at some distance from the general ledger. Such is the case in companies having manufacturing or service facilities in different cities. Also, of course, if a company is divided, legally or organizationally, into several relatively autonomous units, the accounting needs to be subdivided in a similar way. When this is achieved by means of subsidiary ledgers, each such ledger needs to be self-balancing.

SOME DECISIONS REGARDING THE TREATMENT OF CASH DISCOUNT. The matter of discount for prompt payment gives rise to several interrelated questions as follows:

1. At what price should the purchased goods be valued: gross before discount or net after discount?
2. Should cash discounts taken be considered special income or price reductions?

3. Should accounts payable liabilities be carried on the books at the gross invoice price or be reduced by the amount of the cash discount offered?
4. Should cash discounts lost be considered part of the cost of goods or a financial management expense?
5. If discountable invoices are to be recorded prior to the time of payment, which assumption is preferable—that payment will be made in time to take the discount or that the opportunity for discount will be passed?
6. Should the system develop summary information about discounts taken or about discounts lost? Or both?

The answers to these questions depend on three kinds of considerations: management information needs, system operation costs, and accounting theory or philosophy. As with many such decisions the accountant must make, it is necessary to compromise theory with practical considerations and to balance system costs against potential benefits.

For discussion purposes, assume that a purchase invoice is for $1,000 and that terms are 2% 10 net 30. In the following T-account illustrations the entries made at the time of the purchase are shown in bold-faced type; those made at the time of payment are in italics.

The scheme for handling cash discount in the Sport Shop system operated as follows:

Invoice Paid within 10 Days—Discount Taken

Purchases		Accounts Payable		Cash		Purchase Discount Lost	
980		*980*	**980**		*980*		

Invoice Paid after 10 Days—Discount Passed

Purchases		Accounts Payable		Cash		Purchase Discount Lost	
980		*980*	**980**		*1,000*	*20*	

This method illustrates the popular point of view that the appropriate value for the merchandise purchased is the net price. It assumes that discountable invoices normally will be paid in time to earn the discount; if not, the consequence is viewed as a penalty cost associated with the financing of the business. The amount of discounts lost would appear in the income statement of The Sport Shop as a separate item of expense.

One criticism of this scheme is that Accounts Payable is credited at the net price of each invoice and therefore may be understated in some instances. Also, this creates a practical difficulty in reconciling the balance of a specific account payable with the creditor's statement or record, which is almost always at the gross price. Another criticism is that the amount of cash discount earned during an accounting period is not shown in the accounts as a separate figure. These points suggest a *gross-price method,* as follows:

Invoice Paid within 10 Days—Discount Taken

Purchases		Accounts Payable		Cash		Purchase Discount Earned	
1,000		*1,000*	**1,000**		*980*		*20*

Invoice Paid after 10 Days—Discount Passed

Purchases		Accounts Payable		Cash		Purchase Discount Earned	
1,000		*1,000*	**1,000**		*1,000*		

ALTERNATIVE PROCEDURES IN ACCOUNTING. The matter of the treatment of purchase discounts was discussed here in considerable depth, not because it is a vital topic in itself, but to make the point that in accounting many rather ordinary things may be not so clear cut and rule bound as the non-accountant may expect. Even in this elementary presentation of the principles of general accounting and cost accounting, we shall meet many such examples of possible alternative procedures in accounting treatment of common types of business transactions. These examples are particularly frequent in cost accounting.

Usually there is no one right way to handle such problems, and no single criterion for choosing among the alternatives. The accountant is often faced with choices involving conflict among various objectives and requiring compromise.

A REVIEW OF END-OF-PERIOD PROCEDURES. Routine entries are made in the journals and subsidiary ledgers of an accounting system systematically during the accounting period. However, there are many matters that are deferred until the end of the period, including adjustments, accruals, and other special entries and all postings to the general ledger. The things that need to be done at the end of an accounting period and their proper sequence are as follows:

1. Summarize the special journals. Test the totals of each journal for balance: Does the sum of the debits equal the sum of the credits?
2. Post from the special journals to the general ledger accounts. Also post miscellaneous entries from the general journal, if any.
3. Summarize all general ledger accounts.
4. Transfer general ledger account balances to the trial balance columns of a work sheet. Test the trial balance.

5. Develop adjustments, accruals, and corrections on the work sheet, and complete the work sheet, including the income statement and balance sheet sections.
6. Journalize all end-of-period entries developed on the work sheet (including closing entries).
7. Post the end-of-period entries to the general ledger accounts (and to any subsidiary ledger accounts affected) and resummarize the accounts.
8. Determine the total of the account balances in each subsidiary ledger, and compare the total against the balance in the appropriate controlling account in the general ledger.

MORE COMPLEX ACCOUNTING SYSTEMS. The Sport Shop system employs the basic elements present in more complex systems: a general journal and a general ledger supplemented with special-purpose (columnar) journals and one or more subsidiary ledgers. In a larger and more departmentalized enterprise, it is likely there would be additional special journals and more than one subsidiary ledger. Also, the physical form of these records and the methods and equipment used in writing and reading them might be quite different. Nevertheless, the basic principles, techniques, and procedures used in all such systems are essentially the same as those illustrated in the Sport Shop example.

SUMMARY. Some of the important points of this chapter can be restated as follows:

1. Special-purpose columnar journals are commonly used in accounting systems as a means of reducing the cost of ledger posting and the incidence of errors. Such journals also facilitate division of labor and protection against fraud.
2. The design of an accounting system involves many decisions about classifications, methods, procedures, and accounting policy. Such questions are interdependent in various ways.
3. A subsidiary ledger consists of a set of accounts removed from the general ledger and represented therein by a single "control" account. Subsidiary ledgers are particularly advantageous for groups of accounts that must be posted frequently during the accounting period. The control account in the general ledger is up-dated at the end of the accounting period by entries based on summaries of transaction data. The total of the end-of-period balances in the subsidiary ledger accounts will be equal to the end-of-period balance in the control account if no errors have been made. A common example of a subsidiary ledger is one for accounts receivable.
4. The appropriate accounting treatment of many common business transactions is not cut and dried. There are often several plausible alternatives, and a choice involves consideration of conflicting cri-

teria and objectives. A simple example of such a problem is the matter of how to treat discounts for prompt payment.

5. Appropriately, accounting systems vary immensely in complexity, method, procedure, and rules for classification and decision. However, the fundamental accounting principles and basic elements of structure are the same for all such systems.

DISCUSSION QUESTIONS

6-A. What advantages are gained by having special-purpose columnar journals as compared with making all journal entries in a single journal of the type illustrated in Chap. 5?

6-B. A sale on credit is entered in a sales journal such as the one shown in Exhibit 6-2. Explain how and when this journal entry is posted to the various ledgers affected.

6-C. What are the important differences between the subsidiary ledger and the general ledger in an accounting system?

6-D. Explain the use of the Cash Sales Clearing account in Exhibit 6-2.

6-E. What are some representative entries that you would expect to find in a general journal? Assume that the other journals in use are an invoice register, cash disbursements journal, cash receipts journal, and sales journal, just as in the Sport Shop example.

6-F. Explain the purpose of the check-mark column in the sales journal in Exhibit 6-2.

6-G. In the general journal of Exhibit 6-2, there are three columns for check marks. Explain the purpose of each.

6-H. Consider the way in which the problem of allocating advertising expense to accounting periods is treated in the Sport Shop example. Suggest a scheme which would be more appropriate if bills for advertising generally were received and usually were paid prior to the start of the period in which the benefits of the advertising were expected to accrue.

6-I. What is meant by petty cash? Briefly describe a practicable scheme for recording in the accounts all disbursements of petty cash.

6-J. Explain what a "voucher system" is. Define a "voucher" and explain how it is used.

6-K. In the Sport Shop example, suppose that the invoice register is used only for recording purchases of goods and services. If so, how would you make a journal entry to record the payoff of a $5,000 bank loan with current-period interest of $25?

6-L. The journals used in the accounting system of a small merchandising business are cash disbursements journal, sales journal, cash receipts journal, and general journal. The manager frequently makes minor disbursements and uses his automobile on behalf of the business. He keeps track of his expenses and is reimbursed each month by check. Explain how a journal entry would be made for this event and what general ledger accounts you think might be affected.

6-M. If the sales journal and cash receipts journal of Exhibit 6-2 should be combined into a single journal, certain journal entries could be eliminated. Explain the foregoing statement. How would you design such a combined journal? What disadvantages can you see in combining these two journals?

6-N. Assume that the invoice register is to be eliminated in the Sport Shop system. Suggest appropriate column headings for a revised cash disbursements journal for the modified system.

6-P. A purchase of merchandise could be entered into the accounting records (1) when the merchandise is ordered, (2) when the vendor's invoice is received, (3) when the merchandise is received, or (4) when the invoice is paid. Discuss these four alternatives, emphasizing the differences between them, and point out the relative advantages of each.

6-Q. In the discussion of systems in which obligations are generally not recorded until the time of payment, it was pointed out that an adjusting entry is required for unpaid invoices on hand at the end of each accounting period. Explain why this is so. Also explain two or three different ways this might be accomplished.

6-R. Two accounting treatments of discount for prompt payment are referred to as the *net-price method* and the *gross-price method.* In an incorporated merchandising business, in what typical *balance sheet* accounts would you expect to have the balances influenced by the choice between these two methods? For each account that you mention, tell whether the net-price method or the gross-price method would give the higher account balance. Explain your answers.

6-S. What is a "controlling account"? Explain the relationship between the accounts receivable ledger and the controlling account in the general ledger entitled Accounts Receivable.

6-T. What advantages are gained by the use of subsidiary ledgers in combination with a general ledger as contrasted to the plan of having all these accounts in the general ledger?

6-U. How could a *credit* balance occur in an account in the subsidiary ledger for accounts receivable?

6-V. Explain how it is possible for the controlling account Accounts Receivable in the general ledger to have the correct balance even though the sum of the balances in all the accounts in the accounts receivable ledger gives an incorrect figure for the total amount of accounts receivable.

6-W. A business enterprise has five journals, namely, voucher register, cash receipts journal, check register, sales journal, and general journal. It has two ledgers, a general ledger and a subsidiary accounts receivable ledger controlled by the general ledger account Accounts Receivable. There are several hundred customers' accounts in the accounts receivable ledger and approximately 50 accounts in the general ledger. The accounting period is 1 month. Questions: Where are the figures obtained that are posted on the debit side of the controlling account Accounts Receivable in the general ledger? Where are the figures obtained that are posted on the credit side of this account? When are these postings made?

6-X. Sketch a revised cash disbursements journal for the Sport Shop system which would provide for maintaining a running bank balance on a day-to-day basis. Assume that all money (cash and checks) received from Monday through Friday each week is deposited in the bank on Saturday morning (February 7, 14, 21, and 28). Illustrate the use of your new journal, using the data for the first 10 days of February.

6-Y. As a review on the subject of adjusting entries, write out general journal entries for the Sport Shop for the following adjustments that need to be made as of the end of February:

a. Merchandise inventory as of February 28 was $9,900.
b. Insurance expired during February had cost $14 (all policies).
c. Interest accrued for February on the note payable is $6.
d. Interest accrued for February on the note receivable is $4.

PROBLEMS

Problem 6-1. The Shortinch Machine Shop carries outstanding accounts receivable of $4,000 to $6,000. The subsidiary accounts receivable ledger is a file in which a copy of each invoice is placed on the day the job is delivered to the customer and recorded in the sales journal. When a check is received, the payment is recorded in the cash receipts journal and the invoice (or invoices) it covers are removed from the accounts receivable file. At the end of each quarter the billing clerk makes a list of the unpaid invoices in the accounts receivable file and determines the total amount receivable from this list. This figure is then reconciled with the general ledger account.

From the data below, determine whether or not the subsidiary ledger agrees with the controlling account in the general ledger as of June 30.

Balance in general ledger account 04, Accounts Receivable as of March 31	$ 5,302.88
From sales journal, total debit to Account 04 for second quarter	$14,801.05
From cash receipts journal, total credit to Account 04 for second quarter	$15,288.10
Total amount receivable from invoices in accounts receivable file as of June 30	$ 4,722.23

If the subsidiary ledger total does not agree with the general ledger account balance, determine the difference and which is the greater. Explain two or three kinds of mistakes you can think of that might cause such a difference.

Problem 6-2. Set up a subsidiary ledger for the inventory of bicycles for the Hardscelle Sales Co. of problem 4-5. Use a sheet of ledger paper of the double-sided type illustrated in Exhibit 5-2. Divide the sheet with horizontal rulings to accommodate three accounts—one for each model of bicycle. Enter the opening balances, and make the appropriate postings to these subsidiary ledger accounts for the quarter ending September 30. Assume that the bicycles purchased during the quarter were received in one shipment on September 2. Use the following information to make an entry in each account at the end of each month for bicycles sold that month:

	L26	S26	S24
Number sold in July..........	85	80	55
Number sold in August........	80	100	60
Number sold in September....	135	150	85
Total sold during quarter....	300	330	200

Show the balance (quantity and value) in each of the accounts as of the end of each month. At the bottom of the sheet note the total balance in this subsidiary ledger as of September 30.

STATEMENTS APPLICABLE TO PROBLEMS 6-3 THROUGH 6-5. Each of these problems involves keeping the books of a merchandising enterprise for a 1-month period. All the following statements apply to each of the three problems.

The books of original entry consist of an invoice register, a cash disbursements journal, a sales journal, a cash receipts journal, and a general journal. The column headings in the five journals are as shown in Exhibit 6-2.

The general ledger accounts to be used in these problems are the same as in the Sport Shop example, except that additional accounts can be used if necessary. The general ledger can be set up in T-account form. In these T accounts identify the journal from which each figure is posted, as illustrated in Exhibit 6-4.

In each of these systems there is a subsidiary accounts receivable ledger controlled by general ledger account 04, Accounts Receivable. The subsidiary ledger can be set up in T-account form. No more than nine T's are required. The customers' accounts in this subsidiary ledger should be maintained up to date at all times.

Use the net-price method of handling purchase invoices subject to discount for prompt payment.

No perpetual-inventory accounts are kept for any items of merchandise; the cost of goods sold is determined at the end of each month from the initial and final inventories and the purchases.

Problem 6-3. The balances in the accounts of Knight & Dae, Inc., as of February 1 were as follows:

General Ledger Account	*Debit*	*Credit*
01 Cash.................	$ 2,170	
04 Accounts Receivable...	2,390	
10 Merchandise Inventory.	19,100	
16 Prepaid Insurance.....	200	
40 Accounts Payable..............		$ 2,050
50 Capital Stock................		15,000
51 Earned Surplus................		6,810
Totals.............	$23,860	$23,860

Accounts receivable were:

T. Barney..............	$ 310
W. Flook...............	590
P. Gallagher............	180
O. Hollingsworth........	700
B. Pakala..............	610
Total.................	$2,390

The balance in general ledger account 40, Accounts Payable, as of February 1 included obligations for which invoices were received and recorded in the invoice register during January as listed below. In each case, the amount listed is net after the expected cash discount was deducted.

Day	Amount	Vendor	Notes	Date due	Invoice No.
24	$1,470	O'Hara & Co.	2% 15 net 30	2–5	441
28	495	Pollard Supply Co.	1% 10th prox.	2–10	447
30	85	Mercury Service	Jan. deliveries		452
	$2,050				

A. Set up T accounts for the subsidiary ledger, and enter the opening balances in the customers' accounts. Make entries in the appropriate journals for the following transactions that occurred in February. The next unused invoice number is 455; the next check number is 100.

Feb. 2. Sold goods on credit to W. Whitney, $240.
3. Received invoice dated January 30 from Gage & Son for merchandise, $2,000. Terms are 2% 10 days net 30.
4. Paid rent for February to Gorden Realty Co., $200.
5. W. Flook paid his bill in full, $590.
5. Paid O'Hara & Co., invoice 441, $1,470.
5. Received bill from Brown Insurance Co. for 3-year fire insurance policy effective March 1, $390.
6. Paid Community Players $25 for advertising in the theater program during February.
7. Cash sales for week ending February 7 were $1,280.
9. Received bill from Thatcher Print Shop for advertiser printing, $35.
9. Paid Gage & Son bill, $1,960, taking advantage of the discount for prompt payment.
10. Sold goods on credit to A. Blake, $440.
11. B. Pakala paid $250 on account.
11. Paid Mercury Service, invoice 452, $85.
12. Sold goods on credit to J. Martin, $700.
13. Received invoice dated February 10 from Gage & Son for merchandise, $1,200, terms 2% 10 days net 30.
14. T. Barney paid $100 on account.
14. Cash sales for week ending February 14 were $940.
17. Sold goods on credit to B. Pakala, $290.
17. Received invoice from Pollard Supply Co. for merchandise, $700, terms 1% 10th prox. net 30.
18. Allowed J. Martin a credit of $30 on his account because of defective goods.
18. Paid Ace Disposal Co. $12 for trash collection.
19. Received $25 from Romanchak Realty Co. for receiving, unpacking, and assembling a shipment of metal signs.

19. W. Whitney paid his bill, $240.
20. Received bill from the *Daily Sun* for advertising, $60.
20. Paid Gage & Son's bill, $1,176, taking advantage of the cash discount.
21. Cash sales for the week ending February 21 were $1,120.
23. Received invoice dated February 19 from O'Hara & Co. for merchandise, $800, terms 1% 10 days net 30.
23. Sold goods on credit to C. Harrington, $740.
24. Paid Northern Gas & Electric Co. $27 utility bill for the store.
26. O. Hollingsworth paid $100 and gave his promissory note for $600 in settlement of the balance of his open account. The note is due in six monthly payments with interest at 6% per year.
27. Paid the Pollard Supply Co. bill, invoice 447, $500, having passed the cash discount.
28. Received bill from Mercury Service for February deliveries, $75.
28. Cash sales for the week ending February 28 were $1,090.
28. Paid month's salaries: C. Quick, $500; Martha Dae, $600; and A. Knight, $700.

Total the columns in each journal. Check to see that the sum of the totals of the debit columns equals the sum of the totals of the credit columns for each journal.

B. Set up T accounts for the general ledger, and enter the opening balances. Make the end-of-month postings from the journals to the general ledger. Take a trial balance of the general ledger on the first two columns of a 10-column work sheet. Determine the balance in the accounts receivable ledger, and see if it agrees with the balance in the controlling account in the general ledger. From the invoice register, determine the sum of the unpaid invoices as of the end of October. Compare this total with the balance in general ledger account 40, Accounts Payable.

C. Complete the work sheet, making use of the following information:
   a. Merchandise Inventory was $19,300 at the end of February.
   b. Insurance expense for February is $35.

Make general journal entries for these two end-of-period adjustments, and post these entries to the general ledger accounts. Closing entries can be omitted in this problem.

Problem 6-4. The balances in the accounts of the Morris Equipment Co. as of September 1 were as follows:

General Ledger Account	*Debit*	*Credit*
01 Cash	$1,835	
04 Accounts Receivable	1,200	
10 Merchandise Inventory	18,130	
15 Prepaid Advertising	110	
16 Prepaid Insurance	325	
40 Accounts Payable		$ 3,690
50 Capital Stock		10,000
51 Earned Surplus		7,910
Totals	$21,600	$21,600

Accounts receivable were:

W. Atkinson	$ 105
A. Brewer	90
G. Cheever	360
M. Dillon	190
H. Romney	80
W. Thompson	205
M. Vasha	17[illegible]
Total	$1,20[illegible]

The balance in general ledger account 40, Accounts Payable, as of September 1 included obligations for which invoices were received and recorded in the invoice register during August as listed below. In each case, the amount listed is net after deducting the expected cash discount.

Day	Amount	Vendor	Notes	Date due	Invoice No.
12	$1,980	Homan Manufacturing Co.	1% 10th prox.	9–10	134
17	1,470	Linfield & McKee	2% 15 net 30	9–1	138
24	105	Central Transport, Inc.	Aug. deliveries	9–2	142
29	80	Weekly Chronicle	Aug. advertising		144
31	55	Z-I-P Service	Aug. deliveries		149
	$3,690				

A. Set up T accounts for the subsidiary ledger, and enter the opening balances in the customers' accounts. Make entries in the appropriate journals for the following transactions that occurred in September. Assume that sales are on credit unless otherwise specified. The next unused invoice number is 150; the next check is No. 100.

Sept. 1. Paid Linfield & McKee, invoice 138, $1,470, and Central Transport, invoice 142, $105.

2. Sold goods to C. Tallman, $160. H. Romney paid his bill in full, $80. Paid September rent, $220, to SAER Corp.

6. G. Cheever paid $180 on account.

7. Received invoice dated September 3 from Wagner and Sons for merchandise purchased, $1,250, terms 2% 10 net 30.

8. Paid the *Weekly Chronicle,* invoice 144, $80, and the Z-I-P Service, invoice 149, $55.

9. Sold merchandise to W. Thompson, $180.

9. Cash sales for the period September 1 through September 9 totaled $1,320.

11. Sold merchandise to A. Brewer, $125, and J. Millin, $80.

11. Paid Public Services Co. monthly bill for electricity and water, $27.

12. M. Dillon paid $90 on account; M. Vasha paid $50.

12. Received bill from T. V. Ads, Inc., $100, for spot commercials during September.

13. Paid Wagner and Sons invoice, $1,225, taking advantage of the cash discount offered.

14. Sold equipment to H. Romney, $310. Romney paid $100 on account.

15. Paid salaries for first half of September, $825. (In the cash disbursements journal insert the letters PR—meaning "payroll"—in place of check number. This refers to the payroll record for details on the several paychecks issued.)

16. Cash sales for the week ending September 16 were $960.

18. Received bill from Sun Insurance Agency for renewal of 3-year fire insurance policy, $345.
19. W. Atkinson paid his bill, $105.
20. Paid Midstate Telephone Co. $43, of which $15 was monthly directory advertising charge and the balance was for telephone service.
20. Sold goods to M. Vasha, $65.
21. Received invoice dated September 17 from Homan Mfg. Co., $1,000, for merchandise purchased. Terms are 1% 10th prox.
22. Sold goods to G. Cheever, $55, and W. Atkinson, $95.
23. Cash sales for the week ending September 23 were $1,110.
23. Paid Meyer Fuel Service for fuel oil, $25. (Treat this as all September expense.)
25. Sold goods to J. Millin, $225.
25. Received invoice dated September 22 from Linfield & McKee for merchandise, $1,500, terms 2% 15 net 30.
26. C. Tallman paid $145 in full settlement of his account, deducting $15 allowed him for repair of a defective tool purchased September 2. (Make two entries for this.)
27. Paid Homan Mfg. Co., invoice 134, $2,000, having passed the discount; paid Sun Insurance Agency bill, $345.
28. Borrowed $800 from Farmer's Trust Bank on a 60-day 6% note.
29. Received bill from Moore Printing Co. for small circulars, $60. (Assume that the benefits of this advertising will be felt in October and November.)
30. Paid salaries for last half of September, $835.
30. Received monthly bill from Z-I-P Service for September deliveries, $65.
30. Cash sales for the week ending September 30 were $1,270.
30. Paid Central Transport Co. for deliveries during September, $75.

Total the columns in each journal. Check to see that the sum of the totals of the debit columns equals the sum of the totals of the credit columns for each journal.

B. Set up T accounts for the general ledger, and enter the opening balances. Make the end-of-month postings from the journals to the general ledger. Take a trial balance of the general ledger on the first two columns of a 10-column work sheet. Determine the balance in the accounts receivable ledger, and see if it agrees with the balance in the controlling account in the general ledger. From the invoice register, determine the sum of the unpaid invoices as of the end of September. Compare this total with the balance in general ledger account 40, Accounts Payable.

C. Complete the work sheet, making use of the following information:

a. No invoice has been received from the vendor, Porta-Pull Co., for the piece of equipment sold to J. Millin on September 25. The cost is expected to be $150.

b. Insurance expense to be accrued for September is $30.

c. Half of the amount in the Prepaid Advertising account at the start of the month should be charged to September expense.

d. Merchandise inventory September 30 was $18,075.

Make general journal entries for these end-of-month adjustments, and post these entries to the general ledger accounts. Closing entries are not required in this problem.

D. Prepare an end-of-month balance sheet and a profit and loss statement for September.

Problem 6-5. The balances in the accounts of The Furniture Fair as of October 1 were as follows:

General Ledger Account	*Debit*	*Credit*
01 Cash	$ 1,800	
04 Accounts Receivable	4,700	
10 Merchandise Inventory	34,660	
16 Prepaid Insurance	240	
40 Accounts Payable		$ 3,590
50 Capital Stock		25,000
51 Earned Surplus		12,810
Totals	$41,400	$41,400

Accounts receivable were:

M. Black	$ 840
C. Hale	280
S. Horowitz	920
L. Johnson	470
A. Murdock	710
H. Pryor	450
J. Rodriguez	340
P. Shultz	690
Total	$4,700

The balance in general ledger account 40, Accounts Payable, as of October 1 included obligations for which invoices were received and recorded in the invoice register during September as listed below. In each case, the amount listed is net after deducting the expected cash discount.

Day	Amount	Vendor	Notes	Date due	Invoice No.
5	$ 539	Hart Carpet Co.	2% 10th prox.	10–10	792
9	990	Bower Bros.	1% 10th prox.	10–10	798
26	1,782	Minetonka Furniture Co.	1% 10 net 30	10–4	801
30	229	Ad Lib, Inc.	Sept. expense		804
	$3,540				

The other $50 in Accounts Payable is the estimated obligation for delivery truck rental charges for September, which appears in account 40 as the result of an adjusting entry made in the general journal as of September 30.

A. Set up T accounts for the subsidiary ledger, and enter the opening balances in the customers' accounts. Make entries in the appropriate journals for the following transactions that occurred in October.

Oct. 1. Paid S. Stone $200 for October rent of store and fixtures. (Assign invoice number 805. The check number was 401.)

2. Received invoice dated September 30 from Keeler & Co. for merchandise, $2,000, terms 2% 10 days net 30.

3. Received on account $500 from S. Horowitz and $150 from H. Pryor.

3. Sold merchandise to T. Snell on credit, $820.

4. Paid Limited Telephone Company $65, of which $20 was the directory advertisement charge for October. Also included in this

bill was a toll charge of $10 for which reinbursement is expected from an employee.

5. Cash sales October 1 through October 5 totaled $1,100.
7. Paid Hart Carpet Co. $539 (invoice 792), and Bower Bros. $990 (invoice 798), in each case taking advantage of the discount for prompt payment.
7. Sold rug to J. Rodiguez on credit, $180.
8. T. Snell returned for credit furniture he purchased on October 3 for $200.
9. L. Johnson paid his account in full, $470.
9. Received invoice dated October 6 from Hart Carpet Co. for merchandise, $1,250, terms 2% 10th prox. net 30.
10. Paid Keeler & Co. invoice, $1,960, taking advantage of the discount for prompt payment.
11. Received invoice dated October 9 from Valley Furniture Mart for merchandise, $2,500. The payment terms are 2% 10 days net 30.
11. Paid monthly electric bill of the Valley Power Co., $23.
12. Received $240 from A. Murdock on account.
12. Cash sales for the week ending October 12 totaled $950.
14. Received the monthly statement for E-Z-Rents Co. for truck time and mileage (used for deliveries) during September. The amount was $52. This is the obligation that had been estimated at $50 and recorded at the end of September via the general journal. No invoice number has been assigned to this item yet.
15. Sold merchandise to P. Schultz on credit, $270. Schultz paid $200 on his account.
16. Paid the city utilities department the monthly bill for gas, water, and disposal services, $27.
17. Received bill from Rote Insurance Company, $480 for 3-year fire insurance policy effective October 1.
18. Sold merchandise to H. Pryor on credit, $400.
18. Paid Ad Lib, Inc., invoice 804, $229.
19. Cash sales for the week ending October 19 totaled $1,270.
19. Paid Valley Furniture Mart invoice, $2,450.
21. Received $300 from M. Black on account.
22. Received invoice from Modern Van & Storage Co., for delivery of the merchandise sold to H. Pryor, $25.
23. Sold merchandise on credit to A. Murdock, $120, and to L. Johnson, $460.
24. Borrowed $1,900 from the Middle Valley State Bank on a 60-day 6% note.
25. Paid Minetonka Furniture Co. invoice, $1,800, having passed the cash discount.
26. Cash sales for the week ending October 26 totaled $1,090.
28. C. Hale paid his account in full, $280.
28. The employee paid for the $10 telephone toll charge mentioned October 4.

29. Paid the Modern Van & Storage bill, $25, and the Rote Insurance Co. bill, $480.
30. Received bills from the *Daily Times* for $160 and from Ad Lib, Inc., for $130, both for advertising.
31. Cash sales for the period October 28 through October 31 totaled $780.
31. Paid salaries for October, $2,100. (In the cash disbursements journal insert the letters PR in the place of a check number. This refers to the sequence of payroll checks recorded in the payroll record for October.)

Total the columns in each journal. Check to see that the sum of the totals of the debit columns equals the sum of the totals of the credit columns for each journal.

B. Set up T accounts for the general ledger, and enter the opening balances. Make the end-of-month postings from the journals to the general ledger. Take a trial balance of the general ledger on the first two columns of a 10-column work sheet. Determine the balance in the accounts receivable ledger, and see if it agrees with the balance in the controlling account in the general ledger. From the invoice register, determine the sum of the unpaid invoices as of the end of October. Compare this total with the balance in general ledger account 40, Accounts Payable.

C. Complete the work sheet, making use of the following information:
   a. One of the items returned by customer T. Snell was sent back to the Valley Furniture Mart for credit of $38. This item was not included in the end-of-month inventory.
   b. Insurance expired during October, $25.
   c. The delivery truck rental expense for October is expected to be $73.
   d. Inventory of furniture on October 31 is $35,640.

Make general journal entries for these end-of-month adjustments, and post these entries to the general ledger accounts. Closing entries are not required in this problem.

D. Prepare an end-of-month balance sheet and a profit and loss statement for October.

Problem 6-6. The balances in the accounts of the Norris Trading Co. as of September 1 were as follows:

Account	*Debit*	*Credit*
01 Cash	$ 910	
04 Accounts Receivable	4,350	
10 Merchandise Inventory	12,370	
16 Prepaid Insurance	150	
40 Accounts Payable		$ 6,525
44 Notes Payable		2,000
45 Accrued Interest Payable		20
50 Capital Stock		6,000
51 Earned Surplus		3,235
Totals	$17,780	$17,780

Accounts receivable were:	
D. Cooper	$ 530
N. Davis	
R. Greer	710
S. Levin	1,100
R. Rule	100
H. Santos	850
B. Thomas	620
E. Wong	440
Total, Sept. 1	$4,350

Other accounts required for the problem are:

52 Profit and Loss Summary	72 Insurance Expense
53 Sales	73 Office Expenses
54 Sales Returns	75 Salaries
61 Cost of Goods Sold	76 Store Expense
62 Purchases	78 Transportation Expense
63 Purchase Returns	83 Interest Expense
70 Advertising Expense	

A. This part of the problem consists of making certain journal entries and maintaining the accounts receivable ledger during September. Proceed as follows:

1. Set up a sales journal and a cash receipts journal, in the columnar form shown in Exhibit 6-2, and a general journal, using a journal form of the type shown in Exhibit 5-1. Also set up an accounts receivable ledger in T-account form, and head up a T account for each of the eight customers. Enter the September 1 balances in the customers' accounts; identify these figures in the T accounts with the letter A.
2. Following are the transactions to be entered in the sales, cash receipts, and general journals. After entering the transactions for 1 week in the journals, make the appropriate postings to the customers' accounts immediately. As you post each figure to the subsidiary ledger, check it off in the journal to show that this has been done. In the T accounts, indicate the source of each posting as follows: S for sales journal, R for cash receipts journal, and G for general journal.
   a. September 4: Borrowed $1,000 from the Second National Bank on a 60-day note. (Enter this in the cash receipts journal.)
   b. Period of September 1 through September 8:

	Sales on Credit			*Payments Received on Account*	
Date	*Customer*	*Amount*	*Date*	*Received from*	*Amount*
Sept. 1	D. Cooper	$ 95	Sept. 4	R. Greer	$710
4	B. Thomas	260	5	H. Santos	850
4	R. Greer	140	8	B. Thomas	500
5	N. Davis	165			
6	E. Wong	20			
6	N. Davis	75			
7	B. Thomas	45			

Cash sales for the period were $1,125.

   c. Week ending September 15:

	Sales on Credit			*Payments Received on Account*	
Date	*Customer*	*Amount*	*Date*	*Received from*	*Amount*
Sept. 10	R. Rule	$335	Sept. 12	S. Levin	$800
12	D. Cooper	120	13	E. Wong	460
12	E. Wong	70	15	D. Cooper	230
14	R. Rule	185			
14	S. Levin	150			
15	E. Wong	190			

Cash sales for the week were $1,430.

d. Week ending September 22:

Sales on Credit

Date	*Customer*	*Amount*
Sept. 17	R. Greer	$165
18	H. Santos	110
19	D. Cooper	55
19	R. Greer	115
20	B. Thomas	220
20	N. Davis	90
22	S. Levin	210

Cash sales for the week were $1,275.

e. September 21: R. Greer returned goods which he had purchased for $40 and was given a credit slip for that amount. The merchandise was returned to the shelves for resale. (Enter this in the general journal.)

f. Period of September 23 through September 30:

Sales on Credit

Date	*Customer*	*Amount*
Sept. 24	R. Rule	$130
25	E. Wong	80
26	N. Davis	130
26	D. Cooper	175
27	R. Greer	60
28	H. Santos	140
28	R. Rule	200
29	S. Levin	90

Cash sales for the week were $1,350.

g. September 26: Returned to a supplier defective merchandise which had cost $170. That amount will be deducted when paying current merchandise invoices of that supplier. (Enter this in the general journal.)

3. Total the columns in the sales and cash receipts journals. Check the set of totals to see if the sum of the debits is equal to the sum of the credits. Determine and record the customer's end-of-month balance in each account in the subsidiary ledger.

B. Continue from A as follows:

1. Set up T accounts representing the general ledger of the Norris Trading Company, and enter the September 1 balances in the accounts. Identify these figures in the T accounts with the letter A.
2. Post all entries for September from the three journals you prepared in A. Identify the postings in the T accounts as follows: G for general journal, S for sales journal, and R for cash receipts journal.
3. Reconcile the subsidiary accounts receivable ledger with the controlling account (04) in the general ledger. In other words, list the customers' account balances, determine the total, and compare this sum with the balance in account 04. If there is a difference, locate and correct your error.

4. Assume that someone else made the appropriate entries for September in the invoice register and the cash disbursements journal. Make the proper entries in the general ledger directly from the following information. Identify the postings in the T accounts as follows: I for invoice register and D for cash disbursements journal.

   a. The invoice register totals were:

Description	Account No.	Column total
Prepaid insurance	16	$ 90
Merchandise purchases	62	6,060
Freight on merchandise received	62	140
Advertising expense	70	160*
Office expense	73	95*
Salaries	75	2,400*
Store expense	76	380*
Transportation expense	78	75*
Total	...	$9,400

* Assume that these amounts are entirely September expenses.

   b. The cash disbursements journal showed a total of $9,770 paid out, all against Accounts Payable.

5. Determine and record the balance in each of the general ledger accounts. Take a trial balance using the first two columns of a 10-column work sheet.

C. Continue from B as follows:

1. Complete the work sheet started in B, developing appropriate adjustments for the following matters:

   a. Merchandise on hand at the end of September was counted and priced out at a total cost value of $13,040 (freight costs included).

   b. Interest accrued for September is $10 on the $2,000 note and $5 on the $1,000 note.

   c. Insurance having a cost value of $25 expired during the month.

2. Make entries in the general journal for the end-of-month adjustments. Post these entries to the general ledger accounts.

3. Set up closing entries in the general journal. Post these closing entries to the general ledger accounts (identified with the letter d). Balance and rule all accounts.

Submit the work sheet, general ledger, accounts receivable ledger, sales and cash receipts journals, and general journal, assembled in that sequence.

***Problem* 6-7.** This problem is an alternative to the complete-cycle problem 6-6. The company, situation, events, and all data are the same.

A. The first part of problem 6-7 is the same as A of problem 6-6.

B. After completing the journal entries and subsidiary ledger account postings of A, draw a large T (simulating the double-sided ledger form shown in Exhibit 5-2) to represent general ledger account 04, Accounts Receivable. Enter the balance brought forward from the prior month.

Proceed to post to this account the appropriate debit or credit from each journal entry affecting accounts receivable. Compute and record the account balance, and "rule" the account, following the conventions illustrated in Exhibit 5-2. On the lower unused part of this same sheet, "reconcile" the subsidiary ledger with this controlling account as of September 30. In other words, list the customers' account balances, determine the total, and compare this sum with the balance in account 04.

7/ MORE ABOUT END-OF-PERIOD ENTRIES

Some end-of-period entries were introduced in Chap. 4. It was pointed out that the journal entries resulting from systematic handling of repetitive transactions alone do not provide sufficient information. It is necessary to take into account many relevant matters that would not be recorded in the daily and weekly procedures. Therefore, at the end of each accounting period, entries must be initiated for accruals, adjustments, and corrections. These end-of-period entries are essential to the basic proposition of sorting and allocating incomes and expenses among successive accounting periods and providing meaningful valuations for balance sheet purposes. These matters are discussed in this chapter in greater depth than was possible in Chap. 4.

SOME TYPES OF END-OF-PERIOD ENTRIES. The following types of end-of-period entries are discussed in this chapter:

1. Deferred charges (prepaid expenses)
2. Deferred credits (income not yet earned)
3. Accrued expenses and accrued liabilities
4. Accrued income and accrued assets
5. Cost of goods sold
6. Bad debts and sales discounts
7. Depreciation
8. Correction of errors or omissions

The discussion of these various types of end-of-period entries is followed by an example illustrating a variety of such entries.

THE LENGTH OF THE ACCOUNTING PERIOD. Balance sheets are prepared at periodic intervals, and income statements are prepared for successive periods of approximately equal length. In all the examples up to this point, the accounting period has been 1 month. In some enterprises, the shortest accounting period used is 3 months. In others it is 6 months. Sometimes the year is divided into 13 accounting periods of 4 weeks. The longest accounting period in common use is 1 year.

Even where monthly, quarterly, or semiannual financial statements are prepared, the year is likely to be viewed as the most important accounting period. Income taxes are based on annual figures; corporations make annual reports to stockholders. Financial statements at more frequent intervals are frequently viewed as being less accurate than annual statements in the sense that some of the figures in the interim statements are subject to review and modification at year end. Although the accounting year often coincides with the calendar year, it does not necessarily do so. In many seasonal businesses, it is advantageous to start the accounting year on some date other than January 1.

Adjusting entries are always assumed to be made "as of" the final date of an accounting period, even though the physical act of making the entry in the books takes place some days (or even weeks) after that date.

DESIRABILITY OF A SYSTEMATIC PROCEDURE IN TIME DISTRIBUTION OF EXPENSE AND INCOME. It is possible to obtain what appears to be realistic balance sheets and profit and loss statements even though many of the matters discussed in this chapter are disregarded in the accounts. For example, expenses might all be treated as belonging to the period in which the cash is paid and incomes as all belonging to the period in which the cash is received. It should be evident that statements so obtained are much less likely to reflect the true state of affairs than statements obtained after making careful time allotments of expense and income.

Moreover, comparative financial statements are an important tool of management. For instance, a statement showing incomes and expenses for the first quarter of the current year ought to be compared with similar statements for last year and for earlier years. Unless consistent rules are used for identifying incomes and expenses with their appropriate accounting periods, the conclusions drawn from the comparison of financial statements are likely to be misleading.

END-OF-PERIOD ENTRIES AFFECT BOTH THE INCOME STATEMENT AND THE BALANCE SHEET. The existence and operation of an enterprise are continuous through time. For accounting purposes this stream of enterprise life must be divided arbitrarily into a series of successive periods. This is necessary to provide a basis for defining both point-in-time figures (e.g., balance sheet valuations) and sum-for-period figures (e.g., income and expense amounts).

Clearly, to sort and allocate incomes and expenses among accounting periods in a rational and consistent way, many different kinds of accruals, adjustments, and corrections need to be made. Information not available in the during-the-period procedures must be provided and applied, and some of the semiautomatic decisions made in the course of those procedures need to be reviewed and modified. It may be somewhat less obvious that end-of-period entries for such matters affect the balance sheet in the same amount they affect the income statement.

Brief reflection on the balance sheet equation and the rules for debiting and crediting accounts makes it clear that any end-of-period entry that increases or decreases Ownership (e.g., income or expense) necessarily affects also either Assets or Liabilities (or both). More explicitly, if an adjusting entry results in an increase in the net earnings shown on the income statement for the period, it must also cause an increase in the difference between the total assets and the total liabilities of the end-of-period balance sheet (e.g., an increase in an asset or a decrease in a liability). And inversely, an entry decreasing the profit on the income statement must decrease an asset or increase a liability on the balance sheet. Understanding this inherent interrelation between the income statement and balance sheet is important.

DEFERRED CHARGES OR PREPAID EXPENSES. A *deferred charge* or *prepaid expense* is an expense properly chargeable to one or more subsequent accounting periods. Until the appropriate accounting period for the charge arrives, it is carried on the books as an asset. Prepaid insurance and prepaid advertising are two types of deferred charge that were illustrated in the Central Hardware and Sport Shop examples. Some other common expense prepayments which may occur are rents and royalties, interest, certain types of taxes, salary advances, and office and factory supplies.

There are two common methods of making the accounting entries in connection with deferred charges. One method was illustrated by the treatment of prepaid insurance; the other was illustrated by the treatment of prepaid advertising.

In the first method the original debit is made to an asset (deferred charge) account such as Prepaid Insurance. At the end of each accounting period an adjusting entry is made debiting an expense account such as Insurance Expense and crediting the asset account with the amount chargeable to the accounting period just concluded. This is the most convenient method of handling a deferred charge whenever it is evident from the start—as in the case of insurance—that the total outlay is properly divisible among a number of accounting periods.

In the second method, the original debit entries are made to an expense account (such as Advertising Expense). At the end of each accounting period the expense account is reviewed to determine whether a portion of the total debit balance is properly chargeable to subsequent accounting periods. If so, an adjusting entry is made debiting an asset account (such as Prepaid Advertising) and crediting the expense account with the appropriate figure.

DEFERRED CREDITS OR INCOME NOT YET EARNED. The accounting term *deferred credits* applies to income received but not yet earned. Because the services applicable to this income have not yet been rendered, the deferred credit is viewed temporarily as a liability just as the deferred charge was viewed temporarily as an asset.

For example, in leasing property for a year it is a frequent practice to require the prepayment of the final month's rent at the same time that the first month's rent is paid. Thus an owner renting property for $200 a month might receive a payment of $400 at the start of the first month. The $200 applying to the first month is rent income; the $200 applying to the twelfth month is deferred rent income.

If his bookkeeper should credit the entire $400 to Rent Income at the time of the payment, an adjusting entry at the end of the first month would be necessary, debiting Rent Income with $200 and crediting Deferred Rent Income with $200. The Deferred Rent Income will show as a liability (possibly under the general heading Deferred Credits) on the balance sheet at the end of each of the first 11 months of the rental year. Another adjusting entry at the end of the final month debiting Deferred Rent Income and crediting Rent Income with $200 finally puts this income in the month to which it belongs.

In businesses such as magazine publishing which receive a considerable part of their income as prepayments for future services, a recognition of deferred credits is of great importance.

ACCRUED EXPENSES AND ACCRUED LIABILITIES. At the end of an accounting period, an enterprise may owe money for expenses of the period just concluded but, for one reason or another, this liability may not have been recorded on the books. An adjusting entry is required to make the balance sheet reflect such liabilities and to make the income statement reflect the related expenses of the period.

Some common accrued liabilities are accrued wages and salaries, accrued taxes, and accrued interest. If the end of an accounting period does not coincide with the end of a payroll period, there will be accrued wages. If taxes applicable to the past accounting period are not yet payable, there will be accrued taxes. The entries necessary for accrued expenses and accrued liabilities can be illustrated by the following example of accrued interest. In this example, it is assumed that the accounting period is the calendar year.

A corporation borrows $15,000,000 on September 1, 1961, by means of an issue of 20-year 4% bonds with interest payable semiannually on March 1 and September 1. No interest will need to be paid until March 1, 1962, when the first $300,000 of interest comes due. Two-thirds of this first $300,000 payable in 1962 is for the use of the borrowed money during the last 4 months of 1961. At the end of 1961, $200,000 of interest is owed, even though it is not due. To recognize this on the books, the following adjusting journal entry may be made at the end of 1961:

Dec. 31, 1961	Interest Expense	$200,000	
	Accrued Interest Payable		$200,000

Like any other expense account, Interest Expense is closed into Profit and Loss Summary. The recognition of this accrued interest makes the profit shown by the books $200,000 less than it would have appeared to be if the accrued liability Accrued Interest Payable had been disregarded in the accounts.

When the $300,000 interest payment is made on March 1, the entry might be as follows:

Mar. 1, 1962	Interest Expense	$100,000	
	Accrued Interest Payable	200,000	
	Cash		$300,000

In some instances it may not be possible to determine the exact amount of an accrued liability even though there is no question about the existence of the liability. This will usually be true, for example, of the accrued liability for corporation income taxes. In such cases, the adjusting entry showing the accrued liability should be based on the best estimate that can be made at the time of the entry. At the later date when the exact figure is known, the necessary correcting entry can be made.

ACCRUED INCOMES AND ACCRUED ASSETS. Accrued income is income properly credited to the period just concluded but not yet recorded on the books as a result of transactions during the period. Just as accrued liabilities are payables not yet due which are placed on the books by adjusting entries, accrued assets are receivables not yet due. Each adjusting entry involving a debit to an accrued asset account involves an equal credit to some income account. One such adjusting entry occurred in the Central Hardware example, the debit to Accrued Interest Receivable and the credit to Interest Income.

The word accrued is used as part of account titles referring to accrued assets and liabilities, e.g., Accrued Interest Receivable, Accrued Wages Payable. It is not used in the account titles referring to the corresponding income and expense accounts.

RULES FOR THE ALLOCATION OF INCOMES AND EXPENSES AMONG ACCOUNTING PERIODS. In the foregoing discussion, attention has been concentrated mainly on types of situations and on the accounting entries required by each type of situation. Little consideration has been given to rules or criteria for making decisions about the allocation of incomes and expenses among accounting periods.

Just as the division of the life of a business enterprise into separate accounting periods is necessarily somewhat arbitrary, so are the rules governing many of the allocations of incomes and expenses among accounting periods. Frequently, the various objectives that need to be considered lead to conflicting views and the rules adopted are necessarily a compromise. Some of the ideas that influence an accountant's decision on such allocations are as follows:

1. Expenses should be logically "matched," in successive accounting periods, with the amounts of income to which they are most closely related.
2. The relative "materiality," or significance, of a choice between alternative methods needs to be judged in terms of the probable effects on the decisions and actions of people using the accounting information.
3. Simplicity of procedures and minimizing accounting system expense are desirable.
4. Consistency from period to period enhances the opportunity to draw meaningful inferences from the comparison of present and past results and the analysis of trends.
5. It is generally considered desirable to be conservative in the sense of trying to avoid overstatement of current profits.

Frequently, practical considerations are more important than theory and sound logic. Consider, for example, the allocation of the cost of a 3-year fire insurance policy among the 36 months for which it is effective. As illustrated in the Central Hardware example, a common rule is to allocate $\frac{1}{36}$ of the cost of the policy to each month. This rule is simple and easy to apply. It does not introduce distortions in the successive income statements. The fact that the cash surrender value of the insurance policies in force will be less than the balance in the Prepaid Insurance account is not viewed as an important consideration; it is expected that policies will be kept in force for their full periods rather than surrendered for cash before they expire.

DETERMINING THE COST OF GOODS SOLD IN A MERCHANDISING BUSINESS. The Central Hardware example illustrated the end-of-period entry required to establish the cost of goods sold when detailed inventory records are not maintained. As pointed out in Chap. 4, the cost of goods sold is computed for this entry as the inventory at the start of the period plus the net purchases minus the ending inventory. In the following example this matter is explored further, taking into account consideration of the cost of transportation on merchandise purchased, purchase returns and allowances, and discounts for prompt payment.

The following T-account display shows the status of certain accounts of a retail store as of June 30, 1962, the end of an accounting period.

Merchandise Inventory	
10,600	

Purchases	
48,300	

Freight In	
3,500	

Purchase Returns and Allowances	
	1,700

The amount shown in the Merchandise Inventory account is the balance as of July 1, 1961. This inventory value was computed from a physical count of merchandise on hand. We shall assume that the unit values that were applied in pricing the items represented the cost of the merchandise, including freight charges and the net purchase price after discount for prompt payment. The comparable merchandise inventory figure for the end of the year is $13,200. The figures in the other three accounts represent the results of postings from columnar journals for the accounting year ending June 30, 1962. It is assumed that discounts for prompt payment are handled by the net-price method in this system.

Following is an analysis of the foregoing information to determine the cost of goods sold for the year, such as might appear in a detailed income statement:

Merchandise Inventory, July 1, 1961		$10,600
Purchases	$48,300	
Freight In	3,500	
Gross cost of merchandise purchased	$51,800	
Less: Purchase returns and allowances	1,700	
Net cost of merchandise purchased	$50,100	50,100
Cost of merchandise available for sale		60,700
Less: Merchandise inventory, June 30, 1962		13,200
Cost of goods sold		$47,500

The end-of-period entry required to put this information in the accounts is as follows:

Merchandise Inventory	$13,200	
Cost of Goods Sold	47,500	
Purchase Returns and Allowances	1,700	
Merchandise Inventory		$10,600
Purchases		48,300
Freight In		3,500
Totals	$62,400	$62,400

The postings from this entry into the T accounts are shown in the following display in bold-faced type.

Merchandise Inventory	
10,600	**10,600**
13,200	

Purchases	
48,300	**48,300**

Freight In	
3,500	**3,500**

Cost of Goods Sold	
47,500	

Purchase Returns and Allowances	
1,700	1,700

It should be noted that after the above entry has been made, all the temporary accounts except Cost of Goods Sold have zero balances. The Cost of Goods Sold will immediately be closed into Income and Expense Summary, leaving only the $13,200 merchandise inventory figure to be carried forward into the next year's accounts.

The foregoing example illustrates the traditional treatment using separate accounts for Merchandise Inventory, Purchases, Freight In, and Purchases Returns and Allowances. A considerably simplified scheme is used in some systems wherein the above four accounts are replaced by a single account, Merchandise Stock. The initial inventory, the purchases, the purchase returns and allowances, the purchase discounts, and the cost of transportation are all entered in this one account. If this plan had been used in the case cited above, the balance in the Merchandise Stock account (after the end-of-period columnar journal postings) would have been $60,700, the figure previously identified as the "cost of merchandise available for sale." The end-of-period entry required would be as follows:

Cost of Goods Sold	$47,500	
Merchandise Stock		$47,500

In such a system, it would still be possible to develop an analysis of the cost of goods sold calculation as shown in the foregoing example. The detailed information could be obtained by a review of the various debits and credits in the Merchandise Stock account, with reference to the columnar journals if necessary.

IMPORTANCE OF THE INVENTORY VALUATION. It should be emphasized that the amount of profit (or loss) that the books of account allot to any accounting period depends on the valuations that are given to the merchandise inventories at the beginning and end of the period. At the end of the accounting period the initial inventory figure has already been established; therefore, any change in the value assigned to the final inventory will make an equal change in the profit or loss. For instance, if the June 30 inventory value had been $14,200 instead of $13,200, the cost of goods sold would have been decreased from $47,500 to $46,500 and the profit shown for the year would have been increased by $1,000.

There are two elements in the valuation of an inventory, namely, quantity and price. An error in the inventory valuation may occur in the count of the individual items or in their pricing or in both.

An accurate physical count requires a system to ensure that every item is counted and nothing is counted twice. The objective of a count is always to find the quantities on hand at a particular moment, such as at the close of business on June 30. When the period in which the inventory is taken extends over several days, an adjustment must be made for the quantities purchased or sold in the period intervening between the inventory date and the date of the count of any item. Moreover, care should be taken that items sold but not yet delivered be excluded from the count and items purchased but not yet received be included whenever such purchases or sales have been entered on the books before the inventory date.

The objective in pricing an inventory is usually to find the cost of the inventory. In the common situation in which prices have fluctuated, a difficulty is introduced by the fact that there is no single meaning of the word "cost." It becomes necessary to establish a method of defining cost that will be used consistently from one accounting period to the next.

VARIOUS MEANINGS OF COST IN INVENTORY VALUATION. If it were practicable to examine all vendors' invoices and all transportation charges and to identify each item in the inventory with a particular invoice and transportation charge, it would be possible to determine the amount of money spent to acquire the inventory. Often this is out of the question because of the impossibility of determining the time of purchase of each of a number of identical items purchased at different times. Even where it is practicable, this method of pricing an inventory is likely to be time-consuming and expensive.

Various simpler rules for pricing inventories at cost are used by different business enterprises. The pricing may be at the most recent invoice price or at an average price over the past accounting period. Some other common methods are the first-in first-out (FIFO) method and the last-in first-out (LIFO) method. This same problem of valuing inventories under conditions of changing prices arises whenever perpetual inventory accounts are maintained. The problem is discussed at some length in Chap. 12 in connection with the treatment of material costs in cost accounting, and the advantages and disadvantages of the various methods are compared. At this point in our discussion, we shall simply note that different methods exist and that the amount of profit or loss shown by the books will be influenced by the method selected.

"COST OR MARKET, WHICHEVER IS LOWER." If there has been substantial decline in the price of an item since it was purchased, its valuation at cost may be thought to be too optimistic. For this reason, many concerns price their inventories both at cost and at *market*, which is defined as the cost of replacing the inventory at present prices. If *market* is lower than cost, a *loss on market decline* is indicated. Cost of goods sold can be computed in the usual manner based on the final inventory valuation at cost; an additional adjusting entry may debit Loss on Market Decline and credit Merchandise Inventory with the difference between the cost and the market. This reduces the profit (or increases the loss) by the amount of the decline and shows the inventory value on the balance sheet at the current market price.

Although such a decrease in market price is generally shown on the books, a corresponding increase in market price is practically never recorded. If market is above cost, that fact is ignored. This somewhat inconsistent rule of "Cost or market, whichever is lower" is typical of the conservative viewpoint generally adopted in accounting.

THE RETAIL METHOD OF INVENTORY VALUATION. The difficulty and expense of securing unit-cost figures for a large number of merchandise items lead many retail stores to take inventory at the current retail price. Inventories initially valued at retail prices can then be converted to cost price by the application of the appropriate ratio between cost price and retail price for each class of merchandise. Thus it is unnecessary to refer to old invoices and freight bills or other detailed records for unit-cost information.

The trick of this scheme is to find the correct ratio between cost price and retail price in a situation in which revisions of retail prices are frequent. Special techniques have been developed for this purpose, and part of the special terminology of retail accounting is built around these techniques. These techniques not only are aimed at inventory valuation but also serve other managerial purposes in a departmentalized retail store.

INVENTORY VALUATION FOR INTERIM STATEMENTS. In a business having a large number of different items of inventory it may be very expensive to take an accurate physical count of the inventory on hand. For this reason, many merchandising enterprises do this only once a year. In order to develop financial statements for interim periods—quarters or months—it is then necessary to estimate either the cost of goods sold or the value of the inventory on hand. One way to do this is to apply ratios such as those used in the retail method of inventory valuation to the figures for sales of the various classes of merchandise, thereby estimating cost of goods sold as a percentage of retail sales. Under this scheme the merchandise inventory value shown on the interim-period balance sheet is the derived figure; and errors will, of course, be incorporated therein.

ADJUSTING ENTRIES TO DETERMINE COST OF GOODS SOLD IN A MANUFACTURING BUSINESS THAT DOES NOT HAVE A COST ACCOUNTING SYSTEM. In a manufacturing business, the determination of cost of goods sold is more complicated than in a trading or merchandising business. It is explained in Part 2 that this greater complexity is one of the factors that usually leads to the installation of a cost accounting system which uses perpetual inventories to determine cost of goods sold. The manufacturing business without a cost system often must do considerable guessing to arrive at inventory values.

In contrast to a trading enterprise, which typically has only one type of inventory, a manufacturing enterprise usually has at least three inventories. There is an inventory of purchased materials, an inventory of work in the process of being manufactured, and an inventory of finished goods. In the valuation of the inventories of work in process and finished goods, costs of materials, labor, and indirect manufacturing expense should all be included. The difficulties of doing this satisfactorily in the absence of a cost system will become fully apparent to the student only after he has studied the elements of cost accounting.

ADJUSTING ENTRIES FOR PROSPECTIVE LOSSES ON UNCOLLECTIBLE ACCOUNTS. Any concern that grants credit to its customers will find that a certain number of them will not pay their bills. With a consistent credit policy, the percentage of uncollectible bills may be fairly constant. When the end of an accounting period is reached, it will be fairly certain that some of the accounts receivable will turn out to be uncollectible; however, it will not be known definitely which accounts will be the bad ones.

A simple accounting treatment of uncollectible accounts would be to carry each account receivable at its full face value until it is definitely recognized as uncollectible. At that time an entry could be made debiting an account such as Bad Debt Expense and crediting Accounts Receivable with the amount of the bad debt.

Two objections may be raised to such a simple treatment of this matter. One objection is that this treatment of uncollectibles results in an overvaluation of accounts receivable on the balance sheet. For the balance sheet figure to be realistic, the estimated uncollectible amount should be deducted from the total face value of the accounts receivable. A second objection is that it seems more reasonable to consider the uncollectibles as an expense of the period in which the sales were made rather than as an expense of some later period in which the debts are recognized as being bad.

These two objections can be met by using an adjusting entry at the end of each accounting period, charging as Bad Debt Expense the estimated prospective losses on uncollectible accounts for the sales made during the accounting period. If experience has indicated that uncollectible accounts are 0.5% of credit sales, the adjusting entry at the end of a year in which credit sales have been $100,000 will be:

Bad Debt Expense	$500	
Allowance for Bad Debts		$500

The amount thus charged to bad debt expense is of course closed into Income and Expense Summary, reducing the apparent profit for the year by that amount. It should be noted that in the foregoing procedure bad debt expense is estimated for each accounting period as a function of the amount of sales in that period.

The account Allowance for Bad Debts (or Allowance for Doubtful Accounts) is known in accounting language as a *contra* account. This account normally has a credit balance which is viewed as offsetting a portion of the debit balance in the asset account Accounts Receivable. In the chart of accounts the Allowance for Bad Debts account is listed in the group of asset accounts, and the credit balance of this account is incorporated in the balance sheet as a deduction from the total accounts receivable. For example, if the balance in Accounts Receivable was $21,700 (debit) and the balance in the Allowance for Bad Debts account was $900 (credit), these figures would be combined on the balance sheet as follows:

Accounts Receivable	$21,700	
Less: Allowance for Bad Debts	900	$20,800

In effect, this implies that it is estimated that $20,800 will be collected from accounts receivable having a face value of $21,700.

When a particular account receivable is subsequently recognized as uncollectible, the debit is to Allowance for Bad Debts rather than to Bad Debt Expense. For example, if it is decided that the account of John Doe, in the amount of $150, is uncollectible, the general ledger entry is:

Accounts Receivable		Allowance for Bad Debts	
xx,xxx	150	150	x,xxx

Thus the write-off of a particular bad debt does not affect the profit or loss of the period in which it is finally decided that the account is uncollectible. The bad debt expense charged against the income of the current period is an estimate in anticipation of other such write-offs that are expected to occur in the future as a consequence of sales made on credit during this period.

It is often a troublesome matter for the credit department of a concern to determine when any debt should be classified as "bad." In this connection it should be noted that the write-off of a customer's account on the books does not necessarily mean abandoning efforts to collect that account. The implication is merely that the prospects of collection are so poor that it does not seem conservative to include the account receivable among the listed assets any longer. If Doe's account written off the books in January should later be collected, a new entry is required to restore this account receivable to the books. This debit to Accounts Receivable should, of course, be balanced by a credit to Allowance for Bad Debts. The entry to show collection is then the usual debit to Cash and credit to Accounts Receivable.

SALES DISCOUNTS. A discount for prompt payment, called a purchase discount by the purchaser, is a *sales discount* from the point of view of the seller. The questions about how sales discounts should be treated in the books seem to be relatively easier to answer than the comparable questions about purchase discounts. In most systems, Sales is credited and Accounts Receivable is debited at the time of sale at the gross price. No routine entry is made for a sales discount unless the customer takes the discount upon payment of the invoice.

With respect to the income statement the preferred modern treatment of these cash discounts is to show the amount of discount taken by the customers on receivables collected in an accounting period as a deduction from the gross sales for the period. (An alternative treatment that was once quite popular was to show this item as an expense rather than a deduction from gross sales.)

One deficiency of the foregoing treatment is that the discounts taken in one month usually relate to sales made in prior months rather than sales made in the current month. A more important point is that the value of Accounts Receivable shown on the books may be overstated, possibly to a material extent. A correct solution to these two problems is to estimate the probable amount of discount that will be taken by the customers on the credit sales made during the current period and make an end-of-period entry debiting Sales Discounts and crediting Allowance for Sales Discounts. The balance in Allowance for Sales Discounts is then shown in the balance sheet as a deduction from the value of accounts receivable. The estimated sales discounts for the period is shown in the income statement as a deduction from gross sales. Discounts subsequently taken by the customers are then debited to Allowance for Sales Discounts in the cash receipts journal.

This procedure is comparable to that for loss on bad debts explained earlier. It should be noted, however, that, unless sales and collections vary widely from one accounting period to the next, it is unlikely that such a procedure would have any material effect one way or the other on the net income figures for successive periods.

ACCOUNTING FOR DEPRECIABLE FIXED ASSETS. Depreciable fixed assets consist of buildings, machinery and equipment, furniture and fixtures, and other such tangible items used in the production of goods and services. Accounting for such assets was avoided in the examples and problems earlier in the book by assuming that the enterprises rented their stores and equipment.

Experience indicates that all such tangible assets in industry will ultimately be retired. In the classic phrase of Professor Hatfield,[1] "All machinery is on an irresistible march to the junk heap." Experience also indicates that old assets are generally less valuable than the best new ones available for the same purpose, and that there is a general tendency for machines and structures to become less valuable as they get older.

THE PREPAID EXPENSE VIEW OF DEPRECIATION. Accounting for such tangible fixed assets is carried out as if their cost were a prepaid expense to be spread out over their lives by means of depreciation charges. This accounting concept of depreciation is well described in a report of the Committee on Terminology of the American Institute of Certified Public Accountants as follows:[2]

> Depreciation accounting is a system of accounting which aims to distribute the cost or other basic value of tangible capital assets, less salvage (if any), over the estimated useful life of the unit (which may be a group of assets) in a systematic and rational manner. It is a process of allocation, not of valuation. Depreciation for the year is the portion of the total charge under such a system that is allocated to the year. Although the allocation may properly take into account occurrences during the year, it is not intended to be a measurement of the effect of all such occurrences.

This definition emphasizes that accounting views the costs of depreciable fixed assets as prepaid operating expenses to be apportioned among the years of their lives by some more or less systematic precedure. Two

[1] H. R. Hatfield, *Accounting*, Appleton-Century-Crofts, Inc., New York, 1931, p. 130.

[2] Quoted by permission of the American Institute of Certified Public Accountants from *Accounting Research and Terminology Bulletins* (Final Edition—1961), Review and Résumé, p. 25, #56.

important elements in this apportionment are the estimated lives of the assets in question and the scheme for apportioning the difference between first cost and estimated salvage value among the different years of life.

THE END–OF–PERIOD ENTRY FOR DEPRECIATION. Assume that a delivery truck was purchased for $3,200 in mid-1960. The journal entry for this transaction would be a debit for $3,200 to an asset account Delivery Truck and an equal credit to Cash (or to Accounts Payable).

It is decided to write off the cost of this truck at the rate of 20% per year; for the first half year (the remainder of 1960) the depreciation charge is 10%, or $320. Conceivably the depreciation charge each year might be credited to the asset account Delivery Truck, reducing the balance in that account. This would be comparable to the way the insurance expense is credited to the asset account Prepaid Insurance each year. The entry required at the end of 1960 would be a debit of $320 to Depreciation Expense and an equal credit to Delivery Truck. The Depreciation Expense account would be closed into Income and Expense Summary. The Delivery Truck account balance carried forward into 1961 would be $2,880 (i.e., $3,200 minus $320). At the end of 1961 there would be a debit of $640 (i.e., 20% of $3,200) to Depreciation Expense and an equal credit to Delivery Truck. The balance sheet for December 31, 1961, would show the truck to have a "book value" of $2,240. At the start of 1962 the delivery truck account would appear as follows:

Delivery Truck	
3,200	320
	640

Although fixed assets accounts might be kept in the manner indicated above, this is not the usual practice. Instead of the asset account (e.g., Delivery Truck) being credited when a debit is made to Depreciation Expense, the credit entry is usually made to a contra account entitled Accumulated Depreciation or Allowance for Depreciation. If such an account had been used for the delivery truck, the asset account and the contra account would have appeared as follows at the start of 1962:

Delivery Truck	
3,200	

Allowance for Depreciation	
	320
	640

THE ALLOWANCE FOR DEPRECIATION ACCOUNT IN THE BALANCE SHEET. The accumulated depreciation account is generally shown on the asset side of the balance sheet as a deduction from the fixed asset account. Thus the delivery truck would have appeared as follows in the balance sheet of December 31, 1961:

Delivery Truck....................	$3,200	
Less: Allowance for Depreciation......	960	$2,240

This illustrates one of the points mentioned in the definition of depreciation accounting quoted from the American Institute of Accountants. This point is that the $2,240 "book value" shown for the delivery truck has no necessary relationship to the commercial value of the truck on December 31, 1961. The asset and depreciation figures shown in the balance sheet should be interpreted somewhat as follows: "We own a truck that cost us $3,200. Of this $3,200, a total of $960 has already been charged as an operating expense of past accounting periods. The remaining amount to be charged against future accounting periods is $2,240."

WHY USE AN ALLOWANCE FOR DEPRECIATION ACCOUNT? What are the advantages gained by this common practice of putting the investment in a fixed asset in one account and using a separate account to accumulate the depreciation charges against the asset? In general, the answer is that this separation into two accounts provides certain useful information that would not otherwise readily be available. Moreover, it permits more convenient depreciation accounting methods for groups of assets. These answers can be elaborated as follows:

1. It often is desirable for various purposes (e.g., insurance, taxation) to know the original investment in the fixed assets now in service. The use of the contra account makes it possible to preserve this information in convenient form in the asset account.
2. Depreciation charges are based on certain estimates that might reasonably be subject to difference of opinion, such as estimated lives and estimated salvage values. It is also true that the depreciation charges depend on the method used for apportioning the cost of fixed assets among the years of life; different methods can be used for this apportionment, and there is no one right method to select. It is sensible to separate the cumulative figure for past depreciation—based on such matters subject to differences of judgment—from the factual information regarding the investment in fixed assets.
3. For various reasons it is desirable to group similar assets together for depreciation accounting purposes. When such grouping is done, the depreciation accounting procedures are facilitated by using a contra account for the depreciation charged off to date.

SOME COMMENTS ON THE TERM "RESERVE FOR DEPRECIATION." Not many years ago the common name for the contra account in which depreciation is accumulated was Reserve for Depreciation. Similarly, the Accounts Receivable contra account, Allowance for Bad Debts, was commonly titled Reserve for Bad Debts. Although professional accountants are moving rapidly away from the use of the word "reserve" in the titles of such accounts, the terminology is deeply ingrained and still frequently encountered.

In any technical vocabulary, certain words develop meanings somewhat different from their meaning in everyday speech. In this special technical sense, the word reserve refers to an account in which credits are made to show reduced valuations for some asset or group of assets. In contrast, in popular language reserve often means a fund. The difference between these two meanings of reserve has been the source of many misunderstandings of accounting statements by persons who have not had accounting training. Sometimes this confusion has even extended to the courts in litigated matters.

The current trend among professional accountants is to use the word reserve only in connection with ownership accounts that are sometimes used to subdivide retained earnings in accordance with special legal or accounting technicalities.[3]

DEPRECIATION RATES, DEPRECIATION METHODS, AND ENTRIES FOR RETIREMENTS. Many decisions need to be made in connection with depreciation accounting. Which of a number of possible methods shall be used for writing off cost? Different methods result in different rules for making depreciation charges and for entries to show retirements. Within the framework of the depreciation accounting method adopted, what depreciation rates shall be used for each class of assets? Shall these rates be revised from time to time? If so, what evidence shall enter into decisions on rate revision?

In this modern age of high income taxation, the answers to these questions have been greatly influenced by the rules governing depreciation allowances on income tax returns. These rules have differed from time to time and from one country to another.

Moreover, the orthodox accounting approach to depreciation creates certain problems for industry in periods of changing price levels. These problems are particularly serious in periods of rapid inflation. As a result, the orthodox prepaid expense view of depreciation has been severely criticized by certain accountants, economists, and industrialists.

[3] The authors of this book believe the word "accumulated" carries the same unfortunate implication of the existence of a fund that is embodied in the word reserve. However, because the term *accumulated depreciation* seems to be currently the most popular, it is used throughout Part 2 of this book. The use of the other currently popular term *allowance for depreciation* is illustrated in the examples and problems here in Chap. 7 and in Chap. 8. In recognition of its continued use in connection with income taxation the older term *reserve for depreciation* is used in Part 3.

A discussion of all these interesting and important matters is deferred until Chap. 19.

ADJUSTING ENTRIES CORRECTING ERRORS OR OMISSIONS. In reviewing the books it may be discovered that some entry was journalized incorrectly. Possibly the wrong account was debited or credited, or the wrong amount was entered in the journal, or the debit and credit entries were reversed. Or perhaps a necessary entry was omitted completely.

Such errors can be corrected by adjusting journal entries. Each correcting entry must be designed with reference to the error it is intended to correct. The objective should be to establish the same account balances that would have obtained if the entry had been made correctly in the first place.

The preceding paragraphs do not apply to the kinds of errors disclosed by the failure of the trial balance to balance. Postings of incorrect amounts and errors in account balances can be corrected in the ledger without the need for correcting journal entries.

SUMMARY. Some of the important points of this chapter can be restated as follows:

1. If an accounting system is to produce satisfactory statements, end-of-period entries need to be made for many matters that are not provided for in the daily and weekly procedures. These entries deal with prepayments of expense (deferred charges), prepayments of income (deferred credits), obligations for expenses of the closing period not yet entered on the books (accrued liabilities), amounts due for incomes earned in the closing period but not yet entered on the books (accrued assets), adjustments of receivables and income from credit sales (e.g., bad debt expense), depreciation, and other matters.
2. End-of-period entries affecting the net income of an accounting period also affect balance sheet valuations.
3. If the cost of goods sold is derived from information about purchases and end-of-period physical inventories, the inventory valuation policies and procedures may affect income statement results significantly.
4. The cost of tangible assets such as buildings, machines, and furniture can be viewed as a prepaid operating expense to be distributed in some systematic manner over the life of the assets by means of depreciation accounting. For each class of fixed assets, the share of the cost of the fixed assets that has not yet been written off as depreciation expense is the difference between the balance in the fixed asset account and the balance in the contra account Allowance for Depreciation.
5. Some of the considerations involved in deciding how to assign (or allocate) incomes and expenses to accounting periods are the matching of expenses with incomes, the relative importance of the decision, the

alternative accounting costs, and the desirability of being consistent and conservative.

AN EXAMPLE ILLUSTRATING A VARIETY OF END-OF-PERIOD ENTRIES. North & West, Inc., is a wholesale distributor of office supplies and equipment. The company owns a warehouse and office building and employs a force of salesmen calling on retail stores. Deliveries are made by commercial delivery service or motor freight.

The general ledger accounting of North & West is handled on an annual basis; the accounting period is the calendar year. The journals are totaled and posted to the general ledger at the end of each quarter, and interim statements are developed for the first, second, and third quarters using special work-sheet techniques. Closing entries and most of the accruals and adjustments are made in the general ledger only at the end of each year.

The trial balance as of December 31, 1962, is as shown in the first two columns of the work sheet in Exhibit 7-1. Prior to taking this trial balance all routine entries were posted to the accounts. The following matters must be taken into account by means of adjusting entries:

a. Estimated inventories of supplies on hand at the end of the year were $850 for office supplies and $1,600 for warehouse supplies. In this system when such items are purchased, they are charged, respectively, to General Office Expense and Warehouse Supplies and Miscellaneous Expense.
b. The loss on bad debts is estimated at 0.35% of net sales (i.e., Sales minus Sales Returns and Allowances). The estimate is rounded to the nearest $50.
c. Examination of accounts receivable indicated that accounts totaling $2,800 are probably uncollectible and should be written off.
d. Insurance expired during the year totaled $1,800.
e. Wages earned but not yet paid as of December 31 were salesmen's salaries, $1,040; office salaries, $660; warehouse wages, $400; a total of $2,100.
f. Employer's contributions for payroll taxes to be accrued for the year amount to $4,900.
g. Estimated depreciation for the year was $2,200 on the building, $3,200 on warehouse equipment, and $1,900 on office equipment.
h. The $350 charged to Other Sales Expense should be treated as 1963 expense.
i. For each of 12 payments of $400 made on the mortgage during the year, the amount of the payment was debited to Mortgage Payable. Of the total paid during the year, $1,550 was interest.
j. The December 31 inventory of merchandise was $215,000.
k. Federal income tax on the income of the corporation is estimated as 30% of the net income before tax.

SOME COMMENTS ON THE END-OF-PERIOD ENTRIES ILLUSTRATED IN THE NORTH & WEST EXAMPLE. The following discussion is limited to certain matters introduced for the first time in this example, together with an explanation of some details that may not be obvious by inspection of the work sheet.

Entry a. The trial balance showed no balance in the account Office and Warehouse Supplies. The reason for this is that the balance carried forward from 1961 was eliminated from the account by a reversing entry. Similarly, as of January 1, 1963, a reversing entry will be made crediting this account $2,450, debiting General Office Expense $850, and debiting Warehouse Supplies and Miscellaneous Expense $1,600.

Entry e. Accrued wages payable is treated in this system by the reversing entry procedure described in connection with entry a. It may be assumed that the $2,100 figure for accrued wages payable represents wages earned by weekly-paid personnel in the last week of the quarter.

Entry f. The debit balance of $3,700 shown in the account Payroll Taxes Withheld and Accrued in the trial balance presumably reflects debits arising from disbursements made during the year to the state and Federal tax agencies which are to be offset by the credit from end-of-period entry f. The $1,200 credit balance in the account after entry f represents the remaining end-of-year liability to the tax agencies for payroll taxes withheld from paychecks and accrued as the company's expense. The subject of payroll accounting is explored somewhat further in Chap. 13.

Income tax. The presentation of this matter at the bottom of the work sheet reflects the fact that the income tax expense is a portion of the net income before taxes. An adjusting entry would, of course, be required in the ledger, debiting Income Tax Expense and crediting Estimated Income Tax Payable. No prepayment of the 1962 income tax was shown in this example because this would not have been required of a corporation having estimated earnings under $100,000.

Dividends. During the year, $16,000 in dividends was declared payable to the stockholders by the directors of the corporation. Of this, $4,000 remains to be paid and therefore will appear as a liability in the balance sheet.

Retained earnings. The balance in the Retained Earnings account at the end of 1962 will be $56,510—the January 1, 1962, balance of $62,850 plus the net income after taxes of $9,660 and minus the $16,000 dividends declared.

The North & West example is continued in Chap. 8, with the presentation of formal statements and discussion of the analysis of such statements.

EXHIBIT 7-1
WORKSHEET FOR NORTH & WEST, INC.
DECEMBER 31, 1962

ACCOUNT	TRIAL BALANCE DR	TRIAL BALANCE CR	ADJUSTMENTS DR	ADJUSTMENTS CR	INCOME STATEMENT DR	INCOME STATEMENT CR	BALANCE SHEET DR	BALANCE SHEET CR
Cash	21500						21500	
Accounts Receivable	182000			2800 c			179200	
Allowance for Bad Debts		2300	c 2800	3250 b				2750
Merchandise Inventory	225000		j 215000	225000 j			215000	
Prepaid Insurance	2600			1800 d			800	
Other Deferred Charges	750		h 350				1100	
Land	10000						10000	
Building	55000						55000	
Allowance for Deprec., Building		12300		2200 g				14500
Warehouse Equipment	37300						37300	
Allowance for Deprec., Whse. Equip.		19700		3200 g				22900
Office Equipment	17400						17400	
Accumulated Deprec. Office Equip.		7200		1900 g				9100
Accounts Payable		142700						142700
Payroll Taxes With held & Accrued	3700			4900 f				1200
Dividends Payable		4000						4000
Mortgage Payable		28300		1550 i				29850
Capital Stock		250000						250000
Retained Earnings		62850						62850
Dividends Declared	16000						16000	
Sales		943000				94300		
Sales Returns and Allowances	13000				13000			
Cash Discounts on Sales	8000				8000			
Purchases	681500			681500 j				
Freight In	32500			32500 j				

Purchase Returns & Allowances		9000	j 9000					
Sales Commissions and Salaries	57600		e 1040		58640			
Advertising Expense	8700				8700			
Automobile Rental & Operation	7400				7400			
Delivery Expense	16300				16300			
Other Sales Expense	6800			350 h	6450			
Office & Administrative Salaries	37400		e 660		38060			
General Office Expense	7600			850 a	6750			
Telephone Expense	900				900			
Warehouse Wages & Salaries	21900		e 400		22300			
Warehouse Supplies & Misc. Exp.	4700			1600 a	3100			
Building Maintenance	1000				1000			
Utilities Expense	1500				1500			
Property Tax Expense	3300				3300			
Totals	1,481,350	1,481,350						
Office and Warehouse Supplies			a 2450				2450	
Accrued Wages Payable				2100 e				2100
Bad Debt Expense			b 3250		3250			
Insurance Expense			d 1800		1800			
Payroll Tax Expense			f 4900		4900			
Depreciation Expense			g 7300		7300			
Interest Expense			i 1550		1550			
Cost of Goods Sold			j 715000		715000			
Totals			965500	965500	929200	943000		
Estimated Income Tax					4140			4140
Net Income, 1962					9660			9660
Totals					943000	943000	555750	555750

DISCUSSION QUESTIONS

7-A. Why is the year the most important accounting period? What advantages can you see in more frequent financial statements, such as quarterly statements?

7-B. How do deferred charges differ from deferred credits?

7-C. Distinguish between deferred charges and accrued expenses.

7-D. Distinguish between an accrued asset and a deferred charge.

7-E. Distinguish between an accrued liability and a deferred credit.

7-F. Give some illustrations of deferred charges. Of deferred credits. Of accrued assets. Of accrued liabilities.

7-G. Explain why different schemes for determining the "cost" of inventories can result in different figures for the profit or loss of an accounting period.

7-H. What difficulties can you see in the way of taking an accurate physical count for inventory valuation?

7-J. Explain the meaning of the phrase "Cost or market, whichever is lower." What advantage can you see in using this rule for inventory valuation? Do you see any objections that can be raised to its use?

7-K. Sooner or later the same amounts of expense and income that are fed into Income and Expense Summary by means of accrual entries would show up there through entries recording external transactions. Therefore why bother with the expense and trouble of these accrual procedures?

7-L. Why not charge Bad Debt Expense only at the time that it is recognized that particular accounts are likely to be uncollectible? What advantages are gained by using the account Allowance for Bad Debts and charging Bad Debt Expense on an estimated basis?

7-M. In writing off the cost of machinery, buildings, and other depreciable fixed assets, why not balance the debits to Depreciation Expense with credits made directly to the accounts with the assets being written off?

7-N. What is meant by a *contra account?* Explain how such an account can be used in connection with the valuation of certain assets. Could a contra account be used in connection with a liability?

7-P. Explain what is meant by a *reserve for depreciation.*

7-Q. In planning a major overhaul of the accounting system of a wholesale merchandise jobber, an accountant is trying to decide whether to handle bad debt expense on an "actual" basis or accrue it as an estimated percentage of sales each period. He must make a similar decision with respect to cash discounts on sales. He can see that each of these two decisions will have an effect on both the balance sheets and the income statements produced by the system. However, it seems to him that one of these decisions is likely to have a greater effect on future balance sheets than the other decision, and vice versa with respect to the future income statements. Explain his reasoning, and point out any assumptions you think he has made.

7-R. A manufacturing company handles all its sales through manufacturer's representatives who are compensated on a straight commission basis. All sales are on credit; collections follow sales about 45 days on the average. Commissions are paid monthly on all sales for which payment has been received. The commissions average about 10% of the amount billed. Suggest a scheme for handling this matter in the accounting system. Specify the timing and format of all entries that would be made in which these commissions would be involved.

PROBLEMS

Problem 7-1. Callahan & Company, a merchandising business, has the following trial balance taken from its general ledger on December 31, 19___. The accounting period is the calendar year.

Account	Debit	Credit
Accounts Payable		$9,000
Accounts Receivable	$12,000	
Accrued Liabilities		
Advertising Expense	3,000	
Allowance for Depreciation—Furniture and Fixtures		2,500
Allowance for Depreciation—Store Building		4,800
Allowance for Bad Debts		500
Bad Debt Expense		
Capital Stock		20,000
Cash	2,700	
Cost of Goods Sold		
Depreciation Expense		
Freight In	1,600	
Furniture and Fixtures	4,200	
Insurance Expense		
Land	7,700	
Merchandise Inventory	13,700	
Prepaid Advertising		
Prepaid Insurance	800	
Property Tax Expense	600	
Purchases	35,100	
Purchase Returns and Allowances		1,100
Retained Earnings		12,000
Salaries	10,000	
Sales		60,000
Sales Returns and Allowances	2,000	
Store Building	15,000	
Utilities Expense	1,500	
Totals	$109,900	$109,900

Enter the trial balance in the first two columns of a 10-column work sheet. Complete the work sheet, using the following information as a basis for the figures to be shown in the adjustments columns. Use only the accounts shown in the trial balance.

a. The merchandise inventory on December 31 is $11,400. (The inventory figure shown in the trial balance is that of the previous January 1.)
b. An analysis of accounts receivable indicates that $300 of such accounts are very old and should be written off as uncollectible.
c. Depreciation on the store building is estimated as 4% of its cost. Depreciation on furniture and fixtures is estimated as 10% of the cost of furniture and fixtures in service at the end of the year.
d. $450 of prepaid insurance has expired.
e. $200 included in Advertising Expense is really a prepayment of the cost of advertisements that are to appear next year.
f. Accrued property taxes are $650. This is in addition to the $600 already paid.
g. Estimated loss on bad debts on the sales for the year is ½ of 1% of the year's net sales (i.e., of sales minus sales return and allowances).

Problem 7-2. Hull & Company deals in hardware and farm implements. Perpetual-inventory accounts are maintained for farm implements but not for hardware. The following page gives the trial balance taken from the general ledger on December 31, 19___. This trial balance shows all accounts to be used in this problem, including those having zero balances prior to the adjusting entries. The accounting period is the calendar year.

End-of-period adjustments and accruals are required to enter the following information in the accounting records:

a. Hardware inventory December 31, 19___ is $18,200. (The inventory figure shown in the trial balance is that of the previous January 1.)
b. Accrued property taxes payable are $1,600.
c. Interest not yet due but already owed to Hull & Company on notes receivable is $150.
d. It is determined that several accounts receivable, totaling $960, should no longer be shown on the books, as it seems probable that they will prove to be uncollectible.
e. Estimated loss on bad debts from the year's sales of ½ of 1% of the total sales for the year.
f. The interest on the $20,000 mortgage payable is at 6% per annum and is payable semiannualy on April 1 and October 1. The most recent payment was made last October 1.
g. The depreciation to be charged for the year is as follows:

Building	$1,200
Delivery Equipment	700
Furniture and Fixtures	1,000

h. $100 of the amount shown as Rent Income in the trial balance applies to January of next year.

TRIAL BALANCE FOR HULL & COMPANY, DECEMBER 31, 19___

Account	Debit	Credit
Accounts Payable		$ 16,800
Accounts Receivable	$ 40,000	
Accrued Assets		
Accrued Liabilities		
Advertising Expense	3,600	
Allowance for Depreciation—Buildings		9,000
Allowance for Depreciation—Delivery Equipment		2,400
Allowance for Depreciation—Furniture and Fixtures		3,000
Allowance for Bad Debts		600
Bad Debt Expense		
Buildings	60,000	
Capital Stock		80,000
Cash	8,000	
Cost of Goods Sold	64,000	
Deferred Charges	2,200	
Deferred Credits		
Delivery Equipment	4,000	
Delivery Expense	3,800	
Depreciation Expense		
Freight In—Hardware	700	
Furniture and Fixtures	9,600	
Income Tax Expense		
Income Tax Payable		
Interest Expense	900	
Interest Income		200
Insurance Expense		
Inventory—Farm Implements	28,000	
Inventory—Hardware	23,000	
Mortgage Payable		20,000
Notes Receivable	4,500	
Property Tax Expense	3,400	
Purchases—Hardware	38,950	
Purchase Returns—Hardware		850
Rent Income		1,300
Retained Earnings		27,100
Sales		160,000
Salesmen's Salaries	19,400	
Store Expense	7,200	
Totals	$321,250	$321,250

i. \$500 charged to Advertising Expense is for advertising to appear next year.
j. Insurance that cost \$1,200 has expired during the year.
k. \$300 charged to Furniture and Fixtures was for repairs that should correctly have been considered as Store Expense.
m. Corporate income tax for the year is estimated at \$2,550.

Enter the trial balance in the first two columns of a 10-column work sheet. Complete the work sheet. Use only the accounts shown in the trial balance.

Problem 7-3. The general ledger of the Modern Garden Materials Co. is closed at the end of each quarter. The account balances as of June 30, 19——, after all routine entries were made for the second quarter, were as shown in the following trial balance. Enter these balances in the first two columns of a work sheet, listing the accounts in alphabetical order as shown. Complete the work sheet, making appropriate adjusting entries for the matters described below. Use only the accounts listed. Note that the accounting period is a quarter year.

a. A credit of \$98 (\$100 less 2% cash discount) for merchandise shipped back to the supplier just before the end of the accounting period has not been recognized on the books. (Purchase discounts are treated by the net price method in this system.)
b. Two customers' accounts totaling \$190 should be written off as uncollectible.
c. Merchandise inventory at the end of the quarter was \$32,000.
d. Annual depreciation rates are as follows: building, 3% per year; furniture, 10% per year; truck, 30% per year.
e. Insurance expired during the quarter totaled \$160.
f. Property taxes are expected to be \$1,280 for the year, none of which has yet been paid. Business licenses and fees are expected to be \$240 for the year, of which \$190 has already been paid.
g. A local store owner rents the Modern Garden Materials truck at 12½ cents per mile. In June he drove it 200 miles.
h. The employer's contributions for payroll taxes for the quarter are estimated at \$450.
i. Advertising for which \$80 was paid in June should be charged to next quarter.
j. The \$2,000 balance in Notes Receivable represents two 1-year \$1,000 loans, both at 6% interest. On one of these loans the interest was deducted in advance (\$60 for the year); on the other the interest is due at the end of the year.
k. Bad debt expense is expected to be ¾ of 1% of total credit sales, which amounted to \$18,000 this quarter.
m. Wages of weekly paid employees earned but not paid before June 30 were \$420.

In connection with entries d, f, and j, note that the accounting period in this problem is the second *quarter* of the fiscal year.

TRIAL BALANCE FOR MODERN GARDEN MATERIALS CO., JUNE 30, 19____

Account	Debit	Credit
Accounts Payable		$ 9,500
Accounts Receivable	$ 8,800	
Accrued Interest Receivable	10	
Accrued Salaries and Wages Payable		
Accrued Property Tax		320
Accrued Truck Rental Receivable		
Advertising Expense	560	
Allowance for Depreciation—Building		2,160
Allowance for Depreciation—Furniture		1,270
Allowance for Depreciation—Truck		1,620
Allowance for Bad Debts		170
Bad Debt Expense		
Building	24,000	
Capital Stock		40,000
Cash	2,680	
Cost of Goods Sold		
Deferred Insurance Expense	400	
Deferred Interest Income		40
Deferred License and Fee Expense	190	
Depreciation Expense		
Insurance Expense		
Furniture	4,800	
Land	8,000	
Merchandise Inventory	35,500	
Miscellaneous Income		
Notes Receivable	2,000	
Payroll Taxes Withheld and Accrued		390
Payroll Tax Expense		
Prepaid Advertising		
Purchases	22,500	
Purchase Returns and Allowances		600
Retained Earnings		27,630
Salaries and Wages	7,400	
Sales		39,000
Sales Returns and Allowances	900	
Store Expense	1,050	
Tax and License Expense		
Truck	3,600	
Truck Expense	310	
Totals	$122,700	$122,700

Problem 7-4. Suzuki and Komatsu, Inc., is a landscape architect firm. From journals and records maintained in its office, a public accounting firm prepares financial statements and tax reports quarterly. Following is the trial balance taken from the ledger as of March 31, after all the ordinary entries have been made from the various journals. Set up a work sheet with the accounts in the order listed and enter the trial balance figures.

In preparation for end-of-period entries yet to be made in the ledger, make adjustments on the work sheet for the following matters. Use only the accounts listed; do not open any other accounts.

a. This company does not keep an invoice register. The Accounts Payable account is used only at the end of each quarter to record the total of unpaid bills for items affecting that quarter. A list of such bills on hand as of March 31 is as follows:

March blueprinting, art services, and drafting supplies	$300
1-year premium due Mar. 31 on liability insurance	80
Auto service and repair bill	35
Legal and accounting fees payable	125
Total	$540

b. The balance in the Accrued Payroll Taxes account represents the net liability developed through deducting from paychecks the employee contributions for unemployment insurance and FICA and withholding taxes. The additional payroll tax liability of the company (employer's contribution) applicable to this quarter, $960, has not yet been entered in the books.

c. Analyze the following information, and develop entries that will properly distribute salary expenses, payroll tax expense, and supplies and services expense among the following accounts: Job Direct Expense, General Office Expense, and Management and Corporate Expense. On the work sheet, the three entries can be combined into a single compound entry with only one debit or credit to each account.

   1. The $16,000 total salary expense includes $2,400 for the salaries of the office manager and secretary and $12,000 for architect, artist, and draftsman salaries chargeable to jobs worked on during the quarter. The remaining $1,600 represents the portions of the salaries of the president M. Suzuki and vice-president T. Komatsu not included in the $12,000 chargeable to jobs.
   2. Payroll tax expense should be allocated to the various accounts in proportion to salary expense.
   3. $180 of the supplies and services expense should be charged to general office expense; the remainder is properly chargeable to jobs worked on during the quarter.

d. By analogy to the calculation of the cost of goods sold in a merchandising

TRIAL BALANCE OF SUZUKI & KOMATSU, INC., MARCH 31, 19__

Account	Debit	Credit
Cash	$ 980	
Accounts Receivable	7,715	
Allowance for Bad Debts		$ 530
Employee Expense Advances	200	
Jobs in Progress	840	
Prepaid Insurance	460	
Other Prepaid Expenses	220	
Office Equipment	3,660	
Allowance for Depreciation—Office Equipment		910
Automobiles	6,200	
Allowance for Depreciation—Automobiles		2,890
Accounts Payable		
Accrued Payroll Taxes		770
Other Accrued Liabilities		150
Unearned Retainer Fees		670
Capital Stock		10,000
Retained Earnings		3,480
Jobs Billed (i.e., Sales)		20,000
Cost of Jobs Billed		
Job Direct Expense		
Supplies and Services Expense	820	
Salaries	16,000	
Payroll Tax Expense		
General Office Expense	360	
Management and Corporate Expense	140	
Office Facilities Expense	640	
Telephone Expense	210	
Legal and Accounting Fees	50	
Automobile Expense	380	
Insurance Expense		
Depreciation Expense		
Business Tax and License Expense		
Bad Debt Expense		
Entertainment Expense	330	
Other Sales Expense	120	
Miscellaneous Expense	75	
Totals	$39,400	$39,400

business, compute the Cost of Jobs Billed for this service business. An account-by-account comparison is as follows:

Typical Merchandising Business	*Suzuki & Komatsu, Inc.*
Merchandise Inventory	Jobs in Progress
Cost of Goods Sold	Cost of Jobs Billed
Purchases	Job Direct Expense

Assume that, as of March 31, jobs in progress were reviewed and it was estimated that salary, payroll tax, and other expenses associated with jobs that are not yet finished (and not yet billed) amounted to $2,200.

e. Accrue bad debt expense at 1% of sales. Also, write off an account which has been carried on the books at $600 and is now considered uncollectible.

f. Expense accruals to be made for the quarter are:

Prepaid insurance expired this quarter (all policies)	$146
Prepaid license fees and taxes applicable to this quarter	34
Taxes and fees applicable to this quarter but not yet paid	50
Depreciation on office equipment for the quarter	90
Depreciation on automobiles for the quarter	130

g. Set up appropriate correcting entries for the following. An expenditure of $105 for a new table was charged incorrectly to Office Facilities Expense when the bill was paid in March. A bill for $40 paid in February and charged to the Entertainment Expense account should have been treated as a personal expense of M. Suzuki rather than a company expense.

Complete the work sheet, determining the profit or loss and the balance sheet figures. No other statements or papers are required.

Problem 7-5. This problem is a sequel to problem 7-4 concerning the firm Suzuki and Komatsu, Inc., landscape architects. Below are described selected events assumed to occur in April of the same year. Using standard journal paper, set up a journal entry that would be appropriate for each event. Use only the accounts listed in the trial balance of problem 7-4; do not open any new accounts. In your journal entries you may abbreviate account titles and omit entry descriptions.

April 2. M. Suzuki drew an expense advance of $100.

4. M. Suzuki submitted an expense report listing $15 auto expense, $110 entertainment, and $6 telephone. The total is $131.

9. Paid the invoices mentioned in entry a, problem 7-4.

10. Paid a phone bill, $63, and the office rent, $150.

15. Paid half-month salaries of $2,600, deducting withholding taxes of $351, FICA taxes of $78, and unemployment taxes of $26. (Total deducted was $455; net paychecks totaled $2,145.)

16. Received a retainer fee of $100 from a client.

17. A job is finished and billed out at $650. The client previously paid a retainer fee of $150; hence the balance due is $500.

18. Paid quarterly dividend of $600 to the stockholders.

19. Paid U.S. Treasury Department the March withholding taxes ($760), FICA withheld ($165), and employers' FICA taxes ($165), and paid State Employment Department $640 unemploy-

ment insurance premiums for the first quarter, a total of $1,730.

21. A new calculator was purchased for $660. A cash down payment of $180 was made. The balance of $480 is to be paid within 60 days to avoid interest charges.

Problem 7-6. The Best Beverage Company distributes root beer which it purchases from the bottling company packaged in disposable nondeposit bottles. The cost of root beer sold is determined from end-of-month estimates of physical inventory. The company also sells and rents soft-drink coolers. The cost of coolers sold is determined for each such sale by reference to the file of paid purchase invoices. Each customer using a rental cooler owned by Best Beverage is billed for rental charges at the end of the month.

Opening balances on March 1 were as follows:

Account	Debit	Credit
110 Cash	$ 4,976	
120 Accounts Receivable	12,561	
125 Allowance for Bad Debts		$ 120
141 Cooler Inventory	2,400	
142 Root Beer Inventory	3,000	
150 Rental Coolers	10,000	
151 Allowance for Depreciation—Rental Coolers		5,500
152 Plant Equipment	12,000	
153 Allowance for Depreciation—Plant Equipment		5,000
154 Truck	3,500	
155 Allowance for Depreciation—Truck		1,725
160 Deferred Charges	300	
211 Accounts Payable		11,470
215 Accrued Wages Payable		320
216 Payroll Taxes Withheld and Accrued		200
218 Estimated Income Tax Payable		1,200
219 Other Accrued Liabilities		162
241 Deferred Credits		
245 Dividends Payable		
260 Notes Payable		4,000
311 Capital Stock		14,000
312 Retained Earnings		5,040
315 Income and Expense Summary		
Totals	$48,737	$48,737

Other accounts required are listed below.

Income Accounts

410 Root Beer Sales
411 Root Beer Sales Returns and Allowances

420 Cooler Sales
430 Cooler Rental Income
440 Miscellaneous Income

Expense Accounts

510 Cost of Root Beer Sold
515 Cost of Coolers Sold
520 Root Beer Purchases
521 Root Beer Purchase Returns and Allowances
530 Rental Cooler Expense
541 Operating Expenses
543 Truck Expense
545 Salaries and Wages
546 Payroll Tax Expense
550 Tax and License Expense
555 Income Tax Expense
560 Advertising Expense
570 Insurance Expense
571 Bad Debt Expense
575 Depreciation Expense
580 Interest Expense

Set up T accounts and enter the following March transactions directly into these accounts.

A. Enter the opening balances as of March 1.
B. Received $20 in settlement of the account of a former customer that previously had been written off as uncollectible.
C. Paid $240 for a 2-year insurance policy on truck, effective March 1.
D. Purchases of root beer on credit from Boom Bottling Company during March totaled $17,000.
E. Sold a cooler to Ed's Garage for $400. Ed traded in an old cooler for $30, paid $50 in cash, and signed a bank loan agreement for the balance of $320. The bank paid Best Beverage that amount. The old cooler is to be regarded as having no value. The purchase cost of the new cooler was $300.
F. Root beer sales on credit during the month totaled $14,000.
G. The directors declared $2,000 in dividends, payable as of April 30. Consider this as a distribution of past profits.
H. Sports Vending Co., a credit customer, returned root beer from the skating rink, which had closed for the season. Full credit was allowed, $36.
I. Cash sales of root beer for the month totaled $7,000.
J. Refunded $16 to a cash customer for 10 cases of root beer that was found to be flat.
K. Purchased on credit a new cooler for resale, $360.
L. Returned defective root beer to Boom Bottling Company for which full credit of $50 was allowed.
M. Paid Frigid Service Company $100 for repairing and painting a cooler that was damaged in handling at the Best Beverage warehouse. This cooler

originally was purchased at a cost of $400 for resale. Since it can no longer be guaranteed as new, it will now be used as a rental cooler.

N. Received from credit customers $10,340 on account.

P. Paid the following items: $40 for telephone service; $30 to telephone company for monthly classified directory charge; $20 to Sam Cowley for cleaning rental coolers; $200 to state and Federal agencies for February payroll taxes; $50 to city for utilities; $70 to radio station KOOL for spot commercials during March; $120 to Frigid Service for rental cooler repairs; $100 for gas, oil, and service to truck; $60 to *Daily Post* for advertising; $2,100 wages for March 1 through 27; $1,150 salaries for March; $320 wages accrued as of February 28; $15,000 to Boom Bottling Co. on account; $500 rent for March; a total of $19,760.

Q. Received from Sports Vending Co. $40 for use of truck on Sundays.

Summarize the T accounts. Set up a 10-column work sheet, and take a trial balance of the ledger. Complete the work sheet, showing the end-of-period adjustments below. Enter the end-of-period adjustments in the ledger and resummarize the accounts.

a. $45 of the amount paid to the *Daily Post* during March was for advertising which will appear during April.

b. $18 of the truck rental received from Sports Vending Company is for April.

c. Depreciation for March is estimated as follows:

Rental Coolers	$130
Plant Equipment	100
Truck	85
Total	$315

d. Wages for the period of March 28 to 31 are estimated to be $185.

e. Employer's payroll tax expenses for the month is estimated at $220.

f. Customers are to be billed a total of $450 for cooler rental charges for March.

g. $35 worth of cooler rental charges billed to Ace Auto Parts last year have proved to be uncollectible.

h. The closing inventory of root beer is $4,700.

i. Bad debt expense for March is estimated as $70.

j. Interest on the note payable is at 6% per year.

k. Charge 1 month's share of the truck insurance policy cost and $15 of the cost of the previously purchased fire insurance policy against March operations.

m. Property taxes to be accrued for March are $30.

n. Federal income tax on the income of the corporation is estimated as 30% of the net income before tax.

p. Close all income and expense accounts into the Income and Expense Summary account. Then close the net profit into Retained Earnings. Rule and balance all accounts having a nonzero balance.

8/ FUNCTIONS OF FINANCIAL ACCOUNTING SYSTEMS

The preceding seven chapters have dealt with the fundamental concepts and principles of accounting and have introduced the basic accounting techniques such as the work sheet, journals, and subsidiary ledgers. With this background it is feasible to take a broader look at the objectives or purposes of the accounting system of an enterprise and to study more carefully the information it produces, particularly the financial statements.

SUMMARY OF BASIC FUNCTIONS OF ACCOUNTING. An accounting system serves a broad spectrum of purposes. Some important ones can be described in functional terms as follows:

1. Providing information desired by stockholders and creditors
2. Providing information for managerial use
3. Keeping track of assets and liabilities
4. Determining tax liabilities
5. Developing information required by regulatory law

Each of these is an important area of accounting function serving from a few to a large number of purposes. The objective here is to explore these areas briefly but sufficiently to develop some ideas particularly helpful to non-accountants. One such idea is that, in many different ways, accounting is necessary and important for the continued successful operation of an enterprise. Another is that, in making decisions about the design and operation of an accounting system, the accountant must consider a quite complex array of objectives and requirements.

THE PRODUCTS OF ACCOUNTING ARE INFORMATION. An accounting system operates on information of monetary significance to the enterprise. It must be fed information about all events which properly should be reflected in the valuation of assets and liabilities of the system and analysis of changes of ownership. The major classes of events about which the system must receive information are external business transactions, internal conversions and changes of assets, and effects of the passage of time. For all these events, the system must assimilate quantitative data in money units supplemented with a variety of descriptive information necessary for sorting and classifying the money amounts with respect to meaning and time. All this information is collected, recorded, processed, and summarized according to prescribed rules and procedures and digested into preplanned, organized records. These accounting records provide the information from which the benefits of the system are derived in two general ways: direct use of this information for a variety of administrative tasks and distillation of this information into reports for managerial purposes and for satisfying the demands of various agencies and groups outside the organization.

Of all the possible reports an accounting system may produce, the financial statements are the most concise and most broadly useful. They are the primary, most highly distilled products of the accounting system. They present concisely a great deal of information of considerable significance, particularly to the stockholders, to prospective investors and creditors, and to the management. They are important not merely as an accounting end result but because they influence many important decisions both outside and inside the organization. And because of this importance, decisions made in designing and operating an accounting system are strongly influenced by consideration of the effects of such decisions on these basic reports. For good reason, the thinking of professional accountants is strongly oriented toward the production of financial statements that are realistic, truthful, and consistent.

WHO ARE THE FINANCIAL STATEMENTS FOR? Primarily the balance sheet, income statement, and retained earnings statement are reports from the management to the present and prospective investors and creditors.

In a corporation, the principal investors are the buyers of capital shares—the owners of the enterprise. They are interested in learning periodically how the company is doing: the results of recent operations and the current financial status and condition. Essentially their objective in examining the financial statements is to evaluate the prospects of future growth of their investment and of returns in the form of dividends. They are interested in the present status and condition of the enterprise as described by the balance sheet from the point of view of taking a look at the general health and stability of the company as these things may affect future results. And they want a picture of what has happened in the recent past and an explanation of what has been done with newly earned surplus. Also, of course, if the earnings have been poorer than expected, they want to know why and to evaluate the significance of these facts as related to the future.

Institutions and persons providing long-term capital loans to a company are generally critical and careful readers of the financial statements. Their decisions inherently require an evaluation of the likelihood that the company will continue to operate successfully for at least a number of years, because this is prerequisite to judging whether or not the company will meet its long-term obligations as they become due. The picture of present financial condition and the consequences of past operations shown by the financial statements, although historical, provide the primary information which such investors use in making these estimates.

The present and prospective short-term creditors of the company, including loaning institutions, suppliers of goods and services, and the credit information agencies they employ, form a third important group of financial statement readers. Their aim is to evaluate the likelihood that the company will be able to meet its current obligations when due. Their interest is focused more on the short run—present position, relative liquidity, and likelihood of continued successful operation in the relatively near future.

A fourth group of financial statement readers, which is becoming increasingly more important, consists of employees. They are interested in the health and progress of the company because these factors bear directly on job security and possibilities for wage improvement and advancement.

The financial statements included in annual reports of publicly held corporations are, in effect, available to anyone who is interested. Moreover, many companies follow the policy of distributing financial statements to employees, credit agencies, and financial institutions and sometimes to customers and suppliers.

In addition to the external audience, the financial statements also have an important readership within the company—the management. In this realm, the financial statements can be viewed as reports from the accounting group in the organization to the corporate officers and key administrative people.

DISCLOSURE AND CONSERVATISM. The external audience, to whom published financial statements are primarly addressed, uses this information in making relatively important decisions. Customarily it assumes that the statements adequately and truthfully disclose all important facts and that the figures presented are not intentionally misleading. Clearly, there are many decisions made in the operation of an accounting system that can significantly affect the end results appearing on the financial statements. Conceivably, the management of a company might influence these decisions in the direction of making the best reasonable showing of current profit and asset valuation, but there are several reasons why this is seldom true.

One reason is the existence of Federal and state laws that are aimed at guarding the public, particularly investors, against fraud or misrepresentation. Another is the existence of reporting standards (requirements) of the public stock exchanges. But more important are the ethical concepts and accepted practices by which professional accountants employed by corporations guide their decisions and by which public accountants perform their independent audits. In general, professional accountants are extremely careful to avoid concealing facts, biasing figures, or failing to disclose information of significance to the recipients of the statements. Also, it is the accepted practice to be conservative in decisions concerning the balance sheet valuation of the assets and liabilities. In most cases where there is a reasonable choice, the accountant selects the procedure or the basis of valuation that results in the lower stated value of an asset or the higher stated value of a liability and therefore the lower, more pessimistic net ownership.

READING AND INTERPRETING FINANCIAL STATEMENTS. From the brief introduction to accounting presented thus far, it should be clear that the balance sheet and profit and loss statements are technical reports, the nature of which is determined by the basic rules of double-entry accounting. The information they contain is the summary of a large amount of detailed information put into the system and there digested in accordance with a set of technical rules and decisions. However, a large proportion of the readers of accounting statements are non-accountants. This last fact has been given increasing recognition in recent years as evidenced by the trend away from the use of technical terminology that is often obscure in meaning to many readers and in the development of simplified report formats.

Following is an introduction to the subject of reading and interpreting financial statements. Three sets of financial statements are presented, compared and discussed, and then used as the basis for a brief discussion of the analysis of financial statements by means of ratios and comparative figures.

STATEMENTS OF HYPOTHETICAL SMALL MERCHANDISING COMPANY. Exhibits 8-1 and 8-2 are end-of-year statements for the North & West, Inc., example of Chap. 7. These statements are rather traditional in format, except that the balance sheet is arranged vertically in so-called *report form* rather than horizontally.

Both the balance sheet and the income statement are somewhat more detailed than usual. However, assuming that the stock of this small company is held by relatively few people who are closely connected with or engaged in the management of the business, this amount of detail may be quite appropriate. Some simplifications that might be made in statements for wider distribution are combining into one figure the accumulated depreciation amounts shown on the balance sheet, eliminating details of the derivation of net sales and cost of goods sold, and combining various expenses on the income statement.

EXHIBIT 8-1
NORTH & WEST, INC.
BALANCE SHEET
DECEMBER 31, 1962

Assets			
Current Assets:			
Cash		$ 21,500	
Accounts Receivable	$179,200		
Less: Allowance for Bad Debts	2,750	176,450	
Merchandise Inventory		215,000	
Supplies		2,450	
Deferred Charges		1,900	$417,300
Fixed Assets:			
Land, at cost		10,000	
Buildings	55,000		
Less: Allowance for Depreciation	14,500	40,500	
Warehouse Equipment	37,300		
Less: Allowance for Depreciation	22,900	14,400	
Office Equipment	17,400		
Less: Allowance for Depreciation	9,100	8,300	73,200
Total Assets			$490,500
Liabilities			
Current Liabilities:			
Accounts Payable		$142,700	
Payroll Taxes Payable		1,200	
Accrued Wages Payable		2,100	
Dividends Payable		4,000	
Estimated Federal Income Taxes		4,140	$154,140
Long-term Liabilities:			
Mortgage Payable			29,850
Total Liabilities			$183,990
Stockholders' Equity			
Common Stock—2,500 shares outstanding		$250,000	
Retained Earnings		56,510	306,510
Total Liabilities and Stockholders' Equity			$490,500

CORPORATE DIVIDENDS. Near the start of our discussion of accounting principles, we noted that a profit is an increase in Ownership. Our examples and problems have illustrated the point that in a corporation an increase in Ownership as a result of operations finally appears on the books as an increase in Earned Surplus (Retained Earnings).

A formal procedure is necessary to distribute any profits to the stockholders. The first step in this procedure is an action by the board

EXHIBIT 8-2
NORTH & WEST, INC.
INCOME STATEMENT
YEAR ENDING DECEMBER 31, 1962

Sales			$943,000
Less: Sales returns and allowances		$ 13,000	
Cash discounts allowed		8,000	
Estimated bad debt expense		3,250	24,250
Net sales			$918,750
Cost of goods sold:			
Merchandise inventory, Jan. 1, 1962		$225,000	
Purchases	$681,500		
Freight in	32,500		
Total	$714,000		
Less: Purchase returns and allowances	9,000		
Net purchases	$705,000	705,000	
Total		$930,000	
Less: Merchandise inventory, Dec. 31, 1962		215,000	715,000
Gross profit on sales			$203,750
Selling expenses:			
Sales commissions and salaries	$ 58,640		
Advertising expense	8,700		
Automobile rental and operation	7,400		
Delivery expense	16,300		
Other sales expense	6,450	$ 97,490	
General operating expenses:			
Office and administrative salaries	$ 38,060		
General office expense	6,750		
Telephone expense	900		
Warehouse wages and salaries	22,300		
Warehouse supplies and miscellaneous	3,100		
Building maintenance and utilities	2,500		
Property taxes	3,300		
Depreciation	7,300		
Insurance expense	1,800		
Payroll taxes	4,900	$ 90,910	188,400
Income from operations			$ 15,350
Other income and expense:			
Deduct: Interest expense			1,550
Income before taxes thereon			$ 13,800
Deduct: Estimated Federal income taxes			4,140
Net income for the year			$ 9,660

STATEMENT OF RETAINED EARNINGS
YEAR ENDING DECEMBER 31, 1962

Balance, January 1, 1962	$62,850
Add: Net income for the year	9,660
	$72,510
Less: Cash dividends declared, $6.40 per share	16,000
Balance, December 31, 1962	$56,510

of directors declaring a dividend. For example, consider North & West, Inc., having 2,500 shares of capital stock outstanding. Its board of directors, on November 20, passed a resolution that a cash dividend of $1.60 per share is to be paid on January 15 to stockholders of record on December 15 and that this dividend is to be charged to the account Retained Earnings. The accounting entry at the time of the declaration is:

Nov. 20	Retained Earnings	$4,000	
	Dividends Payable		$4,000

On the balance sheet of December 31 (Exhibit 8-1) the $4,000 dividends payable appears as a current liability.

When the actual cash payment to the stockholders is made, the entry will be:

Jan. 15	Dividends Payable	$4,000	
	Cash		$4,000

The declaration and payment of a cash dividend always reduce an Ownership account by the amount of the dividend and make an equal reduction in the asset account Cash.

With certain exceptions, such as the liquidation or dissolution of a corporation, it is not legally permissible for a board of directors to declare a dividend unless the books show undivided profits at least as great as the amount of the dividend. Nevertheless, the existence of profits does not ensure that dividend payments will be made to the stockholders; many corporations expand through the "plowing back" into the enterprise a substantial fraction of the profits. The board of directors decides the extent to which profits will be kept in the business rather than paid out as dividends. Moreover, to pay a cash dividend it is not sufficient that the books show a profit; there must also be cash that is not required for essential business purposes.

In many corporations, the directors act on dividends at regular intervals, such as quarterly or semiannually. The prospect of regular dividend payments, as contrasted to irregular ones, is attractive to many investors in corporate stocks.

Corporations in which a substantial fraction of the profit is used to finance business expansion often declare stock dividends in addition to or as a substitute for cash dividends. For example, the corporation just cited having 2,500 shares of stock outstanding might declare a 4% stock dividend, giving 1 share of stock for each 25 held. The holder of 100 shares of stock would receive a dividend of 4 shares. The proportionate equities of the different stockholders in an enterprise are not changed by such a stock dividend. Prior to the dividend, this stockholder owned 1/25 (i.e., 100/2,500) of the enterprise; after the dividend, he still owns 1/25 (now 104/2,600).

ACTUAL STATEMENTS OF TWO CORPORATIONS. Exhibits 8-3 through 8-5 are the financial statements that were presented in the 1961 annual report of the Aluminum Company of America. Exhibits 8-6 through 8-8 reproduce the financial statements that appeared in the 1961 annual report of King-Seeley Thermos Co. The Alcoa statements are for the year ending December 31, 1961; the King-Seeley reports are for their fiscal year ending July 31, 1961.

All these statements show the previous-year figures alongside the current-year figures. This desirable arrangement makes it easy to see the direction and magnitude of changes that have taken place. Both annual reports also included a comparative summary showing key figures derived from the financial statements and other selected statistics tabulated in columnar fashion by years for the past 10 years. The comparative feature of the statements and the long-run summary are very common in published annual reports.

CONSOLIDATED FINANCIAL STATEMENTS. Both these corporations own subsidiary corporations. In general, where there is a parent corporation and subsidiaries, there are likely to be intercompany obligations; for example, one subsidiary may owe money to another subsidiary or to the parent corporation. Consolidated financial statements such as Exhibits 8-3 to 8-8 eliminate all such intercompany relationships.

In the year ending July 31, 1961, the former King-Seeley Corporation merged with American Thermos Products Company. The financial reports of the new company, King-Seeley Thermos Co., presented in Exhibits 8-6 to 8-8, show consolidated figures for both original companies and all their subsidiaries for 1959–1960 as well as for 1960–1961.

SOME COMMENTS ON THE BALANCE SHEET EXHIBITS. The Alcoa balance sheet, shown in Exhibit 8-3, is a good example of the traditional *account form* balance sheet, with assets on the left and liabilities and owners' equity on the right. Both the assets and the liabilities are arranged in order of liquidity.[1] The King-Seeley balance sheet, Exhibit 8-6, presents the balance sheet information in a form somewhat different from the conventional one illustrated in Exhibit 8-3. The current liabilities are subtracted from the current assets to obtain a figure for net working capital. The fixed assets less depreciation are then added and the long-term liabilities are deducted to give a figure

[1] Public utility companies in the United States customarily use an inverted arrangement, with fixed assets and owners' equity at the top and with current assets and current liabilities at the bottom.

for net assets. This figure for net assets is then reconciled with the ownership figure, which consists of the sum of common stock at par value, capital surplus, and earned surplus. This is the so-called *financial position* form of the balance sheet. A separate statement, shown

EXHIBIT

ALUMINUM COMPANY OF AMERICA *and consolidated subsidiaries*

CONSOLIDATED BALANCE

ASSETS

	December 31 1961	1960
Current Assets:		
Cash	$ 48,147,354	$ 40,748,696
Accounts and notes receivable:		
Customers, less allowances: 1961, $3,068,104; 1960, $3,147,141	124,139,310	108,284,180
Other	12,529,380	6,902,357
Inventories (Note A)	262,509,829	259,997,082
Prepaid insurance and taxes	4,374,746	5,169,387
Total Current Assets	**451,700,619**	**421,101,702**
Investments (Note B):		
Subsidiaries not consolidated	4,452,643	2,812,224
Other companies	34,229,061	28,769,742
Real estate developments	7,830,070	4,372,888
Other	824,705	1,564,912
Total Investments	**47,336,479**	**37,519,766**
Other Assets and Deferred Charges:		
Indemnity and surety deposits	1,277,603	1,106,939
Receivables and advances—noncurrent	25,860,333	32,075,003
Deferred exploration and mining expenses	4,148,522	4,206,119
Other deferred charges	9,206,760	8,504,351
Total Other Assets and Deferred Charges	**40,493,218**	**45,892,412**
Properties, Plants and Equipment, at cost:		
Land and land rights, including mines	66,375,422	65,567,764
Structures, machinery and equipment	1,575,611,225	1,558,727,238
	1,641,986,647	1,624,295,002
Less, accumulated allowances for amortization, depletion and depreciation	854,814,954	797,266,193
	787,171,693	827,028,809
Construction work in progress	52,401,905	41,174,438
Patents and other intangible assets, less amortization	1,440,356	1,417,021
Total Properties, Plants and Equipment	**841,013,954**	**869,620,268**
	$1,380,544,270	**$1,374,134,148**

The appended notes are an integral part of the financial statements.

as Exhibit 8-8, gives details of the inventories and the fixed assets.

The King-Seeley balance sheet shows that the company used government securities as an investment for liquid funds. The cost of these securities is properly included under the heading Current Assets.

The basis used for inventory valuation is of interest in examining financial statements. Both balance sheets give information on this matter. Both companies appear to use the common rule of valuing inventories at cost or market, whichever is lower. In the King-Seeley case, cost

8-3

SHEETS *December 31, 1961 and 1960*

LIABILITIES

	December 31	
	1961	1960
Current Liabilities:		
Notes payable to banks	$ 25,000,000	$ 34,000,000
Accounts payable	32,752,587	28,167,379
Dividends on preferred and common stock	7,639,010	7,631,494
Accrued salaries, wages, vacation allowance and other compensation	21,707,753	21,757,780
Provision for taxes, including taxes on income	24,052,044	9,493,032
Other current liabilities	14,845,601	15,433,629
Long-term debt due within one year	13,602,581	768,837
Total Current Liabilities	**139,599,576**	**117,252,151**
Long-Term Debt, less amount due within one year (Note C)	**385,071,763**	**412,241,602**
Deferred Credits, Reserves and Noncurrent Liabilities	**7,296,748**	**6,686,219**
Reserve for Future Taxes on Income	**73,679,395**	**78,744,005**
	605,647,482	**614,923,977**

SHAREHOLDERS' EQUITY

	1961	1960
Capital Stock:		
Serial Preferred Stock, par value $100 per share: Authorized 1,000,000 shares: $3.75 Cumulative Preferred Stock, redeemable at $100 per share; Authorized 660,000 shares; issued 659,909 shares	65,990,900	65,990,900
Common Stock, par value $1.00 per share: Authorized 50,000,000 shares; Issued: 1961, 21,338,938 shares; 1960, 21,313,857 shares	21,338,938	21,313,857
Additional Capital	44,737,900	44,044,790
Retained Earnings	642,829,050	627,860,624
Total Shareholders' Equity	**774,896,788**	**759,210,171**
	$1,380,544,270	**$1,374,134,148**

is determined by the first-in first-out method; in Alcoa, cost is determined by the last-in first-out method. Note A to the Alcoa statements was as follows:

Note A. Inventories are carried at the lower of cost or market, with

EXHIBIT 8-4
ALUMINUM COMPANY OF AMERICA AND CONSOLIDATED SUBSIDIARIES

STATEMENT OF *Consolidated Income and Retained Earnings*

For the years ended December 31, 1961 and 1960

	1961	1960
Net sales and operating revenues	$ 853,334,514	$ 861,211,772
Income from securities and investments	1,667,472	2,221,562
Gain on sales of capital assets and investments	1,596,188	3,022,531
Other income	2,733,435	3,324,311
Gross revenues	**859,331,609**	**869,780,176**
Cost of goods sold and operating expenses	570,258,468	590,154,919
Selling, general administrative and other expenses	116,960,511	122,048,668
Provision for depreciation and depletion	80,049,923	80,194,803
Interest expense	16,515,708	16,354,802
Taxes, not including social security and United States and foreign taxes on income	14,098,323	13,882,879
Total costs and expenses	**797,882,933**	**822,636,071**
Income before United States and foreign taxes on income	61,448,676	47,144,105
Provision for United States and foreign taxes on income:		
Current	23,464,609	10,248,280
Less, reduction in reserve for future taxes on income	5,064,609	3,148,280
	18,400,000	**7,100,000**
Net income for the year	**43,048,676**	**40,044,105**
Retained earnings, beginning of year	627,860,624	603,443,708
Addition resulting from acquisitions of subsidiaries	—	12,497,427
	670,909,300	**655,985,240**
Dividends declared:		
On preferred stock—$3.75 per share	2,474,680	2,474,688
On common stock—$1.20 per share	25,605,570	25,649,928
	28,080,250	**28,124,616**
Retained earnings, end of year	**$ 642,829,050**	**$ 627,860,624**

STATEMENT OF *Consolidated Additional Capital*

For the years ended December 31, 1961 and 1960

	1961	1960
Additional capital, beginning of year	$ 44,044,790	$ 42,558,078
Addition resulting from acquisitions of subsidiaries	—	562,914
Excess of amounts received over the aggregate par value of common stock issued under Employees' Stock Option Plan	693,110	923,798
Additional capital, end of year	**$ 44,737,900**	**$ 44,044,790**

The appended notes are an integral part of the financial statements.

EXHIBIT 8-5
ALUMINUM COMPANY OF AMERICA AND CONSOLIDATED SUBSIDIARIES
SOURCE AND APPLICATION OF FUNDS DURING 1961

Source of Funds:	
Net income for the year	$ 43,048,676
Add, charges against income which did not require current disbursement of funds:	
Depreciation and depletion.	80,049,923
Book value of properties, plants and equipment retired or sold	12,991,387
Reduction in reserve for future taxes on income	(5,064,609)
Other	1,070,195
Total funds from operations ...	132,095,572
Decrease in other assets and deferred charges, net	5,399,194
Proceeds from sale of common stock	718,191
	$138,212,957

Application of Funds:	
Additions to properties, plants and equipment	$ 64,434,996
Reduction in long-term debt ($14,336,095) and reclassification to current liabilities of portion of debt due within one year ($12,833,744)	27,169,839
Dividends declared:	
Preferred stock	2,474,680
Common stock	25,605,570
Increase in investments, net	9,816,713
Increase in working capital	8,251,492
Other	459,667
	$138,212,957

cost being determined for substantially all inventories under the last-in first-out method. The classification of the inventories follows:

	December 31	
	1961	1960
Finished goods.................	$ 65,439,084	$ 71,252,430
Work in process...............	148,500,973	138,260,447
Bauxite and alumina...........	23,355,219	23,342,917
Purchased raw materials........	14,399,218	15,354,551
Operating supplies.............	10,815,335	11,786,737
Totals......................	$262,509,829	$259,997,082

The problem of valuing inventories (and pricing items out of inventories) when prices vary is discussed in some detail in Chap. 12 in the context of cost accounting. The point of interest here is the common conservative practice of substituting current market value for cost when the unit cost of an inventory item developed in the accounting system is higher than replacement cost.

It was pointed out in Chap. 1 and thereafter that balance sheet valuations of investment assets are ordinarily based on cost and that the market values of such assets may be very different from their costs. If market value exceeds cost, as is often the case with respect to land, securities, and other investments, the generally accepted (conservative) practice is to show these items on the balance sheet at cost.

NOTES TO FINANCIAL STATEMENTS. Both the Alcoa and King-Seeley annual reports included notes to the financial statements explaining details of various matters of interest to investors and creditors. For example, the King-Seeley notes described the merger with American Thermos Products Co. and gave details of the related accounting entries affecting the Capital Stock and Capital Surplus accounts, provided an analysis of long-term debt and information about certain restrictions in the loan agreements on the payment of dividends, discussed the provisions for pension plan costs, and gave facts about the stock purchase

EXHIBIT 8-6

KING-SEELEY THERMOS CO.

CONSOLIDATED STATEMENT OF FINANCIAL CONDITION

	JULY 31	
	1961	1960 (Note 1)
CURRENT ASSETS:		
Cash	$ 3,207,910	$ 3,574,735
U. S. Government securities	5,445,365	5,443,898
Accounts receivable, less $240,000 (1961) and $248,000 (1960) for doubtful accounts	8,081,365	8,285,843
Cost of dies collectible from customers	180,340	1,408,666
Inventories, at lower of cost (first-in, first-out) or market	14,456,034	15,521,949
Prepaid insurance and other expenses	404,390	593,348
TOTAL CURRENT ASSETS	$31,775,404	$34,828,439
LESS—CURRENT LIABILITIES:		
Portion of long-term liabilities payable within one year	$ 138,000	$ 156,000
Notes payable	120,000	2,526,972
Accounts payable	2,940,730	2,785,716
Accrued payrolls, taxes and other items	2,251,951	2,832,078
Estimated liability for income taxes	2,232,978	2,878,253
TOTAL CURRENT LIABILITIES	$ 7,683,659	$11,179,019
WORKING CAPITAL	$24,091,745	$23,649,420
PROPERTY ACCOUNTS, less depreciation and amortization	16,384,261	16,438,940
PATENTS AND TRADEMARKS, at cost less amortization of $209,182 (1961) and $118,221 (1960)	340,512	298,418
	$40,816,518	$40,386,778
LONG-TERM LIABILITIES, less amounts payable within one year (Note 3)	(6,537,000)	(6,691,886)
DEFERRED INCOME TAXES	(140,426)	(59,339)
MINORITY INTERESTS	—	(436,188)
NET ASSETS	$34,139,092	$33,199,365
DERIVED FROM:		
Common stock, $1 par value (Notes 4 and 5) – Authorized 2,000,000 shares Issued 1,649,615 shares	$ 1,649,615	$ 1,649,615
Capital surplus (Note 5)	8,014,517	8,014,517
Income retained for use in the business (Note 3)	24,474,960	23,535,233
	$34,139,092	$33,199,365

options outstanding. Such notes are an integral part of the statements and are used as a means of disclosing facts that are considered to be significant but are too complex to explain adequately in the statements themselves.

COMMON AND PREFERRED STOCK. All preceding examples and problems in this book have assumed the simplest corporate structure

EXHIBIT 8-7
KING-SEELEY THERMOS CO.

CONSOLIDATED STATEMENT OF INCOME

AND INCOME RETAINED FOR USE IN THE BUSINESS

	YEAR ENDED JULY 31	
	1961	1960 (Note 1)
Net sales	$73,655,463	$79,037,885
Other income	406,400	343,073
	$74,061,863	$79,380,958
Costs and expenses (including depreciation and amortization of $2,511,712 in 1961 and $2,606,954 in 1960):		
Manufacturing cost of goods sold	$58,491,980	$62,295,431
Administrative, advertising and other selling expenses	9,491,937	9,718,550
Interest expense	479,788	464,448
	$68,463,705	$72,478,429
Income before income taxes and minority interests	$ 5,598,158	$ 6,902,529
Estimated federal, state and foreign income taxes	2,970,000	3,627,740
	$ 2,628,158	$ 3,274,789
Minority interests	42,699	35,791
NET INCOME FOR THE YEAR	$ 2,585,459	$ 3,238,998
Income retained for use in the business at beginning of year	23,535,233	22,198,694
Cash dividends:		
King-Seeley—$1.00 a share in 1961 and $1.25 a share in 1960	(1,470,556)	(1,166,725)
American Thermos—prior to December 9, 1960 (Note 1)	(175,176)	(735,734)
Income retained for use in the business at end of year (Note 3)	$24,474,960	$23,535,233

with only one class of capital stock. With just one type of stock, each share has one vote for members of the board of directors. All shares have equal rights to the profits of the enterprise and equal rights in the distribution of the assets if the corporation is dissolved. For example, consider the previously mentioned owner of 100 shares in a corporation that has 2,500 shares of capital stock outstanding. This stockholder is entitled to $\frac{1}{25}$ of any profits distributed as dividends and to $\frac{1}{25}$ of the net assets in case of dissolution.

Some corporations have two classes of stock, preferred and common. Preferred stock usually has a prior claim on earnings. This prior claim is made effective by a provision that no dividends may be paid to common stockholders unless a stipulated amount per share is being paid to the

EXHIBIT 8-8
KING-SEELEY THERMOS CO.

DETAILS OF CERTAIN ITEMS

IN CONSOLIDATED STATEMENT OF FINANCIAL CONDITION

		July 31 1961	July 31 1960 (Note 1)
INVENTORIES:	Raw materials	$ 2,667,317	$ 3,050,449
	Work in process and purchased parts	5,755,726	6,514,733
	Finished goods	6,032,991	5,956,767
		$14,456,034	$15,521,949
PROPERTIES—at cost:	Land	$ 530,610	$ 501,700
	Buildings and building equipment	12,963,738	12,147,589
	Machinery and equipment	14,084,346	13,958,539
	Tools, jigs and fixtures	1,797,624	2,364,319
	Construction in progress	1,053,196	1,033,206
		$30,429,514	$30,005,353
	Depreciation and amortization	14,045,253	13,566,413
		$16,384,261	$16,438,940

ACCOUNTANTS' REPORT

To the Stockholders and
Board of Directors of
King-Seeley Thermos Co.

In our opinion, the accompanying statements present fairly the consolidated financial position of King-Seeley Thermos Co. and its subsidiary companies at July 31, 1961 and the results of their operations for the year then ended, in conformity with generally accepted accounting principles applied on a basis consistent with that of the preceding year. Our examination of these statements was made in accordance with generally accepted auditing standards, and accordingly included such tests of the accounting records and such other auditing procedures as we considered necessary in the circumstances.

Price Waterhouse & Co.,
Certified Public Accountants

Detroit, Michigan
September 13, 1961

holders of the preferred stock. For example, consider a corporation that has a 5% preferred stock of $100 par value and pays dividends quarterly. Unless a $1.25 quarterly dividend is paid on the preferred stock, no dividend may be declared on the common stock.

Ordinarily, it is provided that preferred stockholders cannot receive higher dividends than this stipulated amount. Sometimes, this preference right is *cumulative;* if the corporation has failed to pay the stipulated preferred dividends in prior years, the arrearage must be made up before any payments may be made to common stockholders. Preferred stock usually has a prior claim in the dissolution of a corporation; no distribution may be made to common stock until a stated amount per share has been paid to holders of preferred stock. In some cases, preferred stockholders do not have the right to vote for directors except when the corporation has failed to pay preferred dividends at the stipulated rate. Although the provisions governing preferred stock differ from company to company, the general statement can be made that preferred stock is designed to appeal to a more conservative type of investor than is common stock. The common stockholder is the real equity investor, who is in a position to make the greatest gain if the corporation is prosperous and whose dividends are first to be reduced or eliminated when earnings decline.

Some corporations have two or more classes of preferred stock with different stipulated dividend rates or other different provisions. A few corporations have two classes of common stock with voting rights reserved to one class.

Referring again to Exhibits 8-3 and 8-6, Alcoa has two classes of stock, cumulative preferred and common. King-Seeley has only one class of stock, common. Both companies state the maximum number of shares of each class they were legally authorized to issue at the time of the statements. The Alcoa preferred stock carries a stipulated maximum dividend rate of $3.75 per share (per year), with cumulative rights. The company has the right to redeem shares of this preferred stock at specified dates at a price of $100 per share.

PAR AND NO-PAR STOCK. Stock may have a *par* value stated on the stock certificate, such as $100 a share, $25 a share, $5 a share. Although there are exceptions, par value usually indicates the investment per share at the time the stock was first issued. The accounting entry on the issue of 2,500 shares of common stock at their par value of $100 per share would be:

Cash	$250,000	
Capital Stock		$250,000

After a corporation has been operating for a period of time, the valuation per share indicated by the books of account (generally referred to as *book value* per share) may differ considerably from the par value. If there is a surplus, the stockholders' equity per share will exceed par value; if there is a deficit, it will be less than par value.

The market value of the stock of a going concern has no necessary relationship either to par value or to book value Among other matters, market value is likely to be influenced greatly by investors' views on the probable future profits of the enterprise.

Some corporations issue stock without par value. Even with such *no-par* stock, some balance sheet figure for Capital Stock is needed for the accounts. This may properly be the original amount received by the corporation when the stock was issued. Sometimes, however, a lower figure per share, designated as *declared* or *stated* value, will be used. For example, assume that 10,000 shares of no-par stock are issued at $15 per share and that the declared value used for accounting and balance sheet purposes is $10 per share. The accounting entry to record this transaction may be as follows:

Cash	$150,000	
Capital Stock		$100,000
Capital Surplus		50,000

An alternative account title is Paid-in Surplus. Such an account is also used with par-value stock if the corporation receives an amount in excess of par value when the shares are first issued. When an account title such as Capital Surplus or Paid-in Surplus is used for an account showing part of the capital investment made by the stockholders, the undistributed profits or retained earnings are recorded in a separate account.

The Alcoa and King-Seeley statements both list the common stock at par value. In both cases the amount shown under Capital Stock is small in relation to the sum of retained earnings and capital surplus.

Note that the term *earned surplus* is replaced in these statements by the term *retained earnings* or *retained income.* In the Alcoa statement the term *additional capital* is used in place of the term *capital surplus.* The use of these terms, together with the avoidance in both statements of the use of the word *reserve,* illustrates the modern tendency to avoid accounting terms that have technical meaning that differ greatly from the popular concept of these meanings.

The net change in the Alcoa account Additional Capital during each year is explained in the statement of consolidated additional capital in Exhibit 8-4. In both 1961 and 1960 there was an increase in this account arising from the sale of stock at prices in excess of par value. In 1960 there was also an entry made to this account in connection with the acquisition of a subsidiary in exchange for Alcoa common stock. Other examples of events that might result in an entry to capital surplus are mergers, revaluations, and receipt of donations.

THREE DIFFERENT VIEWS OF THE BALANCE SHEET EQUATION. In Chap. 1 and subsequent chapters, emphasis was placed on the important concept that the total value for owners' equity developed in an accounting system is the difference between the book value of the assets and the book value of the liabilities. This derived nature of ownership is demonstrated by writing the balance sheet equation in the form Ownership = Assets — Liabilities. This point of view is emphasized in the *financial position form* of balance sheet illustrated in Exhibit 8-6.

Two other interpretations of the balance sheet equation are brought out by writing the equation in the form Assets = Liabilities + Ownership, which is emphasized in the *account form* of the balance sheet illustrated in Exhibit 8-3. One of these points of view is that the accounts on the right-hand side record the equities, or claims, of various parties against the total assets held by the company at a given point in time. The sequence in which the various equities are listed on the right-hand side indicates the general order of priority: first current-liability creditors, then long-term creditors, then preferred stockholders, and finally the common stockholders. The other point of view is that the right-hand side of the balance sheet identifies the various sources of the total capital invested in the company's assets and shows the amounts "obtained" from each source. In this view, the sum of capital stock, capital surplus, and retained earnings is viewed as the share of the total asset value made available to the company by the common stockholders by direct contribution and by accepting the decisions of the directors with respect to profits (and capital surplus) retained for use in the business.

SOME COMMENTS ON THE INCOME STATEMENTS EXHIBITS. The income statement for North & West in Exhibit 8-2 shows gross profit on sales as the difference between net sales and cost of goods sold and introduces nonoperating incomes and expenses as additions and deductions from net operating income. This is the so-called *multiple-step* format. The current trend is toward a *single-step* format, which is illustrated in the Alcoa and King-Seeley income statements (Exhibits 8-4 and 8-7). All incomes are grouped together, then all costs (including cost of goods sold) are deducted. Estimated income taxes are shown separately, emphasizing the importance of this expense. The relatively low effective tax rate indicated in the Alcoa figures, particularly those for 1960, was the result of a rather unusual combination of circumstances involving product prices, foreign operations, earnings taxed as capital gains, and other matters explained in the text of the 1960 annual report. The King-Seeley figures are much more typical, the estimated tax being about 53% of net income before taxes.

Both companies experienced a drop in sales from the previous year, reflecting the general economic slow-up evidenced in most industries during that time. King-Seeley was apparently somewhat more affected, probably because a major part of their diverse product line was consumer goods and components for automobiles and home appliances.

RETAINED EARNINGS STATEMENTS. Exhibit 8-2 includes a statement explaining the change in retained earnings during the year. Both Alcoa and King-Seeley incorporated this information into a combined statement of income and retained earnings (Exhibits 8-4 and 8-7). The usual sources of change in retained earnings reflected in such a statement are an increase due to earnings (or decrease due to a loss) and a decrease due to cash dividends. Some other events that may affect retained earnings directly are stock dividends, mergers or acquisitions of subsidiaries (see Exhibit 8-4), and unusual gains or losses that have occurred or can be anticipated.

SOURCE AND APPLICATION OF FUNDS STATEMENT. Exhibit 8-5 contains the supplementary statement included in the Alcoa annual report explaining the change in *net working capital,* which is defined as current assets minus current liabilities. The change in net working capital from one balance sheet date to another can be analyzed in terms of the concurrent changes in noncurrent assets and liabilities and Ownership. For any increase in net working capital there is necessarily a corresponding decrease in long-term assets or an increase in long-term liabilities or Ownership. Conversely, any decrease in net working capital is coupled to an equal increase in long-term assets or decrease in long-term liabilities or Ownership.

The usual sources of inflow to working capital during a year are:

1. The net profit for the year adjusted by adding back expenses charged to Profit and Loss that did not involve a current reduction in working capital, such as depreciation and expense accrued from deferred charges
2. Long-term borrowing
3. Capital acquired by the sale of stock
4. Capital recovered by the sale of properties and other noncurrent assets or receipt of payments on long-term receivables

The usual applications (outflows) of working capital are for:

1. Acquisition of long-term assets
2. Dividends declared
3. Payments on long-term debt
4. Redemption of outstanding stock
5. External investments and increases in long-term receivables

In addition to presenting an analysis of the overall change in working capital, such a statement also provides a convenient summary of the changes in all of the noncurrent assets and liabilities and the capital accounts. Some alternative titles for such a statement are Funds

Statement, Working Capital Statement, and Summary of Changes in Working Capital.[2]

SOME ACCOUNTING TERMS USED IN ANALYSIS OF FINANCIAL STATEMENTS. Before proceeding with a brief introduction to the subject of analyzing financial statements from the viewpoint of the investor or creditor, it is necessary to define some terms commonly used in this connection.

The phrase *current assets* was first mentioned in Chap. 2. In general, this phrase refers to the sum of cash, trade accounts and notes receivable, and inventories. As illustrated in Exhibits 8-3 and 8-6, it also includes marketable securities such as government bonds held in lieu of cash. (These bonds are often purchased in order to earn interest on cash balances not required for business purposes in the immediate future.) The phrase *net quick assets* refers to the sum of cash, receivables, and certain marketable securities. *Current liabilities* are short-term liabilities, including accrued liabilities. Often the border line between short-term and long-term liabilities is drawn at 1 year.

Net working capital was defined as the difference between current assets and current liabilities. This figure tells how much money is employed actively in the purchase-conversion-sale-receivable cycle of current operations. It is useful in the analysis of financial statements in various comparisons and ratios. The term is frequently abbreviated to *working capital.*

In addition to current assets and fixed assets (referred to as properties in Exhibits 8-3 and 8-6), there may be other assets. In the Alcoa balance sheet, securities of other companies and other investment holdings are shown in one grouping and other noninvestment assets are shown in a second grouping. The distinction implied by separating other assets and "deferred charges" from the "prepaid insurance and taxes" shown in the current assets category is that the latter are to be chargeable to income in the near future and the former may have a long-run effect.

In the literature dealing with analysis of financial statements, the phrase *net worth* is often used to designate the excess of total assets over total liabilities, as shown by the balance sheet. In the preceding chapters of this book, the word *ownership* has been used with the same meaning. For purposes of financial statement analysis, *tangible net worth* is often used. The addition of the adjective *tangible* implies that intangible assets (such as trademarks or good will) shown in the balance sheet are excluded in the net-worth calculation. The only such assets

[2] Inclusion of a funds statement in the corporate reports is recommended by the American Institute of Certified Public Accountants. See *The Journal of Accountancy,* December, 1961, pp. 66–68.

appearing in the exhibits in this chapter are in the Alcoa balance sheet (in the fixed assets category). The problems of accounting for intangible assets are outside the scope of this book.

For most balance sheet items, there is no doubt whether they are current assets, fixed assets, or sundry assets or whether they are current or long-term liabilities. But there are naturally some borderline items. Moreover, there is sometimes a temptation to misclassify items in order to present a more favorable balance sheet. Professional accountants therefore lay considerable stress on having rules for good practice regarding the classification of items. These rules are particularly important because financial statements are so often used as guides to decisions on the granting of credit and on investments in the securities of business enterprises. For example, consider an enterprise that submits its balance sheet to a banker or prospective trade creditor as a basis for the granting of credit. It would be improper and misleading if the figure shown for notes receivable under the heading Current Assets should include some notes that were given the enterprise by its own officers.

USE OF RATIOS AND COMPARISONS IN FINANCIAL STATEMENT ANALYSIS.[3] A critical examination of financial statements may disclose much more information than meets the eye on casual examination. In general, the interpretation of financial statements is helped by finding a number of ratios that can be calculated from the balance sheet, the income statement, or the two together. Although any ratio taken by itself does not tell a great deal, an examination of the year-by-year trends of certain ratios may indicate favorable conditions or reveal danger signals. It is also significant to compare various ratios for a number of companies in the same line of business.

In judging the probable ability of an enterprise to meet short-term obligations, it is desirable to know the ratio of current assets to current liabilities. This is called the *current ratio.* From the Alcoa 1961 balance sheet, this ratio can be computed to be 3.2 to 1; from the King-Seeley 1961 balance sheet, it can be computed as 4.1 to 1.

An approximate rule that often is used is to view with suspicion any current ratio less than 2 to 1. This rule obviously is an oversimplification of the complex matter of judging the solvency of a business enterprise. In any industry that has a seasonal character, the appropriate current ratio will depend on the time of year; at one season current liabilities will necessarily be much greater than at another season. Moreover, typical current ratios vary considerably among industries. Like all the other ratios used in the analysis of financial statements, a current ratio needs to be examined in the light of all the surrounding circumstances.

[3] A good reference on this topic is Roy A. Foulke, *Practical Financial Statement Analysis*, 5th ed., McGraw-Hill Book Company, Inc., New York, 1962.

Another ratio that is significant in judging the capacity to meet short-run debts is the ratio of net quick assets to current liabilities. Net quick assets includes cash, marketable securities, and current receivables. This is sometimes called the *acid-test ratio*. A standard of 1 to 1 for this ratio is often used. For Alcoa on December 31, 1961, this ratio was 1.3 to 1; for King-Seeley on July 31, 1961, it was 2.2 to 1.

Various figures from the balance sheet and income statement can be compared with net working capital. The ratio of inventory to net working capital is of interest; too high a figure for this ratio may indicate vulnerability to business recession. The ratio of annual net sales to net working capital is a measure of the rate of turnover of working capital.

Other figures can be compared to net worth. The ratios of current liabilities to net worth and of total liabilities to net worth give information on the extent to which the different classes of creditors are sharing in the financing of the enterprise. It obviously is of interest to compare both net sales and net profit with net worth. The ratio of net profit to net sales is also significant. The foregoing ratios computed from the 1961 and 1960 Alcoa figures and the 1960–1961 and 1959–1960 King-Seeley figures are as follows:

	Alcoa		King-Seeley	
	1961	1960	1960–1961	1959–1960
Current ratio	3.2	3.6	4.1	3.1
Quick assets to current liabilities	1.3	1.3	2.2	1.5
Inventory to net working capital	0.84	0.85	0.60	0.66
Current liabilities to net worth	0.18	0.15	0.23	0.34
Total liabilities to net worth	0.78	0.81	0.42	0.55
Net sales to net working capital	2.7	2.8	3.3	3.3
Net sales to net worth	1.1	1.1	2.2	2.4
Net profit to net worth	0.056	0.053	0.076	0.098
Net profit to net sales	0.051	0.047	0.035	0.041

It would be misleading if any standards of comparison for these seven ratios should be given here; the appropriate values will vary with the line of business and with other matters. Standards for many of the above ratios that would be appropriate for Alcoa would not be suitable for King-Seeley, and vice versa. For example, the ratios of net sales to net worth for King-Seeley are double those for Alcoa, and this is to be expected considering the differences in type of industry and size of company.

All nine ratios that have been mentioned are appropriate to compute for sole proprietorships and partnerships as well as for corporations. However, one figure that is appropriate only for corporations is the *book value per share of stock.* This figure is obtained by dividing the common stockholders' equity as shown on the balance sheet by the number of shares of stock outstanding. The book value per share for King-Seeley on July 31, 1960, can be computed to be $20.70. This is the ownership figure of $34,139,092 divided by 1,649,615, the number of shares of stock issued. The book value per share for Alcoa on December 31, 1961, was $33.22.

Any student of accounting will recognize that book value per share may differ greatly from market value per share. In a general way, the book value per share can be viewed as reflecting the investment per share by the stockholders, considering both their original investments and the profits that have been reinvested in the business. The market value per share reflects the opinions of investors concerning future earnings and growth possibilities of the company.

The general field of financial statement analysis has many ramifications and has an extensive literature. This chapter merely provides a brief introduction to the subject, mentioning some of the most common terms and ratios.

MANAGERIAL USES OF ACCOUNTING INFORMATION. The directors, officers, and managers at all levels in a company rely on the accounting system for information that is vital for decision making and planning, for evaluation of results, and for guiding and controlling the many different functions of the organization.

Typically, an accounting system generates a hierarchy of periodic reports, from the highly condensed reports for top management (of which the highest order consists of the annual financial reports) to rather detailed and specific reports for people responsible for repetitive activities. The range of management functions that these various reports support runs from decisions of the directors on such matters as dividends, major capital expenditures, and long-range plans through such areas as financial planning, sales promotion planning, expense control, pricing, budgeting, product cost control, and inventory management.

The detailed information the accounting system continuously assimilates and records is almost entirely factual and historical. The system is therefore committed to the general task of processing this information and deriving from it summaries and analyses of data about events in the past. However, because decisions and events of the past cannot be changed, the only useful application of this historical information is in relation to future events. In a sense, then, the mainstream of accounting function is feedback of sets of information which are of value to the company only if they influence in desirable ways the future decisions and actions of people within the organization or if they fulfill requirements imposed from outside the organization. Accounting systems differ with respect to how well they fulfill the second requirement—satisfying external information demands. They differ even more with respect to how they influence decisions and actions inside the organization.

Internal needs for and uses of accounting information are developed further in subsequent chapters dealing with cost accounting, budgeting, and other accounting topics.

CONSISTENCY IS IMPORTANT. Most uses of accounting information involve comparison of results versus prior plans, both stated in money terms, or comparison of recent results versus prior results. If such comparisons are to be useful and not misleading, the accounting figures must be consistent through time with respect to content (rules of classification) and derivation (rules of processing and manipulation). Changes in the chart of accounts (accounts available), in the decisions about the recording of events and transactions (which accounts are affected and how), and in the rules governing the timing of entries and the sorting of incomes and expenses among successive time periods, all cause discontinuities in the historical data that detract from their value. And the cost of revising prior period figures in accordance with a planned change is often prohibitive. Therefore, in designing parts of the accounting system and making decisions that will be used repetitively, the accountant must try to anticipate future growth and change of the organization's activities and future needs for information, and to make decisions that will turn out to be long-lived.

SOME ADMINISTRATIVE FUNCTIONS USUALLY ASSIGNED TO THE ACCOUNTING UNIT OF AN ORGANIZATION. The functions of timekeeping, payroll, cash disbursement, billing, recording and collection of receivables, and often other activities, including data-processing service and inventory records keeping, may be attached to the accounting section of the organization. These are not inherently parts of the system for *accounting*, as such. However, they are intimately connected with accounting with respect to information flow, and the accounting people are the ones most concerned about the information outputs from such functions. Also, the skills, devices, and knowledge needed to handle tasks of this sort efficiently are similar to those employed in the accounting work. Hence administrative functions such as those mentioned tend to be viewed as accounting functions and are often spoken of as parts of "the accounting system." *Accounting* in this broader common-usage sense usually includes a variety of essential service functions which are really auxiliary to the main accounting functions.

KEEPING TRACK OF LIABILITIES AND ASSETS. A major administrative function of an accounting system is to protect the company against loss and misappropriation of assets and against erroneous or false claims. This responsibility has two sides: keeping track of external rights and obligations and the internal control of assets.

With respect to external relationships, one objective is to avoid losses of receivables and other assets through ignorance, default in action or failure to detect error, nonperformance, or intentional default of customers, suppliers, and other entities the company deals with. A similar objective pertains to liabilities—claims of other entities against the assets held by the company.

The general approach to this problem is, first, to devise and maintain adequate records of all external transactions and, second, to provide for initiating action by the appropriate organizational units as necessary. A somewhat more sophisticated view of these functions is that the *timing* of receipts and disbursements (of cash and other things of value) is important and that the company should be protected not only against outright losses but also against tardiness of receipts and unnecessary prepayments of obligations.

A great deal of thought is usually applied in the design of accounting systems to provide adequate safeguards against embezzlement and unauthorized appropriation of the company's assets by employees and others having internal access. Particular attention is given to the handling of cash and other portable assets readily converted to cash or use by individuals and to the procedures for recording the receipt, location, movement, and disbursement of such assets. A basic requirement in this regard is adequate documentation and records. Procedures are designed to avoid providing any single person access to both attractive assets and the records and documents relating to those assets. Also, a variety of cross-checks are employed so that a discrepancy in one part of the system will cause disagreement with records kept elsewhere (e.g., the accounts receivable subsidiary ledger total should reconcile with the general ledger control account balance). Finally, systematic audits are made by independent, well-trained people to test the records in various ways and to trace and verify the appropriateness and accuracy of entries. Many companies carry on continuous programs of internal audit in addition to having an annual audit by a certified public accounting firm. Annual audit by an independent firm is required by securities control regulations for all companies offering their securities for sale to the public.

In addition to the foregoing purposes of keeping track of assets and liabilities, there is also, of course, the need to value these things for balance sheet purposes and the associated requirement of valuing changes in them that affect profit and loss.

SOME IMPORTANT TAX-DATA REQUIREMENTS. Federal, state, and local government agencies impose demands on the accounting system of any company for information from which tax liabilities are determined as required by law. Some of the important taxes are Federal and state income taxes, property taxes, sales-and-use taxes, excise taxes, and payroll taxes. For each tax applicable to a given company, the accounting system must develop, organize, and document the necessary information for determining the liability in a manner consistent with the law and the current interpretation of the law. But at the same time, the procedures used and the decisions made in developing and organizing such information for presentation properly should be aimed at avoiding unnecessary or excessive tax disbursements. An important point in this regard is that the cost of accumulating, processing, and documenting such information is borne by the taxpaying company.

Tax and insurance matters relating to payroll are discussed in Chap. 13. Income taxes on corporate and partnership income are discussed in Chap. 18. Most other taxes are not mentioned in this book except as they are introduced in the context of examples and problems.

OTHER REQUIREMENTS MAY BE IMPOSED BY LAW. Most private manufacturing service and trading companies are subject to regulatory laws and requirements of public agencies that impose demands on the accounting system. In the case of public utilities and many private manufacturing and service industries, these are very important matters; even small local businesses are affected. In any case, the plan of the accounting system is influenced in various ways by these requirements for prescribed information.

CONFLICTING OBJECTIVES INFLUENCE ACCOUNTING DECISIONS. The demands on an accounting system for information for different purposes are numerous. There are also many different decisions to be made each of which may affect the various accounting outputs in different ways. In many cases there is conflict between what would be best for one purpose and what would be best for another. For example, an expense-versus-capitalization decision appropriate for income tax purposes might be undesirable for financial statement purposes, or a classification of expenses for financial accounting purposes might be poor for internal cost control.

Also, there is always the consideration of the cost of the accounting processes. Many arbitrary allocations and combinations are made to simplify subsequent processing. Compromises are often made between different objectives by selecting and following one of several possible treatments of a particular matter because the cost of doing it one way for one purpose and another way for the other purpose would be exorbitant.

It is conceivable that in the future, high-speed data-processing systems will make it both practicable and economically feasible to consign to machine memory all elementary information inputs for an entire year or more—in pure form, unallocated and unmixed—and then apply a series of programs that will compile and process this information in different ways for different purposes. And if the basic input data were stored on tapes, the reports of any prior year could be regenerated with modifications and new special analyses could be compiled retroactively. Much of the conflict that accountants now face among different objectives and between objectives and data-processing costs would disappear. However, it is likely to be some time before such a scheme becomes practical.

SUMMARY.

1. An accounting system collects and processes information that is factual and historical. This information is processed to produce summaries, analyses, and comparisons that are useful only through their influence on future events.
2. An accounting system must produce information for many different purposes. Some of these information outputs are to satisfy requirements imposed from outside the enterprise; others are for use internally for decision-making, planning, and control purposes.
3. The financial statements are the most highly distilled product of an accounting system. They are important because they influence consequential decisions of investors, creditors, and others as well as the top management of the enterprise.
4. Prospective short-term creditors, present and prospective investors, and management can all obtain useful guidance from a critical analysis of the financial statements of a business enterprise. A number of ratios that can be calculated from the financial statements are useful tools for this type of analysis. For each ratio there needs to be some standard of comparison to provide a basis for judgment. It is desirable to compare the most recent figure for any particular ratio with previous figures for the same enterprise and with figures obtained from other enterprises in the same line of business.
5. Many of the functions of accounting are essential for the continued operation of the enterprise. Others are clearly worthwhile in relation to the benefits gained through the use of accounting information.
6. Many different objectives and requirements must be considered, along with accounting costs, in choosing between alternatives of ac-

counting policy and procedure. The various aspects of such decisions often conflict, and compromise becomes necessary.

DISCUSSION QUESTIONS

8-A. Identify four main classes of readers of the financial statements of an enterprise.

8-B. Explain what is meant by the accounting principles of disclosure and conservatism.

8-C. Why is consistency important in accounting?

8-D. Identify several of the traditional technical accounting terms that are gradually falling into disuse in published accounting reports.

8-E. Indicate briefly how the following figures should be computed: current ratio, net working capital, book value per share of common stock.

8-F. Distinguish between earned surplus and capital surplus.

8-G. The text states that it is improper to include notes receivable from company officers under the heading Current Assets. Do you agree? Why or why not? Why does it make any difference what assets are classified as current?

8-H. A manufacturing company has a current ratio of 2.50 to 1 and an acid-test ratio of 0.60 to 1. What conclusions, if any, can you draw from these two ratios considered together? Why compute the acid-test ratio as well as the current ratio?

8-I. A merchant has a ratio of inventory to net working capital of 1.50 to 1. What conclusions, if any, can you draw from this single statement? In general, does this ratio seem to you to be a useful one to compute? Why or why not?

8-J. On page 185, the ratios of net sales to net worth, net profit to net worth, and net profit to net sales are given for the 1960 and 1961 Alcoa statements and the 1960–1961 and 1959–1960 King-Seeley statements. Discuss the interrelationships of these three ratios. What differences between these two corporations seem to you to be brought out by the differences in these ratios?

8-K. Compute the ratios of depreciation reserves to the cost of properties from Exhibits 8-3 and 8-8. What other information would you need before you could draw useful conclusions from such ratios?

8-L. Distinguish between the *single-step* and *multiple-step* forms of income statement.

8-M. Describe the *financial position* form of the balance sheet. Explain the interpretation of the balance sheet equation that is epitomized in this form of statement.

8-N. Explain the relationships between the retained earnings statement and the comparative balance sheet and between the retained earnings statement and the income statement.

8-P. Explain how the source and application of funds statement supplements the comparative balance sheet and the income statement.

8-Q. Although we should like to get precise measurements of the worth of a business through use of financial statements and comparison from year to year or ratios within a year, this is not possible. The person who regards financial statement ratios as precise measures on a par with measures used in the physical sciences will probably not formulate valid conclusions. Explain the foregoing statement.

8-R. The information assimilated by an accounting system is almost entirely factual and *historical.* Because events in the past cannot be changed, accounting information has value only as its use influences *future* events. Discuss this pair of statements, first with respect to the use of financial statements by present and prospective investors and then with respect to managerial use of internal reports generated by the accounting system.

PROBLEMS

Problem 8-1. For the North & West example (Exhibits 8-1 and 8-2), compute the nine ratios that were calculated from the Alcoa and King-Seeley statements in the text.

Problem 8-2. Assume that a close friend has been offered the opportunity to buy 100 shares of the stock of North & West, Inc. (the example at the end of Chap. 7), at $140 per share, that he has money currently available for such an investment, and that he is specifically interested because he knows some of the employees. He believes that this company, although only ten years old, is well established with its customers and that it handles mainly nationally advertised lines of well-known manufacturers. He also believes that there will be continued future population growth and business expansion in the area served by North & West.

Review and analyze the information he has obtained and made available to you (see Exhibits 8-1 and 8-2). Write a brief report for your friend summarizing the results of your study. Include whatever key facts and figures you think are appropriate. Point out any specific questions you think he should ask and describe any additional information you think he should seek before making his decision.

Problem 8-3. Rewrite the North & West balance sheet, Exhibit 8-1, in *financial position form* as illustrated in Exhibit 8-6. Also, rewrite the North & West income statement, Exhibit 8-2, in *single-step form* as illustrated in Exhibits 8-4 and 8-7. Combine the retained earnings statement with the income statement, and simplify the income statement by combining items and dropping details that might be presented in supplementary internal reports.

Problem 8-4. Prepare a statement of sources and applications of working capital (see Exhibit 8-5) for North & West, Inc. Use the information available in Exhibits 8-1 and 8-2. Assume that the only change in fixed assets during 1962 was the acquisition of equipment costing $1,000, that there was no change in the Capital Stock account, and that payments on the mortgage reduced the principal balance by $1,800. All deferred charges are considered to be current assets.

2/ELEMENTS OF COST ACCOUNTING

9/ OBJECTIVES AND METHODS IN COST ACCOUNTING

The explanation of accounting fundamentals in Part 1 provides a necessary background for the discussion of cost accounting in Part 2. An understanding of the subject matter of Part 2 is desirable for all persons who expect to hold positions of responsibility in connection with any phase of production.

SOME OBJECTIVES OF COST ACCOUNTING. Many different classifications of cost accounting objectives have been made. A convenient classification to provide a basis for discussion is to list the objectives under three general headings, as follows:

1. Valuing inventories and determining cost of goods sold
2. Exerting effective pressure to keep costs as low as possible
3. Setting selling prices and establishing sales policies

These objectives are sometimes in conflict with one another. Cost systems often involve compromises among them or a sacrifice of one objective so that some other objective can be served to better advantage.

FINANCIAL ACCOUNTING REQUIREMENTS. A balance sheet requires inventory values. A profit and loss statement requires a figure for cost of goods sold. Inventory values and figures for cost of goods sold are essential parts of the basic financial statements prepared from the accounts in any merchandising or manufacturing enterprise.

Part 1 illustrated two methods of determining cost of goods sold for a merchandising business. In the first, perpetual-inventory accounts were maintained on the books and the cost of each sale was determined separately. In the second method, inventories were valued only at the ends of accounting periods and the cost of goods sold was determined on the basis of the inventory valuations and the net purchases. If physical inventories can be valued satisfactorily, the second method gives as good a total figure for cost of goods sold as does the first.

In a manufacturing business, it is likely to be difficult to secure a satisfactory inventory valuation merely from a physical count. This is primarily because of the difficulties of assigning unit values to work in process and finished goods. In a trading business, which sells goods in the same form in which it buys them, it is merely necessary to know the purchase price of the goods. In contrast the inventories of work in process and finished goods in a manufacturing business cannot be valued without a distribution of labor cost and indirect manufacturing expense as well as a determination of the cost of purchased materials included in the product. Without a cost system, the valuation of these inventories is likely to involve a good deal of arbitrary pricing and apportionment.

Much of this guesswork is eliminated in a manufacturing enterprise that has a cost accounting system because a cost system usually involves maintaining perpetual inventories of purchased materials, work in process, and finished goods. One of the advantages of keeping these perpetual inventories will be the securing of more accurate and more frequent financial statements. Because inventories are valued on the basis of definite knowledge of the costs of labor and materials plus some systematic apportionment of the overhead expenses, financial statements are more accurate. Because perpetual-inventory figures are available, financial statements are more frequent—perhaps monthly or quarterly instead of annually.

COST CONTROL. In any competitive business, survival may depend on keeping costs to a minimum. This implies a continuous effort toward cost reduction and a guarding against the tendency of costs to increase. For this effort to succeed, it is necessary that costs be measured.

Cost control is the cost accounting objective of greatest interest to production executives and to engineers. In a manufacturing enterprise, it makes cost accounting a tool for judging the efficiency of each part of the manufacturing process and for determining when costs are "out of line" with some standard of comparison. The trends in cost accounting —such as the widespread adoption of standard cost systems and the development of variable expense budgets—are primarily directed at better cost control.

Moreover, certain essential cost accounting procedures tend in themselves to promote cost reduction. For instance, stores control—a necessary part of any cost system—may operate to reduce theft, wastage, and deterioration of materials. Stores control makes possible a more systematic relationship of material purchases to the need for materials; it therefore may greatly reduce the investment in material inventories and the losses through obsolescence of materials. Frequently there is a close relationship between accounting for labor costs and improved production planning.

A cost-control scheme is effective only if it influences decisions in desirable ways and causes worthwhile actions to be taken at appropriate times. Therefore, an accounting report aimed at cost control needs to point out undesirable (and desirable) cost results to someone who is likely to use this information in a beneficial way. The recipient of such a report must perceive the need for action, conceive an appropriate kind of action, be able to do something about it, and be adequately motivated. The report needs to be timely, it needs to interpret recent results in comparison with prior plans (budget estimates) or past results or both, and it must be delivered to someone who can and will influence future results with respect to the costs measured and reported. An important idea here is that the costs reported to an individual at a given level in the organization should relate to activities for which that person is directly responsible. Thus an effective cost-control system will report *controllable* costs organized in a hierarchy of reports that is consistent with the division of responsibility and the distribution of authority in the organization. These matters are discussed further in Chap. 20 in connection with the topic of budgetary control.

Cost accounting is also helpful in judging the comparative economy of various methods of production, although certain limitations on the uncritical use of cost figures in this connection must be recognized. Some of these limitations are pointed out in Chap. 21.

SALES POLICY DETERMINATION. At what price shall manufactured goods be offered for sale? Obviously, something more than a knowledge of production costs is required in order to answer this question. The answer nearly always will be influenced by market conditions and sometimes will be dictated by them.

The extent to which cost accounting may make it possible for sales policies to be based on production costs, either actual or anticipated, is a matter that has been widely debated. Where a manufacturing business produces a diversity of products, it is certainly true that a determination of the direct costs of the various products is necessary for an intelligent determination of sales policy. Moreover, a reasonable distribution of indirect costs may be a great help in detecting unprofitable lines in diversified manufacturing. The measurement of direct costs and apportionment of indirect costs in cost accounting is a great help in determining sales policies, even though it is necessary to recognize that situations occasionally arise where it is advantageous to make sales for somewhat less than the full cost that the cost system has apportioned to a particular product.

Where contracts are awarded on the basis of competitive bidding, cost accounting records furnish information necessary for preparing bids. Where each bid job is unique, as is usually true in job shop manufacturing and construction work, it is necessary that costs be kept for different fundamental operations rather than for completed products in order that they can be useful in bidding on future jobs.

Where laws make the prices at which goods can be sold dependent on their "cost," a cost accounting system provides essential evidence for the determination or justification of selling price. For instance, on certain government contracts, the price is limited to cost plus a fixed fee. On other government contracts, the agreed-on price may later be lowered by renegotiation where the price is too far in excess of "cost" as defined in government regulations.

Not only manufacturing cost records but also distribution cost records may be important in determining and justifying differences in selling prices to different customers of the same concern. Under the Robinson-Patman Act, a Federal law passed in 1936, it is unlawful to discriminate in price among purchasers who are competing with one another, except for price differentials that are due to "differences in the cost of manufacture, sale, or delivery resulting from the differing methods or quantities in which such commodities are to such purchasers sold or delivered."

POSSIBLE CONFLICT BETWEEN DIFFERENT OBJECTIVES OF COST ACCOUNTING. Even in our brief survey of cost accounting, we shall observe a number of instances of alternative possible methods leading to different figures for cost. In many cases, the choice of the method to be used will depend on which of these objectives—financial accounting requirements, cost control, or control of sales policy—are believed to be the most important. For instance, a method that may be best adapted to valuing inventories and determining profits may not be the most satisfactory for judging whether costs are out of line. Or the method that gives the best guide to selling price may not give an acceptable valuation of inventories. Where such different alternative methods are discussed, reference will be made to the way in which the choice among them is likely to be influenced by the objectives that are dominant.

DIVERSITY OF PROCEDURES IN COST ACCOUNTING. Although certain general principles apply to all cost accounting, actual cost systems differ greatly from one another. Some systems are extremely elaborate; in other cases short-cut methods are adopted that may serve only one or two objectives but which may give reasonably satisfactory information at a moderate expense for bookkeeping. For purposes of instruction in cost accounting, it is advantageous to start by examining systems that are artificially simple in the sense of having few materials and products and not many indirect expense accounts or departments but which are "complete" in the sense of fulfilling the objectives of financial accounting by maintaining perpetual-inventory values and costing all sales individually.

TYPES OF COST SYSTEMS. All systems used to obtain manufacturing costs are variants of two general types, *job-order* cost systems and *process* cost systems.

In the job-order method, costs are accumulated by separate jobs. Each job has its own order number. The use of this method is not limited to those cases where each job is unique, as in custom shops; it can also be used where standard product is manufactured for stock. The essential condition for the use of this method is that each job is separately indentifiable throughout all the production operations. Chapter 10 contains a simple example of job-order cost accounting.

In the process cost method, costs are accumulated by departments or processes over a stated period of time. Unit costs of each department or process are obtained by dividing the total cost over the stated time by the number of units produced during that time. Process cost accounting is obviously well adapted to continuous-process industries making a single product or a very few products. It is also widely applicable to many different types of mass production operations wherever suitable product units can be found. Chapter 11 gives a simple example of process cost accounting.

These two methods can both be used within a single manufacturing enterprise, with process costs applied to certain operations and job-order costs applied to others.

THREE CLASSES OF COST. In the operation of systems for finding manufacturing costs, three classes of costs are generally recognized, as follows:

1. Direct-material costs
2. Direct-labor costs
3. All other manufacturing costs

Direct-material costs are the costs of those materials that are included in the final product and are conveniently indentifiable with separate jobs or processes. A cost system requires a systematic plan for stores keeping and for recording the materials used for each job or process. Chapter 12 discusses material costs in general with particular emphasis on direct-material costs.

Direct-labor cost is the cost of the labor applied to separate jobs or processes and identifiable with such jobs or processes. The determination of direct-labor costs will usually be one of the objectives of the scheme of timekeeping used in a manufacturing plant. Chapter 13 discusses labor costs in general with particular emphasis on direct-labor costs.

The sum of direct-material cost and direct-labor cost is sometimes referred to as *prime cost*.

The indirect manufacturing costs are referred to by a number of different names. Some common names are *indirect manufacturing expense*, *manufacturing overhead*, and *factory burden*. These names are abbreviated in various ways, such as IME, manufacturing expense, overhead, expense, and burden. In the remaining chapters of this book, *indirect manufacturing expense, overhead,* and *burden* are used interchangeably.

These indirect costs must be allocated to jobs or processes in some systematic and rational manner. Chapter 14 discusses indirect manufacturing expense.

DISTINCTION BETWEEN SELLING–AND–DISTRIBUTION COSTS AND MANUFACTURING COSTS. Manufacturing costs generally include all costs necessary for the operation of the factory and production of finished product in salable form. These manufacturing costs are (usually) all included in the valuation of finished goods and in the cost of goods sold.

Expenses associated with activities "beyond the factory door," normally including warehousing, shipping, and selling costs, are treated as operating expenses and usually go directly into Profit and Loss rather than through Cost of Goods Manufactured and Cost of Goods Sold.

Packaging materials, labor, and overhead usually are included in the Cost of Goods Maufactured. However, in some cases, packing for shipment may be an integral part of the shipping operations and therefore is treated as selling-and-distribution expense.

HISTORICAL VERSUS PREDETERMINED COSTS. The cost figures used for inventory valuations and for determining the cost of goods sold can be determined from the outlays for direct material and direct labor and from an apportionment of the indirect manufacturing expenses of each accounting period. Costs found in this way are sometimes referred to as *historical* or *actual* costs.

Certain advantages can be gained by estimating unit material costs, unit labor costs, and unit burden costs in advance and using these *predetermined* costs for valuation of inventories and finding cost of goods sold. Where this is done, the differences between the predetermined costs and the historical costs appear in the accounts as *variances.*

For certain reasons of convenience, it is almost universal practice to use predetermined costs for indirect manufacturing expense. All examples and most of the problems in cost accounting in this book recognize this fact by using predetermined burden rates. The example of job-order costs in Chap. 10 and the example of process costs in Chap. 11 both use historical costs for direct material and direct labor.

STANDARD COSTS. Where predetermined costs are based on a careful engineering analysis of the direct materials and the direct labor needed for a product, they may be described as *standard costs.* In a cost system based on standard costs, the variance balances are viewed as important tools of cost control.

Standard costs can be used either in job cost accounting or in process cost acounting. A simple example of standard costs is given in Chap. 15.

PERPETUAL-INVENTORY ACCOUNTS IN COST ACCOUNTING. A manufacturing enterprise usually has three sets of inventories to be valued by the cost system. They are (1) materials, (2) work in process, and (3) finished goods.

The stores department, with its physical control of all materials, will provide the information needed for a perpetual record of the balance on hand of each item of materials. This record is usually kept in a subsidiary stores ledger.

In the job-order method, the maintenance of a perpetual inventory of work in process implies that no production will be undertaken without formal authorization by a job order. All direct production expenses are charged against their respective jobs. The application of the predetermined burden rate of each job aims to apportion the indirect production expenses among the jobs.

When a job is completed, goods in process become finished goods. The unit cost of the finished goods is determined from the charges made against the job. A subsidiary stock ledger[1] must be maintained in which the quantity and cost of finished goods are recorded. Maintenance of a perpetual inventory of finished goods requires posting of goods completed and goods sold.

In some cases, one of the three inventories mentioned can be omitted. For instance, a manufacturer making products only on customers' orders may ship them as soon as completed and thus have no finished goods. In other cases additional inventories will be kept. For instance, a manufacturer may make parts that are not to be assembled into finished product immediately; these will form an inventory of finished parts. Another example is the common case where a significant inventory of factory supplies is maintained.

FLOW OF VALUE THROUGH THE ACCOUNTS. An important concept in accounting, and particularly in cost accounting, is that of flow of value through the accounts. Ultimately, every expenditure becomes an expense. The distinction is a matter of timing. Specifically, the expenditure is associated, in time, with a disbursement of cash or other goods of value. The expense is associated, in time, with a charge to profit and loss. In many cases these events are separated in time, and in some cases one or more expenditures may be associated with one or more subsequent expense charges (i.e., a capital expenditure and subsequent depreciation).[2] The number of such cases is considerably

[1] Throughout these pages, *stores* will refer to materials, *stock* to finished goods. This terminology, although common, is by no means universal in industry. It is adopted here for the sake of definiteness in presentation.

[2] Some expenses are recognized in the accounting system prior to the advent of the associated expenditure; however, in most cases the reverse order of events obtains.

greater in the accounting for a manufacturing business than for a merchandising business.

The following diagram depicts the flow of value through the accounts affected by the manufacturing operations of a company that maintains the three common sets of inventories: raw materials, work in process, and finished goods.

COST FLOW DIAGRAM

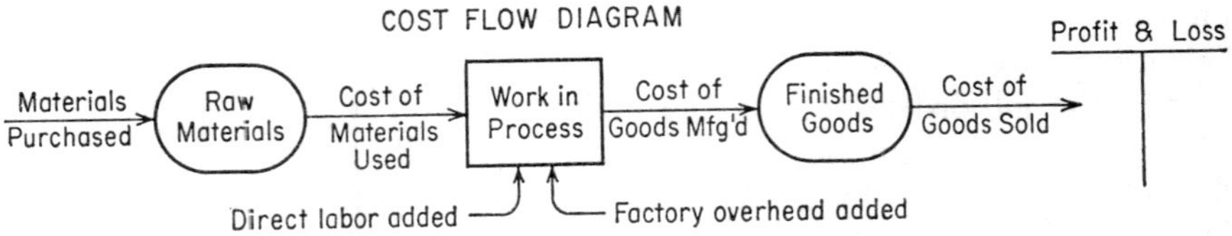

The cost of raw materials purchased goes first into Raw Materials Inventory account. As material is used in production, this value flows from Materials Inventory into the Work in Process account. Direct-labor cost is applied to work-in-process inventory. Overhead, consisting of indirect labor, indirect materials, and all other indirect factory costs, is applied to Work in Process. The cost accounting system associates these costs with products being manufactured. As product is completed and transferred to finished-goods stock, the value associated with that product is transferred from the Work in Process account to the Finished Goods account. As product is shipped out of finished goods, the cost value of those goods flows from Finished Goods Inventory through the Cost of Goods Sold account into Profit and Loss.

The foregoing description of cost flow is considerably abbreviated by ommission of many procedural details and is quite loose with respect to definition of the timing of events. However, these simplifications are intentional so as to focus attention on certain fundamentals. First is the concept of *flow of value,* in a varying but continuous stream, through a series of accounts into the negative side of Profit and Loss Summary (and thence into Earned Surplus). Second is the idea that "costs" become expenses in the periods in which they are debited to Ownership. Third is the observation that these manufacturing costs flow through a series of *asset* accounts en route to ultimate recognition as decreases in Ownership. At first inspection this last statement may seem to be a paradox: How can something be an asset one moment and an expense the next? The answer, of course, lies in the notion that the accounting valuation of assets is based on their original cost and that this valuation carries with it the implied assumption that these assets ultimately will contribute to the earning of income at least equal to their cost. The problem, then, can be viewed as that of matching income with expense wherein expense is defined as the cost of assets dissipated in the process of obtaining that income. As will become apparent through solving simple cost accounting problems in subsequent chapters, this is fundamentally a matter of timing.

APPLYING THE TECHNIQUES OF COST ACCOUNTING TO NONMANUFACTURING COSTS. Some of the concepts and methods originally developed for cost accounting in manufacturing have been borrowed for use in nonmanufacturing activities. Many of these nonmanufacturing applications occur in connection with selling costs and other costs of distribution. Other applications can be made in repetitive activities of various types such as certain clerical activities.

Most nonmanufacturing applications of cost accounting are aimed primarily at cost control. In some instances, they are also aimed at control of sales policies. In contrast to manufacturing cost accounting, no inventory valuations are affected by the accounting procedures adopted for nonmanufacturing activity. That is, either with or without cost accounting, distribution costs and general administrative costs will be charged off in the years in which they occur; they will not be added to valuations of work in process or finished goods.

There are many activities that are sufficiently repetitive to be similar to manufacturing. The clerical operation of billing may be of this type, as may certain distribution operations such as warehousing and packing for shipment. In such operations, the chances of effective cost control are improved if unit costs can be determined. A unit cost is a fraction, with total cost as the numerator and number of units as the denominator. To obtain the numerator, it is necessary to establish the classification of accounts in a way that isolates the particular group of costs that it is desired to control. (Usually only direct costs are involved in this type of cost-control activity.) To obtain the denominator it is necessary to find an appropriate unit and to set up a procedure for measuring the number of units accomplished.

In this type of cost accounting application, the heart of the matter is likely to be the finding of a suitable unit of accomplishment. If a good enough unit can be found, it will be possible to compare unit costs in different places (e.g., unit billing costs in different sales offices) and to compare month-by-month unit costs in each place. Ultimately, cost standards can be established and used to advantage. However, if the unit adopted is not really a valid one, the resulting cost comparisons will be invalid, and the cost-control activity is likely to be ineffective.

SOME SPECIAL ASPECTS OF COST ACCOUNTING FOR DISTRIBUTION COSTS. Distribution includes not only sales promotion activities such as advertising and selling but also activities such as warehousing, packing for shipment, credit investigation, delivery, billing, and collection. In some manufacturing industries the cost of distribution is equal to or greater than the manufacturing cost. When all costs associated with manufactured goods in an industrial society are considered, including wholesale and retail selling, the aggregate costs of distribution are much higher than the aggregate costs of manufacturing. Any contribution that cost accounting can make to the reduction of distribution cost is in the public interest as well as in the interest of the individual firm where the cost reduction is made.

Distribution cost accounting is a much newer field than manufacturing cost accounting. Moreover, distribution cost accounting is not nearly so widely used, and its procedures are much further from being standardized. To some extent, these procedures are aimed at cost control of repetitive operations such as the warehousing and billing activities previously mentioned. But to a much greater extent, the procedures seem to be aimed at helping management to make decisions regarding a host of troublesome questions related to distribution.

To this end, management may want to classify distribution costs by sales territories, by different products or groups of products, by different channels of distribution, by different salesmen or groups of salesmen, by different customers or groups of customers. To obtain such information, the entire cost of distribution needs to be broken down in a number of different ways. The classification of distribution accounts must be drawn in a manner that makes possible the desired breakdowns. The actual analysis of the distribution costs into the many different categories usually is carried out as a statistical procedure apart from the formal books of account. Such analyses generally make use of allocation procedures similar to the ones used for dividing indirect manufacturing expenses among cost centers.

One type of analysis of distribution costs may have legal implications. As pointed out in this chapter, the Robinson-Patman Act is a Federal law in the United States that, in effect, prohibits price differentials that are not based on cost differences. If it is desired to use quantity discounts in pricing or to use other pricing schemes that depend on the method of sale or delivery, a cost analysis is almost essential.

One special application of cost accounting procedures to distribution is found in retail department stores. In such enterprises, management wants to measure the profitableness of each department. The accounts will separate the activities of the different departments with respect to such matters as purchases and sales of merchandise, inventories, and direct selling costs. The techniques of cost accounting are applied to find reasonable ways to allocate all other costs of store operation so that the profit and loss statement can be broken down to give a separate profit and loss figure for each department.

In the following chapters the discussion of cost accounting topics relates to manufacturing costs; details and examples of the application of these techniques to nonmanufacturing costs is beyond the scope of this book.

THE PRESENTATION OF COST ACCOUNTING PRINCIPLES IN THIS BOOK. Various approaches can be used in presenting the principles of cost accounting. The method used here is to start with an explanation of the entries in two simple examples. The first example illustrates job-order costs, and the second illustrates process costs.

These simple examples are designed to concentrate the student's attention on the flow of value through the accounts; they emphasize the use of cost accounting as a device to aid in the preparation of balance sheets and income statements. This initial emphasis on the financial accounting aspect of cost accounting makes the presentation of this subject a logical continuation of the explanation of accounting fundamentals given in Part 1.

These two examples aim to give the student a background for a more critical examination of the three elements of cost—material, labor, and overhead—in the three chapters that follow. In this examination, it is possible to note a number of possible alternative procedures in cost accounting and to recognize the importance of cost control and sales policy control in the decisions that are made in the design of a cost system.

These three chapters are followed by a simple example of the use of standard costs. This example brings out the advantages of using predetermined material and labor costs in inventory valuation and stresses the use of standard costs as an aid to cost control.

Part 2 concludes with a discussion of a number of other problems that arise in the design and operation of some cost accounting systems.

SUMMARY. Some of the important points of this chapter can be restated as follows:

1. A convenient classification of cost accounting objectives is to list them under three general headings: financial accounting requirements, cost control, and sales policy control. It sometimes happens that these objectives are in conflict with one another.
2. There are two general classes of cost systems: job-order and process.
3. Manufacturing costs are generally divided into direct-material costs, direct-labor costs, and indirect manufacturing expenses (otherwise referred to as *overhead* or *burden*). To obtain direct-material costs, it is desirable to have a systematic plan for physical control of stores and for keeping records of material issues. Timekeeping is usually necessary in order to find direct-labor costs. Indirect manufacturing expenses must be allocated among jobs or processes in some systematic manner.
4. The cost figures used to value inventories may be either historical or predetermined. Where predetermined costs are used for inventory

valuation, the difference between historical and predetermined cost appears in the accounts as a variance. It is common practice to use predetermined burden rates even where historical costs are used for direct material and direct labor.

5. Standard costs are predetermined costs that represent an acceptable standard of performance. Standard costs can be used for inventory valuations both in job-order cost systems and in process cost systems.
6. Most cost systems require perpetual-inventory accounts for purchased materials (stores), work in process, and finished goods (stock).
7. The concept of flow of value through the accounts is important for an adequate understanding of cost accounting. In manufacturing companies, costs typically flow through a series of inventory accounts before ultimately entering Profit and Loss as expenses. In such cases, the distinction between *cost* and *expense* is a matter of timing.
8. The techniques of cost accounting are sometimes applied to a number of nonmanufacturing activities, usually with the objective of securing better cost control of these activities.

DISCUSSION QUESTIONS

9-A. Explain how a cost accounting system provides information that is used in the development of financial statements.

9-B. Define the following terms: direct labor, indirect labor, direct materials, indirect materials.

9-C. Define indirect manufacturing cost. What are two alternative terms having the same meaning?

9-D. What is prime cost?

9-E. What is the basic difference between process cost accounting and job cost accounting?

9-F. In the language of cost accounting, what is meant by a *variance?*

9-G. In a manufacturing business what is the difference, if any, between the cost of goods manufactured and the cost of goods sold? (See diagram, page 202.)

9-H. What is meant by the phrase *cost control* as used in this chapter? The text states that this "is the cost accounting objective of greatest interest to production executives and to engineers." Does this statement seem to you to be correct? Why or why not?

9-J. What is meant by *control of sales policy* as this term is used in this chapter? Discuss some manufacturing enterprise with which you are familiar with reference to its possible use of cost accounting to serve the objective of sales policy control.

9-K. In what ways may figures obtained from a cost system be important to a manufacturing enterprise in its dealings with government?

9-L. What are the main advantages of using *predetermined* burden rates?

9-M. Cost accounting is a very important management tool because it helps management make better operating decisions. What general types of decisions are based on the information derived from a good cost system? In answering this, indicate the nature of each type of decision.

9-N. Without a cost system, valuation of work in process and finished goods is likely to involve a good deal of guesswork. Explain.

PROBLEM

Problem 9-1. The Hopi Manufacturing Co. has no cost accounting system. The cost of raw materials used during a fiscal year is derived as follows:

Raw materials inventory value, Jan. 1	$______
Add: purchases	$______
Less: purchase returns	$______
Add: freight in	$______
Less: raw materials inventory value, Dec. 1	$______
Cost of raw materials used	$______

For this calculation (and for balance sheet purposes), the inventory value at the end of each year is determined by taking a physical count and pricing the items according to recent invoices and freight bills.

The figure for cost of raw materials used, from the foregoing calculation, is then used in the following calculation to determine the cost of goods manufactured:

Value of work in process, Jan. 1	$______
Add: cost of raw materials used	$______
Add: direct labor	$______
Add: indirect manufacturing expense	$______
Subtotal	$______
Less: value of work in process, Dec. 31	$______
Cost of goods manufactured	$______

The value of the inventory of work in process at the end of each year is arrived at by taking a physical count of unfinished work on hand in the manufacturing area and applying estimates of the costs of raw materials, labor, and indirect expense represented by the partially completed work.

The cost of goods sold is arrived at by a similar calculation, using the cost of goods manufactured, as follows:

Finished goods inventory value, Jan. 1	$______
Add: cost of goods manufactured	$______
Less: finished-goods inventory, Dec. 31	$______
Cost of goods sold	$______

The value of the finished-goods inventory at the end of each year is arrived at by taking a physical count and applying an estimated average cost for each item.

Using the information listed below, prepare a cost flow diagram for the Hopi Manufacturing Co. for the year 19____ in this form:

COST FLOW DIAGRAM

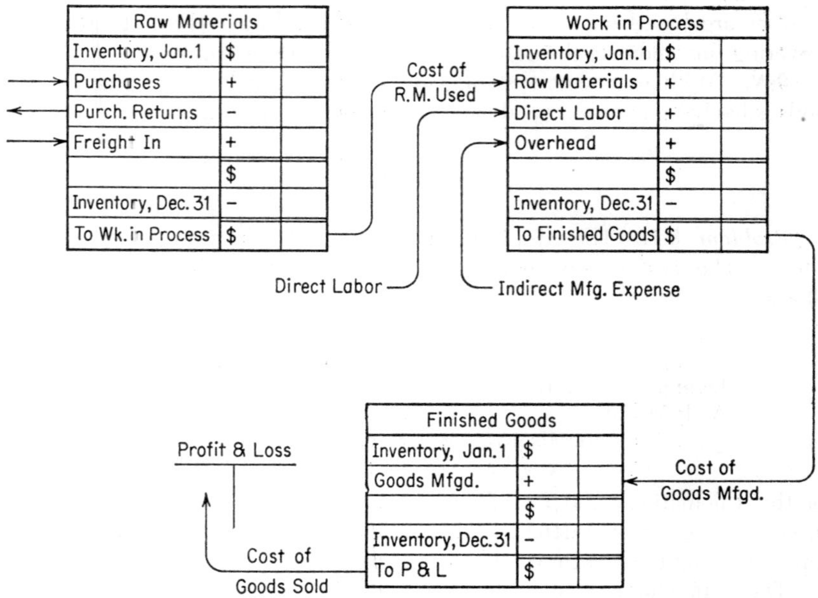

A. Manufacturing and warehouse inventories, January 1, 19____, were:

Raw materials..........	$75,000
Work in process........	$40,000
Finished goods.........	$48,000

B. Raw material purchases during the year totaled $217,500. Purchase returns totaled $6,300. The cost of freight on raw materials purchased was $10,200.

C. Factory costs for the year were summarized as follows:

Direct labor..................................	$182,000
Indirect labor................................	45,600
Factory supervision...........................	27,000
Repairs—machinery and equipment...............	12,000
Repairs—factory buildings.....................	4,500
Manufacturing supplies expense................	12,600
Heat, light, and power........................	44,000
Factory taxes and insurance...................	20,200
Depreciation—machinery and equipment..........	25,200
Depreciation—factory buildings................	9,000
Other indirect expenses.......................	5,500
Total...	$387,600

D. The manufacturing and warehouse inventories on December 31, 19____, were:

Raw materials..........	$64,500
Work in process........	$34,000
Finished goods.........	$66,000

10/ INTRODUCTION TO JOB-ORDER COSTING

This chapter uses a greatly simplified example to explain the essentials of a job-order cost system. In spite of the simplified assumptions in this example, the same general principles of costing apply to complex manufacturing enterprises where many different materials are being converted into a variety of products.

THE JOB-ORDER COST SYSTEM USED IN THIS EXAMPLE. The Modoc Manufacturing Company starts operations on April 1, 19___, following a shutdown. Exhibit 10-1 gives the events of the 3-month period ending June 30. In this exhibit, all transactions of each class are grouped together without regard to their chronological order.

Exhibit 10-2 shows these transactions all entered in one T-account ledger, without regard to the various subsidiary ledgers that are used in job cost accounting. This presentation permits the student to concentrate his attention on the accounts debited and credited as a result of each transaction. It defers any consideration of the formal bookkeeping records that would be used.

This company uses two raw materials, A and B, to make two products, X and Y. During the quarter from April 1 to June 30, four job orders are issued. Of these jobs, two are completed during the period and two remain unfinished at the end of the period.

The company is not departmentalized. There are four accounts recording various types of indirect manufacturing expense, namely, Heat, Light, and Power; Repairs Expense; Indirect Labor; and Depreciation Expense. A single predetermined burden rate is used to distribute indirect manufacturing expense among the jobs. Each job is charged with burden in proportion to its direct labor cost.

The burden rate is established before the period begins by estimating the total indirect manufacturing expense for the period and also estimating the total direct-labor cost for the period. These estimates are $3,900 and $2,600, respectively. They give a ratio of burden to direct-labor cost of 1.50 or 150%. For each dollar of direct-labor cost, therefore, each job will be charged with $1.50 of burden.

The practical problems related to the various journals and subsidiary ledgers that would be needed by the Modoc Manufacturing Company are discussed near the end of this chapter. These matters are illustrated in Exhibits 10-6 and 10-7.

The following explanations apply to the transactions as stated in Exhibit 10-1 and entered in Exhibit 10-2.

EXHIBIT 10-1

TRANSACTIONS FOR MODOC MANUFACTURING COMPANY, APRIL 1 TO JUNE 30, 19___

A. Opening balances are: Cash, Dr., $9,000; Accounts Receivable, Dr., $6,000; Plant & Machinery, Dr., $45,000; Accumulated Depreciation, Plant & Machinery, Cr., $9,200; Accounts Payable, Cr., $3,000; Capital Stock, Cr., $30,000; Earned Surplus, Cr., $17,800.

B. Purchased on credit 20,000 units of material A at $0.21, $4,200, and 5,000 units of material B at $0.45, $2,250.

C–F. Material issues of material A were (C) 4,000 units to job 37, (D) 4,000 to job 38, (E) 6,000 to job 39, (F) 2,100 to job 40.

G–H. Material issues of material B were (G) 2,400 units to job 38, (H) 1,300 to job 40.

I. The direct-labor payroll for the period was $2,840. (Credit Accounts Payable.)

J–M. Analysis of workmen's time cards shows direct-labor cost divided among jobs as follows: (J) job 37, $940; (K) job 38, $880; (L) job 39, $700; (M) job 40, $320.

N. Accounts Payable is credited $5,700 for other obligations incurred as follows: Heat, Light, and Power, $1,100; Repair Expense, $900; Indirect Labor, $1,700; Selling Expense, $1,300; General Office Expense, $700.

O. Burden is charged to the various jobs and credited to Burden Variance at the predetermined burden rate of 150% of direct-labor cost.

P. Job 37 is completed, 10 units of product X.

Q. Job 38 is completed, 40 units of product Y.

R. 7 units of product X are sold on credit at $500 each, $3,500.

S. 20 units of product Y are sold on credit at $150 each, $3,000.

T. Cash receipts on Accounts Receivable for the period are $7,500.

U. Cash disbursements on Accounts Payable for the period are $13,000.

V. Estimated depreciation of Plant and Machinery is $400.

W. All indirect manufacturing expenses (Heat, Light, and Power; Repair Expense; Indirect Labor; Depreciation Expense) are closed into Burden Variance.

X. Burden Variance is closed into Profit and Loss Summary.

Y. All income and expense accounts are closed into Profit and Loss Summary.

Z. Profit and Loss Summary is closed into Earned Surplus.

Entries A to H. Entry A records the balances at the start of the accounting period. This example is simplified by the somewhat unrealistic assumption that, following the shutdown, there are no opening balances of materials, work in process, or finished goods.

Entry B relates to the purchase of materials on credit. Each such purchase is an increase in the asset of materials and calls for a debit to the account with the appropriate material. In Exhibit 10-2, the perpetual-inventory accounts for material A and material B are shown with a space for quantity and unit cost, as well as for total money amount. These T accounts are intended to represent detailed stores ledger forms; examples of such forms are given in Chap. 12.

EXHIBIT 10-2

T-ACCOUNT LEDGER SHOWING ENTRIES IN ACCOUNTS OF MODOC MANUFACTURING COMPANY, APRIL 1 TO JUNE 30, 19___

Cash

Debit	Credit
A 9,000	13,000 U
T 7,500	

Job 38 (40 Y)

Debit	Credit
D 840	4,120 Q
G 1,080	
K 880	
O 1,320	

Plant & Machinery

Debit	Credit
A 45,000	

Accounts Payable

Debit	Credit
U 13,000	3,000 A
	6,450 B
	2,840 I
	5,700 N

Sales

Debit	Credit
Y 6,500	3,500 R
	3,000 S

Accounts Receivable

Debit	Credit
A 6,000	7,500 T
R 3,500	
S 3,000	

Job 39 (15 X)

Debit	Credit
E 1,260	
L 700	
O 1,050	

Accumulated Depreciation

Debit	Credit
	9,200 A
	400 V

Selling Expense

Debit	Credit
N 1,300	1,300 Y

Cost of Goods Sold

Debit	Credit
R 2,233	4,293 Y
S 2,060	

Job 37 (10 X)

Debit	Credit
C 840	3,190 P
J 940	
O 1,410	

Job 40 (20 Y)

Debit	Credit
F 441	
H 585	
M 320	
O 480	

Direct Labor

Debit	Credit
I 2,840	940 J
	880 K
	700 L
	320 M

General Office Expense

Debit	Credit
N 700	700 Y

Burden Variance

Debit	Credit
W 1,100	4,260 O
W 900	
W 1,700	
W 400	
X 160	

Material A

Debit	Credit
B 20,000 at $0.21 = $4,200	4,000 at $0.21 = $ 840 C
	4,000 at 0.21 = 840 D
	6,000 at 0.21 = 1,260 E
	2,100 at 0.21 = 441 F

Heat, Light, and Power

Debit	Credit
N 1,100	1,100 W

Capital Stock

Debit	Credit
	30,000 A

Repair Expense

Debit	Credit
N 900	900 W

Earned Surplus

Debit	Credit
	17,800 A
	367 Z

Material B

Debit	Credit
B 5,000 at $0.45 = $2,250	2,400 at $0.45 = $1,080 G
	1,300 at 0.45 = 585 H

Indirect Labor

Debit	Credit
N 1,700	1,700 W

Profit and Loss Summary

Debit	Credit
Y 4,293	160 X
Y 1,300	6,500 Y
Y 700	
Z 367	

Product X

Debit	Credit
P 10 at $319 = $3,190	7 at $319 = $2,233 R

Depreciation Expense

Debit	Credit
V 400	400 W

Product Y

Debit	Credit
Q 40 at $103 = $4,120	20 at $103 = $2,060 S

The credit in entry B is to the liability accounts increased. In this example and the two following cost accounting examples, attention is concentrated on cost accounting matters, and no individual customers' and creditors' accounts are shown. Accounts Receivable and Accounts

Payable should be viewed by the student as controlling accounts that control omitted subsidiary ledgers. The credit in entry B is therefore to Accounts Payable.

Entries C to H deal with the issues of material to the various jobs. These require credits to the assets decreased, material A and material B, and debits to the assets increased, the work-in-process accounts with jobs 37, 38, 39, and 40.

RECORDING DIRECT-MATERIAL COSTS. Cost accounting requires a physical control of materials, usually under the jurisdiction of a stores department. Perpetual-inventory records are necessary for each material. The quantities, unit costs, and total values of the various materials received must be recorded in these perpetual-inventory records.

A record must be kept of each issue of material to each job. This usually (although not always) means that materials are kept in a storeroom and issued by the storekeeper only after he receives a formal written order of some sort. The written orders, called by various names such as storeroom requisitions or material-issue tickets, constitute part of the accounting records and serve as the basis for charging the jobs with their respective material costs.

All the foregoing points are implied in entries B to H. However, these entries do not indicate all the problems involved in stores accounting. The various methods possible for determining material cost to be charged to successive jobs when material prices vary, the return of materials to stores, the relationship of stores accounting to the systematic purchase of materials, the treatment of discrepancies beween the perpetual-inventory figure and the periodic physical count, and other matters related to control of materials are discussed in Chap 12.

JOB ORDERS. Job cost accounting implies that production will be carried on in accordance with formal production orders (or job orders) which are orders to manufacture a certain number of units of a particular product to certain specifications. Each production order is given a job number; for example, job 37 applies to an order to make 10 units of product X. Each job has its own account or cost sheet. All unfinished jobs are viewed as assets under the general heading of work in process. On each cost sheet will be recorded all direct material, direct labor, and indirect manufacturing expense charged to the particular job. The T accounts for jobs 37 to 40 in Exhibit 10-2 should be thought of as abbreviated versions of the detailed cost sheets that would be used in practice.

Entries I to M. These entries deal with the expenditure for direct labor and the distribution of direct-labor cost among the respective jobs.

All expenditures for direct labor should be viewed as causing increases in the asset of work in process. Nevertheless, for purposes of convenience in accounting, it is usually desirable to debit an account such as Direct Labor, subsequently crediting that account as the various jobs are charged with their direct-labor cost. For this reason, entry I is a debit to Direct Labor and a credit to Accounts Payable and entries J to M are credits to Direct Labor and debits to Jobs 37 to 40 based on the analysis of the workmen's time cards.

ACCOUNTING FOR LABOR COSTS. Where labor is paid on an hourly basis, some form of timekeeping is usually necessary for the preparation of payrolls. Timekeeping is also necessary for purposes of job cost accounting, so that all labor readily identifiable with a particular job is recorded as belonging to that job. If reliance is to be placed on cost accounting figures, it is desirable that the distribution of the total direct-labor cost among the various jobs be as accurate as possible. Some of the problems of obtaining good timekeeping records are discussed in Chap. 13.

Payroll accounting today is a fairly complex and highly specialized affair. Many of the complications are due to laws and government regulations. This example and the following two examples omit the usual complications due to such matters as income tax deductions, payroll deductions and employers' payments under the Federal Insurance Contributions Act, and employers' payments or other provisions for industrial accident insurance. These important practical matters are treated briefly in Chap. 13.

Entries N and O. Entry N involves debits to three separate indirect manufacturing expense accounts. It also involves debits to two other expense accounts not connected with manufacturing, namely, Selling Expense and General Office Expense. The debits to these five accounts are balanced by a credit to Accounts Payable.

Although the entries charging the indirect manufacturing expense accounts seem identical with those charging the other two accounts, the explanations differ for these two classes of entries. The debits to Selling Expense and General Office Expense can be explained on the grounds that these show a decrease in Ownership. In contrast, the debits to Heat, Light, and Power; to Repairs Expense; and to Indirect Labor will be charged into the different jobs by means of the predetermined burden rate, increasing the asset Work in Process.

In entry O, each job is charged with its overhead or burden by using the predetermined rate of 150% of direct-labor cost. These debits are balanced by equal credits to the account Burden Variance. The balances in the various indirect manufacturing expense accounts will later be transferred to the Burden Variance account. In the unlikely event that the total indirect manufacturing expense turns out to be exactly 150% of the total direct-labor cost, these burden charges will turn out to have apportioned the exact amount of the indirect manufacturing expense into work in process.

COST ACCOUNTING TREATMENT OF INDIRECT MANUFACTURING EXPENSE. A manufacturing expense is described as "indirect" because it is not readily identifiable with a particular job or process. In spite of the problems of apportionment, indirect expenses are as necessary to production as are direct-material and direct-labor costs, and they must be recognized as part of production cost. A number of decisions must be made in setting up rules for the distribution of these indirect expenses in any manufacturing enterprise.

One decision is whether to have a single burden rate for the entire enterprise, as in the Modoc Manufacturing Company, or to have a number of different rates for different departments or cost centers. Except in the simplest manufacturing enterprises, it is usually desirable to establish a number of cost centers and to compute a burden rate for each cost center.

It was pointed out in Chap. 9 that one choice to be made in connection with the distribution of burden is the choice between a historical burden rate and a predetermined burden rate. If a historical burden rate should be used, no indirect manufacturing expenses could be allotted against various jobs until the end of an accounting period; after the total indirect manufacturing expenses for the period had been determined from the accounts, the allotment would then be made. With this method, job costs cannot be found until some time after the end of an accounting period even though the product made in many of the jobs may have been sold before that date. The use of a predetermined burden rate eliminates this delay and permits job costs to be computed and entered in the books as soon as a job is completed.

Another choice to be made is the basis of burden distribution. Indirect manufacturing expense must be charged in proportion to something related to the job that is capable of direct measurement. In the Modoc Manufacturing Company example, the basis of burden distribution is direct-labor cost.

In job cost accounting, one practical problem in using a predetermined burden rate is to decide at what time during the accounting period the burden is to be charged to each job. The usual practice is to charge burden for the current accounting period to each job completed during the period at the time the completion of the job is entered on the books. For all jobs remaining unfinished at the end of the period, the burden for the period is charged to the jobs at the end of the period. This matter of the timing of the burden charges is not illustrated in Exhibits 10-1 and 10-2 because these exhibits have grouped like transactions together without regard to their order of occurrence.

Chapter 14 deals with indirect manufacturing expense. Certain other important aspects of the subject are presented, and some of the foregoing matters are discussed at greater length.

Entries P to U. Entries P and Q refer to the completion of jobs 37 and 38, respectively. As soon as the accountant is notified of the completion of a job, he must record on the books that the work in process has become finished goods. This is done by crediting the job with its total recorded cost and debiting an equal number of dollars to the account with the particular product manufactured. At this point, it is necessary to divide the total job cost by the number of units produced in order to find the unit cost of production. As job 37 produced 10 units of product X at a total cost of $3,190, the cost is $319 per unit. As job 38 produced 40 units of product Y at a total cost of $4,120, the unit cost of Y is $103.

Entries R and S refer to the sales made during the accounting period. The unit-cost figures entered in the finished-goods accounts make possible the costing of individual sales.

It was first pointed out in Chap. 3 that each sale implies an entry at the selling price which is a debit to Cash or Accounts Receivable and a credit to Sales and an entry at the cost price which is a debit to Cost of Goods Sold and a credit to an inventory account for the product sold. In a merchandising business, the "cost" of goods sold is simply the price the merchant paid for the goods; in a manufacturing business, the "cost" of goods sold is their manufacturing cost. The cost of the 7 units of product X sold is 7 times the $319 unit cost, or $2,233. The cost of the 20 units of product Y sold is 20 times the $103 unit cost, or $2,060.

No comments are required regarding entries T and U for the receipts on accounts receivable and the payments on accounts payable.

Entry V. The debit of $400 to Depreciation Expense, with its equal credit to Accumulated Depreciation, is the conventional depreciation entry explained in Chap. 7.

One additional aspect of depreciation charges on fixed assets used in manufacturing should be mentioned here. Depreciation Expense is one of the elements of indirect manufacturing expense. As such, it is charged into the product by means of the burden rate. When manufacturing plant and machinery are purchased, it is anticipated that the cost of these assets will eventually be charged into the inventory of work in process and will finally reach the profit and loss statement as one of the cost elements included in Cost of Goods Sold.

Entry W. This adjusting entry closing all the indirect manufacturing expenses into Burden Variance supplements entries N, and V, and O. It will be remembered that in entries N and V, the actual burden for the period was charged to the indirect manufacturing expense accounts Heat, Light, and Power; Repair Expense; Indirect Labor; and Depreciation Expense. In entry O the various jobs were charged with burden at the predetermined rate of 150% of their respective direct-labor costs and Burden Variance was credited with the total of the charges to the jobs. It now remains to find out whether the burden charged to the jobs was greater or less than the burden actually incurred. This can be done by closing the indirect manufacturing expense accounts into Burden Variance and then examining the balance in the Burden Variance account. This entry is a debit to Burden Variance and a credit to the respective expense accounts.

Burden Variance		Heat, Light, and Power		Repair Expense		Indirect Labor		Depreciation Expense	
1,100	4,260	1,100	**1,100**	900	**900**	1,700	**1,700**	400	**400**
900									
1,700									
400									
4,100									

The resulting balance in the Burden Variance account is a credit balance of $160. The total burden charged into the product at the predetermined rate was $4,260, whereas the sum of the actual indirect manufacturing expenses was only $4,100. Such a credit variance is described in the language of cost accounting as an *overabsorbed* burden. If the situation had been reversed and the total of the indirect manufacturing expenses had been greater than the burden charged to the product, the burden would be called *underabsorbed*.

INTERPRETATION OF THE BALANCE IN A VARIANCE ACCOUNT. Entries O and W introduce a variance account. This type of account is used in a variety of situations in modern cost accounting. We shall later meet material variance and labor variance accounts and shall see how a burden variance can be broken down into component elements such as burden budget variance and burden capacity variance. Much of the development of variance accounts has come with the trend toward the use of standard costs.

In general, it can be said that the balance in a variance account somehow measures the discrepancy between an estimate and performance. Wherever an estimate (such as the forecast that indirect manufacturing expense will be 150% of direct-labor cost) is made in advance, it is practically certain that performance will differ from the estimate one way or the other. Therefore, it is almost inevitable that every variance account will have either a debit or credit balance at the end of each accounting period.

The interpretation to be placed on an overabsorbed or underabsorbed burden depends on the intent of the original estimate. If the original intention was merely to estimate the probable indirect manufacturing expense for one accounting period and the probable distribution basis (such as direct-labor cost) for that period, the variance balance at the end of the period may be thought of chiefly as reflecting the errors in these estimates or differences between expected performance and actual performance.

In contrast, if the burden rate is based on the expected volume of production in a normal or average period, the interpretation of a variance balance is not so simple. The matter is complicated by the fact that many of the indirect manufacturing expenses are relatively fixed within a substantial range of variation in volume of production. These expenses do not vary in proportion to direct-labor cost or to any other practical basis of burden distribution. For this reason, the burden variance cannot be interpreted without considering the relationship between the normal production and the actual production during the period. This topic is developed in Chap. 14 in connection with the explanation of the variable budget for indirect manufacturing expense.

Entries X to Z. In these closing entries the $160 credit variance and the income and expense accounts are closed into Profit and Loss Summary, and Profit and Loss Summary is closed into Earned Surplus. The profit shown for the period is $367.

DISPOSITION OF THE BALANCE IN A VARIANCE ACCOUNT. This example illustrates the practice of closing a variance balance into Profit and Loss Summary. An alternative practice which has the same effect on the profit or loss is to close the variance balance into Cost of Goods Sold.

A slightly different figure for profit would have been obtained if the decision had been made to apportion the variance balance among the jobs in process, the finished-goods accounts, and the cost of goods sold. If such adjustments should be made, their purpose presumably would be to give the same inventory values and cost of goods sold that would have been obtained with a historical burden rate. In any complex enterprise, it is hardly practicable to adjust every inventory account in this way. Moreover, there are certain objections to this practice on grounds of principle that are pointed out in Chap. 14 in connection with the explanation of the normal burden rate.

Where monthly, quarterly, or semiannual financial statements are prepared before the end of the fiscal year, intended primarily for the use of management, a common practice is to leave the balances in any variance accounts rather than to close them out. Where this is done, the variance balances may appear in the balance sheet for the time being. It frequently happens—particularly in seasonal industries—that debit variances at one season will be offset by credit variances at another season. Nevertheless, at the end of a fiscal year, when income tax returns and financial statements for stockholders are prepared, it is necessary to close out all variance balances.[1]

POST-CLOSING TRIAL BALANCE. Because so few adjusting entries were involved, it was convenient to complete Exhibit 10-2 without the use of a work sheet. A trial balance taken after the closing entries have been made provides a check to see that debits and credits balance. This trial balance is Exhibit 10-3.

EXHIBIT 10-3
MODOC MANUFACTURING COMPANY
TRIAL BALANCE, JUNE 30, 19___

Account	*Debit*	*Credit*
Cash	$ 3,500	
Accounts Receivable	5,000	
Material A	819	
Material B	585	
Job 39	3,010	
Job 40	1,826	
Product X	957	
Product Y	2,060	
Plant and Machinery	45,000	
Accumulated Depreciation		$ 9,600
Accounts Payable		4,990
Capital Stock		30,000
Earned Surplus		18,167
Totals	$62,757	$62,757

FINANCIAL STATEMENTS. In this simple example, the entries to Profit and Loss Summary give the necessary information for Exhibit 10-4, the profit and loss statement.

The balances shown in the trial balance after closing provide the information for the balance sheet, Exhibit 10-5. In this statement, the individual material accounts are combined as Raw Material, the in-

[1] Although variance balances are not carried on from year to year in the formal books of account, it may be of interest to the management to do so for statistical purposes. For instance, one large manufacturing corporation keeps cumulative burden variance records for each of its many departments; the existence of a cumulative debit burden variance (i.e., underabsorbed burden) in any department puts pressure on the executives of that department to try either to increase the volume of business or to reduce the indirect manufacturing expense.

EXHIBIT 10-4
MODOC MANUFACTURING COMPANY
PROFIT AND LOSS STATEMENT FOR QUARTER ENDING JUNE 30, 19___

Sales		$6,500
Less: Cost of Goods Sold		4,293
Gross Margin on Sales		$2,207
Add: Burden Variance		160
Gross Profit		$2,367
Less: Selling Expense	$1,300	
General Office Expense	700	2,000
Net Profit		$ 367

EXHIBIT 10-5
MODOC MANUFACTURING COMPANY
BALANCE SHEET, JUNE 30, 19___

Assets			*Liabilities and Owners' Equity*		
Current Assets:			Liabilities:		
Cash	$ 3,500		Accounts Payable		$ 4,990
Accounts Receivable	5,000				
Inventories:					
Raw Material	1,404				
Work in Process	4,836		Owners' Equity:		
Finished Goods	3,017	$17,757	Capital Stock	$30,000	
			Earned Surplus	18,167	48,167
Fixed Assets:					
Plant and Equipment	$45,000				
Less: Accumulated Depreciation	9,600	35,400			
Total		$53,157	Total		$53,157

dividual job accounts as Work in Process, and the individual product accounts as Finished Goods.

CONTROLLING ACCOUNTS AND SUBSIDIARY LEDGERS IN COST ACCOUNTING. In Exhibit 10-1 all transactions are listed without regard to the particular journals in which they would be recorded; in Exhibit 10-2 all accounts appear in a single general ledger. This permitted concentration of attention on the accounts to be debited and credited for each transaction without regard to the practical bookkeeping problems involved. The picture of the elements of job-order cost accounting presented in this chapter would not be complete, however, without an illustration of the special subsidiary ledgers required in cost accounting and their relationship to the general ledger and to the various journals.

Exhibits 10-6 to 10-9 illustrate this for the transactions previously studied in Exhibits 10-1 and 10-2. The individual accounts for the dif-

EXHIBIT 10-6
BASIS FOR ENTRIES IN FACTORY SUBSIDIARY LEDGERS
OF MODOC MANUFACTURING COMPANY

Reports of Materials Received showed

(a) 20,000 material A at \$0.21 = \$4,200
(b) 5,000 material B at \$0.45 = 2,250
\$6,450

(This total of \$6,450 appears in the invoice register as a debit to Raw Material. See Exhibits 10-8 and 10-9.)

Storeroom Requisitions showed issues of

(c) 4,000 material A to job 37 = \$ 840
(d) 4,000 material A to job 38 = 840
(e) 6,000 material A to job 39 = 1,260
(f) 2,100 material A to job 40 = 441
(g) 2,400 material B to job 38 = 1,080
(h) 1,300 material B to job 40 = 585
\$5,046

(This total of \$5,046 is the basis for entry G in the general journal. See Exhibits 10-8 and 10-9.)

Payroll Analysis Sheets prepared from time cards showed direct-labor cost distributed as follows: (i) job 37, \$940; (j) job 38, \$880; (k) job 39, \$700; (m) job 40, \$320. (This is summarized in entry H in Exhibits 10-8 and 10-9.)

Burden Distribution Sheet shows indirect manufacturing expense charged to jobs at the predetermined burden rate of 150% of direct-labor cost: (n) job 37, \$1,410; (o) job 38, \$1,320; (p) job 39, \$1,050; (q) job 40, \$480. (This is summarized in entry I in Exhibits 10-8 and 10-9.)

Record of Jobs Completed indicates transfer of respective job ledger balances to the stock ledger.

(r) Job 37 is 10 units of product X (cost is obtained from the total charges to this job).
(s) Job 38 is 40 units of product Y (cost is obtained from the total charges to this job). (These entries are summarized in entry J in Exhibits 10-8 and 10-9.)

Sales of product require transfer of balances out of stock ledger which provides information for recording cost of goods sold in the general books.

(t) 7 product X were sold; (u) 20 product Y were sold.

ferent materials are kept in a subsidiary stores ledger controlled by the general ledger account Raw Material. The individual accounts for the various jobs in process are kept in a subsidiary job ledger controlled by the general ledger account Work in Process. The individual accounts with the different finished products are kept in a subsidiary stock ledger controlled by the general ledger account Finished Goods. Although these subsidiary ledgers are not really necessary in this artifically simple example with its two materials, four jobs, and two finished products, it is obvious that they are necessary in actual situations in which there are hundreds of different material items and many jobs and finished products.

The relationship between each subsidiary ledger and its controlling account in the general ledger is the same as that explained in Chap. 5 with respect to the accounts receivable and acounts payable ledgers. Individual entries are posted to the subsidiary ledger accounts as they take place; summary totals of these individual entries are posted to the controlling account in the general ledger at the end of the accounting period. Thus errors in posting to the subsidiary ledger accounts do not interfere with balancing the general ledger at the end of the period.

THE STORES LEDGER IN EXHIBITS 10-6 TO 10-9. When purchased materials are received, they are counted and a receiving report is made. These reports (illustrated in Chap. 12) provide a basis for the entry of the obligation to pay in the invoice register; they also provide information for the debits to the individual materials accounts

EXHIBIT 10-7
FACTORY SUBSIDIARY LEDGERS FOR MODOC MANUFACTURING COMPANY

Stores Ledger

Material A

Debit	Credit
a 20,000 at $0.21 = $4,200	4,000 at $0.21 = $ 840 c
	4,000 at $0.21 = 840 d
	6,000 at $0.21 = 1,260 e
	2,100 at $0.21 = 441 f

Material B

Debit	Credit
b 5,000 at $0.45 = $2,250	2,400 at $0.45 = $1,080 g
	1,300 at $0.45 = 585 h

Job Ledger

Job 37 (10X)

	Debit	Credit	
c	840	3,190	r
i	940		
n	1,410		

Job 38 (40Y)

	Debit	Credit	
d	840	4,120	s
g	1,080		
j	880		
o	1,320		

Job 39 (15X)

	Debit	Credit
e	1,260	
k	700	
p	1,050	

Job 40 (20Y)

	Debit	Credit
f	441	
h	585	
m	320	
q	480	

Stock Ledger

Product X

Debit	Credit
r 10 at $319 = $3,190	7 at $319 = $2,233 t

Product Y

Debit	Credit
s 40 at $103 = $4,120	20 at $103 = $2,060 u

in the stores ledger. Entries a and b in the stores ledger are based on such reports; they are summarized in a total debit of $6,450 to the general ledger controlling account Raw Material posted from the invoice register.

When the stores department issues materials to the various jobs, each issue is recorded on a storeroom requisition form. Copies of these forms go to the balance-of-stores clerk who makes the appropriate credit entries (entries c, d, e, f, g, h) in the individual materials accounts. At the end of the period the money amounts of these issues are summarized. The total from this summary forms the basis for an entry in the general journal (entry G) debiting Work in Process and crediting Raw Material.

THE JOB LEDGER IN EXHIBITS 10-6 TO 10-9. Copies of the same storeroom requisition go to the cost clerk, who enters them as charges to the respective jobs in the job ledger. This is summarized by the end-of-period journal entry just cited (entry G) debiting the controlling account Work in Process.

Analysis of workmen's time cards supplies the basis for direct-labor

EXHIBIT 10-8
BASIS FOR ENTRIES IN GENERAL LEDGER OF MODOC MANUFACTURING COMPANY

A. Opening balances are: Cash, Dr., $9,000; Accounts Receivable, Dr., $6,000; Plant and Machinery, Dr., $45,000; Accumulated Depreciation, Plant and Machinery, Cr., $9,200; Accounts Payable, Cr., $3,000; Capital Stock, Cr., $30,000; Surplus Cr., $17,800.

B. *Invoice register* totals: Raw Material, Dr., $6,450; Direct Labor, Dr., $2,840; Indirect Labor, Dr., $1,700; Heat, Light, and Power, Dr., $1,100; Repair Expense, Dr., $900; Selling Expense, Dr., $1,300; General Office Expense, Dr., $700; Accounts Payable, Cr., $14,990.

C. *Sales journal* totals: Accounts Receivable, Dr., $6,500; Sales, Cr., $6,500; Cost of Goods Sold, Dr., and Finished Goods, Cr., in amounts determined from Stock Ledger (entries **t** and **u**). Sales were 7 product X at $500 each and 20 product Y at $150 each.

D. *Cash receipts journal* totals: Cash, Dr., $7,500; Accounts Receivable, Cr., $7,500.

E. *Cash disbursements journal* totals: Accounts Payable, Dr., $13,000; Cash, Cr., $13,000.

General journal entries are as follows:

F. Depreciation Expense, Dr., and Accumulated Depreciation, Cr., $400.

G. Work in Process, Dr., and Raw Material, Cr., $5,046 (total of **cdefgh**).

H. Work in Process, Dr., and Direct Labor, Cr., $2,840 (total of **ijkm**).

I. Work in Process, Dr., and Burden Variance, Cr., $4,260 (total of **nopq**).

J. Finished Goods, Dr., and Work in Process, Cr. (total of **r** and **s**).

K. Indirect manufacturing expenses are closed into Burden Variance.

L. The balance in Burden Variance is closed into Profit and Loss Summary.

M. Sales and Cost of Goods Sold are closed into Profit and Loss Summary.

N. Selling and General Office Expense are closed into Profit and Loss Summary.

O. Profit and Loss Summary is closed into Earned Surplus.

charges (entries i, j, k, m) in the job ledger. These are summarized by an entry in the general journal (entry H) debiting Work in Process and crediting Direct Labor.

EXHIBIT 10-9

GENERAL LEDGER FOR MODOC MANUFACTURING COMPANY

Cash	
A 9,000	13,000 E
D 7,500	

Plant and Machinery	
A 45,000	

Indirect Labor	
B 1,700	1,700 K

Sales	
M 6,500	6,500 C

Accounts Receivable	
A 6,000	7,500 D
C 6,500	

Accumulated Depreciation, Plant and Machinery	
	9,200 A
	400 F

Depreciation Expense	
F 400	400 K

Cost of Goods Sold	
C 4,293	4,293 M

Accounts Payable	
E 13,000	3,000 A
	14,990 B

Direct Labor	
B 2,840	2,840 H

Selling Expense	
B 1,300	1,300 N

Capital Stock	
	30,000 A

Raw Material	
B 6,450	5,046 G

Heat, Light, and Power	
B 1,100	1,100 K

General Office Expense	
B 700	700 N

Earned Surplus	
	17,800 A
	367 O

Work in Process	
G 5,046	7,310 J
H 2,840	
I 4,260	

Repair Expense	
B 900	900 K

Burden Variance	
K 1,100	4,260 I
K 900	
K 1,700	
K 400	
L 160	

Profit and Loss Summary	
M 4,293	160 L
N 1,300	6,500 M
N 700	
O 367	

Finished Goods	
J 7,310	4,293 C

When a job is completed, the cost clerk charges it with burden at the predetermined rate of 150% of direct-labor cost (entries in n, o). At the end of the period, uncompleted jobs are charged with burden for the period (entries p, q). These entries in the job ledger are summarized by an entry in the general journal (entry I) debiting Work in Process and crediting Burden Variance.

When a job is completed, the account for that job is closed out. The sum of the total costs on jobs completed during the period appears in an entry in the general journal (entry J) debiting Finished Goods and crediting Work in Process.

THE STOCK LEDGER IN EXHIBITS 10-6 TO 10-9. The total cost on each completed job supplies the basis for an entry in the appropriate product account in the stock ledger (entries r and s). As previously stated, the sum of the total costs of completed jobs provides the basis for the journal entry (entry J) debiting the general ledger controlling account Finished Goods.

The values for the different products as shown in the stock ledger supply the basis for costing all sales, and for entering the debit to Cost of Goods Sold and the equal credit to Finished Goods in the sales journal. The appropriate accounts in the stock ledger must be credited (entries t and u) as goods are sold.

THE GENERAL BOOKS IN EXHIBITS 10-8 AND 10-9. The journals referred to in Exhibit 10-8 serve the same general purposes as those explained in Chap. 6. They have the same titles, namely, invoice register, sales journal, cash receipts journal, cash disbursements journal, and general journal. The sales journal shows the cost of goods sold as well as the selling price. Explanations for the entries in the general books correspond with those given for the entries in the same accounts in the discussion of Exhibits 10-1 and 10-2.

TRIAL BALANCES OF SUBSIDIARY LEDGERS. At the end of the period, it is necessary to check the balance of each subsidiary ledger against the balance in its respective controlling account in the general ledger.

Trial Balance—Stores Ledger

Material A..........	$ 819
Material B..........	585
Total.............	$1,404

This total agrees with the $1,404 balance in the Raw Material account in the general ledger.

Trial Balance—Job Ledger

Job 39..............	$3,010
Job 40..............	1,826
Total.............	$4,836

This total agrees with the $4,836 balance in the Work in Process account in the general ledger.

Trial Balance—Stock Ledger

Product X..........	$ 957
Product Y..........	2,060
Total.............	$3,017

This total agrees with the $3,017 balance in the Finished Goods account in the general ledger.

FACTORY SUBSIDIARY LEDGERS. As pointed out in Chap. 5, a general ledger may contain a controlling account for a subsidiary ledger, that subsidiary ledger may contain a controlling account for another subsidiary ledger, and so on.

A common instance of this is a subsidiary factory ledger controlled by a general ledger account usually called Factory Ledger Control. This ledger will contain the various manufacturing expense accounts. It will also contain accounts Materials and Work in Process that control a subsidiary stores ledger and job ledger, respectively. (The Finished Goods account controlling a subsidiary stock ledger will sometimes be included in the factory ledger and in other cases will be in the general ledger.) The use of a factory ledger is particularly appropriate where the factory and general offices are in different locations. Where there are a number of factories, each will have its factory ledger.

There is no example in this book that illustrates a separate factory ledger with controlling accounts for stores and job ledgers. However, anyone who understands the principles underlying the relationship between controlling accounts and subsidiary ledgers should be able to understand this scheme of organization for the accounts of a manufacturing enterprise.

SUMMARY. The artificially simple example of job-order cost accounting given in this chapter is intentionally concentrated on the financial accounting requirements aspect of cost accounting. It illustrates the flow of value through the cost accounts, showing how cost accounting places continuous valuation on inventories of materials, work in process, and finished goods and how it determines cost of goods sold.

It is desirable that the student should understand this flow of value as a basis for discussion of practical cost problems and for understanding the different results obtained from alternative cost accounting procedures. Nevertheless, he should not get the idea that inventory valuation and determination of cost of goods sold are the most important uses of cost accounting. Various aspects of the managerial use of costs are developed in later chapters.

DISCUSSION QUESTIONS

10-A. Why is timekeeping usually an essential part of job-order cost accounting?

10-B. In a job-order cost system, storeroom requisitions are used in various ways as the original evidences for entries in the formal books of account. Describe the use of these documents in connection with entries in subsidiary ledgers and entries in the general ledger.

10-C. What advantages are there to predetermining the burden rates used in a job-order cost system?

10-D. In the Modoc Manufacturing Company example in this chapter, the predetermined burden rate was 150% of direct-labor cost. What estimates were necessary in order to establish this rate?

10-E. In a merchandising business, expenditures for electric light for the store are viewed as causing a decrease in Ownership. In a manufacturing business, expenditures for electric light for the factory are viewed as causing an increase in an asset. Explain the foregoing statements.

10-F. A manufacturing company ends the first month of its fiscal year with a debit balance of $1,500 in its account Burden Variance. What conclusions, if any, can you draw from this variance balance? What are some possible methods of disposing of this variance balance in the accounts?

10-G. What are the sources of debit and credit entries to the individual material accounts in the stores ledger? What are the sources of debit and credit entries to the general ledger account that controls the stores ledger (usually Materials or Raw Materials)? Explain why an error in an individual material account will not necessarily be responsible for an error in the controlling account in the general ledger.

10-H. What are the sources of debit and credit entries to the individual job-order accounts in the job ledger? Assume that the job ledger is controlled by a single general ledger account Work in Process. What are the sources of the debit and credit entries to this controlling account? Explain why an error made in an individual job-order account will not necessarily be responsible for an error in the controlling account in the general ledger.

10-J. What are the sources of debit and credit entries to the accounts with individual finished goods in the stock ledger? What are the sources of debit and credit entries to the controlling account Finished Goods in the general ledger? Explain why an error in an individual finished-goods account in the stock ledger will not necessarily be responsible for an error in the controlling account in the general ledger.

PROBLEMS

Problem 10-1. This problem illustrates in very simple form the basic entries involved in job-order cost accounting. It is not a complete-cycle problem.

Set up the following T accounts to represent a portion of the general ledger of the Cee-Dee Manufacturing Company, which uses two materials, A and B, in making two products, C and D.

Accounts Receivable	Accumulated Depreciation, Plant and Equipment
*Material A	Accounts Payable
*Material B	Sales
Job C1	Cost of Goods Sold
Job D1	Direct Labor
Job C2	Indirect Labor
Job D2	Heat, Light, and Power
*Product C	Repair and Maintenance Expense
*Product D	Depreciation Expense

* These T accounts should have columns for quantity and unit price.

Make entries in these T accounts for the happenings described below. These include only those events affecting the cost accounts.

A. The opening balances in the accounts are to be omitted.

B. Bought on credit 1,000 units of material A at $2, $2,000, and 500 units of material B at $5, $2,500; a total of $4,500.

C. Incurred obligations to pay for:

Direct labor	$2,000
Indirect labor	1,200
Heat, light, and power	800
Repair and maintenance expense	600
Total	$4,600

D. Materials were issued to jobs as follows:

Job	Material A, units	Material B, units
C1	400	
D1	100	250
C2	200	
D2	50	50
Totals	750	300

E. The time cards showed that direct labor was divided among the various jobs as follows:

Job C1	$1,000
Job D1	400
Job C2	400
Job D2	200
Total	$2,000

F. The depreciation charge on plant and equipment for the period was $400.

G. The total of the indirect manufacturing expenses for the period (Indirect Labor; Heat, Light, and Power; Repair and Maintenance Expense; and Depreciation Expense) is to be apportioned among the four jobs in proportion to their respective direct-labor costs.

H. Job C1 is finished, 100 units of product C. Job D1 is finished, 50 units of product D. The other two jobs are still in process at the end of the period.

I. Sales were made on credit of 80 units of product C at $40 each and 30 units of product D at $60 each. Cost of goods sold should also be entered for these sales.

Entry G illustrated the use of a historical burden rate with direct-labor cost used as the basis of burden distribution. How would this entry and subsequent entries have differed if a historical burden rate had been used with prime cost as the basis of burden distribution? How would these entries have differed if a predetermined burden rate of 160% of direct-labor cost had been used? Each of these two questions may be answered in the form of an adjusting entry that would be required at the end of August if the scheme for burden distribution was to be changed retroactively as of August 1.

Problem 10-2. This is a complete-cycle version of problem **10-1.** A complete general ledger and a subsidiary work-in-process ledger are used. Burden is applied by means of a predetermined burden rate.

The Cee-Dee Manufacturing Company uses two materials, A and B, in making two products, C and D. Production scheduling and control is handled on a job-order basis, and a job-costing system is used for cost accounting.

As of August 1, 19____, when work was resumed after the annual shutdown for vacations, the status of the general ledger was as follows:

Account	Debit	Credit
Cash	$ 3,000	
Accounts Receivable	4,000	
*Material A (250 units @ $2)	500	
*Material B (200 units @ $5)	1,000	
Work in Process		
*Product C		
*Product D		
Plant and Equipment	72,000	
Accumulated Depreciation, Plant and Equipment		$24,000
Accounts Payable		1,000
Capital Stock		35,000
Earned Surplus		20,500
Profit and Loss Summary		
Sales		
Cost of Goods Sold		
Selling and Distributing Expense		
General and Administrative Expense		
Direct Labor		
Indirect Labor		
Heat, Light, and Power		
Repair and Maintenance Expense		
Depreciation Expense		
Burden Variance		
Totals	$80,500	$80,500

* These T accounts should have columns for quantity and unit price.

Set up T accounts representing the general ledger. All the accounts required are listed above. Also, on the same sheet, rule off a set of four T's representing the work-in-process ledger, and title them Job C1, Job D1, Job C2, and Job D2.

A. The opening balances in the accounts are as shown above.

B through F: Same as in problem 10-1.

G. Overhead is to be applied to the jobs at the rate of 160% of direct labor cost.

H and I: Same as in problem 10-1.

J. Incurred obligations to pay $450 for selling and distribution expenses and $550 for general and administrative expenses, a total of $1,000.
K. Collections on accounts receivable totaled $3,500.
L. Paid $5,400 on accounts payable.
M. The indirect manufacturing expense accounts are to be closed to Burden Variance.
N. Entries are required to close the income and expense accounts and the burden variance to Profit and Loss Summary and to close the profit or loss to Earned Surplus.

Rule and balance all accounts with nonzero balances. Take a post-closing trial balance.

Problem 10-3. The Wye-Zee Manufacturing Company uses two materials, W and X, to make two products, Y and Z. It has a job-order cost system using a predetermined burden rate of 150% of direct-labor cost. All cost accounts are kept in the general ledger.

A. Set up T accounts to represent this company's general ledger with account titles and November 1 balances as given in the following table:

Account	Debit	Credit
Cash	$ 4,000	
Accounts Receivable	8,250	
Plant and Equipment	40,000	
Accumulated Depreciation, Plant and Equipment		$ 8,000
*Material W (1,000 at $2)	2,000	
*Material X		
Job 21 (100 Z)	1,200	
Job 22 (100 Y)	350	
Job 23 (200 Z)		
*Product Y		
*Product Z		
Direct Labor		
Indirect Labor		
Heat, Light, and Power		
Depreciation Expense		
Other Factory Expense		
Selling and Administrative Expense		
Burden Variance		
Sales		
Cost of Goods Sold		
Accounts Payable		2,200
Capital Stock		30,000
Earned Surplus		15,600
Profit and Loss Summary		
Totals	$55,800	$55,800

* These T accounts should have columns for quantity, unit price, and total value.

Make entries directly in the T accounts for the following events which took place during November:

B. Bought on credit 800 material W at $2 each, $1,600, and 400 material X at $10 each, $4,000, a total of $5,600.
C. Paid cash for direct labor, $2,000; indirect labor, $1,600; heat, light, and power, $500; other factory expense, $400; selling and administrative expense, $1,500, a total of $6,000.
D. Material W was issued 200 units to job 21 and 400 units to job 23. Material X was issued 160 units to job 22.
E. Direct labor was charged $400 to job 21, $900 to job 22, and $700 to job 23.
F. Burden was charged to the jobs at the predetermined burden rate.
G. Jobs 21 and 22 were completed, 100 Z and 100 Y, respectively. Job 23 remains in process at the end of the month.
H. Sold on credit 70 Y at $60 each, $4,200, and 50 Z at $40 each, $2,000, a total of $6,200.
I. Received on accounts receivable, $7,000.
J. Paid on accounts payable, $3,000.
K. The depreciation charge on plant and equipment for the month is $300.
L. Entries should be made to close out the indirect manufacturing expense accounts and to determine the burden variance.
M. Take a trial balance of the ledger at this point. Then make directly in the T accounts the necessary entries to close the books and determine the profit or loss. In this company Burden Variance is closed into Profit and Loss Summary monthly.

Prepare a profit and loss statement for November and an end-of-month balance sheet.

Problem 10-4. The Piegan Manufacturing Company uses job-order cost accounting. It makes two products, K and N, and also undertakes special jobs to customers' specifications. It has two departments, X and Y. Department X uses a predetermined burden rate of 125% of direct-labor cost. Department Y uses a predetermined burden rate of $2 per machine hour. All cost accounts are kept in the general ledger.

Set up the following T accounts to represent the general ledger:

Cash
Accounts Receivable
Plant and Equipment
Accumulated Depreciation, Plant and Equipment
*Material A
*Material B
Job 91
Job 92
Job 93
Job 94
Job 95
*Product K
*Product N
Accounts Payable
Direct Labor, Department X
Direct Labor, Department Y
Indirect Manufacturing Expense
Selling and Administrative Expense
Burden Variance
Sales
Cost of Goods Sold
Profit and Loss Summary
Capital Stock
Earned Surplus

* These T accounts should have columns for quantity, unit price, and total value.

The company starts operations on June 1 after a temporary shutdown.

A. Record in the ledger the following opening balances:

	Debit	*Credit*
Cash	$ 20,000	
Plant and Equipment	90,000	
Accumulated Depreciation—Plant and Equipment		$ 25,000
Capital Stock		70,000
Earned Surplus		15,000
Totals	$110,000	$110,000

Enter the following June operations directly in the T accounts:

B. Bought on credit 500 material A at a $10 each, $5,000, and 800 material B at $4 each, $3,200, a total of $8,200.

C. Paid cash as follows:

Direct labor, department X	$1,800
Direct labor, department Y	1,600
Indirect manufacturing expense	3,500
Selling and administrative expense	2,000
Total	$8,900

D. Material issues were:

Job	Material A	Material B
91	80	
92		200
93	120	
94		150
95	100	
Totals	300	350

E. Time cards show that the various jobs used direct labor as follows:

Job	Dept. X	Dept. Y
91	$ 800	
92		$ 500
93	400	700
94		400
95	600	
Totals	$1,800	$1,600

F. Burden was charged as required. Machine hours in department Y were as follows: job 92, 350 hours; job 93, 450 hours; job 94, 250 hours, a total of 1,050 hours.

G. Job 91 was completed, 100 units of product K.

H. Job 92 was completed, 200 units of product N.

I. Job 93 was completed. This special order was immediately delivered to the customer for whom it was done, who was billed for its manufacturing cost plus 30%.

J. 20 units of product K were sold on credit at $35 each, $700, and 100 units of product N were sold on credit at $13 each, $1,300, a total of $2,000.

K. Collections on accounts receivable were $900.

L. Depreciation to be charged on plant and equipment for the month is $500.

M. Make all additional entries necessary to close the books. (Burden Variance is to be closed into Profit and Loss Summary.)

Take a trial balance after the closing entries. No work sheet is required in this problem. Prepare a profit and loss statement for June and an end-of-month balance sheet.

Problem 10-5. The May-Bee Manufacturing Company uses job cost accounting. It makes two standard products, P and Q, and also undertakes special jobs made to customers' specifications. Burden is applied to the jobs by means of predetermined burden rates. Items are priced out of inventories at average cost.

Set up a T-account sheet representing the factory ledger. The accounts listed below are the only ones required for this problem.

Factory ledger account	Balance March 1, 19___	
	Debit	Credit
General Ledger—Control		$18,020
Direct Labor		
Factory Supplies	$ 300	
Indirect Manufacturing Expense—Department Y		
Indirect Manufacturing Expense—Department Z		
Burden Variance—Department Y		
Burden Variance—Department Z		
Maintenance Department		
Job P78	2,520	
Job Q43	900	
Job C12		
Job P79		
*Material A (500 @ $3.80)	1,900	
*Material B (120 @ $30)	3,600	
*Product P (60 @ $80)	4,800	
*Product Q (10 @ $400)	4,000	
Totals	$18,020	$18,020

* These T accounts should have columns for quantity, unit price, and total value.

The factory ledger account titled General Ledger—Control is used to record the opposing credit (or debit) whenever an entry is made that involves an increase (or decrease) in the total value recorded in the factory ledger. For example, if a general ledger entry involves a debit to the general ledger account Factory Ledger—Control, the entry in the factory ledger will involve debits to the appropriate factory expense or inventory accounts and a credit to General Ledger—Control. This means that the factory ledger is self-balancing—the sum of the debits should equal the sum of the credits at all times.

Make appropriate entries for March directly into the T accounts using the following information. Identify each figure posted to an account by code letter.

A. The opening balances are as shown above.

B. Charges to the factory ledger from the invoice register were as follows:

	Amount	Departmental allocation		
		Dept. Y	Dept. Z	Maintenance
Repair and maintenance items....	$ 420	....	....	420
Rent....	600	200	320	80
Heat, light, and power....	280	100	130	50
Other factory expenses....	400	150	250	
Subtotals....	$1,700	$450	$700	$550
1,000 units of material A at $4.10..	4,100			
Factory supplies purchased....	1,400			
Total....	$7,200			

C. Charges to the factory ledger from the payroll register were:

Direct labor....	$4,600
Indirect labor, department Y....	950
Indirect labor, department Z....	1,550
Maintenance department....	1,050
Total....	$8,150

D. Materials are to be priced out of inventory and charged to the jobs at average cost, computed on the assumption that all purchases during the month preceded any issues. For example, the 500 units of material A on hand on March 1 were valued at a total of $1,900. The cost of the 1,000 units purchased was $4,100. The average cost to be used for pricing issues to jobs during March is $6,000/1,500 = $4 per unit. The materials issued to the various jobs were as follows:

Job	Material A, units	Material B, units
P78	...	5
Q43	400	40
C12	100	15
P79	300	20
Totals	800	80

E. On the basis of production department time cards, direct labor is distributed to the jobs as follows:

Job	Dept. Y	Dept. Z	Totals
P78	$ 600	$ 360	$ 960
Q43	950	1,400	2,350
C12	......	1,040	1,040
P79	250	......	250
Totals	$1,800	$2,800	$4,600

F. Burden is applied in department Y using a rate of $8 per machine hour and in department Z using a rate of 125% of direct labor cost. The machine time used on the various jobs in department Y was as follows:

Job	*Hours*
P78	105
Q43	205
P79	40
Total	350

G. Job P78 was finished, and 60 units of product P were transferred to finished goods. Job Q43 was finished, and 22 units of product Q were transferred to finished goods. Job C12 was finished and delivered to the customer.

H. Sales of standard products were 70 units of product P and 15 units of product Q. For pricing these goods out of their inventory accounts, use the average-cost method described under entry D.

I. Factory supplies on hand at the end of March are estimated to be $700. The supplies used should be charged 40% to department Y and 60% to department Z.

J. On the basis of work reports, maintenance and repair expenses should be charged to the production departments as follows: $800 to department Y, $500 to department Z, and the remainder allocated one-third to department Y and two-thirds to department Z.

K. The burden variances are closed to Profit and Loss.

Rule and balance each account having an end-of-month balance. Take a trial balance of the factory ledger.

11/ INTRODUCTION TO PROCESS COSTING

This chapter uses a simple example of a single-product manufacturing enterprise to explain the principles of process cost accounting. Comments regarding the problems involved in applying process cost accounting to a diversity of products are made near the end of the chapter.

DISTINCTION BETWEEN PROCESS COSTS AND JOB-ORDER COSTS. It has already been explained that, under job-order cost accounting, all production is part of some job order. Work on a job order may be completed in a day or may extend over many months; it may be done in a single department or spread over many different departments. When a job is completed, the unit cost of the product is computed by dividing the total cost charged to the job by the number of units produced. Generally this number of units is the same as the number originally specified when the job order was issued.

In contrast, process cost accounting is the determination of costs by departments (or processes) for a stipulated period of time, such as a month. All manufacturing costs are charged to some departmental account. At the end of the stipulated period of time, the unit cost for each department is computed by dividing the total cost charged to the department by the number of units produced in the department during the period.

THE EXAMPLE OF PROCESS COSTS IN THIS CHAPTER. Exhibits 11-1 and 11-2 refer to the accounts of the Zapotec Manufacturing Company for August, 19___. This company makes one chemical product called Zapite. The manufacturing process starts with two materials, indicated as materials A and B. These are crushed, ground, and mixed together in a crushing and grinding department. The mixture is then calcined in rotary kilns in a burning department. The result of the burning process is a partly finished product known as clinker. This clinker is not in marketable form but can be stored in a stock pile; in effect, it constitutes a work-in-process inventory that must

EXHIBIT 11-1

SUMMARY OF JOURNAL ENTRY INFORMATION FOR ZAPOTEC MANUFACTURING COMPANY FOR AUGUST, 19___

A. Opening balances were as shown in the T accounts.

B. Invoice register totals for August are: Material B, Dr., $12,000; Packaging Material, Dr., $2,400; Direct Labor, Dr., $8,600; Manufacturing Overhead, Dr., $4,100; Selling and Administrative Expense, Dr., $5,700; Accounts Payable, Cr., $32,800.

C. Sales journal shows Accounts Receivable, Dr., $33,000; Sales, Cr., $33,000; representing sales of 20 tons of bulk Zapite at $460 per ton and 8,500 packages of packaged Zapite at $2.80 per package. Cost of Goods Sold is entered in the general journal at the end of the month after the costs for the month's operations have been computed.

D. Cash receipts journal shows Cash, Dr., $28,500; Accounts Receivable, Cr., $28,500.

E. Cash disbursements journal shows Accounts Payable, Dr., $31,000; Cash, Cr., $31,000.

The necessary entries in the general journal are made to show internal factory operations, as follows:

F. Material issues are: to Crushing and Grinding Department, Material A, $4,940, Material B, $6,800; to Regrinding Department, Material C, $650; to Packaging Department, Packaging Material, $1,240.

G. Direct labor is divided among the departments as follows: Crushing and Grinding Department, $4,200; Burning Department, $1,800; Regrinding Department, $1,600; Packaging Department, $1,000.

H. Overhead is charged to the four departments at the predetermined rate of 50% of direct-labor cost.

I. The entire output of the Crushing and Grinding Department goes to the Burning Department.

J. The output of the Burning Department for the month was 65 tons of clinker. The total of the charges to the department's account is transferred to the inventory account Clinker. The initial balance of $11,060 in the Clinker account represented 35 tons at $316 per ton.

K. During the month, 55 tons of clinker were transferred to the Regrinding Department.

L. In the Regrinding Department, 58 tons of bulk product were made. The total of the charges to the department's account is transferred to the account Bulk Zapite. The initial balance of $7,700 in this account represented 22 tons at $350 per ton.

M. 20 tons of bulk Zapite are sold; Cost of Goods Sold is entered.

N. 40 tons of bulk Zapite are transferred to the Packaging Department.

O. The output of the Packaging Department is 8,000 packages. Departmental charges are transferred to Packaged Zapite. The initial balance of $6,240 in this account represented 3,000 packages at $2.08 per package.

P. 8,500 packages are sold; Cost of Goods Sold is entered.

Q. An adjusting journal entry records $500 of estimated depreciation.

R. Manufacturing Overhead is closed into Overhead Variance.

S. Sales, Cost of Goods Sold, Burden Variance, and Selling and Administrative Expense are closed into Profit and Loss Summary.

T. Profit and Loss Summary is closed into Earned Surplus.

EXHIBIT 11-2
T-ACCOUNT LEDGER SHOWING ENTRIES IN ACCOUNTS OF ZAPOTEC MANUFACTURING COMPANY FOR AUGUST, 19___

General Accounts

Cash

A 30,000	31,000 E
D 28,500	
58,500	

Direct Labor

B 8,600	4,200 G
	1,800 G
	1,600 G
	1,000 G

Accounts Payable

E 31,000	11,000 A
	32,800 B
	43,800

Capital Stock

	80,000 A

Accounts Receivable

A 16,000	28,500 D
C 33,000	
49,000	

Manufacturing Overhead

B 4,100	4,600 R
Q 500	

Sales

S 33,000	33,000 C

Earned Surplus

	64,500 A
	2,090 T
	66,590

Plant and Equipment

A 90,000	

Overhead Variance

R 4,600	2,100 H
	900 H
	800 H
	500 H
	4,300
	300 S

Cost of Goods Sold

M 7,060	24,910 S
P 17,850	

Profit and Loss Summary

S 24,910	33,000 S
S 5,700	
S 300	
T 2,090	

Accumulated Depreciation

	23,000 A
	500 Q
	23,500

Selling and Administrative Expense

B 5,700	5,700 S

Factory Accounts

Material Inventories

Material A

A 10,000	4,940 F

Material B

A 4,000	6,800 F
B 12,000	
16,000	

Material C

A 2,000	650 F

Packaging Material

A 1,500	1,240 F
B 2,400	
3,900	

Process Departments

Crushing and Grinding Department

F 4,940	18,040 I
F 6,800	
G 4,200	
H 2,100	

Burning Department

G 1,800	20,740 J
H 900	
I 18,040	

Regrinding Department

F 650	20,540 L
G 1,600	
H 800	
K 17,490	

Packaging Department

F 1,240	16,860 O
G 1,000	
H 500	
N 14,120	

Product Inventories

Clinker

A 11,060	17,490 K
J 20,740	
31,800	

Bulk Zapite

A 7,700	7,060 M
L 20,540	14,120 N
28,240	*21,180*

Packaged Zapite

A 6,240	17,850 P
O 16,860	
23,100	

be recognized in the accounts. The amount of material actually in process at any time in the crushing and grinding department and the burning department is practically constant and is only a very small fraction of a month's production; this in-process inventory is neglected for accounting purposes.

Clinker and material C are then mixed and ground to a fine powder in the regrinding department. The output of this department constitutes bulk Zapite. Some of this product is sold in bulk; the remainder goes to a packaging department to be placed in packages before marketing.

For the sake of simplicity, Exhibit 11-2 shows all the accounts for this concern in a single ledger. However, this exhibit separates the factory accounts from the general accounts to facilitate study of the example. Accounts Receivable and Accounts Payable should be viewed as controlling accounts for subsidiary ledgers that are not shown.

This example is simplified by the omission of information regarding the numbers of units of materials and their unit prices; the treatment of material unit costs was illustrated in the preceding chapter and will be explained at greater length in the next chapter. Another simplification in Exhibit 11-2 is the showing of all indirect manufacturing expenses in a single account entitled Manufacturing Overhead. Similarly all other expenses are lumped together in a single account, Selling and Administrative Expense.

A predetermined overhead rate of 50% of direct-labor cost is used in all four departments. The balance in Overhead Variance is closed into Profit and Loss Summary at the end of each month. The algebraic sum of the overhead variance figures for the year up to August 1 was a $200 net credit; this cumulative figure is not shown in the T-accounts.

All material and product accounts have opening balances; unlike the example in the preceding chapter, this plant has not been shut down. Unit costs for tranfers of partly finished product between departments are computed by the average-cost method, explained later in this chapter. This method is also used to determine cost of goods sold.

Exhibit 11-1 contains totals from the invoice register, the sales journal, the cash receipts journal, and the cash disbursements journal. It also contains the essential information for the entries in the general journal summarizing the internal factory operations. The journal entries themselves are shown throughout the body of the text in this chapter.

The inventory accounts in Exhibit 11-2 only show the debits and credits in dollars and do not show quantities and unit values in the manner illustrated in Exhibit 10-2. The quantities and unit values for clinker, bulk Zapite, and packaged Zapite are explained in the text of the discussion of this example.

Entries A to E. The postings of totals from the invoice register, sales journal, cash receipts journal, and cash disbursements journal are self-explanatory and require no comment. It should be noted that cost of goods sold is not entered in the sales journal in this example. This cost is computed at the end of the month in a manner explained later in the chapter and is then entered in the general journal.

Entry F. Material issues are: to Crushing and Grinding Department, Material A, $4,940, Material B, $6,800; to Regrinding Department, Material C, $650; to Packaging Department, Packaging Material, $1,240. The foregoing figures are necessarily based on information regarding quantities and unit prices of materials used. This information has been omitted here. The required journal entries are as follows:

Crushing and Grinding Department	$4,940	
Material A		$4,940
Crushing and Grinding Department	6,800	
Material B		6,800
Regrinding Department	650	
Material C		650
Packaging Department	1,240	
Packaging Material		1,240

Stores keeping is usually somewhat simpler in process cost accounting than in job-order cost accounting. It is only necessary to keep track of the materials by departments or processes. In some cases, it even is possible to dispense with the stores department's physical control of certain materials and to place this control in the hands of the departments using these materials. Regardless of the administrative procedure used, the objective must be to obtain an accurate record of the amount of each material used in each department.

Entry G. Direct Labor is divided among the departments as follows: Crushing and Grinding Department, $4,200; Burning Department, $1,800; Regrinding Department, $1,600; Packaging Department $1,000. The distribution of labor costs also is simpler in process cost accounting. It merely is necessary to identify each employee with a department or process. The only timekeeping problems involved in process costs are those arising when employees divide their time among two or more departments. Any employee of a production department can be classified as direct labor in process cost accounting; this contrasts to job cost accounting in which certain service and other employees must be classified as indirect labor even though their full time is spent in a single department.

The journal entry to show the distribution of labor costs is as follows:

Crushing and Grinding Department	$4,200	
Burning Department	1,800	
Regrinding Department	1,600	
Packaging Department	1,000	
Direct Labor		$8,600

Entry H. Overhead is charged to the four departments at the predetermined rate of 50% of direct-labor cost. Just as in the job-order example, the charges of indirect manufacturing expense are to the appropriate work-in-process accounts and the balancing credits are to a variance account.

Crushing and Grinding Department	$2,100	
Burning Department	900	
Regrinding Department	800	
Packaging Department	500	
Overhead Variance		$4,300

As in the job-order example, this illustrates a single predetermined overhead (or burden) rate for the entire enterprise. Comments on the possible effect of departmental overhead rates in this example are made later in this chapter.

Entry I. The entire output of the Crushing and Grinding Department goes to the Burning Department. The total cost in the crushing and grinding department is the sum of the material, labor, and overhead charges to the departmental account, $11,740, $4,200, and $2,100 respectively. As the product of the crushing and grinding department constitutes the material used in the burning department, this total cost, $18,040, must be transferred to that department's account.

Burning Department	$18,040	
Crushing and Grinding Department		$18,040

As previously stated, this accounting procedure disregards the small amount of product in process at the beginning and at the end of the month.

Entry J. The output of the Burning Department for the month was 65 tons of clinker. The total of the charges to the department's account is transferred to the inventory account Clinker. The initial balance of $11,060 in the Clinker account represented 35 tons at $316 per ton. Labor and overhead costs in the burning department were $1,800 and $900 respectively. These costs added to the figure transferred from the crushing and grinding department give a total cost of $20,740 for the 65 tons of clinker produced. The following journal entry transfers this total to clinker inventory.

Clinker	$20,740	
Burning Department		$20,740

It is not practicable to obtain an accurate measure of the physical quantity transferred from the crushing and grinding department to the burning department. For this reason, unit costs of both departments are computed on the basis of the amount of clinker produced in the burning department. These unit costs for August are shown in Exhibit 11-3.

THE AVERAGE–COST METHOD OF INVENTORY VALUATION. At the beginning of August, the Clinker account showed 35 tons on hand at $316 per ton. This unit cost figure of $316 is based on manufacturing costs during previous accounting periods. The unit cost statement, Exhibit 11-3, gives $319.08 as the unit cost of clinker produced during August.

Because variations in unit costs are inevitable, the accountant must adopt some systematic plan for dealing with them. The *average-cost method* is used by the Zapotec Manufacturing Company. This method is illustrated with respect to the Clinker account, as follows:

	Units	Amount	Unit valuation
On hand, Aug. 1	35	$11,060	$316.00
August production	65	20,740	319.08
Total	100	$31,800	$318.00
Transferred in August	55	17,490	318.00
On hand, Sept. 1	45	$14,310	$318.00

In this method, the total dollars already in the account, $11,060, are added to the total dollars transferred into the account, $20,740. The sum, $31,800, is divided by the total units to which it applies, 100. The resulting unit value, $318.00, is used for pricing the transfers out of the account and for valuation of the inventory remaining on hand.

Other systematic methods of dealing with this same problem, such as the first-in first-out (FIFO) method and the last-in first-out (LIFO) method, are explained in the next chapter. In periods of rising or falling prices, different methods give substantially different results which have different influences on financial accounting results, cost control, and sales policy determination. The advantages and disadvantages of the various methods are considered in the next chapter.

Entry K. During the month 55 tons of clinker were transferred to the Regrinding Department. The foregoing calculation of average clinker cost forms the basis for this entry.

Regrinding Department	$17,490	
Clinker		$17,490

Entry L. In the Regrinding Department, 58 tons of bulk product were made. The total of the charges to the department's account is transferred to the account Bulk Zapite. The initial balance of $7,700 in this account

represented 22 tons at $350 per ton. Unit costs in the regrinding department are shown in Exhibit 11-3. The journal entry for the transfer of costs to the inventory account Bulk Zapite is as follows:

Bulk Zapite	$20,540	
Regrinding Department		$20,540

EXHIBIT 11-3

ZAPOTEC MANUFACTURING COMPANY

UNIT COST STATEMENT, AUGUST, 19___

	Output of department	Cost for the month	Cost per unit of departmental output
Crushing and grinding department...	65 tons		
Material...		$11,740	$180.61
Labor...		4,200	64.62
Overhead...		2,100	32.31
Transferred out...		$18,040	$277.54
Burning department...	65 tons		
Transferred in...		$18,040	$277.54
Labor...		1,800	27.69
Overhead...		900	13.85
Transferred out...		$20,740	$319.08
Regrinding department...	58 tons		
Transferred in...		$17,490	$301.55
Material added...		650	11.21
Labor...		1,600	27.59
Overhead...		800	13.79
Cost of bulk Zapite...		$20,540	$354.14
Packaging department...	8,000 packages		
Transferred in...		$14,120	$1.7650
Material added...		1,240	0.1550
Labor...		1,000	0.1250
Overhead...		500	0.0625
Cost of packaged Zapite...		$16,860	$2.1075

Entries M and N. 20 tons of bulk Zapite are sold; Cost of Goods Sold is entered. 40 tons of bulk Zapite are transferred to the Packaging Department. An average cost calculation for the Bulk Zapite account is as follows:

	Units	Amount	Unit valuation
On hand, Aug. 1...	22	$ 7,700	$350.00
August production...	58	20,540	354.14
Total...	80	$28,240	$353.00
Cost of product sold in August...	20	7,060	353.00
Transferred in August...	40	14,120	353.00
On hand, Sept. 1...	20	$ 7,060	$353.00

The required journal entries are:

Cost of Goods Sold	$ 7,060	
Bulk Zapite		$ 7,060
Packaging Department	$14,120	
Bulk Zapite		$14,120

Entry O. The output of the Packaging Department is 8,000 packages. Departmental charges are transferred to Packaged Zapite. The initial balance of $6,240 in this account represented 3,000 packages at $2.08 per package. Unit costs in the packaging department are shown in Exhibit 11-3. The required journal entry is:

Packaged Zapite	$16,860	
Packaging Department		$16,860

Entry P. 8,500 packages are sold; Cost of Goods Sold is entered. An average-cost calculation for the Packaged Zapite account is as follows:

	Units	Amount	Unit valuation
On hand, Aug. 1	3,000	$ 6,240	$2.08
August production	8,000	16,860	2.1075
Total	11,000	$23,100	$2.10
Cost of product sold in August	8,500	17,850	2.10
On hand, Sept. 1	2,500	$ 5,250	$2.10

The required journal entry is:

Cost of Goods Sold	$17,850	
Packaged Zapite		$17,850

Entries Q to T. These entries should be self-evident. The depreciation charge in entry Q is made to Manufacturing Overhead because this example has been simplified by including all indirect manufacturing expenses in this one account.

POST-CLOSING TRIAL BALANCE AND FINANCIAL STATEMENTS. Just as in the job-order example, it has been convenient to complete this simple example without the use of a work sheet. The post-closing trial balance, Exhibit 11-4, provides a check on the equality of debits and credits. It also gives the essential information for the balance sheet, Exhibit 11-5. In the balance sheet, clinker is classified as work in process and bulk and packaged Zapite are both classified as finished product. The needed information for the profit and loss statement, Exhibit 11-6, can be obtained from the Profit and Loss Summary account.

EXHIBIT 11-4
ZAPOTEC MANUFACTURING COMPANY
TRIAL BALANCE, AUGUST 31, 19___

Account	*Debit*	*Credit*
Cash	$ 27,500	
Accounts Receivable	20,500	
Material A	5,060	
Material B	9,200	
Material C	1,350	
Packaging Material	2,660	
Clinker	14,310	
Bulk Zapite	7,060	
Packaged Zapite	5,250	
Plant and Equipment	90,000	
Accumulated Depreciation		$ 23,500
Accounts Payable		12,800
Capital Stock		80,000
Earned Surplus		66,590
Totals	$182,890	$182,890

EXHIBIT 11-5
ZAPOTEC MANUFACTURING COMPANY
BALANCE SHEET, AUGUST 31, 19___

Assets			*Liabilities and Owners' Equity*		
Current Assets:			Liabilities:		
Cash	$27,500		Accounts Payable		$ 12,800
Accounts Receivable	20,500				
Inventories:					
Materials	18,270				
Work in Process	14,310				
Finished Product	12,310	$ 92,890			
Fixed Assets:			Owners' Equity:		
Plant and Equipment	$90,000		Capital Stock	$80,000	
Less: Accumulated			Earned Surplus	66,590	145,690
Depreciation	23,500	66,500			
Total		$159,390	Total		$159,390

EXHIBIT 11-6
ZAPOTEC MANUFACTURING COMPANY
PROFIT AND LOSS STATEMENT FOR AUGUST, 19___

Sales	$33,000
Less: Cost of goods sold	24,910
Gross profit on sales	$ 8,090
Less: Selling and administrative expense	5,700
Less: Burden variance	300
Net profit	$ 2,090

THE UNIT COST REPORT AS A DEVICE FOR COST CONTROL. Exhibit 11-3 breaks down the costs in each department into unit costs of material, labor, and overhead. This breakdown is aimed primarily at cost control, particularly control of material and labor costs. The unit cost report gives management current information regarding the costs in each department and makes it possible to bring pressure for cost reduction whenever the reported unit costs are out of line with past costs for the same operation or with some other standard of comparison. A report such as Exhibit 11-3 will be more useful for this purpose if, in addition to the current unit costs, it also contains the figures to be used as standards of comparison.

Although monthly cost reports are usually sufficient for interdepartmental transfers, for valuation of inventories, and for determination of cost of goods sold, more frequent reports often are desired for purposes of cost control. For certain operations in some industries, it is possible to prepare weekly cost reports or even cost reports that break down certain costs by days or by shifts within a day. It should be kept in mind that such reports require frequent accurate measurements of quantities as well as a more detailed breakdown of costs by time units than is usually needed for financial accounting purposes.

DEPARTMENTAL OVERHEAD RATES IN PROCESS COST ACCOUNTING. In the Zapotec example, all overhead costs were distributed among the departments in proportion to direct-labor cost. This illustrated a simple procedure for overhead distribution but one that may be unsatisfactory for purposes of both financial accounting and cost control. Frequently it is advantageous to have separate overhead rates for each department. This topic is developed in Chap. 14.

DISPOSITION OF OVERHEAD VARIANCE. In the Zapotec example, the overhead variance for the month was closed to the Profit and Loss Summary account at the end of the month. The debit variance of $300 for August was therefore reflected in the profit and loss statement as a decrease in ownership associated with the August operations.

Some indirect manufacturing expenses are subject to seasonal variations unrelated to the volume of production. Also, in certain industries there are seasonal or irregular variations in the volume of production. Where these conditions obtain, it is reasonable to expect to have underabsorbed overhead in some months and to have overabsorbed overhead in other months, even though these debit and credit variances may turn out to be approximately equal at year end. An alternative treatment of overhead variance that is based on this expectation is to carry forward the balance in the Overhead Variance account from month to month, closing out the variance only at the end of the year. In the financial statements for internal use, an accumulated debit variance for the year to date would appear on the assets side of the balance sheet as a deferred charge. If the accumulated variance was a credit amount, it would appear on the liabilities side of the balance sheet as a deferred credit. Although such a variance balance may properly be included in a balance sheet prepared for the use of management, such a variance would ordinarily be eliminated by an adjustment before preparing a balance sheet for submission to stockholders or to bankers or other prospective creditors.

If the policy is to close any variance to Profit and Loss Summary each month, the amount may be considered of sufficient interest to management to be displayed in the profit and loss statement as a separate item. This was illustrated in Exhibits 10-4 and 11-6. However, in a profit and loss statement for external release, such a variance would be incorporated into cost of goods sold or general expense.

THE TREATMENT IN PROCESS COST ACCOUNTING OF WORK PARTLY COMPLETED. In the Zapotec example, the four departmental accounts had zero balances at the beginning of the month and again at month end. The relatively small and relatively constant inventories in process within these departments were disregarded for accounting purposes. The only in-process inventory account at month end was the Clinker account.

In many enterprises using process costs, the matter is not so simple as this; the quantities in process may be substantial and they may change from time to time. To compute costs, it is necessary to make an estimate of the percentage of completion of the work in process in each department at the end of each accounting period. For a given departmental account, this percentage may differ as between material and labor. For example, all the needed material may have been issued to complete the work that is in process but only half of the needed labor may have been applied. Some of the problems of accounting for such partly completed work are illustrated in the standard cost example in Chap. 15.

DIFFERENT DEPARTMENTS USE DIFFERENT UNITS. In the Zapotec example, the unit costs in the crushing and grinding department and the burning department were computed in tons of clinker. Although tons were also used in the regrinding department, it was cost per ton of bulk product, not clinker, that was significant. In the packaging department, costs were computed per package.

It should be emphasized that the units used in process cost accounting are always units of *departmental output.* It is output, not input of materials to the department, that is relevant in computing unit costs. Moreover, it is the output of the department, not the output of final product, that is significant in cost control and in pricing interdepartmental transfers. The appropriate units may properly differ from one department to the next.

CHOOSING BETWEEN PROCESS COSTS AND JOB-ORDER COSTS. In many instances, the choice between process costs and job-order costs will be dictated by the type of manufacturing operation. At one extreme, a single-product plant or process will nearly always use process costs. At the other extreme, where all product is made to customers' specifications on the basis of an order for a specific quantity, job-order costs are the obvious choice. Continuous-process industries generally use process costs. Chemical plants, metallurgical plants, textile mills, flour mills, paper manufacturers, petroleum refineries, and cement plants are some examples. Custom manufacturing, style industries, and heavy industries in the metal trades are likely to use job-order costs. Some examples are job printing, clothing, locomotives, and heavy machine tools. Some manufacturers use process costs for certain operations and job costs for others.

The borderline cases where a decision must be made between job costs and process costs are usually those in which a given manufacturing process produces two or more different items and where these different items have some unit in common (e.g., weight) that might be used to compute the unit cost of all the items. In such cases, a decision to use process costs will ordinarily result in less expense for cost accounting. Both stores keeping and timekeeping are simpler with process costs, and there are likely to be fewer entries to the cost accounts. The critical question for review is whether the proposed unit is an appropriate one or its use will give misleading conclusions regarding the relative costs of the different items made by the process.

DETERMINING UNIT COSTS WHEN A DEPARTMENT MAKES TWO OR MORE PRODUCTS. In process cost accounting, the unit costs in a department are obtained by dividing the total departmental costs for a period of time by the total number of units made during the same period. Where all the units produced in a department are identical, as in Exhibit 11-3, it clearly is appropriate to compute unit costs in this way.

Where two or more different products are made in a department, the products must have some unit in common if a unit cost is to be computed by dividing total departmental costs by total units made. Some examples of possible units are weight in pounds, volume in gallons, length in yards, or numbers of items produced.

Sometimes it will be evident that a proposed unit will be reasonably satisfactory for the purpose for computing the unit costs of a variety of products. For instance, in a foundry making castings that are similar in size and complexity, it may be appropriate for all castings to be valued at the same unit cost per pound. This procedure is illustrated in problem 11-4 at the end of this chapter.

Nevertheless, this simple basis of computing costs clearly will give misleading results in a foundry where some castings are large and simple and others are small and complicated. In general, when a department makes dissimilar products, it frequently happens that there is no one common unit that can be applied to all the departmental products for the purpose of computing unit costs. In such circumstances, a choice can be made among the following procedures:

1. Job-order costs can be used in the department in question even though process costs may be employed elsewhere in the manufacturing plant.
2. Within the department, detailed cost information can be kept regarding the material cost, labor cost, and numbers of items made during the accounting period for each of the different products. Separate costs can then be computed for each of the products for each accounting period. This procedure is illustrated in problem 11-3 at the end of this chapter.
3. Weighting factors can be developed to convert the actual units of different departmental products to a common arbitrary equivalent unit that will be used for the purpose of computing unit costs.

SUMMARY. Like the job-order example in the preceding chapter, the process cost example in this chapter concentrates attention on the flow of value through the cost accounts. In process cost accounting, the total costs in each department for a stipulated period such as a month are divided by the units of departmental output to obtain unit costs. These unit costs are used for inventory valuation; they also form the basis of calculation of cost of goods sold. Departmental unit costs are also important for purposes of cost control.

DISCUSSION QUESTIONS

11-A. Explain the essential differences between job-order costs and process costs.

11-B. In what types of industry would you be most likely to find process costs? Job-order costs? Consider some manufacturing situation for which it is desired to design a cost accounting system. What considerations might enter into the choice between these two types of costs?

11-C. In process cost accounting, what is the *unit cost statement*? What are some uses of this statement?

11-D. At the start of a month, 15,000 units of a certain product were on hand and were valued for inventory purposes at $0.40 per unit. During the month 10,000 units with a total cost of $4,500 were added to the inventory. Apply the average-cost method to determine the unit cost to be used in costing sales or transfers to another department and in valuing the remaining inventory.

11-E. In the Zapotec example, why were the costs of goods sold entered by an end-of-period general journal entry rather than entered in the sales journal at the time of each sale?

11-F. Explain how process costing can be used in a department that processes two or more different products during a typical accounting period.

PROBLEMS

Problem 11-1. The Whammit Manufacturing Company produces a uniform product which passes in succession through four departments, die casting, buffing and cleaning, japanning, and finishing. Process cost accounting is used. A predetermined burden rate of 66⅔% of direct-labor cost is used in each of the four departments. All cost accounts are kept in the general ledger.

Set up a general ledger in T-account form with the following accounts:

Cash
Accounts Receivable
Plant and Equipment
Accumulated Depreciation, Plant and Equipment
*Material A
*Material B
*Material C
Die Casting Department
*Die Castings
Buffing and Cleaning Department
Japanning Department
*Japanned Whammits
Finishing Department
*Finished Whammits
Direct Labor
Indirect Labor
Heat, Light, and Power
Factory Supervision
Depreciation Expense
Selling and Administrative Expense
Sales
Cost of Sales
Burden Variance
Accounts Payable
Profit and Loss Summary
Capital Stock
Earned Surplus

* These T accounts should have columns for quantity, unit price, and total value

The company started business on May 1 after a temporary shutdown. Make entries directly in the T accounts to record the following matters:

A. Opening balances were as follows:

	Debit	*Credit*
Cash	$ 9,000	
Accounts Receivable	4,000	
Plant and Equipment	60,000	
Accumulated Depreciation, Plant and Equipment		$15,000
Accounts Payable		1,000
Capital Stock		50,000
Earned Surplus		7,000
Totals	$73,000	$73,000

B. Purchased the following materials on credit:

Material A—8,000 units at $0.50	$4,000
Material B—1,000 units at $2	2,000
Material C— 800 units at $1	800
Total	$6,800

C. Paid cash as follows:

Direct labor	$2,700
Indirect labor	1,000
Heat, light, and power	300
Factory supervision	500
Selling and administrative expense	900
Accounts payable	3,000
Total	$8,400

D. Materials used in departments were as follows:

Die casting department used 5,000 units of material A.
Japanning department used 450 units of material B.
Finishing department used 500 units of material C.

E. The direct-labor cost mentioned in C was divided among the departments as follows:

Die casting department	$1,200
Buffing and cleaning department	300
Japanning department	600
Finishing department	600
Total	$2,700

F. Burden is applied to the departmental accounts in accordance with the predetermined burden rate.

G. 5,000 die castings were completed in the die casting department. As no in-process material remains in this (or other) departments at the end of the month, transfer all costs in the account Die Casting Department to the account Die Castings.

H. 4,000 of these die castings were delivered to the buffing and cleaning department.

I. After buffing and cleaning, these 4,000 items were also processed in the japanning department.

J. All costs in the account Japanning Department were transferred to the account Japanned Whammits.

K. Of the 4,000 japanned whammits, 3,000 were delivered to the finishing department and there finished. Transfer all costs in the account Finishing Department to the account Finished Whammits.

L. Of the 3,000 finished whammits, 2,500 were sold on credit at $3 each, a total of $7,500. Make also the entry showing cost of sales.

M. Collections on accounts receivable for the month were $5,000.

N. Depreciation to be charged on plant equipment for May is $200.

P. Make the necessary entries to close the indirect manufacturing expense accounts into Burden Variance and to determine the overabsorbed or underabsorbed burden.

Q. At this point, take a trial balance. Then make closing entries necessary to determine the profit or loss, first closing Burden Variance into Cost of Sales.

Prepare a profit and loss statement for May and an end-of-month balance sheet.

Problem 11-2. The Tarascan Manufacturing Company makes a product, Rasca, that passes in succession through three departments: blending, grinding, and packaging. Process cost accounting is used. All accounts are kept in the general ledger.

A. Set up a general ledger in T-account form with the following accounts and account balances as of July 1:

Account	Debit	Credit
Cash	$ 17,000	
Accounts Receivable	40,000	
*Material A (30,000 at $0.60)	18,000	
*Material B (20,000 at $0.80)	16,000	
*Containers (2,000 at $0.20)	400	
*Bulk Rasca (6,000 units at $4.10)	24,600	
*Packaged Rasca (4,000 units at $5.15)	20,600	
Accumulated Depreciation, Plant and Equipment		$ 46,000
Plant and Equipment	120,000	
Accounts Payable		20,000
Blending Department		
Grinding Department		
Packaging Department		
Direct Labor		
Indirect Manufacturing Expense		
Selling and Administrative Expense		
Sales		
Cost of Sales		
Profit and Loss Summary		
Capital Stock		100,000
Earned Surplus		90,600
Totals	$256,600	$256,600

* These T accounts should have columns for quantity, unit price, and total value.

Make entries directly in the T accounts to record the following matters:

B. Purchases on credit during the month of July were:

Material B (10,000 units at $0.80)	$ 8,000
Containers (10,000 at $0.20)	2,000
Total	$10,000

C. Paid cash as follows:

Direct labor	$ 4,500
Indirect manufacturing expense	5,000
Selling and administrative expense	8,000
Accounts payable	15,000
Total	$32,500

D. Storeroom issues during July were:

6,000 units of material A to blending department
8,000 units of material B to blending department
5,000 containers to packaging department

E. The direct-labor cost in each of the three departments was as follows:

Blending department	$1,500
Grinding department	900
Packaging department	2,100

F. Depreciation to be charged on plant and equipment for July is $500.

G. Burden is allocated to the departmental cost center accounts as follows: $1,100 to Blending, $900 to Grinding, $500 to Packaging, and the balance distributed in proportion to direct-labor cost.

H. The materials processed in the blending department were also processed in the grinding department. The grinding department delivered 4,000 units of bulk Rasca to bulk product storage. (At any given moment, the amount of material in process in these two departments is very small in comparison with the total production for a month. Moreover, this in-process material is approximately constant. Hence the material in process in the two departments is neglected for cost accounting purposes.)

I. 5,000 units of bulk Rasca are delivered to the packaging department and there packaged. The average-cost method is used for interdepartmental transfers and for inventory valuation, just as in the Zapotec example in this chapter.

J. Sales on credit are:

2,000 units of bulk Rasca at $5	$10,000
6,000 units of packaged Rasca at $6.50	39,000
Total	$49,000

Use the average-cost method for determining cost of goods sold.

K. Collections on accounts receivable are $32,000.

L. Make all additional entries necessary to close the books.

Take a trial balance after closing. (No work sheet is required.) Prepare a unit cost statement showing the costs of production in the three departments. Prepare a profit and loss statement for July and an end-of-month balance sheet.

Problem 11-3. The Vulcan Forge Company makes railway spikes. It has a forge shop where the spikes are headed and pointed and a packing department where they are inspected, dipped, and packed. It starts operations after a temporary shutdown with no inventories of forgings or finished spikes on hand. The following figures apply to production during the first 3 months of 19____.

Size of spike	No. forged in forge shop	Forged spikes on hand at end of period	Spikes packed and delivered to finished goods	No. sold
A	175,000	15,000	160,000	120,000
B	240,000	40,000	200,000	180,000
C	125,000	25,000	100,000	80,000

Set up the following T accounts to represent the general ledger. All cost accounts are kept in this ledger.

Cash
Accounts Receivable
Steel Bar
Containers
Forge Shop

Forged Spikes—A
Forged Spikes—B
Forged Spikes—C
Packing Department
Packed Spikes—A

Packed Spikes—B
Packed Spikes—C
Plant Equipment
Accumulated Depreciation—Plant Equipment
Direct Labor

Indirect Labor
Repairs and Maintenance
Fuel and Power
Factory Supervision
Factory Taxes

Depreciation Expense
Other Factory Expenses
Selling and Distribution Expense
General and Administrative Expense
Sales

Cost of Goods Sold
Accounts Payable
Notes Payable
Profit and Loss Summary
Capital Stock
Earned Surplus

Show in the ledger all the transactions for the period, determining the valuation of the various inventories and the profit or loss for the period. Burden is to be distributed on the basis of historical costs rather than predetermined costs. Direct-labor cost is to be used in both departments as the basis of burden distribution in allocating burden among the three sizes of spikes. It is also used as the basis for allocating certain indirect manufacturing expenses between the two departments.

A. Opening balances were:

	Debit	Credit
Cash	$ 35,000	
Accounts Receivable	10,000	
Plant Equipment	120,000	
Accumulated Depreciation—Plant Equipment		$ 40,000
Notes Payable		20,000
Capital Stock		60,000
Earned Surplus		45,000
Totals	$165,000	$165,000

B. After 3 months' operations, invoice register totals are:

	Debit	Credit
Steel bar	$44,000	
Containers	1,000	
Direct labor	15,250	
Indirect labor	4,100	
Repairs and maintenance	2,700	
Fuel	4,400	
Factory supervision	4,200	
Factory taxes	1,100	
Other factory expenses	1,900	
Selling and distribution expense	5,000	
General and administrative expense	$ 6,600	
Accounts payable		$90,250

C. The direct-labor cost was $11,100 in the Forge Shop and $4,150 in the Packing Department.

D. Steel bar that cost $33,150 was used in the Forge Shop; containers that cost $600 were used in the Packing Department.

E. Depreciation to be charged on plant and equipment for the period is $2,400.

F. Certain indirect manufacturing expenses are allocated between the two departments as follows:

	Forge shop	Packing dept.
Indirect labor	$ 3,100	$1,000
Repairs and maintenance	2,400	300
Fuel and power	3,800	600
Factory taxes	910	190
Depreciation	2,000	400
Subtotal	$12,210	$2,490

G. Factory supervision and other factory expenses are distributed in proportion to direct-labor cost.

H, I, and J. The following incomplete unit cost statement shows the breakdown of material costs and direct-labor costs among the three classes of spikes on the basis of material usage and labor time kept in the two departments. Complete this statement for the Forge Shop, allocating the burden among the three sizes of spikes in proportion to their respective direct-labor costs and then computing the unit costs for each size. Use these costs for entry H, transferring the balance in the Forge Shop account into the accounts Forged Spikes—A, B, and C. Make entry I, charging the Packing Department account with the spikes used. Complete the packing-department section of the unit cost statement, and transfer the balance in the Packing Department account to the accounts Packed Spikes—A, B, and C. This is entry J.

UNIT COST STATEMENT

	Total	Size A	Size B	Size C
Forge shop:				
Material cost	$33,150	$ 8,750	$14,400	$10,000
Direct-labor cost	11,100	2,800	4,800	3,500
Burden	$	$	$	$
Total cost	$	$	$	$
Quantity produced	....	175,000	240,000	125,000
Unit cost	....	$	$	$
Packing department:				
Forged spikes used	....	160,000	200,000	100,000
Cost of spikes	$	$	$	$
Cost of containers	600	160	240	200
Direct-labor cost	4,150	1,120	1,880	1,150
Burden	$	$	$	$
Total cost	$	$	$	$
Quantity produced	....	160,000	200,000	100,000
Unit cost	....	$	$	$
Spikes sold	....	120,000	180,000	80,000
Cost of goods sold	$	$	$	$

K. Cost of goods sold can be determined from the unit cost statement.
L. The prices at which the spikes were sold were $0.14, $0.17, and $0.23 for sizes A, B, and C respectively.
M. Cash receipts on accounts receivable are $45,000.
N. Cash disbursements on accounts payable are $72,000.
P. Income and expense accounts should be closed into Profit and Loss Summary.
Q. Profit and Loss Summary should be closed into Earned Surplus.

Take a post-closing trial balance of the ledger.

Problem 11-4. The Sure-Fit Food Company makes two products, D (dog food) and C (cat food). The raw meat and fish materials are prepared and precooked in the meat department and delivered to storage. These items, "processed meat" and "processed fish," together with cereal and vegetable materials and additives, are mixed in batches in the mixing department, according to packing orders for products D and C. The single packing line is used alternately for D and C. The same cans, cartons, and (size of) labels are used for packing both products. Sure-Fit uses a process cost system. The

COST FLOW DIAGRAM
SURE-FIT FOOD COMPANY

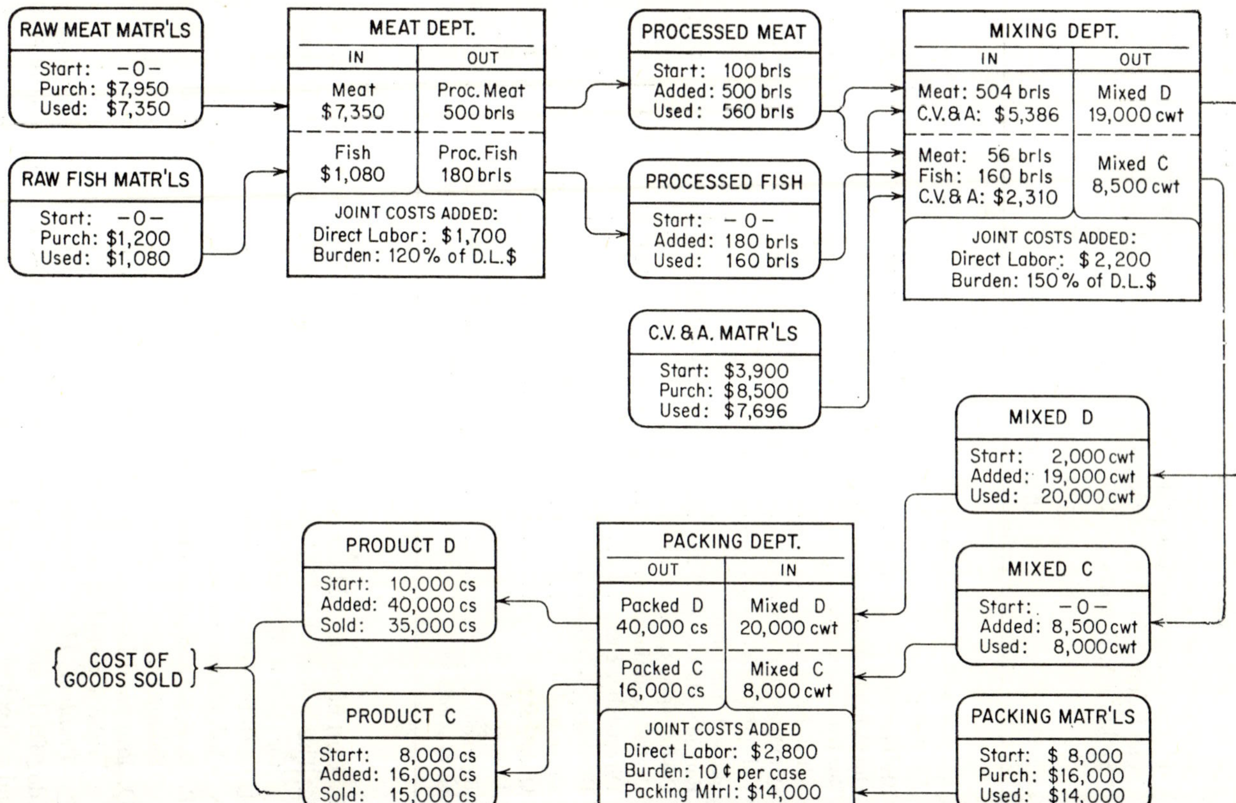

accompanying diagram describes the system and presents data concerning operations for the month of February, 19___.

In each department where joint costs must be allocated, a physical quantity basis is used to do this. In the meat department the basis is barrels of processed material. In the mixing department the basis is hundredweight of mixed food. In the packing department the basis is cases of product (48 cans per case).

Items are valued in the various inventory accounts at *average* cost. A new average unit cost is computed for each item at the end of each month and used to price out the quantity issued during that month.

Set up a T-account sheet representing the factory ledger. The accounts required are as follows:

Work in Process, Meat Department—Meat Processing
Work in Process, Meat Department—Fish Processing
Work in Process, Mixing Department—Product D
Work in Process, Mixing Department—Product C
Work in Process, Packing Department—Product D

Work in Process, Packing Department—Product C
Cereal, Vegetable, and Additive Materials
Packing Materials
Raw Meat Inventory
Raw Fish Inventory

*Processed Meat
*Processed Fish
*Mixed D
*Mixed C
*Product D

*Product C
Direct Labor
Maintenance Department
Indirect Manufacturing Expense—Meat Department
Indirect Manufacturing Expense—Mixing Department

Indirect Manufacturing Expense—Packing Department
Burden Variance—Meat Department
Burden Variance—Mixing Department
Burden Variance—Packing Department
Plant General Overhead

Plant Facilities and Services Expense
General Ledger—Control

* These accounts require columns for quantity, unit price, and total amount.

The opening balances in the factory ledger accounts as of February 1 are as follows:

Account	Debit	Credit
General Ledger—Control		$30,784
Cereal, Vegetable, and Additive Materials	$ 3,900	
Packing Materials Inventory	8,000	
Processed Meat (100 brl @ $19)	1,900	
Mixed D (2,000 cwt @ $0.972)	1,944	
Product D (10,000 cases @ $0.88)	8,800	
Product C (8,000 cases @ $0.78)	6,240	
Totals	$30,784	$30,784

All entries in this subsidiary ledger are to be complete, balanced entries. Any debit (or credit) to a factory ledger account for which the opposing credit (or debit) is to a general ledger account should be balanced by entering the opposing credit (or debit) in the account titled General Ledger—Control. (The balance in this account at the end of a month will therefore be equal and opposite to the balance in the general ledger account titled Factory Ledger—Control.)

A. Enter the opening balances in their respective accounts.

B. Charges to the factory ledger in February from the invoice register were:

Raw meat materials purchased	$ 7,950
Raw fish materials purchased	1,200
Cereal and vegetable materials and additives purchased	8,500
Packing materials purchased	16,000
Plant facilities and services expense	2,000
Maintenance supplies (charge to Maintenance Department)	300
Plant general overhead expense	1,200
Total	$37,150

Note: In entries C, D, and E use the departmental Indirect Manufacturing Expense (IME) accounts to collect the total IME for each department.

C. Charges to the factory ledger from the payroll distribution journal were analyzed as follows:

	Meat dept.	Mixing dept.	Packing dept.	Maint. dept.	Total
Indirect labor	$ 470	$ 400	$ 800	$ 930	$ 2,600
Overtime premium	30	0	40	0	70
Supervision and clerical	600	800	1,000	600	3,000
Department totals	$1,100	$1,200	$1,840	$1,530	$ 5,670
Direct labor (charge to Direct Labor account)					6,700
Total					$12,370

D. Charges to the factory ledger from the general journal (for accrued expenses) were analyzed as follows:

	Meat dept.	Mixing dept.	Packing dept.	Maint. dept.	Total
Depreciation expense.........	$210	$260	$440	$120	$1,030
Taxes and insurance..........	70	100	180	50	400
Department totals.........	$280	360	620	170	$1,430
General plant overhead......					400
Total......					$1,830

E. Make the following departmental distributions of indirect manufacturing expenses:

	Meat dept.	Mixing dept.	Packing dept.	Maint. dept.
Plant facilities expense, %..............	20	25	49	6
Plant general overhead, %..............	25	30	40	5
Maintenance dept. expense, %..........	10	30	60	

Note: For entries F through L, use the data given on the cost flow diagram as necessary. Be sure each entry you make is a balanced "double entry." The data of the problem were chosen so that the average unit prices to be computed for entries H, J, and L come out in whole cents with no remainder.

F. Make suitable entries for direct materials, direct labor, and overhead in the two Meat Department Work in Process accounts. The predetermined burden rate is 120% of direct-labor cost; the credit in this entry is to Burden Variance—Meat Department.

G. There is no work in process in the meat department at the end of the month.

H. Make suitable entries for direct materials, direct labor, and overhead in the two Mixing Department Work in Process accounts. The predetermined burden rate is 150% of direct labor cost.

I. There is no work in process in the mixing department at the end of the month.

J. Make suitable entries for direct materials, direct labor, and overhead in the two Packing Department Work in Process accounts. The predetermined burden rate is 10 cents per case of product packed.

K. There is no work in process in the packing department at the end of the month.

L. Make entries in the Finished Product accounts for the cost of goods sold.

M. Make entries as necessary to determine the departmental burden variances, and close them to Profit and Loss.

N. Compute and record the balance in all accounts, and take a trial balance of the factory ledger.

12/ MATERIAL COSTS

This chapter deals with the accounting problem of valuation of inventories and of the goods withdrawn from inventory and with the matter of charging the cost of materials issued to the proper accounts. This chapter is also concerned with the functions of storeskeeping, inventory management, and purchasing, particularly with respect to accounting requirements and the necessities of integration and coordination between accounting and these other systems.

DISTINCTION BETWEEN DIRECT AND INDIRECT MATERIAL. Direct material is material specifically identified with a job order or a process. In most instances, this is material that enters into the final manufactured product, but it may also be material obviously traceable to a particular job or operation even though used up in the process of manufacture. For example, a polishing material might fall into this latter class.

Indirect material is all other material used in the manufacturing process. The cost of indirect material is treated as one of the cost elements of indirect manufacturing expense. Typical indirect materials are factory supplies of various sorts such as machine lubricants or janitors' supplies. In addition, some materials entering into the final product may be treated as indirect for accounting purposes because of the difficulty or expense of identifying them with specific job orders. For example, although glue used in a furniture factory is part of the finished furniture, the difficulties of its measurement in certain operations may be so great that its cost is more conveniently included in indirect manufacturing expense.

COMPUTING COSTS AND INVENTORY VALUES WHEN PRICES VARY. In the perpetual-inventory accounts in the examples in Chaps. 3 and 10, the difficulties introduced by price variation were avoided because there were no variations in prices in the problem data. In the discussion of inventory valuation in Chap. 7, it was pointed out that there are inherent difficulties in defining "cost" whenever the prices at which goods have been purchased have varied. These difficulties exist whether or not cost accounting methods are used in determining the value of inventory on hand and the cost of inventory used. And they exist with respect to accounting for raw materials, work in process, and manufactured goods, as well as for merchandise purchased for resale.

Three common methods of dealing with these difficulties in a materials cost accounting system are (1) the average-cost method, (2) the first-in first-out (FIFO) method, and (3) the last-in first-out (LIFO) method.

Whenever there are considerable changes in the unit costs at which items enter inventory, these three methods will give substantially different figures for profit as well as different inventory values for balance sheet purposes. This point can be illustrated to best advantage by a numerical example in which there has been a large change in the unit price of a purchased item during an accounting period.

AN EXAMPLE COMPARING THE AVERAGE-COST, FIFO, AND LIFO METHODS. In Exhibit 12-1, it is assumed that 400 units of a material not previously used are purchased on December 15 at $10 per unit for use in the following year. The entries for purchases and issues during the next year are shown using each of these three methods for pricing the issues. The cost of this material rises sharply during the year, with the first purchase at $12 per unit and the second and third purchases at $15 per unit.

The rules for pricing issues and valuing inventories under these three methods should be evident from an examination of this exhibit. Under all three methods, the first two issues (on 1/20 and 2/11) are priced at $10 per unit, the unit cost of the initial purchase of 400 units.

Under the average-cost method, a new average cost per unit is computed every time there is a new purchase. When 100 units are purchased for $1,200 on 2/26, this $1,200 is added to the $3,000 balance in the account to obtain a total account balance of $4,200. This total is divided by the 400 units on hand to obtain an average unit cost of $10.50. In effect, this is a weighted average of unit costs of 300 units at $10 and 100 units at $12. This average cost of $10.50 is used for pricing all issues until a new purchase is made. At that time, a new average is computed to be applied to subsequent issues. And so on. The average-cost method was used in Chap. 11 for valuation of inventories of clinker and bulk and packaged product and for pricing interdepartmental transfers and computing costs of goods sold.

Under the first-in first-out method all issues are priced at $10 per unit until 400 units have been issued. On 10/14 when 100 units are

EXHIBIT 12-1

EXAMPLE OF AVERAGE-COST, FIFO, AND LIFO METHODS APPLIED TO THE SAME DATA ON RECEIPTS AND ISSUES

Date	Received			Issued			On Hand		
	Number of units	Cost per unit	Total cost	Number of units	Price per unit	Value	Number of units	Value	Computed average price
Average Cost Method									
12/15	400	$10	$4,000				400	$4,000	$10.00
1/20				50	$10	$ 500	350	3,500	
2/11				50	10	500	300	3,000	
2/26	100	12	1,200				400	4,200	10.50
4/8				50	10.50	525	350	3,675	
6/23				50	10.50	525	300	3,150	
8/11	200	15	3,000				500	6,150	12.30
9/2				150	12.30	1,845	350	4,305	
10/14				100	12.30	1,230	250	3,075	
10/22	200	15	3,000				450	6,075	13.50
12/9				50	13.50	675	400	5,400	
Totals			$11,200			$5,800			
FIFO Method									
12/15	400	$10	$4,000				400	$4,000	
1/20				50	$10	$ 500	350	3,500	
2/11				50	10	500	300	3,000	
2/26	100	12	1,200				400	4,200	
4/8				50	10	500	350	3,700	
6/23				50	10	500	300	3,200	
8/11	200	15	3,000				500	6,200	
9/2				150	10	1,500	350	4,700	
10/14				50 50	10 12	1,100	250	3,600	
10/22	200	15	3,000				450	6,600	
12/9				50	12	600	400	6,000	
Totals			$11,200			$5,200			
LIFO Method									
12/15	400	$10	$4,000				400	$4,000	
1/20				50	$10	$ 500	350	3,500	
2/11				50	10	500	300	3,000	
2/26	100	12	1,200				400	4,200	
4/8				50	12	600	350	3,600	
6/23				50	12	600	300	3,000	
8/11	200	15	3,000				500	6,000	
9/2				150	15	2,250	350	3,750	
10/14				50 50	15 10	1,250	250	2,500	
10/22	200	15	3,000				450	5,500	
12/9				50	15	750	400	4,750	
Totals			$11,200			$6,450			

issued, 350 units have previously been issued at $10. Therefore only 50 units of this 100 can be priced at $10 and the remaining units must be priced at the next figure of $12. The first-in first-out rule is applied without regard to the physical identity of the units issued.

Under the last-in first-out method, the purchase of 100 units at $12 each on 2/26 causes the next two issues of 50 each to be priced at $12. The purchase of 200 units at $15 each on 8/11 causes the next issues of 150 units to be priced at $15. In the issue of 100 units on 10/14, only 50 units at $15 and no units at $12 remain in the account; the issue requires a pricing of 50 units at $15 and another 50 units at $10. The LIFO method is like the FIFO method in being applied without regard to the physical identity of the units issued.

When prices are stable or when inventories often drop almost to zero balance, the choice among these three methods will have very little effect on the reported figure for profit or loss or on the inventory values shown on the balance sheet. In contrast, the methods gave very different results in Exhibit 12-1 where there was a 50% increase in prices during the year and where the inventory quantity never fell below one-half of the year's consumption of the material in question.

It is evident that the FIFO and LIFO methods are furthest apart in their results; as might be expected, the average-cost method gives intermediate results. Regardless of the method used, $11,200 is the cost of all the materials acquired during the time covered by Exhibit 12-1. In the FIFO method, only $5,200 of this has been charged into work in process; the remaining $6,000 is the book valuation of the end-of-period inventory. In the LIFO method, $6,450 has been charged into work in process; only $4,750 remains as the inventory valuation.

A variation of the LIFO method, not illustrated in Exhibit 12-1, occurs when cost of goods sold is computed from purchases and physical inventories. In this LIFO application, the difference between LIFO and FIFO may be even greater than in the illustration of a perpetual-inventory account in Exhibit 12-1. To illustrate this point, assume that material has been purchased and used as stated in Exhibit 12-1 without benefit of a perpetual-inventory account. Here the end-of-year inventory is 400 units, the same number of units that started the year. Under the LIFO rule as applied to the determination of cost of goods sold from purchases and physical inventories, the 500 units purchased during the year are charged into cost of goods sold at the price of the 500 units purchased during the year and the final 400 units are valued at the price of the initial 400 units. It follows that the amount charged to production cost (and thence to cost of goods sold) is $7,200. This is $750 more than the $6,450 figure shown under the LIFO method in Exhibit 12-1. The final inventory under this application of LIFO is $4,000 rather than the $4,750 shown in Exhibit 12-1.

SOME CONSIDERATIONS INFLUENCING THE CHOICE AMONG AVERAGE-COST, FIFO, AND LIFO METHODS. All three of these methods are widely used. A survey made in 1939 showed the average-cost method to be the most common. However, it happens that 1939 was also the first year in which the general use of the LIFO method, subject to certain restrictions, was permitted for income tax purposes. Since that date, there has been a steady increase in the number of enterprises using LIFO.

Even though these three methods may differ so greatly in their results during periods of changing prices, it should be recognized that no one of the methods is inherently more correct than the others. All three methods will give identical figures for the profit or loss of a terminated enterprise; they differ in their time allocations of the profit or loss figure. A choice among these methods should be based not only on a consideration of their different effects on the financial statements obtained from the accounts but also on a consideration of their probable influences on various business actions based on the accounting reports.

In a period of changing prices, the most realistic cost figures to guide sales policies are figures based on the replacement costs of the materials and goods in question at current market prices. Although none of the three described methods gives such an up-to-date figure for cost, the LIFO method comes the closest. Moreover, the LIFO method usually gives a more realistic figure for current profit or loss. The fact that LIFO gives lower profit figures in a period of rising prices was an important consideration in the many adoptions of LIFO during the period of inflation following World War II. An important factor favoring a change to LIFO during this period of high income tax rates was the fact that lower profit figures resulted in lower current tax payments.

On the other hand, the FIFO method results in the most realistic figure for inventory valuation on the balance sheet—a figure that is nearest to the present replacement cost of the items being valued. The LIFO method may give a figure for inventory value that is badly out of date. Where a large inventory is carried at all times, the inventory valuation under LIFO may actually reflect prices of many years ago; such a valuation is defended on the grounds that this figure is the original cost of a minimum stock that must be on hand for the enterprise to operate at all.

In the introductory remarks about cost accounting in Chap. 9, three general classes of cost accounting objectives were listed, namely, financial accounting, sales policy determination, and cost control. In summary of the foregoing comments about FIFO, LIFO, and average costs, it can be stated that no one of these methods is best from the viewpoint of financial accounting. LIFO gives a more realistic determination of cost of goods sold for use in the profit and loss statement; FIFO gives more realistic inventory valuations for use in the balance sheet; the average-cost method is intermediate between the others in its influence on the two financial statements. However, LIFO is clearly the best of the three methods from the viewpoint of sales policy determination, even though it may fall short of the objective of reflecting current replacement costs.

From the viewpoint of cost control, all three methods are inferior to the use of standard costs.

STANDARD COSTS FOR MATERIALS. FIFO, LIFO, and average costs are so-called *actual* price methods of pricing issues of materials. That is, the pricing of each issue of materials is determined by applying systematic rules to the costs of materials that already have been purchased.

In contrast, where standard material costs are used, the unit prices at which each material item will be issued are *predetermined.* A predetermined standard material cost will be used for a stated period such as 3 months, 6 months, or even longer. In predetermining the standard, it is possible to consider not only the prices at which the material items have been acquired in the recent past but also the prices that are expected in the period to be covered by the standard.

The phrase *standard material cost* may be used with two different meanings. It may be used where material issues are at standard prices but where jobs or processes are charged with the actual quantities of the materials issued. The phrase may also be used where standard material quantities are predetermined for each product or process and where the material costs charged to jobs or processes are computed using standard material quantities together with predetermined standard material prices. The discussion in this chapter is limited to the topic of standard material prices. The topic of standard material quantities is deferred until Chap. 15.

SOME ADVANTAGES OF USING STANDARD PRICES FOR ISSUING MATERIALS. Standard material prices are a great aid to cost control. An essential part of cost control is the fixing of the responsibility for increases or reductions in manufacturing costs. Generally speaking, the manufacturing departments can reasonably be expected to control the quantities of materials used but not the prices at which materials are purchased. With standard prices used for material issues, the unit material costs that the cost accounting system reports for jobs or processes are useful guides to cost control. Such unit material costs measure the effectiveness of the manufacturing departments in controlling material quantities. In contrast, where an actual price system is used for material issues, it is much harder to discover why unit material costs vary from job to job. The prices at which materials are issued may vary from one job to the next one, as illustrated in Exhibit 12-1. The unit materials costs of successive identical jobs are influenced by price changes as well as by changes in the quantities of materials used.

Moreover, where standard prices are used for material issues, it is much easier to put useful information about current material prices into the hands of engineers and other design personnel. In the design of manufactured product, many decisions among different types and sizes of materials must be made. Where information about material prices is readily available to designers, it is likely that designs will be made with greater economy than in those manufacturing plants where designers are insulated from material-price information. Exhibit 12-2 is an example of a standard material cost sheet used by the General Electric Company. Loose-leaf books containing such sheets can be made available in all departments where the information that they contain seems likely to be useful.

An additional advantage of using standard prices for the issuing of material is simplification of the data processing required for stores accounting. With standard costs, the valuation of quantities on hand and the pricing of issues is much simpler than with FIFO, LIFO, or average costs.

THE MATERIAL PRICE VARIANCE ACCOUNT. Whenever charges to jobs or processes are based on predetermined costs, it is practically certain that at the end of each accounting period the actual costs will differ to some extent from the predetermined costs. This difference is recorded in a variance account. The examples in Chaps. 10 and 11 illustrated predetermined burden rates and the use of the account Burden Variance. In a similar manner, an account Material Price Variance can be used where material prices are predetermined. An illustration of the use of such an account is deferred until Chap. 15.

An appropriate aim in setting standard unit costs for materials is to make the material-price variance as small as possible. This requires an estimate of the average cost of each material to be purchased during the period (such as the coming 3 months) for which the standard is to be used.

AN EXAMPLE OF A SIMPLE MATERIALS CONTROL AND COST ACCOUNTING SYSTEM. Exhibit 12-4 is a general diagram of the procedures and information flow of a system of inventory control and cost accounting for raw materials. Many details, particularly those relating to the stock control and replenishment procedures, are omitted to focus attention on the accounting objectives and practices. Exhibit 12-3 presents a brief explanation of each major step in the procedures.

EXHIBIT 12-2

WORKS
ISSUED BY
DATE

STANDARD MATERIAL
COST AND STOCK
HOT ROLLED MACHINE STEEL BAR

B4A2A
ROUND, SQUARE, HEXAGON
PAGE 1

B4A2A is low-carbon hot-rolled machine steel. This is the most common grade and should be used wherever possible. For special conditions use: B4A2C, for parts requiring accurate size and good finish without machining; B4H1, for better machinability; B4B1, for screw machine; B4C1 or B5B1, for high strength.

COST PER 100 LB: (Wt. 0.283 lb/cu in.)

Round and Square			
Dia, Inches	Cost	Dia, Inches	Cost
3/16		2 1/8 to 2 1/2	
1/4		2 9/16 to 3 1/16	
5/16		3 1/8 to 4 9/16	
3/8		4 5/8 to 5 1/16	
7/16		5 1/8 to 5 9/16	
1/2		5 5/8 to 6 1/16	
9/16		6 1/8 to 6 9/16	
5/8 to 11/16		6 5/8 to 7 1/2	
3/4 to 1 1/2		7 9/16 to 7 3/4	
1 9/16 to 2 1/16		7 13/16 to 8	

Hexagon	
Dia, Inches	Cost
1/4	
5/16	
3/8	
7/16	
1/2 to 9/16	
5/8 to 11/16	
3/4 to 1 9/16	
1 5/8 to 3 1/16	
3 1/8 to 3 3/16	

For B4A2A3 (pickled & oil finish) add $.25 per 100 lb to above prices.

ORDER DATA - NOT FOR USE IN BILLING

Specific Length Extra: (All machine cutting - consult Order & Stores Dept.)
5 ft and longer - no charge.
Under 5 ft - Consult Order & Stores Dept.

Straightening Extra:
Bars ordered within a variation from a straight line of not more than 1/8 in. for each 5 ft of length will incur an extra charge - Consult Order & Stores Dept.

Quantity Extras: Calculated on single item basis

Quantity (lb)	Under 1000	1000-1999	2000-3999	4000-5999	6000-49999	50000 & over
Extra (¢ / lb)	+ 1.5	+ 1.0	+ .25	+ .10	0	See O&S Dept.

STANDARD TOLERANCES: VARIATIONS IN SIZE, INCHES

Round and Square			
Dia, Inches		Over &	Out of
Over	Incl	Under	Rd & Sq
-	5/16	±.007	.010
5/16	7/16	±.007	.011
7/16	5/8	±.008	.012
5/8	7/8	±.009	.014
7/8	1	±.010	.015
1	1 1/8	±.012	.016
1 1/8	1 1/4	±.014	.018
1 1/4	1 3/8	±.016	.022
1 3/8	1 1/2	±.018	.026
1 1/2	2	±.022	.030
2	2 1/2	+ 1/16	1/32
2 1/2	3 1/2	+ 5/64	3/64
3 1/2	4 1/2	+ 3/32	1/16
4 1/2	5 1/2	+ 7/64	5/64
3 1/2	8	+ 1/8	3/32

Hexagon			
Dia, Inches		Over &	Diff in
Over	Incl	Under	3 Meas.
-	1/2	±.007	.011
1/2	1	±.010	.015
1	1 1/2	±.021 -.013	.025
1 1/2	2	+ 1/32 - 1/64	1/32
2	2 1/2	+ 3/64 - 1/64	3/64
2 1/2	3 1/2	+ 1/16 - 1/64	1/16

SOURCE: Reproduced by permission of the General Electric Company.

The accounting objectives of these procedures might be identified as follows:

1. To provide for systematically costing materials issued from Stores to jobs (direct materials) and to indirect expense accounts (not illustrated in the diagram)
2. To maintain systematically cost valuation of the materials remaining in stores for balance sheet purposes

3. To provide for various checks on the accuracy of the detailed bookkeeping work, the safekeeping of materials, and the disbursement of cash for materials purchased.

EXHIBIT 12-3

(Explanation of procedures illustrated in Exhibit 12-4)

1. For production order X3711, materials are withdrawn from stores as required for each production operation. Each issue of material is recorded on a stores requisition.
2. For each item on the stores requisition, inventory control posts the quantity issued to the stores record card for that item and copies the current unit price of the item onto the stores requisition. The file of stores record cards is both an inventory control device and a subsidiary ledger of the accounting system. Each "record card" is an account in the stores ledger. This subsidiary ledger is controlled by the general ledger account titled Materials.
3. Cost accounting calculates total cost value on the stores requisition ($83.60) and posts that total to the job cost record for job X3711. Each job cost record is an account in the jobs in process subsidiary ledger.
4. The total amount is determined for all stores issues that are posted to the job cost records each day. The day's total is entered on the monthly summary sheet.
5. At the end of the month, the summary sheet is totaled, providing the total value of materials transferred from stores to jobs in process during the month. The end-of-month entry is posted from the general journal to the two controlling accounts in the general ledger. Note that stores returns and stores issues chargeable to indirect expense were ignored here for simplicity.
6. In this system, when an issue of material brings the quantity remaining below a predetermined point (e.g., 2,000 feet), inventory control initiates reordering of that item. Purchasing selects the vendor and places the order.
7. When the goods and the vendor's invoice have been received, the invoice may be approved for payment and entered in the invoice register.
8. The quantity received and the cost are posted to the stores record card for the item. The new average cost per unit is computed and recorded.
9. Subsequently, payment is made to the vendor and this is recorded in the cash disbursements journal.
10. The column totals for the month are posted from the invoice register to the general ledger accounts Accounts Payable (Cr.) and Materials (Dr.) and to other accounts shown.
11. The column totals for the month are posted from the cash disbursements journal to the general ledger accounts Cash (Cr.) and Accounts Payable (Dr.) and to other accounts not shown.

It is important to note that these procedures also serve other sets of administrative purposes, particularly those relating to inventory management, purchasing, and stores operation. Although theory and practices involved in these other administrative areas are outside the scope of this book, the student should recognize here an example of the need for integration and coordination of interrelated systems in a complex organization.

There are very few repetitive administrative processes in an organiza-

EXHIBIT 12-4
PROCEDURES FOR MATERIALS INVENTORY CONTROL AND COST ACCOUNTING

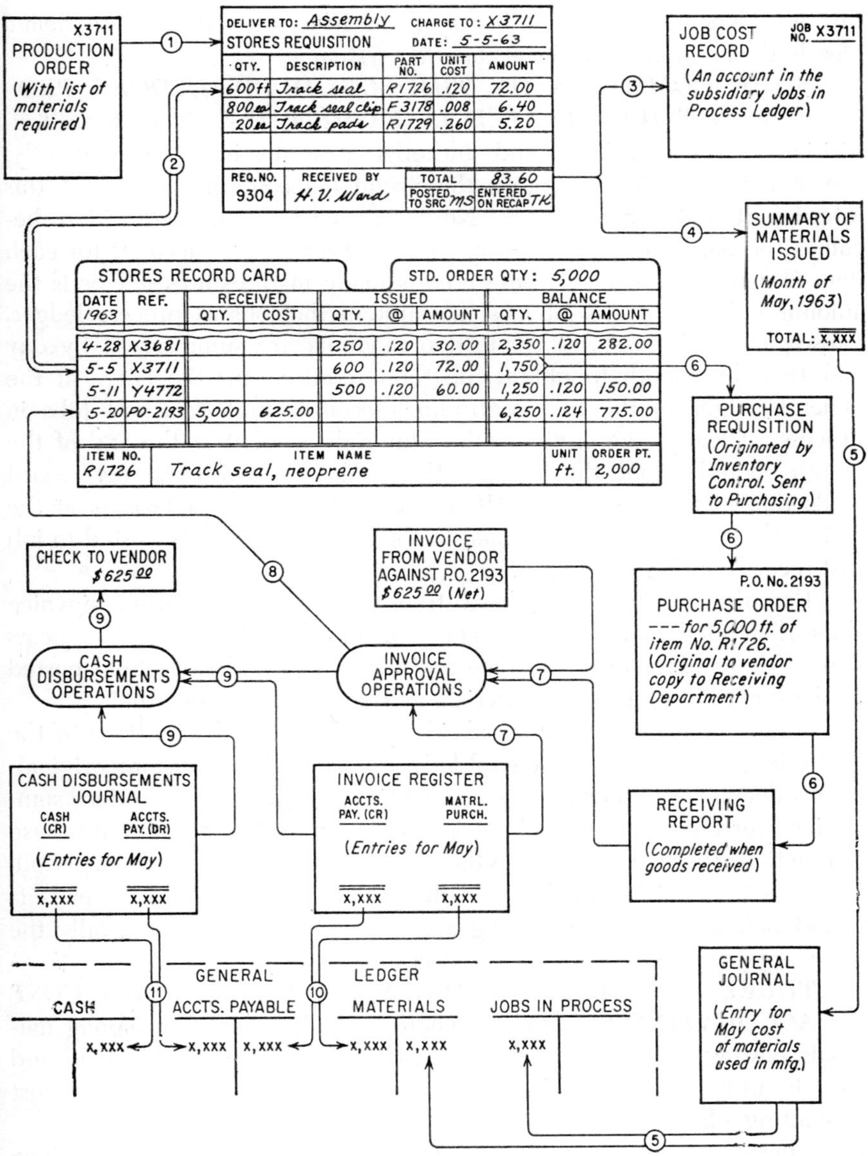

tion that have no interconnection with the accounting system. Many, such as those for inventory management and purchasing, involve the use of information that is also essential for accounting and utilize accounting information for control and decision-making purposes. Because of this interdependence with other systems, it is often difficult to define clearly the boundaries of the accounting system.

SOME COMMENTS ON THE SUBSIDIARY LEDGER PROCEDURES ILLUSTRATED IN EXHIBIT 12-4. The stores requisition serves to initiate and authorize a stores issue; subsequently, the stores requisition becomes the original accounting record of this interdepartmental transaction. Note that each stores requisition becomes the basis for a credit entry to the Stores Ledger account for each item issued. The sum of these credits made in the stores ledger is the amount debited to the job cost account in the jobs in process ledger. Subsequently these stores requisition amounts are summarized by day and then by month to obtain the total required for the entry in the general ledger to the two controlling accounts Materials and Jobs in Process. Clearly, the credit to the Materials account at the end of the month should equal the sum of the credits posted to stores record cards during the month, and the debit made to Jobs in Process at the end of the month should be equal to the sum of the debits posted to job cost records during the month.

For the materials purchase transactions, each approved-invoice amount debited to a Stores Ledger account during the month appears also in the column in the invoice register that provides the total posted to the controlling account Materials at the end of the month.

Clearly, the postings to a subsidiary ledger and the postings to the controlling account in the general ledger are based on the same original-record documents. For any one accounting period, the transactions summarized for the end-of-period entries to the controlling account are those transactions that were posted to the subsidiary ledger during that period. The end-of-period total balance in the subsidiary ledger and the end-of-period balance in the controlling account, although mathematically the same, are developed by divergent processes.

THREE ESSENTIAL FEATURES OF A MATERIALS COST ACCOUNTING SCHEME. There is endless variation among materials costing schemes with respect to the details of what, when, and how information is recorded and used. However, all materials cost accounting plans have the following characteristics in common:

1. A perpetual-inventory record is maintained for each item. The amount of material on hand at the end of each period is developed from information about what was on hand at the start of the period and what was received and issued during the period.
2. The value of the material on hand and the cost of material issued

are determined by means of unit costs that are calculated and applied according to predictable and consistent rules.

3. All materials issued during each period are assigned to specific accounts (normally to processes or jobs in process and to indirect expense accounts).

In the absence of a cost accounting plan, the value of materials in inventory at the end of a period can be determined only by means of a physical count or estimate. Recent-invoice data or estimates must be used in lieu of unit costs for pricing the items. The cost of material used must be derived from starting and ending inventory valuations and a record of purchases. If a material item is used for more than one job (or process) during a period, there is no direct measurement of how much was used for each job.

CHECKING PERPETUAL-INVENTORY BALANCES. Inevitably, errors are introduced into the balance-on-hand quantities shown by perpetual-inventory records. The inventory record for each item should be checked periodically by comparing the balance-on-hand quantity against a physical count of the number of units actually in the storeroom.

Where the perpetual-inventory quantity differs from the physical count, the quantities shown in the stores ledger cards must be corrected to agree with the physical count. The change in quantity also changes the dollar balance in each card corrected. The controlling account Materials must also be corrected so that it will agree with the changed dollar balances in the subsidiary ledger accounts. The correction will be equal to the net dollar shortage or overage. The correcting journal entry for a net shortage is

Inventory Shortage	xxxxx	
Materials		xxxxx

Such a shortage might be viewed as indirect manufacturing expense and the account eventually closed into Burden Variance. Or the account might be closed directly into the Profit and Loss Summary account.

ACCOUNTING TREATMENT OF INCOMING-TRANSPORTATION COSTS. The incoming-transportation cost on each stores item, generally referred to as *freight-in,* is properly viewed as part of the cost of the particular item. Where it is practicable to do so without too much clerical expense, unit costs recorded for materials should include freight-in as well as the purchase price of the materials.

Nevertheless, it often happens that the clerical expense would be excessive if each expenditure for incoming-transportation costs had to be divided among the different items included in the shipment and charged to the respective stores ledger accounts according to this division. Frequently, therefore, freight-in is treated as indirect manufacturing expense. This treatment is made for reasons of convenience, even though it is recognized that, in principle, the cost of acquiring material is the sum of the purchase price and in the incoming-transportation costs.

COST ACCOUNTING FOR MANUFACTURED PARTS AND FINISHED GOODS. Many plants manufacture parts for stock or make other semifinished product (such as the clinker in the process-cost example in Chap. 11). Most manufacturers have inventories of finished product. The accounting problems and control problems in connection with finished parts and finished product are similar to the problems that have been discussed in this chapter with respect to materials.

For example, specific parts or items of product require their own subsidiary ledger accounts. These accounts will need to show information on quantities and values of receipts, issues, and balances on hand. Each subsidiary ledger will have its controlling account (e.g., Manufactured Parts, Finished Goods). Rules must be established for pricing issues of parts and for determining cost of goods sold when production costs increase or decrease; the choice among FIFO, LIFO, average costs, and standard costs is similar to the choice that must be made in accounting for materials. Perpetual-inventory quantities need to be checked from time to time by physical counts. And so on.

One difference between purchased inventory items and manufactured parts or finished goods is that, for the latter, the cost of the items charged into these inventories cannot be determined without systematic analysis of internal transactions and events.

SUMMARY. Some of the important points of this chapter can be restated as follows:

1. Direct material is material specifically identified with a job or process and charged to that job or process. All other material is indirect and is included in cost as one of the elements of indirect manufacturing expense.
2. Different accounting schemes for dealing with price variations are possible. Four common schemes are average cost, first-in first-out (FIFO), last-in first-out (LIFO), and standard costs. No one of these schemes is inherently more correct than the others. In choosing among schemes to use in a particular instance, it is desirable to compare their probable effects on financial accounting, sales policy determination, and cost control.
3. Materials cost accounting involves a perpetual-inventory record for each item and procedures for pricing each issue and charging the cost to a specific job, process, or indirect expense account.
4. Accounting for materials is closely connected with the flow of information among such departments as the purchasing department, receiving department, stores department, accounting department, and the various manufacturing departments.

DISCUSSION QUESTIONS

12-A. With no sheet brass on hand, 200 pounds was purchased at 60 cents per pound on August 1. On September 1, 200 pounds more was purchased at 50 cents per pound. During September, 100 pounds was issued for job 877. What charge would be made to this job under the FIFO method? Under the average-cost method? Under the LIFO method? What can you say about the charge if standard material costs were used?

12-B. A company has on hand 100 transistorized subassemblies which cost $25 each. A shipment of 50 more costing $24 each arrives, and a few days later 30 more identical units costing $22 each are received from a new source of supply.

After several weeks 50 units are withdrawn from stock. Find the unit cost of the withdrawals and the value of the remaining inventory using (1) FIFO, (2) LIFO, and (3) average cost.

12-C. The text states that, where inventories often drop to zero balance, the choice among FIFO, LIFO, and average cost will have little effect on the reported figure for profit or loss. Explain why. Can you see any qualifying limitations that should be made on this statement?

12-D. Explain the statement that FIFO, LIFO, and average cost will all result in identical figures for the profit or loss of a terminated enterprise. Can you see any qualifying limitations that should be made on this statement? Will the three methods also result in identical figures for the cost of goods sold over the life of the enterprise?

12-E. Describe a set of circumstances under which the LIFO, FIFO, and average-cost methods of pricing purchased materials and parts out of inventory of a given item will give identical results. Assume that the quantity on hand at the end of the year is nonzero.

12-F. The text states: "In a period of changing prices, the most realistic cost figures to guide sales policies are figures based on the replacement costs of the materials and goods in question at current market prices." Do you agree with this statement? Why or why not?

12-G. What practical difficulties can you see in the way of pricing all material issues at current market prices (i.e., at their current replacement costs)?

12-H. Why does the FIFO method tend to give the most realistic inventory valuations?

12-J. In the decade following 1945, many enterprises adopted the LIFO method. In many instances, this change was made with several purposes in mind. What do you think were some of these purposes?

12-K. The text describes two types of LIFO method. One, illustrated in Exhibit 12-1, applied to perpetual-inventory accounts. The other applied to the calculation of cost of goods sold from initial and final physical inventories and from purchases. Explain why these two methods can give different figures for cost of goods sold even though both methods can be described as last-in first-out. Under what conditions would the two methods give the same figure for cost of goods sold?

12-L. Discuss the relative merits of FIFO, LIFO, average cost, and standard material cost from the points of view of financial accounting, sales policy determination, and cost control.

12-M. "Different methods of costing disbursements from the various inventory accounts will result in different monthly profit or loss figures." Discuss this statement in terms of the balance sheet equation and the flow of value through the accounts.

12-N. Examine some cost accounting texts for a description of the "base stock" method of inventory valuation. How does this differ from LIFO? In what respect do these two methods seem to be based on the same general philosophy?

12-P. A certain classification of accounts contains the account Material Variance. Explain the purpose of such an account. What is the significance of a credit balance in this account at the end of an accounting period?

12-Q. Considered solely from the viewpoint of cost control, it is desirable to use standard material costs to price the materials issued by the storeroom into production. That is, standard costs are superior to "actual cost" methods such as FIFO or LIFO for purposes of cost control. Give two reasons to support these statements.

12-R. When a perpetual-inventory record is used, the actual quantity of each item in the stock room should be checked against the figure shown on the stores ledger card at least once each year. Explain how the accounting records should be corrected if a shortage is discovered.

12-S. Answer the following questions regarding the procedures illustrated in Exhibit 12-4.

1. Assume that the stores transactions during May involved issues to jobs totaling $15,000, returns to stores of material previously issued to jobs totaling $400, and issues of indirect materials totaling $900. Write out an appropriate end-of-month general journal entry.
2. No formal accounting entry is made at the time a purchase order is issued. Discuss this.
3. The credit to Accounts Payable and the debit to Materials from the invoice register are not likely to be equal. Why?
4. The credit to Cash and the debit to Accounts Payable may be unequal. Explain.

PROBLEMS

Problem 12-1. The stores ledger account for ⅝-inch-diameter cold-drawn machine steel bars shows 20,000 pounds on hand at 18.3 cents per pound on January 1. During the first quarter of the year, issues and receipts were as follows:

Issues January 1 to 21 were 8,000 pounds.
Received on January 22, 10,000 pounds at 19.5 cents per pound.
Issues January 22 to March 2 were 13,000 pounds.
Received on March 3, 10,000 pounds at 20.4 cents per pound.
Issues March 3 to 31 were 11,000 pounds.

A. At what unit prices should the various issues be costed under the first-in first-out method? What should be the valuation placed on the March 31 inventory if this method is used?

B. Answer the same questions using the average-cost method. Round off amounts for issues to the nearest dollar.

C. Answer the same questions using the last-in first-out method.

Problem 12-2. Suppose that all issues of steel bars in the circumstances described in problem 12-1 had been costed at the unit price of the last shipment received and that the final inventory on March 31 was valued in the same way. What apparent profit would the stores department have made on this item during these 3 months?

Problem 12-3. The Moose Jaw Oil Company buys and refines crude oil. At the end of April, Moose Jaw had 60,000 barrels of crude on hand; this oil had been acquired at a cost of $3 per barrel. Another shipment of 40,000 barrels was received May 1 at a cost of $3.50 per barrel. During May, 30,000 barrels of crude oil were processed in the refinery. On June 1, 20,000 barrels of crude costing $4.10 each were received. The refinery used 40,000 barrels during June.

Determine the cost of crude oil used during May and during June, and the value of the crude on hand on May 31 and on June 30, by each of the following methods: (A) first-in first-out, (B) last-in first-out, and (C) average cost.

Problem 12-4. For a certain raw material the *standard cost* is $1.04 per pound. This standard cost is estimated to include freight costs and net purchase price (after cash discount is deducted). The *net-price method* is used with respect to cash discounts. The various events concerning this purchase occur as follows:

Nov. 1. Received 1,100-pound shipment.
Nov. 3. Received invoice for $1,200. Terms are 2% 10 days net 30.
Nov. 5. Received freight bill for $17.
Nov. 11. Paid the freight bill, $17.
Dec. 10. Paid the invoice with a check for $1,200.

A. On a sheet of standard journal paper, set up entries representing the actual entries that would be made in:
   1. The invoice register on November 3 and November 5
   2. The cash disbursements journal on November 11 and December 10

B. Set up T's representing accounts affected by the above events, and show the same entries in this form.

For the purposes of this problem do not use a "purchases" account. Make any entry changing the value of the inventory directly to an account titled Raw Material Inventory.

Problem 12-5. Wilco Manufacturing Company uses job-order cost accounting. It makes two products, J and K, and also undertakes special jobs to customers' specifications. Department A uses a predetermined burden rate of 150% of direct-labor cost. Department B uses a predetermined burden rate of 200% of direct-labor cost. The FIFO rule is used in pricing materials into jobs and in costing sales. All cost accounts are kept in the factory ledger.

Set up a factory ledger in T-account form with the following accounts:

*Material D	Direct Labor—Department A
*Material E	Direct Labor—Department B
*Product J	Indirect Labor
*Product K	Factory Supervision
Job 41	Repair and Maintenance
Job 42	Factory Taxes
Job 43	Depreciation
Job 44	Burden Variance
	General Ledger—Control

* These T accounts should have columns for quantity, unit price, and total value.

Makes entries directly in the T accounts to record July operations as follows:

A. Opening balances on July 1 were:

Account	Debit	Credit
Material D (600 at $5)	$ 3,000	
Material E (100 at $20)	2,000	
Product J (15 at $220)	3,300	
Product K (15 at $500)	7,500	
Job 41	1,600	
Burden Variance		$ 800
General Ledger—Control		16,600
Totals	$17,400	$17,400

B. Charges to the factory ledger from the invoice register were:

For 800 Material D at $6 per unit	$ 4,800
For 200 Material E at $22 per unit	4,400
Direct Labor—Department A	3,200
Direct Labor—Department B	1,600
Indirect Labor	1,200
Factory Supervision	3,000
Repair and Maintenance	3,600
Total (credit to General Ledger—Control)	$21,800

C. Material issues in order were 400 D to Job 41; 70 E to Job 42; 300 D to Job 43; 120 E to Job 44.

D. Time cards show that the various jobs used direct labor as follows:

In Department A		*In Department B*	
Job 42	$2,000	Job 41	$ 400
Job 43	1,200	Job 44	1,200

E. Burden was charged to jobs as required.

F. Job 41 was completed, 20 units of product J. Job 42 was completed. This was a special order that was immediately delivered to the customer for whom it was done.

G. Other sales were 25 units of product J and 10 units of product K.

Take a trial balance at this point. Continue the problem by making the necessary adjusting and closing entries directly in the T accounts, as follows:

H. Depreciation of $600 was charged on plant and equipment.
I. Accrued factory taxes for the current month are $300.
J. Entries are to be made to determine the overabsorbed or underabsorbed burden. The balance in Burden Variance is not closed out but is carried forward into the next month.

Rule and balance all accounts. Take a trial balance of the factory ledger.

Problem 12-6. The Durabel Plastics Company has two departments, Y and Z. Process costs are kept in department Y, which produces a plastic compound Q. Some of this compound is sold directly to customers. The compound is also used for plastic molding operations in department Z, which makes products R, S, and T. Job costs are kept in department Z. The FIFO method is used for costing materials into production and for determining cost of goods sold.

A. Set up a general ledger in T-account form with the accounts and account balances as of July 1, as follows:

Account	Debit	Credit
Cash	$ 7,000	
Accounts Receivable	10,800	
*Material A (300 at $9)	2,700	
*Material B (1,200 at $3)	3,600	
*Compound Q (2,000 at $0.90)	1,800	
*Product R (400 at $5)	2,000	
*Product S (100 at $7)	700	
*Product T (50 at $30)	1,500	
Department Y		
Job 76	700	
Job 77		
Job 78		
Job 79		
Plant and Equipment	70,000	
Accumulated Depreciation—Plant and Equipment		$ 20,000
Deferred Charges	1,200	
Direct Labor		
Indirect Manufacturing Expense		
Selling and Administrative Expense		
Sales		
Cost of Goods Sold		
Accounts Payable		3,600
Accrued Liabilities		1,300
Burden Variance		100
Profit and Loss Summary		
Capital Stock		50,000
Earned Surplus		27,000
Totals	$102,000	$102,000

* Show quantity, unit price, and total value in these T accounts.

Make entries directly in the T accounts to record the following matters related to July operations. Use only the accounts listed above.

B. Purchased on credit 400 units of material A at $10 per unit, $4,000.

C. Collections on accounts receivable were $11,900.

D. Cash paid out for:

Direct labor	$ 4,400
Indirect manufacturing expense	4,500
Selling and administrative expense	2,500
Accounts payable	3,000
Accrued liabilities	900
Total	$15,300

E. Materials used in production in department Y were 540 units of A and 300 units of B.

F. Direct-labor cost in department Y was $1,400. Analysis of time cards in department Z gave direct-labor costs for the various jobs as follows: job 76, $400; job 77, $1,000; job 78, $1,300; job 79, $300.

G. Burden is charged to department Y at 50% of direct-labor cost plus 25% of direct-material cost. The burden rate used in department Z is 100% of direct-labor cost.

H. 10,000 units of compound Q were completed during the month. None of this compound remained in process at the end of the month.

I. Issues of compound Q during the month were to job 77, 1,000 units; to job 78, 1,500 units; to job 79, 500 units. These issues were in the order stated.

J. Job 76 was completed, 200 units of product S. Job 77 was completed, 100 units of product T.

K. Sales during the month, all on credit, were:

4,000 units of compound Q	$ 4,800
200 units of product R	1,600
200 units of product S	2,000
60 units of product T	2,700
Total	$11,100

L. Depreciation charged on plant and equipment was $300.

M. At the end of July, $200 was owed for factory electrical and mechanical maintenance expenses applicable to July but not yet paid. Factory taxes to be accrued for July amount to $250. Prepaid insurance on plant and equipment amounting to $80 was properly chargeable to July.

N. Make the necessary entries to determine the burden variance. The balance in the Burden Variance account should be carried forward into the next month; this account will not be closed out until the end of the year.

P. Make all necessary closing entries. Rule and balance all accounts.

Take a post-closing trial balance. Prepare a profit and loss statement for the month. No balance sheet is required; submit the post-closing trial balance instead.

13/ LABOR COSTS

This chapter deals primarily with the labor-cost aspects of cost accounting. It also deals briefly with the closely related subject of payroll accounting.

PAYROLL ACCOUNTING. If an organization has employees, it must have a payroll system that will:

1. Produce wage and salary payments, on scheduled dates, that are correct, proper, and adequately documented.
2. Produce required state and Federal payroll tax reports and information required for the administration of employee insurance plans and other external relationships affected by employee attendance or pay.
3. Develop and record information required for general accounting purposes.
4. Minimize opportunities for losses due to error, fraud, or embezzlement.
5. Satisfy existing laws, agreements, and policies concerning wage determination and payment.

EXTERNAL REQUIREMENTS AFFECTING PAYROLL ACCOUNTING. Payroll accounting in the United States has become a complex and technical matter. This is largely due to a variety of governmental requirements. Problems are created by the withholding of employees' taxes from their wages, by the calculation and payment of taxes assessed the employer that are based on wage payments, and by the need to comply with laws regarding wage rates, overtime premiums, accident insurance, and other matters.

Employers are required to withhold Federal income taxes from employees' wages and salaries. At regular intervals these withholdings must be remitted to the Director of Internal Revenue. The amount to be deducted from each employee's earnings depends on the length of the payroll period and the employee's earnings during that period, on the number of withholding exemptions claimed by the employee, and on the applicable income tax rates as shown in wage-bracket tables.

Taxes must also be withheld under the Federal Insurance Contributions Act (FICA) which provides for old-age and survivors' insurance. In 1962, employees covered by the act were required to contribute (by withholding) $3\frac{1}{8}$% of the first \$4,800 of annual earnings. The law provided for the rate to go up to $3\frac{5}{8}$% for 1963–1965, to $4\frac{1}{8}$% for 1966–1967, and to $4\frac{5}{8}$% starting in 1968.

Federal law requires that, shortly after the end of each year, each employee must be given a statement showing the total wages for the year, the total income tax withheld, and the total FICA employee tax withheld.

The employer himself must pay an FICA tax equal to the FICA tax paid by his employees and withheld from their wages. The amount to be remitted to the government is therefore double the amount withheld. Employers having four or more employees must also pay Federal and state unemployment insurance taxes. The Federal Unemployment Tax Act (FUTA) rate was 3.5% of the first \$3,000 earnings of each employee in 1962 and 1963. However, a credit of 2.7% was allowed against state unemployment insurance tax paid, resulting in an effective rate of 0.8% at that time. The laws regarding state unemployment taxes vary from state to state; generally they contain provisions whereby the tax rate depends on a merit rating that is based on the stability of employment maintained by each employer. The states determine the rates and the amount of each employee's wages subject to tax. In addition, most states have laws that require many employers to carry workmen's compensation insurance, either with an approved private insurance company or with a state agency. Different occupations vary in the hazard of industrial accidents and therefore carry different insurance rates; it is usually the duty of the payroll department to prepare the statements in connection with this insurance. The cost of the payroll tax and insurance items mentioned in this paragraph is expense of the company; no payroll deductions are involved.

In some states the employees covered by the unemployment tax law also are required to pay a state unemployment tax or "disability insurance contribution." In such cases, the employer is required to deduct the tax or "contribution" from the employee's paychecks. The payroll system may also be required to handle voluntary payroll deductions for such things as union dues, personal insurance, and savings.

The Federal Fair Labor Standards Act establishes a minimum hourly wage, a maximum work week, and an overtime premium percentage for all hours in excess of the maximum work week. The act covers employers directly or indirectly engaged in interstate commerce. There are many technical provisions of the act that govern the determination of which employees are covered and the method of determining the employee's wage rate on which overtime premiums are to be based. It is the responsibility of the payroll department to keep records in sufficient detail so that the employer can prove compliance with the wage and hour regulations. Where the employer is engaged in government work, additional regulations of this general type are applicable. There also may be state regulations or provisions of a collective bargaining agreement that must be followed.

AN EXAMPLE OF PAYROLL AND LABOR-COST ACCOUNTING. The example in this chapter illustrates the payroll system and the labor-cost distribution procedures of a small manufacturing firm, Micro-Drive Corporation, that is assumed to be operating in the United States in 1963.

Micro-Drive, like many other firms, has a dual payroll system: hourly rate, weekly paid employees are handled by the "hourly payroll"; monthly salaried personnel are handled by the "salary payroll." Hourly payroll people are required to "punch in" and "punch out" each day on a time clock. The "clock cards" used for this purpose are of the type shown in Exhibit 13-1. These cards provide the official attendance

EXHIBIT 13-1
AN ATTENDANCE TIME CARD

Warren Wonka
(NAME)

6-15-63 (WEEK ENDING) 1234 (CLOCK NO.)

Lathe (DEPT.) 2 25 (RATE)

MORN IN	NOON OUT	NOON IN	NIGHT OUT	EXTRA IN	EXTRA OUT	HOURS
M 7 29	M 12 00	M 12 45	M 4 17			8
TU 7 25	TU 11 59	TU 12 43	TU 4 15			8
W 7 30	W 12 02	W 12 46	W 4 18	W 8 03	W 10 05	10
TH 7 22	TH 12 01	TH 12 45	TH 4 16			8
F 7 31	F 12 03	F 12 48	F 5 18			9
SA 8 28	SA 12 02					3 1/2
					TOTAL HOURS	46 1/2
					O.T. HOURS	6 1/2

APPROVED BY SUPERVISOR: Mac

data for the calculation of the hourly payroll each week. Hourly payroll people also fill out "daily time report" cards similar to the one shown in Exhibit 13-2. These cards provide the basic data for factory labor-cost distribution.

EXHIBIT 13-2
A DAILY TIME REPORT

W. G. Wonka — EMPLOYEE NAME | 1234 — CLOCK NO. | June 14, 1963 — DATE

DAILY TIME REPORT

JOB NO. OR ACCT. NO.	DESCRIPTION	QTY. PROD.	TIME START	TIME STOP	HOURS	RATE	AMOUNT		✓
7219	Cut-off	190	7 30	10 30	3.0	2 25	6	75	✓
4420	Clean & adjust machine		10 30	11 30	1.0		2	25	✓
9346	Cut-off & groove	250	11 30	5 15	5.0		11	25	✓
CLOCK TIME CHECKED: JJK	COSTED BY: JJK	POSTED BY: BJS		TOTALS:	9.0	2 25	20	25	✓

APPROVED BY SUPERVISOR: Mac

DEPT: Lathe

For each pay period (e.g., each week for the "hourly" payroll), the payroll is computed and recorded on the form illustrated in Exhibit 13-3. This document is a calculation sheet, a means of check and control, and also a journal. When such a document is used as a journal, as in this example, it is usually called a *payroll register.* Each line shows, for a single employee, the derivation of total earnings for the period and the calculation of deductions and net pay. This same information is also recorded on the paycheck stub and on a record of each individual employee's earnings (which are not illustrated here).

The individual earnings records are needed for preparation of reports required by government agencies and also as a means of determining when the earnings of each employee pass the annual limit for each of the payroll taxes and insurance coverages.

Exhibit 13-4 describes the payroll and labor-cost events occurring during the month of July. Exhibit 13-5 shows the general ledger entries for the events set forth in Exhibit 13-4. T accounts are shown only for accounts affected by payroll-related events; all other accounts in the general ledger are represented by a single T account.

SOME COMMENTS ON THE MICRO-DRIVE CORPORATION PAYROLL SYSTEM. In the following paragraphs, some of the

EXHIBIT 13-3

PAYROLL REGISTER

MICRO-DRIVE CORPORATION

Hourly Payroll Period ending *6-15-63* Pay date *6-21-63* No. *63-24*

EMPLOYEE NAME	EMPL. NO.	INC. TAX EX.	TIME: TOTAL HOURS	TIME: O.T. HOURS	RATE	EARNINGS: REGULAR	EARNINGS: O.T. PREM.	EARNINGS: OTHER	EARNINGS: TOTAL	DEDUCTIONS: ST. D.I.	DEDUCTIONS: F.I.C.A.	DEDUCTIONS: W.H. TAX	DEDUCTIONS: OTHER	DEDUCTIONS: TOTAL	PAYCHECK: NET AMOUNT	PAYCHECK: CHECK NO.
A. K. Abel	1010	4	45	5	2.60	117.00	6.50		123.50	1.24	4.48	12.80		18.52	104.98	7122
B. Z. Baker	932	3	40	-	2.75	110.00	—		110.00	1.10	3.99	13.30		18.39	91.61	7123
W. G. Wonka	1234	2	46½	6½	2.25	104.63	7.31		111.94	1.12	4.06	15.60		20.78	91.16	7141
Totals						2,331.50	22.21		2,353.71	23.54	85.32	249.70		358.56	1,995.15	VOU. 2173

EXHIBIT 13-4

(Explanation of entries shown in Exhibit 13-5)

A. The account balances as of July 1, 1963, are identified by the letter A. For simplification, all accounts not directly involved in this example are represented by a single T titled All Other Accounts.

B. July 5: Paychecks for the week ending June 29 were written and distributed. The total earnings for that week were $2,500; deductions totaled $380; the paychecks totaled $2,120.

C. July 6: Paid the insurance company the estimated amount of workmen's compensation insurance premiums accrued for June, $330. The premium deposit of $360 remains unchanged.

D. The hourly payroll for the week ending July 6 was computed. (See Exhibit 13-6 for payroll summary data.) In the ledger entry, overtime premium expense ($50) is separated from the cost of labor at base wage rates ($2,350). These expense debits are offset by credits to Liability accounts totaling the same amount, $2,400. The amount credited to Accrued Hourly Payroll ($2,035) is the net amount to be paid directly to the employees (not the total earnings).

E. July 12: Paychecks for the week ending July 6 are issued.

F. The payroll for the week ending July 13 is computed.

G. July 19: Paychecks for the week ending July 13 are issued.

H. The payroll for the week ending July 20 is computed.

I. July 26: Paychecks for the week ending July 20 are issued.

J. The payroll for the week ending July 27 is computed.

K. July 29: Paid state Department of Employment the disability insurance contributions deducted from employee earnings in the quarter ending June 30. By the same check, also paid the company's contribution for state unemployment insurance for the quarter.

L. July 29: Paid the U.S. Treasury Department $2,470, covering income tax withholding and FICA taxes for the five hourly payrolls for weeks ending in June and the June salary payroll.

M. July 31: The salary payroll for July is computed, and the checks are issued.

N. Hourly payroll wages are computed for July 29, 30, and 31. Overtime premium expense is calculated for this partial-week period on the basis of time worked in excess of 8 hours in any one day.

P. A summary of the factory labor-cost distribution for July (developed from time-report data) provided the basis of distributing the total wages ($10,450) from the Hourly Payroll Wages account to Warehouse and Shipping Wages Expense ($1,200), Factory Direct Labor ($7,000), and Factory Indirect Labor ($2,250).

Q. The company's FICA tax expense is accrued. The rate is equal to the employees' contribution rate (3⅝% in 1963). The amount accrued ($529) includes the tax associated with the partial-week earnings of $1,400. The $529 expense was distributed according to the distribution of taxable wages and salaries.

R. The company's contribution for state unemployment insurance is accrued. The total expense ($435) was distributed according to the distribution of taxable wages and salaries.

S. The company's Federal unemployment tax expense is accrued and distributed at the rate of 0.8% on taxable wages and salaries.

T. Workmen's compensation insurance expense is accrued and distributed by applying the insurance company's rate for each class of employee to the regular earnings.

U. Through the labor-cost distribution system, direct-labor cost was charged to the various jobs in the subsidiary Jobs in Process ledger. The total amount charged to jobs during July ($7,000) is now charged to the controlling account in the general ledger.

EXHIBIT 13-5
GENERAL LEDGER, MICRO-DRIVE CORPORATION
PAYROLL AND LABOR-COST ENTRIES DURING JULY, 1963

Cash	
A 19,000	2,120 B
	330 C
	2,035 E
	1,865 G
	1,950 I
	2,016 K
	2,470 L
	4,800 M

Compensation Insurance Premium Deposit	
A 360	

Jobs in Process	
A 20,000	
T 7,000	

Federal Unemployment Tax Payable	
	384 A
	117 S

State Unemployment Tax Payable	
K 1,536	1,536 A
	435 R

Accrued Hourly Payroll	
B 2,120	2,120 A
E 2,035	2,035 D
G 1,865	1,865 F
I 1,950	1,950 H
	1,950 J
	1,400 N

Accrued Compensation Insurance Premium	
C 330	330 A
	324 T

Employee W.H. Taxes Payable	
L 1,900	1,900 A
	254 D
	233 F
	244 H
	244 J
	620 M

FICA Taxes Payable	
L 570	570 A
	87 D
	80 F
	83 H
	83 J
	145 M
	529 Q

State Disability Insurance Payable	
K 480	480 A
	24 D
	22 F
	23 H
	23 J
	35 M

Hourly Payroll Wages	
D 2,350	10,450 P
F 2,200	
H 2,300	
J 2,240	
N 1,360	

Warehouse and Shipping Expense	
P 1,200	
Q 43	
R 38	
S 10	
T 27	

Factory Direct Labor	
P 7,000	7,000 T

Factory Indirect Labor	
P 2,250	

Factory Overtime Premium Expense	
D 50	
J 60	
N 40	

Factory Compensation Insurance Expense	
T 280	

Factory Payroll Tax Expense	
Q 341	
R 301	
S 75	

General and Administrative Expense	
M 2,400	
Q 51	
R 32	
S 11	
T 5	

Selling Expense	
M 2,000	
Q 54	
R 35	
S 12	
T 6	

Factory Management and Clerical Expense	
M 1,200	
Q 40	
R 29	
S 9	
T 6	

All Other Accounts	
	32,040 A

aspects of payroll accounting introduced in the example are discussed in more detail.

Entry B. It was necessary to include in June costs the payroll for the last week of June, even though payment was deferred until July 5. The entry made as of June 29 was similar to July entries D, F, H, and J.

Entry C. Insurance providing for compensation and medical care of injured employees is required by state law. In this case, the compensation insurance coverage is provided by a private insurance company policy under which Micro-Drive is required to leave on deposit $360 advance premiums and to remit each month the estimated cost of the actual coverage during the prior month. The premiums for each month depend on the amount of regular (base) wages paid for work in each occupational rate group.

Entry D. In the Micro-Drive system, the "payroll register" is used as a journal; the ledger entry for each payroll is made directly from the payroll register. For the week ending July 6 this entry was as follows:

Hourly Payroll Wages	$2,350	
Factory Overtime Premium expense	50	
Accrued Hourly Payroll		$2,035
Employee Withholding Taxes Payable		254
FICA Taxes Payable		87
State Disability Insurance Payable		24

Entry K. The amount deducted from employees' paychecks for state disability insurance during the second quarter ($480) must be paid to the state by July 30. The unemployment tax assessed the employer for the quarter ($1,536) is payable at the same time.

Entry L. Income tax withholding and the FICA taxes are payable monthly (unless the amount is less than $100); hence the balance due on July 1 was for the month of June.

Entry M. Although the FICA and state disability insurance tax rates are the same for salaried and hourly paid people, in this example one or more people in each of the three management salary groups had earned in excess of the amount taxable in any one year. This limit was $4,800 for FICA taxes and was assumed to be $4,100 for the state disability insurance.

Entry N. No payroll deductions are involved in this entry for the partial week; the entire liability is credited to Accrued Hourly Payroll. On August 2 this entry will be reversed and a new entry made for the full week of July 29 through August 2.

Entry P. It should be noted that the cost distributed from Hourly Payroll Wages includes only base-rate wages. The costs of "payroll

EXHIBIT 13-6
MICRO-DRIVE CORPORATION—PAYROLL DATA

Note: For simplicity, all figures are shown to the nearest dollar.

Hourly Payrolls for July

Week ending	Regular earnings	Overtime premium	Total earnings	Deductions				Net pay
				St. D.I.	FICA	W.H. tax	Total	
July 6	$2,350	50	$2,400	$24	$87	$254	$365	$2,035
July 13	2,200	...	2,200	22	80	233	335	1,865
July 20	2,300	...	2,300	23	83	244	350	1,950
July 27	2,240	60	2,300	23	83	244	350	1,950
Aug. 3*	1,360	40	1,400					

* Split week. Data are for the 3 working days falling in July.

Salary Payroll for July

General	Sales	Factory	Total earnings	Deductions				Net pay
				St. D.I.	FICA	W.H. tax	Total	
$2,400	$2,000	$1,200	$5,600	$35*	$145†	$620	$800	$4,800

* Taxable wages for state disability insurance were $3,500.

† Taxable wages for FICA taxes were $4,000.

extras" (fringe benefits and payroll taxes and insurance) are treated as manufacturing overhead in the factory cost accounting system.

Entries Q, R, S, and T. All these entries deal with the accrual of the company's expenses (as distinguished from employees' contributions) for payroll taxes and insurance. Each of these accruals takes into account the fact that the earnings of certain individual employees exceeded the limit for that tax prior to July 31.

At the end of each accounting period, the accounts Factory Indirect Labor, Factory Overtime Premium Expense, Factory Compensation Insurance Expense, and Factory Management and Clerical Expense would all be closed to Burden Variance.

The foregoing example illustrates some of the typical kinds of complications involved in payroll accounting that are generally ignored elsewhere in this book. It is, however, only a brief introduction to these rather technical matters. Also, it should be noted that very little attention is given here to ways and means of capturing, recording, and processing payroll information. These problems of methods, techniques, and devices are very important in the design and operation of an actual payroll system.

DISTINCTION BETWEEN SELLING AND MANUFACTURING COSTS. In the Micro-Drive example, certain hourly rate people were engaged full time or part time in warehouse and shipping activities. The labor cost, at base rates, and the associated cost of labor extras were separated from manufacturing costs and treated as selling expenses.

DISTINCTION BETWEEN DIRECT AND INDIRECT LABOR. Direct labor is the labor that is identifiable with particular jobs in job-order costing or with particular processes in process costing. The cost of direct labor is charged to specific jobs or processes. All other manufacturing labor is indirect. Indirect-labor cost is one of the elements of indirect manufacturing expense and is charged to jobs or processes through the burden or overhead rate.

Some examples of types of labor usually treated as indirect are the following: engineers, supervisors, draftsmen, factory clerical workers, crane operators, lift-truck operators, janitors, watchmen. In an indirect department such as the power plant, all labor is indirect.

LABOR–COST DISTRIBUTION. The problem of labor-cost distribution arises in connection with employees and groups of employees whose time cannot be charged consistently to one account. In the Micro-Drive example, this problem arose with respect to the hourly payroll personnel, many of whom work partly on direct-labor tasks and partly on indirect-labor tasks (and one or two that may work on both manufacturing and selling tasks in the same week). The first requirement of a labor-cost distribution system, then, is to allocate labor costs properly according to the basic classification of accounts. The further requirement is to distribute direct-labor cost satisfactorily to the various jobs or products.

IDENTIFYING DIRECT–LABOR COSTS WITH PARTICULAR JOBS. Consider the case of job-order costing with direct labor paid on an hourly rate. A written record is necessary showing how the time of each direct-labor employee has been divided among the various jobs on which he has worked. The responsibility for making this written record may be assigned to a timekeeper, to a foreman, or to the individual workman.

Exhibit 13-2 illustrates a daily time report such as commonly used to record the time a particular employee spends on each direct-labor job (and/or each different class of indirect-labor work). Each line on such a report is the basis for a charge either to a job in process or to an indirect expense account.

Where a daily time report is used for labor-cost distribution purposes, it is important (1) that the total hours accounted for on each daily time report be equal to the number of hours recorded for that day on the attendance clock card and (2) that the wage rates used for cost accounting be the same as those used for payroll purposes.

For situations in which many employees work on only a few different jobs in any one week, it is often practicable to use a weekly card in place of such a daily card. In these cases, the weekly time report card and the attendance clock card can be combined into one document.

Regardless of the type of form used to record the original information about direct-labor hours spent on different jobs, considerable additional work must be done by the cost accounting department in order to determine the direct-labor costs of each job. Hours must be multiplied by hourly rates to compute the costs for each employee. The figures for the individual employees for each job must be brought together and summarized to determine the total direct-labor cost to be charged to the job for each accounting period.

To facilitate the sorting, collecting, and summarizing of charges to various jobs and indirect accounts, there are many schemes in use that employ the idea of a separate "unit" record for each charge (i.e., a separate record for each *line* on a daily time report). Such unit records are then summarized by sorting and totaling by manual, mechanical, or electronic methods.

THE PROBLEM OF OBTAINING CORRECT FIGURES FOR DIRECT–LABOR COSTS OF INDIVIDUAL JOBS. In principle, the finding of direct-labor cost of a job seems simpler than either direct-material cost or indirect manufacturing expense. No rules such as FIFO or LIFO need to be made; there are no problems of allocations.

Nevertheless, there are administrative problems of making sure that the direct-labor hours reported for each job correspond to the hours actually worked on the respective jobs. Sometimes, where foremen are held to tight budgets on certain jobs but not on others, they may report some of the labor hours spent on the tightly controlled jobs as having been spent on the loosely controlled ones. In other instances, labor-time reports may be so carelessly made that the reported labor hours by jobs bear little relationship to the distribution of the actual hours among the jobs.

Whatever the cause of incorrect distribution of direct-labor costs, it is evident that such errors should be viewed by management as extremely undesirable. They are particularly bad from the viewpoint of effective cost control. The administrative aspects of securing a correct distribution of direct-labor costs among jobs vary greatly from one industry to another as well as from company to company in any given industry.

Certain approximations in identifying direct-labor hours with jobs or operations are justifiable in order to avoid excessive expense for cost accounting. For example, a timekeeper on construction work may record the activities of each employee when he makes his rounds at, say,

2-hour intervals. An assumption for accounting purposes that the observed activity continued throughout a 2-hour period will lead only to minor errors and to errors that tend to compensate.

DIRECT-LABOR COSTS IN PROCESS COST ACCOUNTING. One reason why process cost accounting is generally less expensive than job-order cost accounting is the greater ease of determining direct-labor cost. Because process costs are essentially departmental costs, it is necessary merely to identify each direct worker with the appropriate department. Ordinarily this is a simple matter.

However, process cost systems are sometimes used where different products are processed in the same department and where it is evident that the various products use different amounts of labor. A reasonably satisfactory determination of the direct-labor costs of each product within a department can often be made without a continuous detailed timekeeping to find out how each employee divides his time among the various products. Time studies made by industrial engineers can be used to establish weighting factors that are proportional to the usual direct-labor requirements of each product. The actual direct-labor cost for each accounting period in a department can be divided among the various products in proportion to the quantities produced multiplied by their respective weighting factors. Where this plan of process accounting is used, it is desirable that time studies be made at regular intervals to ensure that the weighting factors are up to date at all times.

COST ACCOUNTING TREATMENT OF LABOR EXTRAS. Each dollar paid for labor is likely to be responsible for a number of other disbursements that are closely proportional to the outlay for wages or salary. Some of these have been mentioned earlier in this chapter, namely, employer's FICA tax, Federal and state unemployment-insurance tax, and workmen's compensation insurance. Other possible labor extras include the costs of paid vacations, sick leave, premium pay for night-shift work or other undesirable duty, and contributions to pension or welfare funds.

In principle, it would seem that, when these labor extras are associated with direct labor, they ought to be treated in the cost accounts as if they were direct-labor costs. As a matter of practice it generally is not convenient to do this; direct-labor extras are usually treated as elements of indirect manufacturing expense and are included in job or process costs through the burden rate.

A special type of labor extra is the premium paid for overtime work. Often this premium is based on "time and a half" for all hours over 40 in any work week. For example, the employee who works 48 hours with a wage rate of $2.25 per hour receives $117 for his week's work, 40 hours of pay for his first 40 hours of work and 12 hours of pay for his final 8 hours of work. In this case, the overtime premium is $9 (i.e., $2.25 times 4).

Where it is clear that a particular job is responsible for the overtime work, it is appropriate to charge that job with the overtime premium. This is particularly desirable whenever the price to be charged for the job is to be based on its cost as shown by the accounts.

Usually it is difficult or impossible to know exactly which jobs have been responsible for any overtime work. Moreover, it should always be recognized that the job that happens to have been worked on during the overtime hours is not necessarily the one that caused the overtime. The most common cost accounting treatment of overtime premiums is to consider them as an element of indirect manufacturing expense and to apportion them to jobs or processes by means of the burden rate.

STANDARD DIRECT–LABOR COSTS. Effective cost control is based on comparisons. Each current cost figure must be compared with some figure that is believed to represent satisfactory performance. This figure used to judge whether or not current costs are satisfactory is, in effect, a standard of comparison. As a practical matter, some standards of comparison used in industry are established on an informal and unsystematic basis; others are established only after formal systematic analysis. Where past cost information is available, standards for labor time and labor cost are likely to be based, in part at least, on past performance. They may also be based on time studies and on a careful industrial engineering analysis of what constitutes good performance.

Any "actual" unit labor cost reported by a cost system should be compared with some standard, formal or informal. But a formal standard can be doubly useful. Its use is not limited to serving as a norm with which current actual figures can be compared. It can be used also to simplify cost accounting procedures and to reduce their expense. Standards used for this purpose provide a basis for valuing inventories of work in process and finished goods and for determining cost of goods sold; the differences between actual and standard costs are entered in the accounts as variances. Chapter 15 illustrates this use of standard labor costs.

INDIRECT–LABOR COSTS. The payroll problems regarding indirect labor are practically the same as for direct labor. In contrast, the problems of cost control of indirect labor are quite different; certain aspects of these problems are discussed in Chap. 14 in connection with the description of the variable budget for indirect manufacturing expense.

Indirect-labor costs may be allocated among cost centers before they are applied to manufactured product through the burden rate. This also is illustrated in Chap. 14.

In some manufacturing companies, direct labor is referred to as *productive labor* and indirect labor as *nonproductive labor*. This is misleading terminology, and its consequences can be most unfortunate. The responsibility for efficient production is shared among all employees, direct and indirect alike. The fact that the cost of the services of design engineers, supervisors, inspectors, and maintenance men cannot conveniently be charged to particular jobs does not make these workers nonproductive. In general, technological progress tends to decrease direct-labor costs and to increase the ratio of indirect to direct labor.

SUMMARY. Some of the important points of this chapter can be restated as follows:

1. In the United States, payroll preparation and accounting are complicated matters because of withholdings, taxes, and various government regulations affecting wage payments and because of the repetitive nature of the tasks involved.
2. The objectives of a system for payroll preparation and accounting are to produce paychecks, tax reports, and information required for general accounting and to protect the company against possible losses and failures to conform to external requirements.
3. Systematic procedures for labor-cost distribution are needed to allocate labor costs according to the basic chart of accounts and to assign direct labor costs properly to the various jobs or products.
4. The effectiveness of a labor-cost distribution system and the costs of operating it depend upon relative success in the solution of problems of human behavior as well as problems of data processing and accounting theory.

DISCUSSION QUESTIONS

13-A. The text mentions certain payroll withholdings. What are they? What are some other payroll withholdings not listed in the text that you might find in industry?

13-B. The text mentions certain costs described as "direct-labor extras." What are they? What are some other direct-labor extras not listed in the text that you might find in industry?

13-C. Briefly explain how the Federal Insurance Contributions Act influences payroll accounting. Identify any payments under this act that enter cost accounting According to the text, what is the most common cost accounting treatment of such payments?

13-D. If you have worked in industry, describe the timekeeping system used for your employer to determine the number of hours of work for which each employee should be paid. If your employer had a cost accounting system, describe the method he used to find the direct-labor hours spent on the different jobs or processes. Do you believe that the method that was used resulted in reasonably accurate figures for these direct-labor hours?

13-E. Each morning the cost accounting department receives time reports for all workers for the previous day from the timekeeping department. Using the current base pay rates of the different workers provided by the personnel department, cost clerks make daily postings of labor costs to the subsidiary ledger accounts. How can a weekly check be made to verify the accuracy of these postings?

13-F. A production worker encounters certain lost-time delays. How is the cost of such delays charged into cost of goods manufactured? (Trace the effect of this cost through the various records, accounts, and cost apportionments from the original evidence to the cost of goods manufactured.)

13-G. In what way can time studies be employed to simplify the charging of direct-labor costs in process cost accounting?

13-H. When a man works a 48-hour week with the last 8 hours considered overtime at time and one-half pay, what is the most common method of handling the cost of the last 8 hours of work? What is another possible method?

13-J. The wage rate of a certain employee in a manufacturing plant is $3 per hour with "time and a half" paid for all hours over 40 in any work week. The employee is engaged in direct labor on two jobs, jobs 109 and 110, during a certain work week. He works 8 hours a day, Monday through Thursday, on job 109 and on Friday and Saturday on job 110. His total pay for the week is $156, including the overtime premium of $12. Discuss the treatment of this overtime premium in the cost accounts. What different treatments are possible? Explain the circumstances under which each treatment appears to be best. What is the most common method of treating overtime premium cost accounting?

13-K. A contractor on large building construction attempts to determine unit labor costs that will be useful in checking performance against estimates and in estimating future jobs. In his classification of different parts of the construction job, he uses a simple mnemonic system, such as E for excavation, C for concrete work, B for brick, W for wood, etc. The timekeeper makes a round of the job every 2 hours. On each round he is required to enter the work being done by each employee at the moment. The primary purpose of his round of the job is to obtain the basis for wage payments on an hourly rate; the information he obtains about unit labor costs is viewed as a by-product.

What differences do you see between the problems of cost control of labor costs on building construction and in repetitive manufacturing carried on in a factory? To what extent do you think these differences should be reflected in differences in cost accounting procedures?

PROBLEMS

Problem 13-1. Wee-Mite Manufacturing Co. has a job cost accounting system in which two subsidiary ledgers are kept for work in process, one for custom jobs and one for standard-product jobs. Shop labor cost is applied to jobs and indirect labor accounts by means of a timekeeping system which also provides the basis for calculating the payroll for all "hourly" personnel. Both salaried and hourly wage employees are paid weekly.

Below is a portion of the chart of accounts for Wee-Mite Manufacturing. This list contains only the accounts required for this problem. No other accounts are to be used.

01 Cash
41 Work in Process, Custom Jobs
43 Work in Process, Standard Products
120 Accrued Wages and Salaries Payable
121 Income Tax Withholding Payable
122 FICA Contributions Payable
123 Federal Unemployment Insurance Payable
124 State Unemployment Insurance Payable
125 State Disability Insurance Payable
126 Compensation Insurance Payable
127 Employee Medical Insurance Payable
401 Shop Administration Expense
411 Direct Labor
421 Shop Indirect Labor
461 Overtime Premium Expense
462 Payroll Tax Expense
466 Compensation Insurance Expense
467 Medical Insurance Expense
601 Administrative Salary Expense
701 Sales Salary Expense
801 Wages and Salaries, Clearing

Accounts 461, 462, 466, and 467 are manufacturing (shop) expense accounts.

For the week ending April 20, 1963, the payroll was computed and summarized as follows:

Base wages earned (including salaries)		$1,567
Overtime premium earned (shop only)		33
Total gross earnings		$1,600
Deduct from paychecks:		
Federal withholding tax	$166	
FICA contributions	58	
State disability insurance	16	
Medical insurance premium	30	270
Net amount of paychecks		$1,330

A. Set up a general journal entry for this. Note that the date for this entry is April 20 and that as of that date the paychecks have not yet been drawn. (In this and the following journal entries, account titles may be abbreviated but account numbers should be shown.)

B. Set up, in general journal form, the entry that would appear in the cash disbursements journal on April 26 when the paychecks are written.

At the end of each week the daily time cards for each hourly wage employee are "costed out," using that employee's wage rate, and summarized to obtain the distribution of the employee's total earnings to the appropriate expense accounts. This information is then combined with an analysis of the earnings of salaried employees on a "labor-cost distribution sheet." The column totals on this sheet provide a breakdown by expense account of the total gross earnings on the payroll for that week.

At the end of each quarter a summary is compiled from these weekly labor-cost distribution sheets (including sheets for the portions of split weeks at the start and end of the quarter, if any). The column totals from this summary sheet for the second quarter of 1963 were as follows:

Shop supervision		$ 1,800
Direct labor		11,200
Custom jobs	$7,200	
Standard products	4,000	
Shop indirect labor		1,600
Administrative salaries		4,500
Sales salaries		1,500
Total base wages		$20,600
Overtime premium		400
Total gross earnings		$21,000

C. Using the above data, set up appropriate end-of-quarter general journal entries, one distributing the labor cost to the various expense accounts and the other applying direct labor to the two Work in Process accounts. Assume that an entry such as the one for A, above, was made for each of the 13 weeks in the quarter.

D. The FICA contributions treated in the weekly entries, such as for A, are the employees' contributions. Assume that the employer also must contribute at the rate of 3⅝% of the gross earnings shown above. Also, in addition to the employees' state disability insurance contributions, the employer must contribute 3.2% of gross earnings for state unemployment insurance and 0.8% for the Federal unemployment tax. Make a journal entry for these matters. Assume that all earnings were taxable; round off all figures to the nearest dollar.

E. Assume that the workmen's compensation insurance premium rates are 3½% (on base wages) for shop direct and indirect labor, 1% for shop supervision, and 0.2 for all other classes of work. Make a journal entry accruing and distributing this expense.

F. Assume that the company pays half of the cost of medical insurance, matching the employees' contributions, which totaled $390 for the quarter. Assume that a logical allocation of this total to shop, administrative, and sales would be $306, $60, and $24, respectively. Make a journal entry accruing and distributing this expense.

Explain when, how, and from what source the labor-cost entries would be made in the two work-in-process ledgers in this system.

Problem 13-2. This is a continuation of problem 13-1 concerning the Wee-Mite Manufacturing Company. Reference may be made to the following accounts in addition to those listed in problem 13-1:

53 Finished Goods, Standard Products
250 Earned Surplus
804 Burden Variance
841 Cost of Goods Sold, Custom Products
843 Cost of Goods Sold, Standard Products
850 Profit and Loss Summary

Assume that the accounting cycle is a calendar quarter and that all accounts numbered 400 or higher are closed out at the end of each quarter.

The following information was transcribed from the time card of A. J. Carlson for September 19, 1963.

Item	Description of job	Job No. or account No.	Hours
1	Blank out base	43-218	3.3
2	Layout and setup	41-302	1.1
3	Fix press clutch	421-05	1.2
4	Form body (2d operation)	41-302	3.9
Total	....	......	9.5

The questions below may be answered in the form of simple diagrams, with supplementary explanation as you think necessary. Use account numbers rather than account names to refer to the various general ledger accounts. You may consider all effects relating to the employer's payroll tax expenses to be outside the scope of each of the questions asked.

A. Consider the debit associated with the 5 hours Carlson spent on custom job 41-302.
   1. Trace the flow of this debit through the various general ledger accounts it would ultimately affect.
   2. Also, assuming that job 41-302 was finished and shipped in September, point out how this debit would be reflected in the balance sheet of September 30 and the income statement for the quarter.
B. Consider the debit associated with the 3.3 hours Carlson spent on standard-product job 43-218. Assume that this product is made to stock (not to customer's order).
   1. Trace the flow of this debit through the various general ledger accounts it would ultimately affect.
   2. Also, assuming that job 43-218 was completed and delivered to stock on September 24, explain how this debit might be reflected in the September 30 balance sheet and the income statement for the quarter.
C. Consider the debit associated with the 1.2 hours Carlson spent fixing the press clutch.
   1. Trace the flow of this debit through the various general ledger accounts

it would ultimately affect. State any assumptions necessary to support your answer.

2. Explain why, in effect, portions of this debit might be reflected in *several* of the balance sheet accounts at the end of the quarter. Identify those accounts.

D. Consider the debit associated with the overtime premium earned by Carlson on this day. Trace the flow of this debit through the various general ledger accounts it would ultimately affect. State any assumptions necessary to support your answer.

E. Consider the credit side of the entries stemming from Carlson's time card(s). Trace the flow through the various accounts on this side. Identify each step in the sequence with an event.

14/ INDIRECT MANUFACTURING EXPENSE

Indirect manufacturing expense is a phrase that can be applied to all manufacturing costs that are not direct materials or direct labor. Many different names have been applied to this group of costs. Some of the more common ones are overhead, factory overhead, manufacturing overhead, burden, factory burden, manufacturing burden, expense, factory expense, and I.M.E., or IME. The terms with modifying adjectives such as *factory* or *manufacturing* are more explicit, as they distinguish the production costs from the indirect costs related to selling and general administration. In the interest of brevity, however, *overhead* and *burden* are frequently used to mean indirect manufacturing expense.

SOME IMPORTANT DIFFERENCES BETWEEN DIRECT AND INDIRECT MANUFACTURING COSTS. In cost accounting for direct materials and direct labor, the problem is to identify the particular material units and labor hours with the jobs or processes on which they were used. For indirect costs, such straightforward identification is not practical. If these indirect costs are to be included in the cost of goods manufactured, they must be *apportioned* among the jobs or processes. Many different schemes of apportionment are possible; different schemes will result in different cost figures reported for the various jobs or processes. Any scheme for apportionment of costs is necessarily more or less arbitrary; it is not reasonable to say that some one scheme is correct and that all other possible schemes are wrong. The objective in each case should be to find a scheme that seems satisfactory for the various purposes of cost accounting, all things considered. A practical limitation is that the scheme adopted should be simple enough that it does not involve excessive expense for cost accounting.

A special difficulty in apportioning indirect costs arises because of the "fixed" element that always is present in manufacturing overhead. Many of the overhead costs are partly or entirely independent of the quantity or product made in a given period of time. The overhead cost per unit of output will depend on the output; the fixed costs will be spread over more units when a manufacturing plant operates at full capacity than when it operates at, say, three-fourths of capacity. For this reason, a predetermined overhead rate cannot be computed without an assumption regarding the rate of plant output.

SOME QUESTIONS ARISING IN APPORTIONING OVERHEAD. It is convenient to discuss the subject matter of this chapter in relation to the following five questions that arise in setting up any plan for the distribution of indirect manufacturing expense:

1. *Shall manufacturing overhead rates be predetermined?* In nearly all cases, they are predetermined. For a number of good reasons it is unusual to wait until the end of an accounting period before setting the overhead rates for the period.
2. *What costs shall be included in manufacturing overhead?* Many different classes of costs of this type are mentioned in this chapter. It is necessary to establish a definite borderline between the indirect costs that are viewed as manufacturing expense and those that are viewed as selling and general administrative expense. It is also important to establish a classification of indirect manufacturing expense accounts that will be useful for purposes of cost control.
3. *Shall indirect manufacturing expenses be apportioned among cost centers before being applied to the product?* Except in the simplest manufacturing operations, this apportionment is desirable. It was not illustrated in the simple examples in Chaps. 10 and 11 but is discussed at some length in the present chapter.
4. *Manufacturing overhead must be applied to jobs or processes in proportion to something measurable about the jobs or processes. But in proportion to what?* In the examples up to this point, overhead has been applied in proportion to direct-labor cost. Other bases for overhead distribution are discussed in the present chapter.
5. *Shall a predetermined burden rate be based on the expected volume of production for the period to which the rate is to apply or on the volume of production for a normal or base period?* In this chapter, the discussion of the normal burden rate is combined with a discussion of the variable budget for indirect manufacturing expense and with a discussion of certain problems related to cost control of these expenses. It also is pointed out how the interpretation of an overabsorbed or underabsorbed burden depends on the way in which this question has been answered.

PREDETERMINED BURDEN RATES VERSUS HISTORICAL BURDEN RATES. There are good reasons why manufacturing overhead rates are nearly always predetermined even in those common instances where direct-material and direct-labor costs are charged on an "actual" or historical basis.

One important reason is the need to determine cost figures promptly. Because of seasonal aspects of certain indirect expenses and seasonal patterns in production rates, a year is generally the shortest period for which it is reasonable to compute any burden rate, either historical or predetermined. If the burden rate is not predetermined, no unit costs of product can be determined during the year; it is necessary to wait until after the year end to apportion the indirect expenses. With a historical burden rate, inventories cannot be valued and cost of goods sold determined at intermediate dates during the year.

The viewpoint underlying the burden rate based on normal output is explained later in this chapter. In many cases, it is desirable to adopt this viewpoint. To implement this viewpoint it is essential that the burden rate be predetermined.

AN EXAMPLE OF A CLASSIFICATION OF ACCOUNTS FOR INDIRECT MANUFACTURING EXPENSE. Exhibit 14-1 shows the indirect manufacturing expense accounts recommended in the uniform accounting manual for the electrical manufacturing industry.[1] The accounts in this exhibit show the many different types of costs that are usually included in manufacturing overhead. In a classification of accounts such as this one, each account title is supplemented by a descriptive statement defining just what items are to be included in the account.

Although most of the account titles in Exhibit 14-1 are self-explanatory, a few of the titles are used in meanings that are somewhat specialized to the particular accounting system. For example, account 522, Make-up, refers to "Wages paid to employees to make up the difference between guaranteed earnings and actual earnings." Account 532, Shift Bonuses, covers "Amounts paid to employees as a bonus for time worked on other than regular day shifts." The descriptive statement for account 520, Indirect Labor, is as follows: "Salaries and wages paid for manufacturing work which is of a service nature to productive operations and not charged to separate accounts. Includes such activities as sweeping and cleaning, material handling, watching and guarding. For control purposes, it may be desirable to set up a subdivision of this account for each activity." Account 526, Down Time, refers to "Wages paid to employees for idle time caused by conditions beyond employees' control, such as machine breakdown and power failure." The descriptive statement for account 540, Employee Welfare, is: "Expenditures incurred

[1] Reproduced by permission from *Uniform Accounting Manual for the Electrical Manufacturing Industry*, amended 7th ed., National Electric Manufacturers Association, New York, 1960.

to promote and maintain the goodwill, health, interest, and morale of employees. Includes cost of group insurance and pension plans; contributions to clubs, sports, outings, meetings, mutual benefit groups which are for the benefit of employees; contributions for medical expenses and special allowances made to employees for which the company is not liable." Account 596, Miscellaneous Expense, covers "Incidental expenses of a minor nature which cannot be otherwise classified."

EXHIBIT 14-1
CLASSIFICATION OF IME ACCOUNTS FOR ELECTRICAL MANUFACTURING INDUSTRY

502	Salaries—Supervision	552	Defective Work and Material
504	Salaries—Professional	554	Dues and Subscriptions
510	Salaries—Office and Clerical	556	Postage
512	Salaries—Inspection	558	Meetings
518	Incentive Payments and Bonuses	560	Traveling and Entertainment
520	Indirect Labor	562	Automobile Expense (Company Owned)
522	Make-up	564	Telephone and Telegraph
524	Machine Setup	570	Depreciation
526	Down Time	572	Rent
528	Training	574	Amortization of Leasehold Improvements
530	Overtime Premium	576	Rent of Equipment
532	Shift Bonuses	578	Repair and Maintenance
534	Social Security Taxes	580	Rearrangement and Alteration
536	Compensation Insurance	582	Property Taxes and Insurance
538	Vacation and Holiday Pay	588	Losses Due to Errors
540	Employee Welfare	592	Professional Fees
544	Supplies Expense	596	Miscellaneous Expense
546	Tool Expense		
548	Fuel		
550	Power, Light, and Heat		

In the interest of simplicity, most of the cost accounting examples and problems in this book either use a single controlling account such as Indirect Manufacturing Expense or use only a few individual accounts such as Indirect Labor; Heat, Light, and Power; Repair Expense; and Depreciation. In all cases the student should view the manufacturing overhead accounts actually used in the examples and problems as representative of a much larger number of accounts that would cover the various types of costs referred to in Exhibit 14-1.

DEFINING THE BORDERLINE BETWEEN INDIRECT MANUFACTURING EXPENSE AND OTHER OVERHEAD COSTS. Indirect expenses allocated to product through the burden rate are, of course, included in the valuation of inventories of work in process and finished goods. Selling expenses should not enter into the valuation of manufactured goods. What is desired in the inventory valuation is the cost to make, not the cost to make and sell. It is sometimes stated that the determination of manufacturing costs should "stop at the factory door."

Nevertheless, there are certain borderline classes of costs that are viewed as manufacturing costs in some instances and as selling costs in others. One example of this is the cost of warehousing the finished product. The decision as to where this cost shall be charged will be influenced by the physical facts and may depend as much on what is convenient as on what is strictly logical. For instance, warehousing costs in a branch warehouse physically separated from the factory are normally viewed as selling costs. On the other hand, consider a case where the stores department handles all finished parts. If some of these parts go into assemblies and others are sold directly to customers, convenience is likely to dictate that the warehousing cost of all finished parts will be treated as a manufacturing expense.

USING COST CENTERS IN APPORTIONING INDIRECT MANUFACTURING EXPENSE. In the job-order example in Chap. 10, the manufacturing plant was not departmentalized and a single predetermined burden rate of 150% of direct-labor cost was applied to all production. Although there were several departments in the process cost accounting example in Chap. 11, all departments used the same predetermined overhead rate of 50% of direct-labor cost. In the introduction to cost accounting in these two chapters, it was desirable to use illustrations that were relatively simple.

Some actual cost systems are similar to these two examples in using only one burden rate to apply to all manufacturing operations. Nevertheless, in departmentalized businesses that make more than one product, the single plant-wide burden rate is the exception rather than the rule. More often, different types of manufacturing operations will use different burden rates.

Generally speaking, an effort is made to charge burden to different products in a way that reflects, as nearly as practicable, the responsibility of the various products for indirect manufacturing expense. Often it is impossible to obtain a sensible burden distribution with a single plant-wide burden rate. To illustrate this point, consider a simple example. Assume that a manufacturing plant has two products. One product requires expensive automatic machinery with a small amount of labor, whereas the other uses inexpensive tools and considerable highly skilled labor. If the same burden rate should be used for both products, the product using the inexpensive tools would—in effect—be charged with part of the depreciation, power, and maintenance cost of the expensive automatic machinery. If a single plant-wide burden rate should be used in this case, the unit cost figures from the accounting system would be likely to mislead management in judging the relative profitableness of the two lines of product. Moreover, such figures for unit cost would give poor guidance in decisions about pricing the different products.

The usual plan for burden distribution requires the division of a manufacturing plant into a number of *cost centers.* In some cases, each department will be a cost center. For example, a certain manufacturer in the metal trades might designate the forge shop as one cost center, the machine shop as another, and the assembly department as a third. However, it often is desirable to break down a department into two or more cost centers. For example, the machine shop might include several cost centers; one center might be a group of lathes, another a group of punch presses, another a vertical boring mill, and so on. Although a department may be broken down into two or more cost centers, it usually is undesirable for a cost center to include two or more departments that are under the supervision of different persons.

Once the cost centers are determined, the various indirect manufacturing expenses are then divided among the centers. Each type of expense is allocated among the centers on some basis that is deemed most appropriate for the particular type of expense. The object of the allocation is to set a separate burden rate for each cost center, to be computed from the total of the indirect expenses allocated to the center.

PRODUCTIVE COST CENTERS, SERVICE COST CENTERS, AND NOMINAL COST CENTERS. The actual charges of burden to product occur in *productive cost centers* such as the punch-press cost center previously mentioned. In allocating indirect manufacturing expenses among centers, all expenses must ultimately be allocated to productive cost centers. Nevertheless, it usually is desirable to make use of certain other cost centers as an aid in carrying out the allocations.

Two other types of cost centers often used are referred to as *service cost centers* and *nominal cost centers.* A service cost center generally is a department that does not carry out manufacturing operations itself but that performs a necessary service to the various productive cost centers. Some common examples are the stores department, the tool room, the maintenance department, and the production-control department. A nominal cost center is one established for bookkeeping convenience to summarize certain closely related expenses. Thus a nominal cost center entitled Space Occupancy might be used to summarize the numerous expenses in connection with the ownership and operation of buildings. Space-occupancy expenses might include building depreciation, real estate taxes, maintenance of buildings and grounds, and building insurance.

The usual procedure is to allocate the total costs from each nominal cost center among both the service and the productive cost centers. The resulting total costs for the service cost centers are then allocated among the productive cost centers.

AN EXAMPLE OF APPORTIONMENT AMONG COST CENTERS. Exhibit 14-2 illustrates the allocation of indirect manufacturing expenses among cost centers.

This exhibit shows how the charges in each of 11 expense accounts (accounts 502 to 570 and account 582) are allocated among three productive cost centers, four service cost centers, and two nominal cost centers. It shows how the costs distributed to these nine cost centers are finally allocated to the three productive cost centers. The final result of the allocation is that the total indirect manufacturing expense of $19,140 is divided among the three productive cost centers, $7,091 to lathes, $6,634 to presses, and $5,415 to mills.

Although allocations among cost centers usually follow the general pattern illustrated in Exhibit 14-2, actual allocation sheets often appear to be much more complex than this exhibit. Usually there are more IME accounts. (For instance, Exhibit 14-1 listed 37 such accounts.) Often there are many productive cost centers.

The student should view Exhibit 14-2 as illustrating both the method of allocating *estimated* costs and the method of allocating *actual* costs. In setting predetermined burden rates, the estimated charges to the respective expense accounts must be used. As explained later in this chapter, the estimates may be either for a specific future accounting period or for a "normal" period. Where separate burden variances are to be computed for each productive cost center, another allocation using actual costs must be made at the end of each accounting period. Actual costs also are allocated in those rare cases where historical burden rates are used.

THE VARIOUS CRITERIA FOR APPORTIONING DIFFERENT TYPES OF EXPENSE AMONG COST CENTERS. For each IME account, a method must be selected for dividing the charges to the account among the various cost centers. A basis of allocation must also be selected to apportion to the productive cost centers the totals assigned to the nominal and service cost centers.

Some of the manufacturing expenses that are *indirect* in the sense that they are not identifiable with specific products may nevertheless be *directly* identified with specific cost centers. For example, each cost center may have certain employees whose wages and salaries are charged as indirect labor. Some other expenses readily identifiable with specific cost centers are incentive-wage payments, machine setup, overtime premiums, social security taxes, compensation insurance, and depreciation on machinery.

Identifying the responsibility of the various cost centers for certain

EXHIBIT 14-2

ALLOCATION OF INDIRECT MANUFACTURING EXPENSES TO PRODUCTIVE-COST CENTERS

Account number	Expense account	Productive cost centers			Service cost centers				Nominal cost centers		Total	Total distributed
		No. 1 lathes	*No. 2 presses*	*No. 3 mills*	*Tool room*	*Stores dept.*	*Maintenance dept.*	*General factory*	*Rent*	*Power heat & light*		
502	Salaries—supervision	......	......	......	.....	....	.....	$800	.....	.....	$800	
510	Salaries—office and clerical	......	......	......	$125	$130	$200	500	.....	.....	955	
520	Indirect labor	$1,642	$1,827	$1,310	418	368	1,943	602	$483	$531	9,124	
530	Overtime premium	106	38	72	.....	....	85	.....	.....	95	396	
544	Supplies expense	560	503	390	106	42	132	96	59	67	1,955	
546	Tool expense	801	752	661	302	....	195	87	.....	103	2,901	
548	Fuel	......	......	......	.....	....	.....	.....	.....	406	406	
550	Power, heat, and light (purchased)	......	......	......	.....	....	.....	.....	.....	542	542	
552	Defective work and material	175	215	163	45	....	.....	.....	.....	.....	598	
570	Depreciation	136	124	102	88	10	114	15	340	116	1,045	
582	Property taxes and insurance	......	......	......	.....	....	.....	.....	418	.....	418	
	Total expenses before allocation	$3,420	$3,459	$2,698	$1,084	$550	$2,669	$2,100	$1,300	$1,860	$19,140	
572	Rent	$300	$200	$150	$100	$200	$250	$100	.....	.....	.....	($1,300)
578	Repair and maintenance	1,265	983	968	.....	....	.....	.....	.....	.....	.....	(3,216)
598	Expenses allocated—debit:											
	Power, heat, and light	419	387	303	283	65	297	106	.....	.....	.....	(1,860)
	General factory	735	852	719	.....	....	.....	.....	.....	.....	.....	(2,306)
	Stores	314	282	219	.....	....	.....	.....	.....	.....	.....	(815)
	Tool room, etc.	638	471	358	.....	....	.....	.....	.....	.....	.....	(1,467)
599	Expenses allocated—credit	......	......	......	(1,467)	(815)	(3,216)	(2,306)	(1,300)	(1,860)	.....	10,964
	Total expenses after allocation	$7,091	$6,634	$5,415	.....	....	.....	.....	.....	.....	$19,140	

SOURCE: Reproduced by permission from the amended seventh edition of the *Uniform Accounting Manual for the Electrical Manufacturing Industry*, 1960.

indirect expenses may require systematic record keeping throughout the year. For instance, whenever indirect materials or manufacturing supplies are issued, the cost center using the supplies may be identified on the storeroom requisition. Similarly the maintenance department and the tool room may keep track of work done for each cost center.

A number of indirect expenses cannot be directly identified with particular cost centers. These expenses must be *prorated* among the centers. For each such expense, a basis for prorating must be found that seems reasonable for the particular expense. The basis selected must be capable of being measured for each cost center.

For example, space-occupancy costs usually are prorated in proportion to the number of square feet of floor area in each cost center. General supervisory costs, welfare costs, and factory clerical costs may be prorated on the basis of the number of employees in each cost center. Stores-department expense may be prorated on the basis of the value of materials issued to each cost center. Fire insurance on machinery and equipment may be prorated in proportion to the value of fixed assets in each center. If social security taxes and compensation insurance are not actually identified by cost centers, they may be prorated in proportion to the total payroll in each center.

In some manufacturing plants, the allocations among cost centers are greatly influenced by the desire of management to make the cost distribution without having it cause any avoidable expense. As an example, assume that electricity is purchased for light and power. If the allocation of the total electric bill is to be based on the electricity used in each cost center, each center must have its own meter to determine the kilowatthours that it consumes. (In principle, because most power bills depend on maximum demand as well as on energy consumed, the amount and time of the maximum demand ought to be measured as well as the kilowatthour consumption.) However, management may be unwilling to buy electric meters that are to be used only for cost accounting and cost control. Where the cost centers are not metered, it frequently happens that the electric bill is divided in proportion to the rated capacities of lights, motors, and other power-using devices in each center. If the electric bill is a relatively minor element in manufacturing cost, or if all devices using electricity have nearly the same hours of use, such an approximate allocation may be good enough for practical purposes. Nevertheless, this type of allocation may sometimes be badly misleading and may be an obstacle to effective cost control. Further comment on this topic is made in Chap. 21.

SOME DIFFERENT BASES FOR CHARGING BURDEN TO PRODUCT. The basis for charging burden to product is often referred to as the *burden vehicle*. Some possible burden vehicles are:

1. Cost vehicles
   a. Direct-labor cost
   b. Direct-material cost
   c. Prime cost (the sum of direct-labor and direct-material costs)
2. Time vehicles
   a. Direct-labor hours
   b. Machine hours
3. Units of output

To obtain a predetermined burden rate, the estimated indirect manufacturing expense is divided by the estimated size of the burden vehicle. Any burden vehicle is necessarily a measure of estimated output.

For example, consider some possible burden rates for cost center No. 1—lathes, in Exhibit 14-2. Assume that the figures in this exhibit refer to estimates for the coming year, and that the plant uses job-order costing. Assume that the following estimates for the year are made for this cost center:

Direct-labor cost, $6,000
Direct-labor hours, 2,700 hours

If the burden rate were to be applied to direct-labor cost, it would be computed as follows:

$$\text{Burden rate} = \frac{\text{allocated IME}}{\text{estimated direct-labor cost}} = \frac{\$7{,}091}{\$6{,}000} = 1.18 \text{ or } 118\%$$

If it were to be applied to direct-labor hours, it would be

$$\text{Burden rate} = \frac{\text{allocated IME}}{\text{estimated direct-labor hours}} = \frac{\$7{,}091}{2{,}700 \text{ hours}} = \$2.63$$

If the rate based on cost were used, 118% of direct-labor cost in the lathe cost center would be entered on each job cost sheet as the burden chargeable to the job in that center. If the hourly rate were used, the job cost sheet would need to record labor hours to permit the calculation of the burden at $2.63 per labor hour.

CHOOSING A BURDEN VEHICLE. It is desirable that a burden vehicle reflect, as nearly as practicable, the responsibility of each job or process for the various indirect expenses that are being allocated by means of the burden rate. Other things being equal, it is advantageous if the burden rate is simple and easy to apply. As already pointed out, a restriction in selecting a burden vehicle is that the vehicle must be some quantity capable of being measured for the job or process to which the burden is to be applied.

No one burden vehicle is best for all circumstances. The choice of a burden vehicle should be influenced by the relative importance of different types of indirect manufacturing expenses in the particular manufacturing situation, by certain aspects of the direct costs, by the extent to which the plant is divided into cost centers, and by the relative convenience of the different vehicles.

If some simple and appropriate unit of product were available to measure the production in each cost center, burden could be charged in each center in proportion to product units. However, in diversified manufacturing it rarely happens that an appropriate product unit can be found. For example, consider the lathe cost center to which references have been made. Many different parts and articles can be machined in such a cost center. Any product unit that it is practicable to use, such as numbers of items or weight in pounds, may be clearly inappropriate for measuring the responsibility of the different products for indirect manufacturing expense.

In a similar way, there may be limitations on the possibility of using certain other burden vehicles. For instance, a machine-hour rate is not practicable unless the plant has been divided into cost centers. Its use is limited to those cost centers that consist of one machine or other piece of production equipment or of a number of closely similar machines. Where practicable, the machine-hour rate is likely to give a more reasonable application of indirect manufacturing expense than any other burden vehicle. It is particularly appropriate where a large fraction of the total indirect manufacturing expense consists of charges associated with machines, such as depreciation, repairs and maintenance, taxes, insurance, and space charges.

Direct-labor cost is one burden vehicle that is always practicable, both when burden is applied in cost centers and when a single plant-wide burden rate is used. Surveys of industrial cost accounting practice disclose that the most common burden vehicle is direct-labor cost. In support of this basis for applying burden, it is pointed out that many indirect expenses are greatly influenced by direct-labor cost and some are almost directly proportional to this cost. Some good examples are the direct-labor extras mentioned in Chap. 13. Moreover, direct-labor cost is a simple and inexpensive basis for applying burden.

Often the choice of a burden vehicle will lie between direct-labor cost and direct-labor hours. If wage rates are approximately the same for all employees, as may frequently be the case in a fairly homogeneous cost center, the two vehicles may give very nearly the same results. If so, direct-labor cost will generally be selected on the grounds of greater simplicity and convenience.

In contrast, where there are wide differences in hourly wage rates for different direct-labor employees, it may be evident that burden charges based on direct-labor hours will not only be different from charges based on direct-labor cost but that, all things considered, the hourly rate will give more reasonable results. For example, consider the case where certain highly skilled employees receiving high wage rates use fairly simple tools requiring a small investment whereas other employees at lower wage rates work at automatic machines that require a large investment. If the same burden rate is to be applied to both groups of employees, the vehicle, direct-labor hours, will charge relatively more burden for the work done on the automatic machines. As these machines are responsible for many indirect expenses, the vehicle, direct-labor hours, is more appropriate than direct-labor cost.

Another burden vehicle that has been mentioned is direct-material cost. Even though this vehicle is simple and easy to apply, particularly when a single plant-wide burden rate is to be used, it may be subject to valid objections. This vehicle will, of course, charge the most burden to the products using the most expensive materials. Because it often is evident that there is little or no relationship between the cost of the materials entering into various products and the responsibility of the products for particular indirect expenses, direct-material cost is not a common vehicle. The same objection may be raised to prime cost (the sum of direct-material and direct-labor costs).

Where overhead costs are apportioned among cost centers, different vehicles may be appropriate in different centers. Thus some centers may use machine hours, others may use direct-labor hours, and still others may use direct-labor cost.

It is possible to use two different vehicles in the same cost center. For example, some indirect manufacturing expenses (such as supervision and direct-labor extras) might be charged to jobs in proportion to direct-labor cost, whereas other indirect expenses (such as space charges, depreciation, repairs, and taxes) might be charged in proportion to machine hours. Although such combined burden rates are occasionally used, their use is not common because of their greater complexity.

SOME REASONS WHY THE YEAR IS THE SHORTEST PERIOD THAT IS APPROPRIATE FOR ESTABLISHING A BURDEN RATE. Any predetermined burden rate may be thought of as a fraction. The numerator of the fraction is a figure for estimated indirect manufacturing expense for a period of time. The denominator is the estimated amount of the direct-labor cost, direct-labor hours, machine hours, or some other burden vehicle for the same period of time. The size of this denominator depends on the estimated output for the period of time in question.

In most cases there will be some indirect expenses that have seasonal patterns of variation. Thus heat and light expense may be greatest in winter; paid vacations may be concentrated in the summer; major repair work may be scheduled during an annual shutdown or period of slack production.

A number of other indirect expenses tend to be relatively constant even when output varies considerably. Some examples are supervisory costs, plant housekeeping, rent, property taxes, insurance, and depreciation. Because output usually varies from month to month for seasonal or other reasons, the indirect expense per unit of output also varies.

If a new burden rate should be established each month, based on the estimated indirect expense and output for the month in question, many manufacturing enterprises would have large fluctuations in their burden rates from month to month. A critical consideration of the matter will show that such fluctuations in burden rates would serve no useful purpose; in fact, they would be undesirable in relation to all the various objectives of cost accounting, namely, sales control, financial control, and cost control. Therefore, when a burden rate is being predetermined, the common practice is to give consideration to the estimated expenses and output for an entire year rather than a single month. In effect, the burden rate used may be viewed as being based on an average month rather than on a particular month.

AN EXAMPLE OF THE VARIATION OF INDIRECT EXPENSES WITH OUTPUT. The relationship between indirect manufacturing expense and the volume of production is an important topic for a number of reasons. In examining the various aspects of this topic, it is helpful to use a set of figures that apply to a specific case. Such figures are shown in Exhibit 14-3.

This exhibit shows the type of estimates that are appropriate in preparing a budget for indirect manufacturing expense. First, some unit to measure volume of output must be selected. In Exhibit 14-3, this unit is direct-labor cost. (Where the product of a manufacturing plant is so diversified that no satisfactory physical measure of output can be found, direct-labor cost is usually the most appropriate measure.) Several different outputs are then chosen, and each indirect expense is estimated for each output. In Exhibit 14-3, it is assumed that $500,000 of direct-labor cost represents the maximum output obtainable from 5-day-a-week single-shift operation. The other outputs are, respectively, 60, 70, 80, and 90% of this maximum plant capacity under the stated conditions.

In estimating the appropriate charges to each indirect labor account at each of the five outputs, a careful study should be made of the numbers of indirect employees really needed at each output. For example, in estimating shop clerical labor, the required numbers of cost clerks, dispatchers, stock clerks, timekeepers, payroll clerks, production-control clerks, and other shop clerical employees are estimated separately. The appropriate wage or salary rates are applied to convert estimated numbers of employees to estimated costs.

Other indirect expenses that depend on total labor costs can be estimated from the direct- and indirect-labor cost; such expenses include social security taxes, compensation insurance, and vacation and holiday pay. Similarly, for other indirect expenses such as power or shop supplies, the physical amounts needed are estimated for the different outputs, and these physical quantities are converted into cost. Still

EXHIBIT 14-3
ESTIMATED MANUFACTURING OVERHEAD FOR THE XYZ MANUFACTURING COMPANY AT VARIOUS LEVELS OF ANNUAL OUTPUT

Direct-labor cost	$300,000	$350,000	$400,000	$450,000	$500,000
Per cent of estimated single-shift 40-hour-per-week capacity	60	70	80	90	100
Estimates of indirect manufacturing expenses:					
Supervisory salaries	$27,500	$27,500	$27,500	$27,500	$27,500
Inspectors	26,600	29,100	31,600	34,100	36,600
Shop clerical labor	51,000	56,500	62,000	67,500	73,000
Service employees	62,800	68,800	74,800	80,800	86,800
Social security taxes	8,000	9,200	10,400	11,600	12,800
Compensation insurance	6,200	7,150	8,100	9,050	10,000
Vacation and holiday pay	13,200	15,200	17,200	19,200	21,200
Shop supplies	17,000	19,500	22,000	24,500	27,000
Tool expense	13,300	14,400	15,500	16,600	17,700
Power, light, and heat	28,400	31,150	33,900	36,650	39,400
Maintenance of machinery	34,700	37,700	40,700	43,700	46,700
Maintenance of buildings	12,000	12,000	12,000	12,000	12,000
Depreciation	94,000	94,000	94,000	94,000	94,000
Rent	25,000	25,000	25,000	25,000	25,000
Property taxes	37,000	37,000	37,000	37,000	37,000
Property insurance	8,300	8,300	8,300	8,300	8,300
Total	$465,000	$492,500	$520,000	$547,500	$575,000

other expenses are controlled by the investment in plant and equipment, by company policies, and by various external matters but are not influenced by moderate variations in output; in Exhibit 14-3 examples of such expenses include rent, property taxes and insurance, depreciation, building maintenance, and supervisory salaries.

GRAPHICAL AND ALGEBRAIC EXPRESSION OF THE RELATIONSHIP BETWEEN INDIRECT MANUFACTURING EXPENSE AND OUTPUT. Exhibit 14-4 is a graph based on the budget figures given in Exhibit 14-3. The vertical scale on this graph shows total estimated indirect manufacturing expense; the horizontal scale shows direct-labor cost (as a measure of output). The five points established by the budget have been plotted on this graph and have been connected by a straight line.

Budgets for indirect manufacturing expense that are based on such an estimated straight-line relationship are common in industry. If the actual behavior of each separate expense were examined for all values

EXHIBIT 14-4

RELATIONSHIP BETWEEN ESTIMATED INDIRECT MANUFACTURING EXPENSE AND ESTIMATED DIRECT–LABOR COST FOR XYZ MANUFACTURING COMPANY

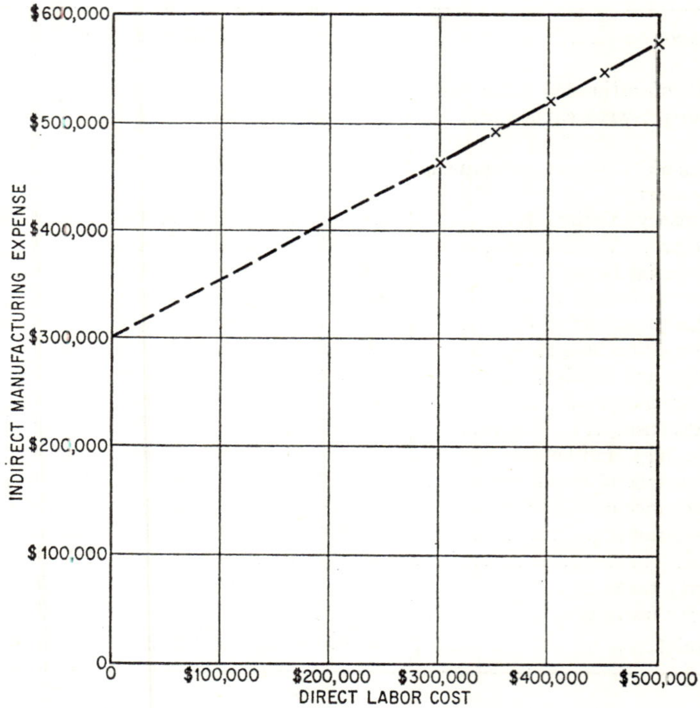

of output, many of the expenses would be found to vary as a series of steps rather than as a straight line. For example, 18 service employees might be needed at 59% of capacity; the nineteenth might be hired at 64%, the twentieth at 69%, and so on. Because the appropriate positions of such steps usually differ for the different indirect expenses, a straight line generally gives an approximation to the total of all indirect expenses that is good enough for practical purposes. Moreover, the assumption of a linear relationship is convenient for use in estimating and budgeting.

This linear assumption has been made for all the individual expenses of Exhibit 14-3 as well as for the total expense.

For certain purposes it is useful to describe the straight-line relationship between indirect expense and output by an algebraic equation. For the figures of Exhibit 14-3, this equation is

$$y = \$300{,}000 + 0.55x$$

where x is direct-labor cost and y is total indirect manufacturing expense.

"FIXED" AND "VARIABLE" ELEMENTS IN MANUFACTURING OVERHEAD. The foregoing equation suggests a possible viewpoint regarding the total indirect manufacturing expense of the XYZ Manufacturing Company. This total expense can be thought of as if it were made up of two parts: One part, $300,000, is not affected by the volume of output; this part can be described as the "fixed" element in manufacturing overhead. The other part varies directly with output and is 55 cents for each dollar of direct-labor cost; this part can be described as the "variable" element in manufacturing overhead.

An examination of the various expenses listed in Exhibit 14-3 shows certain expenses that are unchanged when output varies from full capacity to 60% of capacity. These expenses are as follows:

Supervisory salaries	$ 27,500
Maintenance of buildings	12,000
Depreciation	94,000
Rent	25,000
Property taxes	37,000
Property insurance	8,300
Total	$203,800

The remaining $96,200 of the $300,000 of "fixed" expense consists of "fixed" elements in those indirect expenses that change with output. For example, the equation of a straight line describing the estimated expense for service employees is

$$s = \$26{,}800 + 0.12x$$

where x is direct-labor cost and s is service-employees expense. It is reasonable to expect that, if output increases from 60 to 100% of capacity, certain additional service employees will be hired and that, if output declines from 100 to 60% of capacity, a number of service employees will be laid off. This variability in numbers of employees is responsible for the "variable" element in service-employees expense, the 12 cents of such expense per dollar of direct-labor cost (i.e., the $0.12x$ in the equation). Nevertheless, there are evidently certain kinds of work performed by service employees where it is impracticable or inappropriate to change the numbers of employees when the volume of output changes from 100 to

60% of capacity. In some cases, an employee's full time must be devoted to some one activity that is just as necessary at part capacity as at full capacity. For instance, a crane operator may be essential at 60% of capacity even though he is not so busy as he would be at 100% of capacity. In other cases, the work required from certain service employees may be practically the same at part capacity as at full capacity. For instance, the same number of janitors may be needed even though output declines considerably. Cases such as these create the $26,800 "fixed" element in service-employees expense. In some of the literature of cost accounting, such an expense composed of variable and fixed elements is called a "semivariable" cost.

Throughout this section, the words *fixed* and *variable* have been shown in quotation marks. In discussions of the behavior of manufacturing costs, it is common for these two adjectives to be used with the meanings that have been explained in this section. Nevertheless, it is important for the student to understand that the phrases *fixed costs* and *variable costs* may be used in a variety of meanings which should always be interpreted with respect to the assumed frame of reference. The quotation marks were employed to emphasize that the words were being used with a specialized meaning.

In the long run, all costs are variable in the sense of being subject to change. Costs that appear to be fixed in a given setting may be varied by altering the setting. For example, if new buildings and machinery should be acquired, depreciation, property taxes and insurance, and building maintenance would all be increased. These same costs could be decreased if some of the buildings and machinery now owned should be sold. Some of the costs for personal services that seem fixed when production fluctuates from 60 to 100% of capacity would be eliminated in an extended business recession in which production fluctuated, say, from 30 to 60% of capacity. Still other costs that appear fixed when the plant is operating would be eliminated by an extended complete shutdown.

As already pointed out, the tabulation in Exhibit 14-3 of estimated costs for the XYZ Manufacturing Company assumes single-shift 40-hour-a-week operation with production fluctuating between 60 and 100% of capacity. It should be evident that our breakdown into fixed costs of $300,000 a year and variable costs of 55 cents per dollar of direct labor is valid only under these stipulated conditions. The variable costs per dollar of direct labor would presumably be changed if a second shift should be added or if the plant should be operated 48 hours per week with consequent overtime premiums.

Some other assumptions underlying such a breakdown into fixed and variable costs may be equally important even though they may not be quite so obvious. Any set of estimates such as Exhibit 14-3 must assume certain personnel policies. For example, it may be assumed that any operation at as low as 60% of capacity will not be long-sustained and that it therefore is necessary to employ a number of key personnel at all times regardless of output fluctuations. Moreover, estimates such as Exhibit 14-3 are necessarily based on a particular physical plant; as already pointed out, fixed costs will be changed by plant expansion or contraction.

RELATIONSHIP OF A PREDETERMINED BURDEN RATE TO THE EXPECTED OUTPUT. Consider the problem of setting a predetermined plant-wide burden rate based on direct-labor cost using the estimates shown in Exhibit 14-3. Assume that it is desired to have no overabsorbed or underabsorbed burden at the end of the year for which the rate is to be used. With this objective of a zero burden variance, the rate will depend on the estimated output for the period. For a low estimated output, the burden rate will be much greater than for a high one. This point is illustrated in Exhibit 14-5.

EXHIBIT 14-5
PREDETERMINED BURDEN RATES FOR XYZ MANUFACTURING COMPANY CORRESPONDING TO DIFFERENT LEVELS OF OUTPUT

Output as percentage of capacity	Estimated total IME	Estimated direct-labor cost	Burden rate as percentage of direct-labor cost
60	$465,000	$300,000	155.0
70	492,500	350,000	140.7
80	520,000	400,000	130.0
90	547,500	450,000	121.8
100	575,000	500,000	115.0

In effect, the fixed element in indirect manufacturing expense, which we computed to be $300,000, is spread over more units of product at full capacity than at part capacity. The computed burden rates in Exhibit 14-5 can be viewed as if they were made up of two parts. One part is the variable element in burden which we computed to be 55% of direct-labor cost. The other part is the fixed element, $300,000, divided by the direct-labor cost.

CHOOSING BETWEEN A BURDEN RATE BASED ON EXPECTED ANNUAL OUTPUT AND A RATE BASED ON "NORMAL" OUTPUT. In introducing the topic of the choice between historical and predetermined burden rates in Chaps. 9 and 10 and in the further brief discussion of this topic near the start of the present chapter, the greater convenience of the predetermined rate has been stressed. The historical burden rate was objected to because of the undesirability of waiting until the end of a year to compute the costs of the goods produced throughout the whole year. In our discussion of this topic, it was pointed out that it was almost inevitable that a predetermined burden rate would lead to some burden variance at year end because of the difficulty of making accurate estimates of the total indirect manufacturing expense and of the volume of production. However, the idea was not suggested that a predetermined rate might properly aim at an overabsorbed or underabsorbed burden under certain circumstances.

One possible view on the setting of a predetermined burden rate is that the objective should always be to come as close as possible to the results that would be obtained from a historical rate. In other words, the objective should be to secure a zero burden variance at the end of each year—to absorb into the product all the indirect manufacturing expenses that are charged during the particular year. According to this view, the XYZ Manufacturing Company ought to use a burden rate of 115% of direct-labor cost for a year in which it expects full capacity output and a rate of 155% for a year in which output is expected to be at 60% of capacity. In the early days of cost accounting, this was the common viewpoint.

An alternative view, now widely adopted, is that the burden rate should be based on the average annual output expected over a period of years—on a so-called *normal* output. Assume that the management of the XYZ Company should adopt this view and that it is believed that normal output is 80% of capacity. Exhibit 14-5 shows that a rate of 130% of direct-labor cost should be used at 80% of capacity. The XYZ Company will then use this 130% normal rate even though it is expected that production in the coming year will be, say, at 100% of capacity or at 60%.

A number of sound reasons can be advanced to support the use of a burden rate based on normal output. Some of these reasons are given in the following paragraphs with reference to the specific example of the XYZ Manufacturing Company.

Assume that over a period of years it is reasonable to expect output to vary from 60 to 100% of capacity, with an occasional year at each extreme and most years in between. To simplify the topic, consider only two extreme years, one with output at 60% of capacity and the other with output at 100%. To simplify matters further, assume that 6,000 units of product will be made in the 60% year and 10,000 in the 100% year. Exhibits 14-3 and 14-5 show the respective annual charges to IME as $465,000 and $575,000. Nevertheless, although these two figures are the expected charges *during* the respective years, the figures do not reflect the respective responsibilities of the 2 years for the various indirect expenses. Part of the $465,000 in the 60% year occurs because there are also 100% years.

Some "fixed" expenses charged in the year when 6,000 units are produced can be viewed as costs occurring because sufficient capacity has been provided to make 10,000 units a year rather than 6,000. Such expenses include part of the depreciation charge and part of the property taxes and insurance. Other "fixed" expenses charged during the 6,000-unit year are attributable to the prospect that soon production will again be at a higher level; these expenses would doubtless be eliminated if the XYZ Company management should forecast that production would continue at or below the 6,000-unit level. Such expenses include portions of the fixed elements in the costs of certain personal services as well as the labor extras (social security, paid vacations, etc.) that accompany these services; conceivably this class of expense might also include some of the rent and maintenance costs.

To simplify the example still further, assume that a 6,000-unit year is followed by a 10,000-unit year. Then consider the question of whether it is better to use a 155% burden rate in the first year and a 115% rate in the second or to use a 130% rate for both years. In this special case, the 130% rate can be computed by dividing the total estimated IME for the 2 years ($465,000 + $575,000 = $1,040,000) by the total direct-labor cost for the 2 years ($300,000 + $500,000 = $800,000). In effect, the use of the 130% rate for both years recognizes that 2 years is a more appropriate unit than 1 year for this particular accounting purpose. In general, the use of a normal burden rate contemplates an even longer time unit than 2 years. Some writers on the subject suggest that the time period assumed in setting a normal rate consists of the number of years included in a business cycle.

In this book we have stressed sales policy determination and cost control as two important objectives of cost accounting. In certain respects, these objectives are better served by burden rates based on normal output than by burden rates that vary with each year's expected output.

Consider the matter of sales policy with respect to the specific case of the XYZ Company. If this company uses a 155% burden rate in a 6,000-unit year and a 115% rate in a 10,000-unit year, and if the unit costs based on these rates influence the setting of selling prices, the product will be priced higher in the 6,000-unit year than in the 10,000-unit year. It is probable that such pricing will turn out to be extremely unrealistic. Presumably the year in which the estimated output is 6,000 units is a year of business recession; if so, it is likely that a price increase (based on a 155% burden rate) will be impracticable without a large loss in sales. Presumably the year in which the estimated output is 10,000 units is a year of business prosperity; if so, it is likely that the full capacity output can be sold without lowering prices to a level based on a 115% burden rate. Generally speaking, it is sound sales policy to charge higher prices in periods of business prosperity than in periods of recession. A cost system that seems to give contrary advice is not—in that respect—a helpful guide to sales policy decisions.

DIVIDING BURDEN VARIANCE INTO BUDGET VARIANCE AND CAPACITY VARIANCE. The use of a burden rate based on normal output makes possible an analysis of burden variance that is helpful from the point of view of effective cost control.

A good way to control indirect manufacturing expense is by means of a *variable budget* (sometimes referred to as a *flexible budget*). Exhibit 14-3 illustrated the type of estimates required for such a budget. The budgeted amount for each account can be expressed as a function of output by an appropriate equation. This was illustrated by the equation $s = \$26{,}800 + 0.12x$ that we developed for service-employees expense. The budgeted total IME is also expressed by an equation, illustrated by our $y = \$300{,}000 + 0.55x$.

When a variable budget based on such an equation has been established and when the burden rate is based on normal output, it is appropriate to divide the burden variance into two components: One component is the difference between the actual IME and the budgeted figure determined from the equation. This component is described as the *budget variance* or *controllable variance.* The other component is the difference between the budgeted IME and the amount of IME charged into the product. This is described as the *capacity variance* or *volume variance.* The budget variance is a measure of the effectiveness of the cost control of indirect expenses. The capacity variance can be viewed as attributable to the difference between actual output and normal output.

The difference between this two-variance method and the conventional one-variance method that was illustrated in Chaps. 10 and 11 is shown in T-account form as follows:

One variance:

Burden Variance

Actual IME	IME charged to product at predetermined rate

Two variance:

Burden Budget Variance			**Burden Capacity Variance**	
Actual IME	**Budgeted IME**		**Budgeted IME**	**IME charged to product at predetermined rate based on normal output**

The following numerical illustration assumes that the XYZ Manufacturing Company, using a normal burden rate of 130% of direct-labor cost, actually has $440,000 of direct-labor cost and $545,700 of IME. The entries affecting the burden variance accounts are shown in journal form as follows:

	Debit	Credit
Work in Process	$572,000	
Burden Capacity Variance		$572,000
To charge product with burden at established rate of 130% of direct-labor cost		
Burden Budget Variance	545,700	
Indirect Manufacturing Expense Control		545,700
To close the actual IME into the appropriate variance account		
Burden Capacity Variance	542,000	
Burden Budget Variance		542,000
To enter the budgeted figure for burden based on the budget equation $y = \$300{,}000 + 0.55x$		

The two variance accounts are shown in T-account form as follows:

Burden Budget Variance			Burden Capacity Variance	
545,700	542,000		542,000	572,000

If only one burden variance account had been used, it would have had a credit balance of $26,300, the difference between the $572,000 charged to the product and the actual expense of $545,700. A superficial conclusion might possibly have been that because credit variances are generally viewed favorably by management, this large credit variance reflects good performance in the cost control of indirect manufacturing expense.

The two-variance method permits a more sophisticated view of an overabsorbed or underabsorbed burden. The total credit balance (overabsorbed burden) of $26,300 is now broken down into a $30,000 credit balance in capacity variance and a $3,700 debit balance in budget variance. The $30,000 figure was the credit balance anticipated with operation at 88% of capacity. The budget variance balance is now recognized as a measure of the effectiveness of cost control of this particular class of expenses. In this case, the debit variance shows that the XYZ Company has failed by $3,700 to meet the objective that it had set up in its IME variable budget.

FURTHER COMMENTS ON THE NORMAL BURDEN RATE AND THE VARIABLE BUDGET FOR INDIRECT MANUFACTURING EXPENSE. For simplicity in presentation, the foregoing discussion has assumed a single plant-wide burden rate and has used direct-labor cost as both the burden vehicle and the measure of output. The points made are, of course, valid where burden is applied by cost centers rather than on a plant-wide basis. They also are valid for any burden vehicle and for any measure of output.

The example of estimates for a variable budget was simplified by using annual figures and avoiding consideration of month-to-month fluctuations. It should be recognized that, when costs are controlled by means of such a budget, the comparison of actual expense with budgeted expense should take place at frequent intervals, perhaps monthly or sometimes even weekly. In making such frequent checks of a variable budget, it is necessary to devise procedures that take account of the seasonal patterns of fluctuation in certain indirect expenses (e.g., light, heat, maintenance, paid vacations).

Sometimes, even though a manufacturer recognizes the advantages of basing his burden rate on normal output, the normal rate will not be used because of the difficulties in deciding what level of output shall be selected as normal. Sometimes, also, it may be difficult to adhere to the normal burden rate concept once the concept has been adopted. In principle, the normal output is the average output anticipated over a period of years long enough to cover the expected cyclical fluctuations. Occasionally, this period of years may be so long that it is hard to stick to an accounting procedure based on a belief in the inevitability of substantial fluctuations in output. Even the feast-or-famine industries may once in a while have a long feast or a long famine. For example, many manufacturers had a long period of fractional capacity operation during the depression years of the 1930s and a long period of full-capacity operation during World War II and the years immediately following.

DISPOSITION OF THE BALANCES IN BURDEN VARIANCE ACCOUNTS. The discussion in Chap. 10 of the disposal of burden variance balances pointed out that a common practice is to carry variance balances through to the end of the fiscal year rather than close them out at the end of each quarter or month. This topic now is considered with reference to burden rates based on expected output and burden rates based on normal output.

First, consider the case where the burden rate for each year is based on the expected output for that year and therefore aims at a zero balance in the Burden Variance account at year end. Even though this aim is realized, there are bound to be debit or credit balances in the variance account from month to month throughout the year. These balances will be caused, in part, by seasonal and irregular fluctuations in the various indirect expenses. Fluctuations in level of output throughout the year will be another cause of intermediate debit or credit variances. However, if the estimates used in setting the burden rate turn out to have been reasonably accurate, the net variance for the year will be relatively small. At the end of the year, this overabsorbed or underabsorbed burden will be closed into Profit and Loss Summary (or into Cost of Goods Sold).

In contrast, where a normal burden rate is used, a substantial year-end balance in Burden Capacity Variance often can be expected, even though the aim is to have a zero balance in Burden Budget Variance. Here, also, it is desirable to put off the closing out of variance account balances until the end of the year. However, the interpretation of an overabsorbed or underabsorbed capacity variance at year end calls for special comment.

Because the normal burden rate aims at a net Burden Capacity Variance of zero over a number of years rather than over a single year, it might seem appropriate to carry a balance in this particular account forward from year to year. But considerations related to income taxes and other legal matters make it advisable to close out all variance balances in the formal books of account at the end of each fiscal year, even though a statistical record that is separate from the books may be kept, showing the net variance balance over a period of years.

When the capacity variance balance is closed out each year, it is appropriate to close this particular account directly into Profit and Loss Summary (rather than through Cost of Goods Sold). When production has been above normal capacity, the resulting credit variance can be viewed as an element of profit caused by above normal operations. When production has been below normal capacity, the resulting debit variance can be viewed as a decrease in profit (or increase in loss) caused by below-normal operations.

TREATMENT OF BURDEN VARIANCE IN THE FINANCIAL STATEMENTS. The use of predetermined burden rates and variance accounts is generally viewed as an internal matter that is not of direct interest to the stockholders and creditors. Burden variances, therefore, are not mentioned in annual or quarterly statements for external release.

If a variance for the period is closed to Profit and Loss Summary in the ledger, it will be reflected in the income statement for the period. Although the variance would be reported to management, it would not appear as a separate item in an income statement going outside the organization.

If a variance account balance is carried forward in the ledger from one month or quarter to the next, it may appear on a balance sheet for internal use as a deferred charge or deferred credit. However, for the purpose of quarterly statements prepared for external distribution, such a variance balance either would be treated as a miscellaneous item (the amount integrated with other amounts) or would be adjusted into the profit or loss for the period.

PERIODIC REVISION OF BURDEN RATES. As already pointed out, a burden rate is a fraction. The numerator of the fraction is estimated indirect manufacturing expense at some stipulated output; the denominator is some burden vehicle such as direct-labor cost, direct-labor hours, machine hours, or units of product, at the same stipulated output. Because the circumstances affecting both the numerator and denominator are subject to change, burden rates should be reviewed at regular intervals and revised whenever necessary.

Sometimes an event may occur that obviously calls for an immediate revision of all burden rates. A good example of such an event is a new union contract. Such a contract might call for higher hourly wages (for both direct and indirect labor) and for increased fringe benefits (such as contributions to a special fund for unemployment benefits). The higher wage rates for indirect labor and the new fringe benefits will increase the numerator in the burden calculation. If direct-labor cost is the burden vehicle, the higher wage rate will also increase the denominator. If burden is applied by cost centers, it is conceivable that the new union contract might increase burden rates in some cost centers and decrease them in others, depending on the influence of the contract on the respective numerators and denominators.

An undesirable consequence of revising a burden rate is the discontinuity created in unit costs and other accounting figures affected by the burden rate. This is particularly undesirable with respect to cost figures that are compared from one period to another.

SUMMARY. Some of the important points of this chapter can be restated as follows:

1. Indirect manufacturing expenses are often referred to as IME, burden, or overhead.
2. In contrast to direct manufacturing costs, which can be identified with particular jobs, processes, or products, the best that can be done for indirect costs is to apportion them according to systematic rules.
3. The rates at which burden is to be applied are nearly always established before the start of an accounting period rather than at the end

of the period. In most instances, a full year is the shortest period for which it is appropriate to predetermine the burden rates. The predetermination of a burden rate makes it necessary to use a burden variance account to keep track of the difference between the actual indirect expenses and the amount of indirect expense charged to the product.

4. Except in the simplest manufacturing operations, it is desirable to apportion each indirect manufacturing expense among cost centers according to some basis that seems reasonable for the particular expense. Separate burden rates are then applied in each cost center, based on the total of the indirect expenses apportioned to the center.
5. The actual charging of burden to product must be in proportion to something measurable about jobs or processes, usually direct-labor cost, direct-labor hours, or machine hours.
6. Although some elements in indirect manufacturing expense tend to vary in direct proportion to output, other indirect costs are fixed in the sense that they are unchanged by substantial changes in output. This fixed element in indirect manufacturing expense is the cause of a number of business problems and is a complicating factor in cost accounting.
7. If burden rates are based on the expected output for the coming year, the fixed costs will cause the burden rates to be relatively high for a low expected output and relatively low for a high expected output. There are a number of advantages in basing burden rates on so-called normal output, defined as the average level of output expected over a period of years.
8. The variable budget for indirect manufacturing expense is a useful device for cost control. Where burden rates are based on normal output and a variable budget is used, an underabsorbed or overabsorbed burden can be broken down into two parts: One part, called *budget variance,* is caused by departures from the variable budget. The other part, called *capacity variance,* is caused by the difference between actual output and normal capacity.

DISCUSSION QUESTIONS

14-A. What are some of the names applied to indirect manufacturing expense? Which of these do you prefer? Why?

14-B. Why are burden rates nearly always predetermined? Can you think of any circumstances where you would consider it satisfactory to use a historical burden rate?

14-C. The packaging of finished product for shipment is treated as a manufacturing cost in some accounting systems and as a distribution cost in others. Describe some circumstances in which you think each treatment would be appropriate. Why could it make any difference whether this cost is classified as a manufacturing or a distribution cost?

14-D. Examine in turn each of the account titles in Exhibit 14-1. Which of these expenses seem likely to be fixed in the sense that they will be the same when output is at two-thirds capacity and at full capacity? Which expenses seem likely to have substantial fixed elements even though the expenses will vary to some extent with output?

14-E. There are some classes of manufacturing costs that sometimes are treated as direct costs even though they usually are treated as indirect. Examine the classification of IME accounts in Exhibit 14-1 to identify any types of costs that might conceivably be treated as direct. Discuss the criteria to govern the decision whether each should be treated in the accounts as a direct or an indirect cost.

14-F. What advantages can you see in using cost centers to apportion indirect manufacturing expense? What disadvantages?

14-G. Exhibit 14-2 shows two nominal cost centers. Can you think of any other nominal cost centers that might be appropriate in some circumstances? What is the purpose of using nominal cost centers?

14-H. Exhibit 14-2 shows four service cost centers. Can you think of any other types of service cost centers that might be appropriate in some circumstances? Why is it usually desirable to use service cost centers in apportioning IME among productive cost centers?

14-J. In discussing productive cost centers, the text states that "although a department can be broken down into two or more cost centers, it usually is undesirable for a cost center to include two or more departments that are under the supervision of different persons." Why? What considerations ought to enter into the decision about the productive cost centers that are to be used?

14-K. For each of the IME accounts listed in Exhibit 14-1, discuss the criteria that seem to you to be appropriate for apportioning costs among cost centers.

14-L. Often the choice of a burden vehicle lies between direct-labor cost and direct-labor hours. Under what circumstances is direct-labor cost likely to be preferable? Under what circumstances will it be better to choose direct-labor hours as the burden vehicle?

14-M. Under what circumstances is it desirable to charge burden in proportion to machine hours? What conditions are necessary for a machine-hour rate to be practicable?

14-N. What objections are usually raised to the use of direct-material cost or prime cost as burden vehicles?

14-P. Exhibit 14-3 assumes that 100% capacity is the plant capacity at single-shift 40-hour-per-week operation. This type of operation was implied in the division of the XYZ Company's total manufacturing overhead into fixed cost of $300,000 and variable cost of 55 cents per dollar of direct labor.

Suppose it became necessary to increase output to 120% of capacity and that this increase was obtained by operating a single shift 48 hours per week. Discuss how you would expect the fixed and variable elements of IME to be influenced by this change. Would it be reasonable to extend the straight line shown in Exhibit 14-4?

Suppose it became necessary to increase output to 150% of capacity and that this increase was obtained by adding a second shift with both shifts operating 40 hours per week. Discuss how you would expect the fixed and variable elements of IME to be influenced by this change. Would it be reasonable to extend the straight line shown in Exhibit 14-4?

To what extent, if at all, would the accounting treatment of overtime premiums and shift bonuses influence your answers to the foregoing questions?

14-Q. To establish the burden rate and the variable IME budget for a certain department, the following estimates were developed by an analysis of the behavior of the various indirect expenses in relation to direct-labor cost.

Estimated total annual IME.	$216,000
Estimated annual direct-labor cost.	$120,000

$$\text{Monthly IME budget} = \frac{\$216{,}000}{12} + (0.80)\left(\text{actual DL\$} - \frac{120{,}000}{12}\right)$$

In a subsequent month, the actual IME was $17,000 and the actual direct-labor cost was $8,000. Compute the total burden variance, the burden capacity variance, and the burden budget variance.

14-R. For the case defined in question 14-Q, draw a graph showing burden applied to work in process and the variable IME budget, both in relation to direct-labor cost. Draw vertical lines for the normal monthly direct-labor cost ($10,000) and for the actual direct-labor cost ($8,000); draw horizontal lines for normal monthly IME ($18,000) and for the actual IME ($17,000). Label the line segment representing the burden budget variance and the one representing the burden capacity variance.

14-S. Answer question 14-Q for a subsequent month in which actual IME was $20,000 and actual direct-labor cost was $12,000.

14-T. Even though the text did not include a numerical example, it is common for a burden budget variance to be computed at frequent intervals, for example, monthly. The seasonal variation of certain indirect expenses (such as heat and paid vacations) will obviously be responsible for certain difficulties in computing and interpreting monthly figures for budget variance. Discuss these difficulties, and suggest possible actions to circumvent them.

14-U. What advantages can you see in basing burden rates on normal output? On expected actual output? If rates are to be based on normal output, how would you suggest that normal output be determined?

14-V. The trend of the times seems to be toward more and more automation in industry. In what respects do you think the automatic factory will differ from other factories with regard to the various matters discussed in this chapter?

14-W. In a merchandising business, expenditures for electric light for the store are viewed as causing a decrease in ownership. In a manufacturing business, expenditures for electric light for the factory are viewed as causing an increase in an asset. Explain.

14-X. Consider the following two schemes for disposition of the balance in the Burden Variance account at the end of the fiscal year: (1) close it to Cost of Goods Manufactured, (2) close it to Cost of Goods Sold. As far as the balance sheet and income statement are concerned, might it make a difference which plan is followed? If so, why?

PROBLEMS

Problem 14-1. Prepare the indirect manufacturing expense distribution sheet for the Rapid City Furniture Company. The purpose of this sheet is to apportion the estimated indirect expenses for the coming year among four producing departments, namely: (1) woodworking, (2) finishing, (3) upholstery, and (4) assembly. The apportionment makes it possible to calculate the predetermined burden rates to be used in these departments. The distribution sheet also involves two service departments, (5) power plant and (6) maintenance, the costs of which are finally to be apportioned among the producing departments.

Some of the relevant facts about the departments are as follows:

	Total	(1) Wood-working	(2) Finish-ing	(3) Uphol-stery	(4) Assem-bly	(5) Power Plant	(6) Mainte-nance
Foremen	$ 30,600	$ 9,000	$ 3,600	$ 3,600	$ 4,800	$ 4,800	$ 4,800
Inspectors	14,800	6,000	2,400	2,400	4,000		
Departmental clerical	13,600	6,000	2,000	2,000	2,000	....	1,600
Departmental service	39,600	8,000	2,000	1,600	8,000	12,000	8,000
Total indirect labor	$ 98,600	$29,000	$10,000	$ 9,600	$18,800	$16,800	$14,400
Direct labor	134,400	68,000	14,200	21,800	30,400		
Total dept. payroll	$233,000	$97,000	$24,200	$31,400	$49,200	$16,800	$14,400
Proportion of total floor space, %		42	11	10	21	10	6
Proportion of total investment in machinery and equipment, %		55½	7½	7	10	16	4
Proportion of kilowatthours used, %		64	10	12	7	....	7

Rule a sheet in which the following indirect manufacturing expense accounts are listed in the left-hand column. This should be followed by a column for total cost and columns for each of the six departments. The estimated indirect manufacturing expenses and the rules for the distribution of each expense are given in the following statements. All estimates and distributions should be made only to the nearest $100.

101, General Supervision, $12,000. This should be distributed in proportion to direct labor cost.

102–105, Departmental Indirect Labor: 102, Foreman; 103, Inspectors; 104, Departmental Clerical Labor; and 105, Departmental Service Labor, are all estimated above. The total indirect labor for each department can be copied directly to the IME distribution sheet.

106, General Clerical Labor, $14,000, and 107, General Service Labor, $18,400, are distributed in proportion to total department payroll.

110, Payroll Tax Expense, will be 6½% of the total factory payroll (which includes the general supervision, general clerical labor, and general service labor as well as the departmental totals given in the table above). This total payroll tax expense is to be distributed to the six departments on the basis of total departmental payroll given in the table.

111, Compensation Insurance, is estimated by applying the insurance company's premium rates to the estimated earnings broken down by risk groups. The total estimated in this way is $6,500; the distribution by departments is $3,100 for woodworking, $600 for finishing, $700 for upholstery, $1,100 for assembly, $500 for power plant, and $500 for maintenance.

112, Overtime Allowance, is estimated as 4.4% of direct-labor cost in woodworking, 2.1% of direct labor in varnishing, 2.7% of direct labor in upholstery, 2.6% of direct labor in assembly, and 5% of departmental service labor in the maintenance department.

120, Nondurable Tools, is estimated on the basis of past experience: $1,000 for woodworking, $600 for finishing, $300 for upholstery, $200 for assembly, and $100 for maintenance, a total of $2,200.

121, Shop Supplies and Materials, is estimated at $900 for woodworking, $1,600 for finishing, $1,400 for upholstery, $300 for assembly, $6,000 for power plant, and $300 for maintenance, a total of $10,500.

122, Shop Losses, is estimated as 4% of direct-labor cost in woodworking and 2% in the other three direct departments.

123, Office Supplies and Expense, $3,600. This is to be distributed among the four direct departments in proportion to total department payroll. (The total of the departmental payrolls for the four direct departments is $201,800.)

130–132, Machinery and Equipment Expenses: 130, Taxes—Machinery and Equipment, $4,000; 131, Depreciation—Machinery and Equipment, $8,000; 132 Fire Insurance—Machinery and Equipment, $1,000. These expenses are to be distributed in proportion to the value of machinery and equipment in the six departments.

140–142, Building Expenses: 140, Taxes—Building, $5,400; Depreciation—Building, $3,000; Fire Insurance—Building, $1,600. These expenses are to be distributed among the six departments in proportion to floor space occupied.

Total the expenses allotted to the power plant. Thirty-nine per cent of this total is considered to be the cost of heat and is allocated among the other five departments in proportion to the floor space they occupy. The other 61%

is considered to be light and power expense and is allocated in proportion to the estimated kilowatthour consumption in the other departments.

Total the expenses allotted to maintenance. This total should be distributed 70% to woodworking, 12.3% to finishing, 7.7% to upholstery, and 10% to assembly. These percentages are based on an analysis of the services performed by maintenance for the four direct departments.

Total the expenses allotted to the four direct departments. Find the burden rate for each. In the woodworking department, because the higher priced men use the less expensive machines and vice versa, the burden rate is to be based on direct-labor hours. It is estimated this department will use 25,000 direct-labor hours during the year. In the other departments, the burden vehicle is direct-labor cost. Compute rates to the nearest cent per hour in woodworking and to the nearest per cent in the other three direct departments.

Problem 14-2. This problem provides a review of job-order cost accounting, illustrating the use of subsidiary ledgers in connection with the cost accounts. It also illustrates the application of burden by cost centers.

Set up the following T accounts to represent the general ledger of the Miracle Manufacturing Company:

Cash
Accounts Receivable
Raw Materials
Work in Process
Finished Goods
Land
Plant and Equipment
Accumulated Depreciation—
  Plant and Equipment
Accounts Payable
Capital Stock
Earned Surplus
Profit and Loss Summary
Sales
Cost of Sales
Selling Expense
Administrative Expense
Repair and Maintenance
Factory Office Expense
Heat, Light, and Power
Factory Taxes
Operating Supplies
Depreciation Expense
Direct Labor
Indirect Labor
Factory Supervision
Burden Variance

A stores ledger is controlled by the Raw Materials account in the general ledger. To represent it, set up accounts for Material X, Material Y, and Material Z.

A job ledger is controlled by the Work in Process account in the general ledger. To represent it, set up accounts for job orders 54 to 60, both inclusive.

A stock ledger is controlled by the Finished Goods account in the general ledger. To represent it, set up accounts for the following finished goods: Product A, Product B, and Product C.

Calculation of Predetermined Burden Rate. Before the start of each year, the burden rates are predetermined on the basis of the expected operations in each department for the coming year. To do this, the estimated indirect manufacturing expenses for the year are apportioned between the two productive cost centers, departments S and T, each on some basis that appears to be reasonable.

These estimates for the coming year are as follows:

Repairs and maintenance	$ 18,000
Heat and light	17,000
Power	25,000
Factory taxes	26,400
Operating supplies	47,200
Indirect labor	78,400
Factory supervision	40,000
Depreciation	30,000
Factory office expense	24,000
Total	$306,000

These should first be apportioned among three headings, Building Expense (a nominal-cost center), Department S, and Department T, as follows:

Repairs to Equipment two-thirds to S and one-third to T on the basis of the distribution of past repair costs.

Heat and light is all building expense.

Power 56% to S and 44% to T on the basis of the rated horsepower of the machines in the two departments.

$12,000 of Factory Taxes is building expense. The remainder is apportioned two-thirds to S and one-third to T on the basis of the investment in the machines in the two departments.

Operating Supplies $28,800 to S and $18,400 to T on the basis of past experience of their use in the two departments.

Indirect Labor $37,700 to S and $40,700 to T on the basis of the estimated indirect-labor payroll in the two departments.

Factory Supervision in proportion to the estimated direct-labor cost in the two departments. Direct labor is estimated as $120,000 for department S and $180,000 for department T.

$8,400 of Depreciation is building expense. The balance is apportioned two-thirds to S and one-third to T on the basis of the investment in depreciable assets in the two departments.

Office and Clerical Expense is distributed 45% to S and 55% to T.

Now total the building expense, and divide the total between departments S and T on the basis of the floor space occupied, 50% to department S and 50% to department T.

The burden vehicle is direct-labor cost. The total estimated indirect manufacturing expense apportioned to department S should be divided by the estimated direct-labor cost for S (given above) to compute the predetermined burden rate to be used in S during the year. A similar calculation should be made for T.

Entry of Opening Balances. Following are the account balances on January 1, 19____.

A. Enter the opening balances in their respective accounts in the general ledger.

Account	Subsidiary ledger (debit)	General ledger	
		Debit	Credit
Cash		$ 40,000	
Accounts Receivable		210,000	
Raw Materials:		65,000	
Material X (10,000 at $1)	$10,000		
Material Y (5,000 at $3)	15,000		
Material Z (4,000 at $10)	40,000		
Work in Process:		32,000	
Job order 54 (to make 200 B)	20,000		
Job order 55 (to make 500 C)	12,000		
Finished Goods:		71,000	
Product A (90 at $300)	27,000		
Product B (200 at $160)	32,000		
Product C (300 at $40)	12,000		
Land		75,000	
Plant and Equipment		500,000	
Accumulated Depreciation—Plant and Equip.			$180,000
Accounts Payable			190,000
Capital Stock			400,000
Earned Surplus			223,000
Totals		$993,000	$993,000

Entries in Factory Subsidiary Ledger. The following information relates to manufacturing operations that require entries in the stores ledger, job ledger, and stock ledger.

a. Enter the opening balances in the subsidiary ledger accounts.

b. In the job ledger, set up cost sheets for the following job orders that were started during January:

Job order 56 (to make 100 A)
Job order 57 (to make 120 B)
Job order 58 (to make 400 C)
Job order 59 (to make 200 B)
Job order 60 (to make 200 A)

c. In the stores ledger, enter the following materials received:

Material X, 15,000 at $1 = $15,000
Material Y, 6,000 at $3 = $18,000

d. Compute costs for the following storeroom requisitions, and make the necessary entries in the stores ledger and job ledger.

Storeroom requisition	To job order	Quantity of material issued		
		Material X	Material Y	Material Z
667	56	......	1,100	800
678	57	1,000	.....	110
679	54	4,200	.....	200
680	55	2,400	1,000	
681	57	3,000		
682	58	200	1,000	
683	59	1,000		
684	60	......	2,000	100
Totals.....	...	11,800	5,100	1,210

e. Compute costs for the following storeroom credits (for materials returned to the stores department from various jobs), and make the necessary entries in the stores ledger and job ledger:

Storeroom credit No.	From job order No.	Materials returned
87	56	100 Y
88	57	10 Z
89	54	200 X

f. The payroll analysis sheet prepared from workmen's time cards showed the direct-labor costs during the month to be distributed among the various jobs as follows (this serves as a basis for entries to the job ledger):

Job order	Department S	Department T	Total
54	....	$ 4,000	$ 4,000
55	....	2,000	2,000
56	$ 8,000	....	8,000
57	4,000	3,000	7,000
58	....	5,000	5,000
59	....	3,000	3,000
60	1,000	....	1,000
Totals.....	$13,000	$17,000	$30,000

g. Burden for January should be charged to all jobs at the predetermined rates.

h. Job Orders 54, 55, 56, and 57 are completed during January. These jobs should be closed out in the job ledger and the necessary entries made in the stock ledger.

Entries in General Ledger for External Transactions. The summary totals from the following columnar books of original entry should be posted to the general ledger to reflect the external transactions that took place during January.

B. The cash receipts journal shows the following totals:

Cash—debit	$144,000
Accounts Receivable—credit	144,000

C. The cash disbursements journal shows the following totals:

Accounts Payable—debit	$146,000
Cash—credit	146,000

D. The voucher register shows the following totals:

Raw Materials—debit	$ 33,000
Repairs and Maintenance—debit	2,000
Heat, Light, and Power—debit	4,500
Factory Taxes—debit	2,200
Direct Labor—debit	30,000
Indirect Labor—debit	8,000
Factory Supervision—debit	3,300
Operating Supplies—debit	5,000
Factory Office Expense—debit	2,600
Selling Expense—debit	14,000
Administrative Expense—debit	7,000
Accounts Payable—credit	111,600

Entries for Sales and Cost of Sales. The sales journal shows sales totals by products as follows. All sales were on credit.

Product A: 140 @ $350	$ 49,000
Product B: 300 @ $200	60,000
Product C: 400 @ $ 50	20,000
Total sales	$129,000

E. Make the appropriate entry for total sales.

F. Determine from the stock ledger the appropriate figures for cost of sales for each of the three products and the total. Use the first-in first-out rule. Make an entry in the general ledger for the cost of sales. Also make the necessary entries in the stock ledger.

Entries in General Ledger Summarizing Internal Factory Operations. Summary entries are now required in the general ledger for internal operations that already have been recorded in the factory subsidiary ledger, as follows:

G. To record the total material issues for January

H. To record the total materials returned to stores in January

J. To charge burden to Work in Process

K. To transfer the total manufacturing cost of job orders completed during January from Work in Process to Finished Goods.

Adjusting and Closing Entries. Make the following adjusting and closing entries in the general ledger:

L. To record depreciation on plant and equipment for January, $2,500.

M. To record dividend declared January 15 (payable Feb. 15), $4,000.

N. To close the indirect manufacturing expense accounts into Burden Variance.

P. To close income and expense accounts into Profit and Loss Summary and to close Profit and Loss Summary into Earned Surplus. The burden variance is to be carried forward; this account is closed only at the end of each year.

Trial Balances. Take a post-closing trial balance of the general ledger. Also take trial balances of the stores ledger, job ledger, and stock ledger, and check them against the figures in their respective controlling accounts in the general ledger.

Financial Statements. Prepare a balance sheet as of January 31 and a profit and loss statement for January. On the balance sheet incorporate the burden variance into earned surplus. Also prepare a statement of earned surplus. In this statement show the variance as a separate item.

Problem 14-3. The Plastics Products Company uses a job cost system in which burden is applied by cost centers. In the table below you are given the estimates necessary for computing the burden rates for each of the four cost centers. These estimates are for the year. For each cost center calculate the "estimated normal hours," assuming one 8-hour shift per day per "unit" (machine or employee) and 305 scheduled working days per year. Normal hours is the number of scheduled hours multiplied by the "estimated per cent utilization" given in the table for each cost center. Next calculate the fixed, variable, and total burden rates for each cost center (to the nearest whole cent).

Cost center		Burden vehicle	Estimated normal IME budget for the year			No. of units	Estimated utilization
No.	Name		Fixed	Variable	Total		
1-1	Compression	Machine hr	3,590	3,925	7,515	2	70%
1-2	Injection	Machine hr	22,250	26,050	48,300	8	75%
Dept. 1	Totals		25,840	29,975	55,815		
2-1	Cleanup	DL hr	9,760	21,470	31,230	20	80%
2-2	Assembly	DL hr	9,370	24,990	34,360	16	80%
Dept. 2	Totals		19,130	46,460	65,590		

The balance of the problem consists of analyzing the factory burden variance for one monthly accounting period.

Assume that the rates developed above were used during the month of March to apply burden to the various jobs in process. At the end of the month the actual machine or direct labor hours used (charged to jobs) during the month have been determined from time-keeping records for each cost center as follows.

Cost center	1-1	1-2	2-1	2-2
Actual hours	200	1,000	2,500	2,800

Also the accounting department has arrived at the total actual IME chargeable to each of the two departments for March in accordance with the company's established accounting practice: department 1, $4,000; department 2, $5,400.

A. For each of the two departments compute the burden applied to jobs: fixed, variable, and total.
B. What is the total burden variance for the factory for March?
C. Assume that 25 scheduled working days occur in March, and therefore the normal hours for each cost center for March should be computed as (25/305) × (normal hours per year). An alternative calculation is: Normal hours for March = (25 days) · (8 hours) · (No. of units) · (% utilization). Compute the normal fixed IME budget for each production center for March by multiplying the normal hours by the fixed burden rate, and determine the departmental totals.
D. Compute the total IME budget for March for each of the two departments by adding the variable portion calculated in A to the fixed component found in C.
E. Determine the burden budget variance and the burden capacity variance for each department and the totals for the factory. Check your results against your answer to question B.
F. Show numerically that burden capacity variance can be calculated two other ways: by the differences between normal hours and actual hours multiplied by the fixed burden rates and as the difference between the normal fixed IME budget and the fixed burden applied to jobs.

Problem 14-4. In the job cost system of the Dai Diecasting Co., the IME is applied to jobs through two cost centers, department A and department B, by means of predetermined burden rates. A variable IME budget is employed for each department to permit analysis of the burden variance into budget and capacity variances. The accounting period is a calendar quarter.

The burden rates for the two departments were established using estimates of total IME and direct-labor cost for the year 1963 as follows:

Department	Estimates for coming year, 1963		Burden rate, % of DL$
	IME	DL$	
A	$ 70,000	$28,000	250%
B	90,000	60,000	150%
Totals	$160,000	$88,000	

By analysis of historical data about the variation, from quarter to quarter, of the various components of IME in relation to direct-labor cost, values have been established for r, the variable burden rate, as follows:

For department A: r = 100% of DL$
For department B: r = 60% of DL$

Because of seasonal and calendar variations, the level of production activity is expected to vary from quarter to quarter. Therefore, the IME budget for each department for a given quarter is determined by a variable budget calculation, using the estimate of IME and direct-labor cost for the year together with the variable burden rates mentioned above. The formula is as follows:

$$Y = Y_n + (X_a - X_n)(r)$$

where Y_n is one-quarter of the estimated normal IME for the year, X_n is one-quarter of the estimated normal direct-labor cost for the year, X_a is the actual direct-labor cost for the quarter, and r is the variable burden rate for the department. For the year 1963, the budgets for a given quarter would be arrived at as follows:

$$\text{For department A: } Y = \frac{70{,}000}{4} + \left(X_a - \frac{28{,}000}{4}\right)(1.00)$$

$$\text{For department B: } Y = \frac{90{,}000}{4} + \left(X_a - \frac{60{,}000}{4}\right)(.60)$$

For the first quarter of 1963, assume that actual IME and direct-labor costs were as follows:

Department	IME	DL$
A	$16,200	$ 6,000
B	22,300	13,000
Totals	$38,500	$19,000

A. Calculate the *total* burden variance for each of the two departments A and B and the total for the factory as a whole.
B. Set up T accounts as follows to represent a portion of the general ledger, and show the end-of-quarter balance of $38,500 in the IME account.

Indirect Manufacturing Expense	Burden Budget Variance—A
Work in Process—Department A	Burden Budget Variance—B
Work in Process—Department B	Burden Capacity Variance—A
	Burden Capacity Variance—B

Make appropriate entries in these accounts and derive the balance in each of the variance accounts. Check your results against your answers to A.

Problem 14-5. The problem is a continuation of problem 14-4 concerning the Dai Diecasting Company. The sales of this company are highly seasonal, and even with careful planning the production level will vary considerably with the seasons. Assume that the actual direct-labor costs turned out to be as follows for the four quarters of 1963:

Quarter	Actual direct-labor cost		
	Dept. A	Dept. B	Total
First	$ 6,000	$13,000	$19,000
Second	7,400	15,400	22,800
Third	8,800	18,500	27,300
Fourth	6,600	14,100	20,700
Totals	$28,800	$61,000	$89,800

A. What would be the burden capacity variance for the year for department A? For department B? For the factory as a whole? Identify each as a debit or credit variance.

B. For each of the two departments, calculate the burden capacity variance for each *quarter*. Indicate whether it is a debit or credit variance.

C. Assume that the total IME for the year was $73,900 for department A and $90,400 for department B, a total of $164,300 for the factory. Compute the burden budget variance for each of the two departments for the whole year. Use these results, together with the capacity variances calculated in A, to prepare a table showing an analysis of the total burden variance for the year as follows:

	Burden budget variance	Burden capacity variance	Total variance
Dept. A	______	______	______
Dept. B	______	______	______
Total	______	______	______

D. For this situation, explain briefly how you would interpret a burden capacity variance (1) for a certain quarter and (2) for a fiscal year.

Problem 14-6. The Mistrolite Process Company has three departments. Department D makes a compound, Misto, which is stored in bulk. Department E packages this compound for sale. Department F uses this compound with other materials to make special products to customers' specifications. Process costs are used in departments D and E; job-order costs are used in department F. Material inventories are carried at standard costs; actual quantities issued are charged into production at the standard unit price. The FIFO rule is used in charging Misto into production and in costing sales. A predetermined burden rate of 150% of direct-labor cost is used in all departments; this rate is based on normal output. All cost accounts are kept in the general ledger.

Set up a general ledger in T-account form with the following accounts:

Cash
Accounts Receivable
*Material A
*Material B
*Material C
*Bulk Misto
*Packaged Misto
Job 101
Job 102
Job 103
Prepaid Expenses
Plant and Machinery
Accumulated Depreciation—
Plant and Machinery
Accrued Liabilities
Department D—Work in Process
Department E—Work in Process
Direct Labor Cost
Indirect Manufacturing Expense
Selling and General Expense
Sales
Cost of Goods Sold
Material Price Variance
Burden Budget Variance
Burden Capacity Variance
Capital Stock
Earned Surplus
Profit and Loss Summary

* These T accounts should have columns for quantity, unit price, and total value.

There is no work in process in departments D or E either at the start or at the end of the month. Job 101 is in process in department F at the start of the month; job 103 is in process at the end of the month.

Make entries directly in the T accounts to record January operations, as follows:

A. Opening balances on January 1 were:

Account	Debit	Credit
Cash	$ 15,000	
Accounts Receivable	28,000	
Material A (2,000 at $2)	4,000	
Material B (1,500 at $3)	4,500	
Material C (2,500 at $1)	2,500	
Bulk Misto (22,000 lb at $0.40)	8,800	
Packaged Misto (1,000 packages at $6.50)	6,500	
Job 101	2,200	
Prepaid Expenses	1,200	
Plant and Machinery	100,000	
Accumulated Depreciation—Plant and Machinery		$ 22,000
Accounts Payable		17,000
Capital Stock		90,000
Earned Surplus		43,700
Totals	$155,700	$155,700

B. Incurred obligations as follows:

Direct labor wages	$6,000
Indirect factory labor wages and salaries	4,000
Social security taxes on factory labor	450
Rental of machine tools	1,050
Electric power for factory	900
Repairs to machinery	1,000
Other factory expenses	400
Advertising	1,100
Salesmen's commissions	2,100
General expenses	550
Purchase of 1,000 units of material A at $2.05 per unit	2,050
Total (credit to Accounts Payable)	$19,600

C. Material issues were 1,400 A to department D, 600 B to job 102, 350 B to job 103, and 1,000 C to department E.
D. Time cards showed that direct labor cost was divided as follows: $2,000 to department D; $800 to department E; $600 to job 101; $1,400 to job 102; $1,200 to job 103.
E. Burden was charged to the various departments and jobs as required.
F. In department D, 20,000 pounds of bulk Misto were produced during the month.
G. Issues of bulk Misto were 8,000 pounds to department E, 4,000 pounds to job 102, and 3,000 pounds to job 103.
H. In department E, 1,000 packages of packaged Misto were completed.
I. In department F, job 101 was completed and delivered to the customer, who was billed for the contract price, $4,500.
J. In department F, job 102 was completed and delivered to the customer, who was billed for its manufacturing cost plus 20%.
K. Other sales, all on credit, were 1,200 packages of Misto at $8.50 per package, $10,200.
L. Collections on accounts receivable were $24,000.
M. Cash disbursements against Accounts Payable totaled $21,000.

Continue the problem by making the necessary adjusting and closing entries directly in the T accounts, as follows:

a. Depreciation charged for January on plant and machinery is $450.
b. Of the $1,100 spent for advertising (entry B), $200 is applicable to February.
c. Of the prepaid insurance on plant and machinery in effect at the start of the month, $120 is applicable to January.
d. Accrued factory taxes for January are $150.
e. The monthly budget for indirect manufacturing expense is based on the following formula:

$$\text{IME budget} = \$7{,}500 + 0.60\ (\text{actual direct-labor cost} - \$5{,}000)$$

The predetermined burden rate of 150% was based on a normal production level for which the IME is expected to amount to $7,500 per month and the direct-labor cost is expected to be $5,000. The amount of IME is expected to vary from month to month as output varies, at the rate of 60% of the change in direct-labor cost. Make the necessary entries to determine the burden budget variance and the burden capacity variance.

f. Close the income and expense accounts into Profit and Loss Summary.
g. Close the variance accounts into Profit and Loss Summary.
h. Close Profit and Loss Summary into Earned Surplus.

Take a post-closing trial balance. Prepare an income statement for January. No balance sheet is required; submit the trial balance instead.

15/ STANDARD COSTS

This chapter starts with a brief discussion of the role of cost standards in the control of costs. It continues with an explanation of the use of predetermined standard material and labor costs as a basis for valuation of inventories in the accounts of a manufacturing concern. This is illustrated by a complete-cycle example. The new topic of variance accounts for direct-material and direct-labor costs is introduced in this example. The chapter concludes with a discussion of some different viewpoints regarding the setting of cost standards and with some comments about the use of cost variances as tools for cost control.

THE NEED FOR COST STANDARDS. In a sense, the subjects of cost reduction and cost control in manufacturing are so broad that they include practically all aspects of manufacturing technology and of managerial techniques. Nevertheless, cost accounting should be viewed as one of the most essential tools for cost control. If costs are to be controlled effectively, it is necessary that they be measured.

Moreover, for current measurements of cost to be useful to management, it is necessary to have a basis for judging whether the current costs reflect satisfactory performance. In other words, current cost figures must be compared with something.

In one sense of the word, any figure that is used to judge whether current costs are satisfactory could be referred to as a cost *standard.* The figure might be a cost estimate made before production started; it might be a past cost figure in the same manufacturing plant; it might be a past cost figure elsewhere; it might be a figure believed to represent good performance under favorable conditions.

So defined, a cost standard might conceivably be determined quite informally; perhaps the standard with which actual costs are to be compared might not even be set until after the actual costs have been measured. But cost control is much more likely to be effective if each element of cost is examined carefully and if cost standards are established in advance of production on the basis of a critical analysis. Where standards are predetermined in this way, they can be used to advantage as part of the accounting system. In most cases, the use of standard costs in the accounts has two major purposes, namely, to obtain better managerial control of manufacturing costs and to reduce accounting expense by simplifying the cost accounting.

EXAMPLES OF STANDARD COST CARDS. Exhibits 15-1 and 15-2 show representative tabulations of standard costs in a form suitable for accounting purposes and for use in cost control. Each of these standard cost cards shows costs within a single department and for a particular product. The product in Exhibit 15-1 is needed to make the product in Exhibit 15-2. For this reason, all the costs shown in detail on the first exhibit are shown again in total on the second exhibit as "transferred from other departments."

The analysis needed to prepare such standard cost cards requires separate consideration of direct-material quantities, direct-material prices, direct-labor time, direct-labor wage rates, and IME. For each required material, a standard quantity must be established. This standard should be the quantity of the particular material that is believed to be necessary to manufacture the particular product including any allowance for wastage that is deemed to be appropriate.

Standard material prices have already been discussed in Chap. 12. Where standard material quantities are used in the accounts for inventory valuation, it is essential also to use standard material prices. (In contrast, as pointed out in Chap. 12, where actual material quantities are used in the accounts, either actual or standard prices may be employed.)

Where direct labor is paid an hourly wage, the standard labor cost of each manufacturing operation is the product of the estimated time and the wage rate that is assumed to be applicable. It is obvious that good estimates of labor time are necessary in the development of cost standards. The preparation of such estimates may be an important part of the duties of the industrial engineering department. When a standard cost system is installed to replace some other type of cost accounting system, it often happens that good data on labor times have already been developed for some other purpose such as production planning and control.

USE OF STANDARD COSTS IN THE ACCOUNTS. Cost accounting can be simplified by the use of standard costs for the valuation of inventories of materials, work in process, finished parts, and finished goods. Where standard costs are used in this way, all interdepartmental transfers of inventory items are made at standard cost rather than at actual cost.

Chapters 10, 11, and 14 illustrated the way in which the use of a predetermined burden rate makes it necessary to use a burden variance account and usually results in an overabsorbed or underabsorbed burden at the end of an accounting period. In a similar way, the use of predetermined standard costs for materials and labor requires material and labor variance accounts. The balances in these variance accounts—the

EXHIBIT 15-1

TYPICAL STANDARD COST FILE CARD (SEE ALSO EXHIBIT 15-2)

STANDARD COST CARD
RUBBER-COVERED WIRE

DESCRIPTION: SERVED STRANDED CONDUCTOR — STOCK NO. 1006

SIZE: #18

COST BASIS: 2,050 ft. — DATE: January 1, 19__

Labor and Direct Manufacturing Expense							Materials				Total Std. Cost
Operation or Machine		Cost Center	Labor	I.M.E.	Total						
No.	Description				Oper.	Cum.	Description	Qty.	Std. Price	Std. Cost	
	TRANSFERRED FROM OTHER DEPARTMENTS		—	None	—		TRANSFERRED FROM OTHER DEPARTMENTS	— — —	None	—	
1	STRAND 1						COPPER WIRE	10.30#	289	2 976	
2	STRAND 2		093	419	512	512	COTTON WRAP	.42#	1 770	743	
3	WRAP		077	231	308	820	COMPOUND				
4	COMPOUND MIX						1st COTTON				
5	INSULATE						2nd COTTON				
6	SPARK						JUTE				
7	RESPARK						TAPE				
8	TAPE						JACKET COMPOUND				
9	SERVE						WAX				
10	JACKET						LABELS				
11	BRAID										
12	WEATHERPROOF										
	TOTAL THIS DEPARTMENT		170	650	820					3 719	4 539
	TOTAL STANDARD COST		170	650	820					3 719	4 539

overabsorbed or underabsorbed material and labor costs—constitute an important tool of cost control.

REASONS WHY NUMEROUS VARIANCE ACCOUNTS ARE USED IN STANDARD COST SYSTEMS. In controlling costs, it is not enough to set up good standards to be used as a basis for judging whether actual costs are satisfactory. It also is necessary to fix the responsibility for departures from standards. If control is to be effective, the cost variances must be broken down in a way that permits management to assign these responsibilities to particular individuals. If the causes of high costs are to be corrected, it is essential to know who is responsible for the costs being too high. It also is important to be able to give credit to the persons responsible for good performance in reducing costs or maintaining them at a satisfactory level.

This objective of assignment of responsibility calls for the use of many different variance accounts. For example, the persons who are responsible when materials are used either economically or wastefully rarely have anything to do with the prices at which the materials are

EXHIBIT 15-2

TYPICAL STANDARD COST FILE CARD (SEE ALSO EXHIBIT 15-1)

STANDARD COST CARD
RUBBER-COVERED WIRE

DESCRIPTION PORTABLE CORD — STOCK NO. 1785
SIZE #18
COST BASIS 1,000 ft. — DATE January 1, 19—

Labor and Direct Manufacturing Expense							Materials				Total Std. Cost
Operation or Machine: No.	Description	Cost Center	Labor	I.M.E.	Total: Oper.	Total: Cum.	Description	Qty.	Std. Price	Std. Cost	
	TRANSFERRED FROM OTHER DEPARTMENTS		170	650	820	820	TRANSFERRED FROM OTHER DEPARTMENTS			3 719	4 539
1	STRAND 1						COPPER WIRE				
2	STRAND 2						COTTON WRAP				
3	WRAP						COMPOUND	8.26#	157	1 298	
4	COMPOUND MIX		085	340	425	1 245	1st COTTON	2.00#	912	1 824	
5	INSULATE		652	1 630	2 282	3 527	2nd COTTON				
6	SPARK		244	295	539	4 066	JUTE	4.00#	325	1 300	
7	TWIST		220	550	770	4 836	TAPE				
8	TAPE						JACKET COMPOUND	15.05#	173	2 603	
9	SERVE		119	370	489	5 325	WAX				
10	JACKET COMPOUND MIX		226	870	1 096	6 421	LABELS	4	020	080	
11	JACKET		550	2 475	3 025	9 446					
12	WEATHERPROOF										
13	COIL AND WRAP		171	274	445	9 891					
	TOTAL THIS DEPARTMENT		2 267	6 804	9 071		REMARKS: Made from 2050' #18 served stranded conductor Stock No. 1006			7 103	16 174
	TOTAL STANDARD COST		2 437	7 454	9 891					10 822	20 713

SOURCE: These two exhibits are reproduced by permission from the amended seventh edition of the *Uniform Accounting Manual for the Electrical Manufacturing Industry*, pp. 419 and 420, prepared and issued by the National Electrical Manufacturers Association, New York, 1960.

purchased. Thus it is desirable to have separate accounts for material-price variance and material-quantity variance. In a similar way, it may be desirable to break down direct-labor-cost variance into price and quantity variance. To assign responsibilities to the appropriate supervisors, material- and labor-quantity variance accounts should be kept for each department or cost center. Often it is desirable to keep burden budget variance and capacity variance accounts by departments.

A SIMPLE STANDARD COST EXAMPLE. Exhibit 15-3 summarizes the transactions for a 3-month period for the Bannock Manufacturing Company, which has a standard cost system. Exhibit 15-4 shows this company's ledger in T-account form. Exhibit 15-5 shows the standard cost data used in this example.

EXHIBIT 15-3
SUMMARY OF TRANSACTIONS OF BANNOCK MANUFACTURING COMPANY
JANUARY 1 TO MARCH 31, 19___

A. Opening balances are: Cash, Dr., $65,000; Accounts Receivable, Dr., $50,000; Material X, Dr., $11,000; Material Y, Dr., $7,000; Product A, Dr., $8,000; Product B, Dr., $9,000; Accounts Payable, Cr., $20,000; Plant and Equipment, Dr., $200,000; Accumulated Depreciation, Plant and Equipment, Cr., $45,000; Capital Stock, Cr., $200,000; Surplus, Cr., $85,000. Standard cost data are shown in Exhibit 15-5. Materials and products are valued at standard costs.
B. Purchased on credit 30,000 pounds of X at $0.26, $7,800.
C. Purchased on credit 10,000 pounds of Y at $0.68, $6,800.
D. Cash payments were $108,000, divided as follows: Direct Labor, $32,000; Indirect Manufacturing Expense, $30,000; Selling and Administrative Expense, $29,000; Accounts Payable, $17,000.
E. Material issues, all to department S, were 69,000 pounds of X and 14,800 pounds of Y.
F. Production in department S was 5,000 A on which operations were completed, 200 A on which materials were issued and labor half done, and 8,300 B on which operations were completed.
G. Transfers to department T of units on which work in department S was completed were 5,000 A and 8,300 B.
H. Production in department T was 5,000 A completed, 8,000 B completed, and 300 B on which labor was two-thirds finished.
I. Transfers from department T to finished-goods stock were 5,000 A and 8,000 B.
J. Sales, all on credit, were 4,000 A, $44,000 and 8,400 B, $71,400, a total of $115,400. Cost of sales must also be entered.
K. Collections on accounts receivable were $120,000.
L. Estimated depreciation (charged to Indirect Manufacturing Expense) was $3,000.
M. Direct-labor cost consisted of $18,300 in department S and $13,700 in department T.
N. Analysis of the various indirect manufacturing expenses shows $15,700 applicable to department S and $17,300 to department T.
O. Sales, Cost of Sales, and Selling and Administrative Expense are closed into Profit and Loss Summary.
P. Profit and Loss Summary is closed into Earned Surplus.

Like the earlier cost accounting examples in Chaps. 10 and 11, this example has been made artificially simple in order to permit concentration of attention on particular principles and techniques. The Bannock Company uses two materials, X and Y, to make two products, A and B. There are two departments, S and T. No subsidiary ledgers are shown, although certain accounts, such as Materials and Finished Goods, that would normally be in subsidiary ledgers are shown in the general ledger. Many of the accounts, such as Accounts Receivable,

EXHIBIT 15-4

T-ACCOUNT LEDGER SHOWING ENTRIES IN ACCOUNTS OF BANNOCK MANUFACTURING COMPANY, JANUARY 1 TO MARCH 31, 19___

Cash	
A 65,000	108,000 D
K 120,000	

Indirect Manufacturing Expense	
D 30,000	15,700 N
L 3,000	17,300 N

Material Price Variance	
B 300	200 C

Sales	
O 115,400	115,400 J

Accounts Receivable	
A 50,000	120,000 K
J 115,400	

Work in Process—Department S	
F 27,420	59,880 G
F 18,500	
F 14,800	

Material Quantity Variance	
E 17,250	27,420 F
E 10,360	

Cost of Sales	
J 32,000	82,400 O
J 50,400	

Direct Labor	
D 32,000	18,300 M
	13,700 M

Work in Process—Department T	
G 59,880	40,000 I
H 13,356	48,000 I
H 16,324	

Labor Variance—Department S	
M 18,300	18,500 F

Selling and Administrative Expense	
D 29,000	29,000 O

Material X	
A 44,000 at $0.25 = $11,000	69,000 at $0.25 = $17,250 E
B 30,000 at $0.25 = $ 7,500	

Labor Variance—Department T	
M 13,700	13,356 H

Plant and Equipment	
A 200,000	

Accumulated Depreciation, Plant and Equipment	
	45,000 A
	3,000 L

Material Y	
A 10,000 at $0.70 = $ 7,000	14,800 at $0.70 = $10,360 E
C 10,000 at $0.70 = $ 7,000	

Burden Variance—Department S	
N 15,700	14,800 F

Capital Stock	
	200,000 A

Product A	
A 1,000 at $8.00 = $ 8,000	4,000 at $8.00 = $32,000 J
I 5,000 at $8.00 = $40,000	

Burden Variance—Department T	
N 17,300	16,324 H

Earned Surplus	
	85,000 A
	4,000 P

Product B	
A 1,500 at $6.00 = $ 9,000	8,400 at $6.00 = $50,400 J
I 8,000 at $6.00 = $48,000	

Accounts Payable	
D 17,000	20,000 A
	7,800 B
	6,800 C

Profit and Loss Summary	
O 82,400	115,400 O
O 29,000	
P 4,000	

Accounts Payable, Indirect Manufacturing Expense, Selling and Administrative Expense, and Plant and Equipment, should be thought of as controlling accounts for subsidiary ledgers that have been omitted.

This example illustrates two accounting techniques that have not previously been illustrated. One is the use of standard costs for inventory valuations, interdepartmental transfers, and finding cost of goods sold. The other is the use of material and labor variance accounts. There are four such accounts, namely, Material Price Variance, Material Quantity Variance, Labor Variance—Department S, and Labor Variance—Department T. In this example, it is assumed that all wages for direct labor are paid at the standard rates and that accounts for labor-price variance are therefore unnecessary. Although each department has its own burden variance account, there is no breakdown of the burden variance balances into budget variance and capacity variance. Burden is applied on the basis of standard labor hours (rather than actual hours), $2.00 per standard hour in department S and $2.20 per standard hour in department T.

Explanations and comments regarding the entries in this example are as follows.

Entry A. This entry merely records opening balances. There is no work in process at the start of the period. Materials X and Y are valued at their respective standard costs of 25 and 70 cents per pound. Products A and B are valued at their respective standard costs of $8 and $6 per unit.

Entry B. Purchased on credit 30,000 pounds of X at $0.26, $7,800. At the standard price of 25 cents per pound, the debit to Material X is only $7,500. The credit to Accounts Payable is, of course, the full amount owed for the purchase, $7,800. Any such purchase at a higher price than standard requires a debit to Material Price Variance of the difference between actual and standard price—in this case, $300.

Entry C. Purchased on credit 10,000 pounds of Y at $0.68, $6,800. In this case, the actual price is below the standard price. The debit to Material Y at the standard price is $7,000, whereas the credit to Accounts Payable is only $6,800. The balancing entry is a $200 credit to Material Price Variance.

Entry D. No new concepts are involved in this routine entry for cash disbursements. In this example, all the direct-labor cost is first charged to the account Direct Labor. A subsequent entry will show the division of this cost between the two departments.

Entry E. Material issues, all to department S, were 69,000 pounds of X and 14,800 pounds of Y. The debits for these material issues, all at standard prices, are made to the account Material Quantity Variance. The credits are to the respective material accounts.

Here we meet the account Material Quantity Variance for the first time. The purpose of this account is to measure the difference between the quantity of material actually used and the quantity that ought to have been used according to the standard. The debits of this account—illustrated in entry E—are for the materials actually issued. The credits—illustrated in entry F—are for the predetermined standard quantities of material corresponding to the production that took place during the accounting period.

Entry F. Production in department S was 5,000 A on which operations were completed, 200 A on which materials were issued and labor half done, and 8,300 B on which operations were completed. Before this entry can be made, it is necessary to use the standard cost cards (Exhibit 15-5)

EXHIBIT 15-5
STANDARD COSTS FOR PRODUCTS OF BANNOCK MANUFACTURING COMPANY

	Product A		
Department S	**—Material—4 lb. X at $0.25**	$1.00	
	2 lb. Y at $0.70	1.40	
	Labor—0.8 hr. at $2.50	2.00	
	Burden—0.8 hr. at $2.00	1.60	$6.00
Department T	**—Labor—0.5 hr. at $1.80**	$0.90	
	Burden—0.5 hr. at $2.20	1.10	2.00
Total standard cost per unit			$8.00
	Product B		
Department S	**—Material—5.8 lb. X at $0.25**	$1.45	
	0.5 lb. Y at $0.70	0.35	
	Labor—0.4 hr. at $2.50	1.00	
	Burden—0.4 hr. at $2.00	0.80	$3.60
Department T	**—Labor—0.6 hr. at $1.80**	$1.08	
	Burden—0.6 hr. at $2.20	1.32	2.40
Total standard cost per unit			$6.00

to compute the standard material, labor, and burden cost of the work performed in department S. These standard costs per unit for A are material, $2.40; labor, $2.00; burden, $1.60. For B, they are material, $1.80; labor, $1.00; burden, $0.80. Multiplying the unit costs by the quantities produced, the following figures are obtained:

	Material	Labor	Burden	Totals
5,000 A completed	$12,000	$10,000	$8,000	$30,000
200 A half finished	480	200	160	840
8,300 B completed	14,940	8,300	6,640	29,880
Totals	$27,420	$18,500	$14,800	$60,720

The total standard cost of the work performed in department S, $60,720, is debited to Work in Process—Department S. The total standard material cost of this work, $27,420, is credited to Material Quantity Variance. The total standard labor cost, $18,500, is credited to Labor Variance—Department S. The total standard burden cost, $14,800, is credited to Burden Variance—Department S.

Incidentally, this entry illustrates the estimation of per cent completion for work that is partially finished in a department at the end of an accounting period. Estimates of this type may be needed in many process cost systems and are not limited to systems using standard costs.

Entry G. Transfers to department T of units on which work in department S was completed were 5,000 A and 8,300 B. Obviously the debit is to Work in Process—Department T, and the credit is to Work in Process—Department S. This is an example of transfer of work in process at standard cost. The money amount could be computed as follows, using the standard costs for the two products in department S as shown in Exhibit 15-5:

5,000 A at $6.00 =	$30,000
8,300 B at $3.60 =	29,880
Total..........	$59,880

Of course these two figures, $30,000 and $29,880, are the totals shown in the tabulation of data for entry F by adding the separately calculated standard material, labor, and burden costs for each product. The balance remaining in Work in Process—Department S is $840 (i.e., $60,720 — $59,880), the standard cost of the 200 A that were half finished in department S on March 31.

Entry H. Production in department T was 5,000 A completed, 8,000 B completed, and 300 B on which labor was two-thirds finished. Exhibit 15-5 shows the standard costs in department T per unit of A to be labor, $0.90; burden, $1.10. For B, they are labor, $1.08; burden, $1.32. Multiplying the unit costs by the quantities produced, the following figures are obtained:

	Labor	Burden	Total
5,000 A completed................	$ 4,500	$ 5,500	$10,000
8,000 B completed................	8,640	10,560	19,200
300 B two-thirds finished..........	216	264	480
Totals..........................	$13,356	$16,324	$29,680

The total amount is debited to Work in Process—Department T, and the standard costs of labor and burden are credited to Labor Variance—

Department T and Burden Variance—Department T, respectively. This entry is similar to entry F. However, because no new materials are issued to Department T, there is no entry involving Material Quantity Variance.

Entry I. Transfers from department T to finished goods stock were 5,000 A and 8,000 B. This requires a credit to Work in Process—Department T and debits to the respective finished goods accounts. The money amounts are computed from the standard costs of completed units.

5,000 A at $8 = $40,000
8,000 B at $6 = $48,000

The sum of the debits to Work in Process—Department T is $89,560 and the sum of the credits is $88,000. This leaves a balance of $1,560 in this account. This balance represents the standard cost of the 300 B on which two-thirds of the work required in department T has been completed. This $1,560 figure can be checked by the following calculations:

Standard costs for 300 B in department S	= 300($3.60) =	$1,080
Two-thirds of standard labor cost in department T	= 300($0.72) =	216
Two-thirds of standard burden in department T	= 300($0.88) =	264
Total		$1,560

Entry J. The entries to show sales and cost of sales are routine ones that already have been illustrated many times. The only new point in this example is the use of standard costs in computing cost of sales.

Entries K and L. These entries require no comment.

Entry M. Direct-labor cost consisted of $18,300 in department S and $13,700 in department T. This information, based on payroll records, requires a credit to Direct Labor and debits to the two labor variance accounts. The debit side of each labor variance account now shows the actual departmental labor cost, and the credit side shows the standard labor cost of the work performed. The balance in each account therefore represents overabsorbed or underabsorbed direct-labor cost.

Entry N. Analysis of the various indirect manufacturing expenses shows $15,700 applicable to department S and $17,300 to department T. Presumably this information comes from an apportionment of the various indirect expenses between the departments made somewhat along the lines illustrated in Exhibit 14-2. It is necessary to debit the burden variance accounts with their respective allocated portions of the indirect expenses and to credit Indirect Manufacturing Expense with the total. The balance in each burden variance account now gives the departmental overabsorbed or underabsorbed burden.

Entries O and P. These entries require no comment.

POST-CLOSING TRIAL BALANCE. The balances in the six variance accounts are being carried forward into the next quarter. These variances and the balances in the asset, liability, and ownership summary accounts are all given in Exhibit 15-6, which shows the trial balance after the closing entries have been made.

As no new principles or techniques would be illustrated by the preparation of a balance sheet and profit and loss statement, these financial statements are not shown. Exhibit 15-6 contains all the necessary information for a balance sheet. It is evident from the Profit and Loss Summary account that the books show a profit of $4,000 for this period. However, an inspection of the balances in the variance accounts indicates that the profit figure would have been much less if the variance accounts had been closed out.

EXHIBIT 15-6
TRIAL BALANCE AFTER CLOSING BOOKS MARCH 31, 19___
BANNOCK MANUFACTURING COMPANY

	Debit	*Credit*
Cash	$ 77,000	
Accounts receivable	45,400	
Material X	1,250	
Material Y	3,640	
Work in process—department S	840	
Work in process—department T	1,560	
Product A	16,000	
Product B	6,600	
Material price variance	100	
Material quantity variance	190	
Labor variance—department S		$ 200
Labor variance—department T	344	
Burden variance—department S	900	
Burden variance—department T	976	
Accounts payable		17,600
Plant and equipment	200,000	
Accumulated depreciation, plant and equipment		48,000
Capital stock		200,000
Earned surplus		89,000
Totals	$354,800	$354,800

The topics of the interpretation of variance account balances and their final disposal in the accounts are discussed later in this chapter. These topics are discussed both in general terms and in relation to this specific example.

DIVERSITY OF ACCOUNTING PROCEDURES IN STANDARD COST SYSTEMS. As previously stated, the Bannock Manufacturing Company example should be viewed as a highly simplified illustration of the use of standard costs in the accounts. Moreover, any standard cost example—even a much more complex and realistic one—would give an incomplete picture of the accounting aspects of standard costs as they are used in industry. Standard cost systems differ from one another in many respects.

Certain characteristics that most standard cost systems have in common are illustrated in the Bannock example. Inventories of work in process and finished goods are carried at standard cost in the books, and standard costs are used for interdepartmental transfer and for costing sales. Variance accounts are employed to find the differences between actual and standard costs. In setting up variance accounts, an effort is made to classify the possible causes of failure to meet the cost objectives that have been set up by management. In so far as practicable, this classification follows the lines of personal responsibility of different individuals in the organization. The objective in establishing variance accounts is to provide management with some useful tools for cost control.

But within this general framework, there are many differences among systems. Some systems, like the one in the Bannock example, have only a few variance accounts; others require a great many such accounts. Labor-price variance accounts have already been mentioned, as have burden budget and capacity variances. The more departments there are, the greater the number of variance accounts needed to control costs. Some types of variance accounts are peculiar to particular industries, aiming to isolate certain special influences on costs that may not properly be attributed to manufacturing supervision. For example, in certain industries there are frequent differences in the quality of incoming raw materials (such as ore used in a metallurgical plant); variance accounts can be set up to measure the ways in which these differences influence production costs.

Standard cost systems may differ in the timing of the determination of certain variances. For instance, in the Bannock example, the material-price variance was entered when materials were purchased and the material inventory was carried on the books at standard cost. An alternative treatment is to carry material inventories at actual cost (as determined by FIFO, LIFO, average cost, or some other method) but to issue materials at standard cost, recording the price variance when materials are issued rather than when they are purchased.

MANAGERIAL USE OF VARIANCES IN MATERIAL AND LABOR COSTS. The chief industrial engineer of a manufacturing company was describing some of the favorable results of a standard cost system recently installed in his company. "Under our old system of actual costs," he said, "our vice-president in charge of manufacturing used to receive a tremendous stack of cost reports every month—approximately 5 pounds of paper to examine! Now he receives only a few pages giving him the variance figures. He can concentrate his attention on the particular spots where the debit variances show him that costs are too high."

Authorities on organization and management recognize the soundness of the "exception principle in management." This principle states that, in so far as possible, the time and energy of persons with managerial responsibilities should be directed toward matters that are exceptions rather than toward routine matters. The principle applies at all levels of management. Standard cost systems help to implement this principle with particular reference to cost control, because variance figures concentrate the attention of management on those costs that are out of line.

Although, as pointed out in the quotation from the chief industrial engineer, variance figures can be useful to the vice-president in charge of manufacturing, they are even more valuable at somewhat lower managerial levels. In concentrating managerial attention on matters controllable by manufacturing personnel, material-quantity variances and labor-time (i.e., quantity) variances are particularly helpful. Frequently standard cost systems are organized so that these particular variance figures can be computed at frequent intervals and reported promptly. Labor-time variances often are reported weekly and sometimes even daily.

Consider how management might interpret the following variance figures from the Bannock example:

	Debit	*Credit*
Material Price Variance	$100	
Material Quantity Variance	190	
Labor Variance—Department S		$200
Labor Variance—Department T	344	

In general, of course, it is reasonable to expect debit variances to be viewed unfavorably and credit variances to be viewed favorably. (Debit variances are sometimes referred to as *red* variances.) The debit balance in Material Price Variance tells management that the purchasing department did not succeed in buying materials as cheaply as had been expected. The debit balance in Material Quantity Variance indicates that more materials were used in department S than had been thought to be necessary. On the other hand, the credit balance in its Labor Variance account shows that department S used less labor than estimated. Department T, however, exceeded its standards for labor cost.

In judging variance figures such as these, management should look at their relative magnitude compared with the relevant total costs. Some discrepancies between estimates and performance are inevitable. Most of the variances in the Bannock example are relatively small. For example, the material quantities used were only 0.7% more than standard and the labor used in department S was 1.1% less than standard.

It should be obvious that the conclusions drawn by management from examining variance figures can be no better than the standards on which the variances are based. If a careless job has been done in setting standards, no valid conclusions can be drawn from the variance balances. It is particularly unfortunate if some standards are very tight and others very loose.

POLICY DECISIONS ON THE TIGHTNESS OF COST STANDARDS. An important question in establishing standards for material quantities and labor times is how tight the standards ought to be. One view is that standards should always be based on excellent performance—on the best that can be expected under favorable conditions. If this view is adopted, the variance accounts will almost always have debit balances; frequently the debit variances will be large.

An alternative view is that the aim in setting material and labor standards should be to have variance balances as near zero as practicable. The relatively small variances in our example suggest that this was the objective in the Bannock Manufacturing Company.

The two major objectives of standard cost systems, control of costs and valuation of inventories in the accounts, are somewhat in conflict with each other when the decision is being made regarding the tightness of cost standards. Relatively little pressure for cost reduction will be exerted by standards set at the level of average performance; generally speaking, people are likely to feel that they have done a satisfactory job if they have met the standards that have been established by management. On the other hand, if standards are so tight that variance accounts usually have substantial debit balances, inventories are valued at less than actual costs. This undervaluation of inventories may sometimes cause troublesome accounting problems. Auditors and income tax examiners may take the view that it is improper merely to close the total debit balance in the variance accounts into Profit and Loss Summary (or Cost of Goods Sold). For purposes of audited financial statements and income tax returns, it may be necessary to make adjusting entries that divide the variance balances among the material, work in process, finished-goods inventories, and cost of goods sold. In complex manufacturing enterprises, the analysis to prepare such adjusting entries could be time-consuming and expensive, partially offsetting the saving in accounting costs due to the standard cost system. In effect, such adjusting entries would aim to give the financial statements that would have been obtained if a system of actual costs had been used in the first place.

This dilemma with regard to the tightness of cost standards is inherent in all standard cost systems. Usually the best solution is a compromise between the objective of cost control and the objective of inventory valuation at actual cost. Standards are set at a level believed to represent attainable good performance, somewhat short of the ideal results that could be achieved under the most favorable conditions but better than the average results that have been obtained in the past.

INDIRECT MANUFACTURING EXPENSE IN RELATION TO STANDARD COST SYSTEMS. In cost systems that use actual costs for labor and materials, predetermined burden rates are applied in proportion to some figure reflecting actual performance, such as actual direct-labor cost or actual direct-labor hours. In contrast, in standard cost systems, burden is applied in proportion to a measure of standard performance, such as standard direct-labor cost or standard direct-labor hours.

The burden rate based on normal output was discussed in Chap. 14. So also was the variable budget for indirect manufacturing expense. Both can be used to advantage in standard cost systems as well as in cost systems employing actual costs. In fact, if the burden rate in a standard cost system were not based on normal output, it would be necessary to change the standard cost whenever a change occurred in the expected level of output.

The viewpoint that leads to cost standards as tools for controlling material and labor costs generally leads also to the variable budget as a tool for controlling indirect manufacturing expense. One of the problems in setting up any variable budget is finding a satisfactory measure of output. Standard labor hours or standard labor dollars are likely to be better measures of physical output than actual labor hours or dollars. A standard cost system may therefore make possible a better plan for budgetary control of indirect expense than can be attained with a system of actual costs.

In Chap. 14, it was explained how an underabsorbed or overabsorbed burden variance can be broken down into a budget variance and a capacity variance, using a normal burden rate and a variable IME budget. This two-part analysis of a burden variance is equally appropriate with standard costs. In a standard cost system the burden vehicle is standard hours or standard direct-labor cost rather than actual hours or actual labor cost. Therefore, the variable portion of the IME budget figure for an accounting period is calculated using standard hours (or standard labor cost). It is possible to make a three-part analysis of burden variance, attributing one segment of the variance to the difference between standard labor hours and actual hours. Because this three-part analysis seems of doubtful significance, it is not illustrated here.

CARRYING VARIANCE BALANCES FORWARD TO YEAR END. Balances in burden variance accounts often are carried forward from month to month and closed out only at the end of a fiscal year. This practice was discussed and illustrated in earlier chapters. In the Bannock example a similar practice is applied to balances in material and labor variance accounts.

It often happens that such accounts have debit balances for certain months (or for other short accounting periods) and credit balances for others. In such cases it seems reasonable to give such debit and credit balances a chance to offset each other by carrying variance balances forward throughout an entire year. Nevertheless, the variance balances occurring in each short period should be viewed as tools of cost control and should be reported to management along with the cumulative variance balance for the current year.

NEED FOR FREQUENT REVIEW OF COST STANDARDS. Earlier in this chapter, it was pointed out that it is undesirable to have some standards very tight and others very loose. If standards are to be effective instruments for cost control, the people who are to be controlled must respect the fairness of the standards. This respect will not exist where it is obvious that standards are uneven and have been set carelessly.

But it is not sufficient that standards be good when they are first established. In manufacturing, the conditions influencing costs are continually changing. Unless standards are reviewed at regular intervals and revised whenever appropriate, the standard costs that initially were fair and satisfactory will soon become uneven and a source of trouble and controversy.

SUMMARY. Some of the important points of this chapter can be restated as follows:

1. To judge whether costs are satisfactory, some standards of comparison are necessary. These may be informal standards, or they may be predetermined standards based on careful analysis.
2. If formal predetermined cost standards are established for each product, cost accounting can be simplified by using these standards as a basis for inventory valuations and interdepartmental transfers. A cost accounting system using predetermined standards in this way is referred to as a standard cost system.
3. In standard cost systems, material and labor variance are important

tools of cost control. In setting up the variance accounts, it is desirable to do so in a way that fixes on particular persons the responsibility for departures from cost standards. To this end, price variances usually are separated from quantity variances and separate variance accounts are kept for each department or cost center.

4. Debit balances in variance accounts mean that actual costs have exceeded standards; credit variances mean that actual costs are less than standard.
5. Usually it is desirable to set standards at a level that represents attainable good performance—generally somewhat better than the average performance that is expected. This policy regarding tightness of standards is likely to result in the variance accounts having net debit balances at the end of each fiscal year. These debit variances may occasionally be responsible for accounting problems related to valuation of inventories.

DISCUSSION QUESTIONS

15-A. What are the potential benefits of a standard cost system? What are its disadvantages?

15-B. Why is it necessary to use standard material prices in any standard cost system? Are there any advantages in using standard material prices in a cost accounting system that is based on actual costs?

15-C. The Bannock example in this chapter was simplified by the assumption that all wages paid for direct labor were paid at the standard rates; accounts for labor-price variance were therefore unnecessary. In complex manufacturing operations, any such simple assumption may be incorrect. For this reason, it is common for standard cost systems to include accounts for labor-rate variance. What are some possible causes of a difference between actual wage rates and standard wage rates? When an account for labor-rate variance shows a debit balance, is it ever reasonable to conclude that some one person in a supervisory position is primarily responsible for this variance?

15-D. One aspect of the Bannock example was the estimation of percentage completion for work that was still in process in one of the departments at the end of the period. Explain why it can be appropriate to make different estimates for materials and labor. Discuss the influence of these estimates on the variance balances. The text pointed out that estimates of this type may be required in any process cost accounting, whether inventory valuations are based on actual costs or on standard costs. In what respects will the accounting treatment of such estimates be different when actual costs are used?

15-E. What conclusions can be drawn from a debit balance in the account Material Price Variance? Some writers suggest that management should blame the purchasing department for any debit balance in this account. Do you agree with this suggestion? Why or why not?

15-F. In the Bannock example, all material issues resulted in debts to Material Quantity Variance. Why not make these debits directly to Work in Process accounts? Explain the source of the various entries to Material Quantity Variance and the conclusions to be drawn from a debit or credit balance in this account.

15-G. It would be somewhat simpler to have one plant-wide Labor Variance account than to have different labor variance accounts for each department or cost center. Nevertheless, it is nearly always desirable to keep such accounts by departments or cost centers. Why?

15-H. In the Bannock example, the books showed a $4,000 profit for the 3-month period. What would this profit have been if all variance balances had been closed into Profit and Loss Summary? What advantages can you see in carrying variance balances forward throughout a year in the manner illustrated in the Bannock example? What advantages can you see in closing out variance balances at the end of each month (or quarter) during the year?

15-J. Can you see any advantage in entering the material-price variance when materials are issued rather than when they are purchased? Any disadvantages? Which do you prefer? Which method was illustrated in the Bannock example?

15-K. The text states that "the two major objectives of standard cost systems . . . are somewhat in conflict with each other when the decision is being made regarding the tightness of cost standards." Explain this statement. Discuss the considerations that ought to enter into decisions about the tightness of cost standards.

15-L. Explain the differences between the treatment of IME in actual cost systems and in standard cost systems. Assume that burden is to be charged by means of a predetermined rate in both types of cost system.

15-M. The Bannock example illustrated the application of standard costs to a process cost system. Standard costs are equally applicable to job-order costs. In what respects would you expect a standard cost system to be different where job-order costs are used?

PROBLEMS

Problem 15-1. The Narrow Manufacturing Company produces one standard item. Inventories of raw materials are valued at standard prices. The standard price of material X is 25 cents per pound. This standard includes an allowance for freight-in.

Material X is used only in department B. For each unit of product processed through department B, the standard quantity of material X applied is 4.4 pounds. Thus the standard cost for material X is $1.10 per product unit.

The March 31 inventory balance of material X was 2,800 pounds ($700). During April 3,200 pounds were purchased. The vendor's invoice amounted to $745; the freight bill was $15. Issues of material X during April totaled 5,200 pounds.

Department B processed 1,100 units of product during the month. There was no work in process in the department at the start or at the end of the month.

A. Set up T accounts as follows: Accounts Payable, Inventory—Material X, Work in Process—Department B, Material Quantity Variance—Department B, and Material Price Variance. Enter the April 1 balance of $700 in the inventory account for material X. Also set up one other T headed All Other Accounts, and enter therein the balancing credit of $700. Make all the appropriate entries concerning material X for April. In each of the accounts in which more than one entry is made, derive and show that net end-of-month balance. Take a trial balance to check your work.

Now assume the following: Material X is delivered from the stores department to department B in pallet loads of approximately 500 pounds each. With each pallet there is a tag which is a copy of the materials requisition slip stating the quantity on the pallet to the nearest pound. At the end of any given month there normally is one full pallet plus the balance of the previous pallet waiting at the work station where material X is loaded into the process; in the production equipment, there is either (1) no material X or (2) between 50 and 60 pounds.

B. What would be the undesirable consequences of assuming that this work-in-process inventory of material X is a fixed quantity?

C. Clearly, if physical inventory of material X in department B was taken at the end of each month, proper adjustments could be made in the accounting records. Demonstrate how this might be done using the data given in the problem for April and assuming that the amount of material X in department B was 360 pounds at the end of March and 600 pounds at the end of April.

D. Suppose, now, that the expense of taking physical inventory of material X in the department at the end of each month is viewed as being excessive in relation to the benefits gained. However, assume that production output of the process is being measured for other purposes by an automatic device from which a reading can be taken at any time. How might this information be used to improve the accuracy of the monthly quantity variance for material X?

Problem 15-2. For the Narrow Manufacturing Company of problem 15-1, the following estimates were made as a basis for establishing standard costs for direct labor and overhead:

Direct-labor time per month, hours	1,500
Direct-labor cost per month	$2,250
Fixed overhead expense per month	$ 600
Variable overhead expense per month	$2,400
Production per month, units	1,000

A. Using the normal-month estimates above, compute:
   1. Standard direct-labor rate
   2. Standard direct-labor time per unit

3. Standard direct-labor cost per unit
4. Standard fixed overhead cost per unit
5. Standard variable overhead cost per unit

B. For the month of April, the actual time, cost, and production results were as follows:

Direct-labor time applied, hours	1,700
Direct-labor cost	$2,720
Overhead expense	$3,160
Production, units	1,100

Compute the following variances for the month of April:
1. Total labor variance and total burden variance
2. Labor-rate variance and labor-efficiency variance
3. Burden budget variance and burden capacity variance

C. Set up T's for the accounts listed below. Enter the direct-labor expense, $2,720, and the factory overhead expense, $3,160, and post the balancing credit, $5,880, to the T headed All Other Accounts. Make all appropriate entries in the accounts listed for the month of April. In each of the variance accounts show both the debit and the credit entries, and then derive the variance as the balance in the account. When all entries are completed, take a trial balance to check your work.

Direct Labor	Labor Rate Variance
Factory Overhead	Labor Efficiency Variance
Work in Process	Burden Capacity Variance
All Other Accounts	Burden Budget Variance

Problem 15-3. The Jay-Kay Manufacturing Company has a system of standard costs. During a certain 3-month accounting period at the start of a fiscal year, only two products are made, J and K. The standard costs for these are as follows:

	Product J		Product K	
	Quantity, lb	Standard cost	Quantity, lb	Standard cost
Materials:				
Material G	3	$0.90	2	$ 0.60
Material H	¾	0.60	3	2.40
Labor	...	2.00	...	4.00
Burden	...	2.50	...	5.00
Totals	...	$6.00	...	$12.00

A. Set up a ledger in T-account form and enter the following opening balances:

Account	*Debit*	*Credit*
Cash	$ 6,000	
Accounts Receivable	12,000	
Material G (20,000 lb at $0.30)	6,000	
Plant and Equipment	40,000	
Accumulated Depreciation—Plant and Equipment		$12,000
Accounts Payable		5,000
Capital Stock		30,000
Earned Surplus		17,000
Totals	$64,000	$64,000

From the following information make the necessary entries to find the profit and loss for the period and to find the material price and quantity variances and the labor and burden variances. Open any new accounts that you need.

B. At the close of the period, the voucher register showed the following totals:

Direct Labor—debit	$ 5,160
Material—debit (purchase of 8,000 lb of H)	6,540
Indirect Manufacturing Expense—debit	5,400
Selling and Administrative Expense—debit	3,900
Accounts Payable—credit	21,000

C. Issues from stores into production during the period were 4,500 units of G and 3,200 units of H.

D. Total production during the period was 1,000 units of J and 800 of K. No work was in process at the end of the period.

E. Sales, all on credit, were:

500 units of J at $10 = $5,000
400 units of K at $18 = $7,200

F. The cash receipts journal showed $12,000 as a debit to Cash and a credit to Accounts Receivable.

G. The cash disbursements journal showed $15,000 as a debit to Accounts Payable and a credit to Cash.

H. Estimated depreciation of plant and equipment for the period was $400.

I. Make entries as necessary to determine the labor variance.

J. The IME budget for each quarter is calculated as follows: IME budget = $2,000 + (0.75) (Standard DL$). Make the necessary entries to determine the burden budget variance and budget capacity variance.

K. Make entries as required to determine the profit or loss and close it to Earned Surplus. The variance account balances are to be carried forward; do not close these accounts in the ledger.

Check the ledger for balance. Prepare a balance sheet and an income statement. For the purpose of the balance sheet, incorporate the variance account balances into the figure for earned surplus. Also prepare a report tabulating the manufacturing variances and showing the net amount that was incorporated into earned surplus. On the balance sheet, write a footnote (referenced to the earned surplus figure) explaining the treatment of the variances and referring to the report of manufacturing variances.

Problem 15-4. The Standard Materials Company uses standard costs in their process cost accounting system. Following is the trial balance as of the start of the fiscal year, January 1, 19____. Only the accounts listed are to be used in the solution of the problem.

STANDARD MATERIALS CO.—TRIAL BALANCE, JANUARY 1, 19____

Account	Debit	Credit
Cash	$ 20,000	
Raw Material	29,000	
Work in Process	4,000	
Finished Goods	32,000	
Accounts Receivable	25,000	
Plant and Equipment	200,000	
Accumulated Depreciation—Plant and Equipment		$ 80,000
Material Price Variance		
Material Quantity Variance		
Direct Labor Variance		
Burden Budget Variance		
Burden Capacity Variance		
Sales		
Cost of Goods Sold		
Selling and Administrative Expense		
Accounts Payable		10,000
Capital Stock		120,000
Earned Surplus		100,000
Profit and Loss Summary		
Totals	$310,000	$310,000

The transactions for the entire year are summarized as follows. Set up a T-account ledger, and make the necessary entries.

A. Enter the opening balances given above.

B. Material purchases (all on credit) were $80,000. However, the sum of the standard costs of all the materials purchased was $78,000.

C. Cash outlays during the year were $224,000 distributed as follows:

Direct labor	$46,500
Indirect manufacturing expense	57,500
Selling and administrative expense	45,000
Accounts payable	75,000

D. Issues of material from stores into production at standard prices were $73,000.

E. Standard cost of all work performed during the year, both on completed and on unfinished product, was:

Standard material cost	$74,000
Standard direct-labor cost	45,000
Standard burden	60,000

F. Total standard cost of all work completed and transferred to finished stock was $180,000.

G. Depreciation on plant and equipment for the year was $10,000.

H. The company used a burden rate based on normal output. It is estimated that at normal output the standard direct-labor cost of goods produced in a year should be $60,000. On the basis of a study of the various elements of indirect manufacturing expense, it was determined that burden ought to be $80,000 at normal output. These two estimates gave the standard burden rate used in entry E above. A study to set up a variable budget indicated that the total IME for the year can be expected to vary from the normal-year estimate of $80,000 at the rate of two-thirds of the difference between the standard direct-labor cost for the year and the estimated normal standard direct-labor cost ($60,000). The foregoing analysis makes it possible to separate the total burden variance into budget variance and capacity variance.

I. Sales (on credit) during the year were $250,000. Cost of goods sold (at standard cost) was $185,000.

J. Cash receipts on accounts receivable were $240,000.

K. Dividends declared and paid during the year totaled $15,000.

L. All variance accounts should be closed into profit and loss.

M. Make the necessary entries to close the books and determine the profit or loss for the period.

Take a post-closing trial balance. Prepare an income statement for the year. Also list the variances found in each of the five variance accounts, giving the amount and telling whether it is a debit or credit variance. Write a short interpretation of these five variance balances, telling what conclusions you might draw from them.

Problem 15-5. The Turnwell Wrench Company has a standard cost system. Three sizes of wrench are manufactured with standard costs as follows:

	Large	Medium	Small
Material (at $0.15 per lb)	$0.17	$0.10	$0.06
Forge-shop direct labor	0.12	0.08	0.04
Forge-shop burden	0.15	0.10	0.05
Standard cost of forging	$0.44	$0.28	$0.15
Machine-shop direct labor	0.16	0.12	0.10
Machine-shop burden	0.20	0.15	0.07
Total standard cost of wrench	$0.80	$0.55	$0.33

The standard cost of material is 15 cents per pound. All material is carried in inventory at standard cost. The standard burden rate of 125% of direct-labor cost is based on normal output. At normal monthly output the standard direct-labor cost is $3,200. A study of the fixed and variable elements of burden gives the following equation, which is used as the basis for the variable budget for indirect manufacturing expense:

$$\text{Monthly IME} = \$4{,}000 + 0.75(\text{standard DL\$} - \$3{,}200)$$

Enter the following transactions, which took place during the month of January in the attached T-account ledger. All accounts to be used are listed below with their opening balances on January 1. (Some of these accounts should be interpreted as controlling accounts for subsidiary ledgers that are omitted.) All entries, including adjusting and closing entries, should be made directly in the T accounts.

TURNWELL WRENCH COMPANY
OPENING BALANCES, JANUARY 1, 19___

Account	Debit	Credit
Cash	$ 7,040	
Accounts Receivable	14,000	
Material	2,500	
Forge Shop, Work in Process		
Large Forgings	220	
Medium Forgings	280	
Small Forgings		
Machine Shop, Work in Process		
Large Wrenches	1,200	
Medium Wrenches	1,100	
Small Wrenches	660	
Plant and Equipment	120,000	
Accumulated Depreciation—Plant and Equipment		$ 41,000
Accounts Payable		3,500
Capital Stock		50,000
Earned Surplus		52,500
Profit and Loss Summary		
Sales		
Cost of Goods Sold		
Selling and Administrative Expense		
Indirect Manufacturing Expense		
Material Price Variance		
Material Quantity Variance		
Forge Shop, Labor Variance		
Machine Shop, Labor Variance		
Burden Budget Variance		
Burden Capacity Variance		
Totals	$147,000	$147,000

A. Set up T accounts and enter the opening balances.
B. Purchase of 20,000 pounds of material on credit for $3,090.

C. Cash disbursements as follows:

On accounts payable	$ 3,000
Forge-shop direct labor	1,500
Machine-shop direct labor	2,100
Indirect manufacturing expense	3,800
Selling and administrative expense	4,000
Purchase of new machinery	2,000
Total	$16,400

D. 14,000 pounds of material issued to the forge shop.

E. Production in the forge shop of:
5,000 large forgings
7,000 medium forgings
10,000 small forgings

F. No work in process remains in the forge shop at the end of the month.

G. The following number of forgings are converted into finished wrenches.
4,000 large
6,000 medium
8,000 small

H. No work in process remains in the machine shop at the end of the month.

I. Sales of wrenches (all on credit) are as follows:

3,000 large at $1.20	=	$3,600
5,000 medium at $0.85	=	$4,250
6,000 small at $0.50	=	$3,000
Total sales	=	$10,850

J. Collections on accounts receivable are $12,500.

Make adjusting and closing entries directly in T accounts as follows:

K. Depreciation of $500 is to be charged for January.

L. Entries are necessary to find all variances not previously determined.

M. Entries are necessary to determine the profit or loss for January and to close this into surplus at the end of January. All variance balances shall be carried forward into the next period rather than closed into profit and loss summary. Check the ledger for balance.

Prepare an income statement for January, followed by a statement of the manufacturing cost variances showing the net variance.

Prepare a comparative balance sheet, listing the account balances as of January 31 in one column and the balances as of January 1 in the next column. For the purpose of this interim balance sheet, incorporate all the variances into one figure listed following earned surplus. You may also combine the three sizes of forgings and the three sizes of wrenches into one line each and show one figure for the net value of plant and equipment. Comment briefly on the financial condition of the company at the end of the month as compared with the state of affairs at the start of the month.

Problem 15-6. The Multi-strand Company makes a wide variety of standard and custom insulated electric wire and multiconductor electric cable. The primary production process is extruding insulating material around copper wire. The extrusion department manufactures covered wire for stock and also for custom orders. Accounting-wise, all extrusion department jobs are closed to the Covered Wire Stock inventory account (even though the production of some of the jobs may be in the stock area only long enough to be weighed).

For each extrusion department job, custom or standard, the standard cost is predetermined. Copper wire and plastic compounds are carried in raw materials inventory at standard prices.

At the end of each month the cost record cards for the jobs remaining in process are summarized to arrive at a value for the work in process carried forward into the following month. For this purpose, the value of raw materials in process is determined by costing at standard prices the actual quantities of materials that have been issued to these jobs. The labor cost value is determined by costing at standard labor rates the actual labor time charged to these jobs. The burden cost value is computed at the standard rate of 200% of the direct-labor cost value. The totals of these material, labor, and burden costs for all jobs unfinished at the end of the month, together with similar totals for jobs in process at the start of the month, are used to adjust Work in Process and the variance accounts affected.

Because of the large number of possible combinations of size and finish of wire and composition and color of covering material, there is a very large variety of different jobs to be run each month, and the total time of a job on an extruder seldom is more than 1 or 2 days. The entire production for each job is accumulated and transferred as a single lot from Extrusion of Stock.

Using the data given below, make entries in the cost accounts for the activities of the Extrusion Department for the month of October.

A. Set up T accounts for the accounts listed below, representing a portion of the factory ledger. (Use a long T for the Work in Process account.) Enter the balances in these accounts as indicated. The balance in the Raw Materials, IME, and Direct Labor accounts represent the status of these accounts on October 31 prior to making the entries affecting the variance accounts but after other end-of-month entries have been made. The balances in Work in Process, Covered Wire Stock, and the variance accounts are still as they were after the September 30 closing.

Account	*Amount*
Raw Materials Inventory	$ 40,000 (Dr.)
IME, Extrusion Department	14,500 (Dr.)
Direct Labor, Extrusion Department	7,900 (Dr.)
Work in Process, Extrusion Department	3,600 (Dr.)
Covered Wire Stock	50,000 (Dr.)
Materials Quantity Variance, Extrusion Department	
Labor Rate Variance, Extrusion Department	
Labor Time Variance, Extrusion Department	
Burden Budget Variance, Extrusion Department	
Burden Capacity Variance, Extrusion Department	
All Other Factory Ledger Accounts	116,000 (Cr.)

Entries B, C, and D, following, relate to the extrusion department operations during October. The information given represents summaries of stores requisitions and credit slips, labor time reports, and indirect cost charges.

B. Materials issued to the department totaled $23,800 (actual quantities at standard prices). Materials returned to stores totaled $1,100 (actual quantities at standard prices).

C. The balance of $7,900 shown in the account Direct Labor, Extrusion Department is the actual direct-labor time costed at actual rates. This labor time costed at standard rates totaled $7,600.

D. The balance of $14,500 shown in the account IME, Extrusion Department is the total actual IME charged to the department in October.

E. A summary of the standard costs for all orders completed in extrusion and transferred to covered wire stock during October is as follows:

Materials, total standard cost	$24,000
Direct labor, total standard cost	7,100
Burden (200% of standard DL$)	14,200
Total	$45,300

F. The $3,600 value for work in process at the end of September was established by an adjusting entry based on a summary of orders in process in the extrusion department at that time, as set forth below. All those orders were finished in October. The results of a comparable summary of jobs remaining in process on October 31 are also listed below.

	Work in process	
	Sept. 30	Oct. 31
Materials issued to these orders to date, actual quantity at standard prices	$1,800	$1,500
Actual direct-labor time charged to these orders to date, at standard rates	600	500
Burden charged to work in process for these orders at 200% of actual direct labor (costed at standard rates)	1,200	1,000
Total value of work in process	$3,600	$3,000

Note: The $1,500 figure for materials issued is a portion of the $23,800 total stated in entry B; the $500 figure for direct labor is a portion of the $7,600 total stated in entry C.

G. For the month of October, the IME budget estimate for this department is to be computed using $10,000 as the estimated fixed portion of IME and using 70% of direct-labor cost as the variable burden rate, as follows:

$$\text{IME budget for October} = \$10{,}000 + (0.70)(7{,}100 + 500 - 600)$$

Rule and balance all the accounts. In each of the variance accounts, the balance thus developed will be the net variance for October as it would appear prior to closing the variance to Profit and Loss. At this point, the algebraic sum of the balances in all the inventory and variances accounts should be equal to the total you started with, $116,000. This fact can be used to check your work. No cost reports or statements are required.

16/ DIRECT COSTING

This chapter deals primarily with the matter of overhead costs included in the cost of manufactured product. Previously we have considered only one possibility, *absorption costing*, wherein the objective is to apply all factory overhead to work in process. An alternative is *direct costing*, wherein only variable factory overhead is included in product costs and the nonvariable overhead is charged to expense of the period.[1]

ABSORPTION COSTING. The general approach to product costing considered in prior chapters can be outlined as follows:

1. The cost of manufactured product includes direct labor, direct material, and indirect manufacturing expense.
2. Indirect manufacturing expense (factory overhead) consists of all costs incident to the production of items for sale or for inventory that are not treated as either direct labor or direct material (i.e., that cannot be assigned to specific products or jobs without incurring unreasonable trouble, delay, or expense).

This plan is most often called "absorption" costing; it is sometimes called "full" or "total" costing. These terms all refer to the idea of including all manufacturing expense in product costs. In other words, under absorption costing it is intended that all costs incurred in connection with manufacturing are charged to work in process, are included in the cost of manufactured goods entering inventory, and ultimately are charged against income through cost of goods sold.[2]

[1] Of the source material of value in the preparation of this chapter, the following study was particularly helpful:

Gerald Oren Wentworth, *An Evaluation of Direct Costing*, a dissertation submitted to the Stanford Graduate School of Business, in partial fulfillment of the requirements for the degree of Doctor of Philosophy, Stanford University, 1959.

[2] If predetermined burden rates or standard costs are used that consistently result in debit variances, and if these variances are carried directly to the income statements, then full absorption costing is not truly achieved.

DIRECT COSTING. In the most widely used sense of the term, direct costing means including in the cost of manufactured items only those production costs that vary directly with the number of units produced. These costs include, in addition to direct labor and direct material, the variable portion of the indirect manufacturing expenses. Nonvariable (e.g., "fixed") manufacturing overhead expenses are considered to be *period costs* and are excluded from inventories and carried directly to the income statements.

It should be noted that the word "direct" has quite a different meaning in the term "direct cost" from its meaning in the terms "direct labor" and "direct material." The prime costs, direct labor and direct material, are defined in a practical manner as those labor and material costs that can readily be charged directly to jobs or products. On the other hand, "direct" costs in the direct costing sense are those that vary directly with the amount of product manufactured.

Although *direct costing* is the most commonly used term for this costing scheme, some writers prefer *variable costing* or *marginal costing* as being more explicit. Marginal costing is the term generally used in Great Britain.[3]

TWO IMPORTANT DIFFERENCES BETWEEN DIRECT COSTING AND ABSORPTION COSTING. If the firm maintains inventories of manufactured items—finished goods, finished parts, and work in process—the value of these inventories will be lower under direct costing than under absorption costing. Also, if there is a difference between the total amount of manufactured inventory on hand at the start of a period and the amount on hand at the end of the period, direct costing and absorption costing will give different figures for net income for that period. These points are discussed further in connection with the example comparing the two costing schemes later in this chapter.

THE INCOME STATEMENT UNDER DIRECT COSTING. Two other differences between direct costing and absorption costing are in the format of the income statement and the treatment of nonmanufacturing expenses.

The basic pattern for the income statement based on direct costing is as follows:

[3] In accounting literature, the term *marginal cost* is often used thus synonymously with the term *direct cost,* meaning a cost that varies in a linear relation with short-term variations in production. However *marginal cost* is also used in the economist's sense of rate of change of cost with production.

Sales (less returns and allowances)	$xxx,xxx
Less: direct (marginal) cost of goods sold	xxx,xxx
Manufacturing margin	$xxx,xxx
Less: variable selling and distribution expense	xxx,xxx
Merchandising margin	$xxx,xxx
Less: period costs (fixed expenses)	xxx,xxx
Net operating income before taxes	$ xx,xxx

The period costs, in such a direct-costing income statement, include fixed IME and fixed selling, distribution, administrative, and general expenses.

Analysis of the behavior of nonmanufacturing expenses into variable and fixed components is required for the purposes of this type of statement. However, this separation has no effect on the net income figure, since all such costs are included.

USE OF DIRECT COSTING IN DIFFERENT TYPES OF SYSTEMS. Direct costing can be applied in a job-order cost system or a process cost system. It can be used in a standard cost system or an actual cost system. The essential difference between direct costing and absorption costing is the treatment of the fixed manufacturing expenses as period costs rather than as product costs.

INVENTORY PRICING METHODS IN RELATION TO DIRECT COSTING. Any of the common methods of inventory pricing—FIFO, LIFO, average cost, and standard cost—can be used with respect to goods manufactured to stock that are costed by direct costing. Actual costs will, of course, vary under either direct costing or absorption costing; the use of direct costing does not remove the problem of pricing inventoried items. However, since the inventory values are lower under direct costing, the differences between alternative pricing methods are likely to be somewhat less important.

RELATIONSHIP BETWEEN DIRECT COSTING AND THE FLEXIBLE IME BUDGET. Direct costing requires some systematic means of estimating variable manufacturing expenses and applying them to different products in a consistent way. Direct labor and direct materials, as usually defined in accounting, are normally considered to be variable in proportion to production. To apply variable IME to the products it is necessary to analyze indirect expenses and develop a flexible budget (or a system of departmental flexible budgets), as discussed in Chap. 14. The slope of the flexible IME budget line (see Exhibit 14-4, page 312) is the variable burden rate needed for direct costing purposes.

BURDEN VARIANCE UNDER DIRECT COSTING. In an absorption costing system utilizing a flexible budget, fixed IME is charged into product costs at a rate based on an expected or normal level of production. A deviation of production level from the normal level gives rise to a "capacity" variance. The amount of the burden capacity variance can be calculated as the difference between overhead applied to product and the overhead budget for the period. Deducting the variable overhead from both these figures, it is seen that the capacity variance is the difference between the expected normal amount of fixed overhead and the fixed overhead applied to products through the use of the (total) normal burden rate.

Under direct costing, the fixed overhead is charged directly against income; no fixed IME is applied to the products. Therefore, there is no burden capacity variance. If the amount of fixed overhead charged to period expense under direct costing is the expected fixed IME budget (i.e., a predetermined budget amount), then a burden budget variance may be developed. The budget variance for a given period will be the difference between the total actual IME for the period and the sum of the variable IME charged to products and the fixed IME budget amount.

A COMPARISON OF ABSORPTION COSTING AND DIRECT COSTING. Exhibits 16-1 through 16-4 demonstrate the differences between absorption costing and direct costing in terms of a hypothetical manufacturing enterprise.

In order to focus attention on the basic differences, the following simplifying assumptions were made:

1. Standard costs and a flexible IME budget system are used.
2. Labor and material variances and burden budget variance are all zero in each period.
3. The product mix of goods manufactured to inventory does not change.
4. Work-in-process inventory is negligible. (Or it can be assumed that work-in-process inventory is included in the "manufactured inventories" referred to in the exhibits.)
5. Under absorption costing, burden capacity variance is closed to Profit and Loss Summary at the end of each period.

For the assumed mix of production activities in the various departments, the following overall relationships were established as the basis for calculating manufacturing cost figures shown in the exhibits:

1. Standard direct-labor cost is two-thirds of standard direct-material cost.
2. Estimated normal standard direct-labor cost is $120,000. Estimated total normal IME is $180,000 (150% or direct-labor cost). Variable IME is estimated at 50% of standard direct-labor cost.

Exhibit 16-1 shows that for a period of normal activity, in which there is no net change in manufactured inventories, absorption costing and direct costing give identical results with respect to reported net income.[4] One difference not shown in this exhibit is that, under direct costing, the manufactured inventories would be carried on the balance sheet in this example at 75% of the absorption-costing value of these inventories. For instance, if these inventories were valued under absorption costing at $120,000, they would be valued under direct costing at $90,000, as follows:

	Absorption cost	Direct cost
Direct material..........	$ 45,000	$45,000
Direct labor.............	30,000	30,000
Overhead................	45,000	15,000
Totals................	$120,000	$90,000

Clearly, the difference in asset valuation would be reflected by an equal difference in owners' equity between the two balance sheets. If the manufactured inventories are valued at $30,000 less under direct costing than under absorption costing, then net worth would also be shown at $30,000 less under direct costing than under absorption costing. This follows from the balance sheet equation.

Exhibits 16-2 and 16-3 demonstrate the effects of a change during an accounting period in the amount of manufactured inventory on hand. Any combination of changes in sales and production that causes a decrease in manufactured inventory results in a more favorable net income under direct costing than under absorption costing. This can be seen by comparison of Exhibit 16-2 with Exhibit 16-1. Also, of course, an increase in inventory results in a more favorable net income figure under absorption costing than under direct costing. This can be seen by comparison of Exhibit 16-3 with Exhibit 16-1.

Exhibit 16-4, in comparison with Exhibit 16-3, illustrates the point that the net income arrived at by direct costing is not affected by changes in production level (assuming that these changes are temporary and that the manufacturing costs actually behave as anticipated). On the other hand, the net income arrived at by absorption costing improves with increased production, reflecting the increase in the fixed overhead costs charged into the value of manufactured inventories. Thus under absorption costing, as compared with direct costing, it may appear that a profit is realized through production for inventory.

[4] Minor differences may arise if inventories are priced by an actual-cost procedure, such as LIFO, FIFO, or average-cost.

EXHIBIT 16-1
COMPARISON OF ABSORPTION COSTING AND DIRECT COSTING PRODUCTION AND SALES AT NORMAL LEVELS NO CHANGE IN MANUFACTURED INVENTORIES

	Absorption costing	Direct costing
Manufacturing data		
Cost of goods manufactured during period	$480,000	$360,000
Manufacturing overhead applied to product	$180,000	$ 60,000
Income statement		
Net sales	$720,000	$720,000
Less: Cost of goods sold	480,000	360,000
Gross margin	$240,000	$360,000
Less: Variable selling and general expense	96,000	96,000
Net margin	$144,000	$264,000
Less: Burden capacity variance	0	
Less: Fixed manufacturing overhead		120,000
Less: Fixed selling and general expense	100,000	100,000
Net profit before income taxes	$ 44,000	$ 44,000

EXHIBIT 16-2
COMPARISON OF ABSORPTION COSTING AND DIRECT COSTING PRODUCTION AND SALES ABOVE NORMAL LEVELS DECREASE IN MANUFACTURED INVENTORIES DURING PERIOD

	Absorption costing	Direct costing
Manufacturing data		
Cost of goods manufactured during period	$520,000	$390,000
Manufacturing overhead applied to product	$195,000	$ 65,000
Decrease in manufactured inventories	$100,000	$ 75,000
Income statement		
Net sales	$930,000	$930,000
Less: Cost of goods sold	620,000	465,000
Gross margin	$310,000	$465,000
Less: Variable selling and general costs	124,000	124,000
Net margin	$186,000	$341,000
Add: Credit burden capacity variance	+10,000	
Less: Fixed manufacturing overhead		120,000
Less: Fixed selling and general costs	100,000	100,000
Net profit before taxes	$ 96,000	$121,000

EXHIBIT 16-3
COMPARISON OF ABSORPTION COSTING AND DIRECT COSTING
PRODUCTION AND SALES BELOW NORMAL LEVELS
INCREASE IN MANUFACTURED INVENTORIES DURING PERIOD

	Absorption costing	Direct costing
Manufacturing data		
Cost of goods manufactured during period	$440,000	$330,000
Manufacturing overhead applied to product	$165,000	$ 55,000
Increase in manufactured inventories	$100,000	$ 75,000
Income statement		
Net sales	$510,000	$510,000
Less: Cost of goods sold	340,000	255,000
Gross margin	$170,000	$255,000
Less: Variable selling and general expense	68,000	68,000
Net margin	$102,000	$187,000
Less: Debit burden capacity variance	10,000	
Less: Fixed manufacturing overhead		120,000
Less: Fixed selling and general expense	100,000	100,000
Net profit (loss) before income taxes	($ 8,000)	($ 33,000)

EXHIBIT 16-4
COMPARISON OF ABSORPTION COSTING AND DIRECT COSTING
EFFECT OF INCREASED PRODUCTION WITH SALES UNCHANGED

	Absorption costing	Direct costing
Manufacturing data		
Cost of goods manufactured during period	$480,000	$360,000
Manufacturing overhead applied to product	$180,000	$ 60,000
Increase in manufactured inventories	$140,000	$105,000
Income statement		
Net sales (same as in Exhibit 16-3)	$510,000	$510,000
Less: Cost of goods sold	340,000	255,000
Gross margin	$170,000	$255,000
Less: Variable selling and general expense	68,000	68,000
Net margin	$102,000	$187,000
Less: Burden capacity variance	0	
Less: Fixed manufacturing overhead		120,000
Less: Fixed selling and general expense	100,000	100,000
Net profit (loss) before income taxes	$ 2,000	($ 33,000)

Following is a summary of the results displayed in the four exhibits:

	Exhibit 16-1	Exhibit 16-2	Exhibit 16-3	Exhibit 16-4
Sales	$720,000	$920,000	$510,000	$510,000
Absorption costing:				
Cost of goods manufactured	480,000	520,000	440,000	480,000
Cost of goods sold	480,000	620,000	340,000	340,000
Change in inventory	$ 0	−$100,000	+$100,000	+$140,000
Net income (loss)	44,000	96,000	(8,000)	2,000
Net income/sales	6.1%	10.3%	−1.6%	0.4%
Direct costing:				
Cost of goods manufactured	$360,000	$390,000	$330,000	$360,000
Cost of goods sold	360,000	465,000	255,000	255,000
Change in inventory	$ 0	−$ 75,000	+$ 75,000	+$105,000
Net income (loss)	44,000	121,000	(33,000)	(33,000)
Net income/sales	6.1%	13.0%	−6.5%	−6.5%

In such a comparison between direct costing and absorption costing, the difference in reported net income for a period will be equal to the difference in the change in inventory valuation. This can be illustrated using the data of Exhibit 16-2 and assuming start-of-period inventory values, as follows:

	Absorption costing	Direct costing	Difference
Manufactured inventories, start of period	$120,000	$ 90,000	
Decrease in inventory during the period	100,000	75,000	$25,000
Manufactured inventories, end of period	$ 20,000	$ 15,000	
Net income for period (before taxes)	$ 96,000	$121,000	$25,000

Over a sequence of accounting periods, direct costing and absorption costing may arrive at the same cumulative net income although reporting different net incomes in the individual periods. This can be illustrated by considering the data of Exhibits 16-1 to 16-3 to represent that of three successive accounting periods. The inventory was depleted in the second period but restored to the original amount in the third period. The cumulative net income over the three periods was $132,000 for both costing schemes, even though net income differed by $25,000 in both the second and third periods. The difference between the two schemes was in the allocation of expense among the three periods—a matter of timing.

It should be noted that the differences between direct costing results and absorption costing results, with respect to the measurement of income, depend on the relative size and variation in the inventories of work in process, finished parts, and finished product. If these inventories are small in value and do not change very much in magnitude, as in some custom-order industries, net income will be little affected by the choice between direct and absorption costing.

DIRECT COSTING IN RELATION TO EXTERNAL REPORTING. As compared with absorption costing, the effects on the financial statements of using direct costing are summarized as follows:

1. On the balance sheet, the values of manufactured inventories (and therefore current assets and net working capital) and of net worth are lower.
2. In the income statement, the gross profit on sales is higher and reported net income may be higher or lower for a given period depending on the volumes of sales and production.

Although there is a trend toward the use of direct costing, absorption costing is the most widely used method of costing manufactured product. Public accountants and many industrial accountants hold that consistency with generally accepted practice is desirable for external reporting and therefore are inclined toward the view that direct costing is not appropriate for the purposes of published financial statements. For this reason, some companies using direct costing for internal purposes make a conversion to the absorption-costing basis for external reports.

The permissibility of direct costing for income tax purposes in the United States is not clearly established, although many firms have reported on a direct costing basis for many years. Direct costing is not mentioned in the internal revenue code and therefore is neither specifically permitted nor prohibited for tax purposes. The Internal Revenue Service appears to be reluctant to approve conversions from absorption costing to direct costing where a material write-down of inventory value is involved. Properly, such a change requires prior approval of the Commissioner of Internal Revenue. In some cases such permission has been denied; in other cases permission has been granted subject to certain conditions such as the amortization of the decrease in inventory value over a period of years. As in many other aspects of reporting taxable income, consistency in use of one method is expected.

MANAGERIAL USES OF DIRECT COSTING INFORMATION. Direct cost reporting may provide management greater awareness of and insight into actual cost behavior with respect to the volume of production and the volume of sales and thereby promote a more sophisticated approach to problems of managerial control, policy formulation, and decision making. Also, direct costs may provide information that is directly useful for such purposes.

With respect to sales price determination, direct costs offer a guide as to the minimum attractive pricing for marginal business whereas full absorption costs offer a guide as to the level of prices necessary in the long run to recover all costs and earn a profit. Both are useful in sales policy and price determination, although clearly neither should be given undue weight and both should be viewed as being only systematic measures or estimates of cost.

One potential disadvantage of direct costing is that the unit cost figures developed by the system may be used naïvely in evaluating differences between alternative courses of action. Another is that such unit costs may be unduly emphasized by sales-oriented personnel as an argument for price reductions. These difficulties, of course, arise only if the cost information is carelessly or improperly used. Such matters are discussed further in Chap. 21.

For cost-control purposes, direct costing may be helpful in focusing attention on the importance of fixed costs and the effect of fixed costs on the relationship between sales volume and net income. Also, the separation of variable costs may make it possible to assign responsibility for costs more clearly and to develop more sensitive measures for the control of variable costs.

Some management-incentive bonus plans are based on the accounting figures for profit or on cost accounting figures for the profitability of the different divisions or plants. Under absorption costing, the current-period profit showing can be improved by manufacturing in excess of sales requirements, thereby absorbing additional fixed overhead into the manufactured inventories. Thus a net increase in inventory during one period results in an increase in the immediate bonus. The opposite effect on the bonus will not occur until such time as the inventory is decreased. Also, it is quite possible that the total bonus over a sequence of periods will be greater if inventory readjustment is concentrated in one period, particularly in a low-sales period in which a bonus is not likely in any event. These incentives to overproduce and to oversteer the level of production disappear if a direct costing system is used. Also, whether such a bonus plan is used or not, direct costing figures are likely to provide a somewhat better measurement of performance with respect to the planning and management of production.

It is not possible in this brief book on accounting to consider in depth the theoretical and philosophical arguments on a question such as whether or not direct costing is superior to absorption costing or even the more practical question of whether or not a particular company should use direct costing. This is a controversial topic among professional accountants and accounting teachers. However, one important point regarding the latter question should be noted: It is not clear that a company must use either one of these costing schemes exclusively for all purposes. It is quite possible to devise an accounting system with direct cost capabilities that could readily produce both direct-cost and full-cost figures as desired for different purposes and do this without undue expense.

SUMMARY. Some of the important points of this chapter can be restated as follows:

1. Direct costing is an alternative to absorption costing. Under direct costing, the cost of manufactured products includes only those costs that vary with quantity produced; fixed overhead costs are treated as period costs and charged directly against income.
2. Direct costing places a lower value on manufactured inventories, and therefore on net worth, than does absorption costing. As these inventories vary from period to period, direct costing and absorption costing will give different results with respect to the measurement of income, although over the long run the average results will be the same.
3. The income statement under direct costing emphasizes the point of view that net income is the excess, if any, of the margin between sales income and the variable costs of manufacturing and selling over the fixed (period) costs.
4. Direct costing can be used in a job-order or a process cost system and in an actual-cost system or a standard cost system. If direct costing is used in an actual-cost system, the problem of pricing items out of inventory exists as it does under absorption costing.
5. A choice between direct costing and absorption costing involves consideration of many different and conflicting objectives. In general, the advantages of direct costing relate to managerial problems of control, policy formulation, and decision making. These advantages can be gained without using direct costs for the purposes of external reporting. A change from absorption costing to direct costing for financial accounting purposes may involve a write-off of a portion of the value of manufactured inventories.

DISCUSSION QUESTIONS

16-A. Define direct costing.

16-B. Explain the meaning of the term *period cost.*

16-C. Explain how net income is defined under direct costing.

16-D. "Direct cost includes certain indirect costs." How would you explain the foregoing statement to a person not acquainted with cost accounting?

16-E. Explain the following statement: "The difference between direct costing and absorption costing with respect to the measurement of net income for successive accounting periods is essentially a matter of timing."

16-F. In discussing direct costing, a student has remarked that "There is no difference between direct costing and absorption costing in the long run as far as the reporting of earnings of the company is concerned." Comment on this statement.

16-G. A single-product, single-process plant uses a variable IME budget. The burden rate of 240% of direct-labor cost is composed of a "fixed rate" of 150% and a "variable rate" of 90%. Direct materials average 260% of direct-labor cost. In the last annual report, the finished-goods value was $400,000, the cost of goods sold was $1,600,000, and retained earnings was $4,000,000. Estimate what these figures would have been if direct costing had been used for the past several years.

16-H. Explain the nature of the adjustment that may be required in the balance sheet accounts at the time of a change-over from absorption costing to direct costing. Identify the accounts affected, and for each account state whether it would need to be debited or credited.

16-J. Explain why additional production causes an increase in reported net income under absorption costing but not under direct costing.

16-K. Suggest one or two circumstances under which it might be appropriate to accept an order at a price falling above the direct cost but below the full-absorption cost of manufacturing.

16-L. In a large multiplant manufacturing company, the manager of one of the plants was transferred and replaced by a new man because of persistently unfavorable production cost results for that plant. Coincident with the appointment of the new manager, several other key people were replaced and a management incentive plan was inaugurated. Under this scheme the top executives of the plant were to receive bonus pay dependent upon the cost of the end product. The new "management team" faired very well under this bonus plan. However, 18 months later the "new" manager was relieved of his duties as the result of a study of the plant operations and cost accounting reports by the corporate controller's division. The cost accounting for the plant was handled by a standard cost full-absorption costing system. One recommendation in the controller's division report was that the system should be changed to a direct costing scheme. Discuss this recommendation, pointing out what possible connection this might have with the early success of the ill-fated new management team and how direct costing might be preferable to absorption costing in this situation.

PROBLEMS

Problem 16-1. The Double-Barb Manufacturing Co. makes a single product, barbed wire, that is sold under various brand names. Double-Barb uses standard costs and a flexible budget for factory overhead in their cost system. Following is the income statement for the past year (income taxes ignored):

DOUBLE–BARB MANUFACTURING CO.
INCOME STATEMENT
YEAR ENDED DECEMBER 31, 19__

Sales, less sales returns	$920,000
Other income	12,000
Gross income	$932,000
Cost of goods sold	$600,000
Other factory expenses	32,000
Selling and distribution expenses	170,000
General administrative expenses	120,000
Total expenses	$922,000
Net income for the year	$ 10,000

Assume that "other factory expenses" includes all variances and certain other abnormal expenses.

The standard costs used in costing the product during the year were:

	Standard Cost per Spool
Direct material	$0.40
Direct labor	0.10
Factory overhead	0.25
Total manufactured cost	$0.75

The finished-goods inventory value was $150,000 at the start of the year and $240,000 at the end of the year. Work in process is negligible at both the start and the end of the year. Sales totaled 800,000 spools. The inventory and cost of goods sold are valued at the standard cost of 75 cents per spool. The factory overhead budget estimates provide a breakdown of the overhead cost of 25 cents per spool as follows: 10 cents variable expense and 15 cents fixed expense. The 25-cent burden rate is based on a normal production of 1,000,000 spools per year. Actual production this year was 920,000 spools. In the foregoing income statement, the burden capacity variance was included in the figure labeled "other factory expenses."

A. Calculate what the starting and ending finished-goods inventory values would have been under direct costing.
B. Prepare a revised income statement on the direct costing basis. Assume that an analysis of selling and distribution costs indicates that $60,000 is fixed (period) expense. Treat all the general administrative expense as period expense. Show the miscellaneous income as the last item in the income statement.
C. Show that the difference between the two costing schemes with respect to reported net income is equal to the difference in the change in finished-goods inventory value.

Problem 16-2. The Mulch Manufacturing Company makes a single product in a single-process plant. The cost accounting is handled by a process cost system that employs standard costs. The costing of the finished product is on a direct-cost basis. Work in process at any one time is of negligible value.

The income statement for the last fiscal year was as follows:

MULCH MANUFACTURING COMPANY
INCOME STATEMENT
YEAR ENDED FEBRUARY 28, 1963

Net sales		$540,000
Less direct cost of goods sold:		
Inventory Feb. 28, 1962	$ 55,800	
Direct cost of goods manufactured	248,000	
	$303,800	
Less inventory Feb. 28, 1963	24,800	
Cost of goods sold	$279,000	279,000
Gross margin		$261,000
Less variable selling expenses		41,000
Net margin		$220,000
Less fixed expenses and adjustments:		
Manufacturing expense		83,000
Selling and administrative		96,000
Net income before taxes		$ 41,000

The "manufacturing expense" listed as period cost includes all variances and abnormal expenses as well as the fixed overhead budget.

Standard cost data are as follows:

	Standard Cost per Unit
Direct material	$1.30
Direct labor	1.20
Variable overhead	0.60
Total direct standard cost	$3.10

Sales totaled 90,000 units. The finished product is valued at the above standard cost in inventory. The variable overhead budget is based on a total estimated factory overhead of $112,500 for a normal-production year of 75,000 units.

A. Prepare an income statement for external distribution on the absorption costing basis. Show the beginning and ending finished-goods inventory values and the cost of goods manufactured as in the above direct-costing income statement.

B. Show that the difference between the two costing schemes with respect to reported net income is equal to the difference in the change in finished-goods inventory value.

Problem 16-3. Solve problem 15-6, concerning the Multi-strand Company, using direct costing. Use the same set of accounts as in problem 15-6, except that Burden Capacity Variance is not required. For any entry involving a posting to a general ledger account, that figure should be posted to the T account titled All Other Factory Ledger Accounts (one such account being General Ledger—Control).

For entry A it will be necessary to compute adjusted figures for work in process, covered wire stock, and the balance in the T account titled All Other Factory Ledger Accounts. For this purpose assume that the balance of $50,000 in the account Covered Wire Stock under absorption costing consisted of $26,000 direct-materials cost, $8,000 direct-labor cost, and $12,000 burden, all at standard cost.

Make an additional entry, I, in these accounts for the cost of covered wire stock used (in other departments). Assume that the details for such an entry under absorption costing were $25,000 direct materials, $9,000 direct labor, and $18,000 burden, a total of $52,000, all at standard cost.

Problem 16-4. Solve problem 15-4, concerning the Standard Materials Co., using direct costing. For this purpose, the following additional details of cost results under absorption costing are provided:

	Direct materials	Direct labor and overhead	Total
Work in process, Jan. 1..........	$ 1,900	$ 2,100	$ 4,000
Finished goods, Jan. 1...........	13,100	18,900	32,000
Cost of goods manufactured......	74,300	105,700	180,000
Cost of goods sold..............	76,500	108,500	185,000

Assume that a change from absorption costing to direct costing was made as of the end of the prior year and that the necessary adjustment of inventory values was made as of December 31. Determine the adjusted end-of-prior-year balances for all accounts affected, assuming that the burden rate and flexible budget used in the prior year were the same as used in the current year.

Set up a T-account ledger, and enter the opening balances in the accounts. Make entries as indicated in problem 15-4, modifying those affected by the change to direct costing. In entry L, before closing the variance accounts, transfer the fixed overhead budget amount to Profit and Loss Summary.

Prepare the balance sheet, income statement, and variance report on the direct costing basis. Also, prepare an analysis showing that the difference between the two costing schemes with respect to reported net income is equal to the difference in the change in the value of manufactured inventories during the year.

Problem 16-5. Solve problem 14-6, concerning the Mistrolite Process Co., using direct costing. The variable burden rate, as given in entry **e**, is 60% of direct-labor cost. The T accounts to be used are as specified for problem 14-6, except that Burden Capacity Variance is not required.

For entry A it will be necessary to compute adjusted figures for manufactured inventories. For the purposes of this problem, assume now that the company has been using direct costing for a number of years and that the burden rate and flexible budget used in the prior year were the same as in this year. The following additional details concerning the valuation of opening inventories under absorption costing are provided:

	Materials	Labor	Burden	Total
Bulk Misto	$3,300	$2,200	$3,300	$8,800
Packaged Misto	2,250	1,700	2,550	6,500
Job 101	1,200	400	600	2,200

In the above table, the labor and burden figures shown for packaged Misto include the labor and burden components of the cost of bulk Misto incorporated into the packaged Misto.

For the purpose of the income statement, $2,700 of the selling and general expense is to be considered direct cost; the balance is to be treated as period cost. List the variances in the period cost section of the statement.

Problem 16-6. The Mixup Blending Company specializes in high-quality, low-cost blending of fine-powdered materials into compounds for pharmaceutical and cosmetics manufacturers. The basic materials are normally provided by the customers; Mixup Blending provides only packaging materials and certain common inert ingredients. In the production cost system, actual costs are collected for each job order and compared against standard costs for materials, labor, and overhead. Overhead is applied on the absorption costing basis.

The balances in the factory ledger accounts as of January 1, 19——, were as follows:

Account	Debit	Credit
Packing Materials	$ 4,000	
Ingredient Materials	8,000	
Factory Supplies	2,500	
Jobs in Process	1,000	
Finished Goods	3,500	
General Ledger—Control		$19,000
Totals	$19,000	$19,000

The value of jobs in process represents the sum of actual quantities of materials issued to those unfinished jobs at standard prices, actual direct-labor hours spent on those jobs at standard rates, and overhead on that direct-labor cost at the standard rate of 200%. The finished-goods value is for packaged product accumulated in the shipping department for scheduled future delivery to various customers; these items are valued at standard cost. All variances are carried forward to the end of the fiscal year, December 31.

Part I

Other accounts required for Part I of this problem are as follows:

Factory Overhead Expense
Material Price Variance
Material Quantity Variance
Labor Rate Variance
Labor Time Variance
Overhead Budget Variance
Overhead Capacity Variance

Set up T accounts representing the factory ledger, using the top half of a T-account sheet. (The bottom half will be required for Part II.) Make entries directly into these factory ledger accounts for the following events which occurred during the first quarter. For any entry involving a net increase or decrease in the total value in this subsidiary ledger, post the opposing credit or debit to the balancing account, General Ledger—Control. Identify each entry by transaction letter.

A. Enter the opening balances in the accounts.

B. Debits to the factory ledger from the invoice register in this quarter were:

	Debit amount (actual cost)	Compiled standard cost
Packing materials purchased	$ 4,700	$ 5,000
Ingredient materials purchased	9,800	10,000
Factory supplies purchased	1,300	
Factory overhead expenses	25,800	
Total	$41,600	

C. Debits to the factory ledger from the payroll register for the quarter were:

	At actual rates	At standard rates
Direct labor	$24,600	$25,000
Indirect labor and supervision	14,400	
Total	$39,000	

D. Materials issued to jobs (actual quantities at standard prices) were packing materials, $3,300, and ingredient materials, $9,000, a total of $12,300.

E. The standard costs for jobs completed during the quarter were summarized as follows:

Materials	$11,000
Direct labor	23,000
Overhead	46,000
Total	$80,000

F. Depreciation on the factory and equipment for the quarter totaled $4,800; the cost of supplies used during the quarter is estimated at $2,000.

G. The cost of jobs remaining in process at the start and at the end of the quarter were summarized as follows:

	Jan. 1	Mar. 31	Increase during quarter
Materials (actual quantities at standard prices)	$ 400	$1,000	$ 600
Direct labor (actual hours at standard prices)	200	1,000	800
Overhead at 200% on the above direct labor cost	400	2,000	1,600
Totals	$1,000	$4,000	$3,000

Note: The above added materials cost of $600 is a portion of the $12,300 total stated in entry D; the added direct-labor amount, $800, is a portion of the $25,000 figure given in entry C. The $1,600 increase in end-of-period overhead on jobs in process is in addition to the $46,000 applied to jobs completed (entry E), making a total of $47,600 overhead applied for the quarter.

H. The standard cost of finished product shipped to customers during the quarter amounted to a total of $69,000.

I. Mixup uses a variable overhead budget to obtain a breakdown of the total factory overhead variance into two components—capacity variance and budget variance. The budget figure for a given quarter is determined from the following analysis:

Estimated factory overhead for a normal quarter............ $42,000
Estimated standard direct-labor cost for a normal quarter.... $21,000
Expected variation in overhead: $0.75 per standard direct labor dollar

For unfinished jobs, actual hours at the standard labor rate is used in lieu of standard direct-labor cost.

J. Determine the total actual factory overhead, and make the appropriate entry in the factory ledger.

Rule and balance all accounts, and take a trial balance of the factory ledger.

Part II

On the bottom half of the T-account sheet used in Part I, set up new T accounts as follows:

Overhead Budget Variance
Jobs in Process
Finished Goods
General Ledger—Control

Assume now that a change from absorption costing to direct costing was made as of the start of the year. Resolve the problem using the following information concerning the finished goods, together with the information available in Part I. The accounts affected are those listed above; consider the other eight accounts used in Part I to be part of your new ledger.

Details concerning the postings to the Finished Goods account under absorption costing (Part I) are as follows:

	Balance Jan. 1	Added during quarter	Cost of goods sold
Materials............	$ 500	$11,000	$ 9,000
Direct labor..........	1,000	23,000	20,000
Overhead............	2,000	46,000	40,000
Totals.............	$3,500	$80,000	$69,000

A. Enter the opening (absorption costing) balances in the new Jobs in Process, Finished Goods, and General Ledger—Control accounts. Now determine the adjustments that would be required as of January 1 to make the change to direct costing, and make an appropriate adjusting entry in these accounts. Information required for this is given in entries G and I in Part I.

B through J. Make the appropriate postings that would be required under direct costing to the four new T accounts. Some of the required postings will be the same as in Part I; these should be shown in the accounts along with those that are now revised.

K. Calculate the fixed overhead budget amount, and make an appropriate entry in the factory ledger accounts disposing of this share of the factory overhead as required for direct costing.

Rule and balance the accounts. Take a trial balance of the factory ledger, using columns adjacent to the trial balance taken in Part I so that the results are displayed in comparative fashion.

Part III

Customers were billed $106,000 for the product shipped during the quarter. Selling and distribution expenses totaled $12,000, of which $4,000 is to be considered period expense and $8,000 direct expense for the purposes of direct costing. General and administrative expense totaled $18,000; this is all treated as period expense.

Using this information, together with that developed in Parts I and II, prepare a special comparative income statement displaying the differences between direct costing and absorption costing, in the following format:

	Absorption Costing	*Direct Costing*
Sales	$xxx,xxx	$xxx,xxx
Less cost of goods sold	xx,xxx	xx,xxx
Gross margin	$ xx,xxx	$ xx,xxx
Less direct selling expenses	xx,xxx	xx,xxx
Net margin	$ xx,xxx	$ xx,xxx
Less fixed overhead budget		xx,xxx
Less period selling expenses	xx,xxx	xx,xxx
Less general and administrative expense	xx,xxx	xx,xxx
Net operating margin	$ x,xxx	$ x,xxx
Manufacturing variances	x,xxx	x,xxx
Net operating income	$ x,xxx	$ x,xxx
Inventory cost adjustment		x,xxx
Net income	$ x,xxx	$ x,xxx

Note that, even though the six manufacturing variances are carried forward in the accounts to the end of the year, you are asked to show them in this special-analysis statement as adjustments to net income. The purpose of this is to illustrate the effect of burden capacity variance in a comparison of direct costing and absorption costing.

Following your comparative income statement, show that the difference between the two costing schemes with respect to reported net income (as shown on the "net operating income" line in your statement) is equal to the difference in change in the value of manufactured inventories during the year.

17/ QUALITY COSTS AND JOINT COSTS

In any brief treatment of cost accounting, there are necessarily many aspects of the subject that must be omitted. Nevertheless, there are certain topics that need to be mentioned even though space is not available to discuss them at length. Two such topics are presented in this chapter, namely:

1. The accounting treatment of spoilage and rework
2. Problems created by joint products and by-products

SPOILAGE AND REWORK. Every manufactured article has its particular design specifications, sometimes implied but more often clearly expressed. For example, a dimension such as the diameter of a shaft might be specified as 1.620 ± 0.005 inches; the drained weight of the contents of a can of tomatoes might be specified as at least 18 ounces.

In many manufacturing operations, some product is made that fails to meet the design specifications. Such nonconforming product is referred to as *defective.* Some defective product can be corrected by additional manufacturing operations, referred to as *rework.* For example, an additional machining operation on a shaft with a diameter of 1.630 could bring the diameter within specified limits of 1.625 and 1.615. Other defective product, not subject to correction at any reasonable cost, is referred to as *spoilage.* Some spoilage must be junked or sold for scrap. Other spoilage, defective in the sense of failing to meet its original specifications, may still be useful for some other purpose, possibly an inferior one.

ACCOUNTING TREATMENT OF SPOILAGE AND REWORK. Consider a job calling for the production of 1,000 articles. Experience indicates that the production process is not capable of making all articles to conform to specifications. Assume that, because 40 articles are spoiled, the job requires material and labor sufficient for 1,040 articles rather than for 1,000. Assume also that, of the 1,000 good articles finally produced, 120 were originally defective and were later corrected by rework operations. It is evident that the cost on the 40 spoiled articles and the rework costs on the 120 articles are properly viewed as part of the total cost of making the 1,000 good articles.

In job cost accounting, such costs are sometimes included in total job costs without being separately identified. A job is charged with all materials issued to it whether the materials subsequently appear in the good articles produced or in the spoiled articles. And the job is charged with all labor including the rework labor and that on the spoiled work. In such cases, the reported unit costs for good articles are influenced by the spoilage and rework, even though no one knows how much spoilage and rework have occurred. A similar treatment that includes these costs without identifying them is possible in process cost accounting.

If an accurate record is kept of the amount of spoiled work, it is usually possible to make close estimates of the labor and material costs for which the spoilage is responsible. Rework costs can be measured by identifying all rework operations in the accounts. Even when measured separately, the costs of spoilage and rework are included in the manufacturing costs of the good articles produced. Usually they are charged to the appropriate jobs or processes; sometimes they are treated as manufacturing overhead costs and distributed through the burden rate.

CONTROL OF SPOILAGE AND REWORK COSTS. It is of interest to examine the accounting aspects of spoilage and rework from the point of view of the three general objectives of cost accounting discussed in Chap. 9. For the purposes of inventory valuation and finding cost of goods sold and for the purposes of pricing matters, it is sufficient that the costs of spoilage and rework be included as part of the manufacturing costs of the products on which they were incurred. For these purposes it is not necessary that spoilage and rework costs be known.

In contrast, for purposes of cost control, spoilage and rework costs should be identified separately and should be reported to management at frequent intervals. In many manufacturing enterprises, one of the most effective ways to reduce costs is to decrease the percentages of spoilage and rework. To judge the effectiveness of efforts to control spoilage and rework costs, these costs need to be measured and reported.

A MODERN VIEWPOINT ON THE CONTROL OF QUALITY. Modern statistical methods of quality control have often been spectacularly successful in reducing the percentages of defective product made. This improvement generally occurs, at least in part, because of better diagnosis of the causes of quality troubles. In general, modern quality-control methods are associated with the philosophy that the best way to get good product is to make it right in the first place. It often happens that reductions in spoilage and rework also make it possible to reduce inspection costs by using a scientific sampling inspection plan in place of the previous 100% inspection. Moreover, because of the inevitable inspection errors occurring where 100% inspection is necessary, the same measures that reduce spoilage and rework are likely to improve the quality of outgoing product.[1]

An analysis of the costs associated with quality properly includes spoilage and rework costs, inspection costs, and the adverse effects resulting from delivering unsatisfactory product to customers. These adverse effects may be hard to express in money units, although in some companies the costs of customer service during guarantee periods may give a useful measure. In some instances, also, an analysis of the cost aspects of quality calls for examining certain direct production costs. Such costs may be reduced by quality improvements that reduce the numbers of defectives. For example, consider a manufacturing plant with a forge shop, a machine shop, and an assembly department. Better forgings may reduce labor and overhead costs in the machine shop; better machined parts may reduce labor and overhead costs in the assembly department.

JOINT PRODUCTS. Most manufacturing plants make more than one product. The different products inevitably have certain costs in common. It frequently is the case that the only common costs are the indirect manufacturing expenses; the direct-labor and direct-material costs can be identified for each product. Our examples and problems up to this point have all been based on the assumption that this was true.

In a number of industries, however, an initial raw material is converted into two or more products. Such products are referred to as *joint products;* the material costs and the labor and overhead costs up to the point of division are called *joint costs.*

Joint products seem to be the rule rather than the exception in the chemical and metallurgical industries, the lumber industry, and the food industry. For example, many different petroleum products and chemicals are made from crude oil; many different grades of lumber are

[1] The following references on modern quality control are suggested:

Irving W. Burr, *Engineering Statistics and Quality Control,* McGraw-Hill Book Company, Inc., New York, 1953.

A. J. Duncan, *Quality Control and Industrial Statistics,* 2d ed., Richard D. Irwin, Inc., Homewood, Ill., 1959.

A. V. Feigenbaum, *Total Quality Control,* McGraw-Hill Book Company, Inc., New York, 1961.

Eugene L. Grant, *Statistical Quality Control,* 3d ed., McGraw-Hill Book Company, Inc., New York, 1964.

J. M. Juran, *Quality Control Handbook,* 2d ed., McGraw-Hill Book Company, Inc., New York, 1962.

produced from logs; many different dairy products are made from milk. Numerous similar examples of joint products will doubtless occur to the reader.

ACCOUNTING FOR JOINT PRODUCTS. Most industries making joint products employ process cost accounting. Each product is likely to have its own separable costs after the point of division; these separable costs create no special accounting problems. The really troublesome problem is how to apportion the joint costs at the point of division. A number of different methods are employed, and no method is entirely satisfactory.

AN EXAMPLE OF JOINT COSTS. This type of problem can be illustrated to best advantage by a simple numerical example.

A chemical plant makes two products, Y and Z. The plant has three departments, J, K, and L. In J, certain raw materials are combined and treated to produce two compounds, A and B. Compound A goes to department K where it is combined with other materials to become product Y. Compound B goes to department L where it is processed to become product Z. The following departmental outputs and material, labor, and overhead costs are expected during a normal accounting period. In the analysis of these costs, it is assumed that the amount in process in the three departments can be disregarded on the grounds that this amount is small and constant.

	Department J	Department K	Department L
Material cost......	$10,000	$2,000	
Labor cost.........	2,000	1,400	$1,200
Overhead cost......	3,000	2,100	1,800
Total cost.......	$15,000	$5,500	$3,000
Output...........	40 tons of A and 60 tons of B	50 tons of Y	60 tons of Z

The material costs shown for departments K and L do not include any costs of the compounds A and B delivered from department J. It is evident that the sum of the costs assigned to these two compounds should equal $15,000, the total cost in department J. The problem of joint-cost allocation is to divide this $15,000 between A and B. The division between A and B will, in turn, influence the unit costs computed for products Y and Z.

ALLOCATING JOINT COSTS IN PROPORTION TO QUANTITY. A simple basis of allocation would be in proportion to the respective weights of the two compounds produced in J. Compound A is 40% of the total 100-ton weight, and B is 60%. Such an allocation would result in a charge of $6,000 to department K for the 40 tons of A received from department J; the total cost of the 50 tons of product Y would then appear to be $6,000 + $5,500 = $11,500 or $230 per ton.

Similarly a charge of $9,000 for the 60 tons of compound B would cause the total costs of the 60 tons of product Z to be $12,000 or $200 per ton.

The unit cost figures for final product, such as $230 and $200 per ton, would be used for inventory valuation and for determining cost of goods sold. In many instances, it will happen that such allocations in proportion to quantity will give unit costs that are clearly inappropriate for these or any other purposes.

ALLOCATING JOINT COSTS IN PROPORTION TO MARKET VALUE MINUS SEPARABLE MANUFACTURING COSTS. For example, assume that the market price at which product Z can be sold is only $125 a ton whereas product Y is salable at $520 a ton. It obviously would be misleading to value the inventory of Z at $200 a ton, a figure considerably above its possible selling price. Generally speaking, the prices at which the different joint products can be sold need to be considered in judging the appropriateness of any proposed scheme of allocation of joint costs.

If selling costs of the various final products are to be used as a basis for allocation of joint costs at the point of division, consideration also needs to be given to the separable manufacturing costs of each product beyond that point. The following calculation illustrates a possible method of recognizing selling prices and separable costs in an allocation.

	Product Y	Product Z
Units produced in a representative period	50 tons	60 tons
Expected average selling price per unit	$520 per ton	$125 per ton
Expected gross receipts from sales of units produced	$26,000	$7,500
Separable manufacturing costs	5,500	3,000
Receipts from sales minus separable costs	$20,500	$4,500
Proportion of joint costs allocated to each product	0.82	0.18
Portion of $15,000 joint costs allocated to each product	$12,300	$2,700
Allocated plus separable costs	$17,800	$5,700
Computed unit cost of each product	$356 per ton	$95 per ton

ACCOUNTING TREATMENT OF BY-PRODUCTS. A by-product may be defined as a joint product of minor importance. Generally speaking, none of the joint costs are charged to the by-products. There is no fixed rule regarding how minor a joint product must be before it is treated in the accounts as if it were a by-product.

Some commodities that are the main products of one industry are by-products in another. For those commodities produced chiefly as by-products, the total quantity produced is likely to depend more on the demand for other products (the main products) than on the demand

for the by-product itself. Sometimes this condition results in violent fluctuations in the market price of a by-product.

Different accounting systems treat the income from the sale of by-products in different ways. Sometimes this income (minus separable expenses of by-product production, if any) is treated as a credit to the cost of production of the main products. With this method of treatment, by-product income does not appear separately in the profit and loss statement; the greater the revenue from the by-product, the less the apparent cost of production of the main products. In cases where a by-product price fluctuates greatly, this accounting treatment may be viewed as undesirable because the apparent cost of the main products will be changed at frequent intervals by events unrelated either to the production operations themselves or to the cost of purchased materials.

An alternative accounting treatment is to show by-product revenue in a separate income account included in the profit and loss statement. Any separable costs for manufacturing and handling the by-products will be shown as offsetting expenses.

JOINT PRODUCT COSTS IN RELATION TO THE OBJECTIVES OF COST ACCOUNTING. In joint-product industries, the allocation of joint costs is sometimes viewed as a necessary evil. Allocations are necessary to value inventories for balance sheet purposes and to prepare profit and loss statements and income tax returns. Thus, joint costs must be allocated for financial accounting purposes. But generally speaking, such allocations cannot contribute either to sales policy determination or to cost control.

One common use of product cost figures is evaluation of the profitability of different product lines and items, sometimes leading to a decision to deemphasize or abandon certain commodities. However, in joint-cost situations, such decisions should not logically be influenced by the methods used to allocate the joint costs. As a simple illustration of this point, consider a sawmill that buys logs and saws them into first-grade and second-grade lumber, with the sorting into grades taking place after the boards are sawed. Joint costs include the purchase price of the logs and the sawing and sorting expenses. Assume that these joint costs are allocated in proportion to board feet of lumber produced and that this allocation leads to the conclusion that the second-grade lumber is being sold at less than cost. It should be obvious that this conclusion is meaningless as a guide to a decision about abandoning the production of second-grade lumber. It is not possible to produce the first-grade lumber without also producing the second-grade. Assume that the second-grade lumber is being marketed through the same trade channels as the first-grade and is subject to the same storage and curing. Conceivably, a decision might be made to sell the second-grade at the mill as green lumber at a lower price, or perhaps this lumber might be given away or disposed of by burning. But an analysis to choose between any such alternatives calls for a consideration of differences in costs and revenues and should not be related to any allocation of joint costs.

Thus the extra revenues from selling the second-grade lumber through regular trade channels as compared with selling the lumber green at the mill might properly be compared with the separate costs of handling, curing, shipping, and storing this lumber. If the abandonment of the entire operation involving both grades were to be considered, the total costs and total revenues would be relevant. Generally speaking, although it is essential to know total costs and separable costs as a guide to making decisions on sales policies in joint-cost situations, the allocations of joint costs are of no value as guides to such decisions.

In joint-product industries, just as in other manufacturing, effective control of material and labor costs requires the measurement of the costs of separate operations and the comparison of actual unit costs of material and labor with some type of cost standards. Such comparisons should not be dependent on allocations of joint costs.

STANDARD COSTS IN JOINT–COST SITUATIONS. All industries using process cost accounting are confronted by the problem of pricing interdepartmental transfers of work in process. This statement applies to joint-cost industries as well as to other industries. As pointed out in earlier chapters, accounting for such transfers is simpler with standard costs than with actual costs. This simplification is particularly helpful in joint-cost situations, facilitating cost control in departments located beyond the point of separation of joint products.

SUMMARY. Some of the important points of this chapter can be restated as follows:

1. For purposes of cost control, it is desirable that the costs of spoilage and rework be measured and reported. Nevertheless, in many cost accounting systems these costs are merely included in the cost of the good articles produced but are not identified separately.
2. When two or more products are made from the same raw material (or materials), the costs up to the point of division are referred to as joint costs. In order to value inventories of work in process and finished goods, some scheme for apportioning these joint costs must be adopted. Although no method for this apportionment is really satisfactory, it usually is desirable to adopt a method that gives weight to the prices at which the joint products can be sold and to the separable costs of the different joint products after the point of division.
3. A by-product is a joint product the value of which is relatively small. Usually no joint costs are charged against the by-products.

DISCUSSION QUESTIONS

17-A. Mention some manufacturing operation with which you are familiar that often requires rework. What difficulties can you see in the way of measuring the cost of this rework?

17-B. Mention some manufacturing operation with which you are familiar that often results in spoilage that must be sold for scrap. Discuss the accounting problems that you think are involved in measuring the cost of this spoilage and in disposing of this cost in the accounts. How would you suggest that receipts from the sale of the scrap be treated in the accounts?

17-C. Mention some manufacturing operation with which you are familiar that often results in product that does not meet specifications but is good enough to be sold to the public as "seconds." Discuss the accounting problems that you think are likely to exist in separating the costs of the articles meeting specifications from the costs of the seconds and in valuing the inventories and determining the costs of goods sold for both types of articles.

17-D. In those manufacturing operations in which spoilage and rework are common, why is it important to measure these costs separately? Why not allow them to be merged into the other manufacturing costs without being identified?

17-E. Mention some joint products with which you are familiar. What manufacturing operations take place before and after the point of division? How would you suggest that the joint costs ought to be handled in the accounts?

17-F. Mention some joint product with which you are familiar that is of such minor importance that you think it should be classified as a by-product. Discuss the various accounting problems that you would expect to arise in connection with this by-product.

17-G. The text suggests that commodities produced chiefly as by-products are likely to be subject to substantial price fluctuations. Why? In what ways may this likelihood of price fluctuations influence the method selected for accounting for by-product revenues?

17-H. In a certain pea cannery, peas are graded into several sizes before being canned. Cans containing the smallest sizes are sold for the highest prices, and cans containing the largest sizes are sold for the lowest prices. The manager of the cannery has stated that the cannery makes all its profit on the smallest sized peas and loses money on the large sizes. Comment on this statement.

PROBLEMS

Problem 17-1. The Marvel Manufacturing Co. has a job-order cost system in which all spoilage and rework costs are included in the unit cost of the satisfactory items produced under each job order. Neither spoilage nor rework costs are treated as IME in this system.

A job order was issued for 2,000 widgets for finished-goods stock. Costs charged to the job were direct material, \$320; direct labor, \$240; IME, \$360.

The company produced 2,300 widgets, but 600 of these failed to pass final inspection. Of the rejected widgets, 200 were scrapped and 400 were reworked at additional costs of $40 for direct labor and $60 for IME. Of the reworked units, 300 passed inspection; the other 100 were scrapped.

A. What was the cost per unit of the 2,000 widgets that passed final inspection?
B. What would the unit cost have been if all 2,300 widgets had passed inspection in the first place (without any rework)?
C. What would the unit cost have been if all 600 of the rejected widgets had been reworked successfully at a cost of $60 for direct labor and $90 for IME?

Problem 17-2. The F-G-H Chemical Co. combines several raw materials and processes them in department R. A by-product of this operation is product H, which is sold without further processing to a buyer who takes the product away in his own trucks. From department R the main product goes to department S; here it is treated and divided into two parts. The first part is piped to department T, where, after further processing, it becomes product F. The second part goes to department U, where, after combination with another raw material, it becomes product G. This is a continuous-process industry in which the product in process at any moment is small in relation to a month's output. As this work in process is small and practically constant, it is neglected in computing the unit cost for any period.

The raw material, labor, and burden for the manufacturing departments during a 3-month period were as follows:

	Raw material	Labor	Burden	Total
Department R................	$90,000	$20,000	$40,000	$150,000
Department S................	....	8,000	14,000	22,000
Department T................	....	10,000	20,000	30,000
Department U................	34,000	6,000	10,000	50,000

Department R produced 100,000 pounds of by-product H which was sold at 8 cents per pound. The gross receipts from the sale of this are considered as a credit to the manufacturing cost of the main products.

Department T produced 500,000 pounds of product F; the average gross selling price of this during the period was 48 cents a pound. Department U produced 600 tons of product G; the average gross selling price of this during the period was $200 a ton.

Joint costs of products F and G are divided in proportions to the gross selling price of the total output of each minus the separate costs of each. On this basis, determine the unit cost per ton of products F and G.

Problem 17-3. The Aromatic Lumber Co. manufactures cedar tongue-and-groove lumber. The company buys logs on a delivered-to-the-mill basis. The products are 2- and 4-inch "T-and-G." A by-product is made from the sawdust.

The cost of logs used and the labor and overhead costs up to a certain point in the manufacturing process are joint costs that must be allocated to the two widths of T-and-G produced. After the point of split-off, additional labor and overhead are applied on the basis of time spent on each of the two widths in the subsequent processes.

The sawdust is collected and processed automatically as it is generated. At the end of each day the by-product accumulated during the day is bagged and put into inventory. The selling price of this by-product varies with the local demand and supply, from as low as 30 cents per bag to as high as 50 cents per bag. It has averaged about 40 cents over the past several years. For accounting purposes the by-product is valued in inventory at a standard cost of 25 cents per bag. The direct costs of processing the sawdust and bagging it are charged to an account titled Sawdust Variance. This account is credited for the value of the by-product produced at the standard cost of 25 cents per bag. For any given month the difference is a credit balance in this account. This credit balance is closed each month to the account in which the joint costs of T-and-G are collected.

The following data are for 1 month's operations:

Logs on hand, start of month	$10,000
Logs purchased during month	$30,000
Logs on hand, end of month	$15,000
Production during the month:	
2-in. width	1,000,000 bd ft
4-in. width	800,000 bd ft
By-product	15,000 bags
Production expenses to point of split-off	$40,000
Direct expenses after point of split-off:	
Applicable to 2-in.-width T-and-G	$15,000
Applicable to 4-in.-width T-and-G	$ 8,000
Applicable to the by-product	$ 1,750

A. Allocate the common expenses up to the point of split-off to the two joint products on the basis of board feet (bd ft) produced, and compute the cost per thousand board feet for each width.

B. If the market prices of the two products are 0.092 per board foot for the 2-inch and 0.110 per board foot for the 4-inch, determine the unit costs using the "market price method" of allocating joint costs.

Problem 17-4. The Sunshine Dairy Products Company converts whole milk into two main products: butter and powdered milk. In department A the incoming milk is cooled, filtered, irradiated, and stored; finally the cream and skim milk are separated. In department B the cream is converted into butter, which is packaged. Department B also produces a by-product, buttermilk. Sunshine is able to sell all this commodity to Flopjacks, Inc., a chain of restaurants, for 50 cents per gallon. In department C the skim milk is dehydrated and packaged.

Costs in the three departments for the past month are as follows:

Department	Materials	Labor	Overhead	Total
A	$40,000	$15,000	$17,000	$72,000
B	1,800	11,200	14,000	27,000
C	2,500	10,000	15,000	27,500

Sunshine produced during this month 150,000 pounds of butter, 125,000 pounds of powdered milk, and 15,000 gallons of buttermilk. Department A produced 40,000 gallons of cream and 160,000 gallons of skim milk. Butter is selling at 48 cents a pound and powdered milk for 52 cents a pound; both prices are wholesale.

At present, department A costs are allocated to cream (department B) and skim milk (department C) on the basis of gallons produced. Department B is credited for all buttermilk produced at 50 cents per gallon. However, the management is unhappy with the unit costs of butter and powdered milk arrived at by these calculations.

A. What were the calculated unit costs of butter and powdered milk for the past month?

B. Find unit costs for butter and powdered milk by allocating the joint costs in proportion to market value minus separate costs.

C. Which method of finding costs do you prefer in this case, A or B? Why?

Problem 17-5. The Lottsaw Brass Company produces two items, X and Y. Item X is a specialty item that has a high profit margin and is the main source of revenue. Item Y is a highly competitive item, in which field this company is a small producer. In spite of the separable costs of making item Y, it ordinarily pays to produce this item because it is made from the scrap produced in the manufacture of X.

Because of the competitive nature of item Y, the volume produced fluctuates considerably according to market conditions. It is desired that the joint costs be apportioned in a way that will make the unit costs computed for item X as independent as possible of the production level of item Y.

The plant consists of four main departments as shown in the accompanying diagram. Department R uses a single raw material, A. The product of department R is material B, all of which goes to department S. The main product, X, is made in department S. A hand sorting operation is carried out on the scrap in department S. The scrap that is usable in making item Y goes to department T; in the diagram, this sorted scrap is designated as C.

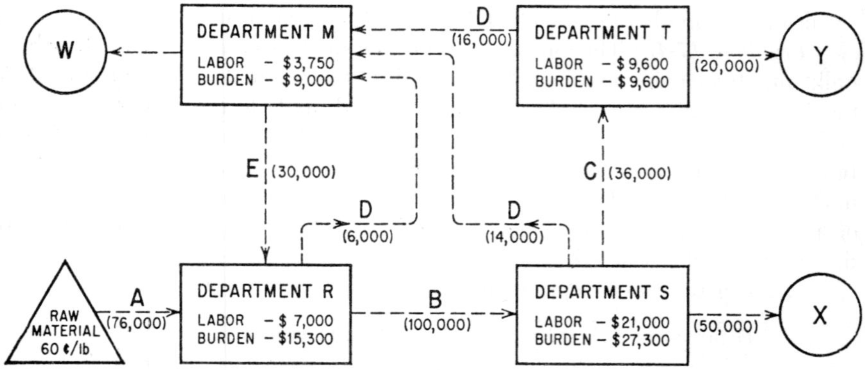

In all three departments, R, S, and T, there is a scrap item D that is reclaimed in department M. All this reclaimed material, designated in the diagram as E, is used in department R in place of equal quantities of new raw material A. Waste W, produced in department M, is accumulated for periodic sale. The proceeds from the sale of W are expected to average ½ cent per pound of material E produced in department M.

Estimates for a normal quarter-year are shown on the diagram. The figures in parentheses are estimated quantities in pounds. Also shown are the standard cost per pound of the raw material A and the estimated weekly direct-labor and burden expenses in each department. It is estimated that the costs incurred in department S that can be attributed to the job of segregating and sorting scrap for department T amount to 5 cents per pound of sorted scrap, C, sent to department T.

Calculate standard unit values in cents per pound for B, C, D, and E. These standard costs are to be used when costing the materials transferred from one department to another. Using these values, calculate standard costs for X and Y.

Hint: Begin by establishing the standard price for E. The correct standard cost for product X is $2.48.

Prepare a table summarizing the standard costs by departments. Use the format shown below. For each department, list the standard costs in terms of dollars per pound of output of the main product of that department.

	Department M	Department R	Department S	Department T
Raw material	D	E, A	B	C
By-product	W	D	D, C	D
Main product	Y	B	X	Y
Standard costs per pound:				
Direct material				
Direct labor				
Burden				
Subtotal				
By-product credit:				
Material				
Labor				
Net standard cost				

Problem 17-6. This problem consists of keeping the factory ledger for the Lottsaw Brass Co. (of problem 17-5) for the third quarter of the fiscal year, using the standard costs calculated in problem 17-5.

The factory ledger accounts required and the opening balances as of July 1 are listed below.

Account	Debit	Credit
Material D	$ 1,050	
Material A	15,000	
Material B	25,500	
Material C	2,000	
Material Quantity Variance, Dept. M		
Material Quantity Variance, Dept. R		
Material Quantity Variance, Dept. S		
Material Quantity Variance, Dept. T		
Labor Variance, Dept. M		
Labor Variance, Dept. R		
Labor Variance, Dept. S		
Labor Variance, Dept. T		
Burden Variance, Dept. M		
Burden Variance, Dept. R		
Burden Variance, Dept. S		
Burden Variance, Dept. T		
Work in Process, Dept. M		
Work in Process, Dept. R		
Work in Process, Dept. S		
Work in Process, Dept. T	1,600	
Material W	150	
Scrap Quantity Variance, Dept. R		
Scrap Quantity Variance, Dept. S		
Scrap Quantity Variance, Dept. T		
Material W Variance		
Price Variance, Material A		
Product X	37,200	
Product Y	9,000	
General Ledger—Control		$91,500
Totals	$91,500	$91,500

A. Enter the opening balances in the accounts.

B. Debits to the factory ledger during the quarter are summarized as follows:

	Department M	Department R	Department S	Department T	Total
Direct labor	$2,650	$ 5,350	$19,000	$10,000	$ 37,000
Indirect labor	1,050	1,850	5,600	3,500	12,000
All other IME	6,000	12,000	20,000	6,000	44,000
Material A purchased: 60,000 lb	....	....	....	....	35,000
Total (enter in controlling account)	....	....	....	....	$128,000

Following are summary figures for actual quantities transferred during the quarter.

	Department M	Department R	Department S	Department T	Total
Production, lb.	20,000 E	80,000 B	45,000 X	20,000 Y	
Raw material used	26,000 D	84,000*	91,000 B	37,000 C	
Material D generated		4,000 D	12,000 D	17,000 D	33,000 D
Material C sorted from scrap			34,000 C		

* 20,000 E plus 64,000 A.

C. Make the necessary entries concerning raw materials used (actual quantities) and direct-material cost applied to work in process (at standard costs).

D. Make the necessary entries applying direct labor to work in process (at standard costs).

E. Make the necessary entries applying factory burden to work in process (at standard costs).

F. Make the necessary entries concerning material D generated, material C sorted from scrap, and material W generated (½ cent per pound of material E produced). When these entries are made, any differences between actual quantities and standard quantities should be reflected in the appropriate variance accounts.

G. The work in process in department T at the end of the quarter was valued at $2,200. A breakdown of this figure and comparative data for the start of the quarter are as follows:

	Material	Labor	Burden	Total
End of quarter	$1,100	$550	$550	$2,200
Start of quarter	740	430	430	1,600
Difference	$ 360	$120	$120	$ 600

Make an appropriate adjusting entry for this.

H. Make the necessary entries concerning material E (i.e., material A) produced, and products X and Y manufactured.

I. Make entries for the cost of goods sold:
Product X shipped during the quarter: 50,000 pounds
Product Y shipped during the quarter: 22,550 pounds

J. By-product W valued at $200 on the books was sold for $250. The entire $250 was credited to the factory ledger.

K. All variances are to be closed out of the factory ledger at the end of the quarter (to Profit and Loss in the general ledger).

Determine and show the end-of-quarter balance in each account. Take a post-closing trial balance of the factory ledger. In addition to the T-account ledger, submit a summary table of the manufacturing variances in the format indicated below. Show credit variances in parentheses; show the material price variance and the material W variance in the column headed Other.

	Department M	Department R	Department S	Department T	Other	Total
Material-price variance...	____	____	____	____	____	____
Material-quantity variance	____	____	____	____	____	____
Scrap-quantity variance...	____	____	____	____	____	____
Material W variance......	____	____	____	____	____	____
Labor variance...........	____	____	____	____	____	____
Burden variance..........	____	____	____	____	____	____
Totals................	____	____	____	____	____	____

3 / SOME ACCOUNTING TOPICS

18/ FORMS OF OWNERSHIP ORGANIZATION; INCOME TAXES

In Parts 1 and 2 of this book, many simplifications were made in order to focus attention on the essentials of general accounting and cost accounting. Also, many important matters were mentioned very briefly or not at all. Two such topics are income taxes and alternative legal forms of business organization. This chapter includes a brief introduction to certain accounting aspects of sole proprietorships and partnerships and some discussion of income taxes in relation to accounting.

SOME LEGAL ASPECTS OF THE CORPORATE FORM OF ORGANIZATION. In a modern industrial society, practically everyone ought to understand the general features of the corporate form of business organization. Presumably most readers of this book will have such understanding. Some well-known aspects of corporations were stated in Chap. 1: The corporation is created by the charter from the state; it is owned by its stockholders; it has continued existence even though its owners may change.

A corporation is a legal entity apart from its owners; it has the right to sue and to be sued in the courts of law. It also is a business entity; the accounts of a corporation record its position as a business enterprise apart from its owners.

An important legal feature of the corporation as a form of organization is the limited personal liability of its owners for its debts. In the usual case where stock is "fully paid and non-assessable," the worst that ordinarily can happen to a stockholder in the event of the failure of his corporation is the loss of his investment; the creditors of the corporation cannot hold him legally liable for its debts.

The governing body of a corporation is its board of directors. The directors are elected by the stockholders to serve for stated terms. The board of directors, in turn, selects the major officers of the corporation, who actually manage the enterprise. The stockholder's influence on management is therefore exerted by means of his vote for members of the board of directors. Depending on circumstances, this influence may be large or small. At one extreme, the major stockholders of a small, closed corporation are likely to select themselves as directors; they may also be the active officers of their corporation. At the other extreme, a small stockholder in a large corporation will usually have a negligible influence on the management.

EXHIBIT 18-1

TRANSACTIONS FOR C. E. WOOD, APRIL TO JUNE, 19____

A. C. E. Wood starts business as a land surveyor, investing $6,000 in cash from his personal funds.

B. For $2,400 cash, the business purchases surveying equipment (considered as fixed assets).

C. Accounts payable incurred for expenses of salaries, rent, expendible supplies, etc., are a total of $4,800.

D. Customers are billed for land-surveying services, $7,500.

E. Collections on accounts receivable are $5,200.

F. Payments on accounts payable are $4,200.

G. During the period, Wood withdrew $2,240 in cash for his personal use.

Adjusting and Closing Entries

H. Depreciation charged on the surveying equipment for the period is $60.

I. Income and expense accounts are closed into Profit and Loss Summary.

J. Profit and Loss Summary is closed into C. E. Wood, Drawings.

K. The balance in Wood's drawing account is closed into his capital account.

A SIMPLE EXAMPLE OF ACCOUNTING FOR A SOLE PROPRIETORSHIP. The simplest form of business organization is the one in which a single individual is the sole owner. No contractual agreements between prospective owners or other formal legal procedures are necessary to start such an enterprise.

The law does not recognize a business conducted as a sole proprietorship as a separate entity apart from the other activities of its owner. Nevertheless, it is desirable that the owner recognize his business enterprise as a separate entity for accounting purposes. The accounts of the enterprise should be kept in a manner that does not confuse the affairs of the enterprise with the personal affairs of the owner.

Asset, liability, income, and expense accounts in a sole proprietorship are governed by the same principles and accounting conventions that have already been illustrated in this book with respect to corporations. The chief differences between the accounts of these two types of enterprise occur in the accounts summarizing ownership, in the accounts recording the withdrawal of profits, and in the treatment of compensation for the owner's services to the enterprise.

Exhibits 18-1 and 18-2 constitute a simple example designed to illustrate these matters. The transactions shown in Exhibit 18-1 summarize the occurrences during the first 3 months of C. E. Wood's land-surveying business. In the T-account ledger, Exhibit 18-2, matters have been simplified by using one account for all expenses rather than using the several expense accounts that actually would be needed.

EXHIBIT 18-2

T-ACCOUNT LEDGER SHOWING ENTRIES IN ACCOUNTS OF C. E. WOOD, APRIL TO JUNE, 19___

Cash

Debit	Credit
A 6,000	2,400 B
E 5,200	4,200 F
	2,240 G

Accounts Receivable

Debit	Credit
D 7,500	5,200 E

Income

Debit	Credit
I 7,500	7,500 D

C. E. Wood, Capital

Debit	Credit
	6,000 A
	400 K

Surveying Instruments

Debit	Credit
B 2,400	

Accounts Payable

Debit	Credit
F 4,200	4,800 C

Expense

Debit	Credit
C 4,800	4,860 I
H 60	

C. E. Wood, Drawings

Debit	Credit
G 2,240	2,640 J
K 400	

Res. for Depr., Surv. Insts.

Debit	Credit
	60 H

Profit and Loss Summary

Debit	Credit
I 4,860	7,500 I
J 2,640	

Some comments on points illustrated by this example are as follows:

1. The account C. E. Wood, Capital, serves the same purpose as the combined Capital Stock and Earned Surplus accounts in a corporation. Thus the $400 net increase in Ownership computed at the end of the period is transferred to the account C. E. Wood, Capital, rather than to an Earned Surplus account. In a sole proprietorship there is no legal necessity to keep a figure for retained earnings separate from the figure for the outside funds invested in the enterprise. (Although Exhibit 18-2 illustrates the common treatment of the matter, a sole proprietor may, of course, introduce an extra account in his books to separate his investment from his retained earnings if he so desires.)
2. Unlike the corporation, the sole proprietorship requires no formal procedure for the withdrawal of profits. The owner is free to withdraw profits (or capital) at any time that his judgment dictates. During the 3 months covered by this example, Wood withdrew $2,240 of cash for his personal use. The resulting decrease in Ownership was shown on the books by debiting these withdrawals to the

account C. E. Wood, Drawings. (An alternative title for this account would be C. E. Wood, Personal.)

3. Even though Wood devotes his full-time personal services to this enterprise, his books do not show him paying a salary to himself. His profit figure of $2,640 for the 3 months therefore does not have the same meaning as a profit figure for a corporation; the corporation must pay for all services performed for it. Wood should properly view this $2,640 as including both the payment for personal services including managerial services and the return that he has made as a result of his investment and risk taking.

Such a disregard of Wood's personal services in entering expenses in the accounts reflects the legal viewpoint that Wood is not separate from his business enterprise. For example, in reporting his business income on his income tax return, Wood could not include as a business expense any salary paid to himself. If a salary that the proprietor of a sole proprietorship pays to himself is charged to an expense account in the books of his enterprise, this item must be eliminated from the expenses in determining business income for tax purposes.

Regardless of the treatment of the proprietor's personal services in the accounts, the proprietor needs to consider a money equivalent of these services in business decisions involving the services. For example, Wood should not set the price for a prospective survey job on which he proposed to work without including a salary figure for his time to be spent on the job.

PARTNERSHIPS. A legal definition of a partnership is "an association of two or more individuals to carry on, as co-owners, a business for profit." Partnerships may be started merely by agreement among the individuals concerned. It is desirable that this agreement be in writing and that it clearly define the rights and duties of each partner. An essential topic for agreement is the method of computing each partner's share of profits and losses.

Certain important features of the partnership as a form of business organization are as follows:

1. **Mutual agency.** Generally speaking, any partner may make agreements that are legally binding on the other partners.
2. **Unlimited personal liability.** In general, the creditors of a partnership may hold any partner liable for the debts of the partnership.
3. **Limited life.** A partnership is dissolved by the withdrawal, death, or legal incapacity of any one of the partners. The admission of a new partner ends the old partnership and starts a new one.
4. **Legal entity.** Even though partnerships are business entities for accounting purposes, a partnership is not a legal entity apart from its owners. In this respect, the partnership is like the sole proprietorship.

In all the foregoing respects, the partnership differs from the corporation.

A SIMPLE EXAMPLE OF ACCOUNTING FOR A PARTNERSHIP. Exhibits 18-3 and 18-4 illustrate certain aspects of partnership accounting. They assume that on July 1, C. E. Wood, the sole proprietor of Exhibits 18-1 and 18-2, takes in one of his employees, L. S. York, as a partner in his land-surveying business. Exhibit 18-3 summarizes the transactions during the first 3 months of the life of this partnership. Exhibit 18-4 is a T-account ledger giving the accounting entries required by these transactions.

Unless the capital contributions made by all partners are in cash, it is necessary for the partners to agree on the valuations to be placed on the assets contributed by each partner. In this example, York agrees to accept the valuations for Wood's assets as shown by Wood's books and Wood agrees on a valuation of $1,600 for surveying equipment furnished by York.

Among other matters, this partnership agreement provides for a division of profits and losses between Wood and York based on (1) monthly salaries of $800 and $600, respectively; (2) at the end of each 3-month period, interest at 6% per annum on each partner's capital at the start of the period; and (3) equal division between the partners of the remaining profits and losses. This division is to be computed quarterly.

On September 30, the books show a profit of $5,660 to be divided according to this agreement. The division is calculated as follows:

	Total	Wood's share	York's share
Salaries	$4,200	$2,400	$1,800
Interest	156	96	60
Balance	1,304	652	652
Profit	$5,660	$3,148	$2,512

Each partner has a drawing (or personal) account separate from his capital account. For example, York's cash withdrawals of $2,100 during the 3 months were debited to L. S. York, Drawings. This account is credited with his $2,512 share of the profits. The net credit balance of $412 in his drawing account is transferred to York's capital account at the end of the accounting period.

Exhibits 18-3 and 18-4 illustrate the viewpoint that the compensation, if any, that the partners receive for their services should be thought of as a part of the profits rather than as an expense of the business enterprise. This is the same viewpoint previously illustrated in the example of accounting for a sole proprietorship. The viewpoint has its origin in the fact that the partnership is not a legal entity separate from the partners themselves. As explained in the discussion of the sole proprietorship, a "profit" figure such as the $5,660 computed for Wood & York does not have the same meaning as a figure for corporate profit, where the costs of all services appear in expense accounts.

EXHIBIT 18-3

TRANSACTIONS FOR WOOD & YORK, JULY TO SEPTEMBER, 19____

A. On July 1, L. S. York becomes a partner in the land-surveying business conducted by C. E. Wood. Before York's entry into the business, Wood's account balances were as follows. York accepts these figures as appropriate commercial valuations for the assets in question and for use in starting the partnership books.

	Debit	*Credit*
Cash	$2,360	
Surveying Instruments	2,400	
Reserve for Depreciation, Surveying Instruments		$ 60
Accounts Receivable	2,300	
Accounts Payable		600
C. E. Wood, Capital		6,400
Totals	$7,060	$7,060

B. York's investment in the enterprise consists of $2,400 in cash and surveying equipment which it is agreed will be valued at $1,600.
C. Accounts payable incurred for expenses of wages (not including partners' salaries), rent, expendible supplies, etc., are a total of $3,800.
D. Customers are billed for land-surveying services of $9,560.
E. Collections on accounts receivable are $8,300.
F. Payments on accounts payable are $3,600.
G. During the period, C. E. Wood withdrew $2,600 in cash for his personal use.
H. During the period, L. S. York withdrew $2,100 in cash for his personal use.

Adjusting and Closing Entries

I. Depreciation charged for the period is $100.
J. Income and expense accounts are closed into Profit and Loss Summary.
K. The partners' shares of the profits are credited to their respective drawing accounts.
L. The drawing accounts are closed into the partners' capital accounts.

An alternative treatment of compensation for partners' services would be for the business to pay the agreed-on salaries at regular intervals, charging them to appropriate expense accounts rather than to the partners' drawing accounts. Although this treatment would not alter the actual division of the earnings among the partners under the terms of the partnership agreement, it would permit the accounts to give a clearer picture of the different elements of cost for guidance in certain managerial decisions. However, such items for partners' salaries could not be treated as business expenses by the partners in reporting the business income for income tax purposes.

THE CORPORATION VERSUS THE PARTNERSHIP OR SOLE PROPRIETORSHIP AS A FORM OF BUSINESS OGANIZATION. Some generalizations are possible about the prevalence of the different forms of business organization. Thus it can be stated that large enterprises are nearly always incorporated; that, although the sole proprietorship is the most common form of business organization, most sole proprietorships are small; that the partnership is a common form of business organization for the sale of services, particularly professional services such as those of accountants, architects, engineers, lawyers, and physicians.

EXHIBIT 18-4

T-ACCOUNT LEDGER SHOWING ENTRIES IN ACCOUNTS OF WOOD & YORK, JULY TO SEPTEMBER, 19__

Cash

Debit	Credit
A 2,360	3,600 F
B 2,400	2,600 G
E 8,300	2,100 H

Accounts Receivable

Debit	Credit
A 2,300	8,300 E
D 9,560	

C. E. Wood, Capital

Debit	Credit
	6,400 A
	548 L

L. S. York, Capital

Debit	Credit
	4,000 B
	412 L

Surveying Instruments

Debit	Credit
A 2,400	
B 1,600	

Accounts Payable

Debit	Credit
F 3,600	600 A
	3,800 C

C. E. Wood, Drawings

Debit	Credit
G 2,600	3,148 K
L 548	

L. S. York, Drawings

Debit	Credit
H 2,100	2,512 K
L 412	

Res. for Depr., Surv. Insts.

Debit	Credit
	60 A
	100 I

Expense

Debit	Credit
C 3,800	3,900 J
I 100	

Income

Debit	Credit
J 9,560	9,560 D

Profit and Loss Summary

Debit	Credit
J 3,900	9,560 J
K 3,148	
K 2,512	

Where equity capital must be secured from many different persons, the corporation is the only practicable form of organization. Although a partnership might conceivably have an indefinitely large number of partners, there are practical limits to the number of persons that are likely to be willing to join any given partnership. Because of the unlimited personal liability of each partner for the debts of the partnership, anyone entering a partnership faces the hazard that, if the enterprise fails, he may lose all his personal capital—not merely his investment in the partnership. Because any partner may make a contract binding the partnership, one does not normally enter a partnership without confidence in the honesty and business judgment of all the other partners.

In many business enterprises, circumstances dictate the form of business organization to be adopted. Often, however, the decision needs to be made whether or not it is desirable to incorporate. A common choice is between the corporation and the partnership where the co-owners' capital contributions will be the same with either form of organization. Here the greater capital-raising possibilities of the corporate form may be of no practical importance in influencing the choice. The limited liability of the owners, the assured continuity of the life of the enterprise, and the ready transferability of ownership interests are all significant advantages of incorporating. A major advantage of the partnership is the avoidance of certain extra costs associated with corporations.

One such cost is the expense of organizing the corporation. More serious than this, in the United States, is the fact that corporations are subject to various forms of taxation not applied to partnerships or sole proprietorships. The most important such tax is the corporation income tax. The remainder of this chapter discusses certain aspects of income taxation in the United States.[1]

CORPORATION AND PERSONAL INCOME TAXES. Corporations organized for profit are subject to a Federal tax on their net incomes. The tax rate changes from time to time. In 1962 the rate was 30% on the first $25,000 of net income and 52% on net income in excess of $25,000.

There is also a Federal individual income tax on personal income in excess of certain stipulated exemptions and deductions. This is a graduated income tax in which the rates increase as the incomes increase. In 1962, the rate varied from 20% on the first $2,000 of "surtax net income" to 91% on surtax net income in excess of $200,000.

In effect, corporation income is taxed twice, first as business income in the year earned by the corporation and then as individual income taxed to the stockholders when they receive dividends. (In 1962, the first $50 of dividends received by an individual could be excluded from gross income. In computing an individual's tax, a "dividends received credit" was also allowed, amounting to 4% of the dividends received in excess of those excluded from gross income but not to exceed 4% of the taxable income.) There is no double taxation of the profits of a sole proprietorship or partnership. The net business income of a sole proprietorship is included in the tax return of the owner. Partners are taxed as individuals on their respective shares of partnership net income. A partnership tax return is required to allow the tax authorities to check

[1] If certain requirements are met, a corporation may elect to be taxed as a partnership. Conversely, under a number of restrictions a sole proprietorship or partnership may be qualified to elect to be taxed as a corporation. These special provisions are highly technical and are ignored in the following discussion for reasons of simplicity.

the income figures reported by the individual partners. The net income to be reported by sole proprietors and partners for any tax year is based on the business earnings for the year in question and does not depend on the withdrawals made during the year by the owners.

The majority of the states of the United States also have corporation and individual income taxes. These are in addition to the Federal taxes. The rates vary from state to state. The specific rules for determination of taxable income also vary, although they tend to be similar in most respects to the rules governing the Federal taxes. The discussion in the remainder of this chapter refers only to the Federal income taxes.

WHY TAX LAWS AND REGULATIONS INFLUENCE ACCOUNTING PRACTICE. Generally speaking, the rules for finding taxable net income of business enterprises are based on the accounting concept of profit, and the books of account supply the figures that are used in tax returns. Nevertheless, many laws and regulations are required to govern the determination of taxable net income. These laws and regulations have a great influence on the accounting practices used by business enterprises.

There are many types of business transactions where two or more different accounting treatments are possible within the general framework of accepted accounting principles. This fact has been evident even in the brief introduction to accounting and cost accounting presented in Parts 1 and 2. These differences in possible treatment generally influence the *timing* of certain expense or income items that will appear in the accounts sooner or later. Some examples have been the treatment of purchase discount (Chap. 6), bad debt expense (Chap. 7), the disposal of variance balances (Chaps. 10 and 15), and the choice among FIFO, LIFO, average-cost, and other methods of valuing inventories and finding cost of goods sold when purchase prices of materials have been changing (Chap. 12). In a more extensive treatise on accounting, many other examples would be presented of alternative treatments leading to differences in timing of incomes and expenses.

In the administration of income tax laws, the timing of income and expense items is an important consideration. Different tax rates may apply to the net incomes of different years. Differences in timing lead to different profit or loss figures for specific years. A treatment that leads to higher immediate taxable income may seem more attractive to the government than one that leads to the possibility of higher taxable income in future years. For these and other reasons, the tax laws and regulations tend to be based on the fiction that there is only one figure that can properly be considered to be the net income of each business enterprise for each tax year.

The government lays considerable stress on consistency in accounting practices from year to year. Also, certain accounting practices are acceptable for tax returns only if they are used in the taxpayer's books and for other business purposes. For example, the use of the LIFO method in tax returns is conditioned upon a requirement that the same method shall be used for inventory valuation for the purpose of reports to shareholders, partners, or proprietors and for credit purposes.

With high income tax rates, many business decisions are naturally influenced by their probable tax effects. When there is an opportunity for a taxpayer to choose among different accounting methods, one matter for consideration is likely to be the probable effect of each method on his reported taxable income and thus on his current income tax payments. As mentioned in Chap. 12, this has been an important element in many decisions made during a period of rising prices to change to LIFO from various other methods of inventory valuation. In this way, tax considerations influence decisions regarding accounting methods.

Moreover, some accounting procedures favored by the managements of certain business enterprises and by their accountants are not acceptable for income tax purposes. Possibly methods viewed by management as giving better cost control or better guidance to managerial decisions are viewed by government as giving too low a figure for current taxable income. One common instance of this—depreciation accounting—is discussed in Chap. 19. In such cases, management must choose between two undesirable alternatives. One alternative is, in effect, to keep two sets of books, one for business purposes and the other to supply the figures that are acceptable in tax returns. The selection of this alternative tends to increase accounting costs and the costs of making tax returns. The other alternative is to make the business accounting practices conform to the rules governing tax returns. This latter alternative seems to be the one usually selected.

ACCOUNTING INCOME AND TAXABLE INCOME. Some revenue and expense items require special treatment for purposes of tax returns. The following are a few examples of this: Gains on the disposal of capital assets held for more than 6 months are taxed at lower rates than items of ordinary income. The deductibility of capital losses is severely limited except for purposes of offsetting capital gains. Deductions from taxable income for the depletion of certain mineral resources may be based on a percentage of the gross income from these resources rather than on their cost. From time to time, permission has been given for a rapid write-off of the cost of certain fixed assets where the government has considered these assets to be necessary for the national defense. These two latter topics—percentage depletion and rapid amortization—are referred to again in Chap. 19.

Generally speaking, Congress is free to define taxable income in any way that it sees fit. Because tax considerations enter into so many business decisions, it is possible to devise tax laws that aim to promote certain economic results (e.g., mineral exploration, defense plant expansion). A number of the discrepancies between accounting income and taxable income have arisen because of the modification of the tax system to eliminate or reduce tax deterrents to certain economic actions.

ACCOUNTING ENTRIES IN CONNECTION WITH CORPORATION INCOME TAXES. Most of the examples and problems that have illustrated corporate accounting in the preceding chapters of this book have omitted certain entries that are always required in profitable corporations in the United States. These are the entries to show income tax liability and later to show the payment of income taxes.

At the end of its fiscal year, a corporation owes the government a tax on the income of the year just concluded. This liability should be shown on the books before they are closed for the year. The formal tax return to the government is not due until the fifteenth day of the third month following the close of the fiscal year. (This is March 15 in the common case where the fiscal year is the same as the calendar year.) Half the tax payment is also due on that date and half 3 months later. Meanwhile the tax liability must be estimated as closely as possible in order that it can be shown on the books.

This estimate requires an application of the appropriate tax rates to the estimated taxable income. The profit before taxes, obtainable from the work sheet, provides a starting point for estimating the taxable income. This profit figure must be modified by any differences between accounting profit and taxable income. Some reasons for such differences have been mentioned in the preceding articles. Taxable income for any year may also be affected by the carrying forward of losses from a previous year (up to 5 years). Moreover, if either of the 2 years immediately preceding had a taxable income and if the current year shows a loss, this loss may be "carried back," and the company may be entitled to a refund of some taxes previously paid.

Assume that the profit of the XYZ Corporation before income taxes is \$75,000 and that this is also the taxable income. Assume that a 30% tax rate applies to the first \$25,000 of this income and that a 52% rate applies to the remainder. The income tax liability can be recorded by the following end-of-year entry:

Dec. 31	Federal Income Tax	\$33,500	
	Accrued Taxes Payable		\$33,500

The tax account is then closed into Profit and Loss Summary:

Dec. 31	Profit and Loss Summary	\$33,500	
	Federal Income Tax		\$33,500

The balance in the Profit and Loss Summary account is now the difference between the profit before taxes ($75,000) and the tax ($33,500). This balance is closed into Earned Surplus.

Dec. 31	Profit and Loss Summary	$41,500	
	Earned Surplus		$41,500

Assume that the actual tax computed in the tax return on March 15 is identical with the end-of-year estimate of $33,500. When the first half of this tax is paid, the entry is:

Mar. 15	Accrued Taxes Payable	$16,750	
	Cash		$16,750

An identical entry will be made when the second half is paid on June 15.

THE INDIVIDUAL INCOME TAX IN RELATION TO ACCOUNTING. In contrast to corporations, partnerships and sole proprietorships show no income tax liability on their books. As previously explained, partners are taxed as individuals on their respective shares of the partnership profits; the business profit of a sole proprietor is one of the items in his individual income tax return. It has already been pointed out that the income from partnerships and sole proprietorships that is subject to taxation is the net income *earned* during the year. No expense deduction for salaries of partners or sole proprietors is permitted in computing net income subject to taxation.

Even though an income tax figure does not appear on the books of a partnership or sole proprietorship, the accounting practices of such enterprises are influenced by income tax rules and regulations in the same way that corporate accounting practices are influenced. The books of all types of business enterprise are subject to tax audit by income tax examiners.

Moreover, income tax considerations enter into business decisions in partnerships and sole proprietorships just as in corporations. The individual income taxes to be paid on dividends received by stockholders may also influence managerial decisions in corporations, particularly in closely held corporations that are managed by their owners.

As mentioned in Chap. 13, the individual income tax enters into all payroll accounting because of the rules requiring the withholding of this tax from wages and salaries.

CASH BASIS ACCOUNTING. Some businesses, particularly smaller ones, which must extend liberal credit to their customers, find it advantageous to keep their books and report their taxable income on the "cash receipts and disbursements" basis. Under this plan, incomes are taken into account in the year in which they are actually or "constructively" received. With certain exceptions expenses are applied to the year in which the actual disbursements take place. Two of the important exceptions are with respect to inventories of materials and merchandise and depreciable assets for which the yearly expense (cost of goods sold and depreciation) must be computed the same as under full accrual accounting. Cash basis accounting is permitted for Federal income taxes provided that the taxpayer keeps his books on the cash basis and is consistent from year to year and provided that the method in the opinion of the commissioner "clearly reflects income for the particular type of business involved."

The advantage of cash basis accounting, where permitted, is the deferral of the income tax on income which is earned but not yet received. Thus, for example, a professional-service business might have accounts receivable as of the end of a particular year of $20,000 which has not been shown in the books as earned income and does not appear on the balance sheet as an asset. Also, under cash basis accounting, many disbursements that would result in prepaid expenses (deferred charges) under accrual accounting are charged to expense immediately. On the other hand, some expenses that would be accrued under accrual accounting appear as expenses in the accounting period in which they are paid rather than the earlier period or periods in which the expense is incurred.

Clearly, the cash and accrual bases will give the same total results over the life of the enterprise, from inception to termination; the differences will be a matter of timing. Of course, use of the cash basis does not permit matching revenue and expense by accounting periods in an adequate and meaningful way. Consequently, financial statements prepared from cash basis accounting books are likely to be misleading and unreliable unless many work-sheet accruals and adjustments are skillfully made in preparing the data for the statements. Without such adjustments, a cash basis balance sheet usually (but not necessarily) understates the owners' equity, and the successive income statements are subject to significant variation depending on the timing of cash receipts and disbursements.

BUSINESS ORGANIZATION AND INCOME TAXATION ARE COMPLEX SUBJECTS. This chapter has explained certain differences between accounting problems of corporations on the one hand and sole proprietorships and partnerships on the other. These differences have been in the accounts summarizing ownership, in the distribution of profits, and in relation to income taxes.

The statements made about the legal aspects of corporations and partnerships and about income taxes have aimed to give the student a general view of these topics as they relate to the accounting matters discussed. A detailed discussion of these topics is beyond the scope of this book. In fact, the topics are so complicated that there are exceptions and qualifications that are appropriate regarding almost any simple general statement about business organization or income taxation. In the interest of simplicity of presentation, many such exceptions and qualifications have been omitted from this chapter.

SUMMARY. Some of the important points of this chapter can be restated as follows:

1. The fundamentals of accounting are the same for sole proprietorships and partnerships as for corporations. The main differences occur in the accounts summarizing ownership and in the interpretation of profit and loss figures.
2. The summary ownership account in a sole proprietorship is designated as the proprietor's capital account. This is supplemented by the proprietor's drawing account. All his withdrawals of profits or capital are charged to this drawing account. The drawing account is closed into the proprietor's capital account at the end of each accounting period.
3. In a partnership, each partner has a capital account and a drawing account. Profits and losses are divided among the partners according to the stipulations in the partnership agreement. In agreeing on the division of profits, it is appropriate to recognize differences in the values of the services of the individual partners to the enterprise and also differences in the amounts of capital they have invested in the enterprise.
4. Income taxes are levied on the net incomes of corporations. Payments of such taxes are therefore shown in corporate accounts. Individual income taxes apply to most types of personal income, including dividends received from corporations and the income earned in sole proprietorships and partnerships. Individual income tax payments by sole proprietors and partners should not appear on the books of sole proprietorships and partnerships.
5. The laws and regulations regarding the determination of taxable income have a great influence on business accounting practice.

DISCUSSION QUESTIONS

18-A. Explain the difference between the accounts Capital Stock and Earned Surplus in a corporation, on the one hand, and the owner's Capital and Drawings accounts in a sole proprietorship, on the other hand. Does the Capital Stock account in the corporation serve the same purpose as the owner's Capital account in the sole proprietorship? Does the Earned Surplus account serve the same purpose as the owner's Drawings account? Explain your answers.

18-B. What is meant by the statement that a corporate enterprise is both a business entity and a legal entity whereas a firm operated as a sole proprietorship or partnership is a business entity but not a legal entity?

18-C. You are entering into the partnership with a friend to own and operate a retail hardware store. What are some of the matters that ought to be covered by your partnership agreement?

18-D. What are the current Federal tax rates on the various brackets of corporate income? What are the current Federal tax rates on the first few brackets of personal income? Does your state have corporate and personal income taxes? If so, what are the tax rates?

18-E. What is meant by the "double taxation" of corporate income?

18-F. To what extent will the personal income taxes of partners be influenced by the partners' decision to leave the profits in the business rather than to withdraw them? Would your answer be the same if the business were incorporated and the decision of the board of directors was to leave the profits in the business rather than to pay dividends?

18-G. Explain why the profit figure in the financial statements of a partnership generally has a different meaning from the profit figure for a corporation.

18-H. What year-end entry, if any, is necessary on the books for a corporation to show the estimated income taxes for the year just ended. Answer the preceding question with respect to a partnership.

18-J. Why is it common for the accounts of sole proprietorships and partnerships to exclude any expense charges for personal services performed for the business by the sole proprietor or the partners? In what ways might this exclusion of the expense of personal services lead to incorrect decisions in the management of an enterprise? If you were a sole proprietor or a partner, would you want to have an item for your personal services included in the accounts? What problems, if any, might be caused by including such an item?

18-K. Discuss the relative advantages of the corporation and the partnership as alternative forms of business organization for the case where the same co-owners will be involved regardless of which form is selected. Assume that the initial capital investments by the respective owners will be the same whether or not the business is incorporated. Also assume that, if the enterprise is a corporation, it will be taxed as such and, if it is not incorporated, it will not be taxed as a corporation.

18-L. Smith and Jones have a partnership. Smith has invested $10,000, and Jones has invested $20,000. Division of the earnings of the business is to be as follows:

1. Smith is to receive $100 per week salary; Jones is to receive $75 per week salary.
2. Both men are to receive interest on their investment at 5% per year.
3. After salary and interest, the remaining profit (or loss) is to be split equally.

Calculate the division of a year's earnings of $9,000.

18-M. What differences between accounting income and taxable income are mentioned in the text? Do you know of some other differences? If so, what are they?

18-N. The text mentions some ways in which income tax laws and regulations have influenced accounting practice. What are they? Do you know of any other examples of this not mentioned in the text?

PROBLEMS

Problem 18-1. On July 1, 19____, A. R. Biggs and T. S. Porter, consulting engineers, enter into a partnership agreement. Set up a T-account ledger for the firm using the following accounts:

Cash	Office Expense
Accounts Receivable	Depreciation Expense
Furniture and Equipment	A. R. Biggs, Drawings
Accumulated Depreciation—Furniture and Equipment	T. S. Porter, Drawings
	A. R. Biggs, Capital
Income from Consulting Fees	T. S. Porter, Capital
Salaries	Profit and Loss Summary

Enter in this ledger the following transactions for the 6-month period from July 1 to December 31:

A. The initial cash investments by the partners were $10,000 by Biggs and $6,000 by Porter.
B. Furniture and equipment were purchased for $7,000 cash.
C. Billed clients for consulting fees, $22,950.
D. Received from clients on account, $15,800.
E. Cash disbursements were $8,000 for salaries (not including any compensation for the partners' services) and $4,000 for office expense.
F. Cash withdrawals for personal use were $6,300 by Biggs and $5,100 by Porter.
G. Depreciation to be charged for the 6 months is $350.
H. Income and expense accounts are to be closed into Profit and Loss Summary.
J. The partners' respective shares of the profits are to be calculated and credited to their respective drawing accounts. The partnership agreement stipulated that the division of the profits or losses shall be computed as follows:
   1. A salary of $1,000 a month to Biggs and $800 a month to Porter
   2. At the end of each 6-month period, interest at 8% per annum on each partner's capital at the start of the period
   3. Equal division between the partners of any remaining profit or loss
K. The drawing accounts are to be closed into the partners' Capital accounts.

Summarize each account, and show the balance forward if any. Take a post-closing trial balance. Submit the T-account ledger, your calculation of the partner's respective shares of the earnings, and your post-closing trial balance.

Problem 18-2. A. Black and B. White formed a partnership and started a retail store on January 1, 19___. White furnished the initial capital, and Black agreed to give full-time personal services to the enterprise. Matters to be recorded in the books for the first year were as follows:

A. The initial cash investment by the partners was $20,000 by White. Nothing was invested by Black.
B. Sales of merchandise for cash during the year totaled $60,000.
C. Merchandise purchases for cash during the year totaled $48,000.
D. Expenses paid in cash during the year were $10,900.
E. Cash withdrawals for personal use during the year were $7,200 by Black and $3,900 by White.
F. On December 31, the final inventory of merchandise was $12,000.
G. Sales, Expense, and Cost of Goods Sold are closed to Profit and Loss Summary.
H. The partnership agreement stipulated that annual profits or losses should be divided as follows:
   1. Each partner receives 8% on his capital balance at the start of the year.
   2. $7,500 a year to Black as compensation for personal services.
   3. Equal division of any profit or loss after interest on investment and salary.
      a. Set up a T-account ledger containing the accounts listed below, and make the necessary entries for the year as indicated above. Any matters not mentioned are to be ignored. Use only the accounts listed below.

Cash	A. Black, Capital
Merchandise	B. White, Capital
Sales	A. Black, Personal
Cost of Goods Sold	B. White, Personal
Other Expense	Profit and Loss Summary

      b. What total income resulting from partnership operations must be reported on Black's personal income tax return for this year? On White's?
      c. If the net earnings of the partnership (before interest and salary) turn out to be $9,600 the following year, how would this amount be divided between the partners? Assume that Black's salary is increased to $8,100 for the year.

19/ FIXED ASSETS AND DEPRECIATION EXPENSE

Chapter 7 dealt with a number of different types of adjusting entries. One of these was the adjusting entry to record depreciation expense. The conventional debit to Depreciation Expense (or other appropriate account) and credit to Reserve for Depreciation or Allowance for Depreciation has been illustrated many times in the intervening chapters.

Up to this point, however, none of the troublesome and controversial aspects of fixed-asset accounting have been presented. The reader is introduced to a number of such topics in the present chapter.

THE IMPORTANCE OF FIXED ASSETS TO INDUSTRY. The modern high standard of living in industrialized countries is made possible by high per capita productivity of labor. This in turn depends on the effective use of capital goods and on skillful management. Improvements in the standard of living result in large measure from improvements in the capital goods used by industry and agriculture, accompanied by improvements in managerial techniques.

The proportion of fixed assets to total assets will vary from industry to industry and from enterprise to enterprise within an industry. Because of the relatively large investment in fixed assets required in public utilities and in many types of manufacturing, it is particularly important that the accounting for fixed assets be well done in these industries.

REASONS FOR RETIREMENT AND FOR DECLINE IN VALUE OF FIXED ASSETS. As pointed out in Chap. 7, experience indicates that the machines and structures of industry eventually will be retired. Moreover, as such fixed assets grow older, they tend to become less valuable to their owners. Retirements and declines in value short of retirement generally occur for one or more of the following reasons:[1]

[1] This is abbreviated from a statement in Eugene L. Grant and P. T. Norton, Jr., *Depreciation,* The Ronald Press Company, New York, 1955, pp. 21–22. Throughout this chapter, a substantial amount of material has been condensed and adapted from this book.

1. *The availability of improved new assets for performing the same service.* If the prospective economies from new methods are sufficient, it will pay to replace old assets with new ones or to relegate the old assets to stand-by purposes or other inferior uses.
2. *Changes in the amount and type of service requirements.*
3. *Changes in the existing assets themselves.* Machines and structures wear out, corrode, and decay because of age and use. The result is an increase in maintenance costs and a decrease in the quality and reliability of performance. It often pays to replace these assets even though they are still capable of rendering service. In some circumstances, wearing out, corrosion, and decay may make retirement imperative rather than merely economical.
4. *Changes in public requirements regarding the assets.*
5. *Casualties.*

These reasons for retirement are not mutually exclusive; often they operate in combination with one another. Thus an old machine might be replaced by a new one that (1) incorporated new automatic features that reduced unit labor costs, (2) provided increased capacity to meet an increased demand for the product, and (3) required initial maintenance costs considerably lower than the current high maintenance costs of the old machine.

The first three reasons for retirement that were cited, namely, improved alternatives, changes in service requirements, and increase of costs with age, tend to make retirements economical rather than imperative. These same causes also operate to decrease the values of assets that it will not yet pay to replace.

Retirements often are deferred beyond the date when they would really be economical. Sometimes this is because decisions on retirements tend to be made on a very conservative basis. Frequently the necessary funds are not available to finance the purchase of replacement assets. In some instances, a misinterpretation of accounting figures operates as a barrier to economical replacements.

SOME QUESTIONS TO BE CONSIDERED IN PLANNING THE ACCOUNTING FOR FIXED ASSETS. In setting up and operating fixed-asset accounts, a number of decisions must be made. The questions to be considered include the following:

1. What rules shall be set up for distinguishing a capital expenditure from an operating expenditure?
2. What classification shall be adopted for fixed-asset accounts?
3. What system shall be established for authorizing the expenditures for fixed assets?
4. What system shall be established for determining the cost of fixed assets?

5. What detailed plant ledger forms shall be maintained?
6. What depreciation accounting method will be used?

DISTINGUISHING BETWEEN FIXED ASSETS AND OPERATING EXPENSES. It is easy enough to see that the cost of a machine tool should be capitalized and that the cost of the lubricants used in its operation should be charged as an operating expense. But many borderline cases arise in which the distinction is not so simple.

The question involved may be clear if it is thought of as: "Shall this be charged entirely to the operations of the current accounting period, or shall it be spread out as an operating expense over a number of accounting periods by means of depreciation accounting?" The answer to this question should be based on the probable effect of the expenditure. If the effect clearly extends over a number of years, the expenditure should be capitalized. If the effect is only in the near future, it is reasonable to treat it as an operating expense.

In addition to the probable effect of the expenditure, consideration should also be given to the inconvenience and bookkeeping expense of capitalizing small items. A common rule is not to capitalize anything that costs less than some stipulated minimum figure. Although this minimum naturally varies from one enterprise to another, $50 is a common figure used in large enterprises.

One important group of borderline cases arises when the design of a machine is changed in the course of an overhaul. An expenditure of this sort that lengthens the prospective life of the machine generally should be capitalized. The same is true of an expenditure that results in substantial operating economies. In contrast, if an overhaul expenditure merely serves to maintain a machine in operating condition, it should be charged to Repairs or Maintenance.

AN EXAMPLE OF A CLASSIFICATION OF FIXED-ASSET ACCOUNTS. Exhibit 19-1 shows the names and account numbers of fixed-asset accounts recommended for electrical manufacturers. This is reproduced by permission from the accounting manual prepared by a committee of the National Electrical Manufacturers Association (NEMA).[2]

The general breakdown of fixed assets into land, buildings and structures, machinery, furniture and fixtures, and assets used for transportation is characteristic of many classifications of fixed-asset accounts. The detail breakdown within each major classification will be influenced by the type of industry and by the size of the company. In a manufacturing company with two or more plants, a further breakdown within each account will be made by location.

[2] *Uniform Accounting Manual for the Electrical Manufacturing Industry*, Amended 7th ed., National Electrical Manufacturers Association, New York, 1960.

Except for Land, all fixed assets are subject to depreciation charges. Where different groups of assets in an account should have different depreciation rates, an additional breakdown within the account may be made. For example, account 152.1, Buildings, may be broken down into Steel and Concrete, Brick and Wood, etc.

EXHIBIT 19-1

PLANT AND EQUIPMENT ACCOUNTS FROM UNIFORM ACCOUNTING MANUAL FOR THE ELECTRICAL MANUFACTURING INDUSTRY

150 Land and Land Improvements
- 150.1 Land
- 150.2 Fees and Damages
- 150.3 Land Improvements

152 Buildings and Structures
- 152.1 Buildings
- 152.2 Structures
- 152.3 General Service Piping and Wiring

154 Machinery and Tools
- 154.1 Machinery
- 154.2 Foundations and Installations
- 154.3 Ovens and Furnaces
- 154.4 Conveyor Equipment
- 154.5 Standard Semidurable Tools
- 154.6 Electrical Accessories
- 154.7 Metal Flasks

156 Furniture and Fixtures
- 156.1 Factory Fixtures and Equipment
- 156.2 Furniture
- 156.3 Office Appliances

158 Transportation System
- 158.1 Roads and Sidewalks
- 158.2 Railway Tracks and Overhead Equipment
- 158.3 Rolling Stock
- 158.4 Automotive Equipment
- 158.5 Electric Vehicles

160 Construction in Progress

DIVERSITY OF ITEMS WITHIN A FIXED-ASSET ACCOUNT. Each fixed-asset account may contain a wide variety of different items. For example, the NEMA manual lists more than 100 different kinds of machines that are included in account 154.1, Machinery, and more than 70 different items included in account 154.5, Standard Semidurable Tools.

AUTHORIZATION FOR PURCHASE OF FIXED ASSETS. Most corporations require a formal authorization for fixed property expenditures. This permits review of two questions that should be answered whenever it is proposed to acquire fixed assets. The first question is,

"Will it pay to make this capital expenditure?" The second is, "How can the expenditure be financed?'"

In large companies the level at which this authorization takes place is likely to depend on the size of the proposed expenditure. For example, in one company a capital expenditure of under $500 may be authorized by the superintendent; one from $500 to $1,000 calls for authorization by the works manager; anything over $1,000 requires authorization by top management.

DETERMINING COSTS OF NEW FIXED ASSETS. For many fixed assets, the total cost to be capitalized will be greater than the purchase price. For example, inbound-transportation costs and installation costs of machinery should be capitalized. Often it is desirable to determine costs of fixed assets by a special job-order cost system similar to the scheme for finding manufacturing costs that was described in Chap. 10.

Account 160, Construction in Progress, in Exhibit 19-1 is an example of a controlling account used for such jobs. When the construction or the installation of the new fixed assets is completed, the total cost is transferred from Construction in Progress to the appropriate asset accounts. No depreciation charges are made against Construction in Progress.

CATALOGUED AND NONCATALOGUED PLANT. The plant ledger is a subsidiary ledger controlled by one or more of the fixed-asset accounts in the general ledger. It consists of a number of sheets or cards each of which refers to one particular asset. Each sheet or card should tell just what the asset is and where it is. It should record the date of acquisition and the initial cost of the asset to the present owner.

For each unit of property, the plant ledger sheet or card should also give (1) the dates and amounts of any capitalized expenditures for additions and betterments, (2) the dates and amounts of partial retirements, (3) the date of complete retirement, and (4) any realization on retirement. In addition, it is common to show the current depreciation rate for the item or for the group, as well as the depreciation rates that have been used in the past. Plant covered by such detailed record for individual assets is referred to as *catalogued plant*.

There are some types of assets for which it is not practicable to keep itemized records and for which there is no satisfactory way to determine the exact time of retirement. These include such things as piping, wiring, and shafting. In addition, there are fixed assets such as small tools and instruments that could be itemized but for which the cost of keeping individual records is often considered not to be worthwhile. All such fixed assets, when not itemized in the plant ledger, are classified under the general heading of *noncatalogued plant*. Where changes in machine location are a common occurrence, it is also advantageous to treat machine foundations and installation costs as noncatalogued plant.

DIVERSITY OF PROCEDURES IN DEPRECIATION ACCOUNTING. As pointed out in the definition quoted on page 143, depreciation accounting is a system of writing off the cost of tangible capital assets "in a systematic and rational manner." Many different systematic methods for this write-off have been used, and there is much room for difference of opinion regarding which method is the most rational. Differences of depreciation accounting practice have occurred among different countries, among different industries, among competing concerns in the same industry, and among different periods of time. In the United States the changes in depreciation accounting practice that have occurred from time to time have been greatly influenced by changes in income tax laws and regulations.

In most depreciation accounting methods, including those commonly used in the United States, the annual depreciation write-off for any fixed capital account is related to the estimated average service life of the assets in the account. The write-off may also be influenced by the estimated average salvage value.

ESTIMATES OF AVERAGE SERVICE LIFE AND MORTALITY DISPERSION. In some industries, statistical studies have been made of the acquisitions and retirements of certain groups of assets. Although the primary purpose of such studies is to give estimates of past average service lives, the studies may also provide mortality curves such as the ones shown in Exhibit 19-2. This particular graph is based on studies made by the Bell Telephone System with respect to certain telephone underground cable. The survivorship and retirement curves that it contains are mathematical curves fitted to actual retirement data.[3]

Some human beings die young and others live to a ripe old age. Statistical studies of property retirements invariably show that property units are like human beings in this respect. It will be noted in Exhibit 19-2 that, although retirements were most frequent close to the average life of about twenty years, some retirements occurred at all ages from the first to the forty-fourth year.

Such statistical studies of property mortality reflect the retirements made for all causes; the influence of obsolescence is measured as well as the influence of wear and tear. Nevertheless, even though the actuarial

[3] For a discussion of mortality curves and the statistical approach to estimates of average service life of property units, see the following: Grant and Norton, *op. cit.*, chap. 5; National Association of Railroad and Utilities Commissioners, *Report of Committee on Depreciation,* Washington, 1943; and Robley Winfrey, *Statistical Analyses of Industrial Property Retirements,* Iowa Engineering Experiment Station Bulletin 125, Ames, Iowa, 1935.

techniques developed for analyzing human mortality are also applicable to property mortality, an examination of many such studies indicates that property mortality is much less predictable than human mortality. As already pointed out, most retirements occur because someone decides that it is economical to make them. In part, retirement decisions reflect the rates of technological progress in each industry; these rates are not always uniform. Moreover, retirement decisions in all industries tend to be influenced by external causes such as wars and business depressions.

EXHIBIT 19-2
RETIREMENT-FREQUENCY CURVE AND SURVIVOR CURVE FOR CERTAIN TELEPHONE UNDERGROUND CABLE

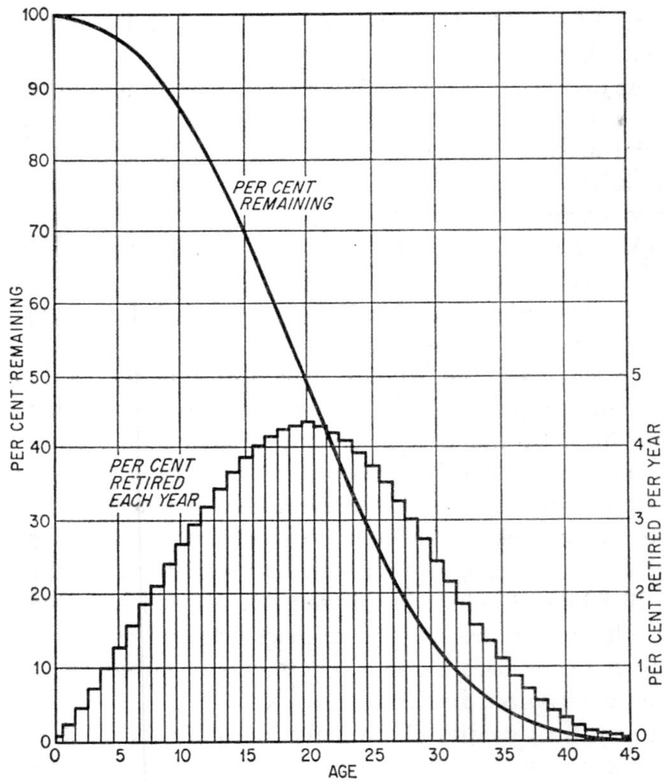

The evidence is conclusive that average service lives of many classes of industrial assets change from time to time. It follows that, wherever depreciation rates are assumed to be based on the best available current estimates of average service lives, it is necessary to review depreciation rates from time to time and to change them occasionally.

Many depreciation rates that purport to be based on service lives and salvage values actually are based on mere opinions or arbitrary assumptions about lives and salvage values rather than on mortality studies or other types of statistical evidence. However, even where there have been no mortality studies, it is possible to apply simple tests to judge whether the realized lives and salvage values to date have been reasonably consistent with the lives and salvage values that were assumed in setting the depreciation rates. Such tests, which acquired widespread importance in the United States starting in 1962, are discussed briefly later in this chapter.

SALVAGE VALUES IN RELATION TO DEPRECIATION ACCOUNTING. Even though all the tangible physical assets of industry may be viewed as being on "an irresistible march to the junk heap," many of these assets will have two or more owners before they reach the junk heap. At least in the hands of the first owners, such assets may have substantial prospective salvage values. Moreover, certain assets that will have only one owner in the form in which they are installed will have prospective salvage value as scrap metal. For many classes of assets, prospective salvage values are negligible.

In principle, the amount to be written off by depreciation accounting is the difference between the cost of an asset and its prospective terminal salvage value to its present owner. In principle, also, it is the *net* salvage value that is relevant; this is the difference between the gross amount received from the disposal of an asset and any expenditures incident to its removal and sale. Presumably, an asset should not be depreciated below a book value that is equal to its prospective net salvage value. (This latter point is stressed in the regulations of the U.S. Internal Revenue Service.)

Motor vehicles are a good example of relatively short-lived assets for which there is always an active secondhand market. For assets of this type, it usually is possible to make a fairly close estimate of the ratio of salvage value to first cost at any age.[4] However, for many other types of assets, actual realized salvage values behave erratically and unpredictably, being high at one time and low at another. Generally speaking, the longer the prospective life of an asset, the harder it is to make a satisfactory estimate of its terminal salvage value.

Actual practices in the use of estimated salvage values for purposes of setting depreciation rates vary considerably from industry to industry

[4] Often old motor vehicles are traded in on new ones. In the United States, there is a special income tax treatment of "nontaxable exchanges" that occur when an old asset is traded in on a similar new one. For such assets, accounting rules are usually adapted to conform to tax regulations. The details of the rather specialized topic of the accounting treatment of trade-ins are not discussed in this chapter.

and from company to company. At one extreme, regulated public utilities often make elaborate studies of realized salvage values and use these studies in the setting of their depreciation rates. At the other extreme, manufacturers arbitrarily assume zero salvage values in setting depreciation rates for all machinery and equipment.

The accounting treatment of net salvage values actually realized at the time of retirement is a different subject from the use of estimated salvage values in setting depreciation rates. The appropriate rules for retirement entries depend on whether single-asset or multiple-asset depreciation accounting is being used. Retirement entries are discussed later in this chapter in connection with the explanation of various types of depreciation accounting.

A DEPRECIATION ACCOUNTING PARADOX. Although there is no best way to apportion the cost of fixed assets among their years of service, it makes a real difference how much cost is written off in any year. The greater the amount of depreciation charged in any given year, the less the profit shown by the books for that year (or the more the loss), and vice versa. The accounting figure for profit may influence many matters, such as the amount of dividends declared by the board of directors, the price investors are willing to pay for a company's stock, and the size of managerial bonuses based on profits.

Moreover, there are various relationships between business and government that may be influenced by the amount of depreciation allotted to any given period of time. In the case of regulated public utilities, the depreciation figures from the accounts influence the rate level permitted by regulatory commissions. Where prices are stipulated to be based on cost, as in government contracts subject to renegotiation or contracts based on cost plus a fixed fee, the price received for a product or service will be influenced by the amount of depreciation allocated to the time covered by the contract. All business enterprises that own depreciable assets and pay income taxes are affected by the rules governing the relationship between depreciation and the calculation of taxable income. In the United States and elsewhere, depreciation accounting for business purposes has been greatly influenced by income tax laws and regulations.

A paradox is that depreciation accounting needs definite formal rules to be applied in any case in spite of the fact that there is no one correct set of such rules. Recourse to formal rules is needed because of the diversity of interests that may be involved—managers, owners, employees, customers, prospective investors, regulatory bodies, tax collectors, etc. Much of the remainder of this chapter deals with various facets of several sets of such formal rules.

INCOME TAX TREATMENT OF DEPRECIATION IN THE UNITED STATES, 1913 TO 1953. During the years 1913 to 1933, the first 21 years of modern income taxes in the United States, the Treasury Department generally accepted the taxpayers' estimates of service lives used in computing depreciation charges. Throughout this period, a common practice in the manufacturing industries was to write off 10% of the cost of machinery each year during the first 10 years of its service. The actual average service lives of machines written off in this way were often 20 to 25 years or even more. At a result, many assets were fully depreciated on the books of account long before they were retired.

Starting with 1934, the Treasury Department placed on the taxpayer the burden of proof of his depreciation rates. In general, the policies of the Treasury Department during 1934 to 1953 were based on the view that the correct way to write off depreciation for tax purposes was by uniform annual amounts over full service life. During the decade or so following 1934, it was a common occurrence for taxpayers to have a reduction made in allowable depreciation rates every time there was a tax audit. Thus many manufacturers who had been writing off assets at 10% per year before 1934 found themselves using a 4 or 5% rate a dozen or so years later.

The 1934 tax rules brought about a substantial change in depreciation accounting practices. In the great majority of cases, the lower depreciation rates that were stipulated for tax purposes were also used by taxpayers in their own accounts.

Before 1940, income tax rates in the United States had not been high enough for the tax treatment of depreciation to have any great influence on decisions regarding the purchase of new fixed assets. The high tax rates in the Revenue Act of 1940, if combined with low allowable depreciation rates, created a large tax deterrent to many plant investments that were in the public interest.

In order to reduce this tax deterrent, the Revenue Act of 1940 permitted the issuance of "certificates of necessity." Taxpayers proposing to acquire fixed assets believed to be important for the national defense could apply for these certificates; if granted, the assets could be written off for income tax purposes in 5 years. During the years 1940 to 1945 many such certificates were granted. With the start of the Korean conflict the issuance of these certificates was again authorized, and the 5-year tax write-off was permitted for many industrial assets acquired in 1950 and for several years thereafter. In some cases, the 5-year write-off privilege was limited to a stated fraction of the investment with the remainder to be written off over an estimated normal service life.

THE CASE FOR DEPRECIATION ACCOUNTING METHODS GIVING A RAPID WRITE-OFF IN THE EARLY YEARS OF LIFE. There is no one correct way to write off the costs of fixed assets in a systematic and rational manner. If one is free to select a depreciation accounting method, a critical question is how rapidly cost ought to be written off, all things considered.

There are many good reasons why the write-off in the early years of life should be more rapid than in the final years.[5] Full service lives are generally longer than economic lives; it is a common experience that the final years of life are spent in stand-by service or other inferior use; because of technological progress there is often a rapid decline in the value of assets to their owners during the initial years of life. Moreover, the combination of high income tax rates and low depreciation rates in the early years of life constitutes an obstacle to technological progress and tends to slow the rate of improvement in the standard of living.

As explained in our brief historical summary, a rapid write-off in the early years of life was common in the United States prior to 1934, when the entire cost of assets with lives of 20 to 25 years was usually written off in the first 10 years. A fast write-off in the early years also occurred after 1940 and after 1950 for the billions of dollars of investments written off under certificates of necessity. However, for the ordinary fixed assets of industry in the United States after 1934, the administration of income tax laws and regulations tended to promote the use of uniform depreciation charges over full service life. This situation was changed by the liberalization of depreciation provisions in the 1954 tax law.

SOME CHANGES IN TAX LAWS AND REGULATIONS IN THE UNITED STATES, 1954 TO 1962. The 1954 Internal Revenue Code gave taxpayers the option of using several methods that permitted from two-thirds to three-fourths of the cost of fixed assets to be written off during the first half of their lives. These methods are discussed later in this chapter. Permission to use the new methods was limited to assets with lives of 3 years or more that were acquired new after December 31, 1953.

The new methods, like the ones stipulated for income tax purposes in 1934 and thereafter, required estimates of the service lives of assets. *Bulletin F*, a Treasury Department publication issued in 1942, gave estimated average service lives for several thousand different classes of assets. In principle, it was the average service life of each class of assets in a taxpayer's own service that was supposed to be used in computing

[5] For a more extended presentation of this viewpoint, see Grant and Norton, *op. cit.*, chaps. 16 to 19.

depreciation rates. In practice, however, many revenue agents used *Bulletin F* lives as the basis for their audits of taxpayers' depreciation rates. There were a variety of reasons why it often was not practicable to base life estimates on each taxpayer's own experience. Some classes of assets were too long-lived for enough assets to have been retired; some taxpayers had been in business too short a time to have had much retirement experience. Moreover, even in the common case where there had been enough retirement experience, most taxpayers had not kept good enough fixed capital records for mortality studies to be made.

A frequent taxpayer complaint (from 1934 through 1961) was that the Treasury Department insisted on too long lives for fixed assets. In 1962, the Treasury issued Revenue Procedure 62-21, containing "guideline lives" for various classes of depreciable assets. In most cases, the new lives were considerably shorter than the corresponding lives in *Bulletin F,* which was superseded by this new document. For many industries, matters were simplified by specifying one guideline life to be used as the average service life in computing depreciation rates for all machinery and equipment. For example, a life of 11 years was given for such assets owned by manufacturers of chemical products, a life of 8 years for manufacturers of electronic equipment, a life of 18 years for producers of ferrous metals. Revenue Procedure 62-21 described certain reserve ratio tests that would be applied by revenue agents to judge whether actual average realized lives were consistent with the lives that had been used to compute depreciation rates.[6]

The following discussion of various depreciation accounting methods is based, in part, on the methods available for income taxes in the United States, considering both the 1954 Revenue Code and Revenue Procedure 62-21. Throughout the discussion the account title Reserve for Depreciation is used rather than Allowance for Depreciation. This usage is adopted to agree with the language of tax regulations and other publications of the U.S. Treasury Department.

[6] We recommend the following two inexpensive government pamphlets for those readers who wish more information about the income tax treatment of depreciation in the United States than the brief explanation given in this chapter:

"Regulations Relating to Depreciation—Treasury Decision No. 6182," *U.S. Treasury Department Internal Revenue Service Publication* 311, Government Printing Office, Washington, D.C., 1956.

"Depreciation—Guidelines and Rules," *U.S. Treasury Department Internal Revenue Service Publication* 456, Government Printing Office, Washington, D.C., 1962.

The 1962 pamphlet includes Revenue Procedure 62-21 as well as considerable explanatory material. The 1962 pamphlet should be viewed as supplementing the 1956 pamphlet rather than as superseding it.

A MATRIX OF DEPRECIATION ACCOUNTING METHODS. Exhibit 19-3 shows a two-way classification of certain depreciation accounting methods that are explained briefly in this chapter. The table is intended to emphasize the point that two separate decisions need to be made in establishing a depreciation method. One is a decision among the various formulas for apportioning the cost of fixed assets among the years of their estimated lives. The other is a decision between having an identifiable depreciation figure for each asset and using one of several possible schemes for grouping assets together for the purpose of computing their depreciation charges.

EXHIBIT 19-3
A TWO-WAY CLASSIFICATION OF CERTAIN DEPRECIATION ACCOUNTING METHODS

Method of combining assets / Depreciation formula	Single-asset or item accounts	Multiple-asset accounts	
		Group	Classified
Straight-line			
Double declining-balance			
Sum-of-the-years-digits			

To apply any depreciation accounting method, it is necessary to know the rules for computing the depreciation rate, the rules for computing year-by-year depreciation charges, and the rules for making entries to record retirements of fixed assets. No two of the nine methods represented by the cells of Exhibit 19-3 are alike in all of these rules.

In addition to the nine methods indicated in Exhibit 19-3, there are a variety of other depreciation accounting methods that are possible. A number of these are mentioned briefly later in this chapter following the explanation of the methods shown in Exhibit 19-3.

THE STRAIGHT-LINE ITEM METHOD. Single-asset or item depreciation accounting is based on the premise that there should be an identifiable depreciation figure for each asset. If life and salvage value for each asset are estimated correctly, the straight-line item method will give a uniform depreciation charge per year.

A characteristic of any straight-line depreciation accounting is that the depreciation rate is applied to the balance in the asset account. That is, neither the balance in the Reserve for Depreciation account nor the estimated salvage value is deducted from the asset account balance when the depreciation rate is applied to determine an annual depreciation charge.

It is convenient to express a straight-line rate as a percentage. In computing a straight-line percentage rate, it is necessary to estimate service life and the percentage of net salvage value to first cost. The depreciation rate is then computed as follows:

$$\text{Straight-line rate} = \frac{100\% \text{ minus estimated net salvage percentage}}{\text{estimated service life in years}}$$

If the estimated life is 10 years and the estimated salvage value is zero,

$$\text{Straight-line rate} = \frac{100\% - 0\%}{10} = 10\%$$

If the estimated life is 10 years and the estimated salvage value is 15% of first cost,

$$\text{Straight-line rate} = \frac{100\% - 15\%}{10} = 8.5\%$$

Consider a $10,000 machine acquired on January 1, 1961. On this date, there is a $10,000 debit to an appropriate asset account, say Machinery. (This debit is balanced by a credit to Cash or Accounts Payable.) If a 10% straight-line rate is to be used (based on an estimated 10-year life with zero salvage value), the depreciation entry at the end of each year will be as follows:

	Debit	Credit
Depreciation Expense	$1,000	
Reserve for Depreciation, Machinery		$1,000

The charge to depreciation expense affects the income statement; each year this expense is closed into Profit and Loss Summary, either directly or indirectly by way of IME and cost of goods sold. In contrast, the credit to reserve affects the balance sheet by reducing the valuation placed on the fixed assets of the enterprise.

Consider the asset and reserve accounts on January 1, 1968, after depreciation charges have been made for 7 years:

Machinery	
10,000	

Reserve for Depreciation, Machinery	
	7,000

The difference between the $10,000 debit figure and the $7,000 credit figure is a net debit balance of $3,000. This $3,000 is referred to as the *book value* of the machine; it is the valuation of the machine that would be used on a balance sheet prepared on January 1, 1968.

Obviously, such a book value has no necessary relationship either to the market value of a fixed asset or to what the asset may be worth to its owner. It is merely that portion of the cost of the fixed asset that has not yet been charged off as depreciation expense.

On January 1, 1971, after depreciation charges have been made for 10 years, the asset and reserve accounts will be as follows:

Machinery			Reserve for Depreciation, Machinery	
10,000				10,000

It is evident that on this date our machine is fully depreciated on the books of account. If it turns out that our estimate of a 10-year life and zero salvage value is correct and the asset is therefore retired at once, the retirement entry will be:

Reserve for Depreciation, Machinery	$10,000	
Machinery		$10,000

Now assume that we have underestimated the service life of the asset and that it is continued in service until it is 25 years old. Obviously, no depreciation charges should be made against it after January 1, 1971. It should continue to be shown on the books as fully depreciated, with its original cost of $10,000 included in the Machinery account and an offsetting $10,000 figure included in the Reserve account. If it is retired without salvage value on January 1, 1986, the entry to show the retirement will be the same as the one that would have been made if the machine had been retired without salvage value 15 years earlier.

A different aspect of straight-line item accounting can be illustrated by considering a retirement before an asset has reached the end of its estimated life. Assume that our machine is sold for $900 cash on January 1, 1968. Because a machine with a book value of $3,000 is exchanged for only $900 cash, our accounting rules require us to record a decrease in ownership. The retirement entry may be shown as follows:

Reserve for Depreciation, Machinery	$7,000	
Cash	900	
Loss on Disposal of Fixed Assets	2,100	
Machinery		$10,000

Although the formal rules of accounting treat this $2,100 "loss" as a decrease in ownership in 1968, it is evident that this $2,100 would not have been assigned to 1968 if the initial estimate of life and salvage value had been correct. An estimated 7-year life and $900 salvage value would have caused a depreciation charge of $1,300 per year. In a sense, this $2,100 expense assigned to 1968 can be viewed as the result of having failed to assign $300 more a year as depreciation expense for the 7 years from 1961 to 1967.

If the cash salvage value at age 7 had been, say, $4,000, the retirement entry in January 1968 would have required a credit of $1,000 to Gain on Disposal of Fixed Assets. In general, in item depreciation accounting any retirement where salvage value differs from book value calls for an entry showing a gain or loss on disposal.

To examine another aspect of straight-line item accounting, let us start with another $10,000 machine acquired on January 1, 1961. This asset also has an estimated life of 10 years. This time, however, we shall estimate a terminal salvage value of $1,500. The depreciation rate is 8.5%, and the depreciation charge is $850 a year. On January 1, 1971, if the asset is still in service, its book value will equal its estimated salvage value, with asset and reserve accounts as follows:

Machinery	
10,000	

Reserve for Depreciation, Machinery	
	8,500

The additional point about item accounting to be brought out here is that any asset is viewed as fully depreciated when its book value equals its estimated salvage value. Therefore, just as in the case of our asset that had an estimated zero salvage value, depreciation charges on this asset terminate on January 1, 1971.

Straight-line item depreciation accounting is really not so important as the reader might assume from the amount of space we have given to it. However, an explanation of this method provides a convenient point of departure for the presentation of many other methods. In our discussion of other methods, we explain only enough to indicate the ways in which they differ from the straight-line item method.

THE DECLINING-BALANCE ITEM METHOD. In the declining-balance method of depreciation accounting, some chosen percentage is applied each year to the book value at the start of the year. Assume that a $10,000 machine is acquired on January 1, 1961, and that a 20% depreciation rate is to be used. The depreciation charge for 1961 is 20% of $10,000, or $2,000. The asset and reserve accounts on January 1, 1962, will be:

Machinery	
10,000	

Reserve for Depreciation, Machinery	
	2,000

The depreciation charge for 1962 is $1,600, 20% of the $8,000 book value at the start of the year. On January 1, 1963, the book value is $6,400 (i.e., $10,000 – $2,000 – $1,600). The depreciation charge for 1963 is $1,280, 20% of $6,400. Similarly, the depreciation charge for 1964 is $1,024, 20% of $5,120 (i.e., of $10,000 – $2,000 – $1,600 – $1,280). And so on.

It is evident that in the declining-balance method the depreciation charge is greatest in the first year and decreases each year thereafter. One characteristic of the declining-balance item method is that, no matter how long an asset is continued in service, it will always have *some* book value. Our $10,000 asset depreciated at a 20% declining-balance rate will have a book value of $1,073.70 at age 10, of $115.30 at age 20, and of $12.40 at age 30.

Retirement entries in the declining-balance item method follow the same general rules as in straight-line or any other type of item accounting. That is, the asset account is credited with the cost of the asset retired; the reserve account is debited with the reserve figure for the asset retired; whenever salvage value differs from book value, it is necessary to show a gain or loss on disposal.

DOUBLE DECLINING–BALANCE RATES UNDER THE UNITED STATES REVENUE ACT OF 1954. For assets acquired new in 1954 and thereafter, the 1954 tax law and its supporting regulations permitted the use of a depreciation rate for tax purposes computed as follows:

$$\text{Declining-balance rate} = \frac{200\%}{\text{estimated life in years}}$$

Such a rate writes off about two-thirds of the cost in the first half of the service life. It should be noted by the reader that this formula does not make use of an estimate of salvage value. The permissible declining-balance rate is double the straight-line rate that would be allowed with zero salvage value. Thus a 20% declining-balance rate would be allowed for an asset with an estimated life of 10 years, whether the estimated salvage value was zero or, say, 15%. This formula gives a remaining book value of about one-ninth of first cost at the end of the estimated life.[7]

[7] There is a "textbook formula" that will make book value equal to any estimated salvage value greater than zero at any given age. For an explanation of this formula and for reasons why it is not appropriate for use in actual accounting, see either of the following:

Grant and Norton, *op. cit.*, pp. 191–192.

E. L. Grant and W. G. Ireson, *Principles of Engineering Economy,* 4th ed., The Ronald Press Company, New York, 1960, pp. 170–171.

Regulations under the 1954 law stipulated that for this method (as well as for all others), an asset should not be depreciated below a reasonable salvage value. Consider this stipulation as applied to our $10,000 machine that had a 10-year estimated life and a $1,500 estimated salvage value. The permissible 20% declining-balance rate would lead to a book value of $1,677.70 at age 8. Therefore, the depreciation charge should be $177.70 (i.e., $1,677.70 — $1,500) for the ninth year rather than 20% of $1,677.70. After the ninth year, there would be no further depreciation charge.

The 1954 law permitted a taxpayer to change from the double declining-balance method to the straight-line method at any time. In cases where declining-balance item accounting is used with an estimated salvage value of zero or nearly zero, it may be desirable to make this change when an asset reaches 50 to 60% of its estimated life. For reasons explained briefly later in this chapter, this provision for change from declining-balance to straight-line is relatively unimportant in declining-balance multiple-asset accounting.

For fixed assets already in service before 1954 and for assets acquired secondhand, tax regulations permitted the use of a declining-balance rate of 150%/(estimated life in years). This provision of the regulations was not widely used.

Most of the use of the declining-balance method in the United States started in 1954. This use has been influenced by various constraints imposed by tax laws and regulations. The reader should recognize that there is nothing inherent in the declining-balance method itself that makes it necessary for a rate to be based on a formal estimate of life. A rate may be chosen on the grounds that the rate is believed to write off cost in an appropriate manner, all things considered. Declining-balance rates so chosen have been widely used in Great Britain and the British Commonwealth of Nations for many decades.

THE SUM-OF-THE-YEARS-DIGITS ITEM METHOD. In this method, the digits corresponding to the number of years of estimated life are added together. For instance, consider a life of 10 years. The sum of the digits from 1 to 10 is 55. The depreciation charge in the first year is $^{10}/_{55}$ of the depreciable cost (i.e., of the first cost minus the estimated salvage value). In the second year, the depreciation charge is $^{9}/_{55}$; in the third, $^{8}/_{55}$; and so on to $^{1}/_{55}$ in the tenth year. For brevity, we shall call this the *years-digits method* throughout the remainder of this chapter.

This method differs from the two methods previously described in having a new rate to be applied every year. It also differs in the depreciation base; the estimated salvage value must be subtracted from the balance in the asset account before applying the depreciation rate. The years-digits item method is like the straight-line item method in terminating depreciation charges at the end of the estimated life. Like all other item methods, a retirement at more or less than book value requires an entry showing a loss or gain on the disposal of fixed assets.

This method, authorized by the 1954 tax law in the United States for assets acquired new in 1954 and thereafter, apparently never was used in actual accounting before 1954. It writes off almost three-fourths of the depreciable cost in the first half of the estimated service life. For assets with estimated salvage values of zero or nearly zero, it gives a slightly more rapid write-off than the double declining-balance method.

MULTIPLE–ASSET VERSUS SINGLE–ASSET DEPRECIATION ACCOUNTING. In single-asset or item accounting, there is an annual depreciation charge and a depreciation reserve figure for each fixed asset. In contrast, in multiple-asset accounting, because fixed assets are considered together in groups, annual depreciation charges and depreciation reserve figures apply to groups of assets; there is no identifiable figure for depreciation charge or for reserve for an individual asset. As we shall see, this difference leads to different rules for making entries to record retirements; in straight-line and years-digits accounting this difference also leads to different rules for computing annual depreciation expense.

For most types of assets, multiple-asset accounting has a number of advantages over item accounting. Some points favorable to multiple-asset accounting are:

1. Where there are a number of assets devoted to the same general purpose, mortality dispersion is almost inevitable. Exhibit 19-2 illustrated this point with respect to certain telephone cable. Lives varied all the way from 1 to 44 years, and only a little over 4% of the cable was retired at the average life of 20 years. It follows that it is reasonable to view most life estimates as applicable to the *average life* of a number of assets rather than to the exact life of any particular asset. Where there are many assets and an average life of, say, 20 years is estimated, it does not seem reasonable to terminate all depreciation charges at age 20. If the estimate of average life turns out to be correct, there will be many unit years of service obtainable after age 20. Moreover, if the average life is estimated correctly, it is inevitable that a substantial proportion (usually nearly half) of the assets will be retired before they reach the estimated average life. Because such retirements are consistent with the life estimate, it does not seem reasonable to view them as "premature" or to assert that they cause a "loss."
2. In the common case where current evidence indicates that the orig-

inal estimates of life and/or salvage value are either too high or too low, the revision of depreciation rates is simpler in multiple-asset accounts than in item accounts.

3. Particularly for manufacturing equipment in the process industries, it may be difficult to divide fixed assets into separate items for the purpose of estimating life.
4. Entries to record retirements are simpler in multiple-asset accounting.
5. Generally speaking, bookkeeping expense will be less in multiple-asset accounting.

Some points favorable to item accounting in certain circumstances are:

1. For some types of assets, an enterprise may have relatively few items or only one item. Often an enterprise will have item accounts for certain major assets even though it uses multiple-asset accounts for most of its assets. For example, an oil company might use item accounting for office buildings and for tankers even though it used multiple-asset accounting for refinery equipment, pipelines and pipeline equipment, and service stations and related marketing facilities.
2. In the United States, certain taxpayers have been able to gain income tax advantages from the reporting of gains and losses on disposal of retired assets. However, the chance for most of these advantages (for depreciable assets other than buildings) was eliminated by certain U.S. Supreme Court decisions in the late 1950s and by certain changes in the Revenue Code made in 1962.
3. The straight-line item method is well adapted to the case where the life used in computing the depreciation rate is considerably shorter than the expected full service life. In this method it is possible for assets to be fully depreciated long before they are retired. Before 1934 in the United States, when a 10% straight-line item rate was common for assets having average lives much longer than 10 years, this method was a good one to use.

COMBINING FIXED ASSETS INTO MULTIPLE-ASSET ACCOUNTS. In all multiple-asset depreciation accounting, policies must be established to determine what fixed assets are to be grouped together for accounting purposes. One grouping may be by location; for example, a manufacturer with several plants might have separate accounts or sets of accounts for the fixed assets at each plant.

Two aspects of the combination of assets influence the rules for computing depreciation charges and for making entries to record retirements. One of these aspects is the extent to which dissimilar assets are included in the same account. The other is the extent to which assets acquired in different years are included in the same accounts.

With respect to the question of the dissimilarity of assets in one account, three general categories of multiple-asset accounts are recognized, as follows:[8]

1. **Group accounts.** Assets similar in kind are grouped together. Examples of group accounts are lathes, punch presses, typewriters, office desks, passenger automobiles, heavy trucks.
2. **Classified accounts.** Assets are grouped together in accordance with their general type of use even though different types of assets in an account have different expected average service lives. Examples of classified accounts are factory machinery and equipment; office furniture, fixtures, machines, and equipment; transportation equipment. The classified account is the most common type of multiple-asset account. The guideline lives in U.S. Revenue Procedure 62-21, previously mentioned, apply to classified accounts.
3. **Composite accounts.** Assets are grouped together regardless of their character or useful lives. For example, all the fixed assets used in a business might be included in one account. Generally speaking, composite accounts give too broad a grouping; they are not discussed further in this chapter.

One possible grouping according to time of acquisition is to have a separate account for each year's acquisitions of each type or class of assets. A single year's acquisitions are sometimes referred to as a *vintage group*. An opposite extreme is to combine all assets of a given type or class, whenever acquired, into an *open-end* account. Sometimes, a series of successive vintage groups are combined into an account that starts out as if it were intended to be an open-end account. Then, for one reason or another, no further additions are made to the account and it is supplemented by a new account that also combines successive vintage groups. For example, a manufacturer may have had one straight-line account for all machinery and equipment acquired before 1954; in 1954, he might start a new double declining-balance account for all machinery and equipment to be acquired in 1954 and thereafter.

Most actual multiple-asset accounts include a great many assets. Nevertheless, for simplicity, our examples will assume relatively few assets in an account. Certain points can be brought out to best advantage assuming vintage-group accounts. To bring out other points, we shall assume open-end accounts.

TWO SIMPLE EXAMPLES OF STRAIGHT-LINE GROUP DEPRECIATION ACCOUNTING. Assume that three machines were acquired on January 1, 1950, each at a cost of $10,000. Assume a straight-line rate of 10% based on an estimated average life of 10 years with zero salvage value. Assume that the average life turns out to

[8] This classification follows the one in "U.S. Treasury Decision 6182," sec. 1.167 (a)–7.

be exactly as estimated but that retirements occur on January 1, 1957, 1960, and 1963. Assume that all salvage values are zero, just as estimated.

The depreciation charge of $3,000 a year during the first 7 years is the same one that would be made under item accounting. After this date, group and item methods give different book values. The difference in book values results from different rules for retirement entries and for annual depreciation charges.

Consider the following account balances on January 1, 1957, just before the first retirement:

Machinery		Reserve for Depreciation, Machinery	
30,000			21,000

Unlike the corresponding entry in item accounting, the entry to record the zero-salvage retirement at age 7 does not involve a so-called loss of $3,000. The Machinery account is credited with the original cost of the asset retired, and the Reserve account debited with an equal amount. This retirement entry is shown in boldface type.

Machinery		Reserve for Depreciation, Machinery	
30,000	**10,000**	**10,000**	21,000

During the next 3 years, the annual depreciation charge is $2,000 (i.e., 10% of the remaining asset account balance of $20,000) just as it would have been under item accounting. Starting at $11,000 after the first retirement, the Reserve account balance increases to $17,000 on January 1, 1960. The account balances on January 1, 1960, before the retirement entry and the retirement entry on that date (shown in boldface type) are:

Machinery		Reserve for Depreciation, Machinery	
20,000	**10,000**	**10,000**	17,000

During the 3 years from January 1, 1960, to January 1, 1963, there is an important difference between the treatment in item and group accounting. Under straight-line item accounting, no further depreciation charges are made after the estimated service life has been reached. In contrast, under straight-line group accounting, the depreciation rate is applied to all assets in an account regardless of their age. Therefore, a depreciation charge of $1,000 (10% of the $10,000 balance in the asset account) is made for 1960, 1961, and 1962. The following T accounts show the account balances on January 1, 1960, after the retirement of the second asset, the credits to the reserve (in italics) that offset the debits to depreciation expense made in each of these 3 years, and the final retirement entry (in boldface) on January 1, 1963.

Machinery	
10,000	**10,000** (1963)

Reserve for Depreciation, Machinery	
(1963) **10,000**	7,000
	1,000 (1960)
	1,000 (1961)
	1,000 (1962)

Now let us change the example by assuming that the depreciation rate is 8.5% based on an estimated average service life of 10 years with an estimated average salvage value of 15% of first cost. Let us assume that the three $10,000 assets have actual lives of 7, 10, and 13 years just as before. Let us assume that the realized cash salvage values for these lives are $2,000, $1,500, and $1,000, respectively. (The total salvage of $4,500 is 15% of the $30,000 first cost, just as estimated.) The 8.5% depreciation charge is $2,550 a year for the first 7 years. The retirement entry on January 1, 1957, is shown in boldface type.

Machinery	
30,000	**10,000**

Reserve for Depreciation, Machinery	
8,000	17,850

Cash	
2,000	

During the next 3 years, the annual depreciation charge is $1,700 (8.5% of the asset account balance of $20,000). The reserve account balance, starting this period at $9,850, will increase by $5,100 to $14,950 on January 1, 1960. The retirement entry on that date is shown in boldface type.

Machinery	
20,000	**10,000**

Reserve for Depreciation, Machinery	
8,500	14,950

Cash	
1,500	

During the 3 years from January 1, 1960, to January 1, 1963, the depreciation charge is $850 a year. The reserve account balance, starting this period at $6,450, will increase by $2,550 to $9,000 on January 1, 1963. The retirement entry on this date is shown in boldface type.

Machinery	
10,000	**10,000**

Reserve for Depreciation, Machinery	
9,000	9,000

Cash	
1,000	

The foregoing two examples have illustrated the following points regarding straight-line group depreciation accounting.

1. The depreciation rate is established just as in the straight-line item method. However, the estimated life is viewed as an estimate of *average* life and the estimated salvage percentage is viewed as an estimate of *average* ratio of salvage to first cost.
2. No gains or losses are deemed to have occurred from retirements that are consistent with the estimates of average life and salvage value. With zero salvage, the debit to the reserve account is equal to the original cost of the assets retired. With a net positive salvage value, the debit to the reserve is the original cost of the asset minus its net salvage.
3. Depreciation charges against an asset do not stop when the asset has reached the average service life used to compute the depreciation rate. They are made against all assets in an account even though some (or all) of the assets are older than the estimated average service life.
4. Where estimates of average service life and salvage percentage turn out to be correct, the investment minus salvage in a vintage-group account will have been exactly written off when the final unit in the vintage group is retired. In other words, no "gain" or "loss" on disposal is entered at any time in the case of correct estimates.

The straight-line group method can be viewed as aiming to write off a uniform amount per service year. In our example of three units with an average service life of 10 years, there were 30 service years. In the zero-salvage example, the write-off per service year was $1,000. In the example where the average salvage was 15%, the write-off per service year was $850. It can be shown that, if estimates of average life and average salvage are correct, the remaining book value at any time is equal to the sum of remaining salvage and the product of the remaining service years and the write-off per service year.

STRAIGHT-LINE GROUP METHOD USING AN OPEN-END ACCOUNT. It has been pointed out that experience indicates that even when all of the assets in a vintage group are of the same general type, there is likely to be considerable mortality dispersion. Experience also indicates that successive vintage groups of assets of the same general type differ considerably in their average service lives.[9] There is a better chance to make a satisfactory estimate of the

[9] Grant and Norton, *Depreciation, op. cit.*, pp. 50–69, report a study made in 1947 of the mortality of steam locomotives of a major railroad. An incidental aspect of this study is that it illustrates the differences that may occur among successive vintage groups. The 1906, 1907, and 1908 vintage groups are a good example. Of the locomotives acquired in 1906, 98%

average life of all assets of a given type than to make such an estimate for a single vintage group or for a single asset. In an open-end group account, life estimates are viewed as applicable to the average of all the assets in the account, regardless of their year of acquisition.

The rules for making depreciation and retirement entries in a straight-line open-end group account are the same rules that were illustrated in our discussion of accounting for a single vintage group. In general, it is simpler to have one open-end account applicable to a given type of class of assets than to have many accounts each applicable to a different vintage group. In multiple-asset accounting, the usual practice is to use open-end accounts rather than vintage-group accounts.

Nevertheless, there is one kind of trouble that may arise with straight-line open-end accounts that is less likely to occur with straight-line vintage-group accounts. This trouble occurs when the average life actually realized turns out to be considerably longer than the life that was used in computing the depreciation rate. Often average life is estimated conservatively at a figure viewed as the economic life in the initial service of an asset, but for various reasons, such as the use of old assets in standby or other inferior service or the difficulty of financing all replacements as soon as they become economical, actual lives are much longer than such economic lives.

In this common type of case, the oldest accounts in a set of vintage-group accounts—like a set of item accounts under similar circumstances—eventually would reach the point where their book values were zero (or, where applicable, the estimated remaining salvage value). At this time, it would become evident that depreciation charges for these accounts would have to be discontinued in spite of the rule in straight-line group accounting that depreciation rates normally are applied to asset account balances regardless of the ages of the assets in an account.

Open-end straight-line accounts do not contain such a convenient built-in check against an underestimate of average life. A disparity between estimated and actual figures may be concealed by the fact that new assets are being added to an account each year. In general, open-end straight-line group accounts do not operate in a satisfactory way unless the actual figures for average life and salvage value are

---

were still in service after 41 years. Of the locomotives acquired in 1907, about two-thirds had been retired by age 40; an extrapolation of the survivor curve indicated that the 1907 group would have an average life of about 34 years. Of the locomotives acquired in 1908, all had been retired with an average life of about 27 years.

fairly consistent with estimated figures.[10] Such open-end accounts therefore require periodic reviews of mortality experience to determine whether the straight-line rates ought to be changed.

Particularly in the public utility industry, such periodic reviews have been based on mortality studies of the types described in the references given in the footnote on page 425. For a mature open-end account (i.e., for an account somewhat older than the estimated service life used to establish the depreciation rate), it is possible to use the reserve ratio to obtain a rough check on whether actual average lives agree with estimated lives.[11] (The reserve ratio is the ratio of the reserve account balance to the asset account balance.)

A DIFFERENCE BETWEEN STRAIGHT-LINE GROUP AND STRAIGHT-LINE CLASSIFIED ACCOUNTS. Certain special aspects of classified accounts can be illustrated to best advantage by examining a particular case. Consider an account Office Furniture, Fixtures, Machines, and Equipment. United States Revenue Procedure 62-21 lists the types of assets appropriate for such an account as follows:

> Includes furniture and fixtures which are not a structural component of the building, and machines and equipment used in the preparation of papers or data. Includes such assets as desks; files; safes; typewriters; accounting, calculating and data processing machines; communications, duplicating and copying equipment.

Different types of assets in such an account may differ greatly in their average lives. For example, typewriters and calculating machines presumably have shorter lives than desks and safes. It follows that there are two different kinds of reasons why mortality dispersion is to be expected in a classified account. One reason is the inherent variability of lives for any given type of asset; for instance, if the average life of a group of desks is 20 years, not all the desks in the group will have lives of exactly 20 years. The other reason is the difference in average lives among the assets in an account.

The following simple numerical example illustrates the setting of a straight-line rate for a classified account containing three types of

[10] For a documentation of this assertion, see Grant and Norton, *Depreciation, op. cit.*, chaps. 7 and 8. See also problem 19-2 at the end of this chapter.

[11] Procedures and tables for making such tests were given in two pamphlets issued in 1962, U.S. Treasury Department Internal Revenue Service Publications 456 and 457, "Tables for Applying Revenue Procedure 62-21." These pamphlets also included rules for revising depreciation rates for income tax purposes whenever a reserve ratio should fall outside a range stipulated in the tables. They dealt with double declining-balance, 150% declining-balance, and years-digits accounts as well as straight-line accounts.

assets, each with a different estimated average service life. Assume an account for Office Furniture, Fixtures, Machines, and Equipment that has a total \$30,000 investment. Of this, \$10,000 is in typewriters that have an estimated average life of 5 years with 20% average salvage value, \$10,000 is in calculating machines that have an estimated average life of 10 years with 10% average salvage value and \$10,000 is in desks, chairs, and bookcases that have an estimated average life of 20 years with zero salvage value. The depreciation for this account is computed in Exhibit 19-4.

EXHIBIT 19-4
EXAMPLE OF CALCULATION OF STRAIGHT-LINE DEPRECIATION RATE FOR A CLASSIFIED ACCOUNT

Type of asset	Estimated average life, years	Investment	Estimated average salvage, %	Annual depreciation charge
Typewriters	5	\$10,000	20	\$1,600
Calculating machines	10	10,000	10	900
Desks, etc	20	10,000	0	500
Total	...	\$30,000	...	\$3,000

$$\text{Initial depreciation rate} = \frac{\text{total annual depreciation charge}}{\text{total investment}}$$

$$= \frac{\$3{,}000}{\$30{,}000} = 0.10 \text{ or } 10\%$$

If estimates of lives and salvage values are correct, and if typewriters and calculating machines are replaced with new ones that have the same first costs, lives, and salvage percentages, and if an open-end account is used, it can be shown that a continuation of this 10% rate for 20 years will exactly write off the first cost minus salvage of the \$70,000 of assets involved (i.e., \$40,000 of typewriters, \$20,000 of calculating machines, and \$10,000 of desks). However, if the assets in Exhibit 19-4 constitute a vintage-group account, a new lower depreciation rate to be applied to the remaining assets must be computed whenever a retirement is made.[12]

In general, it can be said that the depreciation rate used in a straight-line classified account may need frequent review and revision for two kinds of reasons. One reason, not applicable to group accounts, is a change in the relative proportions of the various types of assets in the account. The other reason, applicable to all straight-line multiple-

[12] Problems 19-4 to 19-6 use the data of Exhibit 19-4 to illustrate various aspects of the calculation of straight-line rates for multiple-asset accounts.

asset accounts, is evidence that actual average lives and salvage values are different from the estimated lives and salvage values that were used to compute the depreciation rate.

AVERAGING CONVENTIONS. Up to this point, our numerical examples illustrating various depreciation accounting methods have been somewhat unrealistic in one respect; they have dealt only with acquisitions and retirements taking place on some January 1. We have deliberately avoided the complications that arise when depreciation charges must be made for various different fractions of a year.

The usual condition is for acquisitions and retirements to occur at many different times during a fiscal year. If enough acquisitions and retirements are taking place, it generally is reasonable to assume that they are distributed at random throughout the year. This assumption leads to the use in multiple-asset accounts of some type of *averaging convention,* adopted to avoid the problem of figuring separate depreciation charges for many different fractions of a year.

The most common such convention is the *half-year convention.* Under this convention, one-half of a full year's depreciation charge is applied to an asset in its year of acquisition regardless of the date of acquisition during the year. Similarly, one-half year's depreciation is charged in the retirement year regardless of the retirement date.

The use of the half-year convention in a straight-line multiple-asset open-end account can be illustrated by a numerical example. Assume that the balances in an asset and reserve account in the cement industry are as follows on January 1, 1963:

Machinery		Reserve for Depreciation, Machinery	
107,200			44,100

A 5% straight-line depreciation rate is being used. (This corresponds to the guideline life of 20 years given for the cement industry in Revenue Procedure 62-21.) A new machine costing $18,000 is acquired for cash during 1963. Two machines are retired during the year: One, which cost $5,000 in 1938, is retired without salvage value; the other, which cost $7,000 in 1951, is sold for $1,200 cash.

At year end, before the depreciation expense for the year has been entered, the asset and reserve accounts appear as follows:

Machinery		Reserve for Depreciation, Machinery	
107,200	5,000	5,000	44,100
18,000	7,000	5,800	

It now is necessary to compute the annual depreciation expense for 1963. The easiest way to do this using the half-year convention is to start by noting the figures for the asset account balance at the beginning and end of the year. These two figures are averaged, and the average is multiplied by the annual depreciation rate. In our example, the initial asset balance is $107,200 and the final balance is $113,200. The average, $110,200, multiplied by 0.05 (i.e., by 5%), gives $5,510, the depreciation expense to be charged for 1963. The journal entry to record this expense is

Depreciation Expense	$5,510	
Reserve for Depreciation, Machinery		$5,510

The foregoing simple method of calculation automatically applies half the annual depreciation rate to the assets acquired and retired during the year and applies the full rate to the assets that were in service for the entire year. This statement can be checked by the following calculations:

Assets in service for all of 1963 = $107,200 − $5,000 − $7,000	=	$95,200
5% depreciation charge on the foregoing assets = $95,200(0.05)	=	$4,760
2.5% depreciation charge on assets acquired during year = $18,000(0.025)	=	450
2.5% depreciation charge on assets retired during year = ($5,000 + $7,000)(0.025)	=	300
Total depreciation charge for the year	=	$5,510

An alternate averaging convention is one in which all acquisitions and retirements of fixed assets made in the first half of the year are assumed to have taken place at the start of the year, whereas all during the second half are assumed to have taken place at the end of the year. Under this convention, a full year's depreciation is taken on acquisitions made during the first half of the year and no depreciation on acquisitions made during the second half. Similarly, a full year's depreciation is taken on assets retired during the second half of the year and no depreciation on assets retired during the first half.

YEARS–DIGITS MULTIPLE–ASSET ACCOUNTING. A first impression of the years-digits method might be that it is suitable only for item accounting because a different depreciation fraction must be applied to the depreciable value for each year of the life of an asset. However, the U.S. Internal Revenue Service has devised a scheme for years-digits accounting based on the calculation each year of the weighted average remaining life of all the assets in an account.[13] This scheme makes use of a table that gives decimal equivalents of years-digits multipliers for any given remaining life. The scheme makes possible the use of the years-digits method for multiple-asset accounts.

An explanation of the technicalities of making estimates of weighted

[13] See "Treasury Decision No. 6182," Sec. 1.167(b)–3.

average remaining life of a group of assets having mortality dispersion would require more space than would be appropriate in this chapter. For this reason, we do not give any numerical examples of the use of the years-digits method with multiple-asset accounts. In general, the rules for retirement entries in years-digits multiple-asset accounts are similar to those in straight-line multiple-asset accounts. The differences between group and classified accounts discussed in connection with the straight-line method are also applicable to years-digits accounts.

DECLINING–BALANCE MULTIPLE–ASSET ACCOUNTING USING THE HALF–YEAR CONVENTION. The following numerical example illustrates retirement and depreciation entries with a declining-balance open-end account. Balances in an asset and reserve account on January 1, 1963, are as follows:

Furniture and Fixtures		Reserve for Depreciation, Furniture and Fixtures	
29,400			17,710

A 20% declining-balance rate is being used. New furniture costing $2,200 is acquired for cash during the year. Furniture that originally cost $1,500 is retired without salvage value. The following entries record the acquisitions and retirements:

Furniture and Fixtures	$2,200	
Cash		$2,200
Reserve for Depreciation, Furniture and Fixtures	$1,500	
Furniture and Fixtures		$1,500

It will be noted that the entry for a retirement at zero salvage value is the same in a declining-balance multiple-asset account as in a straight-line multiple-asset account. Entries involving salvage values also are identical in the two methods; for example, if the retired furniture should have a $100 salvage value, the debit to the reserve would be $1,400 rather than $1,500.

In contrast to the retirement entries, the calculations of annual depreciation expense in a declining-balance multiple-asset account are quite different from those in a straight-line multiple-asset account. Where the half-year convention is used, two separate calculations are required, one for the assets that started the year and the other for the year's acquisitions. The full rate is applied to the difference between the asset and reserve account balances at the start of the year.[14] Half

[14] This statement is not strictly correct in calculating declining-balance depreciation for income tax purposes in the United States. Under Treasury regulations, a retirement at a positive salvage value reduces the allowable depreciation for the retirement year by half the product of the salvage value and the declining-balance rate.

the annual rate is applied to the year's acquisitions. The calculations for our example are as follows:

20% depreciation charge on initial book value = ($29,400 − $17,710)(0.20)	=	$2,338
10% depreciation charge on year's acquisitions = $2,200(0.10)	=	220
Total depreciation charge for the year	=	$2,558

The entry to record annual depreciation expense is

Depreciation Expense	$2,558	
Reserve for Depreciation, Furniture and Fixtures		$2,558

In the declining-balance method, the depreciation base is book value (i.e., asset account balance minus reserve balance). A retirement at zero salvage value therefore does not change the depreciation base and does not influence subsequent depreciation charges. This is in contrast to the straight-line multiple-asset accounting in which each retirement reduces the depreciation base (the asset account balance) by the original cost of the asset retired.

SOME ASPECTS OF DOUBLE DECLINING–BALANCE MULTIPLE–ASSET ACCOUNTING. It has already been pointed out that declining-balance depreciation accounting is possible without reference to any stated estimate of average service life or average salvage value. However, the use of this method for income tax purposes in the United States has been based on the assumption that a service life estimate has been made.

One way to relate a declining-balance rate to an estimate of average life is to stipulate that this rate shall be some stated percentage of a straight-line rate computed on the assumption of zero salvage value. Such a stipulation has been used in the income tax laws and regulations in the United States. It should be evident to the reader that any such stated percentage is arbitrary. It might be 200%, the figure specified in the United States for new assets acquired in 1954 and thereafter. Or it might be 150% as specified for used assets and pre-1954 assets. From time to time, writers on depreciation have proposed higher percentages, particularly 250 and 300%.

When the double (200%) declining-balance method was authorized in 1954, a common objection raised by accountants was that this method left an unreasonably high remaining book value at the end of the estimated service life. As applied to any multiple-asset account (the usual type of account), this objection was not valid because it disregarded the common fact of mortality dispersion.

For example, consider a double declining-balance account for a group of assets that have the average life (20 years) and the mortality dispersion shown in Exhibit 19-2. Assume a double declining-balance rate of 10% based on a correct estimate of average life. Consider an account containing only one vintage groups. If all retirements are made with zero salvage value, the remaining book value when half the units have been retired will be about 12% of the first cost; when the final unit has been retired, the remaining book value will be less than 1% of first cost.

Any positive salvage values will reduce the foregoing percentages. The influence of salvage percentage on book values for a vintage group will depend on the mortality dispersion and on the timing of the salvage values. A general statement, subject to exceptions, is that, if typical salvage values are 8% or more of first cost, the book value of a vintage group will fall to zero before the final asset in the group is retired. (In any event, if accounts are kept by vintage groups, any small remaining book value in a vintage group can be written off when the last unit in the group is retired.)

The criticism that the double declining-balance method causes unreasonably high residual book values has even less validity as applied to classified accounts. This assertion is true in part because classified accounts tend to have greater mortality dispersion than group accounts, since they usually include several different types of assets that have different average service lives.

MULTIPLE-STRAIGHT-LINE METHODS. Consider an asset with a $10,000 first cost, an estimated 20-year life, and an estimated zero salvage value. Assume that $500, $\frac{1}{20}$ of $10,000, is being written off each year. If book value is plotted as a function of time on rectangular coordinate paper, a straight line connecting $10,000 at 0 years with $0 at 20 years will show the book value at all times. Hence the name "straight-line method."

It is possible to use depreciation accounting methods where two or more straight lines are used to go from first cost to estimated salvage value at the end of estimated life. For example, at one time it was proposed that half the cost of commercial and industrial buildings should be written off in the first quarter of their estimated lives and the remaining half in the final three-quarters of the life. For a building with an estimated life of 40 years, this would give a 5% rate in the first 10 years and a 1.67% rate in the last 30 years. This may be described as a multiple-straight-line method. The practice, in common use prior to 1934, of writing off the entire cost of machinery in the first 10 years of its life even though it normally continued in service for 20 years or more may be viewed as a special case of the multiple-straight-line method in which a 10% rate is followed by a 0% rate.

Under the 1954 tax law in the United States, multiple-straight-line methods were permitted for new assets subject to the restriction that the amount written off at any time during the first two-thirds of the life could not be more than would have been allowed under the double declining-balance method. Tax laws in many countries, including the United States, have permitted an extra write-off in the year of acquisition of certain assets. If an asset that had, say, an 8-year estimated life with zero estimated salvage value should be written off 30% the first year and 10% each year thereafter, this would be a special case of the multiple-straight-line method.

THE UNIT-OF-PRODUCTION METHOD. Some fixed assets can be identified directly with the production of specific units of output. For such assets, it is possible to charge depreciation in proportion to units of production provided it is reasonable to estimate life in terms of production units. This method is appropriate for assets associated with exhaustible natural resources where the factor that limits the life of the assets is the quantity of the natural resource in question. For instance, the cost of a coal mine tipple might be depreciated at so much per ton of coal mined. Frequently the unit-of-production method is used for motor vehicles with depreciation charged in proportion to miles of operation.

DEPLETION. In most instances, it is appropriate to use the unit-of-production method to write off the cost of the natural resources themselves. A write-off of the cost of exhaustible natural resources is usually referred to as *depletion* rather than as depreciation.

Depletion charges on exhaustible mineral resources are allowed special treatment for income tax purposes in the United States. The depletion deduction for these resources on income tax returns may be based on a stated percentage of the gross income. This percentage method applies to oil and gas wells (27½%), metal mines (in some cases 23% and in others 15%), coal mines (10%), and certain other mineral deposits. The deduction under this method may not exceed 50% of the taxpayer's net income from the mineral property computed without this allowance for depletion.

Even though the percentage method is used in income tax returns, the taxpayer's own books will base depletion charges on the cost of the resource in question. The cost method is also acceptable for income tax purposes; the percentage method will be used only if it gives a higher depletion figure (and hence a lower income tax) than the method based on cost.

DEPRECIATION IS A WORD WITH SEVERAL MEANINGS.[15] It is helpful to distinguish three quite different senses in which the word *depreciation* is used. These may be referred to as:

[15] See J. C. Bonbright, *Valuation of Property*, McGraw-Hill Book Company, Inc., New York, 1937, chap. 10. See also Grant and Norton, *Depreciation*, *op. cit.*, chap. 2.

1. The popular sense—decrease in value
2. The accounting sense—the writing off or amortization of cost
3. The appraisal sense—the difference in value between an existing old asset being appraised and a hypothetical new asset taken as a standard of comparison

The popular sense of the word implies that the value of an asset or group of assets is somehow determined at two dates. The depreciation is computed by subtracting the value at the later date from the value at the earlier date, regardless of the combination of causes that may have been responsible for the value change. If the value has increased, the increase is called *appreciation*. *Value* here may refer to any sort of economic value, such as market value or appraised value for a specific owner.

As pointed out in the definition given at the start of the discussion of depreciation accounting in Chap. 7, the orthodox accounting concept of depreciation is the writing off of cost "in a systematic and rational manner."

Many appraisals of existing assets are based on replacement cost. Such appraisals should answer the question: "How much could one afford to pay for the existing asset in comparison with the most economical new one?" The depreciation deduction from replacement cost should be a measure of the value inferiority of the old asset being appraised to the new one taken as a standard of comparison. Old assets may be inferior to the most economical new one for the many reasons mentioned earlier in this chapter. It should be noted that the appraisal concept of depreciation refers to the difference in value of two different assets on one date, the date of the appraisal. This is in contrast to the popular concept which refers to the difference in the values of a particular asset on two or more dates.

Price level changes do not influence depreciation in the accounting sense which deals with the writing off of *cost*. They obviously do influence depreciation or appreciation in the popular sense. In the appraisal sense, current price levels are recognized in obtaining the appraised values of old assets because the depreciation deduction is made from a replacement-cost figure based on current prices.

RELATIONSHIP OF THE DEPRECIATION CHARGE TO THE FINANCING OF NEW FIXED ASSETS. In a sense, the charge to depreciation expense made in the accounts of a profitable enterprise is closely related to a source of funds for the purchase of fixed assets. That is, an enterprise that does not show a loss collects from its customers a sum that is viewed as recovered capital; this sum is equal to the depreciation charge in the accounts. If no depreciation charge had been entered in the books, this sum would have appeared to be profits available for dividends; one of the effects of the depreciation charge is to force the directors of a corporation to keep this recovered capital in the enterprise. Moreover, if the depreciation charge is acceptable for income tax purposes, this sum is not diminished by income taxation.

In most enterprises, it is sound managerial policy to recognize that a primary use of this recovered capital should be for the financing of new fixed assets, particularly for the replacement of assets that have reached the end of their economic lives. In the many enterprises that cannot readily raise new capital from outside sources, this recovered capital and retained earnings may be the only possible sources of funds to finance such replacements. It has already been pointed out that replacements can generally be put off for a long time after the date when they have become economically desirable. There is great danger that, if replacements are deferred too long, the competitive position of an enterprise will be weakened because of obsolete plant with high operating costs.

SOME CONSEQUENCES OF THE PREPAID-EXPENSE TREATMENT OF DEPRECIATION IN A PERIOD OF RISING PRICES. The unit costs of industrial fixed assets in the 1960s are generally much higher than those prevailing in the 1930s and 1940s. Any such rise in price levels is responsible for many business problems. Certain of these problems are related to limitations of the orthodox accounting treatment of depreciation expense as a time allocation of the cost of fixed assets.

For example, consider industrial machinery 15 years old having an original cost of \$100,000 and a present replacement cost of \$250,000. A fair appraised value for this machinery today is properly based on the \$250,000 replacement cost minus a deduction (depreciation in the appraisal sense) for the value inferiority of the old asset to the replacement asset. Assume that this machinery has an estimated remaining life of 10 years. The prospective decrease in value (depreciation in the popular sense) during the next 10 years will be equal to the present appraised value minus the prospective salvage value, if any, at the end of the 10 years. This depreciation in the popular sense depends on present price levels and is unrelated to the \$100,000 original cost of the asset. It is this prospective depreciation in the popular sense rather than depreciation in the accounting sense that is the appropriate guide to many business decisions, including decisions on the pricing of product. For this reason, unit cost figures that include accounting depreciation may need to be altered before they are used to influence certain business decisions.

Moreover, a \$250,000 replacement cannot be financed solely by the \$100,000 of capital that the accounts will show to have been recovered as a result of the depreciation charge on this machinery. In order to hold its own in machine capacity, this enterprise must find an extra \$150,000 of new equity capital in order to finance the \$250,000 replacement. In many enterprises the only possible way to secure such necessary equity capital is to keep profits in the business rather than to pay them to the owners as dividends. But because of high levels of income taxation, $150,000 of profit before taxes is not enough to supply this needed amount. If, for example, the tax rate is 50%, it is necessary to have $300,000 of profit before taxes if $150,000 is to be retained by the enterprise. If the owners desire to maintain their plant capacity intact, such a $300,000 figure shown by the accounts as "profit" is somewhat illusory; none of it is available either for dividends or for plant expansion.

Even though the preceding example is somewhat oversimplified and some aspects of the subject have not been mentioned, it should be evident to the reader that the prepaid-expense view of depreciation for accounting and tax purpose creates some difficulties in periods of rising prices. Other different problems arise in periods of falling prices. These and other matters have led to suggestions from some industrialists and accountants that depreciation charges for accounting and income tax purposes be based in some way on current price levels.

THE USE OF DIFFERENT DEPRECIATION METHODS FOR BOOK AND TAX PURPOSES. Depreciation in the accounting sense often is described as a *noncash item*. Such a phrase refers to the point that the account Cash is neither debited nor credited when depreciation is entered in the books of account. (Presumably the entry involving Cash took place at the earlier date when the assets in question were acquired.)

Although the mere entry of depreciation in the books does not change the amount of cash on hand, the size of the depreciation figure may influence cash receipts or disbursements in various ways. The larger the depreciation figure, the smaller the profits shown by the books and vice versa. The size of the reported profit may influence decisions by the board of directors regarding the amount of cash to be disbursed for dividends. If there is a system of managerial bonuses based on profit, the depreciation figure will influence the size of the cash disbursement for the bonuses. If product or service is sold at "cost" plus a fixed fee or plus a percentage, and if "cost" is defined to include depreciation as shown in the books of account, the size of the depreciation figure influences cash receipts.

In the many countries that have high income tax rates, perhaps the most important influence on cash flow exerted by the annual depreciation figure is the influence on disbursements for income taxes. However, the depreciation figure used to compute taxable income is not always the same as the figure used in the books of account. The decision on the depreciation method to be used on the books influences the book figure for profit before income taxes but does not affect the available cash. The decision on the method to be used in the tax return influences both the available cash and the after-tax profit shown by the books.

Various ways in which after-tax profit and cash flow can be affected by these two decisions are illustrated in Exhibit 19-5. Because the hypothetical company in this example is assumed to be in competitive industry, gross revenues are assumed to be independent of the depreciation method selected. (This avoids the special complications existing in regulated public utilities, where both the book figure for depreciation and the expected income tax need to be considered by regulatory commissions in determining the prices that may be charged for utility service.) The various assumptions in the example are stated at the top of Exhibit 19-5. As applied to a possible corporate taxpayer in the United States, the assumed 55% tax rate may be viewed as the combined result of Federal and state income taxes. In general, the arithmetic of this exhibit should be self-explanatory to a student of accounting.

A striking conclusion from line K of the exhibit is that the choice of depreciation methods for the two purposes can be responsible for a variation in the profit reported to the stockholders from $11.2 million to $5 million. This difference of $6.2 million exists even though the depreciation figure under DDB is only $4 million more than under SL. Both the relative and absolute differences between the highest and lowest figures in line L are much less than in line K. The after-tax cash flow is either $21.2 million or $19 million in all the cases shown; the $2.2 million difference between these figures is the product of the $4 million difference in tax depreciation and the 55% tax rate.

The most common condition in industry is to use the same depreciation method for book and tax purposes. The first two columns of Exhibit 19-5 illustrate such use with respect to the SL and DDB methods. Here the DDB method gives $2.2 million more cash than the SL but $1.8 million less reported profit.

The third and fourth columns illustrate two different possible accounting treatments of the case where management elects to use more depreciation in computing taxable income than is used in the books of account. The cash flow in line L is the same in both columns. However, the book figure for profit shown in the fourth column is reduced by a $2.2 million allowance for the taxes that have been put off because the lower present taxable income presumably will be offset by a correspondingly higher taxable income at some future date.[16]

The treatment illustrated in the final column of Exhibit 19-5 has

[16] In 1954 and the years immediately thereafter in the United States, the treatment illustrated in the third column was fairly common for corporations that elected to use one of the 1954 methods for tax purposes and to continue to use the straight-line method for book purposes. Many of these corporations later changed to the treatment illustrated in the fourth column when this treatment became recognized as the better accounting practice.

EXHIBIT 19-5

AN EXAMPLE ILLUSTRATING HOW THE SELECTION OF DEPRECIATION METHODS FOR BOOK AND TAX PURPOSES INFLUENCES AFTER-TAX CASH FLOW AND AFTER-TAX PROFITS SHOWN BY THE BOOKS

	SL book and tax	DDB book and tax	SL book DDB tax*	SL book DDB tax†	DDB book SL tax
A. Gross revenue	$100	$100	$100	$100	$100
B. Operating expense (excluding depreciation and income taxes)	70	70	70	70	70
C. Profit (and cash flow) before depreciation and taxes (A − B)	30	30	30	30	30
D. Depreciation for book purposes	10	14	10	10	14
E. Book profit before taxes (C − D)	20	16	20	20	16
F. Depreciation for tax purposes	10	14	14	14	10
G. Taxable income (C − F)	20	16	16	16	20
H. Income tax (0.55G)	11	8.8	8.8	8.8	11
J. Book allowance for deferred taxes (0.55)(F − D)	0	0	0	2.2	0
K. Profit reported to stockholders (C − D − H − J)	9	7.2	11.2	9	5
L. Cash flow before dividends (C − H)	19	21.2	21.2	21.2	19

Note: All figures are in millions of dollars. Straight-line (SL) depreciation is $10 million and double declining-balance (DDB) is $14 million. All revenues and all expenses except depreciation are assumed to be cash items. For simplicity, a tax rate of 55% is assumed to apply to all taxable income.

* No allowance for deferred income taxes made in income statement.

† An allowance for deferred income taxes made in income statement.

not been a common one in the United States since 1954. In the period 1934 to 1953, when allowable depreciation charges for tax purposes often were viewed as being unreasonably low, it was not uncommon for the depreciation figure shown by the books to be greater than the corresponding figure used to compute taxable income.

Space is not available here for an examination of a number of interesting and controversial issues in governmental tax policy that could be introduced by a more extended discussion of Exhibit 19-5.[17] However, the exhibit should help to make the nonaccountant readers of this book aware that an adequate interpretation of many income statements calls for a knowledge of the depreciation methods being used for both book and tax purposes.

SOME ASPECTS OF THE SELECTION OF A METHOD OF DEPRECIATION ACCOUNTING. The following discussion applies to the selection of a method of depreciation accounting in the United States where the decision has been made to use the same method for business purposes that is used for income tax purposes. Under this restriction, there is relatively little range for choice for assets acquired before 1954 or for assets acquired secondhand. In nearly all cases, some variant of the straight-line method will continue to be used for such assets.

For assets acquired new in 1954 and thereafter, it first is necessary to decide whether it is desired to have a more rapid write-off in the early years of life than is possible with the straight-line method. If the rapid write-off is wanted, it then is necessary to choose among the various permissible methods of securing this write-off.

It is the authors' view that a straight-line method based on full-service life will rarely give a write-off that is rapid enough for business purposes, entirely apart from income tax considerations. The rapid write-off is particularly desirable in competitive industry. Most retirements are made for economic reasons; the same factors (i.e., improved alternatives, changes in service requirements, increasing operation and maintenance costs with age) that ultimately cause retirements also cause a rapid decline in the competitive value of fixed assets in the early years of their economic lives. Moreover, full service lives are typically much longer than economic lives. Most business decisions influenced by the depreciation accounts (e.g., decisions on capital conservation, pricing decisions) will be better made if the depreciation write-off is more rapid in the early years of service life.

When income tax rates are high, the case for the more rapid write off in the early years is strengthened by income tax considerations, as

[17] See Grant and Norton, *Depreciation, op. cit.*, chaps. 16–18.

the tax-free recovery of invested capital will occur sooner. This earlier tax-free recovery helps with many aspects of business finance, including the financing of replacement assets.

Once the decision is made to adopt some depreciation accounting method giving a rapid write-off in the early years, the choice among the different permissible methods may properly be influenced by the convenience, simplicity, and accounting costs associated with the various methods. For the usual classified accounts containing many assets, these considerations favor the declining-balance method. For item accounts in which prospective salvage values are zero or nearly so, the years-digits method is preferable if it is desired to obtain the most rapid write-off allowable under the 1954 tax law. Often it will be sensible to employ both methods, using double declining-balance classified accounts for Machinery, Transportation Equipment, and Office Furniture, Fixtures, Machines, and Equipment and using years-digits item accounts for Buildings and similar major assets.

SUMMARY. Some of the important points of this chapter can be restated as follows:

1. The decision whether or not to capitalize a particular expenditure is a decision between distributing the expenditure among a number of accounting periods by means of depreciation accounting or charging it entirely to the current period.
2. The straight-line item method operates as if each item in an asset account has its own reserve balance and book value. Items that have reached the estimated service life are fully depreciated, and no further depreciation charges are made against them. Any retirement in which the net salvage is greater or less than the book value of the asset retired involves an entry showing a so-called gain or loss on the retirement. Although this method is convenient where it is desired to write off the cost of assets over a shorter period than the full service life, such write-offs ordinarily are not permitted for income tax purposes in the United States.
3. The straight-line multiple-asset method of depreciation accounting recognizes the inevitability of a mortality dispersion of the assets in an account. The method aims at a uniform write-off per unit year of service. In this method, the same depreciation rate is applied to all assets in an account, those that are older than the estimated average service life as well as those that are younger. No item in multiple-asset account has an individual book value. Normally, assets are never fully depreciated in this method. Ordinarily no "loss" or "gain" is entered on the disposal of a fixed asset. Depreciation rates need to be reviewed from time to time to check them with actual

mortality experience. This method is not suitable where it is desired to write off the cost of assets in a shorter period than full service life.

4. Actual depreciation accounting practices in the United States have been greatly influenced by what has been allowable for income tax purposes. During the period 1934 to 1953 this influence led to lower depreciation rates and a closer correspondence between estimated lives and actual full service lives.
5. Several different depreciation accounting methods, each permitting the write-off of approximately two-thirds of cost in the first half of service life, were authorized for income tax purposes in the United States by the Internal Revenue Code of 1954. The use of these methods was restricted to new assets with lives of 3 years or more that were acquired in 1954 or thereafter. The simplest of these methods is the declining-balance method, in which the depreciation rate is applied each year to the book value (asset account balance minus reserve balance). The permissible declining-balance rate is double the straight-line rate based on average service life and zero salvage value. There are a number of good reasons in favor of using one of the depreciation accounting methods authorized by the 1954 law.
6. The orthodox accounting rule is to treat depreciation expense as a writing off of the *cost* of fixed assets. When price levels have changed substantially, a number of troublesome business problems are caused by the use of depreciation accounting figures based largely on an earlier price level. These problems are particularly serious when price levels have increased and income tax rates are high.

DISCUSSION QUESTIONS

19-A. What classes of reasons for property retirements are listed in the text? Which of these do you think were the most important when the railroads made retirements of so many steam locomotives in the period 1945 to 1955? Which do you think are the most important in the retirement of motor trucks? Of machine tools? Of personally owned passenger automobiles? Of wooden telephone poles? Of propeller-driven airplanes?

19-B. A laundry company buys a fleet of new delivery trucks. It pays $100 per truck for having the company's name and trademark painted on each truck. Would you recommend that this painting expenditure be capitalized? Why or why not? Would your answer be different if the truck owner were a contractor on earth-moving jobs? In general, what considerations seem to you to be relevant in making decisions in borderline cases on whether or not to capitalize expenditures? What considerations that might be suggested do you believe should be viewed as irrelevant?

19-C. Distinguish between catalogued plant and noncatalogued plant.

19-D. What information is desirable on a plant ledger card?

19-E. What straight-line depreciation rate corresponds to an estimated life of 20 years with zero salvage value? With 25% estimated positive salvage value?

19-F. What is meant by the "half-year convention" in depreciation accounting?

19-G. What is meant by mortality dispersion of physical property?

19-H. With a given straight-line depreciation rate and mortality dispersion, the group and item methods will write off the cost of a group of fixed assets somewhat differently. Why? Explain the differences in the method of obtaining annual depreciation charges under the two methods. Explain the differences between the entries to show retirements. What seems to you to be the underlying difference in point of view between the two methods?

19-I. The Machinery account in an industrial company is increasing its balance year after year; many new assets are being added each year and old assets are being replaced at higher prices. In depreciation accounting for this machinery, the item method has been used with a straight-line 10% rate. Actual average service lives have been about 20 years. Discuss the effect of the discrepancy between the depreciation rate used in the accounts and the actual realized service lives of the assets.

19-J. Answer the preceding question assuming that the straight-line group method has been used with a 10% rate.

19-K. What is meant by the economic service life of an industrial asset? Why are full service lives frequently considerably longer than economic lives? Do you think that this discrepancy between economic lives and full service lives should have any bearing on the choice of a depreciation accounting method?

19-L. Discuss the influence of income tax laws and regulations on depreciation accounting practice in the United States.

19-M. Give an example of multiple-straight-line depreciation accounting.

19-N. What examples of appropriate types of assets for the unit-of-production depreciation method are given in the text? What other kinds of assets can you think of for which this method might be appropriate?

19-P. What is depletion? In what way does the accounting treatment of depletion often differ from the income tax treatment of depletion?

19-Q. The text mentions three senses in which the word *depreciation* is used. These are referred to as the *popular, accounting,* and *appraisal* senses. Explain how these three senses of the word differ from one another. Discuss the influence of price-level changes on the estimation of depreciation in each of these three senses. Relate your discussion to the following numerical example:

A landlord acquired a rental property, paying $10,000 for the land and $40,000 for the building. He owned this property for 10 years, charging off $1,000 of depreciation on the building each year, both in his accounts and on his income tax return. This was a straight-line charge based on an estimated

40-year life for the building. After 10 years he sold the property for $48,000. The buyer's offer was based on an appraisal of $12,000 for the land and $36,000 for the building. The $36,000 figure was based on an estimated $50,000 cost of replacement, from which $14,000 was deducted to reflect the value-inferiority of the existing building to one that was new and modern.

19-R. Explain the relationship between depreciation accounting and the financing of new fixed assets.

19-S. Why have proposals been made to abandon the prepaid-expense concept of depreciation for accounting and income tax purposes and to substitute depreciation figures based in some manner on replacement cost? Can you see any technical accounting problems that might arise if these proposals should be adopted? What advantages and disadvantages can you see from the social viewpoint? From the viewpoint of the owners of fixed assets used to produce income?

19-T. An asset has a first cost of $20,000, an estimated life of 8 years, and an estimated salvage value of $2,000. Compute the annual depreciation charge for each year of life using the sum-of-the-years-digits method.

19-U. The text states that the declining-balance group method is simpler than the other depreciation accounting methods that were newly authorized under the 1954 tax law. Discuss this statement. Compare the declining-balance group method with the sum-of-the-years-digits method and the multiple-straight-line method with respect to (1) calculation of annual depreciation expense, (2) calculations needed for a retirement entry, and (3) the detailed plant records that are required. In your comparison assume an account consisting of many assets acquired in a number of different years.

19-V. A double declining-balance classified account is to be used for Office Furniture, Fixtures, Machines, and Equipment. Discuss the relative advantages of having a single open-end account and having separate accounts for each vintage group.

19-W. In what respects, if any, would your answer to question 19-V be changed if a straight-line classified account were to be used?

19-X. What reasons can you see why management might want to take more depreciation for tax purposes than the amount shown on the books and reported to stockholders in the income statement?

19-Y. The third and fourth columns of Exhibit 19-5 illustrate different possible accounting treatments of the case in which more depreciation is taken for tax purposes than the amount shown on the books. What reasons, if any, can you see for preferring the treatment illustrated in the third column? For preferring the treatment illustrated in the fourth column?

PROBLEMS

Problem 19-1. On pages 440 to 443, two examples of straight-line group depreciation are given, both applicable to three $10,000 assets with an average life of 10 years. Compute book values on January 1, 1956, 1959, and

1962, respectively, for the zero-salvage case and for the case with 15% average salvage value. Show that, as stated on page 443, each of these book values "is equal to the sum of remaining salvage and the product of the remaining service years and the write-off per service year."

Problem 19-2. *Note:* This problem and the next one are designed to illustrate how a reserve ratio behaves under certain simple assumptions. (The reader will recall that this ratio is used as a test to determine whether depreciation rates are too high under U.S. Revenue Procedure 62-21.) To make the calculations as easy as possible, the problem deals with assets that are relatively short-lived and the assets are assumed to have no mortality dispersion.

Assume a straight-line open-end group account using the half-year convention. A 20% depreciation rate is used based on an estimated life of 5 years with zero salvage value. Assume that $10,000 of new assets are acquired during each of the years 1961, 1962, 1963, 1964, and 1965. Each year thereafter, the assets acquired 5 years earlier are retired without salvage value and are replaced with new assets costing $10,000. After 1965, the asset account balance therefore stabilizes at $50,000.

Compute the balance in the reserve account at the end of 1970. On this date, what is the ratio of the reserve account balance to the asset account balance? How would you expect this reserve ratio to behave in the future if the asset account balance remains stabilized at $50,000 and estimates of life and salvage value continue to be correct? How would it behave if the plant expands after 1970, increasing at, say, $5,000 per year?

Problem 19-3. Change the conditions of problem 19-2 by assuming that the actual asset lives are all 6 years with zero salvage value. Continue to use a 20% depreciation rate. (Note that through 1965 the asset and reserve account balances are identical with those in problem 19-2.) Assume that in 1966 there is no retirement and no new asset is acquired. In 1967, 1968, 1969, and 1970, the assets acquired 6 years earlier are retired and are replaced with new assets costing $10,000 each year. Compute the balance in the reserve account at the end of 1970. On this date, what is the ratio of the reserve account balance to the asset account balance? How would you expect this reserve ratio to behave in the future if the asset account balance remains stabilized at $50,000, the 20% depreciation rate is continued, and all asset lives continue to be 6 years with zero salvage values?

Problem 19-4. Use an open-end straight-line classified account for the assets listed in Exhibit 19-4. Assume no mortality dispersion for any of the separate types of assets. Assume that all estimates of lives and salvage values are correct, not only for the initial assets in the account but also for replacement assets. Carry the account through a 20-year period, assuming purchase of $10,000 of new typewriters after 5, 10, and 15 years and of $10,000 of new calculating machines after 10 years. Show that the 10% rate computed in Exhibit 19-4 will exactly write off the cost minus salvage of the $70,000 of assets involved. For the sake of simplicity, assume that all acquisitions and retirements take place on the first day of the year.

Hint: Calculations can be simplified by computing depreciation for 5-year periods rather than for single years.

Problem 19-5. Use a vintage-group straight-line classified account for the assets listed in Exhibit 19-4. Just as in problem 19-4, assume no mortality dispersion for any of the separate types of assets and assume that estimates of life and salvage value are correct. Carry the account through a 20-year period, using a 10% rate for the first 5 years, a 7% rate for the next 5 years, and a 5% rate for the final 10 years. Explain the basis for the 7 and 5% rates. Show that the use of these three rates will exactly write off the cost minus salvage of the $30,000 of assets involved in the vintage group. For the sake of simplicity, assume that the initial acquisitions are all on the first day of the year and that retirements occur at the exact ages indicated.

Problem 19-6. Assume that, for the data of Exhibit 19-4, the average life is calculated as follows:

$$\text{Average life in years} = \frac{5 + 10 + 20}{3} = 11\tfrac{2}{3}$$

The average salvage value obviously is 10%.

The application of the conventional formula for a straight-line rate gives the following result:

$$\text{Straight-line rate} = \frac{100\% - 10\%}{11\tfrac{2}{3}} = 7\tfrac{5}{7}\%$$

(It should be pointed out that the facts have been simplified in Exhibit 19-4 by the assumption of equal investments in the three types of assets. In practice, different types of assets in a classified account usually will have different investments; it therefore is necessary to use averages weighted by investments.)

Show that the consistent application of this $7\frac{5}{7}\%$ rate throughout the 20 years will exactly write off the cost minus salvage of the $30,000 vintage group at the end of 20 years. What objections, if any, can you see to the book values given by the use of this rate?

Problem 19-7. An open-end straight-line classified account is being used for machinery with an 8% depreciation rate and the half-year convention. On January 1, 1964, the balances in the accounts Machinery and Reserve for Depreciation, Machinery, were, respectively, $40,000 and $18,500. Compute the depreciation expense for 1964 and the balances in these two accounts at year end, assuming $5,000 of new machinery is acquired during the year and $3,000 of 10-year-old machinery is retired with a cash salvage value of $400.

Problem 19-8. An open-end declining-balance classified account is being used for Machinery. The depreciation rate is 20%. On January 1, 1963, the balances in the accounts Machinery and Reserve for Depreciation, Machinery, were, respectively, $70,500 and $37,310. The half-year convention is being used. Compute the balances in these two accounts at year end and the depreciation expense for 1963 assuming that $10,000 of new machinery is acquired during the year and $7,000 of 8-year old machinery is retired with zero salvage value.

Problem 19-9. A certain machine acquired on January 1 has a first cost of $150,000, an estimated life of 15 years, and an estimated terminal salvage value of $15,000. Item depreciation accounting is to be used with a full year's depreciation charge in the first year of life. Compute the depreciation charges for each of the first two years of life by (1) the sum-of-the-years-digits method, (2) the double declining-balance method as authorized in 1954 for income tax purposes in the United States, and (3) the straight-line method. Make your calculations to the nearest dollar.

Problem 19-10. In 1963 a corporation has gross revenues of $50 million all in cash. Cash outlays for operating expenses are $32 million. (Of course, the foregoing cash outlays do not include depreciation, a noncash item, or income taxes, which are not viewed as "expenses.") Depreciation would be $8 million calculated by the years-digits (YD) method and $5 million calculated by the straight-line (SL) method. A 50% income tax rate applies to all taxable income. Compute (1) the 1963 profit reported to the stockholders and (2) the 1963 cash flow before dividends under each of the following assumptions:

1. SL method for book and tax purposes
2. YD method for book and tax purposes
3. SL method for book and YD for tax with no allowance in the income statement for deferred taxes
4. SL method for book and YD for tax with an allowance in the income statement for deferred taxes
5. YD method for book and SL for tax with no allowance in the income statement for prepaid income taxes
6. YD method for book and SL for tax with an allowance in the income statement for prepaid income taxes

20/ BUDGETARY CONTROL

This chapter deals with certain aspects of budgets and budgetary control systems and the relationships between these things and accounting.

A BUDGET IS A PLAN. A budget is a plan for future events and courses of action that is stated in money terms. Generally, a budget is a *gross* plan in the sense that it summarizes many detailed estimates and decisions about a variety of future actions and events.

Budgetary planning involves the following steps, which must be completed before the start of the budget period:

1. An estimate for each aspect of the activity being budgeted. If possible, the estimate should be made by the person who will be responsible for carrying out the activity once the budget has been adopted.
2. Assembly and analysis of the various estimates to give an overall forecast of the entire activity for the budget period.
3. An overall review of this forecast based on these estimates. Where necessary, the review will lead to a modification of some of or all the estimates. Finally the modified estimates will be approved as a formal budget.

THE PLANNING INFLUENCE OF A BUDGET. A budget is useful if it exerts desirable influence on the decisions and actions of people in the organization. This can come about in two ways. First, the existence of predetermined decisions, expectancies, and goals incorporated into a budget may directly affect the actual conduct of the activity. This effect is most likely to be significant if the people involved in the budgeted activity are involved in the preparation of the budget and if there is clear evidence that the plans incorporated therein have the support of higher authority. Second, a budget may exert beneficial influence on people in the organization through its use in a managerial control process.

SYSTEMATIC BUDGETARY CONTROL. A budget is most effective if it is used as a standard of comparison in a budgetary control system as well as a guide for operating decisions and actions. The general scheme of such a system is:

1. Measure actual performance as the budget period progresses.
2. At regular intervals, compare actual performance against the budget.
3. Whenever performance does not meet the standard set up by the budget, initiate appropriate corrective action.

These steps can be illustrated by a brief description of an actual budgetary procedure. The following paragraphs describe the operating budget, investment budget, and cash budget of an electric light and power company.

OPERATING BUDGET FOR AN ELECTRIC UTILITY. The operating budget is organized with relation to the accounts that enter into the company's profit and loss statement for a fiscal year. The budget starts with estimates of monthly outputs of electrical energy and monthly incomes from sales. These estimates are prepared by the budget bureau in consultation with a number of other departments. These estimates are based on past sales, on expected growth of the various classes of load, on expected general business conditions, and on any other factors that seem relevant. The estimates are broken down by classes of customers and various divisions of the company.

When these estimates of output and sales have been approved by the appropriate company officers, they are placed in the hands of all department heads. Each department head is responsible for preparing estimates of month-by-month charges for each operating expense account under his jurisdiction. These estimates for the coming fiscal year are, in effect, formal requests for budget allotments of the various amounts. The budget request forms on which they are submitted show the actual monthly figures for the preceding year, the monthly budgeted figures for the current year, and the actual monthly figures to date for the current year.

All these estimates of income and expense are then combined together to give an anticipated profit and loss statement for the coming fiscal year. This statement and the detailed budget requests are then reviewed by a committee of the major executives of the company. This review may disclose that the proposed budget, if adopted, would represent an unsatisfactory goal from the company-wide viewpoint. Budget requests that appear to be out of line are modified after discussion with the department heads concerned. A revised budget is finally approved.

In this company the fiscal year starts on July 1 and ends on June 30. It is necesary that the first budget estimates be prepared in April, nearly 3 months before the start of the fiscal year, to permit time for assembly, review, revision, and final approval. The expense budget as finally approved is thought of as an appropriation for each account that should not be exceeded. However, any budgeted figure may be changed by executive action after the budget period is under way.

Every month, the company's controller prepares a series of statements comparing the actual figures for income and expense with the budgeted amounts. These statements compare both the current month's figures and the totals for the year to date. Statements are made for every account, and summaries are made for each group of accounts under the jurisdiction of a single department head. These are placed in the hands of the major executives of the company as well as in the hands of the department heads concerned. Whenever expenditures exceed budget allotments by more than a specified small percentage, an explanation is required. If revenues turn out to be below budgeted figures, a downward revision in expense budgets for the remainder of the year may be necessary. If output and revenues are above the budget, an upward revision in the budgets for certain expense accounts may be needed. Where discrepancies from the budget occur without satisfactory explanation, steps may quickly be taken to correct the conditions that have given rise to the discrepancies.

INVESTMENT BUDGET. The basis for the investment budget in this utility company is a forecast of growth of load for several years into the future and a comprehensive plan of development to meet the expected load growth. To fit into this engineering plan for the coming budget year, specific estimates are prepared for each new generating station and substation and for additions to present stations. Estimates for the year are made for total additions to the transmission system and to the distribution system by company divisions. Each estimate is made by the engineering group most closely associated with the design of the work being estimated. The estimates are generally part of a study that deals with the economy of the proposed additions.

The budget bureau then assembles the estimates to show the expected cost of each project, the probable date of its start and completion, and the probable expenditure by months. This shows the capital needs of the business during the budget period. The executive review of the proposed investment budget has two separate aspects. One is a review of the merits of the individual projects. The other involves comparing the total budget requests with the funds that can be made available for investment in fixed assets. Before the investment budget is finally approved, some projects may be eliminated and others altered.

Nevertheless, the approval of the budget authorization for fixed-capital additions does not carry with it the final approval of the work. A work order (permitting job cost accounting for all plant additions) is the medium for authorizing the starting of the work and recording commitments and expenditures. A budget project may require several work orders, each for a different division of the work. Except in emergencies, work orders are not issued without a prior budget appropriation to cover them.

As the charges to each work order are entered in the accounts, monthly comparisons are made with the total costs and the unit costs shown in the original budget estimates. In this connection it is necessary not only to examine actual expenditures but also to examine outstanding purchase orders for materials and machinery not yet delivered. Just as in the case of the operating budget, the comparison of estimates and performance is intended to tell when costs are out of line and to permit correcting the conditions if possible.

CASH BUDGET. One important aspect of planning is a forecast of the probable need for cash at all times. Such a forecast discloses any need for financing—either temporary financing through loans from a commercial bank or permanent financing through the issuance and sale of new stocks and bonds.

Both the operating budget and the investment budget contribute to the preparation of the cash budget. This budget consists of a forecast, month by month, of cash receipts from all sources and cash disbursements for all purposes. A number of modifications of the figures from the operating budget must be made to convert them to cash receipts and disbursements. For instance, the operating budget shows sales as income in the months in which the customers are billed; the cash budget shows the same sales as cash receipts in the months—usually later—in which the collections occur. Depreciation shown in the operating budget is omitted from the cash budget, as it is not a current disbursement. Deferred charges and credits and accrued expenses and incomes are treated differently in the two budgets. The cash budget shows dividend disbursements and payments for new fixed assets even though these items do not appear in the operating budget.

A tentative cash budget prepared from the operating budget and the investment budget serves as a basis for planning any necessary financing for the coming year. A final cash budget will include consideration of proposed financing, both short-term loans and their repayments and long-term financing through the issue of new stocks and bonds. Sometimes a tentative cash budget will disclose the need for financing that appears to be impracticable or inadvisable. If so, the investment budget and the operating budget may need to be modified to reflect this limitation in available cash resources.

Problem 20-1 gives a highly simplified example of a cash budget for a company doing a seasonal business.

SPECIAL PROBLEMS OF BUDGETING IN COMPETITIVE INDUSTRY. Competitive enterprises, as well as public utilities, need operating budgets, investment budgets, and cash budgets. However, there are likely to be greater difficulties in the way of successful budgeting in competitive business.

All business operating budgets are similar to the electric utility example in starting the budgetary procedure with an estimate of sales. But a sales forecast for a year or more in advance has a larger margin of error in competitive industry. The demand for electricity or other utility service is likely to be more stable and therefore more predictable than the demand for most competitive products or services. Different companies deal in different ways with the difficulties caused by the uncertainties of sales forecasts.

The planning period may be shorter and new budgets more frequent in competitive industry. For example, every 6 months a month-by-month budget might be prepared for the coming half year. The revision of a budget during a budget period is more likely to be necessary in competitive business.

MANUFACTURING COST BUDGETS. In a manufacturing industry, estimates made to establish predetermined burden rates provide budgets for indirect manufacturing expense. A somewhat more sophisticated type of IME budget is the variable (or flexible) budget discussed in Chap. 14. However, with either a fixed budget or a flexible budget, the actual indirect expenses can be compared against the budget for cost-control purposes. This may be done by departments if the indirect costs are collected and applied by departmental cost centers and may even be broken down also by kinds of indirect expense.

Where standard costs are used, flexible budgets for direct labor and materials costs can be computed for each cost center, providing expense budgets for these primary elements of manufacturing cost.

The variances developed in predetermined-rate burden application schemes and standard cost systems are differences between expected and actual costs. Such systems are, from this point of view, budgetary control schemes.

THE SALES BUDGET IN COMPETITIVE BUSINESS. In competitive industry the sales budget not only gives an estimate of income and establishes the production level on which the expense budget is to be based; it also sets sales quotas that are used to measure the performance of the sales organization. The budgeted figures for total sales will normally be broken down by lines of product and by sales territories as well as by months. The breakdown by product and territories is necessary for budgetary control of sales; the breakdown by product and time is necessary to permit the planning of production schedules and the budgeting of production costs.

In some companies, the sales budget starts with sales estimates made by individual salesmen. Before submission to management as a proposed sales budget, these will be summarized and revised by the sales executives. In other companies, the sales budget may originate with a market-research group in consultation with the sales manager. Whatever the source, the estimates of what can be sold need to give weight to many factors. It is necessary to forecast general business conditions as well as special conditions affecting the industry and the various lines of product. The sales budget as finally adopted by management may require a broader view than the view obtainable from the sales organization. For example, before sales objectives are set, it is desirable to consider the production costs of the various lines of product in relation to their selling prices. Production capacities also need to be considered; an economic study regarding the desirability of expansion should be made whenever a proposed sales budget exceeds present capacity.

There are many industries that have seasonal sales patterns. Wherever practicable, it is desirable that production be relatively stable from month to month even though sales vary. This can be accomplished by production for stock during the off-peak sales months. Such a policy stabilizes employment and reduces the costs that are caused by labor turnover; an offsetting disadvantage may be the hazard that part of the stock cannot be sold. Under these circumstances, an accurate forecast of the total volume of sales is of great importance.

USE OF STANDARD COSTS IN PREPARING OPERATING BUDGETS IN MANUFACTURING. Standard costs are a great help in preparing expense budgets in manufacturing. An important step in estimating the production costs in each cost center is the estimation of labor hours and material quantities for each item of product. If standard costs have been determined, this needed information is available.

Chapter 15 discussed the problem of deciding how tight the cost standards are going to be. In many cases standard costs represent better performance than can be expected on the average. Where such tight standard costs are employed, they may need to be modified to some extent before they are used to prepare estimates of monthly departmental expenses.

BUDGETS IN NONPROFIT ENTERPRISES. The budget is a management device that business has borrowed from government.

Governments have always found budgets essential; the business budget is a modern development.

In any nonprofit enterprise with a limited income and with expenditures that are not directly productive of income, there can be no planning of expenditures without considering prospective income. Most governmental activities are, in this sense, nonprofit. Unless there is deficit financing through borrowing, the governmental expenditures during a fiscal period must not exceed the income from taxes and other sources. A budget for a governmental unit permits an overall look at proposed expenditures in relation to prospective sources of income.

Other nonprofit enterprises such as clubs, hospitals, and universities have a similar problem of planning expenditures so that they do not exceed expected income. This problem also exists for families and individuals. In all such cases, a budget is appropriate.

In many governmental units and other nonprofit enterprises, it is common for budget figures to apply to a full fiscal year with no month-by month breakdowns of estimates or authorizations. In such cases, periodic budgetary statements should show how much of the year's appropriation for each account has not been spent or committed.

RELATIONSHIP BETWEEN BUDGETARY CONTROL AND ACCOUNTING. A budget system relies on accounting records for estimating information and for measuring actual performance. Clearly, to be comparable, the budget figures must be defined in the same way as the accounting figures. Thus the structure and content of a budget must be fully compatible with the classification of accounts if the budget is to be used in a budgetary control process.

One general purpose of budgetary control is to encourage individuals to act in accordance with plans. If the budgeting process is to be successful, the accounting system must be designed to permit measuring the performance of individuals. Accounts should be defined and organized along the lines of personal responsibility. No person should be held accountable for the results in an account unless he has control over the charges to that account. But each account should be the responsibility of some one individual.

SOME OBJECTIVES IN BUDGETING. The chief purposes of financial budgets can be summarized as follows:

1. To give management an overall view of the financial aspects of all the activities of an organization, making it possible to fit each activity into a general plan
2. To set goals of performance for each activity of an organization and to measure the success of each activity in meeting these goals
3. To regulate spending within the limits of income and—in business budgets—to improve the profit position of the enterprise

4. To determine in advance to what extent financing is likely to be necessary and at what time
5. To assist management to anticipate unfavorable situations and to take corrective action without delay

SOME POSSIBLE DIFFICULTIES THAT MAY ARISE FROM UNIMAGINATIVE ADMINISTRATION OF A BUDGET. Like many other good tools, systems of budgetary control are sometimes misused.

One danger is that the overall interests of the enterprise may be lost sight of when decisions are made on the departmental level. The pressure for conformity to budgets may be so great that each department head will view any proposal largely in terms of its probable effect on his own budget. This attitude may be a barrier to sound decisions on certain matters that cross departmental lines. For example, it may be desirable that a certain department initiate changes that will increase its costs but will effect a much greater cost reduction in some other department. Unless the budget is administered in a way that recognizes the interdepartmental aspects of many decisions, proposals for such changes are likely to be vetoed by the head of the department where the costs will increase.[1] Each department head may feel that he may get into trouble if his costs are increased and that he will receive no credit for cost reductions elsewhere.

In addition, there is a danger that an inflexible administration of a budget may indirectly serve as a barrier to certain types of cost reduction that are solely within one department. For example, the funds allotted to a particular activity may be based largely on the amounts recently spent for that activity. A department head may see opportunities for temporary cost reductions but will hesitate to make these reductions if he believes they will make it harder for him to get sufficient funds in the future.

SUMMARY. Budgets are plans stated in money terms. Generally speaking, budgets are prepared so as to separate the various activities of an enterprise along the same lines as the classification of accounts. Accounting information is used in the preparation of a budget. During a budget period, figures obtained from the accounts are used to check actual performance against the goals established by the budget. The use of budgets promotes better planning of the activities of an organization and makes it easier to ensure that activities are carried out according to plan.

[1] For an example of this from the field of industrial quality control, see Eugene L. Grant, *Statistical Quality Control,* 3d ed., McGraw-Hill Book Company, Inc., New York, 1964, chap. 19.

DISCUSSION QUESTIONS

20-A. Do you belong to any nonprofit organization that has a budget? If so, describe its system of budgetary control. Do you think this system could be improved? If so, in what way and why?

20-B. Do you belong to any nonprofit organization that does not have a budget? If so, do you think it would be benefited by having a budget? Why or why not? If you favor a budget for this organization, give your ideas regarding the budgetary-control procedure that you think it should adopt.

20-C. What procedure for budgetary control would you recommend in connection with the administration of competitive athletics in a college or high school? In what respects would such a budget illustrate both the problems of a business budget and of a budget for a nonprofit organization?

20-D. A corporation having approximately a hundred employees manufactures and sells certain patented toys and games. This enterprise, about 5 years old, has operated up to date without a budget but has now expanded to the point where the president believes a budget is desirable. Discuss any problems that you see in setting up a scheme of budgetary control for such an enterprise.

20-E. Tell what you know about the system of bugetary control of some governmental unit, for example, a school district or a small city.

20-F. State two general purposes of an indirect manufacturing expense budget—one accounting purpose and one managerial purpose. Explain how an IME budget might be used for the managerial purpose you have described.

20-G. What is the purpose of an investment budget in business? In what types of enterprise would you expect this budget to be of great importance? In what types might it be of very little importance? Why?

20-H. What are the purposes of a cash budget? Which figures from the operating budget are likely to need to be modified before they can be used in the cash budget? Why? What information not in the operating budget is required for the cash budget?

20-J. The text gives examples of some possible difficulties that may arise from unimaginative administration of a budget. What are these examples? Have you ever observed any similar difficulties? What steps do you think should be taken to minimize the danger of occurrence of such possible adverse effects of budgetary control?

PROBLEMS

Problem 20-1. This problem involves the preparation of a cash budget for the Kootenai Manufacturing Co. As the demand for the products of this company is seasonal, it is necessary for it to borrow large amounts from the commercial banks to finance the production just preceding the seasonal peak of sales. Plans for these bank loans are made as a part of the company's budgeting procedure; the cash budget permits negotiations with the company's bankers in advance of the actual need for funds.

The following estimates are made as a basis for a budget for a 6-month period from July to December, 19___:

Month	Production in units	Sales in units	Advertising expense
July	50,000	30,000	$20,000
August	50,000	30,000	20,000
September	70,000	50,000	40,000
October	70,000	80,000	50,000
November	70,000	100,000	40,000
December	50,000	70,000	30,000
January	40,000		
February	40,000		

All sales are to be assumed at $5 per unit. Variable production costs per unit are as follows: material, $1.50; direct labor, $1.00; variable burden, $0.50. Estimated depreciation is $10,000 per month. Factory taxes for the 6-month period are $60,000 to be paid in November. Other fixed burden is $10,000 a month.

Selling expenses (other than advertising) are $25,000 per month. General administrative expense is $15,000 per month. Dividends of $20,000 will be paid in August and November. New machinery costing $80,000 will be purchased in August.

It is estimated that the company's balance sheet at the start of the budget period (July 1) will be as follows:

Assets			*Liabilities and Ownership*	
Current Assets:			Liabilities:	
Cash	$ 95,000		Accounts Payable	$ 75,000
Accounts Receivable	200,000			
Materials	150,000			
Finished Goods			Ownership:	
(40,000 units)	140,000	$ 585,000	Capital Stock	1,000,000
Fixed Assets:			Surplus	410,000
Plant & Equipment	1,200,000			
Less: Reserve for Depreciation	300,000	900,000		
Total		$1,485,000	Total	$1,485,000

Materials are purchased 2 months in advance of production and paid for in the month following their purchase. Thus the $150,000 Materials inventory is the cost of materials to be used in production in July and August. The $75,000 account payable is for the materials to be used in August; this will be paid in July. Labor and variable burden are paid in the month in which production takes place.

Sales are net, 30 days. For purposes of the budget assume collection in the month following the sale. Assume that the $200,000 Accounts Receivable on July 1 will be collected in July.

The bank requires that the cash balance at all times be at least 20%

of the maximum line of credit (i e., the maximum amount borrowed at one time) and that notes be $50,000 or multiples thereof. Money may be borrowed on 30-, 60-, or 90-day notes with interest at 6% per annum. The interest on a note is deducted in advance as "discount"; for instance on a $50,000 90-day note the company would receive only $49,250, and would pay the full $50,000 at the expiration of 90 days.

Set up a work sheet as indicated below and calculate the total estimated disbursements by months for the 6-month budget period.

Estimated disbursements	July	Aug.	Sept.	Oct.	Nov.	Dec.	Total
Accounts payable (for materials)							
Direct labor							
Variable factory burden							
Taxes							
Other fixed burden							
Selling expense							
Advertising							
General administrative expense							
New machinery							
Dividends							
Total estimated disbursements							

Prepare a preliminary cash budget as follows in order to determine the necessary indebtedness to the bank (required borrowing) each month. In these preliminary calculations neglect discount (i.e., interest) on the notes. Determine the total amount of borrowing required as of the end of each month from the net cash figure, considering the requirements that the minimum cash balance at the start of each month must be 20% of the maximum amount borrowed at any time during the entire 6-month period and that borrowing must be in units of $50,000.

Preliminary cash budget	July	Aug.	Sept.	Oct.	Nov.	Dec.
Net cash—start of month (+ or −)						
Receipts during month (+)						
Disbursements during month (−)						
Net cash—end of month (+ or −)						
Required total borrowing						
Required borrowing this month						
Period of note (days)						
Notes coming due this month						

With the dates and amounts of the borrowings thus established, make the final cash budget calculation as follows. The discount (i.e. interest) on each note is to be deducted from the amount borrowed to arrive at the net amount received from the bank.

Cash budget	July	Aug.	Sept.	Oct.	Nov.	Dec.	Total
Cash on hand—start of month							
Receipts—accounts receivable							
Receipts—notes payable (net)							
Total cash available							
Less: Estimated disbursements							
Less: Repayment of notes due							
Cash on hand—end of month							

Prepare an anticipated income statement for the 6-month period and an anticipated balance sheet as of December 31.

Problem 20-2. The following information deals with the cash budget of the M-C Manufacturing Co., to be prepared late in 1963 for the first 6 months of 1964. This manufacturer makes a single product, Moco. Although there is a year-round demand for this product, a seasonal peak of demand occurs in March, April, and May. Among other purposes, the budget is useful in negotiations with commercial banks for loans to finance operations preceding the seasonal peak of sales.

The estimated balance sheet at the start of the budget period (and fiscal year) on January 1, 1964, is as follows:

Assets			
Current Assets:			
Cash		$14,000	
Accounts Receivable		15,000	
Materials		25,000	
Finished Goods		20,000	$ 74,000
Fixed Assets:			
Machinery & Equipment	$90,000		
Less: Reserve for Depreciation	18,000	72,000	
Office Furniture & Equipment	$10,000		
Less: Reserve for Depreciation	2,000	8,000	80,000
Total			$154,000
Liabilities and Ownership			
Accounts Payable			$ 10,000
Accrued Income Taxes Payable			7,200
Deferred Income Taxes			4,800
Capital Stock			120,000
Earned Surplus			12,000
Total			$154,000

The standard cost of a unit of Moco is as follows:

Direct material	$ 5.00
Direct labor	2.00
IME	3.00
Total	$10.00

The foregoing figure of $3 of IME per unit is based on an assumed normal output of 15,000 units per year with an estimated $45,000 of annual IME at this output. The corresponding monthly variable budget equation is:

Monthly IME = $2,250 + ($1.20) (monthly output in units)

Of the foregoing $2,250 of monthly "fixed cost," $750 is monthly depreciation, $300 is for factory taxes (that are paid $1,800 in March and $1,800 in November), and the remaining $1,200 is made up of a variety of items all involving cash disbursements during the current month.

The following estimates are made as a basis for a budget for the period January 1 to June 30, 1964.

Month	Production, units	Sales, units	Cash disbursements for selling and administrative expense
January	1,500	1,000	$ 4,500
February	2,000	1,000	6,500
March	2,000	2,000	6,500
April	1,500	2,500	6,500
May	1,000	2,000	4,400
June	1,000	1,500	4,400
Total	9,000	10,000	$32,800
July	1,000	1,000	
August	1,000	1,000	

All sales are assumed to be at $15 per unit. For purposes of the budget, it will be assumed that there will be no material or labor price or quantity variances. It will also be assumed that the burden budget variance will be zero; that is, monthly IME will be the figure indicated by the variable budget equation. For purposes of preparing an estimated balance sheet as of June 30, 1964, and an estimated income statement for the first half of 1964, it will be assumed that any balance in the account Burden Capacity Variance will be shown in the mid-year balance sheet. It is estimated that total production and total sales for 1964 will be 15,000 units (the "normal" output used in setting the burden rate).

Materials are purchased 2 months in advance of production and paid for in the month following their purchase. The $25,000 figure for materials shown in the January 1 balance sheet consists of $17,500 required for the expected production in January and February plus $7,500 of base stock. The budget is to be prepared on the assumption that the base stock will continue to be $7,500. The $10,000 account payable is for materials purchased in December and scheduled for use in February; this account will be paid in January.

Sales terms are net 30 days. For purposes of the budget, it is assumed that collection takes place in the month following the sale. It will be assumed that the $15,000 of accounts receivable shown in the January 1 balance sheet will be collected in January.

The accrued income taxes shown in the January balance sheet must be paid in two equal installments on March 15 and June 15. The budget is to assume quarterly dividend payments of $1,800 in February and May.

The bank requires that the cash balance at all times be at least 20% of the maximum line of credit (i.e., the maximum amount to be borrowed at any time during the 6-month period). Notes must be for $20,000 or multiples thereof. Money may be borrowed on 30-, 60-, or 90-day notes with interest at 6% per annum. The interest on a note is deducted in advance as "discount"; for instance, on a $20,000 90-day note, the company would receive only $19,700 and would pay the full $20,000 at the end of the 90 days.

The machinery and equipment and office furniture and equipment were all acquired new when this manufacturer started business in January, 1962. Both accounts are mutliple-asset classified accounts. Both accounts have used depreciation rates based on a 10-year life with zero salvage value. (Depreciation on machinery and equipment is IME; depreciation on office furniture and equipment is selling and administrative expense. Because this manufacturer uses a rented building, there is no building depreciation to be considered.)

The M-C Manufacturing Co. has used straight-line depreciation for book purposes; the estimated balance sheet for January 1, 1964, reflects 2 years of depreciation charges made at 10% per year. However, the double declining-balance method has been used in Federal income tax returns. Therefore, the reserve balances for tax purposes are, respectively, $32,400 for machinery and equipment and $3,600 for office furniture and equipment. The $4,800 shown for Deferred Income Taxes in the estimated balance sheet for January 1, 1964, is 30% of the $16,000 charged as depreciation for tax purposes but not for book purposes. (The income tax rate applicable in 1962 and 1963 has been 30%. By using a higher depreciation charge for tax than for book purposes, the M-C Manufacturing Co. has been able to keep its annual taxable income below $25,000.)

A. Calculate the cash budget for the period January 1 to June 30, 1964, in the manner and form shown in problem 20-1.

B. Prepare an estimated income statement and statement of earned surplus for the period January 1 to June 30, 1964. Prepare an estimated balance sheet for June 30, 1964. All these statements should be based on the budget. If it has been necessary to make any assumptions in preparing these statements, your assumptions should be stated clearly.

Problem 20-3. The X-Y Manufacturing Co. makes two products, X and Y. This company has a standard cost system. The company prepares a semiannual budget. The following preliminary estimates are made in November, 1962, for the period January 1 to June 30, 1963:

Sales of X, 1,000 units at $50 = $50,000
  150 units per month, January through April
  200 units per month in May and June
Sales of Y, 100 units at $300 = $30,000
  20 units per month, January through April
  10 units per month in May and June
Production of X, 1,200 units at 200 units per month

Production of Y, 90 units at 15 units per month
Selling expense, $12,000 at $2,000 per month
General administrative expense, $9,000 at $1,500 per month
Dividends to be declared and paid during the 6-month period, $4,800
Standard costs for the two products are as follows:

	X	Y
Direct material	$10	$ 50
Direct labor	8	60
Indirect manufacturing expense	12	90
Total	$30	$200

The IME rate of 150% of standard direct-labor cost used in the foregoing standard costs is based on a normal annual output of $30,000 of standard direct-labor cost. The variable budget for annual IME is based on the following equation:

$$\text{Annual IME} = \$21{,}000 + (0.8)(\text{standard direct-labor cost})$$

Of the $21,000 fixed element of IME, $6,000 is depreciation.

The estimated balance sheet on January 1, 1963, is as follows:

Assets			*Liabilities and Ownership*		
Current Assets:			Current Liabilities:		
Cash	$20,500		Accounts Payable	$ 2,750	
Accounts Receivable	13,500		Accrued Income Taxes	6,000	$ 8,750
Inventories:					
Materials	5,500				
Finished Goods	13,500	$ 53,000			
Fixed Assets:			Ownership:		
Plant and Equipment	$80,000		Capital Stock	$60,000	
Less: Reserve for Depreciation	20,000	60,000	Retained Earnings	44,250	104,250
Total		$113,000	Total		$113,000

Some comments regarding certain items in the foregoing estimated balance sheet are as follows:

Accounts receivable. All sales are on credit. It is assumed that, on the average, the collection period is 1 month from the date of a sale. The $13,500 figure for accounts receivable on January 1 is based on the following estimated December sales:

150 units of X at $50 = $7,500
20 units of Y at $300 = $6,000

Material. On the average, materials are purchased 2 months in advance of production. Materials expected to be on hand are based on the anticipated production schedules for January and February (i.e., for 400 units of X at a material cost of $10 per unit and 30 units of Y at a material cost of $50 per unit).

It is assumed that there will be no inventories of work in process either on January 1 or June 30.

Assume that the rate of production of X and Y in June will continue throughout July and August.

Finished goods. Inventories expected for January 1 are:

250 units of X at $30 = $7,500
30 units of Y at $200 = $6,000

Fixed assets. Straight-line group depreciation is used with an annual rate of 7.5%. It is not expected that any new fixed assets will be purchased or that any fixed assets will be retired during the first half of 1963.

Accounts payable. These apply to materials purchased during December. All materials are paid for in the month following purchase.

Accrued income tax. The $6,000 is the income tax expected to be due on an estimated $20,000 of 1962 taxable income. None of this 1962 tax will have been paid in 1962. All of it must be paid during the first 6 months of 1963.

On the basis of the foregoing preliminary estimates, prepare an estimated balance sheet on June 30, 1963, and prepare an income statement and a retained earnings statement for the period January 1 to June 30, 1963. Assume that material purchases will be at standard costs. Also assume that all production will use standard amounts of labor and material so that there will be no labor or material cost variances at the end of the 6 months. Base your estimate of IME for the period on the variable budget equation; compute the rate of annual output for the 6-month period and assume that half of the IME for the year will occur in the first 6 months. Assume that income tax liability will accrue at 30% of the net income before taxes to be shown by the books of account; however, no income taxes for 1963 will actually be paid during 1963.

Show any computations that you have made to obtain your financial statements. If you find it necessary to make any assumptions in addition to those given in the problem statement, explain these assumptions. You are expected to ignore payroll expenses, property taxes, insurance, and other such matters that are not mentioned in the problem.

21/ SOME HAZARDS IN THE UNCRITICAL USE OF ACCOUNTING FIGURES

The first chapter of this book stressed the importance of accounting as a means of business control. This topic has been expanded throughout the intervening chapters. Without the use of modern accounting techniques, it would be difficult or impossible for our complex modern industry to function.

Nevertheless, information from the accounts often is misused as a basis for making managerial decisions. One of the reasons why nonaccountants need to understand accounting is to make them less vulnerable to the incorrect use of accounting figures. However, it is not always true that people with accounting training fully realize the limitations of accounting figures.

A GENERAL PRINCIPLE REGARDING DECISION MAKING. In business, just as in all human activities, decisions are between alternative courses of action. One aspect of decision making is a clear definition of the alternatives to be considered. To secure a rational basis for choice, it is necessary to predict the consequences of choosing each of the various alternatives. In this connection, it is only the prospective difference in consequences that influences the choice. Matters that are unaffected by the choice should logically be viewed as irrelevant.

It should be noted that, in decision making, all relevant differences are necessarily future differences, starting from the moment of decision. Past events cannot be changed by a decision made today.

SOME SOURCES OF INCORRECT INFERENCES FROM ACCOUNTING FIGURES. In business decisions it is natural to express the probable consequences of proposed alternatives in terms of money. It is desirable to have a basis for judgment as to the way in which each decision will affect the profits of the enterprise. It is natural to look to the accounts as the source of any estimates made in money terms.

In some cases, however, the allocations and omissions in accounting may interfere with clear reasoning about differences between alternatives.

Allocations that need to be viewed with a critical eye are of two kinds, namely, allocations among activities (such as allocations of indirect manufacturing expense) and allocations among time periods (such as depreciation charges). Omissions of relevant matters in decision making (such as interest and income taxes) arise out of the conventions of accounting.

The following discussion illustrates the misuse of accounting allocations by four examples of actual cases. Two matters are then discussed that are relevant in many business decisions but are normally omitted from accounting costs.

AN EXAMPLE OF MISUSE OF AN OVERHEAD ALLOCATION. Paul T. Norton, Jr., writing in the "Engineering Economy" section of the *Handbook of Industrial Engineering and Management,* tells the following story:[1]

> This example records an actual experience of the writer some years ago when he was being shown by the plant manager through a large mass-production furniture factory. . . .
>
> In a lean-to off the machine room were four carving spindles which had evidently not been used for some time. In answer to a question, the plant manager stated that the same four men who had formerly operated these spindles on a time wage basis were still producing the ornaments used by this company, utilizing second-hand rented spindles in a rented shed located in the same city. Further questioning developed the information that without working any harder than previously these four men were making more money, while the company was buying the ornaments cheaper than they had manufactured them. When asked how this could be, the plant manager stated that it was because they had a high overhead rate in this highly mechanized factory, whereas the four men had very little overhead in their operations with rented spindles in a rented shed.
>
> Naturally, the writer then asked how the decision to discontinue manufacturing the ornaments had reduced to the slightest extent the *total overhead expense* of the factory. The factory manager replied that this had been bothering him, but that the head of the cost accounting department had assured him that their method of figuring costs was correct and that they really were saving money by buying the ornaments. From further information furnished the writer by the plant manager,

[1] W. G. Ireson and Eugene L. Grant (eds.), *Handbook of Industrial Engineering and Management,* Prentice-Hall, Inc., Englewood Cliffs, N.J., 1955, pp. 151–152.

it was apparent that there had been no real decrease in the total overhead expense as a result of this decision to buy the ornaments. Even the supervision had not been reduced to any great extent, because one of the four men had previously acted as a subforeman over the group. It seemed that the expense in the office incident to buying the ornaments was at least as great as the former expense in the production control department.

There was one feature of this cost accounting system which, while satisfactory for the main purpose of the system, made it almost certain that any decision of this sort would be an incorrect decision. Because no repair parts had to be costed separately and all complete articles utilized the facilities of each department approximately to the same degree as their direct labor cost in each department, this company followed a rule quite common in the furniture industry of basing the charge for factory overhead on direct labor cost, using a single plant-wide overhead rate. This practice made the overhead cost of manufacturing the ornaments seem much greater than it actually was, because the wage rates of the highly skilled men who operated these carving spindles were much higher than the average for the plant, while the overhead expense per man-hour for these inexpensive spindles was very much less than the overhead rate per man-hour for the many very expensive automatic machines that were used in this highly mechanized factory.

ANOTHER EXAMPLE INVOLVING THE INTERPRETATION OF AN OVERHEAD RATE. A manufacturing company in the electrical manufacturing industry had an active cost-reduction program. One facet of this program was an effort to stimulate the engineers who designed the company's products to alter designs in ways that would reduce direct costs without affecting quality.

One ingenious designer proposed a change in the design of a mass-produced article that was made in large quantities. This proposed change would reduce direct-material cost by $2.45 per unit of product. In order to obtain the same structural strength of the product with a reduced quantity of material, an additional fabrication operation would be needed; it was estimated that this operation would increase the direct-labor cost by $1.10 per unit.

This particular product carried a predetermined overhead rate of 230% of direct-labor cost. From the viewpoint of the cost accounts, it therefore seemed as if the proposed design change would alter unit costs as follows:

Direct-material cost	$2.45 decrease	
Direct-labor cost	1.10 increase	
Overhead cost	2.53 increase	(i.e., 230% of $1.10)
Total cost	$1.18 increase	

If the managerial review of the proposal had been limited to the foregoing tabulation of costs, the change would have been vetoed. Fortunately, management recognized that the 230% overhead rate used in the accounts did not mean that every change of direct-labor costs by $1.00 would change total overhead expenditures by $2.30. In this case, the real question was the extent to which the total overhead costs would be altered by the proposed design change. No sensible answer to this question could be obtained without examining each specific overhead cost and considering how the particular cost would be influenced by the proposed change. The overhead accounts were similar to those shown in Exhibit 14-1. Each account was examined in turn, and it was finally concluded that the proposed change in design would increase total overhead costs by approximately 50 cents per unit. The estimated net effect of the change was therefore to decrease production costs by 85 cents per unit. On this basis, the design change was approved.

AN EXAMPLE INVOLVING THE ALLOCATION OF OVERHEAD COSTS AMONG COST CENTERS. Billy E. Goetz discusses some possible misleading conclusions from traditional methods of allocating power costs among cost centers, as follows:[2]

> Purchased power is customarily allocated to departments in proportion to kilowatt-hours consumed by each or, if sufficient meters are not available, in proportion to connected horsepower loads of the several departments. Either method ignores the laws of behavior of this cost.
>
> A typical industrial rate is composed of four separate charges:
>
> 1. A charge per kilowatt-hour. This component is correctly apportioned by traditional costing technique.
> 2. A demand charge based on maximum power used in any 15-minute period during the preceding 12 months.
> 3. A peak charge based on maximum power used in any 15-minute period between 4:30 and 6:00 P.M. on any day during the preceding 12 months.
> 4. A penalty for low power factor.
>
> The demand charge is erroneously allocated by traditional

[2] Billy E. Goetz, *Management Planning and Control,* McGraw-Hill Book Company, Inc., New York, 1949, pp. 131–132.

costing technique. Many plants shut down certain pieces of equipment at certain times to avoid increasing the demand charge for the entire ensuing 12-month period. One such plant has assigned to the engineer in charge of its heating and power plant the duty of maintaining a watch on a demand meter. Whenever, the maximum demand level is approached, he telephones a department operating a large metal saw and orders the saw shut off. Later, when demand drops, he telephones again to give permission to start the saw. Consequently, this saw never contributes to the demand charge. Yet, following custom, the cost accountant allocates a considerable fraction of the demand charge against the metal-sawing department because of the large proportion of total kilowatt-hours used by the department. The department is given no relief from extra costs of disrupted schedules and idle labor and machine time caused by such shutdowns.

The peak charge is often misleadingly allocated to departments. The metal saw discussed above was always shut down from 4:30 to 6:00 P.M. to keep down the peak charge. It never contributed to these charges but bears a considerable portion because of its high kilowatt-hour usage. Nor is relief accorded from costs arising from difficulties of coordination with other departments.

A large electric furnace uses many kilowatt-hours but improves the over-all power factor of a plant. Under the customary allocation, this department would bear a large share of the power factor penalty because total power costs are usually allocated in proportion to kilowatt-hours. These errors are misleading and important when management faces problems of choice. Suppose management is deciding whether to install an electric heat-treating furnace or to send material out to be heat-treated. The kilowatt consumption of the proposed furnace is known and the hours it will operate are estimated. The resulting kilowatt-hour load is typically multiplied by the average rate experienced by the company as reported in its cost records. Yet the power factor penalty portion of electrical cost should not be charged to the furnace at all. In fact, the unit power factor of the straight resistance load of the furnace may decrease this portion of the electric bill, and the furnace should receive a credit instead of a charge. Management may deliberately plan to operate the heat-treating department from 8 to 4 instead of from 9 to 5 to avoid the peak charge. If so, the plan to install heat-treating equipment should not be burdened with any part of the peak load charge. Operation of the furnace may not permit avoidance of periods in which new demand charges are set, and consequently this element may be chargeable to the department—rarely in proportion to kilowatt-hour consumption. Other equipment may be shut down during such periods, vitiating the kilowatt-hour ratio for this purpose. Demand charge should be allocated on its own ratio: connected horsepower likely to be in operation at the time new demand charges are set.

A COMMON INCORRECT PROCEDURE IN ANALYZING THE ECONOMY OF PROPOSED RETIREMENTS OF FIXED ASSETS. As pointed out in Chap. 19, in modern industry most retirements of fixed assets take place for reasons of economy. Assets that are physically capable of rendering service for additional years are retired because someone decides that it no longer pays to own them. The rational basis for analyzing the economy of a proposed retirement is therefore a matter of some importance.

A retirement decision involves a choice between two alternatives, namely, (1) disposing of the asset in question and (2) continuing the asset in service for an additional period of time. In estimating the cost of alternative 2, one element of cost is depreciation. An uncritical person estimating this cost might be inclined to use the depreciation charge that will be made in the accounts if the asset is continued in service. However, analytical thinking about this matter will lead to the conclusion that this accounting figure is not relevant in a retirement-economy study. The accounting figure for annual depreciation of an asset represents the writing off of a past expenditure; the past expenditure for an asset cannot be influenced by a present decision on the question of whether or not to retire the asset. In estimating the depreciation cost of extending the service of an asset for, say, another year, the relevant estimates apply to future matters. It is necessary to estimate the net receipts, if any, from disposing of the asset immediately and also one year hence. If the net salvage value of the asset today is zero and the prospective net salvage a year from now is also zero, there is no depreciation cost to consider in an economy study to judge whether or not to keep the asset 1 year longer. If the net salvage value today is $5,000 and the prospective net salvage value next year is $3,500, the relevant depreciation figure is $1,500.

As explained in Chap. 19, *depreciation* is a word with several meanings. In a retirement-economy study, the appropriate meaning is the popular meaning, decrease in value, rather than the accounting meaning, amortization of cost. The relevant value is net salvage value.

Many proposed retirements involve replacements. Here an economy study involves a comparison between the alternatives: (1) dispose of an old asset and acquire a new one in its place and (2) continue the old asset in service. Often the same uncritical viewpoint that uses accounting depreciation for the old asset in computing the costs of 2 also leads to a similar error in computing the costs of 1. If the old asset is carried on the books at a figure greater than its net salvage value, a "loss of disposal" is computed and added to the first cost of the proposed new asset for purposes of the economy study.

Both these errors were made in a set of formulas contained in a paper published by the American Society of Mechanical Engineers in 1923.[3] For thirty years or so after the publication of this paper, hardly a year passed without the reproduction of these so-called ASME formulas (or similar formulas adapted from them and containing the same errors) in technical articles, textbooks, and handbooks. The frequency with which these formulas have been published supplies convincing evidence of the common occurrence of these errors.

OMISSION OF THE TIME VALUE OF MONEY IN THE USUAL COST DATA FROM THE ACCOUNTS. Money has a time value. If money is borrowed, it is necessary to pay interest. If money is available for investment, it may be loaned at interest or otherwise invested in a way that earns a return.

No rational decision regarding proposed investments of money can be made without recognizing the time value of money. The foregoing statement applies, for example, to engineering economy studies relative to the acquisition and replacement of proposed industrial plant and equipment. In such studies, interest is properly recognized as a cost even though equity capital rather than borrowed money is to be used in the financing. This is *cost* in the economist's sense of *opportunity cost*. The investment of funds in any particular fixed assets involves an opportunity forgone; there is a sacrifice of the interest (or other return) that might have been obtained elsewhere from some other available investment for the same funds.

In the accounts of an enterprise, interest is not recognized as a cost unless money is borrowed. No interest on equity capital is recorded in the accounts. One of the objectives of accounting is viewed as the determination of whether or not equity capital has earned a return and, if so, how much; the profit and loss statement purports to give an answer to this question. Therefore, interest on equity capital does not appear in the accounts as an element of manufacturing cost. (Neither does interest on borrowed capital in most cases, because interest paid is

[3] "Formulas for Computing Economics of Labor-saving Equipment," *Mechanical Engineering*, vol. 45, p. 564, September, 1923.

generally classified as a financial expense rather than a manufacturing expense.)

Many managerial decisions, therefore, require the modification of accounting figures in a way that gives consideration to the time value of money.

OMISSION OF INCOME TAX CONSIDERATIONS IN THE USUAL COST DATA FROM THE ACCOUNTS. In our modern age of high income taxes, one of the elements influencing many managerial decisions is the probable income tax effect of each decision. In many instances a choice must be made between alternatives that will differ both in the probable timing and the probable total amount of income taxes.

Income taxes do not appear as manufacturing costs in the accounts; there is no income tax liability until it has been determined that taxable income has been earned. Consider a study in which prospective income tax differences enter into the choice between alternatives. The times and amounts of prospective income tax payments influenced by the choice will need to be estimated as separate items in the study; to the extent that the data of the study come from the accounts, the data will not include income taxes. It is, however, necessary to have an understanding of accounting in order to understand the income tax laws and regulations that are the basis of estimating the income tax effect of business decisions.

RELATIONSHIP BETWEEN THE DESIGN OF AN ACCOUNTING SYSTEM AND THE AVOIDANCE OF INCORRECT INFERENCES FROM THE ACCOUNTS. Many persons, hearing illustrations of incorrect inferences from the accounts, have concluded that the fault lay with the particular accounting system rather than with the persons who drew the incorrect inferences. Often it is suggested that the way to prevent such mistakes is to design an accounting system in a way that will make it practically impossible to draw incorrect conclusions from the accounts.

Persons who make this suggestion have completely missed the point that it is prospective differences between alternatives that are relevant in the comparison of alternatives; the diversity of sets of alternatives to be compared in industry is so great that *no* formal record-keeping scheme can measure all kinds of relevant differences. The matter is well stated by Joel Dean, as follows:[4]

> . . . it is clear that cost is a relative matter. What is cost depends upon what sacrifices are really produced by a par-

[4] Joel Dean, *Managerial Economics,* Prentice-Hall, Inc., Englewood Cliffs, N.J., 1951, pp. 271–272.

> ticular business decision. These different cost concepts do not necessarily correspond to any accounting category. Financial accounting has a specific task—namely, to determine the overall asset status (balance sheet) and the origin and disposition of funds (operating statement) during a specific and arbitrary time period. To do this well, accountants need unchanging and conventional definitions of costs. This approach wars with the notion that a particular item is a cost under some circumstances and not under others.
>
> It is better to use a rough approximation of the concept of cost that is correct for a particular decision than to have an accurate estimate of an irrelevant concept. The unsophisticated executive is in danger of taking the easier course of using conventional accounting costs as though they were appropriate for all purposes. Instead, it is better to modify reported costs as necessary to make the best guess at the concept theoretically relevant for each decision.
>
> Since it is usually impractical to keep cost records in sufficiently flexible and detailed form to give off estimates of various concepts of cost by established routine, back-of-the-envelope guesses are typically needed to give management the right cost tools for its decisions.

One possible way out of this dilemma was suggested by Billy Goetz in 1947.[5] The central idea of Professor Goetz' paper was that an accounting system might be designed to collect and retain all the basic input data in pure form, unallocated and unmixed. Then such basic data could be used selectively for whatever purposes arose, including those of financial accounting, cost control, and decision making. Whereas these suggestions were entirely valid, in 1947 they were startlingly at odds with current practice and thinking. Also, such a system was generally impracticable, because suitably economical means of data storage and processing were not then available. However, it is likely that these technological barriers can now (or in the near future) be transcended, permitting accounting systems to be essentially general-purpose and not fettered by merging, allocating, and time-period division that cannot be equally appropriate for many different purposes.

Even if the Goetz idea was fully implemented, the typical accounting mergings, distributions, and allocations would be necessary in the processes leading to accounting statements and control reports. Because

[5] Billy E. Goetz, "Tomorrow's Cost System," *Advanced Management,* Quarterly Journal of the Society for the Advancement of Management, December 1947.

such statements and reports do affect many kinds of decisions, it is desirable to minimize misinterpretations and misuses of such information. This applies not only to decisions that rationally ought to be based on accounting figures but also to possible decisions by the "unsophisticated executives" mentioned in the Dean quotation. For example, in the case described by Norton, an incorrect decision would have been less likely if the furniture factory had used direct costing instead of absorbtion costing or had applied overhead by cost centers rather than by one plant-wide overhead rate. As another example, the errors in reasoning that were cited as being common in replacement-economy studies would be less likely to cause incorrect conclusions with declining-balance depreciation accounting than with straight-line depreciation accounting.

It should not be concluded from the furniture factory and electrical manufacturing cases, and the subsequent discussion, that direct costing will necessarily lead to sounder decisions about differences between alternatives than will be reached under absorption costing. One possible disadvantage of direct costing was mentioned in Chap. 16: Sales personnel are likely to misuse cost figures to support their inclinations to justify sales whenever marginal revenue exceeds marginal cost.

Moreover, even the most elaborate analysis of indirect manufacturing costs cannot be expected to give "fixed" and "variable" rates that are appropriate for all kinds of decisions. As pointed out in Chap. 14, all costs are variable in the long run in the sense of being subject to change. Any breakdown of costs into fixed and variable requires assumptions and arbitrary allocations.

One danger in having an "official" variable burden rate is that the assumption and the methods of allocations may be unknown to (or forgotten by) many of the persons who make decisions using this rate. The convenience of having an official rate may lead to its careless use. It should be kept in mind that a typical analysis of IME variability is single-dimensional (normally only one burden vehicle is used), is dependent on the general assumption that deviations from normal are transient, and is based on historical data that have been affected by merging and allocating in the accounting processes. The variable burden rate developed by such an analysis may serve excellently the accounting purpose for which it was made and, at the same time, may be a very poor measure of differences between two alternatives with respect to indirect manufacturing expenses.

THE USE OF STATISTICAL SAMPLING IN SECURING ACCOUNTING DATA FOR MAKING DECISIONS. It frequently happens that information desired as a guide to decision making is available only by going to such accounting records as sales slips, customers' orders, purchase orders, storeroom requisitions, time cards, job-order sheets, or plant ledger cards.

In many instances, the cost of examining *all* the available records turns out to be excessively high, and it is practicable to look at only a small fraction. In such cases, it is advantageous to use some scheme for randomization to make sure that each record has an equal chance of being included in the sample selected. Such a scheme makes it more likely that the sample will fairly represent the large bulk of records from which the sample is taken. Moreover, the use of random samples makes possible the use of the techniques of mathematical statistics to judge the reliability with which the sample represents the larger bulk.[6]

Sampling procedures and the techniques of statistical analysis are also very useful for auditing, internal control systems, and many cost accounting problems.[7]

SOME SUGGESTED READINGS FOR NON-ACCOUNTANTS INTERESTED IN ACCOUNTING. This book is intended to be introductory in scope and compact in size. Many topics have been treated only briefly, and many specific accounting problems have not been mentioned at all. In order to focus attention on the fundamentals a non-accountant ought to know, it was necessary to present many viewpoints and practices without adequate discussion of the supporting philosophy or theoretical justification. Exploration of the administrative systems design aspect of accounting was restricted primarily to brief consideration of techniques widely used in accounting systems to provide for error detection and for adequate safeguards and controls. Virtually no attention was given to data-processing methods and technology. Also largely bypassed were the areas of accounting history, organization, professional ethics, public accounting, and auditing, which were considered to be of less importance to non-accountants than other material.

It is hoped that the readers of this book have been stimulated to explore the field of accounting further. With this in mind, we have included, following this chapter, a list of works selected to provide reinforcement of the material covered in this book and to offer additional depth and wider coverage of the range of accounting topics.

[6] A good illustration is contained in an operations research example by C. W. Churchman, "The Application of Sampling to LCL Interline Settlements of Accounts of American Railroads," pp. 1051–1057 in Ireson and Grant, *op. cit.* Another good example is given in a paper by E. T. Magruder, "Statistical Methods for Appraising Public Utility Property," pp. 27–41 in *Quality Control Convention Papers—1954*, American Society for Quality Control, New York.

[7] A good reference on this topic is Lawrence L. Vance and John Neter, *Statistical Sampling for Auditors and Accountants*, John Wiley & Sons, Inc., New York, 1956.

SUMMARY. Although a major objective of modern accounting is to supply management with information that will guide business decisions, incorrect decisions are sometimes made as a result of the uncritical use of accounting figures. Generally speaking, a rational decision between business alternatives requires estimates of the way in which future receipts and disbursements will be influenced by the choice between the alternatives. Accounting allocations among different activities and among different time periods may interfere with clear thinking about the differences between alternatives. Moreover, the conventions of accounting may omit certain financial matters that are relevant in decision making.

DISCUSSION QUESTIONS

21-A. In order to have specific figures for the example quoted from Norton, assume that the furniture factory was buying ornaments (the products of the carving spindles) at a price 10% below the unit costs that had been shown on the books when the factory produced its own ornaments. Assume also that the four former employees were making 50% more money without working any harder or producing any more ornaments per day. (These assumptions are close to the actual facts of the case.) Explain how it was possible for both these events to have occurred at the same time.

21-B. In the Norton example, the profits of the furniture factory really were decreased by the decision to shut down the carving spindles and purchase the ornaments from the former employees. Explain this statement. In what way would the influence of this decision on the profits have appeared in the books of account? Why is it unlikely that the normal accounting reports submitted to top management would have identified the influence of this decision? Why do you suppose the head of the cost accounting department felt justified in assuring the plant manager that money was being saved by buying the ornaments?

21-C. Explain the statement that, if the furniture factory in the Norton example had applied overhead by cost centers rather than on a plant-wide basis, the incorrect decision to purchase ornaments would have been less likely. Does this statement necessarily mean that, all things considered, it would have been desirable to apply overhead by cost centers? Explain your answer. Suppose overhead had been applied by cost centers. Could the resulting overhead rates for the carving spindles then have been used in an economy study to determine whether it was better to buy the ornaments or to produce them? Why or why not?

21-D. Consider the example of the proposed design change in the electrical manufacturing plant. In this example, overhead rates were applied by products rather than by cost centers. Management finally decided to approve the change in design even though an application of the current 230% overhead rate to the prospective increase in direct-labor cost seemed to indicate that the sum of the increases in direct-labor and overhead costs was greater than the prospective decrease in direct-material cost. Discuss the question of how the cost reduction from the design change would appear in the accounts, assuming that management was correct in its estimate that the increase in total overhead costs would be 50 cents per unit. Consider the classification of overhead expenses shown in Exhibit 14-1 in Chap. 14. Which of these expenses do you think likely to be increased by a design change that increases direct-labor cost? Are there any overhead expenses that you think might be decreased by a design change that decreases direct-material cost?

21-E. In the example of the proposed design change in the electrical manufacturing plant, the overhead vehicle was direct-labor cost and the overhead rate was 230%. An uncritical application of this overhead rate would have led to the incorrect conclusion that the proposed design change would increase total costs. However, if the overhead vehicle had been prime cost, this incorrect conclusion would not have been reached by an uncritical application of overhead rates. Why not? Does it follow that prime cost would have been a better overhead vehicle for this manufacturer, all things considered? Explain your answer.

21-F. A large company manufactures its product in a number of different cities. The product is distributed in most of the 50 states. Comparison of the unit costs of production of plant A and plant B, located 400 miles apart, has led to executive action reducing the production at plant A and transferring that production load to plant B, where the unit cost is lower. The controller protested this proposal and the subsequent decision with great vigor. Why do you think the controller opposed this action??

21-G. The foregoing questions suggest ways in which the existing accounting procedures might have been modified so that it would have been less likely for an uncritical use of accounting figures to have resulted in wrong conclusions in these particular cases. Discuss your answers to these questions in relation to the general problem of designing accounting systems in a way that will minimize the danger of drawing wrong conclusions from an uncritical use of figures from the accounts.

SUGGESTED REFERENCES

GENERAL ACCOUNTING. The following are standard introductory texts:

A. W. Holmes, G. P. Maynard, J. D. Edwards, and R. A. Meier, *Elementary Accounting*, 3d ed., Richard D. Irwin, Inc., Homewood, Ill., 1962.

H. S. Noble and R. Niswonger, *Accounting Principles,* 8th ed., South-Western Publishing Company, Cincinnati, 1961.

Perry Mason, Sidney Davidson, and James S. Schindler, *Fundamentals of Accounting*, 4th ed., Holt, Rinehart and Winston, Inc., New York, 1959.

H. A. Finney and Herbert E. Miller, *Principles of Accounting—Introductory,* 5th ed., Prentice-Hall, Inc., Englewood Cliffs, N.J., 1957.

The following are good elementary texts in first edition:

Walter B. Meigs and Charles E. Johnson, *Accounting*, McGraw-Hill Book Company, Inc., New York, 1962.

Lawrence L. Vance, *Accountinng Principles and Control,* Holt, Rinehart and Winston, Inc., New York, 1960.

Committee on Accounting (collaborative writing group), *Principles of Accounting*, Pitman Publishing Corporation, New York, 1959.

Two "intermediate" texts that presume prior knowledge of accounting fundamentals are as follows:

H. A. Finney and Herbert E. Miller, *Principles of Accounting—Intermediate,* 5th ed., Prentice-Hall, Inc., Englewood Cliffs, N.J., 1958.

A. W. Holmes, G. P. Maynard, J. D. Edwards, and R. A. Meier, *Intermediate Accounting*, 3d ed., Richarl D. Irwin, Inc., Homewood, Ill., 1958.

The following three books are addressed to non-accountants and emphasize managerial needs for accounting information and the use of accounting information for planning, control, and policy-formulation purposes:

R. N. Anthony, *Management Accounting,* rev. ed., Richard D. Irwin, Inc., Homewood, Ill., 1960.

C. A. Smith and J. Ashburne, *Financial and Administrative Accounting,* 2d ed., McGraw-Hill Book Company, Inc., New York, 1960.

Thomas M. Hill and Myron J. Gordon, *Accounting—A Management Approach,* rev. ed., Richard D. Irwin, Inc., Homewood, Ill., 1959.

COST ACCOUNTING. The first three of the following books are good standard works on cost accounting. The fourth one, by Nickerson, explores cost accounting in relation to cost control and managerial economics by means of the case method. The fifth one, by Shillinglaw, also includes material on managerial economics. The sixth one, by Henrici, is devoted entirely to standard costing. The last one, by Brummet, is an excellent study of overhead costing, including a thorough analysis of direct costing.

J. J. W. Neuner, *Cost Accounting,* 6th ed., Richard D. Irvin, Inc., Homewood, Ill., 1962.

Lawrence L. Vance, *Theory and Technique of Cost Accounting,* rev. ed., Holt, Rinehart and Winston, Inc., New York.

Cecil Gillespie, *Cost Accounting and Control,* Prentice-Hall, Inc., Englewood Cliffs, N.J., 1957.

Clarence B. Nickerson, *Managerial Cost Accounting and Analysis,* 2d ed., McGraw-Hill Book Company, Inc., New York, 1962.

Gordon Shillinglaw, *Cost Accounting: Analysis and Control,* Richard D. Irwin, Inc., Homewood, Ill., 1961.

Stanley B. Henrici, *Standard Costs for Manufacturing,* 3d ed., McGraw-Hill Book Company, Inc., New York, 1960.

R. Lee Brummet, *Overhead Costing—The Costing of Manufactured Products,* Bureau of Business Research, School of Business Administration, University of Michigan, Ann Arbor, Mich., 1957.

ACCOUNTING SYSTEMS. Following are five works dealing with the design of accounting systems. The first three deal mainly with procedures, methods, and devices for recording, storing, and processing accounting data; producing accounting reports; and carrying on accounting-connected functions such as billing, receiving and disbursing cash, and paying wages and salaries. The fourth, by Bennett, is a case-study approach to some of the basic problems of accounting systems design. The last, by one of the authors of this book, treats the fundamental concepts applicable to the design and improvement of repetitive administrative processes, of which accounting systems are an important example.

Cecil Gillespie, *Accounting Systems: Procedures and Methods,* 2d ed., Prentice-Hall, Inc., Englewood Cliffs, N.J., 1961.

John J. W. Neuner and Ulrich J. Neuner, *Accounting Systems,* 3d ed., International Textbook Company, Scranton, Pa., 1959.

Eldred A. Johnson, *Accounting Systems in Modern Business,* McGraw-Hill Book Company, Inc., New York, 1959.

Earl D. Bennett, *Cost Administration: Cases and Notes*, Prentice-Hall, Inc., Englewood Cliffs, N.J., 1960.

Lawrance F. Bell, "Factory Systems and Procedures," sec. 6 in *Handbook of Industrial Engineering and Management* (Ireson and Grant, eds.), Prentice-Hall, Inc., Englewood Cliffs, N.J., 1955.

READINGS RELATING TO DECISION-MAKING USES OF ACCOUNTING FIGURES. The first four books in this group are suggested for the non-accountant who has not had an opportunity to do much reading in the area of engineering economy (or managerial economics). These books deal with making decisions where the monetary differences between the alternatives are important, particularly where investments in long-lived assets are involved. The other books in this group, by Goetz, Thomas, Solomons, and Braun, deal primarily with the purposes and uses of accounting information, with particular reference to economy decisions. All the books in this group relate to the subject matter of the last chapter of this book.

E. L. Grant and W. G. Ireson, *Engineering Economy*, 4th ed., The Ronald Press Company, New York, 1960.

E. L. Grant and P. T. Norton, *Depreciation*, The Ronald Press Company, New York, 1955. See particularly Chap. 16.

Joel Dean, *Managerial Economics*, Prentice-Hall, Inc., Englewood Cliffs, N.J., 1951.

Ezra Solomon (ed.), *The Management of Corporate Capital*, Graduate School of Business, The University of Chicago, The Free Press of Glencoe, New York, 1959. A carefully chosen collection of articles on internal investment theory and policy determination.

Billy E. Goetz, *Management Planning and Control*, McGraw-Hill Book Company, Inc., New York, 1949. A classic in constructive criticism of accounting.

William E. Thomas (ed.), *Readings in Cost Accounting, Budgeting, and Control*, 2d ed., South-Western Publishing Company, Cincinnati, 1960. An excellent collection of articles by well-known writers in the fields of applied economics and accounting. Includes classics such as the article by Jonathan N. Harris referred to in Chap. 16 and "Tomorrow's Cost System" by Billy Goetz referred to in Chap. 21.

David Solomons, *Studies in Costing*, Sweet and Maxwell, London, 1952. A collection of articles concerning the history and theory of cost measurement and the use of cost data in planning, administrative control, and decision making.

Carl F. Braun, *Objective Accounting*, C. F. Braun & Co., Alhambra, Calif., 1953. Presents the challenging views of an industrialist with respect to the actual and potential contributions of accounting toward the success of an organization.

REVIEW PROBLEMS

Problem R-1. The Blue Ox Logging Company does not have a cost system. Its trial balance on December 31, 19___, after its first year of operation is as follows:

	Debit	*Credit*
Cash	$ 240,000	
Standing timber (210,000 M ft at $8)	1,680,000	
Railroad	630,000	
Logging machinery and equipment	720,000	
Accounts receivable	84,000	
Accounts payable		$ 32,000
Notes payable		200,000
Capital stock (30,000 shares)		3,000,000
Felling and sawing	52,000	
Loading and hauling	90,000	
Sales		320,000
Taxes on railroad and logging machinery	12,000	
Camp superintendence	18,000	
City office expense	9,200	
Selling expense	16,800	
Totals	$3,552,000	$3,552,000

The 210,000 M ft of standing timber shown in the trial balance is the total amount that was acquired at the start of the year. Out of this total, 13,000 M ft were cut during the year. Of the logs cut, 8,000 M ft have been sold at $40 per M ft. In addition to this, 4,000 M ft are in pond ready for sale and 1,000 M ft are lying in the woods felled and sawed. These latter are to be valued for inventory purposes at their stumpage cost (i.e., at the figure at which they were carried on the books as standing timber) plus their direct felling and sawing costs, with no other costs included. The logs in pond are to be valued at the same unit figure used in determining cost of logs sold.

Logging machinery and equipment are to be depreciated on a straight-line time basis assuming a 10-year life and no salvage value. As these assets were acquired at the start of the year, a full year's depreciation is to be charged for this first year. All logs are to be hauled over the railroad; depreciation on the railroad is to be charged on a unit-of-production basis in proportion to its production in haulage of logs. Accrued interest on notes payable is $1,000.

Make the necessary calculations to determine the cost of logs sold during the year. In so far as practicable, apply the principles of absorption cost accounting to these calculations. Estimate the corporation income tax for the year on the basis of 30% of the first $25,000 of taxable income plus 53% of income in excess of $25,000.

Prepare a profit and loss statement for the year and a balance sheet as of December 31.

Problem R-2. This problem consists of preparing a balance sheet for the Zero Manufacturing Company as of the close of business on December 31, 1960, and a profit and loss statement for the year 1960. These financial statements are to be derived from the following information. To prepare these two financial statements, it may be necessary for you to make certain assumptions or certain decisions regarding the accounting methods to be employed in the future by this company; if so, you should state your assumptions or decisions as a part of your solution.

Several years ago, Alonzo Smith invented a new game which he named "Zero." As the game was popular with his friends, he decided to manufacture some of the games in his home workshop in his spare time and to market them through a local department store. Because the games sold readily, he finally decided to incorporate a business to engage in the manufacture and marketing of his game. The Zero Manufacturing Company was incorporated early in January, 1960. It rented space, commenced manufacturing operations, and sold 15,000 games during 1960 at a price of $2.50 each.

The actual manufacturing operations that were carried out in this small plant consisted of woodworking, painting, and assembly. The woodworking consisted of cutting, drilling, and sanding the game board. Each board required 4 square feet of plywood. Several painting operations on the board were required. Each game required three dice, 24 plastic pegs, a rule book, and a printed cardboard box; these items were purchased from outside vendors. The assembly operation consisted of placing the game board, the dice, the plastic pegs, and the rule book in the game box. As the orders were received, the games were packed for shipping in cartons containing 24 games each.

The following bill of materials shows the quantities and most recent prices for the various component items:

Plywood, 4 sq ft @ 9¢	36¢
Dice, 3 @ 2¢	6¢
Plastic pegs, 2 dozen @ 5¢ per dozen	10¢
Rule book, 1 @ 10¢	10¢
Box, 1 @ 17¢	17¢
Total (exclusive of paint)	79¢

Prices for plywood, dice, plastic pegs, and boxes were unchanged throughout 1960. The first purchase of rule books during the year was 3,000 books for $480, a unit price of 16 cents per book. The second purchase was 15,000 books for $1,500 and was responsible for the foregoing unit price of 10 cents. All the first 3,000 books were used before the 15,000 arrived.

Inventories on hand December 31 were:

1,000 assembled games of Zero (not yet packed in shipping cartons)
3,000 square feet of plywood

2,000 sets of rules
175 shipping cartons

Also on hand are office supplies that cost approximately $100. The average-cost method is to be used for inventory valuation.

All sales have been made through a selling agent, Avery Horton, on a commission basis of 40 cents per game sold. Horton has undertaken responsibility for all sales promotion activities and has agreed to pay for these activities from his own funds.

The only liabilities at year end are to the Internal Revenue Service for income taxes withheld and for FICA taxes withheld and accrued during the final quarter of the year and to the Federal and state governments for income taxes on the year's corporate income. The applicable Federal tax rate is 30% of net income before taxes, and the applicable state tax rate is 4% of net income before taxes.

The accounts receivable at the end of the year totaled $7,500. All these customers have excellent credit ratings; no bad debts are anticipated.

Depreciation on all fixed assets is to be charged using the double declining-balance method permitted under the U.S. Internal Revenue Code and Regulations. A 16-year life to be assumed for woodworking machinery and a 10-year life for all other fixed assets. Because all fixed assets were purchased at the start of the year, a full year's depreciation charge is applicable to 1960.

Smith did not keep formal double-entry books for his business. However, he did make a complete record of all cash receipts and disbursements during 1960. A summary of this record follows, with comments on a number of the disbursements.

Receipts

Alonzo Smith (50 shares no par stock)	$ 5,000
Mary Smith (10 shares no par stock)	1,000
Avery Horton (40 shares no par stock)	4,000
Receipts from sales of Zero to various customers, 12,000 games @ $2.50	30,000
Total cash received by the corporation during 1960	$40,000

Disbursements

Rent of factory and office space	$ 2,250
(This $2,250 consisted of a deposit of $450 applicable to the last 3 months' rent under a 2-year lease, plus $150 per month for the 12 months of 1960. 80% of the building space was used for manufacturing operations.)	
Expenditures necessary for incorporation	350
(Under income tax regulations, a corporation may write off such expenditures uniformly over the first 5 years of its life.)	
Checks drawn to employees for wages and salaries	8,452
Checks drawn to Internal Revenue Service	1,354
(Total wages and salaries for the year were $10,000. Much of this was to Alonzo and Mary Smith as full-time employees; there were	

also several temporary part-time employees from time to time. An analysis of the various duties of the employees indicates that $8,000 of this is properly chargeable as manufacturing cost and the remaining $2,000 is shipping and general administrative cost. Total withholdings were $1,548, consisting of $1,248 income taxes withheld and $300 of FICA taxes withheld. The payment of $1,354 to the Internal Revenue Service consisted of $924 of income taxes withheld for the first three quarters, $215 of FICA taxes withheld for the first three quarters, and $215 of employer's FICA taxes for the first three quarters. A sum of $494 for the final quarter is presently owed to the Internal Revenue Service, consisting of $324 of income taxes withheld for the final quarter, $85 of FICA taxes withheld, and $85 of employer's FICA taxes due. In this state the unemployment insurance tax program does not apply to a company such as Zero Manufacturing wherein the only full-time employees are major stockholders.)

Purchases of 67,000 sq ft of plywood @ 9¢	$ 6,030
Purchases of paint	800
Purchases of 32,000 dozen plastic pegs @ 5¢ per dozen	1,600
Purchases of 48,000 dice @ 2¢	960
Purchases of 3,000 rule books	480
Purchase of 15,000 rule books	1,500
Purchase of 16,000 game boxes @ 17¢	2,720
Purchase of 800 shipping cartons @ 40¢	320
Shipping expenses on games	700
*Electric light and power	480
*Industrial accident insurance	350
*City and county property taxes	70
*Fire insurance	420
Woodworking machinery	1,200
Painting equipment	800
Worktables	300
(Depreciation on these assets is a manufacturing cost.)	
Office furniture and fixtures	500
(Depreciation on these assets is not a manufacturing cost.)	
Repairs to woodworking machinery	250
Copyright expenditures on rule book	280
(These are to be written off at a uniform rate over the 28-year life of the copyright.)	
Sales commissions to Avery Horton	4,800
(This is 40 cents per game on the sale of 12,000 games. Horton is still owed for commissions on 3,000 games.)	
Postage and mailing expense	80
Office supplies	220
Total cash disbursed by the corporation in 1960	$37,266

* These four items should be considered as applicable solely to manufacturing. Fire insurance payment was for a 3-year policy starting January 1, 1960. The other three items are completely applicable to 1960.

Problem R-3. This problem involves a direct-costing solution of problem 17-6, which was based on problem 17-5 concerning the Lottsaw Brass Company.

The standard costs for departments R, S, and T, as developed in problem 17-5, need to be modified to a direct costing basis, using the following burden rate information. The figures in the table are dollars per pound produced.

	Dept. R	Dept. S	Dept. T
Absorption costing burden rate........	0.153	0.546	0.480
Direct costing (variable) burden rate....	0.063	0.246	0.280

Department M is to be treated, as in the prior problems, as a "nonprofit" service department. Therefore, in this direct costing solution, full-absorption costing is to be used in connection with department M and the standard costs for materials E and D will be the same as before (E, 60 cents per pound; D, 15 cents per pound).

A. Using the normal-quarter production quantity data given in the diagram of problem 17-5, compute the fixed-burden budget for departments R, S, and T. Also, prepare a table as specified in problem 17-5, showing the revised standard unit costs to be used for direct costing.
B. The opening balances given in problem 17-6 for those accounts containing burden as an element of cost must be revised to a direct costing basis, and the balance in the control account must be adjusted accordingly. Show, in general-journal form, the adjusting entry that would be required as of the end of the previous quarter if a change from absorption costing to direct costing was made at that time. For Work in Process—Department T, round off the adjustment to the nearest $10. Thus the burden included in this account at the start of the quarter will be $250 under direct costing.
C. Set up a T-account factory ledger as in problem 17-6, enter the opening balances, and make entries B through K. Determine and show the end-of-quarter balance in each account, and take a post-closing trial balance of the ledger.
D. Given the following data abstracted from the general ledger, prepare an income statement for the quarter comparing the two costing schemes:

Net sales..................................	$215,000
Variable selling and general expense..........	18,500
Fixed selling and general expense............	25,000

Follow the general format illustrated in Exhibit 16-1. The variance may be shown in the period-cost section of this report on two lines, one reporting the total burden capacity variance for the factory and the other reporting all other manufacturing variances. For this purpose, the absorption costing burden variance for the four departments must be split into budget and capacity variances. For department T the burden budget for the quarter is \$9,670 (not \$9,600) because of the net increase in work in process during the quarter. For department M, the equation for determining the burden budget for the quarter is \$3,600 + (0.18) (pounds of E produced). The capacity variance for department M will appear in the direct-costing income statement because absorption costing is still used for this service department. The fixed manufacturing expense shown in the direct-costing statement should therefore not include the fixed burden budget of department M. Also, note that the department S material-quantity variance to be included in "other manufacturing variances" is less under direct costing than under absorption costing.

E. Show that the difference between the direct costing and absorption costing results with respect to reported net profit before taxes for the quarter is equal to the difference between the two schemes with respect to the change in the value of manufactured inventories during the quarter.

Problem R-4. In the standard cost system of the Technical Products Company, job-order costs are used. The standard costs at which materials are carried in the stores' accounts are intended to cover the purchase price of the materials plus inbound transportation charges to the plant. Standard direct labor costs and standard material quantities are established for each product. The standard burden rate is based on the normal volume of output (measured in standard direct-labor cost) and is 175% of standard direct-labor cost.

To simplify this problem, no books of original entry are to be used. All entries are to be made directly into the T accounts representing the general ledger. The accounts for the different finished products (normally in a subsidiary ledger) are included in this general ledger. Many of the general ledger accounts, such as Accounts Receivable, Materials, Jobs in Progress, Accounts Payable, Indirect Manufacturing Expense, Selling Expense, Buildings, and Machinery, should be viewed as controlling accounts for subsidiary ledgers that have been omitted from the problem. Accounts required in addition to those listed in the opening trial balance (entry A, below) are as follows:

Deferred Income
Dividends Payable
Sales
Other Income
Cost of Goods Sold
Bad Debt Expense
Interest Expense
Income Tax Expense
Office Expense
Selling Expense
General and Administrative Expense
Wages and Salaries
Indirect Manufacturing Expense
Burden Budget Variance
Burden Capacity Variance
Material Price Variance
Material Quantity Variance
Direct Labor Variance
Profit and Loss Summary

A. Enter the April 1, 1962, opening balances in the accounts as follows:

Account	Debit	Credit
Cash	$ 27,000	
Accounts Receivable	42,000	
Allowance for Bad Debts		$ 900
Materials	37,000	
Jobs in Progress	13,700	
Product RZ (1,600 @ $7)	112,000	
Product XT (800 @ $23)	18,400	
Product NU (100 @ $46)	4,600	
Product CL (200 @ $11)	2,200	
Prepaid Insurance	880	
Prepaid Property Taxes	1,320	
Buildings	192,000	
Reserve for Depreciation, Buildings		40,800
Machinery (A)	240,000	
Reserve for Depreciation, Machinery (A)		112,600
Machinery (B)	24,000	
Reserve for Depreciation, Machinery (B)		8,000
Land	40,000	
Accounts Payable		9,000
Accrued Interest Payable		1,000
Income Taxes Payable		1,200
Accrued Payroll		2,915
Employee Withholding Tax Payable		1,875
FICA Taxes Payable		940
FUTA Taxes Payable		360
State Disability Insurance Payable		1,215
State Unemployment Tax Payable		450
Mortgage Payable		80,000
Capital Stock		300,000
Earned Surplus		93,045
Totals	$654,300	$654,300

B. Production materials were purchased (all on credit) during the quarter for $24,000. The total standard cost of these materials was $25,500.

C. A summary of the 13 weekly payrolls falling in this quarter is as follows:

Total wages		$48,000
Deductions:		
Employees' withholding taxes	$6,000	
Employees' FICA taxes	1,500	
State unemployment insurance	480	7,980
Net wages payable		$40,020

D. Timekeeping analysis provided the following distribution of total wages for the quarter:

Factory direct labor	$18,000
Overtime premiums	300
Factory indirect labor	8,200
Factory supervision	9,000
Total manufacturing wages	$35,500
Sales department salaries	6,600
General administrative salaries	5,900
Total wages and salaries	$48,000

E. During this quarter the payrolls for the 13 weeks including the week ending March 31 through the week ending June 23 were disbursed. The total of these paychecks was $39,600. (The payroll for the week ending June 30 was not disbursed as of the end of the quarter but was included in the summaries given in entries C and D.)

F. Other disbursements during the quarter were:

For factory indirect expenses	$ 6,400
On accounts payable	23,400
For freight on raw materials	2,000
For freight on product sold	1,600
For rental of office equipment	1,500
For other office expenses	2,100
For advertising	3,480
Employee withholding taxes	5,755
FICA taxes	2,880
State disability insurance	1,215
State unemployment taxes	450
Total	$50,780

G. The value of jobs in progress at the end of each quarter is determined by summarizing the cost of the actual materials issued (at standard prices) and the actual direct labor expended (at standard rates) from the job cost records of the unfinished jobs remaining in the shop. These figures for March 31 and June 30 were as follows:

	March 31	June 30
Direct material	$ 3,800	$ 4,200
Direct labor	3,600	3,800
Burden (175% of DL)	6,300	6,650
Total	$13,700	$14,650

The total standard cost of jobs completed during the quarter was summarized from the subsidiary job cost records as follows:

Product	Quantity	Direct material	Direct labor	Burden	Total
RZ	4,000	$10,400	$ 6,400	$11,200	$28,000
XT	500	3,250	3,000	5,250	11,500
NU	300	3,900	3,600	6,300	13,800
CL	1,600	4,400	4,800	8,400	17,600
Total		$21,950	$17,800	$31,150	$70,900

Make appropriate entries for the foregoing matters.

H. Issues of materials to production jobs (actual quantities at standard prices) totaled $22,500.

I. Sales of finished products during the period totaled $100,000. The items sold were 3,600 RZ, 600 XT, 350 NU, and 1,400 CL.

J. Collections on accounts receivable were $98,000.

K. Paid 3 months' interest on the mortgage payable, $1,200. This was the quarterly interest payment for the period January 16 to April 15. The interest rate is 6% per annum.

L. Paid $1,800 for a 3-year fire insurance policy on the factory building and its contents, starting May 1.

M. A quarterly dividend of $3,000 ($1 per share for the 3,000 shares of capital stock outstanding) was declared by the board of directors in April and paid on May 15.

N. Received $600 from W & H Construction Co. for 6 months' rental of a portion of the Technical Products Company's land for the period April 1 to September 30.

P. A former customer whose account had previously been written off as uncollectible paid $180, the total amount he owed.

At this point, take a trial balance of the ledger. (Provide additional columns for a second trial balance, to be taken after closing. No work sheet is required in this problem.)

Make the following adjusting and closing entries directly in the T accounts:

a. The depreciation charge for buildings is to be made for the quarter. This charge is one-quarter of the total depreciation charge anticipated for the year. Straight-line item depreciation accounting has been used for buildings with an annual depreciation rate of 2.5% based on a 40-year life. There are two buildings in this account. One, used for factory purposes, had a first cost of $144,000. The other, used for office purposes, had a first cost of $48,000.

b. The depreciation charge for each of the machinery accounts for the quarter is one-quarter of the total depreciation charge anticipated for that account for the year. The Machinery (A) account includes all machinery acquired before 1954. This account uses straight-line group depreciation accounting with an annual depreciation rate of 5%. The Machinery (B) account includes the machinery acquired since 1954 and will include all machinery acquired in the future. It carries a declining-balance group rate of 10%. The half-year convention has been used.

c. Estimated loss on bad debts applicable this quarter is $500. Accounts totaling $600 should be written off as uncollectible.

d. The property tax expense applicable to this quarter is $1,320. Distribute this $1,100 to factory expense and $220 to general and administrative expense.

e. Interest has accrued on the mortgage payable (see entry K).

f. Insurance that cost $270 expired during the quarter. Treat this as $200 factory expense and $70 general administrative expense.

g. The company's expenses in connection with payrolls for the quarter must be accrued as follows:
FICA taxes equal to the employees contributions
FUTA tax at 0.8% of total wages
State disability insurance at 2.7% of total wages
These expenses should be distributed according to the distribution of total wages (see entry D). Round off each figure to the nearest $10.

h. Office expenses should be distributed one-third to selling expense and two-thirds to general and administrative expense.

i. Make any other adjusting entries that you think are necessary.

j. Make any additional entries necessary to determine the balances in the variance accounts. For separating burden budget variance from burden capacity variance, a variable budget analysis has developed the following equation: IME (indirect manufacturing expense) for a quarter should equal $19,000 plus 75% of the standard direct-labor cost of the quarter. The normal burden rate of 175% of standard direct-labor cost is based on the assumption that normal output involves a standard direct-labor cost of $19,000 per quarter. Close the variance account balances into Profit and Loss Summary.

k. Close income and expense accounts into Profit and Loss Summary.

m. Enter in the books the estimated income tax liability that has accrued because of the operations of the quarter. Assume that an income tax rate of 30% is applicable and that taxable income is the same as the profit before income taxes shown by the books.

n. Close the account Income Tax Expense into Profit and Loss Summary.

p. Close Profit and Loss Summary into Earned Surplus.

Take a trial balance after closing. (Use additional columns on the sheet used for the trial balance taken after entry P.)

Prepare a profit and loss statement for the quarter, a balance sheet as of June 30, and an earned surplus statement showing the changes in Earned Surplus that occurred during the quarter.

In addition to the foregoing financial statements, submit the following papers:

1. The T-account general ledger showing all entries including adjusting and closing entries
2. The trial balance taken after entry P and the post-closing trial balance

Problem R-5. The Rainbow Ashtray Company makes two sizes of dyed aluminum ashtrays which are stamped from coil stock in the punch press department and then anodized and dyed in the finishing department. An inventory of stampings is maintained between the two departments. The finished ashtrays are sent to the warehouse building where they are packed for shipment. The costs of packing, warehousing, and shipping are treated as nonmanufacturing expenses.

In the factory, a standard cost system is used. Coil aluminum is the only direct material. It is carried in inventory at a standard cost of 50 cents per pound. Scrap aluminum from both departments is returned to stores at a standard value of 12½ cents per pound. Burden is applied at standard rates; the burden vehicle in both departments is direct-labor cost. A variable budget is established for the IME of each department, permitting an analysis of burden variance into two components.

Dept.	Dept. name	Standard burden rate, %	Standard DL$ at normal production	Formula for monthly IME budget (expected IME)
A	Punch press	150	\$3,200	Budget = \$2,400 + (0.75)(Std. DL\$)
B	Finishing	100	\$2,500	Budget = \$1,000 + (0.60)(Std. DL\$)

Standard costs per piece for the two sizes of ashtray are as follows:

	Large ashtray	Small ashtray
Department A—punch press department:		
Direct-material quantity	0.06 lb	0.04 lb
Direct-material cost	\$0.030	\$0.020
Direct-labor cost	0.032	0.024
Burden (150% of DL\$)	0.048	0.036
Total cost per stamping	\$0.110	\$0.080
Department B—finishing department:		
Direct-labor cost	\$0.025	\$0.020
Burden (100% of DL\$)	0.025	0.020
Total cost per finished ashtray	\$0.160	\$0.120

The factory inventory and cost accounts are in a subsidiary factory ledger controlled by the general ledger account titled Factory Ledger. This problem involves operation of the accounting system for the month of January, the first month of a new fiscal year. For simplicity, only illustrative transactions are mentioned. Neglect any accruals, disbursements, or receipts that are not specifically, indicated, or assume they are included in summary figures given. Use only the accounts listed below. Any necessary calculations should be accurate to the nearest whole dollar.

GENERAL LEDGER, RAINBOW ASHTRAY COMPANY
TRIAL BALANCE, DECEMBER 31, 19___

Account	Debit	Credit
Cash	$ 10,000	
Accounts Receivable	20,400	
Finished Ashtrays	4,400	
Factory Ledger	4,300	
Notes Receivable	8,000	
Accrued Assets		
Deferred Charges		
Land	10,000	
Buildings	144,000	
Accumulated Depreciation—Buildings		$ 45,000
Office Equipment	32,000	
Accumulated Depreciation—Office Equipment		10,000
Plant Equipment	360,000	
Accumulated Depreciation—Plant Equipment		126,100
Accounts Payable		1,800
Accrued Liabilities		1,200
Deferred Credits		
Capital Stock		250,000
Earned Surplus		159,000
Profit and Loss Summary		
Cost of Goods Sold		
Sales		
Other Income		
Office, Selling, and Administrative Expense		
Packing, Shipping, and Warehouse Expense		
Land and Building Expense		
Totals	$593,100	$593,100

FACTORY LEDGER, RAINBOW ASHTRAY COMPANY
TRIAL BALANCE, DECEMBER 31, 19____

Account	Debit	Credit
General Ledger—Control		$4,300
Aluminum Coil	$1,000	
Stampings	2,700	
Scrap Aluminum	200	
Work in Process, Dept. A—Labor and Burden		
Work in Process, Dept. A—Raw Material	300	
Work in Process, Dept. B—Labor and Burden	20	
Work in Process, Dept. B—Stampings	80	
Material Price Variance		
Material Quantity Variance, Dept. A		
Labor Variance, Dept. A		
Labor Variance, Dept. B		
Burden Capacity Variance		
Burden Budget Variance, Dept. A		
Burden Budget Variance, Dept. B		
Indirect Labor		
Indirect Mfg. Expense—Dept. A		
Indirect Mfg. Expense—Dept. B		
Totals	$4,300	$4,300

Part I—General Ledger Entries

Set up a T-account sheet representing the general ledger, and make entries in the T accounts for the following matters:

A. Enter the opening balances in the general ledger accounts.

B. Purchased on credit, 6,000 pounds of aluminum coil for $2,820.

C. Cash disbursements for the month are summarized as follows:

Paid on accounts payable	$ 2,000
Land and building expenses	800
Packing and shipping expense	600
Selling and administrative expense	2,820
Accrued wages for December	600
Packing and shipping labor	880
Charges to factory ledger	8,300
Total	$16,000

D. Collections on accounts receivable were $19,000.

E. 2,000 pounds of scrap aluminum was sold for 14 cents per pound cash. This material is valued in the factory ledger at 12½ cents per pound. *Note:* This sale of scrap should *not* be reflected in the Sales or Cost of Goods Sold figures.

F. Ashtrays completed in the factory and delivered to the warehouse in January were 40,000 large and 47,500 small.

G. Sales, all on credit, were:

40,000 large ashtrays at 24 cents each
50,000 small ashtrays at 18 cents each

H. The cost of goods sold is calculated at standard cost.

I. Accrued wages payable at the end of January were:

Factory labor	$800
Packing and shipping labor	120
Total	$920

J. A punch press which cost $2,000 12 years ago was sold for $300 cash. A local drayage company has submitted a bill for $50 for moving and loading the machine onto a flatcar. The straight-line depreciation rate used on such equipment has been 6⅔% per year. This company uses group depreciation accounting for such machinery.

K. Depreciation charges for the month are:

	General office	Factory	Warehouse	Total
Office equipment	$100	$ 40	$ 20	$ 160
Plant equipment	....	1,360	240	1,600
Totals	$100	$1,400	$260	$1,760

Total depreciation on buildings, $300, is to be charged to Land and Building Expense.

L. Land and building expense is distributed as follows: General office, 5%; factory, 60%; warehouse, 35%.

M. One month's interest has been earned on the $8,000 note receivable. The interest rate is 6% per year.

N. $120 which was charged to selling and administrative expense is really a prepayment for an advertisement which is to appear in February.

P. Dividends for the previous quarter declared and paid in January amounted to $4,000.

Q. An order for 1,000 special ashtrays was received and accepted along with a check for $200 representing an advance deposit of 50% of the agreed total price. The order will be manufactured and shipped in February.

R. Make the necessary entries to determine the profit or loss for January, and close it to Earned Surplus. No general ledger entry is required at the end of this month with respect to the factory cost variances because they are carried forward to the end of the year. Rule and balance all the general ledger accounts, and take a post-closing trial balance.

Part II—Factory Ledger Entries

Make the necessary entries directly into the factory ledger T accounts for the following matters:

a. Record the purchase of aluminum mentioned in general ledger entry B.
b. A breakdown of the charges to the factory ledger mentioned in general ledger entry C is as follows:

Freight on raw material shipment received	$ 60
Direct labor, department A	2,400
Direct labor, department B	1,600
Factory indirect labor	1,080
Indirect manufacturing expense, department A	2,360
Indirect manufacturing expense, department B	800
Total	$8,300

c. The accrued wages charged to the factory ledger in general ledger entry I is to be distributed as follows: department A direct labor, $360; department B direct labor, $320; factory indirect labor, $120.
d. 5,400 pounds of coil aluminum was issued to department A.
e. Production in department A was 45,000 large stampings and 50,000 small stampings. All these stampings were delivered to stores. The only work in process in department A at the end of any month is unused aluminum coil on the press stock reels. At the start of January there were 600 pounds of such material in the department; at the end of January there were 900 pounds.
f. Production data for department B is given in the table below. Assume that the stampings in process at the start of the month and those in process at the end of the month were 50% finished with respect to the necessary processing in department B and that all finished ashtrays are transferred to the warehouse. Make the appropriate entries relating to production accomplished in this department this month. (See entry g concerning the matter of stampings spoiled.)

	Large ashtrays	Small ashtrays
Stampings in process Jan. 1	0	1,000
Stampings delivered from stores	43,000	48,000
Subtotal	43,000	49,000
Stampings spoiled (see entry g)	1,000	1,500
Ashtrays delivered to warehouse	40,000	47,500
Stampings in process Jan. 31	2,000	0

g. In department B a certain amount of spoilage is expected. The standard direct-labor and burden costs for department B are set high enough to compensate for the direct labor and burden spent in that department on normal amounts of spoiled work. Therefore, for each good ashtray produced in the department the standard labor time provides a small incremental labor time allowance to offset time expected to be spent on stampings that end up in the scrap tub. Similarly, actual indirect manufacturing expense incurred in working on stampings that are subsequently scrapped is offset, on the average, through the allowance of burden at the standard rate on standard direct-labor cost. However, the foregoing allowance does not cover the cost of the stampings spoiled—the cost of material plus the direct labor and burden costs applied in department A. This element of the loss due to spoilage is treated in department B as an indirect manufacturing expense. To determine the amount of this expense for a given month and for quality-control purposes, a record is kept of the number of stampings of each size spoiled during the month. These quantities, costed at standard (0.11 and 0.08, respectively), provide the basis for the necessary factory ledger entry. In January the spoilage was 1,000 large stampings and 1,500 small stampings, as shown in the table entry f.

h. The production departments receive credit for their scrap at the standard price of 12½ cents per pound. In January, department A generated 960 pounds of scrap (trim material) and department B developed 104 pounds (spoiled stampings). Assume that no scrap remained in either department at the end of the month.

i. Record the sale of scrap mentioned in general ledger entry E.

j. Factory indirect labor is to be distributed $830 to department A and the remainder to department B.

k. The $1,400 factory depreciation expense charged to the factory ledger in entry K should be distributed $960 to department A and $440 to department B.

m. The factory share of land and building expense (general ledger entry L) should be distributed two-thirds to department A and one-third to department B.

n. Make the entries as necessary to determine all cost variances not previously found. Rule and balance all accounts in the factory ledger, and take a trial balance.

Part III—Direct Costing

Assume that it has been proposed that Rainbow Ashtray change from absorption costing to direct costing as of the start of January. For this purpose, the following details about the January 1 opening inventories are provided:

	Large	Small
Finished ashtrays..........	14,000	18,000
Stampings..................	14,000	14,500

1. Prepare a table, similar to the one in the third paragraph of the problem statement, showing the standard costs as they would be modified for direct costing.
2. Write out the general journal entry that would be required as of January 1 to adjust the general ledger accounts. Assume that any net change in the valuation of assets is to be charged directly to Earned Surplus.
3. Write out, in general journal form, the appropriate adjusting entry to be made in the factory ledger as of January 1.

4. Make the necessary cost calculations for January using the direct costing scheme. Prepare a post-closing trial balance of the general ledger showing the January 31 account balances as they would be under direct costing.
5. Prepare a report comparing the income statements that would be developed for January under direct costing and absorption costing, following the format indicated below. For this purpose, assume that $2,000 of the office, selling, and administrative expense and $1,000 of the packing, shipping, and warehouse expense are fixed and that the remainders represent variable expenses.

Direct Costing		*Absorption Costing*	
Sales	______	Sales	______
Cost of goods sold	______	Cost of goods sold	______
Manufacturing margin	______	Gross margin on sales	______
Less: Other variable expenses	______	Less: Other expenses	______
Merchandising margin	______	Unadjusted operating profit	______
Less: Fixed period costs	______	Less: Burden capacity variance	______
Net operating profit	______	Net operating profit	______
Add: Other income	______	Add: Other income	______
Net profit	______	Net profit	______

INDEX